ETHICS, INTEGRITY AND APTITUDE

Preface

This publication titled, "Ethics, Integrity & Aptitude" is written in such a way that it would excel as the most referred book for The Civil Services Mains Examination, General Studies, Paper IV. This book provides aspiring IAS candidates with not only basic study material for the complete Paper but also with elaborate Case Studies and previous years' solved question papers.

This publication provides readers with an overview of ethics including the in-depth human interface; areas of ethical study/branches of ethics; philosophical and psychological basis of ethics. Focus also lies on metaethics; normative ethics; and applied ethics. Various fields of application of ethics are described, such as, bioethics; business ethics; organizational ethics; machine ethics; military ethics; political ethics; development and environmental ethics; and descriptive ethics. Multiple ethical theories are analyzed. Similarities and differences among morality, values and ethics are discussed. The determinants of ethical behavior and ethics in governance are presented. The dimensions of ethics in private and public relationships and contemporary implications of ethics are evaluated in detail with highlights on current state of ethics in public relations and codes of ethics. An overview of ethical concerns in public administration is given with focus on accountability; ethics in government; code of administrative ethics; work ethics in public administration; and hindrances to ethical accountability in public administration.

A brief analysis of human values is made with highlights on characteristics of values and moral values; classification of values; principle of preference of values; significance of human values; etc. Focus also lies on positive and negative value; intrinsic value; instrumental value; direct and indirect value; and positive and negative instrumental value. The application of human values and role of various factors in inculcating values are discussed with focus on empathy and compassion.Various lessons emanating from the lives and teachings of great leaders, reformers and administrators from India and abroad are described. A brief analysis of attitude is done with highlights on implicit and explicit attitudes; components of attitude; functions of attitude; attitude formation; influence of attitude and relation with thought and behaviour; and difference between attitude and behavior; and beliefs, values and moral attitudes.

The theme of emotional intelligence is covered in detail with special focus on the eight competencies of emotional intelligence and various models of emotional intelligence. The difference between emotional quotient vs intelligence quotient is analyzed. The use of emotional intelligence in administration and governance is discussed with focus on themes like emotional intelligence and leadership; emotional intelligence and team building; emotional intelligence and conflict; emotional intelligence and profession; and significance of emotional intelligence in the workplace. Special chapter is dedicated to elaborate upon the importance of problem-solving approach to issues faced while dealing with society with highlights on problem-solving strategies; role of eight disciplines in problem solving; and problem-solving tools.

This book also covers the details of contributions of moral thinkers and philosophers from India and world, such as, Socrates; Plato; Aristotle; Immanuel Kant; John Rawls; Jeremy Bentham; John Stuart Mill; Rousseau; Dalai Lama; Gautam Buddha; Vardhmana Mahavira; Swami Vivekananda; Raja Ram Mohan Roy; Mohandas Karamchand Gandhi; Sarvepalli Radhakrishnan; etc.

The theme of corporate governance is discussed in detail with focus on ethical leadership; ethics, transparency and accountability; corporate social responsibility (CSR); ISO 26000: social responsibility; and training and advisory services in corporate social responsibility (CSR). The Indian CSR situation is discussed with focus on the Companies Act, 2013; and Clause 135: CSR committee requirements.

The theme of administrative ethics is covered in great detail with focus on its three basic components; special ethical requirements for the civil service; and need for administrative ethics. The ethical concerns and dilemmas in government institutions are described with highlights on the context of ethics and its significance for public administration. The new dimensions of ethics are described. Focus also lies on the laws, rules, regulations and conscience as sources of ethical guidance; politics and ethics; ethics in public life; international approaches such as United Nations Public Service Awards, ASPA code of ethics in USA; various legal provisions to guide ethical behavior of internationalcivil servants; Article 153 of the Polish Constitution; civil service values in the United Kingdom; etc. Special emphasis is on civil services of India with highlights on code of ethics for civil servants; constitution of ethics committees, such as, the Vohra Committee, the committee on ethics of the Lok Sabha; etc.

The issues of corruption in India and international cooperation; menace of corruption in public life; enhancing development through better use of public resources; international measures to combat corruption; legal framework for fighting corruption in India; evolution of the anti-corruption laws in India; and training Indian officials on ethics, values in public governance; are critically evaluated. In addition, the theme of probity in governance is discussed in detail with highlights on good governance and e-governance; tools for good governance; civil society participation; citizens' charters;

right to information (RTI); transparency; importance of systemic reforms; and slew of measures in India.

This book also provides a concluding overview of the significance of themes of ethics, integrity and aptitude with renewed focus on subject areas of ethics; moral psychology; principles of sociology and ethics; role of social psychology; social psychological ways to understand the world; social beliefs and judgments; relationship between attitudes and behaviours; other assorted social psychology concepts; ethical considerations in sociological research; morality; social code and morality; integrity; testing of integrity; integrity in ethics; other integrities; impartiality; nonpartisan; safeguarding non-partisanship in the public service; non-partisanship in staffing; objectivity; aptitude; intelligence; combined aptitude and knowledge tests; aptitude and foundational values for civil service; attitude; measuring attitudes; attitude structure; attitude function; attitude formation; attitude change; emotion and attitude change; attitude-behaviour relationship; approach to issues relating to attitude, integrity and probity in public life; characteristic of attitude; functions of attitudes; ethics in governance; transparency and credibility; integrity in public service; ethics and human interface; ethics in human actions; modern moral philosophy; social and ethical acceptability of NBICs for purposes of human enhancement; professional responsibility and codes of conduct; probity in governance; integrity in public life; work culture; probity in public life; culpability; scapegoating; bribe payers index; corruption perceptions index; whistleblower; whistleblower protection in India; importance of classified information and citizen's charter; and the Indian experiences.

This book boasts of presenting IAS aspirants with maximum number of case studies presented at one place in this Paper till date. The right way to answer case-study questions are also given so as to facilitate the UPSC candidates to the maximum for scoring best possible marks in this rather difficult paper. Various appendices are given to acquaint UPSC candidates with primary sources of information on this theme, such as, Right to Public Services Legislation in India; The Right of Citizens for Time Bound Delivery of Goods and Services and Redressal of Their Grievances Bill, 2011; India's Citizen's Charter and Grievance Redressal Bill, 2011; Official Secrets Act of India, 1923; and the International NGO Accountability Charter. Previous years' questions of IAS GS Mains Paper IV on "Ethics, Integrity & Aptitude" are given with focus on model questions of IAS GS Mains Paper IV: Ethics, Integrity & Aptitude for 2018.

Contents

Appendix 5.

A Synopsis of Ethics

1 CHAPTER

DEFINITION OF ETHICS

- In general, ethics refer to a system of moral principles, which affect the decision-making ability of the people and act as guiding principles for them to lead their lives.
- Ethics takes into consideration the moral values that are favourable to the individuals and the society he lives in and is also interpreted as moral philosophy.
- The term ethics originates from the Greek word ethos meaning character or disposition, custom and habit.

Ethics are the guiding principles to overcome the following dilemmas:

- Way to live a good life
- A person's rights and responsibilities
- Knowledge of the language of right and wrong
- Taking moral decisions over what is good and bad

Our religions, philosophies and cultures have played a major role in shaping our concepts of ethics. They inculcate values in people to indulge in debates on topics like human rights, abortion and professional conduct.

Hence, ethics refer to a system of moral principles or a branch of philosophy, which set the criteria for the good of an individual and society.

Ethics specifies which elements are necessary for human well-being and proposes the principles to be followed as guidelines for introducing an ethical culture. The specific values, standards, rules, and agreements adopted by the people to conduct their lives also come under ethics.

Generally, Ethics could be defined as the study of human behaviour and its outcome in view of the ideal possibility. For example, the study of the morals of a society could help an ethicist to find out their possible effects on humankind in case they are used as universal standards.

Ethics are not just social conventions to be followed like table manners, but these specify the social conditions, which are essential for human beings to prosper.

How do we know what is Ethical?

The struggle for existence over a long time led to shaping of ethical wisdom in human beings. Societies learned by employing various trial and error methods and discovered the ways to create mutually enhancing relationships. *The reality-producing function of the mind* is also a factor contributing to the origination of ***ethics.***

The human beings lead their life not only by their learning from the events of the past, but also by keeping in view the outcomes possible in future. When people sense the possibility of happening of an event and act that way they behave as such to make it a self-fulfilling prophecy.

The challenge lies in realizing the conditions that led to human well-being to visualize an ideal ethical culture, and then evolve the principles to create a good life.

What does it Mean to Act Ethically?

Ethical Culture asserts that the state of spiritual-ethical harmony could be created when people imbibe the following three guidelines taken together to lead their life.

- When a person behaves as if he is living as a member of an ideal ethical culture and is having a sense of interdependence with humanity and nature.
- When people behave in a manner so as to achieve their full and unique potential.
- When people behave so as to extract the best and the most distinctive qualities in others and thereby in oneself.

APPROACHES TO ETHICS

According to philosophers, ethical theories in current time could be divided into three areas: meta-ethics, normative ethics and applied ethics.

- ***Meta-ethics*** addresses the nature of moral judgment by focusing on the origins and meaning of ethical principles.
- ***Normative ethics*** takes into account the content of moral judgements and the criteria for judging right or wrong.
- ***Applied ethics*** is concerned with controversial topics such as war, animal rights and capital punishment.

APPLICATIONS OF ETHICS

To prove their validity in practice, ethical theories need to affect the behaviours of human beings.

According to some philosophers, ethics do have impact on human behaviours. They opine that it would be quite irrational for an individual not to do what he understands as morally good for him to do.

However, in actual practice, it is seen that human beings behave quite irrationally and they often follow their ***'gut instinct'*** even when they have a different course of action in their minds. However, ethics equip one with good tools to think about moral issues.

Some significant uses of ethics are as follows:

I. Ethics can Present a Moral Map

Most moral issues, such as abortion and euthanasia for beginners, arouse conflicting views in our mind. These emotional issues almost drain us as though our hearts do all the arguing but our brains just go with the flow.

However, philosophers role become prominent to help us make decision to choose another way of tackling these issues. The ethical rules and principles, which they offer, enable us to take a relaxed approach to overcome moral problems.

Hence, ethics offer an individual with a moral map, a framework for him to follow to find a way through difficult issues.

II. Ethics can Determine a Discord

The people having arguments over a moral issue can follow the framework of ethics to find out that their point of disagreement lies about just one particular part of the issue, otherwise mostly they agree on every other points related to the issue.

This can significantly reduce the intensity of heat out of the argument, and sometimes even suggest a way to arrive at a solution to the problem.

However, sometimes even ethics are unable to offer the people the kind of help that they really want.

III. Ethics does not Provide Right Answers

Sometimes ethics also fail to provide the right answer to moral problems.

In truth, many people have their viewpoints that for many ethical issues a single right answer is not available. It contains just a set of principles to be applicable to particular cases to offer those involved some clear choices.

Some philosophers bring another angle to this argument and opine that ethics can only eliminate confusion and clarify the issues. However, it is for the individuals to take their own decisions and arrive at a conclusion.

IV. Ethics can give Several Answers

Most of the people expect the ethical questions to have a lone right answer. For them it is hard to live with moral ambiguity as they carry a genuine desire to do the 'right' thing. Despite having no possibility of figuring out the right thing, they have a craving for the idea that one right answer is there somewhere for such questions.

However, one right answer is not possible most of the time and an individual will have to choose from several right answers, or just some least bad answers.

Some people find moral ambiguity hard to live with as they are compelled to bear the responsibility of their own choices and actions, instead of falling back on convenient rules and customs.

Ethics: The In-Depth Human Interface

2 CHAPTER

Ethics is that segment of philosophy, which includes standardizing, safeguarding and proposing concepts of right and wrong conduct. It is also known as moral philosophy. Derived from the Greek word ethos, the term ethics means "character". While it is a counterpart to Aesthetics in Axiology, in philosophy, ethics studies the moral behaviour in humans and the way they should act.

DOMAINS OF ETHICAL STUDY/BRANCHES OF ETHICS

There are Three Extensive Fields of Ethical Study

a. *Meta-ethics*: The focus of this branch of ethics is on the meaning of ethical terms themselves (for instance, 'what is goodness?') and to get the answers to questions for attaining ethical knowledge, instead of focusing on the question of common usage. For example, it will focus on the nature of questions such as 'how can I distinguish what is good from what is bad?' instead of 'what should I do in a particular situation?' Thus, meta-ethics deals with the nature of ethical properties, attitudes, statements, and judgments. It studies such themes for exploring the meaning attached with moral questions and the basis for people to know what is 'true' or 'false'.
b. *Normative ethics is* that branch of ethics, which analyses the ethical acts. Thus, generally, it focuses absolutely on questions of 'what is the right thing to do?' It deals with questions of what people ought to do when faced in ambiguous situation, and on how to make decision on what 'correct' moral actions need to be taken.
c. *Applied ethics* deals with the way adopted by the people to achieve moral outcomes in specific situations. Hence, it takes into account the philosophical examination of peculiar and generally complex issues involving moral judgments. Applied ethics covers areas such as bioethics, business/corporate ethics, development ethics, and environmental ethics. However, discriminating between the normative and applied ethics is getting increasingly difficult.

META-ETHICS

Meta-ethics is that branch of ethics that deals with the nature of goodness and badness and what it is to be morally right or wrong instead of dealing with what acts or what kind of acts are good or bad, right or wrong, and thus it is regarded as the most abstract area of moral philosophy.

Meta-ethics is often associated with philosophical ethics, but in this specific sense, it became more noticeable with G.E. Moore's Principia Ethica from 1903. In Principia Ethica, he first describes about the naturalistic fallacy. In his open-question argument, Moore discarded naturalism in ethics. This caused the thinkers to reconsider the second order questions about ethics. The Scottish philosopher David Hume had expressed a similar opinion on the difference between facts and values, previously.

The biggest dispute in metaethics might be the difference of opinion that divides ***moral realists*** and ***antirealists.***

Moral realists are of the opinion that moral facts are objective facts that already exist in the world. Things termed as good or bad do not depend on our interpretation, and then we appear and discover morality.

Antirealists on the contrary are of the opinion that without our involvement in their interpretation, moral facts are non-existent in the world and that the facts about us determine the morality. Holding this viewpoint, morality is something, which is invented and not something that is discovered.

The disagreement between ***cognitivism and noncognitivism*** is quite close in relation to that of moral realists and antirealists..

Cognitivism holds the value that moral statements express the world. If a person considers lying as wrong, then in the cognitivist' viewpoint that person has said something about the world, and that person has assigned a property wrongness to an act of lying. It is an objective matter that whether lying has that property, and so the statement made by the person might objectively either true or false.

Non-cognitivists holds a contrary opinion and do not approve this analysis of moral statements. From the view point of noncognitivists, someone making moral statements are expressing their feelings or telling people what to do and are not describing the world. Non-cognitivism holds the opinion that moral statements are non-descriptive and are neither true nor false. It relates that for something to be true, it is described as being the way that it is, and to be false it is described as being other than the way that it is; statements that are not descriptive cannot be either.

NORMATIVE ETHICS

Normative ethics is that branch of philosophical ethics, which analyses the ethical acts. It enquires into the set of questions that emerge in view of how one ought to act. It is dissimilar to meta-ethics because it analyses the criteria for the rightness and wrongness of actions. Meta-ethics in comparison analyses the meaning of moral language and the metaphysics of moral facts. Normative ethics also differs from descriptive ethics, as the latter is an empirical study of people's moral beliefs. In other words, descriptive ethics would focus on determining the proportion of people who believe killing to be always wrong, whereas normative ethics focuses on whether holding such a belief is correct. Thus, normative ethics is sometimes referred to as prescriptive, rather than descriptive. However, the nature of moral facts could be both descriptive and prescriptive at the same time on certain versions of the meta-ethical view called moral realism.

APPLIED ETHICS

Applied ethics is that branch of philosophy that is concerned with application of ethical theory to real-life situations. The discipline is bifurcated into many specialized domains, such as engineering ethics, bioethics, geo ethics, public service ethics and business ethics.

Applied ethics finds usage in some facets of determining public policy, and is also used by individuals facing difficult decisions. It addresses questions such as: "What are human rights, and how do we determine them?" "Is affirmative action right or wrong?" "Is getting an abortion immoral?" "Is euthanasia immoral?" "Do animals also have rights?" and "Do individuals have the right to self-determine?" A more explicit question could be "If someone else can make better out of his/her life than I can, is it then morally justified to sacrifice myself for them if needed?" These questions are necessary to balance law, politics, and the practice of arbitration. In fact, no common assumptions could be made of all participants. Hence, it is a pre-requirement to formulate the questions prior to rights balancing. However, it is not necessary that all questions studied in applied ethics concern public policy only. For example, To make ethical judgments regarding questions such as, "Is lying always wrong?" and, "If not, in which situations is it permitted?" Generally, people feel more comfortable with dichotomies (two opposites). However, in ethics, there are multifaceted issue to look out for and the best-proposed actions should address many diverse areas at the same time. While making ethical decisions, answers are almost never a "yes or no", "right or wrong" statement. Many buttons are pushed to improve the overall condition so that it does not benefit any particular faction.

3 CHAPTER

Philosophical and Psychological Basis of Ethics

The field of ethics or moral philosophy is that segment of philosophy, which includes standardizing, safeguarding and proposing concepts of right and wrong conduct. Modern philosophers, in general, bifurcate ethical theories into three general subject areas: meta-ethics, normative ethics and applied ethics. *Meta-ethics* analyses the origination of our ethical principles, and the meaning they carry. Are they simply social inventions? Do they involve more than expressions of our individual emotions? Meta-ethical answers to these questions are concerned on the issues of universal truths, the will of God, the role of reason in ethical judgments, and the meaning of ethical terms themselves. *Normative ethics* are concerned with a more practical task to arrive at moral standards that determine right and wrong behaviour. This may involve formulating the good habits for us to acquire, the duties to be followed by us, or the consequences of our behaviour on others. Finally, *applied ethics* is concerned with analysing specific controversial issues that includes abortion, infanticide, capital punishment, environmental concerns, animal rights, homosexuality, or nuclear war.

Discussions in applied ethics make use of conceptual tools of meta-ethics and normative ethics to decide on these controversial matters. The thin lines of differences between meta-ethics, normative ethics and applied ethics are often indistinct. For example, the issue of abortion comes under applied ethics as it involves a peculiar type of controversial behaviour. However, it also relies on more general standardizing principles, such as the right of self-rule and the right to life, which are litmus tests to determine the morality of that procedure. Meta-ethical issues such as, "where do rights come from?" and "what kind of beings have rights?" are also the factors on which this issue depends.

META-ETHICS

"Meta" is the term that refers to *after* or *beyond*, and, accordingly, the concept of meta-ethics includes a removed or panoramic view of the entire project of ethics. Meta-ethics may be referred to as the study of the origin and meaning of ethical concepts. The field of meta-ethics in comparison to normative ethics and applied ethics is the least accurately defined area of moral philosophy and covers issues from moral semantics to moral epistemology. However, two issues, metaphysical issues and psychological issues, are prominent. While the former is concerned withexistence of morality in relation to humans, whether morality exists independently of humans, the latter is concerned with the underlying mental basis of moral judgments and conduct of humans.

a. Metaphysical Issues: Objectivism and Relativism

Metaphysics is that branch of philosophy which studies about the kinds of things existing in the universe. The universe consists of some things in physical form, such as rocks, while some other things of nonphysical nature, such as thoughts, spirits, and gods. The metaphysical component of metaethics is concerned with finding out particularly about the moral values, whether these exist as eternal truths in a spirit-like domain, or simply human conventions. Discussions on this topic will take two general directions, *other-worldly* and *this-worldly*.

People advocating for the other-worldly view generally hold the moral values to be objective in the sense, existing in a spirit-like domain beyond subjective human conventions. They hold moral values to be absolute, or eternal, which are inalterable as well as universal to that extent as they are applicable to all rational creatures around the world and throughout time. Plato, inspired by the field of mathematics, was the most suitable proponent of this view. For example, if we consider numbers and mathematical relations, such as $1 + 1 = 2$, they are timeless concepts that are unalterable and are applicable everywhere in the universe. Numbers are not invented by humans and cannot be changed by them. This eternal character of mathematics was explained by Plato who stated them to be *abstract entities* existing in a spirit-like realm. He noticed moral values also to be absolute truths, and hence considered them as abstract, spirit-like entities. According to Pluto, in this sense, moral values are spiritual *objects*. All moral principles were commonly grouped together by the medieval philosophers under the heading of "eternal law", which were also frequently seen as spirit-like objects. Instead of spirit-like objects, they were described as spirit-like *relationships* by Samuel Clarke, the 17th century British philosopher. Though, in both the cases, they exist in a sprit-like realm. Another other-worldly approach considers the metaphysical status of morality to be *divine commands* that are issued from God's will. It is also called as *voluntarism* or divine command theory. The belief of an all-powerful God controlling everything in the universe inspired this notion. Proponents of this view claim that God simply wills things, and they become reality. He wills the existence of physical world, infusion of human life into existence, and all moral values into existence. People advocating this view, such as medieval philosopher William of Ockham, are of the belief that moral principles are wills of God and exist in God's mind as commands, such as "murder is wrong". God by implanting the humans with moral intuitions informs them of these commands or reveals these commands in scripture.

The second this-worldly approach to the metaphysical status of morality believes in following the sceptical philosophical tradition and denies the objective status of moral values, such as that enunciated by Greek philosopher Sextus Empiricus. According to the facts, skeptics did not rule out the existence of moral values themselves, but only refused to accept the existence of values as spirit-like objects, or as divine commands in the mind of God. According to them, moral values are purely human inventions, a position that has been acknowledged as *moral relativism*. Moral relativism is divided into two distinct forms, *individual relativism* and *cultural relativism*. The first approach holds the view that individual people create their own moral standards. Friedrich Nietzsche, for example, made an argument that the superhuman builds his or her morality distinguishing from and in response to the slave-like value system of the masses. The second approach holds the view that morality is based in the approval of one's society instead of individual preferences of people. Proponents of this view are Sextus, followed by Michel Montaigne and William Graham Sumner in more recent centuries. This-worldly approaches to the metaphysical status of morality follows skepticism and relativism and also refuse to accept the absolute and universal nature of morality and instead believes in moral values differing from society to society throughout time and throughout the globe. They often try to prove their point by referring to examples of values differing greatly from one culture to another, such as attitudes about homosexuality, polygamy and human sacrifice.

b. Psychological Issues in Meta-ethics

Another area of meta-ethics takes into consideration the psychological basis of our moral judgements and conduct, specifically realizing what motivates us to be moral. A person might further dig into this subject by asking the simple question, "Why be moral?" Getting aware of basic moral standards, such as do not kill and do not steal, does not ensure that one would be psychologically compelled to act on them. Responses to the question "Why be moral?" may vary just as to avoid punishment, to attain happiness, to gain praise, to be dignified or to fit in with society.

I. Egoism and Altruism

Selfishness inherent in humans is another significant area concerning the moral psychology. According to Thomas Hobbes, the seventeenth century British philosopher, selfish desires of humans are the root cause of many, if not all, of their actions. Even the actions considered selfless, such as donating to charity, have hidden selfish motives, such as experiencing power over other people. This view is acknowledged as *psychological egoism*, which asserts that self-oriented interests ultimately act as motivating force behind all human actions. Another view that is closely related to psychological egoism is called *psychological hedonism*, which considers pursuit of *pleasure* as the particular driving force behind all of our actions. Joseph Butler, the eighteenth century British philosopher, agreed that much of our conduct is the outcome of our instinctive selfishness and pleasure-seeking outlook. However, Butler argued that humans also possess an innate psychological capacity to show kindness to others. This view is referred to as *psychological altruism* and asserts that instinctive benevolence stimulates at least some of our actions.

II. Emotion and Reason

Another area of moral psychology calls for a dispute in relation to the role of reason to motivate moral actions. If a person makes a statement "abortion is morally wrong," then it is to be find out whether he is making a rational assessment or only expressing his feelings. David Hume, the eighteenth century British philosopher, made supportive argument favouring one side of the dispute that moral assessments involve our emotions and not our reason. One can accumulate all the reasons one want, but that will not be sufficient in constituting a moral assessment. Making a moral pronouncement require a precise emotional reaction. Reason might be useful in giving us the appropriate data, but, in Hume's words, "reason is, and ought to be, the slave of the passions." Taking inspiration from Hume's anti-rationalist views, some twentieth century philosophers, in particular A. J. Ayer, similarly refused to consider moral assessments as factual descriptions. For example, the statement "it is good to donate to charity" may seem to be a factual description about charity, but in reality it is not. On the contrary, a moral utterance like this takes two things into consideration. First, the speaker expressing his or her personal feelings of approving the charitable donations and basically saying "Hooray for charity!" As the person expresses his or her emotions about some specific behaviour, this is called the *emotive* element to such an extent. Second, the speaker is imposing his will to donate to charity by essentially giving the command, "Donate to charity!" It is known as the *prescriptive* element in the sense that the person is prescribing some particular behaviour.

Moving forward since Hume's days, more rational-minded philosophers have argued about moral assessments to be acts of reasonindeed and denied the emotive theories of ethics (see non-cognitivism in ethics). The case in point is of Immanuel Kant, the eighteenth century German philosopher. He made the argument that even though emotional factors frequently influence our conduct, inspite of that we should resist that kind of sway. Rather than emotions, only reason, when free from emotions and desires, prompts true moral action. Contrary to the emotivist and prescriptivist theories of Ayer and others, a recent rationalist approach, offered by Kurt Baier (1958), was proposed. Baier, when making moral choices, emphasizes more generally on the reasoning and argumentation process that takes place. All of the moral choices a person makes are, or at least can be, supported with some reason or justification. A person making a claim that it is wrong to steal someone's car, should be able to put forth some kind of arguments to justify his or her claim. For example, argumentsmay be made that stealing Smith's car is wrong since she would get upset because of this, her ownership rights would be violated, or thief would be at a risk of getting caught. In Baier's opinion, providing the best reasons in support of one course of action versus anotherlead to proper moral decision making.

III. Male and Female Morality

One more area of moral psychology emphasizes on whether there is a precisely female approach to ethics that is based in the psychological differences between men and women. Discussions of this issue emphasizes on two claims: (1) male-centred traditional morality and (2) a unique female perspective of the world that could be moulded into a value theory. Many feminist philosophers are of the opinion that traditional morality is male-centered since it is shaped after practices that have been traditionally male-dominated, such as acquiring property, governing societies and engaging in business contracts. The inflexible systems of rules that were formulated to run the trade and government were later adopted as models for the introduction of equally rigid systems of moral conventions, such as lists of rights and duties. On the contrary, the role of women was limited to traditionally having a nurturing role by raising children and overseeing domestic life. Though, these exercises demanded more spontaneous and creative action but required less rule following. The woman's experience when used as a model for moral theory provides the basis of morality to be spontaneously caring for others as would be appropriate in each unique circumstance. This model involves the agent as a part of the situation and assigns him the role to act caringly within that context. On the contrary, in the male-modelled morality, agent is a mechanical actor who performs his required duty, but can be less attached and unaffected by the situation. The feminist ethicists suggest that the traditional male-modelled moral systems should either be replaced by care-based approach to morality or be supplemented by them.

NORMATIVE ETHICS

Normative ethics is concerned with attaining moral standards that influence right and wrong conduct. Theoretically, it is exploring for an ideal litmus test of appropriate behaviour. A classic example of a normative principle is the Golden Rule, which says that we should do to others what we would want others to do to us. It would be wrong for me to steal the car of my neighbour if I want my car not be stolen by my neighbour. Similarly, I should help in feeding starving people since I would want the same act of generosity from people if I were starving. Applying the same reasoning, the right or wrongful conduct for any possible action could be theoretically determined. Hence, on the basis of the Golden Rule, it would be wrong for a person to lie, harass, victimize, assault, or kill others. The Golden Rule, which lays down a *single principle* to judge all the actions, is one example of a normative theory. In the same manner, other normative theories emphasize on a *set* of foundational principles, or a set of good character traits.

Normative ethics primarily believes in only *one* ultimate criterion of moral conduct, whether it is a single rule or a set of principles. Three strategies to be taken notice of include (1) virtue theories, (2) duty theories and (3) consequentialist theories.

a. Virtue Theories

Many philosophers express similar opinion about morality consisting of following precisely defined rules of conduct, such as "do not kill," or "do not steal." Theoretically, people must learn these rules, and ensure that each of their actions meet the requirements of the rules. On the other hand, virtue ethics emphasizes more on the importance of developing *good habits of character*, such as benevolence (see moral character), and less on learning rules. Having acquired benevolence, a person will habitually act in a benign way. Historically acknowledged as being among the oldest normative traditions in Western philosophy, virtue theory has its roots in ancient Greek civilization. Four virtues in particular, which were later known as *cardinal virtues*, were prioritized by Plato to follow. Cardinal virtues include wisdom, courage, temperance and justice. Other important virtues that should be followed are self-respect, fortitude, generosity, good temper and sincerity. Virtue theorists not only advocate for adopting good habits of character, but also hold the belief that one should restrain from acquiring bad character traits, or *vices*, such as cowardice, injustice, insensibility and vanity. Virtue theory puts emphasis on moral education from the initial stage itself since virtuous character traits are developed in one's youth. Thus, it is the responsibility of the adults to instil virtues in the young.

According to Aristotle, virtues are good habits, acquiring which helps to regulate our emotions. For example, people should develop the virtue of courage to allay their natural feelings of fear. This helps them to stay firm when faced with danger. Aristotle analysed 11 specific virtues and argued that most virtues lie in the middle of more extreme character traits. Consider an example of courage, a person not having enough courage develops the tendency of cowardice, which is a vice. A person having too much courage also develops a tendency towards rashness, which is also a vice. From the point of view of Aristotle, finding the perfect mean between extreme character traits is not an easy task to perform. In reality, our reason provides the assistance to do this task. Following Aristotle, medieval theologians incorporated three Christian ones, or *theological virtues*: faith, hope and charity in the Greek lists of virtues. The ascension of alternative moral theories resulted in the declining of interest in virtue theory that was there through the middle ages. Virtue theory drew significant attention from philosophers in the mid-twentieth century, who were of the opinion that more modern approaches to ethical theories were misled for focusing too much on rules and actions, rather than on pure character traits. The primary role of virtues in moral theory was well defended by Alasdaire MacIntyre (1984) who argued that virtues are based in and emerge from within social traditions.

b. Duty Theories

It is a common belief among many people who feel that as human beings they have clear responsibilities to care for their children, and to not commit murder. Duty theories, also called as *deontological*, evaluate morality on specific, foundational principles of obligation. The term *deontological* is derived from the Greek word *deon*, or duty, and these theories are called so by virtue of the foundational nature of our duty or obligation. These principles are obligatory in nature, irrespective of the consequences that might follow from our actions and, therefore, they are also called *non-consequentialist*. For example, even if a person stands to gain significant benefits by not taking care of his or her children, such as financial savings, it is wrong for him or her to not care for children. Four key duty theories have been determined by the philosophers.

Samuel Pufendorf, the seventeenth century German philosopher, advocated for the *first* theory and classified dozens of duties under three headings: duties to God, duties to oneself and duties to others. According to him, one should perform two kinds of duties towards God:

- A theoretical duty to know the existence and nature of God.
- A practical duty to both inwardly and outwardly worship God.
- Similarly, there are two kinds of duties with regard to humans for themselves also. These are as follows:
- Duties of the soul, which is concerned with developing one's skills and talents.
- Duties of the body, which is concerned with not harming our bodies, as we might through gluttony or drunkenness, and not killing oneself.

In relation to people's duties towards others, Pufendorf classified them as absolute duties, which are universally binding on people, and conditional duties, arising out of the result of contracts between people. Absolute duties are of three types given as follows:

- Avoid wronging others
- Treat people as equals
- Promote the good of others

Conditional duties take into account various types of agreements, the main among them is the duty to keep one's promises.

Rights theory is regarded as the *second* duty-based approach to ethics. Usually, a "right" is defined as a justified claim made by a person against another person for intruding upon his or her rights so as to ensure that rights of the former is not harmed by the latter (see also human rights). There exists a relationship between rights and duties and the two are related in such a way that the rights of one person becomes the duties of another person. Consider the situation when a person has a right to payment of $10 by Smith, then it becomes the duty of Smith to pay the person $10. This is referred to as the correlativity of rights and duties. John Locke, the seventeenth century British philosopher, gave the most influential early account of rights theory, arguing that the laws of nature mandate that one should avoid harming anyone's life, health, liberty or possessions. According to Locke, these are the natural rights granted by God to humans. After Locke's version of rights theory, the United States Declaration of Independence authored by Thomas Jefferson acknowledges three basic rights: life, liberty and the pursuit of happiness. It was further advocated by Jefferson and others rights theorists to derive other more specific rights from these, including the rights of property, movement, speech and religious expression. Traditionally, moral rights include four features. First, rights are *natural* to such an extent as they are neither invented nor created by governments. Second, they are *universal* to such an extent as they do not vary from country to country. Third, irrespective of gender, race, or handicap, rights are the same for all people, and hence they are *equal* in the sense. Fourth, rights are *inalienable* as these cannot be handed over from one person to another person, such as by selling themselves into slavery.

Kant proposed a *third* duty-based theory, which puts emphasis on a single principle of duty. Kant getting inspired from Pufendorf supported the view that people have moral duties towards themselves and others, such as developing one's talents, and keeping their promises to others. However, according to Kant a more fundamental principle of duty is there which encompasses our particular duties. He named a lone, self-evident principle of reason as "categorical imperative." According to him, a categorical imperative is basically different from hypothetical imperatives that are associated with some personal desire that one have, for example, "If a person wants to get a good job, then he or she ought to go to college." On the contrary, a categorical imperative merely authorizes an action, regardless of one's personal desires, such as "You ought to do X." At least four versions of the categorical imperative were proposed by Kant. Among these, one is especially direct: Treat people as an end, and never as a means to an end. It implies that people should always be treated with dignity, and should never be used as mere instruments. According to Kant, people are treated as an end by a person whenever his or her actions towards someone reflect the inherent value of that person. Donations for charitable causes, for example, is morally correct because this recognizes the inherent value of the recipient. On the other hand, a person is treated as a means to an end whenever that person is used as a tool to achieve something else. For example, it is not acceptable that a person steals somebody's car since it would be treated as a means to his or her own happiness. The morality of actions affecting us individually are also regulated by the categorical imperative. For example, suicide would be wrong because he or she would be treating their life as a means to the alleviation of their misery. From the point of view of Kant, the morality of all actions can be determined by invoking this single principle of duty.

W.D. Ross, the British philosopher proposed a *fourth* and more recent duty-based theory, which emphasizes *prima facie* duties. Following his seventeenth and eighteenth century counterparts, Ross argues that people's duties are "part of the fundamental nature of the universe." However, the list of duties provided by Ross is much shorter, which he believes reflects people's actual moral convictions, given as follows:

- *Fidelity*: the duty to keep promises
- *Reparation*: the duty to make up for others when we harm them
- *Gratitude*: the duty to thank the people who help us
- *Justice*: the duty to acknowledge merit
- *Beneficence*: the duty to make the conditions of others better
- *Self-improvement*: the duty to enhance our virtue and intelligence
- *Non-maleficence*: the duty to not impart injury to others

According to Ross, situations will arise when we will have to choose between two conflicting duties. Consider an example when a person borrow his neighbour's gun, promising him to return it when he asks for it. One day, out of temper, the neighbour pounds on his door asking for the gun so that he can take vengeance on someone. The point of conflict arises here that on the one hand, the duty of fidelity obligates him to return the gun to the neighbour while on the other hand, the duty of non-maleficence obligates me to avoid harming others and thus not return the gun. From the viewpoint of Ross, he will intuitively know which is his actual duty out of these duties, and which is his apparent or prima facie duty. In this particular case, his duty of non-maleficence emerges as his actual duty and he should not return the gun.

c. Consequentialist Theories

It is natural for us to decide upon our moral responsibility by weighing the consequences of our actions. According to consequentialism, a cost-benefit analysis of the consequences of an action could help in determining the correct moral conduct.

Consequentialism: A morally right action would have more favourable consequences than unfavourable ones.

Consequentialist normative principles demand that people should first tally both the good and bad consequences of an action. Second, they must then decide whether the total good consequences overcome the total bad consequences. An action is considered morally appropriate if the good consequences are greater, whereas it is considered morally inappropriate if the bad consequences are greater. As the end result of the action is the sole determining factor of morality in consequentialist theories, these are also known as *teleological* theories, derived from the Greek word *telos*, or end.

Consequentialist theories gained popularity in the eighteenth century by philosophers searching for a quick way to morally assess an action by appealing to experience, instead of invoking gut intuitions or long lists of questionable duties. In reality, the most desirable feature of consequentialism is that it is appealing to publicly observable consequences of actions. Consequentialism has most of its versions more precisely formulated than the general principle mentioned above. Particularly, by comparing these consequentialist theories with each other, it can be determined that which consequences for affected groups of people are relevant. Consequentialism could be further classified into three subdivisions:

- *Ethical Egoism*: In ethical egoism, if the consequences of an action are more favourable than unfavourable *only to the agent* performing the action, the action is considered morally right.
- *Ethical Altruism*: In ethical altruism, if the consequences of an action are more favourable than unfavourable *to everyone except the agent*, the action is considered morally right.
- *Utilitarianism*: In utilitarianism, if the consequences of that action are more favourable than unfavourable *to everyone*, the action is considered morally right.

The area of emphasis of all these theories is on the consequences of actions for different groups of people. However, similar to all normative theories, the three aforementioned theories are rivals of each other, yielding different conclusions. Let us take the following example. In a developing country, a woman came as a tourist. She took a taxi and while she was traveling through the country, she witnessed that a car in front of her skidded on the road and rolled over several times. Immediately assessing the situation, she asked the taxi driver to pull over to assist, but, contrary to her expectations, the driver accelerated nervously past the scene of the accident. After driving a few miles down the road, the driver explained to the tourist his helplessness that in his country if someone assists an accident victim, the police often holds the assisting person accountable for the accident itself. In case of death of such victims, the police could held the assisting person responsible for the death. The driver further explained to her that the road accident victims were therefore generally left unattended and often died from exposure to the country's harsh desert conditions. From the point of view of the principle of ethical egoism, in this situation, the only concern of woman would be in the consequences of her attempted assistance as *she* would be affected. Obviously, the morally appropriate choice would be the decision to drive on. Taking into account, the principle of ethical altruism, only the consequences of her action would be of concern to her, as *others* are affected, particularly the accident victim. Analysing only these consequences reveals that the morally correct choice would be to assist the victim, irrespective of the negative consequences that follow for her. Taking into account the principle of utilitarianism, she must consider the consequences for both herself and the victim. The outcome here is less clear, and the woman need to precisely calculate the overall pros and cons arising out of her action.

I. Types of Utilitarianism

One of the earliest fully developed systems of utilitarianism was presented by Jeremy Bentham. The two features of his theory are noteworthy and presented as follows. The first aspect of the theory as proposed by Bentham was that we tally the consequences of each action we perform and thereby determine on a case by case basis whether an action is morally right or wrong. This feature of Bentham's theory is acknowledged as *act-utilitarianism*. The second aspect of the theory as proposed by Bentham was that we tally the pleasure and pain which results from our actions. According to Bentham, the only consequences that matter in determining whether our conduct is moral are pleasure and pain. This facet of Bentham's theory is acknowledged as *hedonistic utilitarianism*. According to critics, both of these aspects have limitations.

First, in accordance with act-utilitarianism, wasting time on leisure activities such as watching television would be morally wrong, because our time could be spent in ways that brought out a greater social benefit, such as charity work. However, restraining leisure activities does not seem reasonable. More importantly, act-utilitarianism states that peculiar acts of torture or slavery would be morally permissible in case the social benefit of these actions outweighed their harm. *Rule-utilitarianism*, which is a revised version of utilitarianism, deals with these problems. The rule-utilitarianism approach states that for a behavioural code or rule to be morally right, the consequences of adopting that rule should be more favourable than unfavourable to everyone. Contrary to act utilitarianism, which takes into account each particular action and weighs the consequences of each one of them, rule-utilitarianism takes into account only morality of moral rules and offers a litmus test only for them, such as "stealing is wrong." Clearly, there are more favourable consequences than unfavourable consequences for everyone when a rule is adopted against theft. The same approach is applicable for moral rules against lying or murdering. For evaluating conduct, rule-utilitarianism offers a three-tiered method. When a specific action violates a moral rule, it is judged wrong, for example, stealing somebody's car, which defies the moral rule against theft. In turn, adopting this rule against theft is of favourable consequences for everyone and, thus, is morally binding to everyone. John Stuart Mill considers utilitarianism as rule-oriented.

Second, hedonistic utilitarianism considers pleasurable consequences as the only factors that matter, morally speaking. However, this appears to be quite restrictive since it overlooks other morally important consequences that are not necessarily pleasing or painful. Take for instance acts that promote loyalty and friendship; though such acts are valued but they are not always pleasing. G.E. Moore came out with another theory *ideal utilitarianism* to overcome such problems. It considers tallying any consequence that is intuitively recognized as good or bad, and not simply as pleasurable or painful. Moreover, R.M. Hare also came out with *preference utilitarianism*, which considers tallying any consequence that fulfils our preferences.

II. Ethical Egoism and Social Contract Theory

It is already known that Hobbes was an advocate of the meta-ethical theory of psychological egoism according to which all of our actions are selfishly motivated. On that basis, a normative theory was developed by Hobbes known as social contract theory, which is a type of rule-ethical-egoism. In Hobbes opinion, for purely selfish reasons, it is better for a person to live in a world which is run with moral rules than one without moral rules. Without moral rules, a person may be subjected to the whims of other people's selfish interests and people face continual risk of their property, their families, and even their lives. Hence, selfishness alone could be a motivating factor for each person to adopt a basic set of rules, which allows for a civilized community. Keeping with the expectations, these rules would impose various constraints to prevent lying, stealing and killing. However, to ensure the safety of people, it is necessary to enforce these rules. As man by nature is selfish and will always look for an opportunity to plunder the property of other people once they are vulnerable or not vigilant enough. Every person will feel a sense of insecurity from the person living nearby. Hence, to safeguard their selfish interests, humans formulated a means of enforcing these rules by creating a policing agency that punishes us on violation of these rules.

APPLIED ETHICS

The analysis of specific, controversial moral issues such as abortion, animal rights or euthanasia comes under the branch of ethics known as applied ethics. In the past few years, applied ethical issues have been bifurcated to convenient groups such as medical ethics, business ethics, environmental ethics and sexual ethics. In a broad sense, two aspects are required for an issue to be considered an "applied ethical issue". First, there should be some sort of controversy attached to the issue so that there are significant groups of people both in favour of and against the issue at hand. Take for instance the issue of drive-by shooting. This is not considered an applied ethical issue because everyone has the same view that this practice is grossly immoral. On the contrary, the issue of gun control would be considered an applied ethical issue because there are significant groups of people both in favour of and against gun control.

Another necessary condition for an issue to be considered an applied ethical issue is that it must be a precisely moral issue. Every day, the media keeps us abreast with a lot of sensitive issues such as affirmative action policies, capitalistic versus socialistic business practices, gays in the military, involuntary commitment of the mentally impaired, energy conservation and public versus private health care systems. Although some or other kind of controversy is associated with these issues and they have an important impact on society, all of them cannot be considered as moral issues. Few of them are only issues of social policy. The social policy is devised with the objective to help make a given society run efficiently and thus various conventions are framed, such as traffic laws, tax laws and zoning codes. On the other hand, moral issues are not limited to individual societies but are concerned with more universally obligatory practices, such as our duty to avoid lying. The issues of social policy and morality often coincide, as the case of murder which is both socially prohibited and immoral. However, there are often dissimilarities between the two groups of issues. For example, sexual promiscuity is considered immoral by many people, but they may not advocated for devising social policies that regulate sexual conduct, or laws punishing people for promiscuity. In the same manner, certain social policies prohibited residents in certain neighbourhoods from having yard sales. However, as far as the neighbours remain unaffected, there is nothing immoral in itself about a resident having a yard sale in one of these neighbourhoods. Hence, an issue should not only be one of mere social policy but morally relevant also in order to meet the requirement of being an applied ethical issue.

In principle, it should be easy to resolve specific applied ethical issues. Take for instance the issue of abortion, where we would simply refer to our normative principle of choice, such as act-utilitarianism, to determine its morality. In case, carrying out an abortion produces greater benefit than harm, then, applying the theory of act-utilitarianism, one could find out that having the abortion would be morally acceptable. However, hundreds of rival normative principles are there to choose from, many among which yield opposite conclusions. It becomes very difficult to use a single decisive procedure for determining the morality of a specific issue because of the deadlock arising between conflicting theories in normative ethics. This stalemate could be resolved by consulting several representative normative principles on a given issue and determine where the weight of the evidence lies.

a. Normative Principles in Applied Ethics

It is quite a challenging task to prepare a short list of representative normative principles. The chosen principles must not be too barely centred, such as a version of act-egoism that might concentrate only on the short-term benefits arising out of an action. It is necessary that the principles hold merit from the point of view of the individuals on both sides of an applied ethical issue. Hence, principles that appeal to obligation to God are generally not referred to since this would have no effect on a nonbeliever involved in the argument. The principles which are most often involved in applied ethical discussions are as follows:

- *Personal benefit*: This principle acknowledges the extent to which an activity produces beneficial results for the individual in question.
- *Social benefit*: This principle acknowledges the extent to which an activity produces beneficial results for society.

- *Principle of benevolence*: This principle helps those in need.
- *Principle of paternalism*: This principle assists others in following their best interests when they cannot do to themselves.
- *Principle of harm*: This principle does not harm others.
- *Principle of honesty*: This principle does not deceive others.
- *Principle of lawfulness*: This principle does not violate the law.
- *Principle of autonomy*: This principle recognizes a person's sovereignty over his/her activity or physical body.
- *Principle of justice*: This principle recognizes a person's right to due process, fair compensation for harm done, and fair distribution of benefits.
- *Rights*: This principle recognizes a person's rights to life, information, privacy, free expression and safety.

The aforementioned principles correspond to a range of customary normative principles and are obtained from both consequentialist and duty-based approaches. The initial two principles, personal benefit and social benefit, are consequentialist because they invoke the outcomes of an action as it influences the individual or society. The rest of the principles are duty-based. The principles of benevolence, paternalism, harm, honesty and lawfulness are based on a person's obligation towards others. The principles of autonomy, justice and the various rights depend on moral rights.

A living case will help clarify the role of these principles in an applied ethical discussion. A baby with severe mental and physical disabilities was born to a couple from Bloomington, Indiana in 1982. Among other complications, the stomach of the newborn baby, known as Baby Doe, was detached from its throat and was thus unfit to get sustenance. In spite of the fact that this stomach deformation was correctable through surgery, the couple did not have any desire to bring up a badly disabled child and hence denied it surgery, food, and water. Local courts upheld the decision of the parents, and Baby Doe died after six days. The question arises here whether the corrective surgery should have been performed for Baby Doe. Arguments in support of corrective surgery were inferred from the new-born baby's right to life and the principle of paternalism which specifies that we should follow the best interests of others when they are unequipped of doing so themselves. Arguments against corrective surgery arise from the individual and social damage which would be cause due to such surgery. Even if Baby Doe had survived, it would have been living a poor quality of life and anyhow it presumably would have died at an early age. Similarly, from the parent's viewpoint, the child's survival would have been a substantial emotional and financial burden. Taking into consideration both sides of the issue, the parents and the courts concluded that the arguments against surgery were more substantial than the arguments for surgery. To begin with, relinquishing surgery seemed to be in the best interests of the child, given the low quality of life it would live. Second, the status of child's right to life was not clear given the severity of its mental disability. For, to have moral rights, merely having a human body is not enough, an individual must also have presence of certain cognitive functions. The issue that needs addressing here includes what is often referred to as moral personhood, and is vital to many applied ethical discussions.

b. Issues in Applied Ethics

As noticed, there are numerous disputable issues examined by ethicists in present days, few of which are briefly mentioned as follows:

Biomedical ethics concentrates on an array of issues which emerge in clinical settings. Health care workers are in a bizarre position of ceaselessly managing circumstances of life and death. No wonder, then, that medical ethics issues are more intense and varying in nature than other areas of applied ethics. Prenatal problems emerge about the morality of surrogate mothering, genetic handling of foetuses, the status of unused frozen embryos, and abortion. Various issues emerge about patient rights and physician's obligations, for instance, the secrecy of the patient's records and the physician's obligation to reveal the truth to the dying patients. The AIDS crisis has brought up the particular issues of the compulsory screening of all patients for AIDS, and whether physicians can decline the treatmentof AIDS patients. Added issues concern therapeutic experimentation on humans, the morality of instinctive commitment, and the privileges of the mentally impaired. At last, end of life issues emerge about the morality of suicide, the reasonability of suicide intervention, physician-assisted suicide, and euthanasia.

The area of *business ethics* analyses moral disputes concerned with the social obligations of capitalist business processes, the moral status of corporate entities, deceptive advertising, insider trading, fundamental employee rights, job discrimination, affirmative action, drug testing and whistle blowing.

Issues in *environmental ethics* frequently covers business and medical issues. These incorporate the rights of animals, the morality of animal experimentation, preservation of endangered species, controlling pollution, administration of environmental assets, whether ecosystems are entitled to direct moral consideration, and human's responsibility towards future generations.

Disputable issues of *sexual morality* incorporate monogamy versus polygamy, sexual relations without love, homosexual relations, and extramarital intimacies.

In the end, there are issues of *social morality* which analyse capital punishment, nuclear war, gun control, the recreational use of medications, welfare privileges, and racism.

Fields of Application of Ethics

4 CHAPTER

BIOETHICS

Bioethics is the investigation of disputable morals caused due to advances in biology and medicine. Bioethicists deal with the moral queries emerging in the relationships among life sciences, biotechnology, medicine, politics, law, and philosophy.

It additionally incorporates primary care ethics which is the study of the routine choices that primary care clinicians make, for example, the time to spend with a particular patient, the way to accommodate their particular values and those of their patients, when and where to specify or examine, to the ways to maintain confidentiality when dealing with patients, relatives and third parties.

Bioethics similarly needs to treat rising biotechnologies influencing basic biology and future generation. These advancements include cloning, gene therapy, human genetic engineering, bioethics and life in space, and control of basic biology through altered DNA, etc.

Numerous religious associations have their own histories of investigations into bioethical issues and have devised rules and guidelines on the way to handle these issues from within the perspective of their particular beliefs.

BUSINESS ETHICS

Business ethics also known as corporate ethics is a type of applied ethics or professional ethics that investigates ethical principles and moral or ethical problems that emerge in a business environment. It is applicable to all facets of business conduct and is of relevance to the conduct of people and whole institutions.

Business ethics additionally has both prescriptive and descriptive properties. The field is basically normative in terms of corporate practice and career specialization. Academicians endeavouring to realize business behaviour utilize descriptive methods.

The scope and amount of business ethical issues mirrors the communication of profit-maximizing behaviour with non-economic concerns.

There was a dramatic rise towards interest in business ethics among academicians or corporations during the 1980s and 1990s. Take for example, the present scenario where most major corporations elevate their dedication with regard to non-economic values under headings, for example, ethics codes and social responsibility charters. Governments utilize laws and regulations to specify business conduct in what they realize to be advantageous directions. Ethics implicitly controls territories and particulars of conduct that lie outside governmental control. The rise of big corporations with restricted relationships and sensitivity to the societies in which they work increased the growth of formal ethics authorities.

ORGANIZATIONAL ETHICS

The ethical approach adopted by an organization is known as organizational ethics. An organization use this approach to respond to an internal or external stimulus. Organizational ethics is mutually dependent with the organizational culture. In spite of its similarity to both organizational behaviour (OB) and business ethics, organizational ethics is neither OB nor exclusively business ethics, which includes corporate governance and corporate ethics. Organizational ethics convey the values of an institution to its workers and/or other entities regardless of governmental and/or regulatory laws.

An organization takes shapes when people with different interests and varying backgrounds combine on a common platform and work united to achieve predefined goals and objectives. An array of standards that is utilized to provide directions to the organization in its decisions, programs, and policies within an organization is known as a code of ethics.

A minimum of four elements are required to accomplish the objective of creating an ethical culture and conduct of employees inside an organization. These elements are as follows:

- A written code of ethics and standards, i.e. ethical code
- Ethics training for managers, executives and employees
- The availability of ethical situational advice, i.e. advice lines or offices
- Confidential reporting systems

MACHINE ETHICS

Machine Ethics is that section of the ethics of artificial intelligence which is related to the moral conduct of artificially intelligent beings. Machine Ethics differentiates with robo-ethics, which is related to the moral conduct of people as they design, construct, utilize and treat such beings. It would be wrong to consider machine ethics as computer ethics, which concentrates on professional conduct towards computers and data.

The attempt to actually program a machine or artificial agent to act as if ingrained with a feel of ethics needs new specificity in our normative theories.

MILITARY ETHICS

Military ethics refer to queries in relation to the application of force and the ethos of the soldier and are often interpreted as applied professional ethics.

Various areas incorporated under military ethics include the following among others:

- Determining the laws of war
- Justification for the introduction of military force
- Decisions about the potential targets in warfare
- Decisions on choice of weaponry, and what indirect effects such weaponry may have
- Standards for treating military captives
- Methods of tackling with infringements of the laws of war

POLITICAL ETHICS

The act of making moral judgements about political activity and political agents is known as political ethics also termed as political morality or public ethics.

It takes into account two areas. One is the ethics of process or the ethics of office, which addresses public officials and the methods used by them. Another is the ethics of policy or ethics and public policy which deals with judgements about policies and laws.

Some critics, the so called political realists, opine that ethics has no role in politics. To be compelling in the real world, the politicians need to be free from any boundations of moral rules. They need to seek after the national interest.

Another type of criticism is made by those who contend that instead of paying much attention to politicians and policies, people should look more carefully at the bigger structures of society where the most genuine ethical issues lie. People advocating for political ethics react that while structural injustice should not be neglected, giving too much priority on structures disregards the human agents who are authoritative for evolving them.

DEVELOPMENT AND ENVIRONMENTAL ETHICS

The two areas of applied ethics which are of direct concern to us are development ethics and environmental ethics.

The former, **development ethics**, rose as an area of investigation in the second half of the twentieth century. It enquires and analyses the ethical consequences of ideas such as 'progress' and at the consequences of various kinds of social change. It takes into account the costs and gains arising from key socioeconomic changes, and whether those in wealthier nations have an obligation to help those in poorer parts of the world. Similar to most areas of applied ethics, the objective of development ethics is to help in recognizing, considering and making ethical choices about societal 'development', and in distinguishing and evaluating the explicit and implicit ethical theories. In other words, it intends to give clearer interpretation of the key issues encompassing socioeconomic development, and to unravel the many secret presumptions about what is the 'right' or 'good' thing to do. Major issues involve social and human rights, poverty diminution, the disparity between rich and poor, and deliberated international interference by some countries in the development of others.

The latter field of applied ethics is **environmental ethics**. Environmental ethics rose as a distinct field of philosophical study during the 1970s. The methods of environmental philosophers are different, but many of them hold the convictions from the very beginning that we are confronting a critical point in our association with the non-human world, and that in order to deflect (or overturn) an ecological disaster, we need to reevaluate the ways in which we assess the non-human world. While not all environmental philosophers propose to adopt an innovative approach to the ethical values we assign to nature, many different proposals have been made for making a choice among various alternative frameworks that should be used for assessing nature.

These two vital subjects of applied ethics are crucial to recognizing numerous imperative contemporary issues, for example, those concerned with sustainable development, climate change, and environmental management. The environmental and developmental ethicists have also raised issues concerning with another vital area of applied ethics: corporate ethics (while some would consider business/corporate ethics as an advanced area of applied ethics in its own right).

DESCRIPTIVE ETHICS

A value-free approach to ethics, which characterizes it as a social science instead of humanity is known as descriptive ethics. Its analysis of ethics does not begin with a preconceived theory, but instead analyses observations of real choices made by moral agents in practice. Few philosophers bank on descriptive ethics and choices made and unopposed by a society or culture to infer categories, which generally change by context. This could result in situational ethics and situated ethics. Such philosophers frequently perceive aesthetics, etiquette, and arbitration as more fundamental, permeating 'bottom up' to denote the existence of, rather than explicitly prescribe, theories of value or of conduct. The investigation of descriptive ethics may involve analysis of the following:

- Ethical codes utilized by different groups. Few philosophers view aesthetics itself as the basis of ethics and an individual moral core developed through art and story telling as very effective in one's later ethical choices.
- Informal theories of etiquette having the tendency to be less rigorous and more situational. Some view etiquette as an uncomplicated negative ethics, such as, where can one evade an uncomfortable truth without doing wrong? One noteworthy advocate of this view is Judith Martin ('Miss Manners'). In accordance with this view, ethics is more a brief of common sense social choices.
- Practices in arbitration and law, for example, the assertion that ethics itself involves balancing 'right versus right,' such as, prioritizing two things that are both right, but that must be determined precisely in every circumstance.
- Observed choices made by common individuals, without expert help or guidance, who vote, purchase, and choose what is worth valuing. This is a key affair of sociology, political science, and economics.

Ethical Theories 5 CHAPTER

THE EXTREMES OF ETHICAL THEORIES: RELATIVISM AND ABSOLUTISM

There are various ethical theories doing the rounds, but, before discussing them, we first consider the two extremes of the normative ethical theories. One point of view is concerned with normative relativism. According to it, all moral points of view are relative. The ethics of one individual are not essentially equivalent to the ethics of another individual. Following this, it is also not possible to comment on the worth of certain norms and values in comparison to other norms and values. The issue with this philosophy is that presently it is difficult to discuss normative ethics: all norms and values are allowed.

Another point of view is concerned with absolutism, also known as universalism. According to this theory, a system of norms and values exists that is universally applicable to everyone, everywhere at every time. Absolutism makes no special cases: a rule is a rule under absolutism. However, every set of norms and values is somewhere contrary to itself . Hence, even absolutism generally does not work.

We realize that both relativism and absolutism do not work. Any choice/judgment made on the basis of any one of these theories is ethically suspected.

Ethical pluralism is another option to absolutism and relativism. Discarding the absolutist's opinion of there being only one correct solution in ethics, pluralists also dismiss the relativist assertion that there can be no correct answer. Rather, moral pluralists uphold the view that there is a majority of moral truths that cannot be accommodated into a single principle.

Deontological (Non-Consequentialism)

Deontological ethics or deontology is a method of dealing with ethics that ascertains goodness or rightness from analysing acts, or the rules and obligations that the person doing the act endeavoured to accomplish. This is in contrary to consequentialism, in which rightness depends on the outcome of an act instead of depending on the act by itself. According to deontology, an act which pursues the rule "one should do unto others as they would have done unto them" may be considered right even if it produces a bad outcome. and even if the individual doing this act lacks virtue and had a bad intention in performing it. In deontology, we have an obligation to act in a manner that does those things that are intrinsically good as acts ("truth-telling" for example), or pursue an objectively obligatory rule (as in rule utilitarianism). For deontologists, the ends or outcomes of our activities are not crucial in and of themselves, and our desires are not crucial in and of themselves. Fore several different reasons, Immanuel Kant's theory of ethics is considered deontological. First, from Kant's point of view, to act in the morally correct manner, people must act from duty (deon). Second, he opined that it was not the outcomes of actions that make them right or wrong but the intentions of the person who performs the action.

All deontological ethics theories are non-consequentialist in nature so that they emphasize on the decision or action itself, for example, on the motivations, principles, or ideals underlying the decision or action, instead of being concerned with the outcomes or consequences of that decision or action. This arguing is based on the desirability of principle (usually duties or rights) to act in a given circumstance. The two major non-consequentialist theories are ethics of duties and ethics of rights and justice. Both of these are established in suppositions about general rights and wrongs and obligations. The this approach means that people who promote these types of ethical principles generally believe that they should be applied to everyone, everywhere in the world. Let us take the example of a child having the right to education in one country, then this means that all children, everyone in the world, should have a right to an education.

Duties

Many of the people have the viewpoint that all human beings have some duties to other human beings. Duties can be constructive, such as the duty to take care of one's children, or negative, for example, the duty not to kill another person. When individuals utilize the language of duties, they generally do so in a way that entails that the duty is worldwide to all the people or at least to all grown-up humans of sound mentality. The basis of theories of duties is the theory established by Immanuel Kant (1724–1804), the German philosopher. Instead of depending on religion to interpret our duties to us, Kant believed that people can rely on their powers of reason to do so. At the focal point of the Kant's theory of duty is what he named categorical imperatives. A few activities and decisions are based on our personal desires. For example, one could state, 'If you want to live in a beautiful house, you ought to work hard'. However, this is not a categorical imperative, as it is founded merely on satisfying our intentions. A categorical imperative instructs people to do something, regardless of their personal desires: for example, 'You ought to look after your parents'.

The core principle of the categorical imperative is that people should be treated as an end, never as a means to an end. This implies that individuals should be dealt with dignity. Regarding someone as a medium to an end implies using them as a tool to accomplish something else. Purchasing products produced by workers who have been paid unsatisfactorily low wages in order to ensure a cheap price for the items they manufacture, is treating the workers as a means to an end and it does not accomplish the duties we have towards those workers. Purchasing assured 'fair trade' products, in opposition, realizes our duty to make certain that the workers who make our items earn reasonable wages. The notion of duty is not only utilized in terms of secular opinions. The urging to 'do to others as you would have them do to you' is a text taken from Christian sacred scriptures, yet it has similarities with numerous other religious traditions. Both secular and religious concepts of duty offer us various obligations, for example, those to keep promises, not to harm others, compensating others when we do them harm, to uphold justice, improving the living conditions of others, etc. Duties are frequently often firmly associated to the concept of rights. When an individual has a right, generally this indicates that others have a duty to maintain this right.

Rights

Rights theory is a specific obligation-based theory of ethics. A right is an advocated assertion against another individual's conduct. Hence, rights and duties are associated in that the rights of one person indicates the obligation of someone else to protect that right. As Traer describes, the most widely accepted explanation for ethical rights depends on Kant's deontological argument that we have an obligation to regard every person as an end, and not as a means to our ends, because every person is self-reliant and reasonable, and thus has inherent worth'.

The notion of individual human rights is elementary to Western legal frameworks, and has formulated both from the opinion that all humans have certain essential rights and from religious concepts that rights originate from God. According to The American Declaration of Independence, 'all men' are 'endowed by their creator with certain inalienable rights'. The 'French revolution exclaimed that the "rights of man" are natural rights intrinsic to the humanity of each person'. Throughout the nineteenth century, the rationale for rights became more secular, but rights were generally limited to the country. However, the notion that rights were freedom assured to inhabitants of a country was questioned in the twentieth century by the recognition that Nazi Germany acted lawfully under German law when it perpetrated what were later classified as crimes against humanity. The United Nations' Universal Declaration of Human Rights of 1948 is grounded on the rationale that justice and equal treatment of humans should be applicable universally.

The Universal Declaration of Human Rights

- *Article 18:* According to Article 18, everyone has the right to freedom of thought, conscience and religion; this right incorporates freedom to change his [sic] religion or belief, and freedom, either alone or in community with others and in public or private, to manifest his religion or belief in teaching, practice, worship and observance.
- *Article 19:* According to Article 19, everyone has the right to freedom of opinion and expression; this right incorporates freedom to hold opinions without interference and to seek, receive and impart information and ideas through any media and regardless of frontiers.

Consequentialism

Consequentialism is concerned with ethical theories that maintain that the consequences of a specific action form the basis for any reasonable ethical judgment about that action (or creates a structure for judgment, see rule consequentialism). Hence, according to a consequentialist, a morally right action is one that produces a good outcome, or consequence. This point of view is often expressed as the aphorism "The ends justify the means". Introduced by G.E.M. Anscombe in her essay "Modern Moral Philosophy" in 1958, the term "consequentialism" was brought out to explain what she observed as the central error of certain moral theories, such as those put forward by Mill and Sidgwick. Afterwards, the term has turned out to be frequent in English-language ethical theory. The characterizing feature of consequentialist ethical theories is the weightage given to the consequences in assessing the justness and inappropriateness of actions. In consequentialist theories, the outcomes of an activity or rule usually outweigh other considerations. In addition to this basic outline, there is very little that can be unambiguously said about consequentialism as such. One approach to separate various consequentialisms is by the kinds of consequences that are taken to be of utmost importance, that is, which consequences consider as good states of affairs. Hedonistic utilitarianism views a good action as one that leads to enhanced pleasure, and the best action is one that leads to the most pleasure for the greatest number. Firmly related to this approach is eudaimonic consequentialism, which states that a full, flourishing life, which may or may not be the same as enjoying a great deal of pleasure, is the ultimate aim. In a similar way, one might follow an aesthetic consequentialism, the ultimate aim of which is to produce beauty. Nevertheless, one might settle on non-psychological goods as the suitable effect. Hence, one might follow an increase in material equality or political liberty rather than something similar to the more transient "pleasure". Other theories endorse a package of various goods, for equal promotion. Whether a specific consequentialist theory concentrates on a single good or many, conflicts and tensions between various good states of affairs are to be anticipated and must be resolved.

Utilitarianism

One need not focus on actions always. One can also concentrate on consequences. If a person does this, he or she ends up with consequentialism. One kind of consequentialism is utilitarianism, instituted by Jeremy Bentham. The term utilitarianism originates from the Latin word 'utilis', meaning 'useful'. In utilitarianism, the outcome of activities are weighed against one value. This 'useful' value can be something similar to happiness, welfare or pleasure. It ought to be escalated.

Utilitarianism is a hedonistic ethical theory that opines that the sound course of action is one that amplifies overall "happiness". Jeremy Bentham and John Stuart Mill are leading exponents of this school of thought. Bentham states 'it is the greatest happiness of the greatest number that is the measure of right and wrong' and expresses this as a key axiom. In An Introduction to the Principles of Morals and Legislation he speaks of 'the principle of utility' but afterwards chooses "the greatest happiness principle". Hedonistic utilitarianism is the typical case of a consequentialist moral theory. According to this type of utilitarianism, what matters the most is the aggregate happiness, that is, the happiness of everyone instead of happiness of any particular person. John Stuart Mill, in his description of hedonistic utilitarianism, suggested a hierarchy of pleasures, implying that following certain types of pleasure is more highly valued than pursuing for other pleasures.

Utilitarianism has three integral elements detailed as follows:

1. The validity of an action to be right or wrong is determined solely by its consequences.
2. The value of the outcomes of an activity is evaluated in terms of the amount of happiness or well-being caused.
3. For an assessment of the total happiness caused to a number of people, equal amounts of happiness are to have equal value, none of the person's happiness should have greater value than another's.

Egoism

Egoism holds the opinion that an activity is right if it amplifies good for the self. Hence, egoism may permit activities which are beneficial for a person, but damaging to the general wellbeing. Individual Egoism believes that all individuals should do whatever advantages them. Personal Egoism advocates for an individual to act in his own self-interest, yet makes no claims about what any other person should do. Universal Egoism holds the view that each person ought to act in ways that serve their best interests.

VIRTUE ETHICS AND CARE ETHICS

Virtue ethics is a theory that believes that the matter of importance is the character of the actor and by suggestion the motivations of the actor, instead of the act itself or its outcomes. Though the utilitarian and Kantian ethics create general guidelines to be connected to conditions irrespective of their specifics, virtue ethics works the other way. It views individuals' particular responses to particular conditions, and adjudicates the characters these disclose. In similarity to other approaches, it winds up by making general as opposed to specific judgements, but inductively instead of deductively. To evaluate the extent to which a fictional character is ethical, we need to read the entire novel, not just a few pages, and the same holds true of real life. Generally, the basis to judge the virtue of a person is not only a single act, but his or her overall behaviour, over a period of time, which could sometimes be a whole lifetime, and in a variety of circumstances.

Virtue ethics concentrates on the nature of the person performing the act. The performer should act on the basis of right virtues. Hence, the main theme in virtue ethics is moulding individuals into ethically good and responsible creatures.

Dissimilar to utilitarianism or Kantian ethics, virtue ethics generally makes no strong theoretical assertions. It does not look to get the virtues from first principles, yet usually acknowledges those that are characteristic of, and realized within, a specific culture or community. In a few forms, it serves primarily to systematize or justify our instituted social norms. The first and most notable virtue ethicist, Confucius, reasoned that the conventional virtues of ancient Chinese society, such as the virtues of loyalty and obedience, should be moderated by the basic human virtues of kindness, justice and human-heartedness. After a few generations, the founder of Western virtue ethics, Aristotle, cast the virtues of ancient Athenian society as the moderate means between excessive vices. Some contemporary virtue ethicists have created lists of virtues that are expected to bring together and systematize the different virtues found in various cultures, religions and traditions.

Virtue ethics is heavily affected by Aristotle. He asserted that each ethical virtue is located somewhere between two extremes. In reality, the right ethical virtue equates the optimal balance between these two extremes. For instance, to be courageous, you must find an the best balance between the two extremes of cowardice and recklessness. Tragically, there are negative aspects of this idea. The maximum balance frequently depends upon the circumstances which a person is facing. Similarly, moral virtues are subjective: one cannot normally state that the gallantry of one person is better than the valiancy of the other.

Virtue ethics moves the analytical emphasis away from rule-based decision-making (of deontological ethics) or of the outcomes of an activity (e.g., in utilitarianism) towards the morals of individuals and the morals of human character. Hence, for instance, while a utilitarian would reason that giving to a charity optimizes prosperity in society, and a deontologist would reason that people have a duty to help others, a virtue ethicist would hold the view that helping others showcases desirable virtues, for example, being charitable or benevolent. Other required virtues are courage, honesty, friendship, loyalty, mercy, modesty, patience, and so on. Contrary to virtues are vices.

Care ethics is a fairly innovative ethical theory. It stresses that the development of morals does not result from learning moral principles. Rather, people should imbibe norms and values in particular contexts. Other individuals are of key importance here. People learn what is good or bad at a particular time for them by connecting with other people, and by placing himself in their position. The answer to moral problems need to be always concentrated on preserving the relationships between people. Hence, the association of people is the key.

Virtues and Vices

It is likely to see the ethical cogency or rightness of an activity in terms of compliance to certain types of conduct. Cases or forms of behaviour that are morally right, good and proper are virtues, whereas those that are wrong, bad or improper are vices. This form of moral evaluation lends itself specifically to expressions of ethical judgement that put emphasis on the character of the performer, so that the act as well as the person who reliably acts in ethical ways is also virtuous.

ANCIENT PHILOSOPHERS AND VIRTUE ETHICS

Socrates

Virtue ethics depicts the character of an ethical agent as an impetus for ethical conduct, and is used to depict the ethics of Socrates, Aristotle, and other early Greek philosophers. Socrates (469 BC–399 BC) was one of the principal Greek philosophers to inspire both scholars and the general public to shift their attention from the outside world to the condition of mankind. In this context, knowledge having an effect on human life was given priority, all other knowledge being of lesser importance. Self-information was viewed important for success and innately an essential good. A self-conscious individual will act entirely within his capabilities to his maximum, whereas an uninformed person will struggle and encounter hardship. According to Socrates, an individual must be cognizant of every fact (and its context) applicable to his existence, if he desires to accomplish self-awareness. He stated that people will normally do what is good, in case they are aware of what is right. Sinful or awful activities are the outcome of ignorance. In the case of a criminal being truly aware of the mental and spiritual aftereffects of his activities, he would neither perform nor even consider performing those activities. Any individual who recognizes what is truly correct will automatically do it, according to Socrates. While he equated learning with virtue, he similarly likened virtue with happiness. The genuinely learned man will recognize what is right, do what is good, and hence be happy.

Aristotle

Aristotle (384 BC–322 BC) postulated an ethical system that may be termed "self-realizationism." According to Aristotle, when an individual acts in accordance with his nature and realizes his full potential, he will do well and be content. When a baby is born, it is not a person, but a potential person. To grow into a "real" person, the child's innate potential must be actualized. Sadness and disappointments are the result of the unfulfilled potential of a person, resulting in failed goals and a miserable life. Aristotle said, "Nature does nothing in vain." Hence, it is necessary for people to act in conformity with their nature and develop their potential talents in order to be satisfied and accomplished. Happiness was viewed as the final goal. All the remaining things, for example, civic life or wealth, are simply ways to the end. Self-recognition, the realization of one's nature and the development of one's talents, is the most certain way to happiness.

Aristotle claimed that humans had three natures: vegetable (physical/metabolism), animal (emotional/appetite) and rational (mental/conceptual). Physical nature can be appeased through exercise and concern, emotional nature through gratification of instinct and urges, and mental through human rationality and evolved potential. Rational development was visualized as the most important, as necessary to philosophical self-knowledge and as differently human. Restraint was encouraged, with the extremes viewed as debased and indecent. For example, courage is the temperate virtue between the excess of cowardice and rashness. Humans should not merely live, but live well with behaviour governed by moderate virtue. This is considered as arduous, as virtue implies doing the right thing, to the right person, at the right time, to the appropriate extent, in the accurate manner, for the right reason.

SOME OTHER FORMS OF ETHICS

PRAGMATIC ETHICS

Correlated with the pragmatists, Charles Sanders Peirce, William James, and specifically John Dewey, pragmatic ethics holds the view that moral correctness develops in a similar manner as scientific knowledge: socially over the course of several lifetimes. Thus, we should assign priority to social reform over efforts to account for outcomes, individual virtue or duty (although these may be worthy efforts, in case social reform is provided for).

ROLE ETHICS

Role ethics is a moral theory grounded on family roles. Dissimilar to virtue ethics, role ethics is not individualistic. Morality is inferred from an individual's association with their community. One such example of role ethics is Confucian ethics. The focus of Confucian roles revolved around the concept of filial piety or xiao, a respect for family members. In the opinion of Roger Ames and Henry Rosemont, "Confucian normativity is defined by living one's family roles to maximum effect." Morality is decided through an individual's accomplishment of a role, such as that of a parent or a child. Confucian roles are irrational, and arise through the xin, or human feelings.

PUBLIC SECTOR ETHICS

An array of principles that directs public officials in their service to their constituents, which includes their decision-making on behalf of their constituents, are known as public sector ethics, including. Central to the notion of public sector ethics is the concept that decisions and actions are grounded on what better suits the public's interests, in opposition to the official's personal interests, which includes financial interests, or self-serving political interests.

EVOLUTIONARY ETHICS

Evolutionary ethics is concerned with ideas to ethics (morality) grounded on the part of evolution in moulding human psychology and behaviour. This kind of approaches may be grounded in scientific fields, for example, evolutionary psychology or socio-biology, with an area of focus centred on realizing and explaining observed ethical preferences and choices.

6 CHAPTER

Morality, Values and Ethics

Ethics is frequently utilized in relation to the activities of organizations and with professional codes of behaviour, such as, medical and business ethics, which are regularly formalized in terms of exhaustive sets of rules or guidelines directing the employees how they should behave in their workplaces, for example, with reference to a duty of care or confidentiality that health-care professionals owe to their patients; or the medical ethical principles of benevolence, non-maleficence, respect for autonomy, and justice.

Ethics describes the a set of rules that a society or group of people follow while morality introspects right and wrong at a much deeper level, in terms of both individual and spiritual forms. The ethics that a person follows are influenced by external factors such as the nation, society, peer group, religion and profession, and could vary with a variation in any of these influencing factors.

Morality, on the contrary, is more frequently utilized in relation with how people conduct their individual, private lives, frequently in connection with personal financial integrity, legitimate behaviour and acceptable criteria of interpersonal behaviour, which includes truthfulness, honesty, and sexual correctitude.

Values are notions that a person follows about things and facets of life. These are guiding principles that shape an individual's conduct all his life. Mainly the values an individual carry with him are evolved by the company he keeps, and the first values he imbibes are bestowed by his parents. Afterwards he learns more about values in school. Societies have various value systems and individuals inhabiting these societies are guided by these values.

Values are guiding principles which a person follows when faced with a quandary as to what direction he should take at any specific moment in his life, it is these values that he pursues to determine his action and behaviour.

Individuals also possess their own value systems acting as the lens through which they look at the world around them and make assessments on the basis of this value system. This causes the situation to become complicated as when there is conflict between what are values for the society and personal values held by a person.

Common Difference between Ethics and Morality

- Ethics concern with a set of principles; the philosophy or theory in relation to principles. Morals are more similar notions than principles, grounded on teachings and often led by societal or religiously driven criteria.
- Ethics deals with social standards; morality deals with personal beliefs.
- Ethical judgments are complete and objective; moral judgments are relative to some specific standpoint and subjective.

In easiest terms

- Ethics account for a generally accepted set of moral principles.
- Morals account for the goodness or badness or right or wrong of actions.
- Values account for individual or personal standards of what is valuable or important.

FACTORS INFLUENCING ETHICAL BEHAVIOUR

There are three Major Factors that Influence the Ethical Behaviour and Decisions:

A. Individual Personality Traits: These are traits such as individual value system, upbringing, education, religious beliefs, experiences, etc.

- *Personal values and morals*: A person's values and morals will also influence his or her ethical standards. A fundamental variable which impacts the ethical behaviour is "locus of control". A person with an inner locus of control considers that he/she can control the events in his/her life. A person with an external locus of control considers that fate or luck or other people influence his life.
- *Family influences*: People begin to form moral standards as children in response to their understanding of their parent's behaviour and are expected to embrace high moral standards if they visualize that their family members hold to high moral standard. They evolve lower moral standards if their family members are engaged in unethical behaviours.
- *Peer influences*: Peers are co-workers always around us in carrying out our routine work. The conduct and attitudes of peers affect a person's decisions in his or her life. They are important to a person for ethical decision making. Hence, an employee need to build good relationships with fellow workers. Without there being any good relations among colleagues, no harmonious atmosphere develops between them which further results in failure in achieving one's goal.
- *Life experiences*: People's life experiences examine important ethical concepts such as "right", "wrong" and "permissible." It helps us investigate possible sources of ethical obligation, for example, God, human reason or the will to be happy. It asks for establishing principles of right conduct that may act as action guides for people and groups.

B. Culture/Society of a Person: On certain occasions, the culture and the nation in which a person inhabits affect his moral decisions/conduct. For example, Arab Muslim Countries has given women permanent and inalienable privileges, and has never distinguished against minorities on any basis.

C. Legal Provisions: Legal Interpretations are based upon modern and frequently short-lived values and standards. The call for controlling, legislating and regulating the moral conduct at the government, individual, and corporate levels has origins traced back to the ancient world. One such example is of ancient Babylon, where one of the earliest law codes developed, the Code of Hammurabi, that made Bribery a crime in Babylon during the eighteenth century BC. Many of the ancient societies' share common moral codes, for example, against murder, resulting in injury to fellow people, and assaults on honour and reputation of a person. In contemporary world civilizations, law and justice to the people are closely related to ethics and they impose certain rights and duties in an effort to suppresss and penalize variations from these standards.

DETERMINANTS OF ETHICS IN GOVERNANCE

The stages of ethics in administration rely on the social, economic, political, cultural, legal-judicial and historical circumstances of the country. These particular aspects affect ethics in public administrative systems. Ethics both in a complete society, or in a social sub-system, develops over a long period of time and is affected, during its nurturance and development, by a diversity of environmental factors, for example, historical, socio-cultural, legal-judicial, political and economic.

DIMENSIONS OF ETHICS IN PRIVATE AND PUBLIC RELATIONSHIPS

Private or personal Ethics refers to an individual's life outside his work domain, and professional, which is also called public ethics, is concerned with one's work life.

In certain cases, personal and professional ethics may coincide and result in a moral conflict. A few examples are given as follows:

- A police officer may have an independent opinion that a law that he is required to impose is wrong. However, keeping with the Indian law, he needs to conform to all lawful and rational instructions to impose that law unless there is good and ample reason to do otherwise.
- The personal opinion of a doctor may be contrary to the choice made by a patient whether the chosen course of medical treatment is the right one. However, under the Code of Ethics for the Indian Medical Association, he or she need to respect the rights, autonomy and freedom of choice of the patient.

Contemporary Implications of Ethics

Ethics generally is the analysis of right and wrong. It can view descriptively at ethical conduct and judgements; it can provide practical advice (normative ethics), or it can examine and hypothesize about the nature of morality and ethics. Modern analysis of ethics has various connections with other disciplines, in philosophy itself and other sciences. Normative ethics has a decrease in the number of followers, while meta-ethics is increasingly followed. Abstract theorizing has been replaced by more experience-based research in various fields.

PRACTICAL AND THEORETICAL AREAS

Psychology, sociology, politics, medicine and neurobiology are the domain which have assisted and been assisted in progress in ethics. Within philosophy, epistemology or the study of how we know has pulled closer to ethics. This is partially due to the realization that knowledge, similar to value and goodness, can be visualized as a normative concept. The customary examinations and descriptions of knowledge have been established to be unsound by the Gettier problem. Fresh concern has prospered in meta-ethics. This has over the years evolved as a recognized category continuing from the work of Hume, G. E. Moore and the error theories of J. L. Mackie who looks for a real basis, if any, for talk of values and right and wrong. Mackie is doubtful about resolving the quandary presented by the differentiation between values and facts.

REASON VERSUS INTUITION

The authorization of rationality has come under enhanced challenges from various quarters. Heidegger's work has been more and more translated and interpreted in the Anglo-American sphere and the acumen of forever pursuing reason is widely interrogated. The ethics of care, and environmental ethics are other expanding domains of research. These indicate to a universal enhanced cultural awareness of the so far authority of reason and male-based values in society instead of a relational, contextual and communitarian aspect of the social world. Reason and emotion are viewed as more alike associates in human activities. There stays major deviations of viewpoint, such as, between continental and analytic approaches, and process/pragmatism versus logical, *a priori* approaches. Edmund Gettier wrote a brief but influential piece of writing demonstrating that knowledge is not acquired by a customarily accepted reason-based definitions. Pragmatism, and process philosophy, generally, is gradually being adopted as an answer to a constantly altering perception of a dynamic world, both physically and in the domain of experiment and investigation.

CHANGED FOCUS

Mackie (1977) describes that growing secularization implies that religion is not viewed by many as the basis for determining the way we should act. Quine's review of the analytic-synthetic distinction has inferences for ethicality, such as in the work of Kant. Logic is a distinct and evidently adaptable branch of thought, instead of being the base for mathematics and reasoning, as thought of previously. Postmodernism and its aftereffect has left behind the inspiration for an overarching theory of ethics, single concepts which were renowned to explain or rationalize entire aspects of human experience and wisdom, such as Marxism, religion, Freudianism or nationalism. Various writers such as Jean-François Lyotard and J. L. Mackie (1977) indicate the decline in grand narratives. Mackie (1977), specifically, viewed this drop as undermining the authenticity of customary morality. This has induced the growth of both error theory and meta-ethics as attempts to either assess or to strengthen the foundation of our inherited value systems. In consequence, there is increasing acknowledgement of the plausibility of making decisions based on the circumstances, and the specific situation being considered, instead of by reference to principles. This act drifting from grand theory substantiates earlier views of Adam Smith, who believed that moral theories originated from moral actions rather than conversely.

CHALLENGES REMAINING

Major hurdles for ethics involve the fact/value characteristics, the error theory which seems to weaken the reality of ethical claims and evident relativism across cultures and eras. Some philosophers think that the tenacity of problems in ethics theory has resulted in an overall decrease in the curiosity in working in the domain of pure ethics as more chances come up in applied ethics and meta-ethics. Stephen Darwall *et al* made reference to "a genuinely new period in twentieth Century ethics, the vigorous revival of metaethics coincidental with the emergence of a criticism of the enterprise of moral theory itself".

DESCRIPTIVE ETHICS

Descriptive ethics, also known as comparative ethics, is the analysis of people's notions about morality. It is contrary to the prescriptive or normative ethics, which is the analysis of ethical theories that advocate for how people should act, and with meta-ethics, which is the analysis of what ethical terms and theories actually mention. Descriptive ethics is a type of empirical research into the viewpoints of people or groups of people. Those working on descriptive ethics aspire to reveal people's notions about such things as values, which activities are right and wrong, and which traits of ethical agents are righteous. Investigation into descriptive ethics may also examine people's moral ideals or what activities societies denounce or penalize in law or politics. The thing to take note of is that culture is generational and non-static. Hence, a new generation will develop its own set of ethicals and that fits as their ethics. Descriptive ethics will thus endeavour to keep tabs onwhether ethics still retains its place in a new generation. Since descriptive ethics includes empirical investigation, it is a domain that is generally examined by the people working in the fields of evolutionary biology, psychology, sociology or anthropology. Knowledge that arises from descriptive ethics is, nevertheless, also utilized in philosophical arguments. Value theory could take either normative form or descriptive form but generally it is of descriptive form. Descriptive ethics does not clearly distinguish between good and bad moral theories. This form of ethics can be described in two ways.

- Descriptive ethics asserts, indirectly or overtly, that amorality, which should not be mistaken as immorality, is moral. Descriptive ethics therefore embraces moral relativism. Or,
- Descriptive ethics does not assert that amorality is moral. Its inherent amorality is exclusively because of a practical division of labour between descriptive ethics and normative ethics.

The first perspective views descriptive ethics to be in contention with normative ethics, while the second views it as complementary to normative ethics.

PROFESSIONAL ETHICS

Professional ethics is a segment of the extensive domain of applied ethics and evaluates the ethical attribute of human activity in professions that have professional status. These professions involve law, medicine, ministry and by extension higher education, journalism, engineering and management. Professional ethics refers to moral conduct and standards administering the profession and its members. This field of research investigates issues, problems and the social responsibility of the distinct practitioners and of the occupation itself in view of philosophical principles, including duty and obligation. Groups comprised of occupational set criteria in order to ensure the competency and unity of members involved in secret practices. In some areas, for example, medicine and law, there are also systems that keep an eye on their conduct. In many instances, civil law also strengthens these criteria through a process of evaluation and licensing. In addition to providing guidelines that govern the relationship between professional and client, professional ethics also define rules governing the professional's responsibility to colleagues and the public as a whole. Many occupations have a code of ethics or other statement of their occupational practice's rules, but such arguments are only limited representations of the occupation's rules and duties. The complete content of these rules is ascertained in an ongoing negotiation between the expert group and the larger community. Hence, it is difficult to ascertain an occupation's rules and well-known ethical groups, for example, autonomy, beneficence and justice are only an initiating point. One of the theoretical matters invoked by professional ethics is the level to which an occupation's rules and principles outweigh a professional's peculiar rights and other moral principles.

Ethics in Digital Age

In reducing the disparity between our personal and professional lives, the Internet brings up difficult ethical questions. Our Ethics Code differentiates between our professional and our personal lives. The code's second paragraph in the "Introduction and Applicability" section describes, "This Ethics Code applies only to psychologists' activities that are part of their scientific, educational, or professional roles as psychologists. These activities shall be distinguished from the purely private conduct of psychologists, which is not within the purview of the Ethics Code." The Internet is offering plentiful chances to reveal the association between the private and the professional by providing in the public domain what has traditionally been regarded as private conduct. When information shifts from the private to the public sphere, there is an increased possibility of its having an effect on our occupational lives. From one point of view, more instead of less data is usually better; psychologists are trained to evaluate the utility of data for a given intent; data on the Internet is publicly existing information, almost equal to what is posted on the bulletin board of a local coffee shop or supermarket; and Internet searches may be evolving into the criterion of practice in the private sector. From the other point of view, working upon information that a trainee or applicant has not provided to a programme may not be in agreement with a respect for that person's privacy and autonomy; information on the Internet is extremely unreliable; and there is a "slippery slope" to seeking and trusting on such information that runs a risk of turning psychologists into private investigators.

The vision of culture may be of great help in our assessment about this issue, with regard to how different generations view their association to the Internet and what information they opt for presenting it as a consequence. Culture is also of significance with regard to determining the ways in which our values play a part in reacting to and evaluating information about our current and future colleagues that is available in a public forum and, even 10 years ago, would almost for certain have remained exclusively private. Ethics, values, culture and competence will therefore be key to our ongoing discourse about psychology and the Internet.

Ethical Relationship

An ethical relationship, in most theories of ethics that utilize the term, is a fundamental and reliable relationship that one has with another human being, which cannot necessarily be described with regard to any abstraction other than trust and common protection of each other's body. Honesty is very frequently a foremost centre of attraction.

Generally, the most fundamental of these relationships analysed is that between the mother and the child, and second most fundamental is between sexual partners—the focus of feminism and Queer theory, respectively, where relationships are crucial. Family role theory expands this to investigate paternalistic, maternalistic and sibling characters, and proposes that one's later associations are formed mostly so as to occupy the roles one has grown to find contented as part of one's family environment—the family of origin thus determining blueprint for the family of choice.

Mohandas Gandhi, Confucius, Menno Simons and Baruch Spinoza are such figures in moral philosophy and political philosophy whose area of focus was primarily on the moral choices made in the real framing and encounter of moral interpositions. Two such examples of modern movements are Greens and New Confucians that are originated in part from relational traditions.

PUBLIC RELATIONS

Public relations (PR) is the way of administering the expansion of knowledge between an individual or an organization and the public. Public relations may involve an establishment or a person attaining exposure to their audiences utilizing issues of public interest and news items that do not call for direct payment. The objective behind establishing public relations by a company often is to influence the public, investors, partners, employees, and other stakeholders to uphold a specific point of view about it, its leadership, products, or of political decisions. Common endeavours include speaking at conferences, winning industry awards, working with the press, and communication with the employees.

Tactics of PR

Public relations professionals represent the public appearance of an establishment or individual, generally to enunciate its aims and official opinions on topics of relevance, chiefly to the media. Public relations play a role to the way an organization is realized by influencing the media and sustaining relationships with stakeholders. In the opinion of Dr. Jacquie L'Etang from Queen Margaret University, public relations professionals can be regarded as "discourse workers specializing in communication and the presentation of argument and employing rhetorical strategies to achieve managerial aims."

Particular public relations disciplines include the following:

- Financial public relations—It is concerned with communicating financial results and business strategy.
- Consumer/lifestyle public relations—It is concerned with gaining publicity for a particular product or service.
- Crisis communication—It is concerned with responding in a crisis.
- Internal communications—It is concerned with communicating within the company itself.
- Government relations—It plays a part in engaging government departments to influence public policy.

Each domain deals in standard activities involving publicity events, speaking opportunities, press releases, newsletters, blogs, social media, press kits and outbound communication to members of the press. Video and audio news releases (VNRs and ANRs) are often produced and dispensed to TV outlets with the perspective of using it as regular programme content. Establishing and administering associations with those who impact an organization or a person's audiences has a crucial role in doing public relations. After a public relations practitioner has been functioning in the domain, they amass a list of associations that become an advantage, specifically for those in media relations.

Audience Targeting

A basic technique employed in public relations is to recognize the target audience, and to customize messages to drew interest in each audience. Occasionally, the concerns of diverse audiences and stakeholders generic to a public relations attempt require the creation of various discrete but complementary messages. In contrast, stakeholders theory recognizes individuals having a stake in a given establishment or issue. Though all audiences are stakeholders (or presumptive stakeholders), yet all stakeholders are not audiences. For instance, in the case of a charity which authorizes a public relations agency to produce an advertising campaign to amass money to find a treatmentfor a disease, the charity and the individuals infected with the disease are stakeholders, but the audience is someonewho is expected to contribute money.

Messaging

Messaging is the method of producing a coherent story involving a product, person, company or service. Messaging aims to eliminate the chances of readers receiving conflicting or confusing information that will implant suspicion in their purchasing choice or other decisions that can affect the company. Brands aspire to have the same issue statement, industry perspective or brand assessment shared across sources and media.

Social Media Marketing

Digital marketing is the usage of Internet tools and technologies, for example, search engines, Web 2.0 social bookmarking, new media relations, blogging and social media marketing. Interactive PR is helpful for companies and organizations to publicize information without depending entirely on conventional publications and to have direct communication with the people, clients and prospects.

Other Techniques

Litigation public relations is the administration of the communication method during the course of any legal dispute or adjudicatory processing in order to affect the consequence or its impact on the client's overall reputation (Haggerty, 2003).

ETHICS

The field of public relations is usually extremely unstructured, yet most professionals willingly follow the code of conduct of one or more professional bodies to escape revelation for moral violations. The Chartered Institute of Public Relations, the Public Relations Society of America and The Institute of Public Relations are a few institutions known to publish a moral code. However, Edelman's 2003 semi-annual trust survey showed that only 20 percent of survey respondents from the public had faith on paid communicators within a company in terms of their credibility.

SPIN

Spin has been explained generally to refer to open deceit intended to influence the people, but since the 1990s has altered to describing a "polishing of the truth." At present, spin implies providing a certain perception of information meant to strongly influence public opinion. Companies may utilize spin to build the appearance of the organization or other events taking a slightly different direction than they actually are. Within the field of public relations, spin is viewed as an offensive term, explained by professionals as refereeing to blatant deceit and manipulation. Expert practitioners of spin are occasionally called "spin doctors." The methods of spin involve selectively producing facts and quotes that promote ideal positions (cherry picking), the so-called "non-denial denial," phrasing that in a way postulates unproven truths, euphemisms for taking attention away from items viewed as distasteful, and vagueness in public statements. Another spin technique requires cautious choice of timing in the publication of certain news so that it can benefit from the prominent events in the news.

Negative PR

Negative public relations, also referred to as dark public relations (DPR) and in some previous writing "Black PR", is known as a practice of damaging the target's reputation and/or corporate identity. The DPR aims to harm the reputation of someone else, who may present a risk to the client's business or could emerge as a political rival. DPR may depend on IT security, industrial espionage, social engineering and competitive intelligence to accomplish its objective. Generally employed techniques involve using dark secrets from the target, coming out with misleading facts to dupe a competitor. Some of the philosophers are of the view that negative public relations may turn out to be highly ethical and advantageous for the general public since companies, organizations and individuals get disciplined, perceiving the threat of losing their reputation. In addition to this, negative public relations enables to unmask lawful claims against one.

POLITICS AND CIVIL SOCIETY

In *Propaganda* (1928), Bernays claimed that controlling the public opinion was an essential component of democracy. In public relations, lobby groups are formed to manipulate government policy, corporate policy or public opinion, generally in a way that is beneficial for the sponsoring organization. When a lobby group conceals its true motive and support base, it is referred to as a front group. Front groups are a type of astroturfing, since they aim to influence the public or the government without revealing their financial link to corporate or political interests. They initiate a bogus grass-roots movement by assuming the appearance of a reliable institution that serves the interests of the public, when they in reality serve their sponsors. In the early 1900s, Ivy Lee and Edward Louis Bernays came out with the first definition of public relations as follows:

"A management function, which tabulates public attitudes, defines the policies, procedures, and interests of an organization... followed by executing a programme of action to earn public understanding and acceptance."

In August 1978, the World Assembly of Public Relations Associations interpreted the field as follows:

"The art and social science of analysing trends, predicting their consequences, counselling organizational leaders, and implementing planned programmes of action, which will serve both the organization and the public interest."

In 1982, the Public Relations Society of America (PRSA) interpreted public relations as follows:

"Public relations helps an organization and its publics adapt mutually to each other."

The PRSA developed a crowd-sourced definition in 2011 and 2012, which is given as follows:

"Public relations is a strategic communication process that builds mutually beneficial relationships between organizations and their publics."

Public relations can also be described merely as the system of administrating communication between an organization and its publics.

The European view of public relations observes that in addition to a relational form of interactivity there is also a reflective prototype that pertains to publics and the public sphere; not only to relational, which can in standard be private, but also with public outcomes of organizational behaviour.

Spin in PR

In public relations, spin is a type of hype, realized through presenting a description of an event or campaign to sway public opinion in favour or against a certain institution or public personality. Though customary public relations may also depend on innovative presentation of the facts, "spin" frequently, though not always, implies artful, deceptive and/or highly devious tactics.

Politicians are frequently charged by their adversaries of professing to be upright and look for the truth while using spin tactics to influence public opinion. Because of the recurrent relationship between spin and press conferences (especially government press conferences), the room in which these are held is sometimes described as a spin room. A faction of people who create spin may be referred to as "spin doctors" who evaluate "spin doctoring" for the person or group that employed them.

The techniques of spin include the following:

- Selectively producing facts and quotes that boost one's position (cherry picking)
- Non-denial denial
- Non-apology apology
- Mistakes were committed
- Phrasing in a way that adopts unproven truths, or avoiding the question
- "Burying bad news": declaring one popular thing simultaneously with several unpopular things, anticipating that the media will emphasize on the popular one.
- Misdirection and diversion

For long time, businesses have used bogus or misguiding client declarations by editing/spinning a customer's/client's to manifest a much more contented experience than was the case in reality. In 2009, the Federal Trade Commission (FTC) modified their laws to incorporate methods to prohibit this type of 'spinning' and have been imposing these laws as of late. In addition, for the past 5–6 years several companies have originated that affirm the veracity of the testimonials businesses present on the marketing materials in an endeavour to entice one to become a customer. Another spin technique includes a delay in the publishing bad news so it can be concealed in the "shadow" of more significant or favourable news or events.

ETHICS IN PUBLIC RELATIONS

Public Relations identify a longstanding obligation and attempt to sway and to accomplish common understanding by acquiring the willing approval of attitudes and ideas. It can thrive only when the fundamental policy is ethical, and ways to achieve itare truthful. In Public Relations, the conclusions can never justify the use of false, harmful or questionable means to achieve its objective.

However, describing ethical and unethical is a difficult task. It would be easier to describe it as a matter of choice between the right and wrong options in keeping with morality. Anything that leads to discord in the mind gives rise to a notion of guilt and dishonesty. And deceitful communication cannot be helpful in to binding relationships.

Public also should not be underrated as fools. As the famous saying from Abraham Lincoln goes, 'you can fool some people all the time, and all of the people some of the time, but you cannot fool all the people all of the time.'

A lot of acts could be categorized as unethical, ranging from suppressing of news hoodwinking the audience. Immoral act in public relations may include the following:

- Censoring unfavourable news
- Distorting facts
- Deferring to serve a cause but in reality serving some other interest
- Assuring results that cannot be obtained
- Use of unwanted method towards putting pressures on editors for carrying publicity material

With the spread of education, the consumers as well as the public have become aware of their rights and a public Relations person may have to tackle different such as, trade unions, consumer protection groups, environment protection activities, etc. Hence, it is compulsory for a public Relations practitioner to be self-regulating and morally contended s also be cautious about the legal aspects of communication.

The Internet Encyclopaedia of Philosophy states: "The field of ethics, also called moral philosophy, involves systematizing, defending, and recommending concepts of right and wrong behaviour". Description of ethics generally share the elements requiring some form of systematic analysis, differentiating ethical from unethical, and ascertaining the nature of what should be valued. In the public relations field, ethics involves ideals, for example, honesty, openness, loyalty, fair-mindedness, respect, integrity and candid communication. This description of public relations ethics goes deep beyond the past of "flacking for space" or spinning some convincing message, but not everyone endorse this view. Present study aids an ancient trend of linking public relations with all things immoral—lying, spin-doctoring, and even spying. Numerous critics reason that ethical public relations cannot exist because the exercise itself is similar to control and information. A disappointing conviction among many journalists, policy makers, and laymen is the notion that the term 'public relations ethics' is an oxymoron: either an unreal possibility, or smoke and mirrors to conceal fraud. Groups like the Center for Public Integrity condemn the public relations industry for an absence of morals, considering the impact of public relations and lobbying as one of the main perils to truthful journalism. Various groups like Corporate Watch are less controlled in their reproach and consider public relations firms and professionals as purposefully immoral: There is a substantial body of evidence evolving to propose that modern public relations exercises are having a very noteworthy injurious effect on the democratic practice... by giving personal stakes the chance to purposefully conceal, deceive, and disrupt public debate on important matters the public relations industry diminishes society's competence to answer efficiently to crucial social, environmental and political challenges.

Current State of Ethics in Public Relations: Codes of Ethics

The present condition of ethics in public relations practice rely to a great extent on codes of ethics viewed by the key professional associations. Membership in these groups is intentional, which implies that one is not required to be a part of such a group in order to practice public relations. Members concur to follow a code of ethics that is drafted for the entire group. Few codes of ethics are created in terms that prohibit a list of certain actions; other codes of ethics advocate a set of ethical standards which should be followed. Most of the professional associations in public relations have a code of ethics, no matter it is written in positive or negative terms. Although codes of ethics can be formulated which fulfil general conditions or standards (Kruckeberg, 1993), they have been reviewed by scholars (Parkinson, 2001; Wright, 1993) for falling short of the principles adopted in the codes, or even in being internally conflicting. Practitioners often proclaim that codes of ethics are too ambiguous to be beneficial in their own careers or that they do not give sufficient specific counselling to be anything other than fundamental (Bowen et al., 2006). Study found that some practitioners state that they see a code of ethics once and then do not make reference to it or see it again (Bowen, 2002a). Most codes of ethics offer no execution monitoring or option for their violation, leaving them ineffective other than the occasional cancellation of association membership. These issues with codes of ethics are not new and they are not restricted to the domain of public relations. Some researchers (Kruckeberg, 2000) of public relations contend that if professionals are ethical then no authorization is required for the codes of ethics. Various researchers (Bowen, 2004a; Parkinson, 2001) add further, contending that a simple ethics statement is all that is required because noble motive is a more strict rule than a code of ethics. This argument reflects the basis of Plato, as quoted in Parsons (2004): "Good people do not need laws to tell them to act responsibly, while bad people will find a way around the laws". Given the reviews against codes of ethics, public relations researchers have worked to devise other methods of comprehending, analysing, and administering ethical conflicts. These methodoloiges are founded on the basis of differing schools of thought from philosophy to sociology.

Pushing the Frontiers in Public Relations Ethics

To meet the request for ethics training from the expert front, training in ethical decision making is being provided by various employers, universities, and professional associations. In the recent past, public relations scholars have consolidated a significant amount of ethical philosophy into the group of knowledge known as communication. The incorporation of this insightful literature in our own field can effectively prolong the ethical reasoning capacities of public relations experts. These methodologies, which are assessed further, provide fundamental ethical guidelines for analysing deadlocks.

Dialogical Ethics Versus Advocacy Ethics

Dialogue as a philosophy was initiated in ancient Greece, with the traditional debate of philosophers such as Aristotle, Plato and Socrates. Dialogue is a usual involvement of ethics in any discussion because some scholars (J. E. Grunig, 2001; Habermas, 1984) contend that dialogue is intrinsically ethical. They view dialogue as ethical since it involves in a give and take review of public relations issues with the option for all stakeholders to have input. The talk is finally expected to arrive at truth or to disclose the basic truth to which the parties can be in accord. Beliefs are analysed on merit alone instead of on a positional ground. It should be noticed that this difference is a subtle one that isolates advocacy from dialogue—genuine dialogue reasons based on values until the achievement of truth. Advocacy contends positionally, which implies as per the opinions coming from the side of the client or employer, instead of coming from any or all sides. The advocate's perspective may or may not be in line with the truth, but it begins with a partial approach in the discourse and thus fails the trial of being truly ethical. A dialogue can possibly arrive at a truth that could be discouraging to an employer or client simply grounded on creditable arguments, and is seen as ethical because it is not biased towards any particular party ignoring the views of others. Public relations philosophers such as Heath (2006) view dialogue as the way in which a noble institution involves in open communication with its people. The merit or good character of the institute is upheld through its attempts to communicate with people, deliberating issues in a dialogue of give and take. This "wrangle in the marketplace" (Heath, 2001) leads to the best opinions emerging to the top, irrespective of their origin. Heath (2006) stated, "What was needed...was not more articulate advocates, but advocates who had achieved higher standards of corporate responsibility". This higher standard is to involve in dialogue for accomplishing the realization of the truth, and truth can emerge from any viewpoint. One thing to be taken into account is that engagement of dialogue must be with good intentions; Kent and Taylor (2002) sensibly noticed that "If one partner subverts the dialogic process through manipulation, disconfirmation, or exclusion, then the end result will not be dialogic".

Pearson (1989a) examined the notion of dialogue as a moral basis for public relations. He believed that public relations was best expressed as "the management of interpersonal dialectic" (Pearson, 1989b) laying emphasis on the personal relationship preservation and forming functions of public relations with individuals from publics. An entire strain of study (Ledingham & Bruning, 2001, 2000) has realized that relationship building functions are the most important facet of public relations, and Pearson's connection to the utility of dialogue in doing that creates perfect logic. Dialogue is best visualized as a continuous process of looking for knowledge and association, with the potential to put an end to ethical dilemmas through a mutual production of truth. Kent and Taylor (2002) provide a broad record of elements to take notice of while engaging in the process of dialogue, and it is an important resource for public relations experts looking for building that process into the communication of their institution. Many individuals who consider public relations as assistance would differ with the dialogical perspective since they consider that the institution can best describe details in connection with an issue and influence people to comprehend or approve those interpretations (Pfau & Wan, 2006). These philosophers (Fitzpatrick & Bronstein, 2006; Miller, 1989; Peters, 1987) give their consent over the belief that the advocate role of public relations is alike that of an attorney, in which Pfau and

Wan pointed out that "persuasion plays an integral role". Nevertheless, this method lacks genuineness since it puts emphasis on one-sided influence and does not allow for the validity of conflicting facts arising outside the institution or from other people.

Advocacy can occasionally be problematic since it can baffle credibility to the client or employer with credibility to the truth. For example, a longstanding moral approach might be to enable the client change or amend procedures to ensure future feasibility, but this view can be neglected in favour of temporary success or commitment to management's explanation of issues. While some advocates uphold that an ethically responsible approach is sufficient (Fitzpatrick & Bronstein, 2006) numerous executive-level professionals state that they require more authoritative ways of evaluations for ethical issue determination (Bowen, 2002b, 2006). Equivalent perceptions see public relations as the association's aim or balanced advisory voice in strategic management, as discussed further.

Strategic Management Methodologies to Ethics

Strategic management looks to boost institutional competence and profitability by taking decisions that steadily make every effort towards that goal. Public relations executives working as strategy advisors and ethics counsellors to senior management is a part that is aided in research outcomes with regard to the practice and in theory. The way to execute this obligation ethically and with coherent approaches has been examined from different strategic management viewpoints. J. E. Grunig (1992b) recommended that associations with people could be used to expedite organizational decision making in a steady, commensurate manner. Grunig's notion of symmetry is that institutions realize more of their longstanding objectives when they coordinate some of what publics want, implying that administration takes part in a continuous relationship of mutual concession with publics. Grunig and his colleagues (Dozier, L. A. Grunig, & J. E. Grunig, 1995; L. A. Grunig, Grunig, & Dozier, 2002) in this line of study upheld that symmetrical communication is intrinsically moral. They clarified "The two-way symmetrical model avoids the problem of ethical relativism because it defines ethics as a process of public relations rather than an outcome" (J. E. Grunig & L. A. Grunig, 1992). These sholars (J. E. Grunig & L. A. Grunig, 1996) upheld that a strategic management methodology is in harmony with teleological ethical philosophy, generally termed as utilitarianism, because of its underlying emphasis on consequences. Both utilitarian philosophy and associations with people are visualized with regard to their consequences and potential outcomes. In utilitarianism, the ethical decision is described as that which optimizes positive outcomes and limits negative consequences. In the utilitarian approach to ethics, a measure of possible decisions and their anticipated outcomes is the ethical analysis utilized to conclude right or wrong. Strategic management also endeavours to forecastpossibleoutcomes of administrative decisions and thus is a characteristic fit with utilitarian ethics. Bivins (1992) also created a systems model for ethical decision making based on the strategic management approach. General systems theory considers the institution as an open and interdependent system reliant on intercommunication with its environment for survival. Publics are considered as a crucial part of the environment giving information inputs and feedback to the administration. He contended that preserving a method of ethical decision making in administration could enable an institution to have fruitful interactions with its environment. As a standard role of the management system, moral concerns could have more exhaustive and regular examination than when left to risk. Following the same approach, Tilley (2005) supported incorporating ethical standards in the strategic management of public relations campaigns including "formalizing ethics as part of campaign measurement". Developing on a strategic management prototype, Bowen's (2004a) investigation looked for strengthening ethical analyses by incorporating deontological philosophy into public relations. She associated this philosophical methodology to Grunig's research on two-way symmetrical communication explained above. Deontological moral philosophy, based on the work of German philosopher Immanuel Kant (1724–1804) looks to determine fundamental ethical principles upon which any reasonable decision maker would opt for the same choice. The useful Internet Encyclopaedia of Philosophy states, "Deontology is the study of duty" and believes ethical only works with a purely noble intention. It is a precious expansion to the knowledge of a public relations expert since it produces more reasonable, level-headed, and continuing decisions instead of less-demanding analyses. To execute a deontological evaluation of public relations ethics an individual must endeavour to be asself-sufficient, impartial and objective as possible. Potential judgement must be analysed from all view points. Study (C. B. Pratt, Im, & Montague, 1994) exhibits that public relations experts engage this form of analysis more often as they progress to higher levels in their careers. Bowen (2008) provides a good synopsis of executing deontology.

Ethical Resolution: Practical Recommendations and Guidelines for PR Practitioners

In case of ethical issues emerging in an organization, it is the responsibility of public relations experts to alert senior management. Public relations advocates should also have the knowledge of values of both internal and external people, and utilize these in sharp analyses and final resolutions of ethical conflicts. At any stage of an individual's profession it is never too early or too late to enforce the following guidelines:

- The foremost action to be inferred from examining ethical cases is that communication experts need to pay attention to ethics before seeking it desperately. Once an issue of disputable ethics or high media interest arises in an organization, it is too late to start looking for moral counselling. Expert communicators need to be familiar with the value systems of their institutions before these values openly raise doubts. Counselling the prevailing alliance demands great consideration to research, input, institutional values, information of the values of strategic communities, possible consequences, and the skill to implement severe forms of ethical analyses. Public relations experts should start examining ethics at the earliest before addressing an issue. Doing so will add to the decision-making ability in their public relations department and will permit and promote advancement in their career. Individuals should know their own values. Analysing the values a person hold and embraces in a systematic way will enable the person to deal well when they are staring down the barrel and are under extreme pressure by a supervisor, client, or someone else.

Taking note of the most imperative virtues of an appreciated individual or mentor is a beneficial exercise, as well as registering the values that you hold most dear. Scholars (Ladkin, 2006) call this activity "attending to one's own values" and it is imperative to enable the individuals to express their notions and reasoning, as well as stay firm when their reasoning is tested. Coordinating their own values to those embraced by their employer or customer implies that they have a strong rapport on which to build their expert practice. Otherwise, they might have to become an "activist" for morals in their institution or look for occupation in an environment more compatiblewith their own values (Berger & Reber, 2006).

- Spot and talk about ethical issues. Issues management (Heath, 1997), as the principal task that looks for and resolves issues before they turn disasters, is a region with a natural tendency to recognize difficult ethical circumstances. Public relations experts should examine the academic research and best practices of issues management to equip themselves best to tackle ethical issues. Study (Bowen, 2002b) has discovered that determining issues that will end up as ethical problems is one of the most testing facetsof issues management. Neglecting to recognize a moral problem before taking action for its resolution can lead to exorbitantdisappointmentsfor the institution, where it is bound to face loss both in terms of operational cost as well asreputation as an ethical institution. Being hyperattentive on the recognition of moral issues in the beginning permits more time for their investigation, research, discussion, and resolution than does holding up until one is recognized by people or by the media. Early recognition of an ethical issue also permit the organization to adopt a proactive perspective to characterizing and handling the issue, instead of a reactionary viewpoint when it is characterized by others. Moreover, self-attentive understanding of such issues is the morally reliable approach for an organization, exhibiting a desire to resolve difficult issues as an accountable organization and ethically good objectives.
- Over and over again investigation discovers that organizational culture significantly impacts moral analyses and decision-making ability of an organization (Bowen, 2004b; Goodpaster, 2007; Sims, 1994; Sims & Brinkman, 2003). Public relations experts should recognize the core values in the institution's mission statement, code of ethics, or additional policy record. One should recognize the approach in ethics nearest to prevailing institutional values. Those specifying the better good, advantage of society, or outcomes of functioning are most probably utilitarian. Assertions reverberating obligation, justice, fairness, responsibility, or objectives are deontological. Recognizing these underlying values of the institution is essential in inculcating a more broadlymoral institutional culture. They additionally suggest the ways of moral analysis that will be extremely valuable in resolving predicaments for administration since it is compatible with the values of the institution. The public relations function can promote moral argumentand understanding through the institution by using internal interaction to concentrate on these issues. Spearheads should endeavour to demonstrate and work on moral values (Berger & Reber, 2006; Goodpaster, 2007). Investigation (Bowen, 2004b) in this domain exhibits that in order to promote brilliance in ethics, the internal

correspondences of the public relations function should explain to employees the things to be considered when faced with moral dilemma, recompense moral conduct, promote the characterizing of issues in ethical terms, and support an environment of open moral contest. Facing management with proof that an organizational culture promoting ethics prevents crises of the Enron type might earn renewed assistance for an institutional ethics initiative.

- Alerting administrators in the establishment, particularly the CEO and dominant association, of the capabilities of the public relations function to involve in ethical deliberation by utilizing issues management, research, associations with people, and dispute resolution should be one of the key obligations of communication executives. Most leading administrators come from financial or engineering environments, and have little or no knowledge about the competencies of public relations other than media relations. Hence, it is the duty of the public relations expert to instruct them about the numerous ways that public relations can influence the accomplishment of the corporation, together with resolving and preventing moral quandaries. Alerting the CEO and other authoritative individuals in the alliance in the corporation is one of the chief routes through which experts in the IABC study alleged they accomplished membership in the strategic decision making group. Therefore, this proposal also helps in authorizing the public relations function within a corporation and promoting advanced career opportunities for specialists.
- Engage in organized and investigative ways of deliberating moral quandaries. The utilization of ethical philosophy offers arduous, orderly, and dependable ways of moral analyses and choices in public relations. The measurement or "yard stick" for measuring what is value or good in the corporation should be judiciously described before participating in moral analyses. Mission statements are generally the best manual to find out what is valued, rewarded, or looked for. A mission statement is generally the best place to start characterizing the moral values existing in the corporation. These moral beliefs can then be formulated in the kind of an ethics statement, a code of conduct, an ethics code, an ideology, or other codified rules. To raise the consistency of administrative policies, dispute resolutions, and enhance the longevity of administrative decisions, moral analyses should always start with the fundamental values mentioned in the corporation's mission. Ethical counsel of the leading alliance frequently requires what ethicists call 'moral courage' (Parks, 1993) in the way that they must be eager to contend for their evaluation even when it does not find favour with other organizational operations. Despite their solution not being enforced, the advice of public relations will be regarded and looked for in the future. Disapproving solutions to moral quandaries often show their acumen over the period, as well. Offering regular dependable analyses is a way to improve both individual trustworthiness and that of the public relations operation inside the corporation. The skill to participate in moral reasoning in public relations is increasingly sought after, in obligation, and in significance. Academic research, university and ongoing learning, and professional training are all focusing with greater reason to matters of ethics.

The public relations function stays at a crucial and defining point: whether to choose ethics counselling to top management or to stay outside the domain of the strategic management body. Our reaction to the crisis of creditability among our public will characterize the public relations in the coming years.

Inspite of it being a fact that a single individual or function cannot be the whole "ethical conscience" of a corporation, the public relations function is preferably told to instruct top administrators about moral issues. Public relations experts understand the values of important publics engaged with moral quandaries, and can conduct severe moral analyses to control the policies of their corporations, as well as in interactions with people and the news media. Thorough and regular moral analyses enable trust, which improves the building and preservation of relationships—after all, that is the eventual objective of the public relations function.

ADMINISTRATION OF ETHICS AND CORPORATE SOCIAL RESPONSIBILITY (CSR) ISSUES IN PR

At various stages of their careers, public relations (PR) experts are expected to confront decisions that are moral in nature. This type of choices exhibits an array of moral quandaries between, such as, truth versus loyalty, justice versus mercy, short-term versus long-term consequences, and the individual versus the collective (Kidder 1995, Stacks & Wright 1989). Public relations experts, by nature of their rank and employment obligations, are regularly in a junction of an array of conflicting interests. Frequently, the stress might be between the expert's own ethics and the culture of the corporation. In other instances, it may be a dispute between the expert's professional code of ethics and organizational standardsand anticipations. In yet other situations, they may be confronted with contending concerns between the corporation and its different publics. In any case, experts will regularly face conflicts between business requirements for economic operation and public anticipations for moral behaviour.

Concerns over these contending obligations and the moral quandaries they give rise to for public affairs are the focus of this article. An array of problems confronted by public relations experts in connection with issues of ethics and corporate social responsibility (CSR) are investigated. It is reasoned that CSR has, in many ways, changed the anticipations and requirements assigned on the profession.

As an occupation, public relations have a long and contended association with ethics and as of late with corporate social responsibility (McBride 198). However, public relations has been considered as a fledgling profession that is wanting of basic principles to lead moral, dependable exercises that get across structural and cultural limits (Olasky 1985, Rampton& Stauber 2001; Stauber & Rampton 1995).

Synopsis of Ethical Concerns in Public Administration

7 CHAPTER

It is not possible to define 'ethics' as it is a complex term, and with the time, its meaning, nature and scope have become wide also. In this chapter, we will discuss about ethical concerns in public administration. It is not possible to separate ethics and public administration by saying that ethics is all about morals and values, and public administration deals with actions and decisions. Ethics is the essential part of public administration. If we talk about public administration, ethics focuses on the smooth functioning of public administration. Ethics, in public administration, is important for good business conduct on the basis of the needs of a particular town, state or country. The ethics, in governance, depends on the social, economic, political, cultural, legal-judicial and historical situations of the nation. The term ethics can be explained as a system of accepted beliefs, morals and values that influences any person's behaviour. Ethics is a Latin word 'ethicus' and its meaning is character. Thus, specifically, ethics is based on morals and it helps individuals to decide on what option to take in case of an ethical dilemma. It is about differentiating between wrong and right and ethical and unethical. In the early 17th century, 'ethics' has been defined as the 'Science of morals; the rules of conduct, the science of human duty'. Hence, ethics is considered as moral codes that administers a person's or a group's behaviour/actions. The science of the good and the nature of the right, both are included under this wide term. Indian scriptures and other treatises, like *Ramayana, Mahabharata, Bhagvad Gita, Buddha Charita, Arthashastra, Panchatantra, Manusmriti, Kural, Shukra Niti, Kadambari, Raja Tarangani and Hitopadesh*, etc., are some examples of ethical concerns of governance. At the same time, it is not possible to ignore the sayings on ethical governance given by the Chinese philosophers, like Lao-Tzu, Confucius and Mencius. There are three well-known and reputed schools of ethics in the Western philosophy. The first school is inspired by Aristotle holds that virtues, like justice, charity and generosity, are a person's natural quality to act in ways that benefit the one who owns these qualities and the society of which he is a part. The second school, inspired by Immanuel Kant, makes the concept of duty central to morality, human beings are duty-bound, from the knowledge of their duty as rational beings, to obey the moral principle to respect other rational beings with whom they communicate. The last is inspired by the Utilitarian which states that the guiding principle of conduct should be the greatest benefit of the greatest number.

In a monarchy, i.e., a country ruled by king or queen or a democratic country, the Western thought is full of ethical codes to rulers. These points can be found in the literatures of Plato, Aristotle, Thomas Jefferson, Alexander Hamilton, Thomas Penn, John Stuart Mill, Edmund Burke etc. According to Rawl's theory of justice, it revolves around the adaptation of two basic principles of justice, which assure a morally acceptable society. The first principle assures the right of each individual to have the widebasic liberty well-suited with liberty of other individuals. According to second principle, social and economic positions are to be: (a) to everyone's advantage and (b) open to all. A major question arises for Rawls is to show how such principles would be universally accepted. Rawls introduces a theoretical 'veil of ignorance' in which all 'players' in the social game would be put in a situation, which is referred as 'original position'. Having only general information about the facts of 'life and society', each player is to make a 'rationally' sensible choice regarding the kind of social institution they would enter into contract with. Denying those players access to any specific data about themselves compels them to embrace a summed up viewpoint that has high similarity to the moral perspective. This point of review revolves around moral conclusions that can be achieved without abandoning those prudential viewpoint and presenting an ethical standpoint just by seeking after one's own sensible analysis under certain procedural haggling.

The sense of acumen on administrative ethics is that the public administrators are 'guardians' of the Administrative State. They are supposed to respect public trust and not flout it. In this circumstance, two important and critical questions raised: 'Why guardians should be guarded?' and 'Who guards the guardian?' The administrators need to be careful against their tendency to misinterpret public interest, encourage self-interest and indulge in corruption and treason of national interest. They need to be protected by the external institutions like the judiciary, legislature, political executive, media and civil society organizations. These modes of control become tools of responsibility.

ETHICS IN PUBLIC ADMINISTRATION

In the public sector, ethics is a wide term. Simply, ethics is a branch of philosophy that seeks to solve questions of human morality by explaining concepts like right and wrong, virtue and vice and justice and crime. Ethics provide responsibility between the public and the administration. In the public sector, ethics refers the fundamental principle of a public administrator's duty as a 'steward' to the public. In addition, it is the moral explanationand consideration for decisions and actions taken during the completion of day-to-day duties when working to provide the general services of government and non-profit organizations. Ethics builds standards of professionalism that workmates, in the public sector, can expect from each other. Decisions are based upon ethical principles and these principles are the opinion of the public that they view as right. Different views ensure that public administrators are not functioning on an internal set of ethical principles without first interrogative whether these principles would hold to public scrutiny. Also, it has put an extra load upon public administrators related to the behaviourof their personal lives. Public sector ethics is an effort to establish a more open environment within governmental actions.

The concept of ethics has developed itself to involve all major spheres of human existence. Here, some salient features of ethics in public administration are outlined which are summarized as following maxims:

- ***Maxim of Legality and Rationality***: An administrator should obey the law and rules that are framed to administer and guide different categories of policies and decisions.
- ***Maxim of Responsibility and Accountability***: An administrator would not hesitate to accept responsibility for his decision and actions. Additionally, he would be willing to be held accountable to higher authorities of governance and even to the people who are the ultimate beneficiaries of his decisions and actions.
- ***Maxim of Work Commitment***: An administrator would be dedicated to his liabilities and perform his work with dedication, intelligence and skill. As Swami Vivekananda said, 'Every duty is holy and devotion to duty is the highest form of worship'. This would also involve respect for time, punctuality and fulfilment of promises made. Work cannot be considered as a load but it can be viewed as an opportunity to serve and fruitfully contribute to society.
- ***Maxim of Excellence***: In administrative decisions and actions, an administrator would ensure the highest standards of quality, and would not compromise with standards because of convenience or self-satisfaction. In a competitive international environment, an administrative system should faithfully follow the fundamentals of Total Quality Management.
- ***Maxim of Fusion:*** To develop union, an administrator would wisely bring about a fusion of individual, organizational and social goals to and imbibe in his behaviour a commitment to such a fusion. On circumstances for clashing goals, a concern to ethics ought to govern the decisions constructed.
- ***Maxim of Responsiveness and Resilience***: For the demands and challenges from the external as well as internal environment, an administrator would respond efficiently. He would adapt to environmental change and yet sustain the ethical norms of conduct. Clinched alongside circumstances about deviation starting with the proposed moral norms, the regulatory framework might show adaptability and ricochet back under the acknowledged moral mould in the soonest good fortune.
- ***Maxim of Utilitarianism***: It is the responsibility of an administrator to ensure happiness and benefits of the greatest number while framing and implementing strategies and decisions.
- ***Maxim of Compassion***: An administrator, without violating the recommended and specified laws and rules, would demonstrate sympathy for the underprivileged, the disabled and the weak while using his will in making decisions. He would not give any benefits to the stronger section of society only because of their power and might not deny those expected attention of the weak, notwithstanding their shortcoming.

- ***Maxim of National Interest***: Though universalistic in orientation and liberal in viewpoints, a civil servant would keep in view the impact of his action on his country's strength and prestige. Those Japanese, the Koreans, the Germans and the Chinese subjects (including civil servants), same time performing their official roles, need a concern and appreciation to their nation over. This naturally raises the level from claiming administration given and the items conveyed.
- ***Maxim of Justice***: It is the responsibility of administrator to ensure respect towards the principles of equality, equity, fairness, impartiality and objectivity during formulation and execution of strategies and decisions of governance. In addition, they are not expected to provide any special supports on the criteria of status, position, power, gender, class, caste or wealth etc.
- ***Maxim of Transparency***: There should be transparency in decision-making and in implementation of those decisions, so that those affected by the decisions and those who wish to evaluate their rationale, will be able to analyse the motives behind such decisions and the sources of information on which these decisions were made.
- ***Maxim of Integrity***: The administrative action taken by the administrator should be based on the honesty and not on his power, position and discretion to serve his personal interest and the illegitimate interests of other individuals or groups.

ETHICAL CONCERNS IN ADMINISTRATION

Political Science and the science of Management has been broadly influenced the field of Public Administration at the initial levels of its development. The philosophical bases of Public Administration were shaped primarily by Political Science and its technological part was designed by Management Sciences. Moral Philosophy and Political Economy were part of the early Political Science, while its current programme is the product of secular, practical, empirical and scientific tendencies of the past century. In the early years of the last century, the American students of Political Science were disappointed at the insufficiencies of the ethical approach in the gilded age. After students' interaction with the German universities and the influence on their thinking by scholars, like J. N. Burgess, E. J. James, A. B. Hart, A. L Lovell, and F. J. Goodnow, they wanted to re-form Political Science as a true science. They started showing great interest in observing and analysing 'actual governments', and Natural and Social Sciences had greatly influenced their ideas and approaches. After some time, Logical Positivism of the Austrian School motivated scholars, like Herbert Simon, and thus there emerged a faith in developing a Science of Politics and a Science of Administration, that would be capable to 'predict and control' political and administrative life. According to Dwight Waldo comments, the old idea that good government was the government of moral men was replaced by a morality that was irrelevant, and that proper institutions and expert personnel were the determining factors in shaping good government. 'The new amorality became almost a request for professional respect'. Until the mid-1960s, the ethical issues, in the study of Political Science and Public Administration, were further marginalized by the eminence of Behaviouralism. It was only after the arrival of Post-behaviouralism in Political Science and of the emphasis on New Public Administration in Public Administration, that the scientific methods of Behaviouralism and ethical values struck a homogenous chord with administration, and the issues between facts and values were resolved considerably. The current discipline of public administration gives importance to the values of equity, justice, humanism, human rights, gender equality and compassion. In 1992, the initiative taken by the World Bank, the movement of Good Governance, focuses, among others on the ethical and moral conduct of administrators. On another side, the New Public Management movement deals with administrative effectiveness, in addition, this movement also focuses on administrative ethics in its broader manifestation. It can be said from the above that both the movements are opposite to each other. This complementarity also exists hundred years ago, as it was today, when the industrial world was experiencing the rise of Scientific Management among the strong acceptance of the views of administrative responsibility. John Kennedy, during his Presidency (1961-1963) had stated, 'No responsibility of government is more fundamental than the responsibility of maintaining the higher standards of ethical behaviour. The ideal-type construction of bureaucracy, propounded by Max Weber also highlighted an ethical imperative of bureaucratic behaviour. Weber (1947) observed: In the rational type, it is a matter of principle that the members of the administrative staff should be completely separated from ownership of the means of production and administration. Officials, employees and workers attached to the administrative staff do not themselves own the non-human means of production and administration .... These exists, furthermore, in principle complete separation of property belonging to the organization, which is controlled within the sphere of office, and the personal property of the official, which is available for his own private uses'. Weber's analysis emphasizes the need to avoid the misuse of an official status for personal benefits, although, his ideal-type concept on bureaucracy is not practical, but it has a practical idea. Weber was not normative in his ideal-type concept but his message is clear that do not misuse official assets for personal advantage. Harold Laski, Carl Friedrich, Victor Thompson and Warren Bennis, some critics of real-world bureaucracies, have criticized bureaucrats for disobeyingthe recommended rules of moral conduct. While discussing the qualities of a prismatic society like 'formalism' and 'nepotism', Even Fred Riggs mentioned the wide differences between the 'ideal' and the 'real' in administrative activities. The deviances from the norms and values have become so much transparent to be ignored and thus, immoral behaviour has become an essential part of 'bureaupathology'.

ETHICS: SIGNIFICANCE FOR PUBLIC ADMINISTRATION

In the entire society or in a social sub-system, ethics has taken a longer period of time for its development, and during its development and growth, it was shaped by various environmental factors. Administrative ethics is the combination of numerous contextual structures and it never stops to grow and change. Here is mentioned some of the related factors that influence ethics in the public administrative systems: the history of a nation marks a great influence on the ethical character of the governance system. The Spoils System in the United States, during the initial phase of the American nation, reduced the ethical environment of the American Public Administration. Jackson, American President, stated, 'To victor belong the spoils'. Things would have remained the same had not anannoyed job seeker assassinated President Garfield in 1881. Garfield's assassination had encouraged the process of improving civil service in the United States. The setting up of the US Civil Service Commission, in 1883, was the first important step taken in this direction. India has seen unethical practices in the governance system, in the past. Many examples of corrupt practices, in which the administrators of past times were involved themselves, are mentioned in Kautilya's Arthashastra. The corrupt practices of the courtiers and administrative functionaries also affected the Mughal Empire and the Indian princely rule, and 'bakashish' was one of the accepted means of selling and purchasing services. The impact of morality and immorality co-exist in all phases of human history, and out of both these forces, which force is stronger depends upon the support these get from the political administrative system. The long legacy of unethical practices in governance functions as a supporting factor in increasing the easiness level for administrative corruption. In most developing countries having a colonial history, the gap between the citizens and the government continues to be broad. During colonial period, the justice of the governance was not accepted happily by a majority of population and consequently, true loyalty to the rulers was an exceptional phenomenon. It is true that the gap between the governing elite and the citizens has been decreased a lot in the transformed democratic government, still the affinity and believe between these have not been totally smoothed. The legacy of competitive cooperation between the people and the administrators still exist, and the nature of this bond has a contrary influence on 'administrative ethics'.

The nature of governance system is determined by the values that influence the social order in a society. Presently, the Indian society seems to give more preference to wealth in compare to any other values, and in the process of creating wealth, the means-ends debate has been ignored. Sadly, ends have obtained supremacy and the means do not command an equal value. A search for wealth is not bad in itself, in fact, it is a symbol of civilizational growth. What is important is the methods adopted while being engaged in this search. We seem to be living in an economic society where one-dimensional progress of individuals seems to be accepted and even appreciated, where ends have been controlled by means, and ideals have been suppressed under the weight of more practical concerns of economic growth. The question arises; can we change this social order? Mahatma Gandhi was very much interested in transforming the priority order of the Indian society, but there were few supporters of his thinking that was steeped in a strong moral order. After Mahatma Gandhi, there was no one in independent India to challenge the supremacy of 'teleology and unidimensionalism'. No one questioned this unilinear growth of society, neither have our family values nor has our educational system made sincere efforts to bring morality into the minds of the youth. We have totally failed on these fronts. There is the need to develop new viewpoints on what kind of the Indians we want to evolve and what is the procedure and till then, efforts will have to be aimed on the non-social fronts. The issues of morality may or may not be rooted in the religious culture of a society. Indian religious scriptures do not support quest of wealth through dishonest methods. Thiru Valluvar's Kural, written two thousand years ago in Tamil Nadu, emphasizes that earning wealth gives fame, respect and an opportunity to support and serve others, but it should be earned through honest methods only. Can this statement form the base of our socio-moral positioning? Some belief that the level of honesty among Protestants and Parsees is relatively developed when compared to other religions, and one can find the base of such honesty and unity in the well-established morals of these religions. However, it is only one point of view, as there are many other religious and secular groups, which are famous for their high moral behaviour. The cultural practice of a nation, including its religious orientation, has played a key role in influencing the work ethics of its citizens. For example, focus on hard work has helped various Christian societies to improve their efficiency. Judaism has given importance to the physical work by its supporters. On the other side, Hindu and Islamic societies have generally considered physical labour to be of lower rank and have given more importance to the mental work. Work ethics may or may not be linked with religious moorings. The family system and the educational system are motivational tools of socialization in its gullible days. If the family and the school taught honesty and ethics, then the mind-set of citizens is likely to be extremely positive and influential.

The judiciary of a nation determines the effectiveness of the ethical concerns in the governance system. A neatly framed law focuses on the norms of fair conduct and honesty in the ethical universe. On the contrary, nebulous laws, with confusing description of corruption, will only support corruption. It would not be able to instil the fear of law among those disobeying the laws of the land and morals of the society. Apart from above, an efficient and effective judiciary, with fast-track justice system, will prove a barrier to corruption in public activities. But, a slow-moving judiciary, with a concern for letter rather than the spirit of the law, will delay and even support the executors of crimes by providing them freedom through lengthy trials and benefits of doubt. Similarly, the anti-corruption machinery of the government will unintentionally grants relief to the accused who are indirectly assisted by its slow and complex procedures. In India, there is very few, actually hardly, effective anti-corruption institution.

In power or outside the power-domain, the political leadership is, may be, the most effective influence on the morals and values of citizens. The leaders do rule the minds, but in a democratic system, all political parties, powerful groups and the media also influence the beliefs and approaches on moral questions. As happens in the Scandinavian countries, if politicians act as true examples of honesty, or as examples/models of gross self-interest, as found in most South Asian countries, the administrative system cannot remain unaffected to the levels of political morality. In India, the election system is considered the largest record of political corruption. A candidate spends millions on the elections that compels him to refund his expenses through fair or foul means, which is more foul than fair, and it is well-known that fair has limits, foul has no limits. Generally, it is argued that the administrative class, comprising civil servants at higher, middle as well as lower levels, emerges from the society itself. Of course, the morals, values and behavioural patterns widespread in the society, are expected to be reflected in the actions of administrators. It is completely unrealistic to expect that the administrators will be insulated from the beliefs and norms evidenced in the society. The argument, proposed here, has a convincing logic, yet there can be a contrast that the rulers are expected to possess stronger moral character than the followers do. As, there are hardly any tools to protect and support administrative morality in respect of the general social morality, such an expectation remains at the most an elusive ideal. Therefore, there is an obvious necessity to understand the problem sincerely. The behaviour of politicians has a demonstrative effect on civil servants. Also, the less honest political masters have the great capability to control civil servants. It is ironical that in a country like India, the moral environment is shaped more by its politicians than by other social group. The role of media can be supportive in preventing corruption if the responsibilities are fulfilled with impartiality and fearlessly and media can even function as a catalytic agent in the promotion of ethical behaviour among administrators. Thus, the person who owns and manage the media can clearly understand their wider social and moral responsibilities. Many television channels have taken initiatives in this direction and regularly expose the various malpractices practiced in the system. This role of the media is valuable and worthy if they perform their duties with the intention of social responsibility rather than sensationalism.

The nation's economic development is likely to have a positive link with the level of ethics in the governance system. In fact, in the lack of causal relation between the two, a correlation cannot be ruled out. A lower level of economic development can create a void among social classes and groups. The less privileged sections of society may forget the principles of honest conduct while fulfilling their basic needs of existence and safety. It cannot be said that the rich will necessarily be more honest, yet what is apprehended is that the poor may find it an easy way to compromise with the principles of honesty. It can be seen that with the beginning of liberalizing economic system in developing countries, there is developing concern about following the norms of integrity in industry, trade, management and the governance system due to the international pressures for higher level of integrity in the WTO rule. Fred Riggs would describe it as 'exogenous' inducements to administrative change.

Major Focus and Concerns

Is the administrative system limited to acting morally in its conduct or does it also share the responsibility of protecting and promoting an ethical order in the society? This is an important question arises in connection with the moral responsibility of an administrative system. While, within the administrative system, mostly focus on administrative morality is on the aspect of honesty, so, there is a need to consider the issue of responsibility of the governance system, of which the administrative system is an integral part, to create and maintain an ethical atmosphere in the socioeconomic system that would develop and protect the basic moral values. According to moral political philosophy, the rulers will not only be moral themselves, but would also be the protectors of morality in a society. The fact is, being moral is a criterion to being a guardian of wider morality. Both the responsibilities are connected.

It is a saying that ethical decision-making is the core of administrative morality. It is not possible to separate questions of facts and values from ethical decision-making. Thus, the science of administration gets integrated with the ethics of administration, and in this united system, only that empirical concern is valued, which respects the normative concerns in the delivery of administrative services. There is a list of value that is required in an administrative action. However, one has to focus on the most crucial values, in case of being selective. Now focus on the values of justice, fairness and objectivity. Woodrow Wilson, 'The Study of Administration' (1887), in his inaugural address stated that justice was more important than sympathy and he placed justice at the top of value-hierarchy in a governance system. Since then, there has been a lot of discussion on the formal-legal features of administrative law, but few analyses have been made of the philosophical dimension of administrative justice. The other two issues of ethical decision-making, fairness and objectivity are, in fact, important components of administrative justice. Administrators, who are loyal to their profession, are expected to be unbiased and fair and not get influenced by nepotism, favouritism and greed in decision-making process of governance. Objectivity should not be misinterpreted as a mechanical and inflexible loyalty to laws and rules. From the decision-making perspective, it has wider results including a set of positive orientations. Presently, the concept of ethics has expanded itself to all major areas of human existence. The salient aspects ethics in public administration has already mentioned in the 'Ethics in Public Administration' column.

The overall objective of these maxims is to ensure 'Good Governance' with a prime focus for ethical principles, practices, orientations and behaviour. There is no code of belief involved in defining administrative ethics and the main concern is the positive consequence of administrative action and not just ostensibly rational modes of administrative processes. A few of the salient concerns and foci of ethics are briefly discussed in the following section.

ACCOUNTABILITY

As in most of the nations, there is a severe crisis of legality, and ethics and accountability have become important themes for modern government. In ethics and governance, accountability is defined as answerability, blameworthiness, liability, and the expectation of explanation. As a part of governance, it has been central to discussions related to issues in the public sector, nonprofit and private/corporate sectors. In the role of leadership, accountability is the affirmation and acceptance of accountability for activities, items, decisions and approaches, including the organization, administration and execution, inside the extent of the part or employment position and encompassing the commitment to report, clarify and be liable for resulting outcomes.

In governance, it is described as an account-giving relationship between individuals, for example 'A is accountable to B when A is obliged to inform B about A's (past or future) actions and decisions, to justify them, and to suffer punishment in the case of eventual misconduct'. Without proper accounting practices, accountability cannot exist. Simply, an absence of accounting means an absence of accountability.

"Accountability" term is derived from Latin *accomptare* (to account), a prefixed form of *computare* (to calculate), which in turn derived from *putare* (to reckon). The word is first time used in 13th century, Norman England. The concept of account-giving has old origins in record keeping activities related to governance and money-lending systems.

Types

Moral, administrative, political, managerial, market, legal/judicial, constituency relation and professional: these are eight types of accountability, which were listed by Bruce Stone, O.P. Dwivedi, and Joseph G. Jabbra.

Political Accountability

The accountability of the government, civil servants and politicians to the public and legislative bodies, like a congress or a parliament, are included in the political accountability. In some cases, recall elections can be used to revoke the office of an elected official. Normally, electors, during the term of their election, do not have any straightforward way of holding elected representatives to account. In addition, some officials and legislators may be appointed rather than elected and Constitution, or statute, can give power toa legislative body to support their own members, the government, and government bodies to account. This can be possible by holding an internal or independent inquiry and inquiries are usually held in response to an allegation of misconduct or corruption. The powers, procedures and sanctions vary from nation to nation. The legislature may have the authority to put on trialthe individual, remove them, or suspend them from office for a time-period. The accused person has the authority to resign before trial. In parliamentary systems, the government trustson the support or parliament, which gives parliament authority to hold the government to account.

It was found by the researchers, at the Overseas Development Institute, that empowering citizens in developing nations to have the ability to hold their domestic governments accountable was difficult in practice. The complex state-citizen dynamics can be better understood by developing explicit processes that generate change from individuals, groups or communities (theories of change), and by combining political economy analysis and outcome mapping tools.

Ethical Accountability

The objective of principles and practices of ethical accountability, within an organization, is to develop both the internal standard of individual and group conduct as well as external factors, like sustainable economic and ecologic approaches. Ethical accountability plays an important role in academic fields, like laboratory experiments and field research. Norma R.A. Romm had researched on the practice of ethical accountability in the social field, professional or others, in her work on *Accountability in Social Research*, including her book on *New Racism: Revisiting Researcher Accountabilities*, reviewed by Carole Truman in the journal *Sociological Research Online*. It is recommended that researcher accountability implies that researchers are awareof, and take some responsibility for, the potential impact of their ways of doing research on the social fields of which the research is part. Accountability is related to one's choices concerning how research plansare framed and the styles in which write-ups of research 'results' are formed.

Administrative Accountability

Internal rules and norms as well as some independent commission are methods to control civil servant within the administration of government accountable. Within department or ministry, behaviour is bound by rules and protocols; civil servants are assistants in a hierarchy and accountable to seniors. However, there are independent 'watchdog' units to examineand hold departments accountable. Legality of these commissions is built upon their independence.

Individual Accountability in Organizations

As in large organizations, many different individuals contribute in decisions and policies in several ways, so it is difficult to identify the person who should be responsible for the results. It creates a problem for accountability. If individuals are considered responsible, individuals who could not have prevented the results are either unfairly punished, or they 'take responsibility' in a symbolic ritual without suffering any consequences. On the other side, if only organizations are considered accountable, then all individuals in the organization are equally responsible or all are excused. There are many solutions have been suggested. The criteria should be broader for individual responsibility so that individuals are considered responsible for failing to prepare for failures in the organization. Another recently suggested by Thompson is to consider individuals responsible for the design of the organization.

Constituency Relations

According to this perspective, a particular agency or the government would be responsible if voices from agencies, groups or institutions, which is outside the public sector and representing citizens' interests in a particular field, are heard. Additionally, those administration will be obliged to enable parts from claiming organizations for political privileges to run for races and be elected, or, name them under general society part as an approach to hold those legislature illustrative and guarantee voices from all the constituencies would incorporated to policy-making methodology.

Public/Private Overlap

As public service provision has increased by private entities, over the last several decades, particularly in Britain and the United States, some have requested for political accountability methods to be applied to otherwise non-political bodies. Legal scholar Anne Davies says that the line between public institutions and private entities, like corporations, is becoming unclear in specific areas of public service provision in the United Kingdom, and that this can compromise political accountability in those fields. She and others said that some administrative law improvements are necessary to reduce this accountability gap.

In the United States, with respect to the public/private overlap, public interest over the contracting out of government, including military, services and the resulting accountability gap has been emphasized recently following the shooting incident involving the Blackwater security firm in Iraq.

Contemporary Evolution

Accountability includes either the expectation or assumption of account-giving behaviour. The study of account-giving as a sociological act was formulated in a 1968 article on 'Accounts' by Marvin Scott, Stanford Lyman and Stephen Soroka. Although, it can be foundas well to J. L. Austin's 1956 essay *A Plea for Excuses* in which he used excuse-making as an example of speech acts.

This work has been extended by communications scholars through the examination of strategic uses of excuses, justifications, rationalizations, apologies and other forms of account-giving behaviour by individuals and corporations. Even, in the studyof how individuals behave under various scenarios and situations that demand accountability, Philip Tetlock and his teammates have applied experimental design techniques.

Recently, in the discussion about the legitimacy of international institutions, accountability has become an important topic. As, there is no global legitimately elected body to which organizations must account, global organizations, from all sectors bodies, are often criticized as having large accountability gaps. The Charter 99 for Global Democracy, led by the One World Trust, first suggested that cross-sector principles of accountability should be researched and monitoredby institutions that affect people, independent of their legal status. One typical issue arising in the global situation is that institutions like the World Bank and the International Monetary Fund who are founded and supported by wealthy nations and provide aid, in the form of grants and loans, to developing nations, should those institutions be accountable to their founders and investors or to the persons and nations they support.

In the argument over global justice and its distributional outcomes, Cosmopolitans like to support greater accountability to the disregarded interests of traditionally marginalized populations and developing countries. On another side, those in the Nationalism and Society of States traditions deny the theories of moral universalism and argue that beneficiaries of global development initiatives have no substantive right to call international institutions to account. In order to measure the potential of global organizations to be accountable to their stakeholders, the One World Trust Global Accountability Report has been published in a first full cycle 2006 to 2008.

In the non-profit world, accountability is becoming an increasingly important issue. In 2005, several NGOs signed the 'accountability charter'. In the Humanitarian field, initiatives like the Humanitarian Accountability Partnership International (HAPI) appeared. Many individual NGOs, for example, the ALPS, Accountability, Learning and Planning System of ActionAid, have set their own accountability systems.

Accountability in Education

Traditionally, student accountability is based on having school and classroom rules, combined with penaltiesfor breach.

But some educational bodies like Sudbury schools believe that students are personally responsible for their activities, and that traditional schools do not allow students to decide their course of action fully. Once chosen, they do not allow students to embark on the course and they do not permit students to suffer the outcome of the course, once taken. The three great freedoms that constitute personal responsibility are: Freedom of choice, freedom of action, freedom to bear the results of action. Sudbury schools claim that 'Ethics is a course taught by life experience'. They cited that the essential elementfor acquiring values and for moral action is personal responsibility. The schools will be involved in the teaching of values when they become communities of people who respect each other's right to make choices, and the only method the schools can become meaningful sources of ethical values is, if they provide students and adults with real-life experiences that are carriers of moral import. The school is run by a direct democracy in which students and staff are equivalents and students are given complete responsibility for their education.

ETHICS IN GOVERNMENT

Ethics is not only a part of public interest but also an important area of study in the academics field of politics and government. This article introduces the basic concepts, issues and debates covering government ethics, the meaning and importance of government ethics, different types of unethical conduct in the context of government and issues and debates covering the establishment of ethical codes in government. The term 'government ethics' is often heard in the media by politicians and political pundits, but the exact meaning of this term is still unclear. A useful way to understand this term is by examining the word 'ethics'. Simply, ethics is related to the study of right and wrong behaviours. Generally, we face some important questions, in our day-to-day life, as given below:

- Should I keep my promise or should I not?
- Should I report a lost wallet, or simply keep the money inside?
- Should I give to the panhandler or keep my change?
- Ethics, as a field of study, try to find principles and rules for answering such questions.

Professional Codes of Conduct

A Professional code of conduct is an important field of study in ethics. Many professions, for example the fields of medicine, law and education, have introduced sets of rules or guidelines that govern members' conduct. These codes of conduct have outlined very clear guidelines of what are considered ethical and unethical behaviours within the particular profession. One of the most famous examples of a professional code of conduct is the Hippocratic oath of doctors in which medical students after completing graduation take this oath that usually contains a promise to serve sick persons selflessly.

Many times, it can be seen easily when things go wrong in the government such as dishonesty among elected officials, candidates lie about their rivals and city officials make important public decisions in secret meetings. Sometimes, the right thing is not so obvious, such as is it acceptable for a governor to assigna family member for the cabinet if the appointee is the suitable person for the job?

Ethical issues are easier to address, whether they are recognizable or complicated, if public servants have given some thought to the kinds of dilemmas they will meet before occurring a crisis. The objective of the resources in this 'primer' on government ethics is to provide elected officials, government workers and ordinary citizens with an introduction to the basic questions that are included in the managementof public business.

Each section of the primer discusses definitions, ethical issues and an explanation of the unavoidable ethical dilemmas that arise in government. One of the centres that provide training on these issues is The Markkula Center for Applied Ethics. For additional information, links are provided to the selected websites.

Ethics in Civil Service

The ethics and values for the civil services should be different and well-structured for the public or other sectors of the society because civil servants have special responsibilities towards the society. Civil service will be function effectively if ethics and values go along in the given categories of relationships and behaviours:

- With the government, legislature and political system.
- With the community.
- In the way the civil servants function and
- In the workplace.

The Second Administrative Reforms Commission, 2007, quotes US Senator Fulbright on the issue of those government's employees who commit ethical mistakes but which is not equal to criminal conduct: *What should be done about men who do not directly and blatantly sell the favours of their offices for money and so place themselves within the penalties of the law?*

How do we deal with those who, under the guise of friendship, accept favours, which offend the spirit of the law but do not violate its letter?

It is well-known thought that each new swindle seems to come up with its share of names of civil servants, and these are the persons who have held responsible positions in Union and State governments. There is no doubt that most, if not all, of them will go scot-free in a judicial trial, not because of their power but because the law fails to punish them. The criminals know this more than others that their activities might be morally unforgiveable, but legally it is not possible to recognize them.

Conduct rules deal with the problems, which can be conclusively proved beyond reasonable doubt and these rules are legal in nature. It has included few ethical issues by notify against partying with interested persons, receiving expensive gifts and funding relatives for jobs with companies who have relations with the officer. These rules were initially framed at that time when the government's role was regulatory and the role of private sector was comparatively limited. But the role of government as a facilitator has very much improved the scope for malfeasance in office after liberalization. Conduct rules do not deal with conflict of interest in many occasions because these are difficult to be proved in the court of law.

Actually, we need a code of ethics for civil service which would deal such moral issues. Also at the same time, the higher authorities will judge the officers by their previous record in moral uprightness.

For example, some civil servants who are involved into such issueswould not have reached positions of power had there been an efficient system of filtering. The President of India has the authority to suspend/remove civil servants who have been appointed to legislative positions. Definitely, a more effective system of scrutiny of the ethical conduct of such officers would have brought out their past offenses and prevented such appointments that cause embarrassment everywhere.

The code of conduct also deals with retired civil servants. Presently, they are required to providea certificate to the pension disbursing authority that they are alive. In the same way, retired senior civil servants, above a certain grade, may be required to file an annual return regarding their professional work in which they were involved. For such statements, there should be random scrutiny. This will control their indulging in unethical politicization, often by using their past contacts in government, euphemistically known as 'environment management'.

DIFFERENCE BETWEEN CODE OF ETHICS AND CODE OF CONDUCT

Code of Ethics

A code of ethics helps professionals to run business honestly and with integrity. A code of ethics can be defined as a set of principles usually issued by the board of directors that affect decision-making. A code of ethics explains about what is right and what is wrong. Code of ethics can be written or unwritten. It is sometimes referred as 'value statement'. Letus understand this term by an example, a code of ethics specify that XYZ Corporation is committed to environmental protection and green initiatives. The code of ethics expect the employees that individual employee, in the case of given option, will select the greenest solution. In situation of ethical dilemmas or controversial situations, the code of ethics can help in decision making.

Code of Conduct

A code of conduct is issued by the board of directors that outlines specific behaviours that are prohibited as criteria of ongoing employment. A code of conduct might bansexual harassment, racial intimidation and watching inappropriate or unauthorized content using company computers. The codes of conduct have helped some companies to pull out of the scandals, and have helped many companies to create a healthier work environment and reputation. A code of conduct is applicable to the code of ethics to a host of relevant situations. A specific rule in the code of ethics states that employees will follow the law and the codes of conduct might list several specific laws applicable to various areas of organizational operations that employees need to obey.

Similarities

Both codes are similar in some ways as both codes attempt to encourage specific forms of behaviour by employees. The guidelines mentioned in the ethics try to provide guidance about values and choices to influence decision-making, and conduct regulations emphasizethat some specific actions are appropriate or inappropriate. In both cases, the company expects to obtain acceptable behaviours from employees.

Differences

People often get confused between code of ethics and code of conduct. As these two terms are very similar, but still there is a slight difference between them. Code of conduct is acceptable by law and ethics is acceptable to the society. Codes of ethics deals with decision-making, and codes of conduct deals with actions. These terms represent two of the most common ways that companies self-regulate. These codes provide direction to employees and establish a public image of ethical behaviour, which benefit businesses of any size. Codes of conduct are rules and regulations that are respected and obeyed strictly by the employees of a company, and could lead to their removal in case of violating these codes. Codes of ethics are not specific, and there is no rule of punishment, but these codes of ethics are expected to be obeyed.

Codes in Harmony

In large companies, both types of codes are included, in simple words, they are combined into a general ethics document that contain principles for the right action with a list of actions that are required or prohibited. Sometimes, large companies like hospitals experience tension when the corporate compliance leadership issues a code of ethics that is a code of conduct and another business unit, such as the medical staff, issues a genuine code of ethics. This tension is minimum for small businesses, because it is easier for all employees to share the same basic expectations.

Ethics and Government

Government ethics deals with a specific professional code of conduct for those people who work in and for government. Government ethics gives the detail of rules and recommendationsabout right and wrong behaviours for a host of different groups, including elected leaders like the Prime Minister and Cabinet Ministers, elected representatives like members of Parliament, political staff and public servants. These groups deal with a variety of difficult and unique ethical questions such as:

- Should a public official be able to hire his/her own company to work for the government?
- Should elected representatives be allowed to accept expensive gifts from lobby groups?
- When can a public official divulge personal information about citizens?
- How should public servants treat their co-workers and subordinates?
- Government ethics identifies what are correct behaviours in each of these situations and establishes rules of conduct for public officials to follow.

Government Ethics and Democratic Participation

Here is a question arises that why should we care about government ethics? The reason is the importance of government ethics in the democratic participation. As a democratic nation, the political system of Canada only functions effectively if its citizens are actively involved in the democratic process. If, in case, Canadians supposed that politicians and governments were unethical or corrupt, they might develop a sense of lack of interest towards their democracy. The consequences may be negative as the people may withdraw from democratic participation altogether. Many times, we have heard comments like 'Why bother voting they are all crooks anyway'.

Government ethics plays a key role in preventing all these from happening. By outlining clear rules that public officials must standby considering persons responsible in case of violating the rules, Canadians can have assurance in their elected governmentsand political system. It is understood that there will always be scandals that violate ethics and when unethical behaviour does occur, suitableactions will be taken to punish the responsible person.

Government Ethics and Effective Public Administration

Government ethics and effective public administration are the pillars for a nation. Another common argument for government ethics focuses on effective public administration. Governments provide important services to citizens, for example social services, public utilities, police services and national security. Therefore, citizens have to ensure that the public money and property, as well as services upon which they depend, are used efficiently and effectively as possible. For this, precautions should be taken against activities that cause widespread government waste and inefficiency. On properly enforcing government ethics among the citizens, it can be proved as a valuable means for protecting against government waste and ensuring effective public administration. Such a code helps in prohibiting many of the activities that cause waste, including theft by public officials and use of government assets for personal benefit. It can also focuson problems like corruptionand conflicts of interest activities that can lead public officials to sacrifice the public interest in the administration of programmes and services for personal advantages.

Unethical Conduct by Public Officials

Several different kinds of conduct are often considered as unethical with respect to government and public officials. Some are given below:

Theft and Fraud by Public Officials

Canada's government manages billions of dollars in public money yearly and own billions more in physical property, which includes everything from land and buildings, to vehicles and aircraft, to office equipment and furniture etc. One of the major ethical issues in government is theft of public property by public officials. Such theft could be from the minor, like taking home office supplies, to the greater, like theft of millions of dollars from the public purse. Fraud is considered as the most common forms of theft by public officials, which occurs when an individual intentionally deceives others to unfairly gain money, property or services. There are several ways in which public officials try to deceive government and taxpayers. They may submit false expense reports for costs or provide overestimated work invoices for services.

Improper Use of Government Property

Apart from theft and fraud, another important issue is the use of public assets by public officials for personal benefit. Using one's office telephone for personal long-distance conversation and using government vehicles for personal transportation are some examples of improper use of government property. These misuses of government property are not considered as theft as the public official is not stealing the office telephone or the government vehicle. In fact, the issue is all about the reason for which the government asset is utilized. It is expected from everyone that equipment and transportation will be used for the performance of public duties, and not for only personal reasons or for personal advantages.

Bribery and Influence Peddling

Bribery is also an important issue in government ethics. When a person of authority is offered, and the person accepts, any personal gain in exchange of performing some action, then bribery occurs. The personal gain which is offered may include money, property or free services etc. In exchange, if the person agrees to take some action that benefits the person who is offering the bribe, like voting a certain way on a piece of legislation or approval of any illegal activity.

A particular form of bribery in which a public official sells his/her ability to influence the decision-making of government is known as influence peddling. Other forms of bribery involve a private individual or group approaching a public official and attempting to buy interests. However, in the case of influence peddling, it is the official him/herself approaches others to sell access to government, services etc. Bribery and influence peddling can be very harmfulto public perceptions of government, as well as effective public administration. In a democratic nation, we view our officeholdersand elected officials as being responsible to, and servants of, the citizens. Accordingly, we expect from these public officials that they will act honestly and objectively in the functioning of their official responsibilities, with the aim of achieving the public welfares. When a public official involves in a bribe, then the person is no longer working in the direction of public's welfare, but rather in the welfare of the person or group who is paying the bribe.

Conflict of Interest and Self-Dealing

In this point, we will discuss about another common problem in government ethics, conflict of interest. The issue of conflict of interest occurs when a public official's personal interests influence the performance of his or her public responsibilities. Here, the concern is same as with bribery and influence peddling, as given above. When performing official duties, public servants and elected officials are expected to follow fairness and objectivity and should act in the public's welfare. But, when there is conflict of interest, there is a concern that the public official may favour person interest other than the citizens.

There are many situations in which conflict of interest can occur and self-dealing is one of the factors. The situation of self-dealing occurs when a person's activities in his/her official capacity involve dealing with personal benefit for himself/herself. For example, if a public official is using his/her office to hire their own private company to work for the government, then this is the situation of self-dealing. The reason is that the public official may choose his/her own company instead of other because they want benefits from the government contract. The conflict of interest can also arise when public officials deal with persons with whom they have familiarrelations, such as family members, close friends and business partners. Here, the concern is that for the public official, the priority will be the interests of particular individual above the greater interests of the citizens.

As conflict of interest is a major issue so, many countries have applied conflict of interest rules. Public officials may be required to divest their business interests before taking office. This may include selling the interest or placing it under the control of someone else, for example, placing it in a trust, for the short term. While dealing with situations that, possibly,involve conflict of interest, officials may be required to take certain precautions. They may be required to excuse themselves from specific government decisions where they have a personal interest at stake.

Divulging Confidential Information

Public servants and elected officials are aware of all kindsof sensitive information, like military/security secrets and personal information about citizens, like, criminal records, tax information and medical histories. An important area of government ethics is relatedwith the controllingof public officials about the sensitive information. It is the real fact that the public officials are always expected to keep this information confidential and will not reveal the information.

There are lot of reasons for which confidentiality is important, depending on the situation. For instance, confidentiality in military secrets is essential for the physical security of the country and its citizens. Disclosingsuch secrets is referred as 'treason' and it is considered unethical which is punishable by long prison terms or even execution in some countries. On the other side, in the case of personal information, confidentiality is important for personal privacy and pride. In many nations, citizens have the right to privacy means they can keep their information personal.

Improper Conduct Post-Employment

In this text, much of the discussion has focused on unethical acts by public officials during the office. Another issue of government ethics focuses on the conduct of public officials as they make the transition from the public service to private employment. There are many possible issues are included such as conflict of interest, improper use of confidential information and bribery and influence peddling.

Before leaving office, a public servant or elected official may ask for favour to certain persons as a means of securing future employment. Again, the basic matterhere is the impartiality of the public official in the performance of his/her public responsibilities. The desire to secure future employment may create the situation of conflict of interest or in the situation of bribery or influence peddling.

Another concern is the activities of government officials who may take advantage of secret information she/he obtained in performing public service responsibilities, information that is unavailable to the citizens. This information could offer the former public servant advantage in the marketplace with respect to investing.After leaving office, former officials may also use their links to gain special treatment to government. The issue may be serious if the former official joins a private lobby group and uses his/her connections to gain unfair advantages for others. Many nations enforce a 'cooling down' period in which former government officials have to wait for a period of time after leaving office before becoming a private lobbyist. This is different from those peoples who have worked in private enterprise, with a particular firm and then resigned to 'set up shop', either with another company or individually.

Immoral Conduct by Public Officials

The personal moral conduct of public officials is one of the more controversial areas of government ethics. This includes issues like sexual harassment, discrimination, drug abuse and extramarital affairs etc. Here, the concern is whether the public servant or elected official is a person of good moral character and is able to perform public office responsibilities. In many countries, law has prohibited some forms of immoral conduct, particularly those directly related to the performance of one's public duties. For instance, it is expected to public officials to treat their associatesand juniorswith a certain level of respect, and is prohibited from involving in certain immoral activities like sexual harassment or discrimination based on gender, race, religion or sexuality etc. Public officials are also expected to be honest in relations with superiors and the public.

A more controversial topic is the regulation of other methods of immoral conduct, especially those that do not have a direct connection to one's official duties. In many nations, public officials are expected to follow high moral codes in all phases of their lives. In fact, in Western democracies, the people often consider that elected politicians should be of high moral values. Some people may argue that persons who engage in extramarital affairs in their personal lives or who have had past drug abuse issues, have bad moral character, and should not be considered as public officials. On the other side, some argue that judgement of public officials should be limited to their professional qualifications and work, not their personal lives. According to this view, public officials can secure a certain level of privacy in their private lives.

Regulating Ethical Conduct

During analysing government codes of ethics, it is important to consider major issues like which ethical rules are being included or excluded and what procedures and toolsare in place to ensure suitable responsibility and transparency. These important issues and debates are introduced in the following section.

Establishing a Code of Ethics

To regulate the ethical conduct of public officials, it is important to establish code of ethics. A government code of ethics should include prohibitions against cases of unethical conduct, for example theft, fraud, treason, bribery, self-dealing etc.

Some debate that in case when no actual unethical behaviour has occurred then in that case which ethical guidelines for public officials should go much further, prohibiting specific activities. The example could be complete banon public officials accepting gifts from private individuals and irrespective of whether or not it involves an actual case of bribery, influence peddling or conflict of interest. This ethical code of conduct could be supported by some people because permitting any sort of gift accepting encourages more serious unethical act. It is also argued that these ethical codes are important in maintaining the positive image of government amongst public. Only supposing that government is corrupt or unethical is just as harmful to society as actual cases of corruption.

Whether or not government codes of ethics should include rules of good moral character for public officials and elected officials is another controversial issue. This may include not engaging in morally frowned upon activities, for example drug use, frequenting establishments of disrepute or involving in sexual act. For some people, the need of government codes of ethics for public officials is to be 'good employees' and from this perception, such codes should only regulate the work-related activities of related officials. For some others, code of ethics is required by public servants and elected officials to be 'good persons', and further that it should outline rules governing the officials behaviour both at and outside the office.

Setting Out a Code of Conduct

A second issue deals with how a code of ethics for public officials should be lay out. There are various options available, as given below:

- *Criminal law*: One method of laying out ethical rules for public officials is through criminal law such as, Criminal Code of Canada. Under such law, violation of an ethical rule is considered as criminal offence, and punishment for the offence could be strict penalties like imprisonment.
- *Formal ethics legislation*: Ethical rules for public officials may also be in the form of legislation passed by the government. Generally, ethics legislation of this kind is very broad, define various ethical offences, methodsfor investigating and prosecuting unethical conduct, and various penalties for violating an ethical law.
- *Informal ethics guidelines*: At last, ethical codes of conducts may be outlined as informal guidelines. These rules are not formal in nature but are, simply, internal policy createdby the government to guide public officials.

Out of the above-mentioned rules, government can use any methods in setting out ethical rules for public officials. Generally, governments consider criminal activities more serious ethical offences, like theft, fraud, bribery or treason, and will prohibit these offences under criminal law. Other less serious activities, for example conflict of interest, improper use of government assets, might be regulated through formal ethics legislation or an informal ethics guideline. In addition, a government may also use various different pieces of legislation and guidelines for different groups of public officials. For example, elected politicians may have different ethics legislation leading their conduct than public servants and officeholders.

Which method will be used is decided by the government. If the government has a desire to have a huge control over ethics investigations, especially, investigations of its own people, then a particular government may prefer informal ethics guidelines. As these guidelines are not formal laws, but only internal policy, they have the advantage of being easily changed or disregarded whenever the government thinks it is necessary to do so. On the other hand, if a government wants regularized and stable ethical rules, then, the government may prefer criminal legislation or a formal code of ethics lay out in detail in legislation that is passed by the elected officials of a given legislature.

Accountability and Ethics Commissions

Presently, accountability is another common issue in government ethics. Here code of ethics can be considered as a rulebook that details what is expected from public officials. The rulebook lay out the rules and on the other hand, accountability refers to what happens when the rules of the law are broken. It includes 'holding the person/s accountable' when they involve in unethical activities.

In addition, accountability includes a number of important topics, as given below:

- How are allegations of unethical conduct made and investigated, and who has the responsibility of such investigations?
- Should a separate ethics agency be created, or should the police handle it?
- Who has the authority to take legal actionand resolveethics cases?
- Should it be an ethics commissioner, the government or the courts?
- Finally, what should the punishment(s) be for violating ethical rules?
- Should there be fines, jail time or other forms of disciplinary action?

The structure of the agency that is responsible for controlling government ethics is one of the most important issues related to accountability. Many governments, including the Canadian federal government, have set up an ethics office or commission, which is regulated by an ethics commissioner. Some say that an ethics commission should be responsible for investigating and monitoring public officials' activities, and should be giveninvestigative and prosecutorial rights. Some of the rights include the power to demand evidenceand documents from public officials, as well as to charge those officials who have violated an ethical rule. Also, ethics commission should be independent from government to investigate and prosecute ethical offences, especially in investigation of government bodies.

According to others, the function of an ethics commission should be to advice the government on how to deal with ethical issues, and to guide individual public officials in the situation of ethical dilemma. This view also states that traditional institutions, like public inquiries, the police and the courts, should be trusted in investigating and prosecution unethical act. According to this view, there would be no requirement to appoint strong investigative or prosecutorial authorities to an ethics commission.

Transparency, Disclosure and Public Awareness

Among the various issues, one more issue exist, issue of transparency. As we seen above, ethical codes of conduct are the rules of the game, accountability deals with the steps when these rules are violated and transparency is capable in monitoring when and where violation of the rules are taking place. If there are procedures and mechanisms to warn us when an ethical rule is violated, then we say that there occurs a high level of transparency. But, if public officials are able to hide their secret behaviour(s), then there is little or no transparency. At the point, when these guidelines are made necessary and people are to be considered responsible, at that point we can awarethat at which level these guidelines are abusing.

There are various ways to encourage transparency. One way is the formation of some ethics supervision body to monitor the actions taken by public officials on the regular basis. The body may be a formal ethics agency or commission, or a series of legislative committees regulated by elected politicians. Another means of providing transparency could be disclosure requirements for public officials, for example, it is requiredfor public servants and elected politicians to divulgefinancial properties and other important information before entering office, as well as it is important for them to reveal any possible conflict of interest situations during the course of carrying out their official responsibilities.

There is also a method to ensure transparency, whistle blower legislation. There are many situations when public officials become aware of the unethical acts of other public officials, but, due to some reason like fear of losing job or being ignored from their respective professional groups, they do not initiate to report against those officials. Many nations have approved whistle blower legislation to protect these public officials and make it easier for them to take initiative against the unethical activities.

To encourage transparency, public awareness and attention is very important. It is important for public to find out when unethical conduct has taken place as well as it is also required for them to know what steps has taken against those public officials who are responsible for such unethical behaviour. There are various methods to encourage such public awareness. The government should reveal important information widely available to the public, like the financial properties of public officials and the results of government reviews and investigations. In fact, the media and the public should be allowed by government to access government documents, such as, through freedom of information legislation. Public access to government documents has proved an important way to prevent unethical activities.

CODE OF ADMINISTRATIVE ETHICS

Public administration has included the concept of ethics after a long time. It is interesting to know that in the United States, the original city managers' and federal code of ethics placed significant stress on efficiency as ethical concept. In 1924, the International City/Country Management Association approved the public sector's first code of ethics. In 1958, the US Congress applied a code of ethics on the Federal Government and in 1978, set up the

Office of Government Ethics as an outcome of the Ethics in Government Act of 1978. The Office of Government Ethics released the Federal Government's first comprehensive set of standards of ethical conduct in 1992 that includes standards relating to gifts, conflicts of financial interest, impartiality, misuse of office, seeking outside employment and outside activities. Most of the American states have also publicized their respective codes of ethics, though they are less comprehensive in compared to the federal initiative. Presently, codes of ethics, ethics boards and ethics training have been accepted as essential attributes of public administration in the United States. The National Association of Schools of Public Affairs and Public Administration have made ethics education an important module of a Public Administration Programme and have recommended that all introductory textbooks in public administration should include ethics education. Famous professional associations of public administration also provide training programmes on ethical conduct for public managers. In our nation, India, there are few training programmes on administrative ethics offered by the Indian Institute of Public Administration and other institutions for civil servants. In 1984, the American Society for Public Administration (ASPA) had adopted a Code of Ethics for its members and the code was again revised in 1994. Here are some important points of the ASPA's Code of Ethics mentioned below:

- Exercise of discretionary authority to promote public interest
- Recognition and support to the public's right to know the public business
- Exercise of compassion, benevolence, fairness and optimism
- Prevention of all forms of mismanagement of public funds by Establishing and maintaining strong fiscal and management controls, by supporting audits and investigative activities
- Protection of Constitutional principles of equality, fairness, representativeness, responsiveness and due process in protecting citizens' rights
- Maintenance of truthfulness and honesty and not to compromise them for advancement, honour, or personal gain
- Guarding zealously against conflict of interest or its appearance: e.g. nepotism, improper outside employment, misuse of public resources or the acceptance of gifts
- Establishment of procedures that promote ethical behaviour and hold individuals and organizations accountable for their conduct.

There are many other 'commitments' that shape the ASPA's Code of Ethics. In India, the document can help as a model for various public sector organizations. It would be a great step if all public administrative agencies, such as ministries, departments, boards, commissions, public enterprises, urban administrative authorities, rural administrative organizations and other public institutions, implement and respect such codes of ethics. The entire idea has to turn into a movement, which will definitely take some time for its acceptance among the public. In this situation, it has been said that while dealing with critical moral contradictions in administrative decisions and actions, though no ethical code can provide exactly answer for every decisional dilemma, then such a code can definitely provide broad guidelines (Dhameja, 2003). Certainly, it may not be possible to outline complete ethical codes for administrative decision-making, but efforts can be made in this direction. More importantly, such codes should be formulated by the administrators themselves and not by someone from the senior level. These have to make a balance between what is ideal and what is possible. tends to always resist extremities. The conduct rules should not be limited to the 'don'ts' of administrative behaviour, in fact it should also be helpful in solving ethical dilemmas. In complex decisional situations, cases and illustrations can be helpful in directing administrators. However, it is very difficult to draft a specific conduct rule as some issues are bound to creep during the formulation of such rules. is the most important thing is to examine and analyse them on regular basis and modify them accordingly with the changing social priorities, modified economic parameters and the existing cultural environment. While defining morality, we are not supporting negligencein the enforcement of codes of ethics, but only emphasizingthe essentiality of 'realism'. In maintaining ethical order, combination of 'ought' and `possible' will make the ethical code a helpful tool.

WORK ETHICS IN PUBLIC ADMINISTRATION

Work ethics is an important elementof ethics in public administration. Work ethics is a commitment to the fulfilment of one's official responsibilities with dedication, discipline and sincerity. According to work ethics, a government functionary should be dedicated for his work and should not consider it as a burden. Efficiency, productivity and punctuality are the qualities of their administrative behaviour. Efficiency means doing one's best in his/her job, with a concern for maximum possible utilization of human, material and financial resources and even for time to achieve the advisedand desired goals. Efficiency can be treated as ethics. An efficient person has a regard for the higher goals of governance including public welfare, and he is dedicated towards those goals. Therefore, it can be said that an efficient person is also an ethical person. He or she holds administrative morality that is actually rooted in a belief in the desirability of ethical behaviour. Here, efficiency is not equating with mechanical efficiency, but with higher levels of performance that compares the ideal with the applied aspects of organizational functions. This raises another question: why is the quality of services and goods produced by the government organizations comparatively poorer than normally observed in non-governmental sector? The services provided by the government schools, government dispensaries and government offices provide disappointing services. Actually, in India, the general work culture in public systems is comparatively lower than that exist in the public sector and in the government systems in most developing nations. In fact, on comparing per capita productivity with China, South Korea and Japan, India has very low per capita productivity. The reason for this result lies in systemic flaws, such as poor infrastructure, sloppy monitoring, lacklustre control and evaluation and an absence of reward and punishment rule. But, the mainreason behind the poor quality of output of public systems is the negligence and insensibility on the part of government officials and representative. Lack of the feeling of 'oneness' with their organization and their job is a major issue. They are not fully dedicated towards their responsibilities. Impracticablepolicies, irrational decisions, unpredictablechanges in government systems and an indifference towards the beneficiaries of the system are some consequences of the issue. It may be possible that not all these are illegal, yet it is consider as extremely immoral. If we accept that work ethics is important to organizational morality, and sound time management and a respect for punctuality in work disposal is a valued trait, then we can plan for the improvement of work ethics in developing nations including India. For organizational units including individuals, there should be recommended specific norms of productivity and work performance and a completely and broad performance appraisal system should be accepted. This would be practically possible only if job is factual and role and responsibilities of each position has been specified. At every level, there should be maximum allocationof powers with a synchronizedsystem of effective monitoring and work review. In administrative affairs, punctuality and promptness must be valued along with the quality of work performed. These should make as the criteria for reward and punishment in organizations. The seniors should motivate their juniors to take initiative and responsibilities by setting an ethical example. On the other hand, from the person with idleness, indecision, inefficiency and dishonesty should be penalized which would help in creating a healthy work environment. The same spirit pervades the pronouncements of public leaders at the helm of governments in most nations. Thus, ethics has got back its status as a unique attributeof good governance. The trend is not likely to reverse in the nearfuture. Positively, there would be a great focus on the quality in public affairs and public service. The movement of Total Quality Management (TQM) will permeatethe governmental functioning and influence the functioningof governmental structure. Good service is a major attribute of ethics and this principleapplies most to public systems. The main responsibility of public administration is to serve 'public' and it is designed for the same purpose. It should be people-oriented and even people-centred. It is expected from bureaucracies to follow the laws and rules, but it not compulsory to make them systematically rule-centric. As Public administrative organizations are human organizations and they should be civilizedin their policies, decisions, orientation and behaviour, etc. Being reactive to individual's requirements enjoins upon civil servants to be reactive to their psychological requirements of being cared for, nurtured, and helped. Administrators have to acquire and show a higher level of emotional as well as spiritual intelligence in this situation that would make them caring as well sympathetic towards the emotions of citizens.

Despite the visible huge success and wealth in India, it is impossible to ignore worst and unacceptable poverty in the nation. As long as a single poor person exists in the nation, the moral responsibility of administration remains to support him. But, the issue of sympathyand humanityis not limitedto showingpositive behaviour towards the less-privileged sections of society, even, a single person having access to administration should be given a treatment of respect. This treatment should not be apparent, but in real, it should be reliableand intense. Ethical behaviour originatesfrom a pure and kind heart, and therefore, those who are serving people should make their heart sensitive and caring. Compassion contains a sense of sympathy and it does not end with disappointment. Compassion needs sensibilities to realize the grief of others and motivates one to overcome from his pain. Thus, administrative ethics in public affairs visualizes that the realmof feelings and the universe of wisdom should bring together in thought as well as actions of civil servants. For a positive and healthy approach to services, courtesy and politeness are required in in administrative behaviour, a wish to resolve their problems, and satisfy them even when extra help cannot be provided and issues have to be dealt accordingly with legal and formal requirements of the system. Two areas where administrator's have to show a thoughtful and caring attitude is to provide accurate and useful information to clients when they need it and to redress the citizens' complaints. In case, if a grievance cannot be rectified, then at least a citizen needs be given an explanation as to why it cannot it be rectified. The most important thing is a positive approach in dealing with people, being helpful to them and not ignoring them. Ethics involves a respectful behaviour towards the societies.

NEW DIMENSIONS OF ETHICS

Adopting and encouraging 'sunshine' in public administration is one of the best ways of ensuring higher standards of administrative ethics. Openness is the foe of corruption. Most of the nations of the world have Freedom of Information or Right to Information Acts. In the United States, at the federal level, right to information and open hearing provisions are an essential part of the Administrative Procedure Act. In India, the Freedom of Information Act of 2002 was reshaped as Right to Information Act, which was legislatedin 2005. Also, many state governments including Goa, Rajasthan, Tamil Nadu and Maharashtra have passed legislations that help in securing accountability of public employees. For the implementation of legislation requires a determination on the part of the State, commitment on the part of administrators and an initiative united with courage on the part of citizens themselves. The civil servants, who hinder the implementation of Right to Information Act, should be punished by State machinery. The old belief to treat information as 'secret', must give way to openness and clarity. For this, administrators have to change their mindsets in order to reorient the thinking of administration at all levels, particularly at the progressive level. For the successful implementation of the right to information, citizens have to motivate themselves and ask for the advantage of the right. Although, it has concluded in the Right to Information Act, but still it will take a long time before we can ensure its effective functioning. There is the requirement to take initiatives at a massive level in this direction by people's group such as the one led by Aruna Roy. For its effective implementation, even the educational system and the media have to contribute in this area. In the American law, 'whistle blowing' by public employees is considered as legitimate protected. It is expected from public employees that they would use their voice against the administrative activities that are illegal or unethical and they can even choose to resign from their positions to give voice to their protests. In fact, these acts are considered ethical and appropriate. In the American federal government, for the prevention of fraud, waste and abuse, there works a hotline which is called 'Fraud Net'. By using fraud net, employees and others can secretly report cases of misconduct for investigation to the General Accounting Office. In addition, the American federal government provide Constitutional protection to those public employees who raise their voice on the public issues like dangers to public health or safety. In Britain, a new appeals procedure for civil employees has come into effect and under this system, a civil servant could raise issues, secretly, with a person outside his normal hierarchy. Even, the person, who raises the concern, may report the issue to the Civil Service Commissioner if he/she feels that the response is not satisfactory or reasonable. In India, the Constitutional Review Commission has considered the possibility of whistle blowing a constitutional activity, but it was not accepted as a feasible choice. But, India needs to develop a new and clear perspective on this concern.

HINDRANCES TO ETHICAL ACCOUNTABILITY IN PUBLIC ADMINISTRATION

Accountability and ethics are interconnected. Effective accountability plays an effective role in the achievement of ethical standards in the governance system. Legislative or parliamentary control provides plenty of opportunity to the people's representatives to raise issues of ethics and morality in the governance system. In India, the Public Accounts Committee comments on the report of the Comptroller and Auditor General of India in its reports and raises issues,which are related, directly or indirectly, with ethics and good governance.

In the United States, the Office of Government Ethics helps the governing body in the process of confirming or rejecting Presidential appointments, especially on the matter of financial decisions. 'Ethics can be considered a form of self-accountability, or an "inner-check" on public administrators' conduct'. Self-accountability and external accountability are interrelated. Still, there are certain time-tested standards of moral conduct that define the character of self-accountability, and these principlesof moral philosophy may be considered as internal checks. Essentially, it is the fusion of external and internal checks that shapethe parameters of administrative ethics. The higher the level of morals, the lower the requirement for solid instruments of outer responsibility and control. Then again, bring down the level of morals, higher the requirement for powerful outer means for ensuring responsibility. Max Weber had mentioned that the outside checks on public administration were unequal. That's why, self-accountability is very important. The craving of being ethical in one's profession emerge from inside. In 1936, John Gaus in his book, *The Frontiers of Public Administration*, had stated that public employees were expected to practice the 'inner check', rooted in professional standards of administration and principles. David Rosenbloom and Robert S. Kravchuk asked a relevant and important question: 'Why is it difficult to guard the guardians?' There are some important characteristics of the administrative system that make it challenging for the external regulating institutions to control it. Few of these enigmas are mentioned below:

Generally, public administrators have experiences in their specific area of functioning, and it is tough and problematic for any outside agency to beat them in their areas. Besides, they generate and control critical information that may be difficult to figure out by law controllers. Although, many nations have adopted the Right to Information Act (or similar legislations), but still, there is cost to be paid for obtaining such information and verifying its legitimacy. The administrators do not easily part with such information, and are too eager to let their citadels remain invincible.

The majority of public administrators are full-time, while for outsiders such as legislators, judiciary, Comptroller and Auditor General of India and even the media, it is not possible to give equal amount of time for supervising their actions or behaviours on the regular basis. They cannot get all the vital information from administrators and even if they become successful in getting that information, they are not capable to process that information and use it efficiently.

The role of public administration has been increasing continuously in many countries like India. Its regulatory, developmental, promotional and entrepreneurial responsibilities are also growing along with its size. It is difficult for the political executive or the legislature to effectively control over them, as the number of public personnel as well as the agencies they work for has also increased so much. Similarly, in large-sized organizations such as Public Works Department, Income Tax Department, Police Department, etc., it is impossible for higher officials to supervise the activities of their subordinates. The geographical distribution of government agencies also become an issue in effectively handling the situation. Even computerization of all personnel records fails in ensuring the supervision over the activities of all administrators.

To ensure integrity in public administration, agencies have also been increasing frequently. For example, the Central Bureau of Investigation, the Central Vigilance Commission, State Lok Ayuktas, State Vigilance Bodies and Anti-Corruption Departments co-exist in India, without effective coordination among them. There are voids in the functioning of the vigilance machinery and lack of coordination among the various anti-corruption agencies. For many years, the permission to take legal action against government officials is not allowed to the Anti-Corruption Departments. The Lok Pal is yet to be appointed at the national level, and there is no agency that is fulfilling the responsibility undertaken by him. There is lack of fast-track courts for dealing with cases of corruption. As we have seen in the above, in the United States, the Ethics in Government Act of 1978 set upan Office of Government Ethics (OGE) in the Office of Personnel Management. The Ethics Reforms Act of 1989 fortified the OGE, which is presently an autonomous office inside the executing branch. But, in India or in other developing countries, no such institution exists.

There are many nations that allow protection to civil servants and desist from punishing them for the common mistakes in the functioning of their responsibilities. Also, there is no rule of punishments recommended for non-performance or for low production. According to Article 311 of the Indian Constitution, it is almost impossible to remove a civil servant. Too much over-security permeates in the personnel system, and the inquiry system is very slow and bulky that it lacks of any threat. Finally, a low level of discipline in most government organizations can be clearly seen, and when corruption affects all the levels of administrators in the organizations, then the potential efficacy of internal control becomes worst.

Civil servants often involve themselves in activities that are unethical and against public welfare. In addition, they define their role and responsibilities in a manner that is either self-centred, group-centred or organization-centred and but never people-centred. As important professional groups, including the politicians, adopt a tunnel vision in comprehending social reality, there are hardly any forces for the prevention of parochial interpretation of public interest by the administrative personnel. Due to this, both ethics and accountability suffer. The administrators have a general tendency to view public interest from a narrow angle and tunnel vision, and their specialization and the specific goals of their organizations provoke them to focus on the achievement of narrow organizational objectives. In this process, there are the chances that the concern of public interest may get suppressed under organizational interest. For example, the Excise Department of a state may be interested in opening more wine and beer shops in order to earn more profits, and thus may avoid the negative impact on the physical and moral health of citizens. The political pressures forced from above also influence the vision of administrators. One can notice that the Police Department is caught between the pressure of hierarchy and the obligation of duty because of pressure from its political heads. In order to save their own safeties and that of their families, the police officials often surrender in front of political pressures. Sometimes, 'inconvenient' civil servants are punished with transferred to 'difficult' locations that may cause issues to their families.

In most developing countries as well as in India, public employees are dedicated to contribute into developing loyalty towards the organization that they serve as well as to the superior authority under which they work. It is very normal in the Indian society to show respect to the superior and to desistfrom criticism of one's boss in a public organization. If any voice is raised against the superiors, then it is considered as an act of disobedience. In this kind of environment, it is very difficult for the honest and hard-working employees to speak out against unethical practices of their colleaguesand seniors. And sometimes, the unnecessary sympathy shown to the subordinates on their errors of omission and commission tend to strengthen the sinews of a 'soft state'. All the above-mentioned represent the lost loyalty and generosity that have disturbed the ethical order very much in public administrative system. With the coming time, as the Indian democracy is developing, it is expected that 'whistle blowing' will be considered as a legitimate and an intellectual activity in the future, and will be protected under the law.

The conduct rules, for civil servants, emphasize upon the rules of good conduct in which some rules have not changed and now appear to be nonsensical. As well, there is an emphasis that official property, equipment and stationery should not be used for personal needs. This is also related to the use of official vehicles and phone. These rules are conspicuous, more in their violation than in their implementation, and when compared to wider issues of ethics and morality, these are at best cases of petty morality. They must not be allowed to replace the more important ethical concerns of duty, fairness, objectivity and dedication. Sometimes, in matters of administrative ethics, we tend to be 'penny wise and pound foolish' which means we search into the trivial in compare to more relevant and serious issues of ethics. There is the requirement to guard against this tendency.

Many times, the employees' unions oppose the managerial action against their members even when they have violated the ethical rules which is consider as the another drawback in the way of implementing discipline and codes of conduct is. Aggressive unions can take any action, even a legitimate one, against their members. Consequently, in public systems, the supervisory level leadership gets infuriated and starts avoiding the unethical actions of their juniors. In a political system, where employees' unions are associated with powerful political parties, administrative leadership avoids from taking any strict stand against the perpetrator because of the fear of compulsive back-tracking or mortification. It has been seen that collective bargaining agreements seriously endanger the authority of managers to control their employees. Sometimes, the courts also show extreme concern for the safety of the 'Constitutional rights' of the employees than of the citizens. Corruption is considered as the violence of official powers for personal advantages. Also, corruption is disloyalty of public belief for protecting private goods. Currently, corruption is a universal issue, although the nature and quantum of corruption may differ among various nations. The international and the Indian national press are full with cases of corruption in government. Generally, politicians and administrators work together in perpetuating corruption. Thus, citizens become the victims of immorality in governance. It also indicates the existence of corruption in cross-national settings. In the middle-east and in India, because of the Mughal influence, baksheesh is used to seek the favours of an administrative functionary at the lower level, and in Western Africa, its name changes to dash. 'Speed money' in India meansa fee to speed up the processing of a governmental favour; in the Latin America, la mordida or 'the bite' are popular forms of bribes; in Russia, its name changes to shtraff; 'protekzi' refers to the exploitation of personal contracts to achieve a favourable treatment from administrators in Israel. In the United States, a country rated high on the integrity index of the Transparency International, terms like Watergate, Iran-Contragate and White-Watergate exist which refer to carrying favours and bribery. Unfortunately, in India the standards of ethics in the governance system have varied extremely in proclamations and in practice. The Constitution, laws, policies, and manifestoes of political parties and speeches of politicians are full with references to ethical basis of governance, but in practice, there is an awful violation of moral principles in the functioning of the politico-administrative system. The major reasons behind administrative corruption are the lack of what people want from public administrators and the problems involved in the normal channels of administrative decisions. In 1982, Michael Johnston explained. the demand for government's rewards frequently exceeds the supply, and routine decision-making processes are lengthy, costly, and uncertain in their outcome. Consequently, legally approved decision-making processes form a 'bottleneck' between what people want and what they get. The desire to get around the bottleneck is built into the relationship between government and society, to speed things up and make favourable decisions more possible. To get around the bottleneck, the person has to use political influence and corruption. Because of the lack of what people want from the government, they pay bribes in exchange for jobs, land, licences, quotas, admissions, passports etc. or even for getting them speedily or illegally.

Other reasons include escaping arrests, punishments, fines or major inconveniences which are examples of transactional corruption. This gets terrifying proportions when it turns into an acknowledged characteristic of the socio-cultural framework. President Dwight D. Eisenhower, former American President from 1953 to 1961, had once warned his country of the existence of a 'military-industrial complex', which supportedand encouraged the culture of 'transactional corruption' based on quid pro quo. *The Power Elite,* 1956, an epic work by C. Wright Mills had also raised the issue of such alliances and their impact on the decision-making of government. In 1995, the former Home Secretary of India, B.B. Vohra, had presented a report on the activities of crime syndicates/mafia organizations which were associated with government bodies as well as them. Some Asian countries have already proven that it is possible to fight and control corruption. And fort his, there is the requirement of effective political and administrative determination.

Administrative corruption had affected almost all levels of political systems. In totalitarian societies and military governments, corruption might be focused at the higher levels of party, military or civilian bureaucracy, while in democratic system, it might spread throughout the system. Particularly, in 'Soft States', political as well as administrative corruption has greater capability of permeatingthe governance system. It is not possible to prevent corruption by weak control and supervisory mechanisms and thus, these become its catalysts. In a democratic society like India, politicians who are elected on people's support and vote, are mostly concerned with strengthening their constituencies, and thus are keen to serve those who are their supporters. On the other hand, administrators follow the prescribed procedures. In case of conflict between the politicians and administrators, there is either a deadlock or ultimately, the politicians win. But, the most suitable optionfor the politician is to win over administration and make them partners in corruption. With a temptation for gaining extra or illegitimate benefits, administrators associate with their political leaders and indulge in corruption. It is very rare case when honest and strong administrators stand up against the corrupt politician. Similarly, there might be few government officials who really apply brakes of the fleeting trend from claiming managerial defilement. 'Weather-cock' syndrome can generally be seen in relation to government corruption. When the top-level political or administrative executive gets strict on corruption, the middle and lower level hierarchy get careful about issues of ethics. Greed is controlled by fear only if fear is genuinely feared.

While corruption is common in government organization, there is another ethical flaw which badly affects the administrative system. There are the chances that few government servants who works in sensitive organizations such as ordinance factories, nuclear energy establishments and defence forces, in exchange for monetary benefits or for the sale of extra-territorial loyalty, may pass on critical secrets to enemies. Subversion is also possible in modern days of global competition within the government, one can attempt to destabilize friendly relations with foreign nations. In worst scenario, civil servants may undermine certain government programmes, for example family planning or prevention of illegal migration. There can be many other examples of ethical issues are involved in public administration. Attempts should be made to devise strategies to combat such subversions. To fight against such corruptions, plan should be develop and it is also important to implement them properly.

TOWARDS NEW PUBLIC MANAGEMENT

The old public administration had put great emphasis on efficiency and economy. Similarly, conventional management science was very much concerned with productivity and performance. The modern public management, with its Neo-Taylorism orientation, has completely focused on performance and outcomes. Al Gore, the US Vice President, during Bill Clinton's presidency, urged through the National Performance Review's (NPR) version of the New Public Management (NPM) that ethics means achieving high level of customer satisfaction. It believed that people, in government or outside, were mostly trustworthy and well intentioned and there was no requirement for misusing time and energy on focusing on corruption. Trusting them is bound to conduct friendly atmosphere for ethical behaviour. The expense of deterring defilement is too high in terms of formalities that such efforts make. The NPR underlined that reinventing government required innovations, which in turn involved deviations from the grooves of tradition. Doubting and accusing people for their innovative initiatives reduces their passion for innovation. For creating a more effective administrative system in the self-governing democracy, trusting the employees as well as the people would help a lot in this process.

It seems that Al Gore has exceeded Douglas McGregor's 'Theory Y' and created an image of a human being who is creative and trustworthy. Certainly, this kind of person in government would not need any external control over him as the person has adopted very well the principle of self-accountability. In fact, if we consider Al Gore's description of government personnel to be too optimistic, it has a lesson to offer. Should we not question our unnecessary concern with prevention of corruption and in its place,adopt a more balanced view on the issue of ethics? Does not an extreme concern with corruption take our mind away from the more critical issues of people's interest through innovative and well-intentioned initiatives on the part of public employees? Such awareness should not bring slackness in tackling corruption, in fact, it should encourage the value of promoting trust in public system. Trust brings trust. Optimum acuity is a requisite to the accretion of an altitude of assurance for they are complementary and mutually supportive. It seems that such an emphasis on trust and de-emphasis on control would be more applicable to societies having a higher level of honesty and morality in public life in compare to those, which have low standards of morality and principles. Therefore, there cannot be any consistent approach to deal with corruption in the governance system.

Training is an important part of bureaucratic socialization. An administrator undergoes three types of training. Primarily, we are concerned with training that is taught after a person enters the administrative service. First, administrator's career starts with induction training which comprises of foundational, institutional and field training. Second is in-service training that is taught throughout the service career in the form of refresher courses, orientation programmes, seminars and conferences. The third is on-the job training that is intelligently provided by job performance and observation. Despite a great deal of conversation on ethical trait of administration, the emphasis on ethical training in the induction training as well in-service training is insufficient and inadequate.

There is a general thought that in the administrative circles, it is not possible to teach morality through training. As, there is no certain organized research has gone into it, so, it may be true, but there is no method to prove or disprove it. However, to make ethics an essential and main part of induction as well as in-service training, it is necessary that the option of ethical training is not discarded and systematic initiatives are adopted. National and international training institutions have already prepared the modules on this topic. The requirement is to establish our faith in this type of training and implementation of idea with proper intelligence and talent.

The impact of the immediate work-environment on the mind of a government functionary is immense for the on-the-job training. Principled and honest leaders and members of the peer group are duty-bound to promote morality in the behaviourof a government employee. On the other hand, if the official environment encourages ethical slackness and compromises, then it becomes easier for the personnel to join the immorality. Certain departments like Income Tax, Excise, Customs, Commercial Taxes, Public Works Department and Police are famous for their low ethical values. The question is that can this situation change? The answer is, yes, it can. However, the will and the efforts must meet with the challenge. Many countries, whether Kamal Pasha's Turkey or contemporary South Korea have shown resistance in transforming their governmental order and its attendant mind-set.

In 1951, A. D. Gorwala, in India, presented his report on Public Administration in which he had emphasized that honesty was one of the basic philosophical principles of good administration. It is contradictory that despite visible failure of moral standards in public life, the mainstream reports on administrative remodels have not focused on ethical issues. The Santhanam Committee report on the Prevention of Corruption in India in 1964 and a specific segmented report on the theme, the Railway Corruption Enquiry Committee by Acharya Kriplani in 1955 were the only that had focused on such issue. Otherwise, there have been no major attempts at recommending strategies for integrating moral values with the administrative system. In 1966, the ARC report on Lok Pal and Lok Ayukta was published on the issue, but again, it was limitedto structural changes rather than developing any new ethical order in public systems. In 2005, it was expecting that ethical matters of public services were given a respectable place in the emergent inquiry on administrative reforms in India with the announcement of the intention of appointing a second Administrative Reforms Commission by the Manmohan Singh government. The requirement is to go beyond the typical statements of administrative morality and be more careful and accurate in suggesting modifications in laws, rules, structures and behavioural patterns in the particular context of individual departments or organizations. For instance, issues of ethics in the Police Department carry a unique character and possible solutions than in the Education Department. Further, this would require a thorough modification in the laws and procedures belong to specific functional areas.

The administrative ethics of the twenty-first century is different from that of the twentieth century because of the increasing unionof ethical concerns at the cross-national level. Globalization of governance issues will likely be achieved byglobalization of the economic order. But, with the alleviation of gulf among countries in the area of the goals, philosophy and strategies of governance, the ethical affairs are likely to go beyond international boundaries. These will reflect the usual concerns of public administration such as efficiency, responsibility, accountability and integrity along with the growing beliefs in equity, justice, openness, compassion, altruism, responsiveness, human rights and human dignity. Expectantly, this would be influential in developing a new citizenship committed to the nourishment of administrative morality. In fact, public administration institution will have to act as facilitators and educators for nurturing such a positive citizenship. That is considered as the biggest challenge as well as an opportunity for the administrative system in the future.

Ethics is a wide-ranging concept, comprising all aspects of administration, and emphasis on moral and ethical norms has been an essential part of our tradition. Although, immoralities of corruption, malpractices and bureaupathology have slowly developed in our system. It is important to adopt holistic administrative reforms procedures to cater to purview questions on nature of work ethics, foci and concerns of ethics, various dimensions of ethics, and also the nature of obstacles to ethical accountability.

For the transparent, accountable, efficient and sensitive government system, a code of ethics in the form of service rules, procedural norms and administrative strategies is required. It is not possible to adopt a code of ethics that is self-serving and is area of constant external interference and manipulation. A certain amount of liberty is required for any code to be successful. We have seen a change in the pattern of authority, discipline and obedience. In addition, globalization trends have created universalization of ethical norms and values. Philosophy of governance has exceeded international boundaries. Almost each step of administration is involved in decision-making. The conflict between individual values, organizational standards and societal norms can be clearly seen. In spite of the fact that, the code may not recommend an accord on moral issues, but it can still provide direction and advice with respect to ethical conduct and help the administrators in analysing their options in the right perspective. This Unit has emphasized these relevant and important qualities.

Human Values

8 CHAPTER

COMPREHENDING THE SIGNIFICANCE OF HUMAN VALUES

Human values are regarded as the virtues that help understand the human element upon interaction of one human with other human beings. These values go a long way in creating bonds of humanity between people that are of great value for all human beings. These virtues instil a strong positive feeling of human essence towards other human beings. These attributes are so valuable that are liked by all and we expect others to follow the same as human beings. (Do unto the other what you wish for yourself). These human values create a sense of belongingness, reassurance, warmth and peace of mind.

Values are 'things that have an intrinsic worth in usefulness or importance to the possessor', or 'principles, standards, or qualities considered worthwhile or desirable'.

Human values form an important aspect of self-concept that proves to be a guiding principle for every individual.

Human values form the basis for any viable life to perform day-to-day activities in the society: they help create space for a drive, a movement towards one another, thus create an atmosphere of peace.

Human values are considered to be universal in nature which are shared by all human beings, irrespective of their religion, nationality, culture or personal history. By very character, they inject a sense of consideration towards others.

Human Values, for Instance, Induce a Feeling of

- Civility, respect, consideration;
- Honesty, justness, trustworthiness, sharing, fellowship, unity;
- Broadmindedness, acceptance, receiving, acknowledgment, admiration; fraternity, kinship, warmth, sympathy, affection.

DIFFERENT WAYS TO DEFINE VALUES

'Values mean whatever is actually liked, prized, esteemed, desired, approved, and enjoyed by anyone at any time'.
—Brightman

'Values are conscious or unconscious motivators and justifiers of the actions and judgments'.
—T.W. Hipple

'The term value means the relative prominence of the subject's interest or the dominant interest in personality'.
—Allport

A *'value system'* is described as a universal institution comprising of beliefs with regard to desired modes of conduct which are of high importance. Thus the significance of various values co-varies with the significance of other values in the value system. For instance, a person can have preference towards one value (for example, 'honesty') over other value (for example, successes).

ATTRIBUTES ASSOCIATED WITH VALUES AND MORAL VALUES

Max Scheler talks about four attributes associated with values in his theory of values.

1. They are highly pure qualities.
2. They are fair or unbiased and surpass the emotional feelings.
3. They are dependent, relative and hierarchical among themselves and the perceiver.
4. They are always depicted in pairs, indicating a positive value will always exist with its corresponding counter value.

Attributes Associated with Moral Values

- A value is regarded to be moral when it is considered to be reasonable and chosen freely by a person.
- They are quite noticeable as compared to other human values.
- They are known to be absolute which means they are independent of other values and preferred for their own sake.

CATEGORIZATION OF VALUES

Based on different thought process, educational thinkers have categorized values in different ways.

- Plato categorized values as:
  - Truth
  - Beauty
  - Goodness
- Classification made by Parker
  - Biological value
  - Economic value
  - Affective value
  - Social value
  - Intellectual value
  - Aesthetic value
  - Moral value
  - Religious value
- Classification made by Spranger
  - Theoretical values
  - Economic values

  - Aesthetic values
  - Social values
  - Political values
  - Religious values
- Classification of values made by Walter G. Everett
  - Economic value
  - Recreational value
  - Bodily value
  - Association value
  - Intellectual value
  - Character value
  - Aesthetic value
  - Religious value
- Recent categorization made by Brubacer
  - *Immediate value*: These values go a long way in satisfying the biological and psychological needs of a person.
  - *Remote value*: These values are significant in fulfilling the intelligent and rational needs of a person.
  - *Instrumental or extrinsic values*: These values are considered to be good because they are good for something. Organic values, in other words, can also be referred as instrumental values (Recreational value, Bodily value, Economic value).
  - *Intrinsic values*: Intrinsic values are ultimate and permanent values considered to be end in themselves.

Intrinsic and Extrinsic Values

- An intrinsic value refers to a value that one has of itself, and is independent of other things, including its context. For instance, fundamental form of consequentialism refers to whether an action is morally right or wrong is completely dependent on whether its consequences are intrinsically better than those of any other action performed under a specific situation.
- An intrinsic value refers to something that is good in and of itself. The thing that has true intrinsic value is happiness or pleasure. Intrinsic value is not contained in any physical things.
- An extrinsic (or relational) value is an attribute that is dependent on relationship of a thing with other things. It refers to the value, which is dependent on how much it creates intrinsic value. It is a way to reach a destination which means money has extrinsic value as it can be a means to purchase something you desire.
- The reason behind the fact that things have extrinsic value is that they themselves are the cause of happiness or pleasure or they can result in a number of other things ultimately causing happiness.
- Pleasure (Intrinsic Value) is the final goal for which all things of extrinsic value are the means.

OTHER WAYS TO CLASSIFY VALUES

- ***Personal Values***: These are principles and ideologies that are followed by a person in personal life.
- ***Universal Values***: These refer to principles that are expected to be followed by all people across the world.
- ***Human Values***: These values refer to principles and ideologies that are quite fundamental to human nature with an aim to make life easy and cheerful.
- ***Religious Values***: As per these values, people regard a particular thought to be the guiding force to differentiate good from bad.
- ***Civic Values***: These are principles that create the dos and don'ts for the people of a country.
- ***Moral Values***: These are principles and directives which prove to be the guiding light to adhere to the path of righteousness.
- Spiritual Values: These refer to principles that guide people to have faith in some philosophical thoughts.
- ***National Values***: These are principles, which motivate a person to assimilate the feelings of nationalism and national integration.
- ***Social Values***: These refer to certain principles and ideologies, which motivate people to live and work together in peace.
- ***Scientific values***: These values refer to principles and directives which compel people to test, investigate, interpret, validate or explore etc.

Indian Constitution as a Source of Values

The values that are contained in the Indian constitution are mainly based on four principles like ***Equality, Justice, Liberty and Fraternity.***

Principle of Preference of Values

1. ***Preference for permanent values***: Permanent values are preferred as compared to transitory values. Sensuous happiness is temporary; happiness due to association and character are comparatively stable and long-lasting. If the happiness due to association and character is compared, the values of truth, beauty, goodness and religion are always considered to be long-lasting.
2. ***Preference for productive values***: Productive values are shown preference over non-productive values. The intrinsic values go a long way in enriching the self which in turn help bring harmony and peace. These values play an important role in taking self to greater elevation while extrinsic values are used up in the process. These values when more extensive and universal, they tend to become more productive.
3. ***Preference for intrinsic values***: Intrinsic values are given preference over extrinsic values.

IMPORTANCE OF HUMAN VALUES

A personal value is regarded to be absolute or relative and ethical value can be assumed to be the foundation of ethical action. A *value system* is defined as a set of consistent values and measures. A *principle value* is the base for other values and measures of integrity. The determination of some values can be done physiologically and are usually objective in nature, for instance a wish to overcome physical pain or explore pleasure. Other values are regarded to be subjective, which can vary from individual to individual or from culture to culture, and get aligned with belief and belief systems in different ways. Different types of values are ethical/moral values, doctrinal/ideological (religious, political) values, social values along with aesthetic values. It is argued if those values that cannot be determined physiologically clearly, for instance altruism, are intrinsic in nature, and if some values, for instance acquisitiveness, can be categorized as vices or virtues. The study of values has been done in sociology, anthropology, social psychology, moral philosophy as well as business ethics. Values can be explained as broad preferences associated with appropriate courses of action or results. Fundamentally, values reflect a sense of right and wrong of a person or what "ought" them to be. 'Equal rights for all', 'Excellence deserves admiration', and 'People should be treated with respect and dignity' are representative of values. Values have a nature to affect attitudes and behaviour. For instance, if you are of the belief that all people should have equal rights and you get a chance to work for an organization that gives preferential treatment to its managers as compared to its workers, you may get compelled to form an opinion that the company is not a suitable place to work; this can affect your actual potential or productivity or you may think of leaving the company. Had the company an unbiased policy, your attitude, opinion and behaviours would have been different and more positive.

Values are usually derived through cultural means, these are particularly transmitted from parents to children. Parents can have different values in different cultures. For instance, parents in a hunter-gatherer society or those who are dependent on subsistence agriculture give more importance to practical survival skills from the very beginning of their birth. Many such cultures start training children to use different mechanical tools which may range from sharp tools like knives to many other such tools from the beginning of their childhood ages. Italian parents give importance to social and emotional abilities including even composure. Spanish parents expect their children to be more socially oriented. Swedish parents show more importance to security and happiness. Dutch parents give more emphasis on aspects like freedom, longer attention time, and foreseeable schedules. American parents are unusual for strongly valuing intellectual ability, especially in a narrow 'book learning' sense. The Kipsigis people of Kenya admire those children who are not only good-looking but also make use of their intelligence in a responsible and helpful way, which is referred to as*ng'om*.

Value Theory

Value theory comprises of a number approaches so as to understand how, why and to what extent people give importance to different things; whether the thing is a person, idea, object or anything else. This type of investigation can be found in ancient philosophy, where this is described as axiology or ethics. Early philosophical investigations required an understanding of the concept of good and evil. Today value theory is more or less scientifically empirical, which cites what type of values people give importance to and tries to comprehend the reasoning behind it in the context of psychology, sociology and economics. In general, distinction between moral and natural goods is made. Moral goods are described to be those that are associated with the conduct of persons, which usually brings admiration or blame whereas natural goods are associated with objects and not persons. For instance, to say that 'Mary is a morally good person' may contain a different sense of 'good' as compared to the one used in the sentence 'That was some good food'. The primary focus of ethics is on moral goods instead of natural goods, while economics is more concerned about what is economically good for the society and shows interest in natural goods as well but no single person. However, the relevance of both moral and natural goods can be related to goodness and value theory, which is more general in scope. In sociology, value theory has more to do with personal values which are commonly held by a community, and also take note of how those values show changes under specific situations. Various groups of people may follow or give preference to different kinds of values which may an impact on social behaviour. A large number of Western theorists such as Max Weber, mile Durkheim, Talcott Parsons and Jurgen Habermas underline the significance of values as an analytical independent variable. Classical examples of sociological traditions include institutionalism, historical materialism (including Marxism), behaviourism, pragmatic-oriented theories, postmodern philosophy along with various objectivist-oriented theories which negate or lessens the significance of the question associated with values.

Methods of study may include surveys in the form of questionnaire to simple observation of participant.

Ethics and Axiology

If thought with intuition, theories of value are crucial to ethics. Philosophers have made a number of vital distinctions in the treatment of value.

Intrinsic and Instrumental Value

There have been many people who find it highly useful to differentiate *instrumental value* from *intrinsic values* which was first explained by Plato in the 'Republic'. An instrumental value can be useful as a means to acquire something else that is good (for instance, as an instrument, a radio is good so far as hearing music is concerned). A thing that is of intrinsic value is worth having for itself, and not as a means to something else. This offers value intrinsic and extrinsic characteristics. Intrinsic and instrumental goods are not mutually exclusive categories. There are some things that are good not just in themselves but also good in getting other things that are considered to be good. 'Understanding science' may be such a good, being both worthwhile in and of itself and may become a great way to achieve other goods. An important point that is made by writers like Aldo Leopold and Holmes Rolston III in environmental ethics is that wild nature and healthy ecosystems have intrinsic value, prior to and apart from their instrumental value as resources for humans, and should therefore be preserved. The articulation of this type of reasoning has further been done in recent years by Canadian philosopher John McMurtry in the *Encyclopaedia of Life Support Systems* published by UNESCO.

Pragmatism and Contributory Goodness

In the book *Theory of Valuation,* John Dewey (1859–1952) has shown goodness as a result of ethic valuation, a regular balancing of 'ends in view'. An end in view was described as an objective potentially accepted which may be refined or denied depending on its consistency with other objectives or as a means to objectives already held, almost identical to an object having comparative intrinsic value. His empirical approach was associated with absolute intrinsic value denial, not accepting intrinsic value as an innate or long-lasting characteristic of things. He considered it as a misleading product of our regular valuing activity as purposive beings. Dewey absolutely rejected the existence of anything like intrinsic values and had same opinion in regard to moral values—a learning process was the basis of moral values; these moral values were never considered to be 'intrinsic' either absolutely or relativist. (In reality, a relative intrinsic value is a self-contradictory term; intrinsic values are either absolute or else they can be intrinsic by definition). Another improvement relates to making distinction of contributory goods having a contributory conditionality. These are provided with the same qualities as is found with the good thing, but require some emergent characteristics of a whole state-of-affairs so as to be good. For instance, salt has got the characteristic of food on its own, and at the same time can be described to be good, but its goodness gets far better when it becomes a part of a cooked meal. Offering a good out of this context is not the result that is expected. In other words, such goods are only good under certain conditions. This is opposed to other goods, which may be treated 'good' in a wider range of situations.

Kant: Hypothetical and Categorical Goods

Moral philosophy was greatly influenced by the thinking of Immanuel Kant (1724–1804). He considered moral value to be a distinctive and invariable characteristic that can be identified, and is considered to be an absolute value instead of a relative value. He exhibited that a large number of practical goods are good only in states-of-affairs explained by a sentence with an 'if' clause, for instance, in the sentence, 'Sunshine is only good if you do not live in the desert'. Further, the 'if' clause usually relate the category with which the judgment was associated (art, science, etc.). Kant considered these as 'hypothetical goods,' and made an attempt to discover a 'categorical' good that would operate across all categories of judgment irrespective of an 'if-then' clause. A significant outcome of Kant's search was the concept of a *good will* which is treated as the only intrinsic good. Besides, Kant considered a good will to be acting as per a moral command, the 'Categorical Imperative': 'Act according to those maxims that you could will to be universal law' but should not be confused with the Ethic of Reciprocity or Golden Rule, e.g. Mt. 7:12. Whereas the golden rule states that 'One should treat others as one would like others to treat oneself', Kant is of the view that we should analyse if an act can be executed at the same time by all without any exclusion. For instance, murder cannot be executed at the same time by everyone, one set of people would have to live while the other would have to die. That disparity is an exception. The act cannot be operated without exception, hence it fails the categorical imperative. Compare this with the golden rule which shows subjectivity to different individuals. If the logic of the golden rule were considered, I would kill other person only if it would be acceptable for me to kill others. This important point has to be kept in mind, because categorical imperative proposed by Kant ignores this flaw. Based on this and a few other axioms, Kant came up with a moral system that can be applicable to any "praiseworthy person."

Kantian philosophers are of the view that any common definition of goodness must be in a position to define goods that are absolute so far as Kant's intention is concerned.

MEANING OF VALUE IN TERMS OF ETHICS

In ethics, value refers to degree of importance of something, with a purpose to determine what type of action is best to be performed or what kind of life is best to be lived (deontology), or at least make an effort to elaborate the value of different actions (axiology). It may be described as treating actions themselves as abstract objects, putting value to them. It concerns right conduct and good life, in the context that a highly, or at least relatively highly, valuable action may be considered as ethically 'good' (adjective sense), and an action of low, or at least relatively low, value may be considered as 'bad'. Things that make an action valuable depend on the ethical values of the objects it increases, reduces or changes. An object with 'ethic value' may be called as an 'ethic or philosophic good' (noun sense).

- Ethical value may be viewed as a study under ethics, which may, in turn, be classified as philosophy. Similarly, ethics may be considered to be a subfield of philosophy, *ethical value* may be considered to be a subgroup of the more broad (and vague) philosophic value. Ethical value refers to degree of importance of something, with the aim to determine what action or life is best to perform, or at least make an effort to explain the value of various actions. It may be described as treating actions themselves as abstract objects, putting value to them. It concerns right conduct and good life, in the sense that a highly, or at least relatively highly, valuable action or may be regarded as *good,* and an action of low, or at least relatively low, value may be regarded as *bad.*
- Value theory also comprises of the study of ethical value.

On some occasion, the use of ethical value is synonymous with goodness. However, goodness has a number of other meanings also and may thus be considered to be more ambiguous.

Absolute or Relative

The meaning of personal and cultural values is relative in nature as they differ from person to person and in broader sense, between people of different cultures. Whereas theories of the existence of *absolute values*, which can also be called as *noumenal values* (not to get puzzled with mathematical absolute value). An absolute value can be explained as philosophically absolute which are not dependent on individual and cultural views, and are also independent of whether it is known or apprehended or not.

Relative value may be considered as an 'experience' by subjects of the absolute value. Relative value thus shows variation depending on individual and cultural interpretation, while absolute value stays constant, irrespective of its individual or collective 'experience'.

Intrinsic or Extrinsic

Philosophic value may be classified into *instrumental value* and *intrinsic values*. An instrumental value is significant as a means to acquire something else that is good for instance, a radio as an instrument is good so as to hear music. An intrinsically valuable thing is worth for itself, not as a means to something else. It gives intrinsic value and extrinsic characteristics. An *ethic good* with *instrumental value* may be described as an ethic mean, and an *ethic good* with *intrinsic value* may be described as an end-in-itself. An object may be identified with both a mean and an end-in-itself. Intrinsic and instrumental goods are not recognized as mutually exclusive categories. Some objects are both good in themselves, and also good to get other good objects. 'Understanding science' may be such a good, being both worthwhile in and of itself, and as a means to achieve other goods. In such cases, the sum of instrumental (specifically the all instrumental value) and intrinsic value of an object may be used while that object is put in value systems.

Average and Instantaneous Value

Keeping time in mind, a distinction between *average ethic* or *philosophic value* and *instantaneous ethic* or *philosophic value* is drawn.

- The *average ethic or philosophic value* refers to the average of the ethic or philosophic value of an object during a certain time period. If not else specified it is supposed to be the value duration of the object in mind. It can, however, also denote a chain of events duration or other specific time period.
- The *instantaneous ethic or philosophic value* refers to the ethic or philosophic value of an object at a specific point of time. If may refer to a point of time in *present*, *past* or *future*.

Total Value

The total ethic or philosophic value of an object can be considered to be the product of its average value, average intensity and *value duration*. It may vary from being absolute or relative or both.

Any reduction in the whole value, intensity or duration of an object reduces its total value and vice versa. For instance, again while considering a fictional life-stance for waffles as of ends-in-themselves, it still does not create any total value if there are no waffles, no intensity, despite how much average value a waffle has. In other words, the total value can be explained as being the sum of the total intrinsic value and total instrumental value. Still, it may vary from being relative or *absolute*, or both.

Economic and Philosophic Value

A distinction between philosophical value and economic value can be made, as philosophical value is not dependent on some other desired condition or commodity. The rise in economic value of an object may be due to the high supply of exchangeable desired condition or commodity, for instance money and may have an opposite effect when there is low supply of money. Nevertheless, economic value may result due to philosophical value. In the subjective theory of value, the personal philosophic value that a person puts in possessing something is reflected in what economic value this person puts in it. The limit where a person thinks of purchasing something may be considered as the point where the *personal philosophic value* of possessing something surpasses the personal philosophic value of what is given up in the form of exchange for it, e.g. money. In this context, everything can possess a 'personal economic value' in contrast to its 'societal economic value'.

Equality

Philosophic or ethic value equality pertains to the concept of two objects with the same philosophic value. Depending on the value, it can have different types:

- ***Philosophic or ethic intrinsic value equality***: Under this, the objects possess the same *intrinsic value.*
- ***Philosophic or ethic instrumental value equality***: Under this, the objects possess the same *instrumental value.*
- ***Philosophic or ethic whole value equality***: Under this, the objects possess the same *whole value.*
- ***Philosophic or ethic total value equality***: In this case, the objects possess the same *total value.*

VALUE SYSTEM

A *value system* is defined as a collection of consistent ethic values and measures which is used with an aim to ensure ethical or ideological integrity. A precise and well-organized *value system* can be identified with a moral code.

Positive and Negative Value

A difference between positive and negative philosophic or ethic value can be observed. While positive ethic value is usually correlated with something that is pursued or maximized, negative ethic value can be correlated with something that is avoided or minimized. Negative value may be referred as both intrinsic negative value and/or instrumental negative value.

Intrinsic Value

Intrinsic value refers to an ethical and philosophic property. It is the ethical or philosophic value that an object has 'in itself' or 'for its own sake', as an intrinsic property. An object with intrinsic value may be considered to be an end or (in Kantian terminology), end-in-itself. It is in contrast with instrumental value (or extrinsic value), the value of which is dependent on how much intrinsic value is generated by it. For a eudaemonist, happiness has intrinsic value, while having a family may not have intrinsic value, yet be instrumental as it gives rise to happiness. Intrinsic value is a term that is used in axiology, which can be described as the study of quality or value. Intrinsic value is primarily used in ethics, however its concept can also be utilized in philosophy, with terms that may necessarily be referred to the same concept.

- As 'ultimate importance' it is associated with a sentient being so as to forma life stance.
- It is identical with the meaning of life, as this may be expressed as what is meaningful or valuable in life. However, *meaning of life* is vaguer, with other uses as well.
- *Summum bonum* is fundamentally its equivalent in medieval philosophy.
- The relative intrinsic value is almost identical with the ethic ideal.
- Inherent value may be considered as a first grade instrumental value when the intrinsic value is associated with a personal experience.

Instrumental Value

Instrumental value (or extrinsic value, contributory value) is the value of objects, both physical objects and abstract objects, not as ends-in-themselves, but as means of achieving something else. It is often in contrast with items of intrinsic value. It is studied in the field of value theory.

An ethic good with instrumental value may be considered as an ethic mean, not necessarily being an end in itself.

An *ethic mean* is usually only used as a plurale tantum, so it is expressed as ethic means or just *means*.

Direct and Indirect Value

An instrumental value may be directly valuable or more or less indirectly so. For example, in the context of a hedonist with pleasure as end-in-itself, then music may be viewed as something directly instrumentally valuable by directly creating pleasure. A guitar, on the contrary, may be considered as something indirectly instrumentally valuable, since it creates end-in-itself by creating music which, in turn, creates the end-in-itself pleasure in this instance. Often, irrespective of what is the meaning of having intrinsic value, the instrumental values may be considered to have different grades of instrumental value, the first grade instrumental value is the direct instrumental value, the second grade instrumental value is the degree something generates this, etc. etc. until the infinite grade instrumental value. The universe may be associated with a series of events of objects, possibly finally producing the end-in-itself. More than one thing may produce something of the next grade value—both a guitar and a piano may produce music. Besides, a thing may produce many other things in the chain-reaction—money, for instance, may result in producing both guitars and pianos. Thus, the causality may be described as a fabric of events, with a number of series of events intertwined, on some occasion splitting while on other joining. It may sometimes be designated as more or less self-generating, when an object with instrumental value generates itself somewhere later in the series of events.

Positive and Negative Instrumental Value

Instrumental value may be both positive and negative value. An object associated with positive instrumental value may be termed a *positive mean* or a *posmean*. Whereas an object associated with negative instrumental value may be regarded as a *negative mean* or a *negmean*. A *posmean* may be described as something that directly or indirectly produces a posend. A *negmean*, on the contrary, may be described as something that generates a negend either directly or indirectly.

Difference Instrumental Value

Usually, any object can have more or less both positive and negative instrumental value. In such instances, the *difference instrumental value* of the object is the difference between the positive and negative value, with the positive value as minuend and the negative value as subtrahend and the resulting difference value relates to the mathematical difference between them. It may also be called the *all-ponetivities instrumental value*, so as to be homologous to other types of instrumental values.

The rise of such multiple positive or negative values may be because of multiple grades, ends or parallels of instrumental value.

All Instrumental Value

The *all instrumental value* of an object is the instrumental value for all ends, all grades for each of these ends and all parallels for each of these grades, and regarding both positive and negative value. In a way, it is the *all-grades, all-ends, all-ponetivities and different instrumental value* of an object.

The *all instrumental value* and the intrinsic value of an object both when combined form the whole value of the object.

Total Instrumental Value

The total instrumental of an object is described as the product of its *average all instrumental value*, average value intensity and value duration. It may be either absolute or relative.

The *total instrumental value* and total intrinsic value when combined together form the total whole value of an object.

Application of Human Values

When the values construct is applied in the social sciences, it suffers from the absence of an agreed-upon conception of basic values, of the content and structure of relations among these values, and of reliable methods to measure them. This article takes into account the data from more than 70 countries by making use of two different instruments so as to ascertain a theory aiming to bridge apart of this gap. It is associated with the fundamental values that are recognized by individuals in all cultures. The theory identifies 10 motivationally distinct values and specifies the dynamics of conflict and congruence among them. These dynamics produces a design of relations among values common to groups that are culturally diverse, indicating a universal organization of human motivations. Individuals and groups show difference in their priorities to these values. The article evaluates sources of individual differences in value priorities and behavioural and attitudinal consequences that result due to these priorities for particular values. While doing this, it takes into account the processes through which values get affected and through which they affect action. Since their inception, values have been regarded to be a central concept in the social sciences. For both Durkheim (1893, 1897) and Weber (1905), values were highly important so as to explain social and personal organization and change. The role of values has not just been important in sociology, but also in psychology, anthropology along with other related disciplines. Values can go a long way in characterizing societies and individuals, tracing change over time and explaining the motivational bases of attitudes and behaviour. Despite or, perhaps, due to the extensive application of values, multiple concepts of this construct have emerged (e.g., Boudon, 2001; Inglehart, 1997; Kohn, 1969; Parsons, 1951; Rokeach 1973). It has been observed that the application of the values construct in the social sciences has suffered, however, from the absence of an agreed-upon conception of basic values, of the content and structure of relations among these values, and of reliable empirical methods to measure them (Hitlin & Piliavin, 2004; Rohan, 2000). This article talks about a theory that aims to remove the part of this gap associated with the values of individuals (Schwartz, 1992, 2005a).

The theory is associated with the fundamental values that are taken note of by people across all cultures. It takes note of10motivationally distinct value orientations and specifies the dynamics of conflict and congruence among these values. Some values oppose other values (for instance, benevolence and power) whereas others show great compatibility (for instance, conformity and security). The 'structure' of values pertains to these relations of conflict and congruence among values, not to their relative significance. If the structures of value were similar across groups that are culturally diverse, this would mean that there is a universal organization of human motivations. Of course, even if the types of human motivation that values express and the structure of relations among them are universal, individuals and groups show substantial difference in the relative importance they offer to their values. This means individuals and groups are known to have different value 'priorities' or 'hierarchies'. Individuals do not show successful adaptation with these requirements of human existence on their own. Rather, people must look for right goals to adapt with them, inform others about them and receive necessary assistance in their pursuit. Values are considered to be socially desirable concepts that are used to represent these goals mentally and the vocabulary is used to express them in social interaction. Based on evolutionary viewpoint (Buss, 1986), these goals and the values that express them are of crucial survival significance.

- ***Self-Direction***: Explaining goal: independent thought and action—selecting, generating and searching. Self-direction is derived from organismic requirements for control and mastery (e.g., Bandura, 1977; Deci, 1975) and interactional requirements of autonomy and independence (e.g., Kluckhohn, 1951; Kohn & Schooler, 1983; Morris, 1956) (creativity, freedom, selecting own goals, inquisitive, independent)[self-respect, brilliant, secrecy].

- ***Stimulation***: Explaining goal: elation, novelty and hurdles in life. Stimulation values are derived from the organismic need for variety and stimulation so as to ensure an optimal, positive, instead of threatening, level of activation (e.g., Berlyne, 1960). This need is possibly related to the needs associated with self-direction values (cf. Deci, 1975) (a life filled with variety, a life filled with enthusiasm, courage).
- ***Hedonism***: Explaining goal: pleasure or sensuous gratification for oneself. Hedonism values are derived from organismic needs and the pleasure that help satisfy them. There are many theorists from different disciplines (e.g., Freud, 1933; Morris, 1956; Williams, 1968) who are known to cite hedonism (pleasure, enjoying life, self-indulgent).
- ***Achievement***: Explaining goal: individual success by showing competence as per social standards. Competent performance that creates resources is required for the survival of individuals, groups and institutions to achieve their goals. Achievement values can be found in a number of sources (e.g., Maslow, 1965; Rokeach, 1973). As explained here, achievement values give emphasis on demonstrating competence in the form of existing cultural standards, thereby acquiring social approval (ambitious, successful, capable, influential) [intelligent, self-respect, social recognition].
- ***Power***: Explaining goal: social stature and prestige, command or supremacy over people and resources. The operation of social institutions seemingly requires some level of status differentiation (Parsons, 1951). A dominance/submission dimension arises in almost all empirical analyses of interpersonal relations both within and across cultures (Lonner, 1980). To substantiate this fact of social life and to inspire group members to ensure its acceptance, groups must consider power as a value. Power values may also result due to the transformations of individual needs for dominance and control (Korman, 1974). Value analysts have also made reference to power values (e.g., Allport, 1961) (authority, wealth, social power)[preserving my public image, social recognition]. Social esteem has been the focus of both power and achievement values. However, achievement values (e.g., ambitious) stress the active exhibition of successful performance in concrete interaction, whereas power values (e.g., authority, wealth) stress on attaining or preserving a dominant position within the more general social system.
- ***Security***: Explaining goal: safety, harmony and stability of society, of relationships, and of self. Security values are derived from fundamental individual and group requirements (cf. Kluckhohn, 1951; Maslow, 1965; Williams, 1968). Security values are of two subtypes. Some mainly aid individual interests (e.g. clean), while some others aid wider group interests (e.g., security of a nation). Even the latter, however, expresses the goal of security for self (or those with whom one identifies) to a significant level. So, the two subtypes can be combined together into a more inclusive value (social order, family security, national security, clean, reciprocation of favours) [healthy, moderate, sense of belonging].
- ***Conformity***: Explaining goal: restraint of actions, inclinations, and impulses possibly disturb or harm others and disregard social expectations or norms. Conformity values are derived from the requirement that individuals curb inclinations that might upset

and weaken smooth interaction and group functioning. Virtually all value analyses make a mention of conformity (e.g., Freud, 1930; Kohn & Schooler, 1983; Morris, 1956; Parsons, 1951). As they are explained by me, conformity values give emphasis on self-restraint in daily interaction, often with close others. (obedient, self-discipline, politeness, honouring parents and elders)[loyal, responsible]

- ***Tradition***: Explaining goal: honour, commitment and acceptance of the customs and ideas that one's culture or religion offers. Groups everywhere create practices, symbols, ideas and beliefs that are representatives of their shared experience and fate. These are accepted as valued group customs and traditions (Sumner, 1906). They stand for the group's solidarity, expression of its unique worth and play a role to its survival (Durkheim, 1912/1954; Parsons, 1951). They generally take the form of religious rites, beliefs and norms of behaviour (regard for tradition, humble, devout, accepting my portion in life)[moderate, spiritual life]. Tradition and conformity values are particularly close motivationally; they share the goal of subordinating the self in favour of expectations that are socially imposed. They mainly show difference in the objects to which one subordinates the self. Conformity comprises of subordination to persons with whom one makes constant interaction—parents, teachers and bosses. Tradition pertains to subordination to more abstract objects in the form of religious and cultural customs or ideas. This means conformity values exhort responsiveness to current, possibly changing expectations. Tradition values require responsiveness to unchangeable expectations from the past.
- ***Benevolence***: Explaining goal: preserving and improving the welfare of people with whom one is in constant personal touch (the 'in-group'). Benevolence values are derived from the fundamental need for functioning of smooth group (cf. Kluckhohn, 1951; Williams, 1968) and from the organismic need for affiliation (cf. Korman, 1974; Maslow, 1965). Among the most critical relations are the relations associated with family and other essential groups. Benevolence values give emphasis on voluntary concern for the welfare of others. (helpful, honest, forgiving, responsible, loyal, true friendship, mature love)[Sense of belonging, meaning in life, a spiritual life]. Both benevolence and conformity values infuse a sense of cooperative and supportive social relations. However, benevolence values offer an internalized motivational base for such behaviour. On the contrary, conformity values infuse a sense of cooperation so as to overcome negative outcomes for self. Both of these values may stimulate the same helpful act, either separately or together.
- ***Universalism***: Explaining goal: comprehending, admiration, tolerance, and protection to ensuring welfare of all people and nature. This is in contrast with the in-group focus of benevolence values. Universalism values are derived from needs for survival of individuals and groups. But people do not take note of these needs till they come across others beyond the extended primary group or till they understand the low level of natural resources. People may then become aware of the failure to accept others who are different and treat them fairly which lead to fatal struggle. They may also become aware of the failure to protect the natural environment causing depletion

of the resources that are crucial for life. Universalism integrates two subtypes of concern—to ensure the welfare of people in the larger society and world and nature (broadminded, social justice, equality, world at peace, world of beauty, unity with nature, wisdom, protecting the environment)[inner harmony, a spiritual life]. The fundamental social function of values is to motivate and control the behaviour of group members (Parsons, 1951). There are two mechanisms that are critical. First, values can be identified as internalized guides for individuals; they give relief to the group of the necessity for continuous social control. Second, people make use of values to explain specific behaviours as socially acceptable, to substantiate their demands on others, and to evoke desired behaviours. Socializers attempt to instil values either consciously or unconsciously so as to enhance the survival and prosperity of the group. To describe the meaning of the pan-cultural value hierarchy, we must make an attempt to explain why particular values are seen to be more or less desirable across societies.

Three demands of human nature and requirements of societal functioning are particularly significant to explain the observed hierarchy of pan-cultural value. (1) The most important is to promote and preserve cooperative and supportive relations among primary groups' members. The most crucial thing associated with value transmission is to generate commitment to positive relations, establishing identity with the group along with loyalty to its members. (2) Second thing is that individuals must be encouraged so as to invest the time, the physical and the intellectual effort required to carry out productive work with an aim to solve problems that arise at the time of performing task and develop new ideas and technical solutions. (3) Third, it is socially functional to legalize gratification of self-oriented needs and desires till the time this does not undermine the goals of group. Rejecting all such gratification would cause frustration among individuals, leading them to hold back their energies or efforts from the group and its tasks. The high significance of benevolence values (1st) arises from the core of positive, cooperative social relations in the family, the main setting for initial and continuing value acquisition. Benevolence values offer the internalized motivational base for such relations. They are reinforced and modelled early and frequently. Universalism values (2nd) also play a vital role to establishing positive social relations. They are mainly significant in operations when group members relate to those with whom they do not readily recognize in schools, work places and the like. They may even create problem to in-group solidarity at the time of intergroup conflict. So, universalism values are less significant as compared to benevolence values. Security (4th) and conformity (5th) values also strengthen harmonious social relations. They do this by preventing conflict and breach of group norms. But these values are commonly realized in response to demands and sanctions to overcome danger, manage prohibited impulses and limit the self. This limits their significance as it combats with pleasing self-oriented needs and desires. Besides, these values put stress on preserving the status quo conflicts with innovation in finding solutions to the tasks of the group. Action on tradition values (overall 8th) can also assist in strengthening group solidarity and therefore ensuring smooth functioning and survival of the group. But tradition values show little expression in the behaviour that interaction partners have a vital interest in controlling. They are mostly associated with commitment to abstract beliefs and symbols. Pursuing power values (10th) may harm or exploit others and spoil social relations. Still, they have some value because power values help to encourage individuals to work for the interests of the group. They also explain the social hierarchical arrangements in all societies. Self-direction (3rd) values act as the second and third fundamental functions of values without underestimating the first. They go a long way in enhancing creativity, innovation and coping with challenges the group may come across in critical situations. Behaviour based on these values is intrinsically enhanced. It meets the requirements of an individual without causing any problem to others. Therefore, it seldom causes any problem to positive social relations.

The moderate significance of achievement values (7th) may show a kind of compromise among the bases of value importance. On the positive side, these values encourage people to make investment in group tasks. They also legalize self-enhancing behaviour, till the time it makes its contribution to the well-being of the group. On the negative side, these values are highly significant in making efforts so as to achieve social consent that may hamper harmony in social relations and hinder the goal attainment of the group. The significance of hedonism (6th) and stimulation (9th) values are deduced from the needs to legalize inborn requirements to obtain pleasure and arousal. These values are possibly more significant as compared to power values because, unlike power values, their effort does not essentially cause problem to positive social relations. Each value seems to express one drive or a combination of two. Values convert drives into desirable goals available to awareness and can thus be useful in conscious planning and decision-making. The matches are as follows: benevolence—to bond; universalism—to bond + to learn; self-direction—to learn; stimulation—to learn (+ to obtain enjoyable experience); hedonism—(to learn) + to obtain enjoyable experience; achievement—to obtain; power—to obtain+ to protect; security—to protect; conformity and tradition—to protect+ to bond. This mapping of values onto drives goes around the value circle. The oppositions between values co-exist with the conflicts between drives that Lawrence and Nohria (2002) recognize. The matching of values to drives exhibits that an innate basis may assist in accounting for the near-universality of the value structure.

CONTRIBUTION OF DIFFERENT FACTORS IN INSTILLING VALUES

Contribution of Family in Instilling Values

Parents or family contributes significantly in providing education to a child. Parents are the most accessible members in a family to the child as compared to any other family members: 'Mother is the first teacher and Home is the first school'. The newly born baby shows almost complete dependency on parents who are committed to ensure their children's nourishment and upbringing. The elder members of the family train the developing baby about good behaviour, dress codes, traditions and expectations etc. Thus, it can be asserted safely that the children's minds develop prominently through the process of non-formal education in the homely atmosphere.

According to Pestalozzi, 'Home- A centre of love and affection is the best place for education and first school of child'. The most appropriate solution for the existing value crisis relates to dynamic parenting. If the country as a whole has to blossom, must show flexibility to improve. Without a harmonious atmosphere at home, peace in the country cannot be thought of.

It is really unfortunate that parents themselves are responsible for getting their children spoilt as 90% of children get excess pampering. It is the duty of parents that they teach their children the value of inner peace, contentment and achievement which would help them go beyond external indices of success like huge earnings or wealth. If the whole family is filled with fragrance sense of contentment and peace, all its members will remain hale and hearty. The role of elders thus becomes crucial in ensuring the right upbringing of the future generations. For a desired upbringing of our children, we have to teach them the significance of human values and a feel of spirituality based on self-control.

Parents should help their children comprehend certain components like understanding truth, a sense of responsibility, emotional maturity, communication skills, understanding the development of intellect, sense of judgment and observation, awareness of culture, personality development, religious and spiritual values and leadership qualities. Parents contribute significantly in transforming the character of a child. During the developmental stages of children, parents should help their children develop skills, attitude and emotions that can go a long way in building or spoiling the children's future. The mother and father are the first examples for their children in social behaviour because children watch them and try to follow. Therefore, the parents should make their children learn the right behaviour from the early childhood days.

Role of Family in the Development of Moral Values Among Children

- The family and society contribute significantly in cultivating the moral values among children. The relationship between the parents and children is crucial in determining the personality of child. Family is the best place where values can be learnt.
- Moral values in the form of truthfulness, happiness, peace, justice are inculcated in the thoughts, feelings and actions of children and function as ideals and standards important for their actions in their life. For the value system that is practiced in the family, it becomes quite natural for the young family members to learn if they are taught moral values systematically.
- The family plays an important role in shaping the attitude child with regard to people and society. It contributes in ensuring the mental growth and ambitions and values among children. A very good atmosphere of bliss and cheerfulness in the family helps ensure the development of love, kindness, affection and tolerance. A child always tries to learn his behaviour based on what he observes around him.
- Family contributes immensely in assisting a child socialize that has a great bearing in ensuring the development of the child. The role of joint family system and the presence of elders in the family are significant in ensuring social and moral development of the

children. This will also assist the young generation of the family inculcate human values and remove the negative tendencies of mind as they stay among elders.

- Children have a nature to identify themselves with their parents and other elder members of the family and therefore, consider them as their ideal to emulate and imitate. The correction in behavioural problems is made only by the involvement of family members in the life of children as most of their time is spent with the parents during their young ages.
- Family is regarded as the first social organization providing immediate proximity to children from where they can learn good behaviour.
- The emotional and physical aspects of a child are supported by social standards and customs defined by a family. The development of values by a family becomes the foundation based on which children learn, grow and perform in the society. These beliefs are crucial in providing children a way of life and help them transform into an individual in a society. These values and morals give a direction to the individual in his actions on a regular basis. Children can be transformed to be a good person because of the learning of values that are taught by their family members. Family values take a shape based on the ideas that are passed down from generation to generation. The family teaches the customs and traditions which are followed and by children. This enables children to lead a disciplined and organized life.
- Families values give a sense of strength to children with the help of which they stand strong on his views despite others trying to oppose their beliefs. A child is believed to have a strong sense of what is right and wrong and is less likely to get affected by opposing forces.

Contribution of Society in Cultivating Values

The child, being a bonafide member with all facilities at disposal, is initiated into learning in the society. The society may be offered new roles so as to contribute effectively and vigorously towards development and inculcation of values of different types. The expectations of society are in:

- Creating homogeneous environment so that the learners could take up valuable lessons on ethics, behaviour, adjustment, togetherness, sympathy and service.
- Reflecting simplicity, honesty, kindness and fairness in the conduct of children, so as to ensure the development of positive habits, attitude, inner strength and feeling and wish to live.
- Providing required freedom to ensure complete growth with experiences (Spencer) and with assistance of desired suggestion and persuasion (Stuart Mill).
- Explaining its customs, rituals, mythical stories, outcomes and contribution to the modern order of society.
- Taking the valuable lesson from Gandhian thoughts, 'do not hear ill, do not speak ill and do not see ill of others'.
- Narrating the cultural-socio-economic life patterns and the values the members of society should keep providing quality lessons taken from the scriptures like Vedas,

Upanishads, Geeta, Koran, Bible along with the teaching of the great souls and the saints.

- Making the children emotionally integrated for exercising the values like oneness, unity, neighbourhood, code-conduct, love and sympathy for the down-trodden or poor. The significance of values like co-operation, sincerity and commitment can be comprehended and inculcated in the society itself.
- As in real sense the children are considered to be the working force and asset to the society with relation to the nation, they need to learn the 'value of dignity of labour'.

Contribution of Educational Establishments in Teaching Values

Values Associated with Education

With no doubt in mind, it can be said that education is one of the most potential agencies that help mould the individuality and determine the future of individuals and nations. Thus, the whole sphere of education is based on the development of the morality among men and women. Plato led an emphasis on educational effort that should be aimed at promoting virtues. Herbert made a declaration that the entire work of education, which aims to provide a long and complex training, should target one very important concept called 'Morality'. Mahatma Gandhi opines, 'Education of heart, or Moral Education is the prime function to provide. If we succeed in building character of the individual, society will take care of itself'. In words of Bertrand Russel, the primary goal of education is the 'formation of character'.

Education is a medium for ensuring the cultivation of values; the end product is ensuring the development of character, individuality and humanness. The whole emphasis of education is on developing values in the conduct of people.

The University Education Commission (1964-66) lays emphasis on the Indian concept of education in following words:

'Education according to Indian tradition is not merely a means of earning a living; nor is it only a nursery of thought or a school for citizenship. It is the initiation into a life of spirit, a training of human souls in pursuit of truth and the practice of virtue'.

Educational values are the activities that are not just good or useful but also valuable from the perspective of education. These are crucial to every sphere of life. It goes a long way in generating the capacity of livelihood, professional performance, character and strong personality. It helps in promoting social efficiency by cultivating skills of social adjustments. The contribution can be experienced from the views of some of the following experts.

'The greatest use of education is not merely to collect facts, but to know man and make one self-know to man'.

—R. N. Tagore

'Education should be for the hand, head and heart. Education for the heart means spiritual training. The aim of education is self-realization, the summum bonum of life and education'.

—M. K. Gandhi

'Education is not limited to the imparting of information or training in skill. It has to give the educated a proper sense of values'. **—Radhakrishnan**

Contribution of Educational Institutions

In school, children are considered members of a small society that has great impact on the development of morality. Teachers are considered to be role models for students in school; they contribute an important role in cultivating their ethical behaviour.

Peers at school show courage in activities like cheating, lying, stealing and consideration for others. Despite rules and regulations, the educational establishments inculcate the value education to the children in an informal way. They play a significant role in promoting ethical behaviour among children. Some of the steps are as follows:

- ***Liability***: The children should be motivated to be accountable for their own deeds and should get a sense to respect and treat other people with kindness.
- ***Setting example***: The teachers have to set example for their children as outside their family they are the guide. When the children observe the role model exhibiting concern for others, inspiring them for their good action and assisting and guiding with their academic issues, the children inculcate the value of helping others just by watching it with fellow peers.
- ***Cooperation***: School teaches children some of the fundamental morals and values. They should be provided lessons on the importance of values like helping others by means of different activities like stories and tales which will motivate them to indulge in more helping behaviours.
- ***Admiration***: An appreciation of children by the teachers motivates them to develop pro-social behaviour, particularly for any specific activity they have engaged in to help others.

Cultivation of Values through Education

With an aim to underline the prominence of values in our educational programmes, the incorporation of following ideas in the educational programmes are necessary:

- Developing a sense of self-respect, self-growth, uniqueness and self-confidence.
- Enhancing selflessness, spirit of helpfulness and sharing.
- Inculcating respect for one's own property along with others.
- Comprehending the role of home in ensuring physical, emotional, cultural and spiritual progress of young people.
- Providing clear direction on sanitation, punctuality, using refined language, manners and respect for elders.
- Infusing a sense of awareness towards the needs of others.
- Enhancing civic sense and becoming aware of oneself as a member of a community in performing civic duties.
- Becoming more aware of the Constitution and rights along with duties.

- Becoming aware of the provision for promoting human dignity and justice, patriotism, national integrity and international understanding.
- Protecting the environment.
- Passing down the cultural heritage to younger generation.
- Spreading the philosophy of values.

Contribution of Teachers

A teacher is not just a mentor, facilitator or communicator but also a manager of the teaching or learning activities. She/he is the source of motivation filled with action, thought, vision and wisdom. A teacher is believed to perform the duty as assigned:

- A teacher is one who acts as the friend, philosopher and guide and teaches the skills for spending whole life successfully.
- Honesty, morality, truth along with non-violence should be considered the foundation of life for which learners look upon the behaviour of their teachers.
- Competency, methodology, strategy, technique of teaching and innovative skills should be imbibed by him so as to organize learning.
- The significance of the social and the national heritage, culture, civilization and its useful values to the modern adolescents should be explained by him.
- The values associated with the teacher's habits, behaviour, actions and thoughts must exhibit the real face in front of the students.

EMPATHY

Empathy is an ability to identify emotions being experienced by other fictional being. A person may require having a certain amount of empathy before one experiences the right feeling of kindness or compassion. The coining of the English word was done in 1909 by the psychologist Edward B. Titchener in an effort to translate the German word '*Einfühlungsvermögen*', a new phenomenon discovered at the end of 19th century primarily by philosopher Theodor Lipps. Later, its re-translation was done into the German language as '*Empathie*' which is still used there.

The origin of the English word is from the Greek word (*empatheia*), 'physical affection, passion, partiality' which comes from (*pathos*), 'passion' or 'suffering'. The term was made in use by Hermann Lotze and Robert Vischer to develop the German word *Einfühlung* ('feeling into'), which was translated into the English term empathy by Edward B. Titchener.

Alexithymia from the Ancient Greek words (*lexis*) and (*thumos*) modified by an alpha-privative—literally 'without words for emotions'—is a term that is used to specify a state of shortage in comprehending, processing or describing emotions in oneself. It should be noted that in Modern Greek, the term 'empathy' translates as 'hatred' or 'spitefulness' (a condition of causing passion, rather than mutual relation to one's passion); is the right modern equivalent of empathy. Empathy comprises of a number of different definitions that include a wide range of emotional states, from caring for other people and having an eagerness to help them, to having emotional experiences that match emotions of other person, to knowing the thinking or feeling of other person, to obscuring the line between self and other.

Since empathy comprises of comprehending the emotional states of other people, the way it is portrayed is derived from the characteristics of emotions themselves. For instance, if emotions are considered to be centrally identified by bodily feelings, then understanding the bodily feelings of another will be crucial to empathy. On the contrary, if emotions are primarily characterized by a combination of beliefs and desires, then understanding these beliefs and desires will be highly crucial to empathy. The ability to consider oneself as another person is a complex process involving an intense feeling of creativity and imagination. However, the fundamental ability to identify emotions is probably innate and may be attained unconsciously. Yet it can be trained and attained with different levels of intensity or accuracy. Empathy essentially refers to a 'more or less' quality. The paradigm case of an empathic interaction, however, comprises of a person disseminating a right identification of the importance of continuing intentional actions, related emotional states and personal traits of another person in a way that the recognized person can bear. Both accurate and tolerable recognitions are important features of empathy. The human ability to identify the bodily feelings of another is associated with one's imitative capacities and appears to be present in an innate capacity to relate the bodily movements and facial expressions one sees in another with the proprioceptive feelings of creating those corresponding movements or expressions oneself. Humans appear to create the same immediate connection between the tone of voice and other expressions associated with voice and inner feeling.

Empathy is different from sympathy, pity and emotional contagion. Sympathy or empathic concern refers to the compassionate feelings or concern for others, a desire to see them better off or cheerful. Pity refers to feeling that other person is in trouble and in need of assistance as they are unable to resolve their problems themselves, often referred to as 'feeling sorry' for someone. Emotional contagion is a situation when an individual (especially an infant or a member of a mob) imitatively 'catches' the emotions that other people are exhibiting without essentially noticing this to be occurring.

EMOTIONAL AND COGNITIVE EMPATHY

Empathy Associated with Emotion and Cognition

Empathy can be categorized under two major components:

- *Emotional empathy or affective empathy*: This refers to a drive to reciprocate with a right emotion to mental states of others. Our capability to identify emotionally is believed to be based on emotional contagion: being influenced by emotional or arousal state of others.
- *Cognitive empathy*: It refers to drive to take note of mental states of others. The term cognitive empathy and theory of mind are usually used as synonyms.

Despite the fact that these constructs have not been defined, there is no dispute about this distinction. In different psychiatric disorders, there is a distinction in disturbance of affective empathy against cognitive. Psychopathy, schizoid identity issue, depersonalization and narcissism are portrayed by weaknesses in passionate compassion however not in subjective sympathy, whereas bipolar disorder, borderline, and, according to a few accounts, autistic traits are related with deficiencies in psychological sympathy yet not in enthusiastic sympathy. Likewise in individuals without mental scatters, the harmony amongst emotional and cognitive empathy fluctuates. A meta-investigation of late fMRI investigations of compassion affirmed that distinctive cerebrum territories are initiated amid affective—perceptual sympathy and cognitive—evaluative compassion. Additionally an examination with patients with different kinds of brain damage affirmed the difference between emotional and cognitive empathy. In particular, the inferior frontal gyrus gives off an impression of being in charge of enthusiastic compassion, and the ventromedial prefrontal gyrus appears to intervene intellectual sympathy. Emotional empathy can be further classified as:

- ***Personal agony***: It refers to the tendency to encounter egotistical sentiments of inconvenience and nervousness because of another's misery.
- ***Empathic concern***: The tendency to have sympathy and compassion for others on account of their suffering.

There is no agreement with respect to the inquiry if individual misery is a fundamental type of sympathy or in the event that it falls outside of compassion. There is a formative viewpoint to this subdivision. Newborn children react to the trouble of others by getting bothered themselves; just when they are 2 years of age they begin to react in other-situated courses, endeavouring to help, solace and share.

DEVELOPMENT

By the age of two years, kids ordinarily start to show the major practices of sympathy by having a passionate reaction that compares with someone else's enthusiastic state. Considerably prior at one year of age, newborn children have a few fundamentals of compassion as in they comprehend that much the same as their own particular activities, other individuals' activities have objectives. Some of the time, little children will comfort others or exhibit caring behaviour for them at as early an age as two. Additionally amid the second year, little children will play diversions of lie or 'imagine' with an end goal to trick others, and this requires the youngster comprehend what others accept before he or she can control those convictions. As per specialists at the University of Chicago who utilized functional magnetic resonance imaging (fMRI), kids between the ages of 7 and 12 years give off an impression of being normally disposed to feel sympathy for others in torment. Their discoveries are steady with past fMRI investigations of pain empathy with grown-ups. The exploration likewise found that extra parts of the brain were activated when adolescents saw someone else purposefully hurt by another individual, incorporating reasons associated with moral thinking.

In spite of having the capacity to hint at some compassion, for example, endeavouring to comfort a crying infant, from as early as a year and a half to two years, most youngsters don't demonstrate a completely fledged theory of brain until around the age of four. Theory of brain includes the capacity to comprehend that other individuals may have convictions that are not quite the same as one's own, and is thought to include the psychological segment of compassion. Youngsters normally end up passing 'false conviction' undertakings, thought to be a test for a theory of brain, around the age of four. People with autism (a mental imbalance) frequently discover utilizing a theory of mind extremely troublesome (e.g., Baron-Cohen, Leslie & Frith, 1988; the Sally-Anne test). Compassionate development is cognitive structural theory created at the Yale University School of Nursing and addresses how grown-ups consider or comprehend the personhood of patients. The hypothesis, first connected to medical attendants and since connected to different callings, hypothesizes three levels that have the properties of intellectual structures. The third and most elevated level is held to be a meta-ethical hypothesis of the ethical structure of care. Those grown-ups working with level-III understanding blend frameworks of equity and ethics based on care.

NEUROLOGICAL BASIS

Research as of late has concentrated on conceivable brain forms underlying the experience of compassion. For example, functional magnetic resonance imaging (fMRI) has been utilized to explore the practical life systems of sympathy. These examinations have demonstrated that watching someone else's enthusiastic state initiates parts of the neuronal system engaged with preparing that same state in oneself regardless of whether it is disgust, touch or agony. The investigation of the neural underpinnings of sympathy has gotten enhanced interest following the objective paper published by Preston and Frans de Waal, following the revelation of mirror neurons in monkeys that fire both when the animal watches another play out an activity and when they themselves perform it. In their paper, they made an argument that attended perception of the object's state naturally activates neural representations, and that this activation naturally primes or produces the related autonomic and somatic reactions (thought of observation activity coupling), unless inhibited. This component is like the regular coding hypothesis amongst observation and activity. Another current investigation gives confirmation of isolated neural pathways activating reciprocal suppression in various regions of the brain related with the execution of 'social' and 'mechanical' assignments. These discoveries propose that the comprehension related to thinking about the 'state of another person's mind' and 'causal/mechanical properties of inanimate objects' are neutrally suppressed from happening simultaneously.

ANGER AND DISTRESS

Anger

Empathic anger is a feeling, a type of empathic pain. Empathic anger is felt in a circumstance where another person is being harmed by someone else or thing. It is conceivable to see this type of outrage as a pro-social feeling. Empathic outrage affects both aiding and punishing desires. Empathic outrage can be categorized into two sub-classifications: trait empathic outrage and state empathic outrage. The connection amongst compassion and outrage reaction towards someone else has likewise been explored, with two investigations essentially finding that the higher a man's point of view taking capacity, the less outraged they were in light of an incitement. Empathic concern did not, notwithstanding, essentially anticipate outrage reaction, and higher individual pain was related with enhanced outrage.

Distress

Empathic trouble is feeling the apparent torment of someone else. This inclination can be changed into empathic outrage, sentiments of treachery or blame. These feelings can be seen as pro-social, and some say they can be viewed as thought processes in moral conduct.

Atypical Empathic Response

Atypical empathic reactions are found in individuals on the autism array, those with specific personality disorders, for example, borderline personality disorder, psychopathy, narcissistic personality disorder, and schizoid personality disorder, besides individuals with conduct or bipolar disorder, and those encountering depersonalization.

Autism Spectrum

The cooperation amongst compassion and the autism spectrum is a perplexing and progressing field of research. A number of distinct variables are proposed to be impacting everything here.

Alexithymia

Research recommends that 85% of ASD people have alexithymia, which includes not only the powerlessness to verbally express feelings, but particularly the failure to identify emotional states in self or others. As indicated by late fMRI studies, the disorder of alexithymia, a condition in which an individual is rendered unequipped for perceiving and articulating emotional excitement in self or others, is in charge of an extreme absence of emotional empathy. The absence of empathic attunement inborn to alexithymic states may diminish quality and fulfilment of connections. As of late, a research has demonstrated that high-functioning grown-ups with autism seem to have a scope of reactions to music like that of neurotypical people, including the intentional utilization of music for the management of mind. Clinical treatment of alexithymia could include utilizing a basic cooperative learning process between musically incited feelings and their cognitive correlates.

Theory based on Mind

Past investigations have proposed that people with autism have a debilitated theory of brain (ToM). ToM and compassion are usually used as synonyms, however these capacities talk of various capacities that depend on various neuronal circuitry. ToM is the capacity to comprehend mental states, for example, aims, objectives and convictions, and depends on structures of the temporal lobe and the pre-frontal cortex. Be that as it may, sympathy is the capacity to share the sentiments of others and depends on the sensorimotor cortices and also limbic and para-limbic structures. Francesca Happe demonstrated that autistic children who exhibit an absence of brain theory (cognitive empathy) lack theory of mind for self and also for others.

Mirror Neuron Activity

One investigation found that, in respect to typically developing youngsters, high-functioning children with autism indicated diminished mirror neuron movement in the brain's inferior frontal gyrus (pars opercularis) while impersonating and watching expressions of emotions. The evidence of EEG uncovered that there was altogether more prominent mu suppression in the sensorimotor cortex of people with autism. Action around this area was contrarily identified with symptom seriousness in the social area, proposing that a dysfunctional mirror neuron framework may underlie the social deficiencies seen in people with autism.

Cognitive Versus Affective Empathy

Rogers' examination, following the differentiation between cognitive empathy and affective empathy, recommends that individuals with Asperger disorder have less capacity to find out others' emotions (as far as theory of mind), yet exhibit equal compassion when they know about others' perspectives (in terms of affect). As to subdivision of emotional empathy into individual pain and empathic concern, people with an autism spectrum disorder (ASD) self-report bring down levels of empathic concern, and they indicate less or truant ameliorating reactions towards somebody who is undergoing suffering. Be that as it may, people with ASD likewise report equivalent or more elevated amounts of individual pain contrasted with controls. The blend of diminished empathic concern and enhanced individual pain may prompt the general lessening of compassion in ASD. Social psychology research came with the findings that when a man is overpowered by his or her own particular sentiments while watching a man who needs assistance, he or she is probably not going to participate in soothing or helping other people.'As regards the failure of empathic response, it would appear that at least some people with autism are oversensitive to the feelings of others rather than immune to them, but cannot handle the painful feed back that this initiates in the body, and have therefore learnt to suppress this facility'.

Sex Differences and Autism

It has been demonstrated that guys are by and large less compassionate than females. The 'Extreme Male Brain' (EMB) hypothesis recommends that people on the autistic spectrum are portrayed by weaknesses in compassion because of sex contrasts in the brain: particularly, individuals with conditions of autism-spectrum demonstrate an overstated male profile. An investigation demonstrated that a few aspects of autistic neuroanatomy appear to be extremes of typical male neuroanatomy. One of the major questions that should be addressed is: if autism is an extreme of the male brain, at that point is it the aftereffect of enhanced foetal testosterone (FT), variations from the norm in androgen receptors or the genes controlling FT or expression of sexually dimorphic gene irrelevant to FT? Future research should outline parts of autistic neuroanatomy that are hypermasculinized and in addition consider how to clarify those perspectives that are most certainly not. In the event that the EMB theory applies to autism, and the male brain is a hazard factor for autism, this may clarify the lower predominance in females. In any case, another investigation has proposed that Alexithymia, a co-morbid condition common in up to 85% of individuals on the Autism Spectrum, is connected to the sympathy debilitation rather than Autism.

PERSONALITY DISORDERS

Atypical empathy is an attribute of some personality disorders which also include borderline personality disorder, psychopathy, narcissistic personality disorder as well as schizoid personality disorder.

Borderline Personality Disorder

Borderline personality disorder is portrayed by broad behavioural and relational troubles that emerge from dysfunction associated with emotion and cognition. Dysfunctional social and relational conduct has been assumed to play a critical part in the extremely emotional individuals with borderline personality disorder response. While people with borderline personality disorder may demonstrate their feelings excessively, a number of authors have recommended that they may have a reduced capacity to think about mental states (intellectual compassion), and additionally a disabled theory of brain. Individuals with borderline personality disorder are great at perceiving feelings in individuals' appearances, proposing enhanced empathic capacities. It is, hence, conceivable that reduced cognitive empathy (the ability with respect to understanding someone else's involvement and viewpoint) may represent borderline personality disorder people's tendency for interpersonal dysfunction, while 'hyperemotional empathy' (the ability to share the passionate condition of someone else) may represent the overreactivity of emotions seen in these people. One of the major investigations affirmed that patients with borderline personality disorder were altogether impeded in cognitive empathy, yet there was no indication of impairment in affective empathy.

Psychopathy

Psychopaths show introverted and forceful conduct, and in addition some passionate and relational qualities as shallow feelings, manipulation of others and absence of guilt and sympathy for victims. It has been recommended that children having psychopathic characteristics and grown-up psychopaths have specific hindrances in perceiving trouble prompts (e.g., facial and vocal articulations of fear and sadness), yet match control groups at perceiving other facial and vocal articulations of feelings like happiness. People with psychopathy do not process others' signs of pain as repulsive, which brings about an absence of sympathy which at that point neglects to anticipate conduct that creates problems in others.

People with psychopathy have biological contrasts from controls when they verifiably process facial feelings. The underlying biological natural surfaces to process outward appearances of bliss are practically in place, albeit less responsive than those of controls. Interestingly, people with psychopathy show a response of atypical pattern to frightful appearances as against neutral faces, including diminished initiation of the fusiform and extrastriate cortical regions. This in part may represent hindered acknowledgment of and decreased autonomic responsiveness to expressions associated with fear, and impedances of compassion.

Narcissistic Personality Disorder

One demonstrative paradigm of narcissistic personality disorder is an absence of compassion and an unwillingness to perceive or relate to the sentiments and requirements of others.

Schizoid Personality Disorder

Attributes of schizoid personality disorder incorporate emotional coldness, detachment, and weakened influence comparing with a powerlessness to be sympathetic and touchy towards others.

Conduct Disorder

An investigation led by Jean Decety and associates at the University of Chicago exhibited that subjects with forceful conduct disorder evoke atypical empathic reactions by observing others in torment or pain. Subjects with conduct disorder were at any rate as responsive as controls to the agony of others, however dissimilar to controls, subjects with conduct disorder demonstrated solid and particular activation of the amygdala and ventral striatum (regions that empower a general exciting impact of reward), yet hindered activation of the neural areas associated with auto-regulation and metacognition (including moral thinking), apart from lessened processing between the amygdala and the prefrontal cortex.

REALISTIC ISSUES

Appropriate empathic engagement enables a person to comprehend and anticipate the conduct of another. Aside from the programmed propensity to perceive the feelings of others, one may likewise purposely participate in empathic thinking. Two general techniques have been recognized here. An individual may recreate imaginary renditions of the convictions, wants, character qualities and setting of another person to perceive what emotions it incites. Or, on the other hand, an individual may recreate a passionate feeling and afterward get to the environment for a reasonable explanation behind the emotional feeling to be suitable for that particular condition. Some studies recommend that individuals are more capable and willing to feel for those most like themselves. Specifically, empathy enhances with likenesses in culture and living conditions. Compassion will probably happen between people whose interaction is more on a regular basis. A measure of how well a man can gather the particular content of someone else's considerations and emotions has been created by William Ickes (1997, 2003). Ickes and his associates have created a video-based strategy to gauge empathic precision and have utilized this technique to make a study about the empathic error of maritally forceful and harsh mates, among different topics.

There are worries that the empathizer's own emotional background may influence or misshape what feelings they see in others (e.g. Goleman 1996: p. 104). Empathy is not a procedure that is probably going to convey certain judgments about the emotional states of others. It is an expertise that is bit by bit created all through life, and which enhances the more contact we have with the individual with whom one identifies. Following that any knowledge picked up of the feelings of the other must be revisable in light of additional data.

ISSUES ASSOCIATED WITH ETHICS

The degree to which a man's feelings are openly detectable or mutually identified as such has critical social outcomes. Empathic acknowledgment could not be possibly invited or socially alluring. This is especially the situation where we perceive the feelings that somebody has towards us amid continuous communications. In view of an allegorical proclivity with touch, logician Edith Wyschogrod claims that the vicinity involved by compassion expands the potential weakness of either party. The proper part of empathy in our dealings with others is profoundly subject to the situations. For example, Tania Singer asserts that clinicians or parental figures must take mind not to be excessively touchy, making it impossible to the feelings of others, to overcontribute their own feelings, at the danger of depleting endlessly their own genius. Moreover an attention to the confinements of empathic exactness is reasonable in a caregiving circumstance.

DISCIPLINARY APPROACHES

Psychotherapy

Heinz Kohut is the primary introducer of the principle of compassion in psychoanalysis. His guideline applies to the technique of collecting unconscious material. The likelihood of not applying the technique is conceded in the cure, for example when you figure another guideline, that of reality. Creating aptitudes of compassion is usually a focal topic in the recuperation procedure for drug addicts. In transformative brain research, endeavours at clarifying pro social conduct frequently specify the presence of compassion in the person as a possible variable. Though correct thought processes behind complex social practices are hard to recognize, the 'ability to put oneself in the shoes of another person and experience events and emotions the way that person experienced them' is the authoritative factor for really unselfish conduct as indicated by Batson's empathy-altruism hypothesis. In the event that sympathy is not felt, social trade (how might this benefit me?) supersedes pure altruism, however in the event that compassion is felt, an individual will help by activities or by word, paying little heed to whether it is to their greatest advantage to do as such and regardless of the possibility that the expenses exceed potential rewards.

Education

A vital focus of the strategy Learning by Teaching (LbT) is to provide systematic training and, in every lesson, impact teachings on sympathy. Students need to transmit new content to their friends, so they need to think persistently on the mental procedures of other students in the classroom. Thus, it is quite likely to create well-ordered feelings of students for responses of group and networking.

Evolution of Empathy

A large number of research studies associated with animal conduct and neuroscience guarantee that sympathy is not limited to people, and is in certainty as old as or even older than the mammals. Instances of dolphins saving people from drowning or from shark assaults, and a huge number of practices can be seen in primates, both in bondage and in the wild, and specifically in bonobos, which are accounted for as the most compassionate of all the primates. A current report has shown prosocial conduct evoked by compassion in rodents. Rodents have been shown to be compassionate for cagemates (but not outsiders) in torment. A standout amongst the most broadly read investigations on the advancement of compassion, which talks about a neural perception-action mechanism (PAM), is the one by Stephanie Preston and de Waal. This study proposes a bottom-up model of compassion that ties together all levels, from state matching to perspective-taking. For University of Chicago neurobiologist Jean Decety, empathy is not specific to people. He contends that there is solid proof that compassion has profound transformative, biochemical, and neurological underpinnings, and that even the most developed types of sympathy in people are based on more essential structures and stay associated with central mechanisms related to affective communication, social connection and parental care. Central neural circuits that are engaged with empathy and caring consist of the brainstem, the amygdala, hypothalamus, basal ganglia, insula and orbitofrontal cortex.

Fiction

A few rationalists, (for example, Martha Nussbaum) propose that novel reading generates a sense of compassion among readers and helps them to practice better world citizenship. For an analysis of the use of this empathy-altruism hypothesis to experiences of narrative empathy, see Keen's Empathy and the Novel (Oxford, 2007). In a few works of science fiction and fantasy, empathy is comprehended to be a paranormal or psychic capability to get a sense of the feelings of others, instead of telepathy, which enables one to perceive thoughts also. A person who has that capacity is also referred to as an 'empath' or 'telepath' in this unique situation. Sometimes these empaths are likewise ready to extend their own particular feelings, or to influence the feelings of others.

History

Some postmodern historians, for example, Keith Jenkins as of late have put forth their arguments on whether it is possible to empathize with individuals from the past. Jenkins contends that empathy has such a favoured position in the present as it compares concordantly with the prevailing liberal talk of current society and can be associated with John Stuart Mill's idea of complementary opportunity. Jenkins contends the past is an outside nation and as we do not approach the epistemological states of by gone ages we can't sympathize. It is difficult to predict the impact of compassion on what's to come. A past subject may participate in the present by the supposed historic present. When we see from an imaginary past, we can talk about the present with the future tense, as it occurs with the trick of the false prophecy. There is no chance to get of telling the present with the methods of the past.

Business

In the book Wired to Care written in 2009, strategy consultant Dev Patnaik contends that a noteworthy drawback in contemporary business practice is an absence of empathy inside huge organizations. He expresses that without any feeling of sympathy, individuals inside organizations battle to settle on instinctive choices and frequently get fooled into trusting they comprehend their business if they have to depend on quantitative research. Patnaik claims that the real opportunity for organizations working together in the 21st Century is to make a broadly held feeling of sympathy for clients, pointing to Nike, Harley-Davidson and IBM as big examples of 'Open Empathy Organizations'. Such organizations, he asserts, see new opportunities more rapidly than contenders, adjust to change all the more effortlessly and make work environments that offer employees a more noteworthy feeling of mission in their employments. In the book The Empathy Factor written in 2011, organizational consultant Marie Miyashiro comparably contends the benefit of conveying sympathy to the working environment, and offers Nonviolent Communication as a viable system for accomplishing this.

Philosophy

In the book *The Ethics of Care and Empathy* written in 2007, thinker Michael Slote presents a theory of care-based ethics incorporating compassion. His claim is that ethical inspiration does, and should, originate from a premise of empathic reaction. He asserts that our common responses to circumstances of high moral significance are clarified by compassion. He clarifies the points of confinement and commitments of sympathy and thus views morality to be natural. These natural commitments incorporate a more noteworthy empathic and good commitment to family and companions, alongside a record of fleeting and physical separation. In circumstances of close worldly and physical separation, and with family or companions, our ethical commitment appears to be more grounded to us than with outsiders at a separation normally. Slote clarifies this is because of compassion and our common empathic ties. He additionally includes that activities arenot right if they reflect or show an insufficiency of completely created empathic concern for others on the part of the agent. In phenomenology, compassion portrays the experience of something from the other's perspective, without any confusion between self and other. This is drawn on the sense of agency. In the most fundamental sense, this is the experience of the other's body and, in this sense, it is an experience of 'my body over there'. In most other cases, nonetheless, the experience is altered with the goal that what is experienced will be experienced similar to the other's understanding; in experiencing empathy, what is experienced isn't 'my' experience, despite the fact that I encounter it. Compassion is additionally thought to be the state of intersubjectivity and, thus, the source of the constitution of objectivity.

MEASUREMENT

Research into the estimation of compassion has looked to answer various queries: who should be making the estimation? What should go for compassion and what ought to be marked down? What unit of measure (UOM) should be followed and to what degree each occurrence should accurately match that UOM are additionally major inquiries that analysts have tried to examine. Researchers have moved towards the estimation of empathy from various viewpoints. Behavioural measures typically include raters examining the appearance or nonappearance of certain either predetermined or ad-hoc behaviours in the subjects under investigation. Both verbal and non-verbal practices have been caught on video by experimenters, for example, Truax (1967b). Different experimenters, including Mehrabian and Epstein (1972), have expected subjects to remark upon their own sentiments and practices, or those of other individuals associated with the test, as indirect methods of estimating their level of empathic functioning to the raters.

Physiological reactions have a tendency to be caught by expound electronic device that has been physically associated with the subject's body. Analysts at that point draw inferences about that individual's empathic responses from the electronic readings created (e.g., Levenson and Ruef, 1992; Leslie et al., 2004). Bodily or 'somatic' measures can be looked upon as behavioural measures at a micro level. Their concentration is on measuring compassion based on facial and other non-verbally communicated responses in the empathizer. These progressions are apparently supported by physiological changes achieved by some type of 'emotional contagion' or reflecting (e.g., Levenson and Ruef, 1992; Leslie et al., 2004). It should be brought to the notice that these responses, while seeming to mirror the inward passionate condition of the empathizer, could likewise, if the stimulus occurrence kept going more than the shortest period, be mirroring the consequences of enthusiastic responses that depend on more bits of thoroughly considering (perceptions) related with role-taking ('if I were him I would feel...'). Paper-based indices include one or more variety of techniques for reacting. In a few investigations, subjects are required to watch video scenarios (either arranged or real) and to make composed reactions which are then evaluated for their levels of empathy (e.g., Geher, Warner and Brown, 2001); scenarios are on some occasions depicted in print (e.g., Mehrabian and Epstein, 1972). Measures likewise most of the time need subjects to self-report upon their own capacity or limit with respect to sympathy, utilizing Likert-style numerical reactions to a printed survey that may have been intended to take advantage of the emotional, cognitive-affective or to a great extent cognitive substrates of empathic working. A few surveys claim to have possessed the capacity to take advantage of both cognitive and emotional substrates (e.g. Davis, 1980). Latest paper-based devices consist of The Empathy Quotient (EQ) developed by Baron-Cohen and Wheelwright which contains a self-report questionnaire comprising of 60 things.

For the extremely youthful, picture or puppet story indices for sympathy have been embraced to empower even very youthful, pre-school subjects to react without requiring to read questions and compose answers (e.g., Denham and Couchoud, 1990). Subordinate variables (factors that are observed for any change by the experimenter) for more youthful subjects have included self-reporting on a 7-point smiley face scale and taped facial responses (Barnett, 1984).

A specific measure of perplexity exists about how to do measurement of sympathy. These might be inherent in another problem: choosing what compassion is and what it isnot. In general, researchers have as of recently been quick enough to come up with a particular meaning of empathy which would enable them to plan a measure to evaluate its presence in an exchange, in somebody's collection of practices or inside them as a hidden characteristic. Therefore they have been much of the time compelled to disregard the abundance of the empathic procedure for catching surface, express self-report or third-party data about whether sympathy between two individuals was available or not. Most of the time, instruments have sadly just yielded data on whether somebody could exhibit compassion (Geher et al., 2001). Gladstein (1987) abridges the position taking note of that compassion has been measured from the perspective of the empathizer, the beneficiary for empathy and the outsider onlooker. He proposes that since the numerous measures utilized have given outcomes that bear little connection to each other, researchers should abstain making any sorts of comparisons between scales that are in reality measuring diverse things. He proposes that scientists ought to rather stipulate what sort of compassion they are embarking to measure as opposed to straightforwardly expressing that they are embarking to quantify the unitary marvel 'empathy'; a view of late supported by Duan and Hill (1996). In the medical field, a measuring instrument for carers is the Jefferson Scale of Physician Empathy, Health Professional Version (JSPE-HP). No less than one investigation utilizing this instrument with the students of health sciences has discovered that levels of empathy are more noteworthy among females as compared to males, and furthermore these are also more prominent among older students as compared to younger counterparts.

DIFFERENCES ASSOCIATED WITH GENDER

The question of differences associated with gender in relation to empathy is largely disputable. It is usually supposed that females are more empathic as compared to males. Proof for sexual orientation contrasts in sympathy are vital for self-report surveys of compassion in which it is clear what was being recorded (e.g., effect of social allure and sex generalizations) however are smaller or non-existent for different sorts of indexes that are less self-obvious concerning their purpose. By and large female subjects score higher than males on the Empathy Quotient (EQ), while males tend to score higher on the Systemizing Quotient (SQ). Both males as well as females with Autistic Spectrum Disorders generally exhibit higher SQ (Baron-Cohen, 2003). In any case, a number of latest research studies, utilizing a number of different neurophysiological measures, including MEG, spinal reflex sensitivity and electroencephalography have noted the existence of a difference in gender in the human mirror neuron framework, with female members showing more robust motor resonance as compared to male members. Furthermore, these previously mentioned studies found that female members scored higher on empathy self-report dispositional measures and that these measures emphatically showed strong correlation with the physiological reaction. On the other hand, different investigations demonstrate that women donot have more noteworthy empathic capacities than men, and sexual orientation contrasts are the consequence of motivational contrasts. Utilizing fMRI, neuroscientist Tania Singer demonstrated that empathy-related neural responses are altogether lower in men while watching an 'unfair' individual feeling pain.

ETHNOCULTURAL EMPATHY

Ethnocultural sympathy means the comprehension of people's sentiments that are ethnically or culturally unique in relation to ones' self. This concept throws questions on worldwide empathy, which expect that empathy is "feeling in oneself the feelings of others" and isn't particularly focusing on any one group (e.g., age, sexual orientation, and ethnicity) or setting. Ethnocultural compassion, then again, expect that sympathy towards others presumably enhances if the other is like oneself as far as ethnicity, sex, age or social background. The application of Ethnocultural compassion is generally connected with cross-culture as well as cross-ethnics examination. The levels of ethnocultural sympathy were accounted to show variation based on demographic and societal components. Past research demonstrated that women will probably report more elevated amount of ethnocultural compassion than men, Non-White people were found to have essentially larger amounts of general and particular ethnocultural sympathy than their White partners. Racisms was contrarily connected with ethnocultural compassion. Individuals with different levels of ethnocultural empathy were also found to react differently to individuals who are similar with themselves and those who are not. For instance, individuals with more elevated amount of ethnocultural sympathy had been found to work all the more effectively with people from different societies. Ethnocultural empathy not just worked in of ethnocultural empathy were found to predict positive attitude towards minority groups, namely rape victims, domestic violence victims, female leaders and so on. Ethnocultural social sympathy has been utilized as a part of numerous other research subjects, for example, racialism, woman's rights, multiculturalism, ethnic character and so forth.

SIMULATION THEORY OF EMPATHY

The simulation hypothesis isnot essentially a hypothesis of sympathy, but instead a hypothesis of how we comprehend others—that we do as such by method for a sort of compassionate reaction. The hypothesis holds that people suspect and understand the conduct of others by activating mental procedures that, if carried into action, would deliver comparable conduct. This incorporates purposeful conduct and in addition the statement of feelings. The hypothesis expresses that children utilize their own particular feelings to anticipate what others will do. Along these lines, we anticipate our own particular mental states onto others. This hypothesis utilizes more organic confirmation than different speculations of brain, for example, the hypothesis.

Compassion

Compassion is the feeling or empathy for the sufferings of others. Compassion is regularly viewed as emotional in nature, and there is an aspect of sympathy which considers a quantitative measurement, with the end goal that person's sympathy is frequently given a property of 'depth', 'vigour' or 'passion'. The historical background of 'empathy' is Latin, signifying 'co-suffering'. More involved than simple sympathy, empathy generally offers surge in a dynamic desire to ease another's suffering. It is frequently, however not definitely, the main component in what shows in the social setting as altruism. In moral terms, the different articulations down the periods of the purported Golden Rule frequently encapsulate by suggestion the rule of sympathy: Do to others what you would have them do to you. The English noun sympathy, which means to suffer together with, originates from Latin. Its prefix *com* comes straightforwardly from com, a bygone form of the Latin relational word and join cum (= with); the enthusiasm portion is gotten from passus, past participle of the deponent verb patior, patî, passus aggregate. Sympathy in this manner is related in birthplace, shape and importance to the English noun patient (= one who undergoes suffering), from patiens, exhibit participle of the same patior, and is much the same as the Greek verb (= paskhein, to endure) and to its cognate noun (= tenderness). Considered a great virtue in various philosophies, empathy is considered in all the significant religious customs as among the best of ideals.

RELIGIOUS AND SPIRITUAL VIEWS

Hinduism

In the different Hindu conventions, sympathy is called daya, and alongside philanthropy and self-control, is one of the three focal qualities.The significance of empathy in the Hindu conventions comes to as far back as the Vedas. The focal idea especially pertinent to empathy in Hindu deep sense of being is that of ahimsa. The correct meaning of ahimsa differs starting with one convention to the next. Ahimsa is a Sanskrit word which can be interpreted most specifically as 'refraining from harmfulness'. It is a deviation of himsa which implies *harmful*, or having the purpose to cause hurt.

The prayers made by Vasudeva Datta, for instance, a sixteenth century Vaishnava sacred man or sadhu, represent empathy inside Gaudiya Vaishnavism.

He offered prayers to the Lord Krishna asking him to 'deliver all conditioned souls' because his 'heart breaks to see the sufferings of all conditioned souls'.

Judaism

In the Jewish custom, God is the Compassionate and is conjured as the Father of Compassion: consequently Rahmana or Compassionate turns into the typical assignment for His uncovered word (compare, beneath, the regular utilization of rahman in the Quran). Distress and pity for one in trouble, making a desire to relieve, is an inclination credited alike to man and God: in Biblical Hebrew, ('riham', from 'rehem', the mother, womb), 'to pity' or 'to show mercy' in perspective of the sufferer's vulnerability, hence also 'to forgive' (Hab. iii. 2); 'to forbear' (Ex. ii. 6; I Sam. xv. 3; Jer. xv. 15, xxi. 7). The Rabbis speak of the 'thirteen attributes of compassion'. The Biblical origination of empathy is the sentiment of the parent for the kid. Subsequently, the prophet's appeal in affirmation of his trust in God conjures the sentiment a mother offers for her children (Isa. xlix. 15). An exemplary explanation of the Golden Rule originated from the main century Rabbi Hillel the Elder.

Eminent in the Jewish convention as a sage and a researcher, he is related with the improvement of the Mishnah and the Talmud and, thus, a standout amongst the most essential figures in Jewish history. Requested an outline of the Jewish religion in the 'while standing on one leg' meaning in the most concise terms, Hillel stated: 'That which is hateful to you, do not do to your fellow. That is the whole Torah. The rest is the explanation; go and learn'. Post 9/11, the expressions of Rabbi Hillel are much of the time cited out in the public addresses and meetings around the globe by the noticeable author on similar religion Karen Armstrong.

Many Jewish sources highlight the significance of sympathy for animals. Important rabbis who have done so include Rabbi Samson Raphael Hirsch, Rabbi Simhah Zissel Ziv and Rabbi Moshe Cordovero.

Buddhism

Sympathy is what makes the core of the great move at the pain of others. It crushes and demolishes the distress of others; subsequently, it is called sympathy. It is called sympathy since it provides shelter and embraces the persons in distress- The Buddha. Sympathy or karuna is at the supernatural and experiential heart of the teachings of Buddha. He was supposedlyasked by his personal attendant, Ananda, 'Would it be true to say that the cultivation of loving kindness and compassion is a part of our practice?' To which the Buddha replied, 'No. It would not be true to say that the cultivation of loving kindness and compassion is part of our practice. It would be true to say that the cultivation of loving kindness and compassion is all of our practice'.

The first of what in English are known as the Four Noble Truths is reality of suffering or dukkha (unsatisfactoriness or stress). Dukkha is recognized as one of the three recognizing attributes of all conditional existence. It emerges as a result of the inability to adjust to change or anicca (the second characteristic) and the deficiency, absence of settled personality, the frightful absence of sureness of anatta (the third characteristic) to which this consistent change arises. Sympathy mentioned conceivable by objective fact and exact discernment is the fitting functional reaction. A definitive and sincere wish, shown in the Buddha, both as original and as chronicled substance, is to mitigate the misery of every living being all over the place.

According to Dalai Lama, 'If you want others to be happy, practice compassion. If you want to be happy, practice compassion'. The American monk Bhikkhu Bodhi proposes that compassion 'supplies the complement to loving-kindness: whereas loving-kindness has the characteristic of wishing for the happiness and welfare of others, compassion has the characteristic of wishing that others be free from suffering, a wish to be extended without limits to all living beings. Like metta, compassion arises by entering into the subjectivity of others, by sharing their interiority in a deep and total way. It springs up by considering that all beings, like ourselves, wish to be free from suffering, yet despite their wishes continue to be harassed by pain, fear, sorrow, and other forms of dukkha'. Simultaneously, it is stressed that in order to show effective compassion for others, it is first of all necessary to be able to experience and fully appreciate one's own suffering and to have, as a consequence, compassion for oneself. The Buddha is reported to have said, 'It is possible to travel the whole world in search of one who is more worthy of compassion than oneself. No such person can be found'. Compassion is considered the remedy to the self-chosen poison of anger.

Christianity

The Christian Bible's Second Epistle to the Corinthians is but one place where God is considered the 'Father of compassion' and the 'God of all comfort.' It reads as follows: 2 Corinthians 1:3-7 'Praise be to the God and Father of our Lord Jesus Christ, the Father of compassion and the God of all comfort, who comforts us in all our troubles, so that we can comfort those in any trouble with the comfort we ourselves received from God. For just as the sufferings of Christ flow over into our lives, so also through Christ our comfort overflows. If we are distressed, it is for your comfort and salvation; if we are comforted, it is for your comfort, which produces in you patient endurance of the same sufferings we suffer. And our hope for you is firm, because we know that just as you share in our sufferings, so also you share in our comfort'. Jesus embodies for Christians, the very essence of compassion and relational care. Christ challenges Christians to forsake their own desires and to act with sympathy towards others, especially those in need or distress. Jesus assures his listeners in the Sermon on the Mount that, 'Blessed are the merciful, for they shall obtain mercy'. In the Parable of the Good Samaritan, he holds up to his followers the ideal of compassionate conduct. True Christian compassion, say the Gospels, should include all, even loving one's enemies.

Islam

In the Muslim tradition, foremost among God's attributes are mercy and compassion or, in the canonical language of Arabic, *Rahman* and *Rahim*. In the Muslim custom, first among God's qualities are mercy and sympathy or, in the authoritative dialect of Arabic, Rahman and Rahim. Each of the 114 parts of the Quran, with one special case, starts with the verse, 'In the name of God the Compassionate, the Merciful'. The Arabic word used for compassion is *rahmah*. As a cultural influence, its roots are found in the Quran. A good Muslim is to begin the day with prayer and perform all the important activities by invoking God the Merciful and Compassionate, i.e. by reciting *Bism-i-llah a-Rahman-i-Rahim*. The womb and family ties are portrayed by compassion and named after the magnified property of God 'Al-Rahim' (The Compassionate). The Muslim scriptures give a lot of emphasis on compassion towards captives, widows, orphans and the poor. *Zakat*, a toll tax has been mentioned to help the poor and needy which is obligatory for all Muslims deemed wealthy enough to do so (calculation is done based on assessing the total wealth of an adult by a year-end) (9:60). One of the real purposes of fasting or sawm during the month of Ramadan is to help one empathize with the hunger pangs of those less fortunate, to enhance sensitivity to the suffering of others and develop compassion for the poor and destitute. The Prophet is referred to by the Quran as the Mercy for the World (21:107); and one of the sayings of the Prophet informs the faithful that, God is more loving and kinder than a mother to her dear child'.

Jainism

Empathy for all life, human and non-human, is key to the tradition of Jainism. Despite the fact that all life is viewed as holy, human life is considered the most noteworthy type of physical existence. To murder any individual, regardless of their wrongdoing, is considered unfathomably despicable. It is the main substantial religious convention that requires both the priests and people to be vegetarian. It is recommended that specific strains of the Hindu tradition progressed towards becoming veggie lover because of solid Jain impacts. The Jain convention's position on peacefulness, be that as it may, goes a long way beyond vegetarianism. Jains reject sustenance acquired with superfluous savagery. Many practice veganism. Jains run shelters for protection of animals all across India: Delhi has a bird health centre being run by Jains; each city and town in Bundelkhand has shelters for animals run by Jains. Jain priests go to lengths to abstain from slaughtering any living animal, clearing the ground before them with a specific end goal to avoid killing creatures, and even wearing a face mask to avoid inhaling the smallest fly.

PSYCHOLOGY

Compassion has been related and researched in the field of Positive Psychology. Compassion is a way of making association by identifying another process. This identification with others through compassion results in enhanced motivation to do something with a purpose to relieve the suffering of others. Compassion is considered as a sentiment that is essential in assisting professions. Compassion comprises of three major requirements, which include: People must have feelings that troubles that infuse their feelings are serious, people require that sufferers' troubles are not self-inflicted, and that people must be ready to face those problems.

Theoretical Accounts

Three theoretical points of view on sympathy have been proposed, which are differentiated by their predictions and methodologies of empathy.

- Compassion as an equivalent word of empathic trouble, which is portrayed by the sentiment of pain associated with the sufferings of other people. This point of view on empathy depends on the finding that individuals now and again copy and feel the feelings of individuals around them.

- Compassion simply refers to a variation of love or sadness, not a distinct emotion.
- Based on evolutionary psychology, compassion can be described as a state of distinct emotion, which can be distinguished from distress, sadness and love.

The Fundamentals of Compassion

Relating to someone else is a fundamental procedure for people. It is normally observed all through the world as individuals adjust and change with new styles of garments, dialect, conduct and so forth, which is outlined by newborn children that start to reflect the facial expressions and body movements of their mothers as early as the first days of their lives. This process is highly associated with compassion because having sympathy with others is possible with people from different countries, cultures, locations and so on. A conceivable source of this procedure of relating to others originates from an all-inclusive class called, 'Soul'. Around the late 1970s, altogether different societies and countries around the globe took a swing to religious fundamentalism, which has once in a while been ascribed to 'Soul'. The more an individual thinks about the human condition and the related experiences is another route to identification. The significance of relating to others for empathy is differentiated by the negative physical and mental impacts of deserting. Empathy is by all accounts normal for majority rule social orders. The part of sympathy as a factor adding to individual or societal conduct has been the point of nonstop verbal confrontation. As opposed to the way towards relating to other individuals, a total nonappearance of sympathy may require overlooking or objecting distinguishing proof with other individuals or gatherings. This idea has been delineated all through history, for example, The Holocaust, Genocide, European colonization of the Americas, and so on. The apparently fundamental advance in these barbarities could be the defining of the victims as 'not human' or 'not us'. The different abominations that have been submitted all through mankind's history have just been assuaged by following the path of empathy. Suffering has been characterized as the impression of a man's approaching obliteration or loss of uprightness, which proceeds until the point when the danger is gone or the individual's respectability can be re-established. Identity Psychology concurs that individuals are naturally different and distinct from each other, which should prompt the conclusion that human suffering is constantly individual and one of a kind. Experiencing suffering can come about with mental, social and physical injury. Suffering seems to occur in acute forms very frequently. There is an inalienable trouble in realizing that another person is undergoing suffering because of a direct result of its forlorn nature, which prompts the conclusion that many individuals may not know they are suffering. They may rather point to their outer conditions with the beginning times of suffering being peaceful or not examined. The later stages may include the individual communicating their exploitation and searching for assistance. Sympathy is perceived through relating to other individuals, the information of human conduct, the impression of agony, exchange of sentiments, learning of objective and reason of changes in sufferers and the nonappearance of the sufferer from a gathering. A new global review recommends that empathy towards animals is related with sympathy towards people. Prior investigations likewise settled the connections between interpersonal violence and cruelty towards animals. Empathy may be able to incite sentiments of thoughtfulness and pardoning, which could offer sympathy to be able to stop circumstances that often prompt brutality.

Utilizations of Compassion

Credible authority and general initiative might be the keys to expanding empathy in the work environment. Likewise, Acting in concordance with one's valid self-idea is basic for the expression of care and empathy.

Self-sympathy may affect subjective Happiness, Optimism, Wisdom, Curiosity, Agreeableness and Extroversion positively.

Practice of Compassion

Particular exercises may build sentiments of and preparation to hone sympathy, some of these exercises include: making a wake-up routine, honing compassion, rehearse irregular demonstrations of generosity and making evening schedules.

HISTORICAL

'Greek and Roman philosophers distrusted (feeling) compassion. In their view, reason alone was the proper guide to conduct. They regarded compassion (a virtue) as an effect, neither admirable nor contemptible'. Thomas Szasz from his book 'Cruel Compassion'. On the other hand, a current investigation of the historical Jesus has guaranteed that the founder of Christianity looked to hoist Judaic empathy as the incomparable human excellence, equipped for lessening distress and satisfying our God ordained objective behind changing the world into something more deserving of its maker.

Lessons to be Learnt Based on the Lives and Teachings of Great Leaders, Reformers and Administrators

9
CHAPTER

Uncertainty in any part of our lives can evoke numerous sentiments that can incredibly influence individual, group and authoritative execution. Pioneers in settings as differing as business, government, not-revenue driven associations, training and the military can take in numerous lessons from the activities of great leaders from ancient and present day history.

The following is the list of some of critical lessons which we can draw from the lives, activities and expressions of four leaders—Nelson Mandela, Abraham Lincoln, Margaret Thatcher and Mahatma Gandhi.

- Vision, motive and values
- Strategy and execution
- Courage, persistence and resilience
- Inspiration and engagement
- Coalition building amongst diverse stakeholders
- Overcoming supposedly unachievable obstacles
- Grace under fire

LESSONS TO BE LEARNT FROM SOME GREAT PERSONALITIES

MOHANDAS KARAMCHAND GANDHI

One of the best figures of the twentieth century, and maybe of the thousand years, Mohandas Karamchand Gandhi was born in Gujarat on October 2, 1869.

He was charismatic, yet he was likewise analytical and pondering in his approach. Gandhi became great particularly as a result of his own circumstances, yet one of his most noteworthy sources of motivation was the Bhagavad-Gita, composed a number of years ago. He was a politician, a writer, a scholarly and a speaker. Undoubtedly, he was an exceptionally complex man, however a man who trusted in basic things. Gandhiji proclaimed that 'Action is my domain'.

He was called both 'Mahatma', which means extraordinary soul, and 'Bapu', which means Father.

Gandhi spent his time of about 21 years in South Africa. A critical event in his life during his stay in South Africa was of one week where he was made a request to leave the First Class compartment of a train by a European. Regardless of having the correct ticket, he was coercively expelled from the train. He endured other racial insults in those early months.

His two focal thoughts were conceived in South Africa. These were

- 'Swaraj' (freedom for India and individual spiritual recharging of all Indians)
- 'Satyagraha' (truth, love and non-violence)

The life of Mahatma Gandhi is loaded with lessons that still motivate individuals all over the world.

Valuable Learning from Mahatma's Life

- ***Change should be made at individual level before you desire to see the change in others:*** According to Gandhi, before we expect to see our desired qualities in others, we should absorb them in ourselves. We all are awesome and extremely elegant from the inside and the more we will see the same thing in others, we shall get the same in return. We should love and be kind towards others and then only we can be able to see the wonderful world outside.
- ***Strength of mind is more critical than physical strength*:** Strength can occur in different forms. In life it is more critical to have strength of mind—additionally called will power—than a well-built strong body. A man with a strong will can actually move mountains regardless of the possibility that he may not be a Hercules. Quality is picking what is appropriate in spite of the decision being troublesome. Gandhi was not a physically tough man but rather it was his sheer will power that compelled the British to get on their knees.
- ***Forgiveness is the quality of strong and not of weak*:** To pardon the person who in some way has inflicted pain on you is not easy. It is a matter of great courage to exonerate and move forward in life. But one who is able to act that way can be truly considered a man of great and strong values. If we don't forgive then we make a fence of disapprobation around us and it becomes tough to move on in life. We should not focus too much on the mistakes of other people. This will ensure an uncomplicated life.
- ***Happiness is doing work with harmony*:** In today's world, happiness and harmony are very unimaginable and superlative. Living in harmony is something that we can achieve and it is something that is composed with our values. If our own values show difference then in such situation, we will be in no position to reach the level of harmony. In sum, Mahatma Gandhi viewed that only when there is a balance in our thoughts, actions and wordsthat are connected to each other, we can attain harmony in true sense.
- ***Peace is inside us and not influenced by external conditions*:** Do we truly look for peace inside ourselves? The appropriate response will, most presumably, be 'No' in light of the fact that we have characterized peace by outside and deceptive

components. We meet somebody out of the blue and his feeling matters to us so much that our certainty beats. Rather we should endeavour to do thoughtfulness and tune in to our inward voice and discover peace inside unaffected by outside powers.

- ***A genuine 'No' is superior to a deceptive 'Yes'***: Individuals frequently say 'Yes' rather than 'No' out of impulse or just to conciliate the other. They regularly confabulate or participate in exercises and dealings without an individual interest. Gandhi said that saying yes when you actually don't mean it can have no meaning. Then again it causes a drift, anger and offense among the general population whom you have been close once. In this way, a yes should be communicated with a solid conviction at all times.
- ***Path to goal is as divine as goal itself***: Mahatma Gandhi was a man who was known for his strong character. He didn't devise any method for achieving independence which was against his conscience. He upheld non-violence as the most potent weapon for the freedom of India. Gandhi always considered his inner conscience above everything. We, too, should abide by the path of morality so as to fulfil our dreams and reach our destination and not follow that path which could bring any ingloriousness.
- ***Priority is expressed through action***: In the event that the objective in our life is very important and we are not making any move to finish or satisfy that objective then we have to reassess our needs. This delineates we are not serious in achieving our goals and we have not assessed our goal closely. In the event that this is the reason then we should go through the needs and make the important move to achieve those goals.
- ***Don't give up and be steady***: Mahatma Gandhi never gave up; his imprisonment on several occasions didn't deter him from fighting consistently for freedom. Similarly, we should continuously pursue those goals that we have set for ourselves till the time we get closer to our intended destination and attain our dreams. It is highly desired to have a great plan so that we can realize the success through it. And consistency always goes a long way in realizing our dreams.
- ***As we think so we become***: Gandhi opined that we as persons assert our personalities based on what our own thoughts are. If we keep thinking of our failure all the time, it is certain that we will fail and will not achieve our goal and will never realize our success. Both positive and negative thoughts pass across our minds, but our effort should have focus on eliminating the negative ones and retain the positives. Our very nature is shaped by thoughts and, therefore, we become what we think.

NELSON MANDELA

'I was not a messiah, but an ordinary man who had become a leader because of extraordinary circumstances'.

—Nelson Mandela

In 1918, Nelson Mandela was born in Transkei of South Africa. He spent his childhood in a customary tribal society in which he would have been conceded a high-office position by right of his heritage. Rather than picking a comfortable life, in any case, he picked up the path of struggle and sacrifice with the end goal to secure the essential human rights of the people of his nation.

Mandela spent his initial adulthood as an individual from the African National Congress (ANC), making progress towards political and social change in an atmosphere of extraordinary racial mistreatment coming about because of the apartheid laws of the South African government.

In June 1961, Mandela and his associates arrived at the conclusion that it would be ineffective for African leaders to keep lecturing passive resistance when the administration took care of their peaceful demands using force. This choice to participate in more forceful types of political battle prompted the arrest of Mandela.

The trial brought about a lifelong incarceration for Mandela and seven of his co-workers. Amid his detainment, Mandela emerged as a symbol of the anti-apartheid movement and development by constantly declining to yield his beliefs in return of liberty.

Indeed, even in jail, Mandela declined to compromise his values and convictions, until in 1990, after discourses with the then president of South Africa; following his release from jail, and soon moved towards becoming leader of his nation.

He was a man known for his courage and ethics, who kept up his vision for change, and drove his people to another democratic government.

Nelson Mandela has become a prominent voice against the AIDS epidemic because of which a number of deaths are reported in his country which also included his son. He has also utilized his global stature to enhance awareness to solutions of global poverty. The latest project of Mandela is called as The Elders. Launched in 2007, The Elders is a group of well-known and independent world leaders working publicly and behind the scenes to' support courage where there is fear, foster agreement where there is conflict, and inspire hope where there is despair'.

We are motivated by the patience, intelligence and trustworthiness with which Mandela drove his country in their quest for equality and freedom. He is an extraordinary leader and we as a whole could gain much from his sacrifices towards individual and national freedom.

Moral values that can be learnt from Nelson Mandela

- Patience, intelligence and readiness to sacrifice for others.
- Learn from the mistakes committed instead of repeat them.
- Integrity.

MOTHER TERESA

'There is more hunger in the world for love and appreciation in this world than for bread. We think sometimes that poverty is only being hungry, naked and homeless.

The poverty of being unwanted, unloved and uncared for is the greatest poverty. We must start in our own homes to remedy this kind of poverty'. **—Mother Teresa**

In 1910, Mother Teresa was born in Yugoslavia. She got the name 'Teresa' when in 1928, she joined the Sisters of Loreto, an Irish community of nuns.

Mother Teresa was offered consent to live as an autonomous nun. She dedicated her life to poor people. She established a school for destitute kids in Calcutta and set up her own order, which turned into the Missionaries of Charity. She extended this order to other nations in 1965, making a worldwide system of more than 517 missions all across the globe.

Mother Teresa's projects have included hospices for those with lethal or crippling illnesses, soup kitchens, counselling programs, relief activities in natural disasters, and shelters for orphans. In 1982 at the height of the siege in Beirut, she persuaded the Israelis and Palestinians to cease fire sufficiently long to permit the protection of 37 kids from a hospital.

Her work has been perceived and acclaimed throughout the world and she has been the beneficiary of various honours, which include the Nobel Peace Prize, the Nehru Prize and the Pope John Paul XXIII Peace Prize.

Some have criticized parts of Mother Teresa's work, for example, her lack of worry over the source of donations and resource priorities. However these reactions can't eclipse her huge accomplishments. It can be said with certainty that she was an inspiration for many, pulling in supporters, devotees and volunteers wherever she went. Her battle for dignity for poor people gave the world a moral perspective, crossing over social and religious partitions. Mother Teresa, who passed away in 1997, is a person of untiring commitment and showing others how it's done. She is probably one among the most respected ladies ever.

Her legacy and message of peace and love are something that we require desperately in our today's life.

Important Learning

- ***Take up a work for higher cause***: Mother Teresa put in more than 60 years of her life in the streets and slums of Calcutta and committed every last bit of her life to serve poor people, particularly untouchables, the wiped out, the withering and the deserted.

  It took a great deal of resolve, determination and faith to keep going despite innumerable troubles and difficulties.
- ***Begin with your own home and people around***: You don't have to visit a remote place to do something. Begin with your own home and people around. Likewise, you don't have to make enormous sacrifices or spend huge amount of money. Figure out how to make contribution from the heart and don't rely completely on your pocket to help others.

  In you cannot do much, simply invest a little bit of time with those who are desolate, dependent and have no support of others.

  Everyone today is by all accounts in such a terrible hurry that all seem to be concerned for their developments, advancements and greater wealth because of which parents do not even have much time for their children.

  Even parents don't have much time for each other which becomes the common cause of disturbance at home and in turn in the whole world.
- ***Have a strong individual foundation***: Mother Teresa had a strong foundation that propped her up through all the turmoil and difficulties throughout her life – her determined faith.

It has been well documented how for the whole of her life she confronted individual questions about her faith and how she ran her missions. Be that as it may, her core value of love and desire to serve others kept her on the go.

- ***Inculcate the habit of smiling and loving***: Mother Teresa's most charming and consistent qualities were her nature to smile and love others all the time and even tempered in the most unfavourable times of difficulties.

SWAMI VIVEKANANDA

If you are a person filled with the quality of love and have a mind-set to help, then under any circumstances you will discover the internal capacity and resources to help others.

—**Swami Vivekananda**

Swami Vivekananda, also called by the name Narendranath Datta in his pre-ascetic life, was born in a princely family in Kolkata on 12 January 1863. His dad, Vishwanath Datta, was a successful lawyer with interests in an extensive range of subjects, and his mom, Bhuvaneshwari Devi, was blessed with profound devotion to God, strong character and many other qualities. An intelligent kid, Narendra was good in music, acrobatics and studies. When he moved on from Calcutta University after graduating, he had gathered a vast knowledge in various subjects, particularly Western philosophy and history. Conceived with a yogic temperament, he used to meditate even from his childhood, he made important contribution to Brahmo Movement for quite a while.

Swami Vivekananda ended up becoming one of India's driving social reformers of the modern time and was a champion of philanthropy and service to God through service to mankind. He is adored both in the East and the West as a rejuvenator of humanity by understanding the eternal truths of Hinduism. He talked about Hinduism and its actual significance as written in the Vedas all across the world and established the Ramkrishna Mission, one of India's leading charitable foundations.

Ramakrishna Paramhansa underlined the essence of all religions and the need to lead a life based on spirituality. He was of the belief that the different religions are just different methods to attain god.

Selected Teachings on Morality by Swami Vivekananda

- Education is the way to manifest flawlessness inherent in man.
- We should focus on education as it is through this, character is formed, strong mind is resulted, intellect is expanded and one can stand on one's feet.
- As long as the million people live in hunger and ignorance, I consider every man a backstabber who having been educated at their expense, pays not minimal attention to them.
- You become what you think. You become powerless if you think so but you feel yourself filled with power if you think you have the power and you actually become powerful or strong.
- There can be no salvation if a person has faith in all the three hundred and thirty million mythological gods but no faith in himself. Inner faith is essential to be strong, this is what is required.

- Strength is a quality that we need the most in our life, for what we call sin and distress have all one reason, and that is our weakness. Due to weakness, ignorance is resulted which in turn causes distress.
- My new Gospel says that the older I become, everything appears to be in more manliness.
- Purity, patience and diligence besides love are the three fundamental components required for success.
- Religion is not about sermon or theory how much ever excellent they may be. It is being and becoming, not hearing or acknowledging; it is the entire soul getting changed to what it has firm faith in.
- Religion is for divinity inside us to manifest.
- Teach everybody his genuine nature, learn the ways to awaken the resting soul and experience how it gets awakened. Power, purity, glory and goodness, all that is considered magnificent will dawn upon you when this resting soul is stirred to a state of self-conscious.
- They live alone who live for others, the rest are more dead than alive.
- This is the essence of all forms of worship—to be pure and to perform good action for others. I preach love which is at the core of the great Vedantic truth of omnipresence and oneness of the Soul prevailing all across the Universe.

MARGARET THATCHER

Margaret Thatcher left behind a brand of politics and a set of convictions which still resound across the world. The quintessence of Thatcherism was a solid state and a free economy. Her system was moral as much as economic.

Her convictions were adjusted in the political battles of the 1970s and 1980s. However, as a result they made little changes from what she imbibed at her home in Grantham, a provincial town in eastern England, where she was born in 1925. The most critical impact in her life was her dad, Alfred Roberts, who ran the merchant's shop above which she was brought up. He made preachings of values like the thrift, self-help and diligent work. Youthful Margaret, ever sincere, got inspiration inspired by his example.

ABRAHAM LINCOLN

Abraham Lincoln, with the nickname 'Honest Abe' or 'Father Abraham', was by far one of the strongest and greatest Presidents that America has ever seen.

Though he rose from a modest and humble beginning, his sheer determination and honest effort led him to the highest office of the nation. A sharp legislator and capable legal counsellor, he played a role in unifying the states and contributed significantly to the cause of removing slavery from the nation, in the long run giving individuals equal rights, irrespective of caste, colour or creed.

Abraham Lincoln was a man of intense feeling, principles of firmness and justness, and morally sound honesty. As an American and America's pioneer, Lincoln was a symbol of values and virtues for his nation. He was so humble by nature that he was always ready to walk behind any man who desired to walk before him.

Mr. Lincoln's own philosophy depended on reason and regard for the law. Mr. Lincoln had confidence in laws that imperiously ruled matter as well as brain. With him there does not exist any supernatural occurrences outside of law.

There were no accidents in his rationality. There was a cause for each event. The past to him was the reason for the present and the present including the past will be the reason for the excellent future. Everything to him was the aftereffect of the powers of Nature, playing on matter and mind from the very starting point of time and will to its finish, play on matter and mind giving the world other, further and more amazing outcomes. Because of its basis in reason, there was a consistency in the philosophy of Mr. Lincolnalong with a consistent focus on morality.

Lincoln had an extraordinary respect for truth. Fellow lawyer Samuel Parks wrote that 'the great feature in Mr. Lincoln's character was his integrity in the longest sense of that term – his devotion to truth and justice and freedom in every department of human life and under every temptation'.

For Lincoln, honesty was a key value for the whole of his life.

JAWAHARLAL NEHRU

Jawaharlal Nehru, who was the first Prime Minister of free India, laid the foundation of India's foreign policy. He was a man who grew from an anglicized child to a devoted patriot.

Jawaharlal, Motilal and Gandhi

Jawaharlal, Motilal Nehru and Gandhi maintained a kind of relationship that was unique and their joint contribution to the Congress prompted them to be called the 'Holy Trinity' by a few columnists. For sure the incorporation of the Nehru into the National Movement had much to do with the connection amongst father and child and Jawaharlal's faithfulness to Gandhi. When Jawaharlal was in England, he had turned into the scholarly accomplice of his dad Motilal. Motilal Nehru, born a posthumous child, had from the age of 26 years, supported his wife and child and the widow and seven children of his brother. A tough, fearless, clever legal advisor, Motilal cleared his way to the highest point of the legal profession with gigantic diligent work and respect. His home, 'Anand Bhavan', at Allahabad was the focal point of attention and Motilal declined to follow the tradition of eating independently like other Brahmins or purifying himself after outside visits and so on. His kids (Jawaharlal, Swarup Kumari and Krishna) got the most ideal education required. Practical and gritty, Motilal was an important member of the Moderates in the Congress but by 1920, he took after his careless child to become a staunch supporter of Gandhi. Amid the 1920 Non Co-operation development, Motilal came to limelight when he got rid of his horses, cars, carriages, servants, precious stone and Seville Row suits and embraced sudh Khadi and the Gandhi cap. Both father and child left prospering legal profession to follow the national development and in the words of B. R. Nanda:

'What seemed a tryst with destiny in 1947 was, 28 years earlier, a leap in the dark?'

The connection between Gandhi and Jawaharlal was as yet harder to describe, as despite numerous differences they stayed faithful to each other. Jawaharlal initially met Gandhiji at the 1916 Lucknow Session of the Congress and became a part of the Satyagraha Sabha by 1919. Jawaharlal identified Gandhi's wonderful capacity to energize the majority and Gandhi considered Nehru like a son.

1920s and 1930s:

The Jallianwala Bagh massacre (1919) affected Jawaharlal and his mom's ties with people in Lahore, made Nehru come closer with official butchery. While the Non-Co-operation Movement (1920) was on, Nehru became staunch Nationalists.

In 1926, Jawaharlal and his family (spouse Kamala and little girl Indira) put in a year in Europe during which Nehru got associated with Socialism. At the Congress of Oppressed Nationalities in Brussels (1927), Nehru was chosen to a member of executive committee consisting of 9 members like Romain Rolland, Mme Sun Yat Sen and Albert Einstein of the Russian Revolution.

Coming back to India, Jawaharlal dedicated himself completely to the anti-Senior Commission Satyagraha and was beaten badly in a lathi-charge. At this crossroad, a letter to Jawaharlal by Gandhi dated Dec 3rd, 1928 stated,

'May God spare you for many a long year to come and make you his chosen instrument for freeing India from the yoke — a truly prophetic vision'.

In 1929 Jawaharlal Nehru was chosen President of the All India Congress Committee and was given the reception equivalent to a lord at the Lahore session of 1929. As the Civil Disobedience movement started, Jawaharlal and Motilal spent long stretches in prison (starting in 1921, Jawaharlal was captured many times - spending roughly 10 years under arrest between 1920 – 1947), however the ladies of the Nehru family devoted themselves completely to the nationalists movement. A big tragedy came in the life of Jawaharlal when his dad passed away in 1921 and his wife Kamala passed away in 1936, both after prolonged ailments.

India's Freedom and After

Jawaharlal stayed at the front line of the National movement and turned into the Chief Negotiator of the Congress for the Transfer of energy. A dear friend of Lord Mountbatten, Nehru turned into the P.M. of the Interim government and on fifteenth August 1947, turned into the first Prime Minister of Independent India. Alongside Vallabhai Patel as Interior minister, Jawaharlal Nehru guaranteed the accession of the Princely states to India and stretched out a hand of fellowship to other Afro-Asian Countries. The architect of India's foreign policy, Nehru described it as anti-imperialist, anti-apartheid as well as anti-colonial. Likewise, Nehru was of the belief that the recently free states in Asia and Africa had the right either to join the Soviet or Capitalist Power Blocs. In this manner he alongside Tito (Yugoslavia) and Nasser (Egypt) established the Non-Aligned Movement. Nehru did not consider the 'Non-Aligned Policy' to be impartial yet he trusted it enabled

Nations to acknowledge aid and keep up friendly relations with Nations from both Power Blocs. The only blot on the foreign policy of Nehru was the breakdown of the 'Panchasheel' accord signed with China—in 1962, the Chinese Aggression on India was huge blow to Nehru. But, Nehru's various outings abroad, India's enrolment in the commonwealth and sense of commitment against apartheidism and anti-imperialism were generally welcomed.

In December 1929, Nehru had announced that 'our economic programme must be based on a human outlook, and must not sacrifice men to money'. With regards to this, Nehru's economic policy was inclined towards communist, leading India to a mixed economy and an arrangement of five year plan. Not at all like Gandhi who trusted that village advancement was more essential, Nehru focused on industrialization, refuelling to dams and power units as new Temples of India. Nehru passed away in 1964, putting India into grieving. In no way a perfect leader, he can be described as a thoughtful, some of the time impetuous man. As he was very fond of children, his birthday is celebrated as children's Day in India. Many have talked about some of aspects of Nehru in negative sense which include Nehru's economic or foreign policy along with his relationships with Edwura Mountbatten. Be that as it may, few who knew him were invulnerable to Jawaharlal's profoundly enthusiastic love for India and his fantasies for her future. But few who knew him were immune to Jawaharlal's deeply passionate love for India and his dreams for her future. In the expressions of Rabindranath Tagore, Nehru was 'the Rituraj speaking to the period of youth and triumphant delight of a strong soul of battle and uncompromising dependability to the reason for flexibility'.

SARDAR VALLABHBHAI PATEL

Sardar Vallabhbhai Patel was an Indian nationalist leader who was born in the state of Gujarat. After completing the studies of law in England, he returned to India in 1915 and started his legal practice in Ahmadabad. He was greatly influenced by the nationalist leader Mohandas Gandhi and joined the civil disobedience movement and successfully prepared the landowners of Bardoli to fight against the increase of British duties in 1928. In 1931 he worked in the capacity of president of the Indian National Congress. The British detained Patel so many times for his fight against the British atrocities.

As home minister, minister of states and deputy prime minister (1947–50) under Jawaharlal Nehru, Patel competently accomplished the peaceful unification of the princely Indian states into the Union. His quick, cool response to Gandhi's assassination in 1948 is broadly accepted to have thwarted a probable civil war.

BAL GANGADHAR TILAK

Bal Gangadhar Tilak (29th Couplet) was explained by British as 'The Father of Indian Unrest'. Tilak was born on 23.07.1856. His trademark, 'Swaraj (Self-Rule) is my birthright', motivated a large number of Indians. His book 'Geetarahasya', a great treatise on Geeta in Marathi was composed by him, in jail at Mandalay. He is popularly known as a great journalist-editor, an expert on Vedas, Sanskrit Scholar, mathematician and a natural leader of India. When he passed away on 01.08.1920, 'Swaraj is my birthright', thundered Tilak, the Lion of India. He established schools and published daily papers, just for his country. He spent a life of misery in a far off prison at Manda lay in Burma. He kept writing continuously till the end of his life to awaken the people of his country.

Swaraj—Our Birth-Right

After completing the visit to Lucknow, he came down to Kanpur.

'Swaraj is our Birth-Right' 'We want equality. We cannot remain slaves under foreign rule. We will not carry for an instant longer, the yoke of slavery that we have carded all these years. Swaraj is our birth right. We must have it at any cost. When the Japanese, who are Asians like us, are free, why should we be slaves? Why should our Mother's hands be hand- cuffed'?

Swaraj's alter blazed. The government was again frightened and grieved.

As days passed, Tilak started to stamp the slogan 'Swaraj is our birthright' on each Indian's mind. The popularity of Lokamanya Tilak grew far and wide very quickly.

LAL BAHADUR SHASTRI

Little in stature, simple and calm by nature, Lal Bahadur ended up being one of the great personalities in the history of India. He was a wonderful general in Gandhi's army whose motto was to gain freedom through peace. He was considered to be the symbol of India's valour and sense of pride. After the demise of Nehru, the biggest question before the country was who will assume the responsibility of leading the country forward. At last all leaders agreed on the choice of Lal Bahadur Shastri as they believed Shastri to be the only leader to lead the country at such a critical time. He was person with short stature and lean body with eyes wide as the wheels of a truck. His attires were simple and soft voice that was practically inaudible. But he always had a smiling face that overarched his words. There was not even a small trace of pride or authority in his bearing. Some even doubted if he would be able to administer a country of five hundred million individuals.

Lal Bahadur never boasted himself. On the contrary he was of the belief: 'I am an ordinary man and not a very bright man'. He had no aspiration to gain power. He never sought to control it. Despite that power and authority came behind him. Fame set a crown on his head. The short man turned into a colossus. He showed through his work that though he was delicate like a blossom, he could be hard as diamond as well. He spread the name and fame of India across all the four corners of the world. When the world sang his glory and recognized him as a legend, an exceptional nationalist leader and as the architect of peace, and just as he touched the pinnacle of his life, Lal Bahadur passed away all of a sudden. He came to administer the country out of the blue, and he left the world on similar note. The 27th of May 1964 became an exceptional day ever as on that day the people went for their normal work and amid the day came shocking news from Teen Moorti Bhavan.

SUBHASH CHANDRA BOSE

'Patriot of Patriots', this is the thing that Mahatma Gandhi portrayed Subhash Chandra Bose. Subhash Chandra Bose was a splendid young fellow set for a sparkling future in the Indian Civil Services when he committed himself to the Indian National movement. Starting as youth Congressman, Bose tired of Gandhian politics, formed the Azad Hind Fauj to vanquish the British during World War II. Despite the defeat of the Azad Hind Fauj, Subhash Chandra Bose would always find an immortal place in the history of India. 'Jai-Hind' was his rallying call and he stirred the country to an extraordinary enthusiastic statures. Subhash had a deep interest of reading and was attracted towards religious truth and self-control. He was fond of doing social services. Subsequent to perusing Vivekananda's compositions, social service turned to be the long-term aim of his life.

Subhash Chandra Bose was even ousted from the school which proved to be the defining moment of his career. Considering the intellect of his child, Subhash Chandra Bose's dad was resolved that Bose should become an Indian Civil Servant of high repute. He went to England to pursue his higher studies. After released from jail on September 25, he was Mayor of Calcutta. In 1920, Bose passed the Civil Service open examination and stood fourth. Despite the fact that Bose excelled at all the prescribed courses in India and England, he was resolved to join the India's freedom struggle. Bose got associated with the Congress and was especially active in its youth wing. He left the Indian Civil Service in April 1921. Subsequent to coming back to India, Subhash went to Gandhiji. However, his thoughts did not go well with that of Gandhiji's faith in non-violence. So he left and came back to Calcutta to work under CR Das, the Bengali freedom fighter. In 1921, Bose organized a boycott of the festivals to mark a protest to the visit of Prince of Wales in India. This led to his detention.

In April 1924, Bose was chosen the Chief Executive Officer of the Calcutta Corporation which was newly constituted. Afterwards, in October, Bose was captured as one of the suspected militants. To begin with, he was in Alipore Jail and later banished to Mandalay in Burma. In June 1925, Bose was deeply struck by the sudden loss of his leader CR Das. In 1926, he was selected as a contender for the Bengal Legislative Assembly. On May 16, 1927 he was discharged from prison because of prolonged sickness. The two years in Mandalay gave him a chance to rejuvenate and regain his strength and confidence. By December 1927, Bose with Jawaharlal Nehru got to work as the General Secretary of the Congress. In January 23, 1930, Bose was once again captured to lead an 'Independence' procession. After discharged from prison on September 25, he was appointed as the Mayor of Calcutta. In 1932, Bose went to Vienna for medical treatment and there he was profoundly impacted by Vithaldas Patel, another Indian freedom fighter. They identified the requirement for coordinated effort between Indian nationalists and nations opposed to Britain and in their joint statement they announced, 'Non-co-operation cannot be given up but the form of non-co-operation will have to be changed into a more militant one and the fight for freedom waged on all fronts'. In October 1933, Vithalbhai Patel passed away and left Bose with lots of money for spreading the knowledge of India abroad.

BHAGAT SINGH

He is the symbol of the valour of the adolescents of India. He was a revolutionary who hurled a bomb when the Legislature was in session to caution the British Government. He was hanged but his memories always lived in the hearts of the people of India. One night a kid of 3 years was out for a stroll with his dad. An elderly man walked with the father. They walked while chatting and went past the town. Green crops pleased the eyes. The elders were on a walk along a field's edge. Not hearing the strides of the kid, the father looked back. The boy was found sitting on the ground and appeared to plant something. The father became inquisitive. 'What are you doing?'said he. 'Look, father, I shall grow guns all over the field' was the innocent answer of the kid. His eyes were shining with the self-belief that firearms would develop in the field. Both the elders were amazed at the utterances of the boy.

The boy was none other than Bhagat Singh who later battled like a legend for India's independence and relinquished his life for this cause.

Indeed, even at home, Bhagat Singh couldn't sit idle. Around that time the Akali Dal began a procession. But with a specific goal to avoid it, the District Collector Dil Bagh Singh passed an order to everyone that no one should supply anything to eat or drink to the members from the Akali Dal. The Collector who passed the order was in fact from Bhagat Singh's family. But being a government officer, he had hatred for the revolutionaries.

Bhagat Singh thought of aiding the Akali Dal members by making a visit to his village. He disclosed the situation to the villagers and masterminded to supply food in a secret way to the Akali Dal members during the night time. In this manner seven days passed. The Dal's activities went on a regular basis successfully and effectively. For the whole day, there used to be discussions on the country's freedom and the responsibilities that people should take up. Bhagat Singh was also one among many to share his thoughts. The Collector got furious that the common people had helped the Dal against his requests. He issued a warrant to capture Bhagat Singh. At that point Bhagat Singh was just seventeen. So he was a minor and couldn't be captured. The Collector became angrier. 'Bhagat Singh may be too young but his brain is not too young!' he grumbled.

Arrest and Release

Bhagat Singh was a fountain filled with enthusiasm. His village was very small to carry out his activities. He moved to Lahore. In Lahore, a union of revolutionaries by name 'Naujavan Bharat Sabha' was established. Bhagat Singh was given the responsibility of becoming the Secretary. Like the Kranti Dal in Bengal, the new union began imparting lessons of transformation to the common people of Punjab.Just to say its objectives were to spread Indian culture, to make the youth of country strong, confident etc., but, the actual motto was to ascertain revolution for the independence of India. Within a couple of days, it began branches in different places. The celebration of the birthday events of revolutionaries got a priority in the list of the programme of the union. The members would take out pictures of revolutionaries, decorated with Khadi garlands, in processions. They used to make a cut in their fingers and put a mark of blood on the foreheads of the heroes in the photos. They would address the gathering about their heroes. It was during these days that Bhagat Singh got a good practice in public speaking. Within a couple of days, he turned into a decent speaker. He later got in contact with the students' unions of universities. He started spreading the message of revolution all over the place.At this point, Bhagat Singh had gotten the attention of the police. His movements were carefully tracked by spies. Once, as he was simply leaving the train at Amritsar, the spies got after Bhagat Singh. Endeavouring to escape from them, he started to make fun. But, any place he went he couldn't get away. Finally he raced into a legal counsellor's home and got away from the police. At that point he ventured out to Lahore. At the point when the train reached Lahore, the police caught him and pushed him into the Lahore Fort Jail.

Bhagat Singh was surprised as why he was captured. A couple of days later, it came to be known that a few rogues had hurled a bomb on a procession during the Dussara Festival which killed a few people. The police suspected the hand of revolutionaries in it. That was the reason they captured Bhagat Singh and pushed him into the prison. To find the secret details of different revolutionaries, they tortured him in different ways. They lashed him with a knot and gored with a spear. Despite all these, Bhagat Singh did not open his mouth. At long last, a Magistrate chose that Bhagat Singh could be discharged just on a bail of sixty thousand rupees. Out of sheer love for Bhagat Singh, two rich people approached. They were Duneechand and Daulatram. On their surety, Bhagat Singh was released. It was decided that if Bhagat Singh took an interest in revolutionary activities during the bail period, the two well off men would have to pay sixty thousand rupees to the Government. Bhagat Singh did not wish that others get caught because of him. That was the reason he chose to stay silent during the bail period. At this point of time, his dad built a cowshed for him in his native place, with the goal that Bhagat Singh could run a small dairy. Bhagat Singh took up that work earnestly. Consistently he got up at four. At that point he sustained the cows, expelled the bovine compost and cleaned the shed. Next he fed the dairy animals and sold the milk. It was all efficient, and flawlessly done. Whatever work he took, he made a decent showing in that.

The whole day he was occupied with his dairy, however the night brought contemplations of revolution. He joined his companions for talks. In the meantime, he got in contact with the daily newspapers, 'Kirtee' and 'Akalee'. He composed articles for them. A journal drew out an extraordinary issue to respect fighters who had been hanged; Bhagat Singh himself made an introduction of some of the revolutionaries. The Dussara Bomb case including Bhagat Singh was all the while going on. Finally he was discharged. He was not even on bail. Now Bhagat Singh chose to shut down the milk centre and returned to his revolutionary work. Subsequent to a meeting of revolutionaries in Delhi in 1928, he stayed away from home forever.

Vengeance

In Delhi, Chandrasekhar Azad, a youth revolutionary was acquainted with Bhagat Singh. It was as though fire and wind were joined together. The activities of the revolutionaries got a new strength and vigour. Bhagat Singh removed his beard and had a closer crop with the goal that the police won't identify him. All these days he had been a hero for the Sikhs but now he turned into a national hero. There was a revolutionary party called the 'Hindustan Prajatantra Sangha' (The Indian Republic Party) whose name was now changed to 'Hindustan Samajvadi Prajatantra Sangha' (The Indian Socialist Republican Party). Its aim was to build up a republic in India using armed revolution.

When a bomb is thrown to the ground, it explodes causing a deafening sound, and destroys everything nearby. The revolutionaries needed any number of bombs to drive out the British. But where could they get them? Bhagat Singh went to Calcutta to learn to make bombs. There he bought as many bombs as he needed. He also learnt from Jatindranath Das, a revolutionary, how to make bombs. At the point when a bomb is hurled to the ground, it detonates causing a stunning sound, and decimates everything close by. The revolutionaries required any number of bombs to drive out the British. But, where would they be able to get them? Bhagat Singh visited Calcutta to learn the methods to make bombs. There he purchased the same number of bombs as he required. He also learnt the methods to make bomb from a revolutionary named Jatindranath Das.The revolutionaries set up a factory covertly at Agra to make bombs. But, how could they get the cash they required? Once in a while for three days together they lived just on some cup of tea. They didn't have beds or floor coverings even though it was gnawing cold. They sometimes had to starve for many days. And at the same time the possibility of the police torment always plagued them. Amidst this they went ahead with their hallowed work. Also, for cash they would at times plunder government offices. Finally they could design bombs. The bombs were tried at Jhansi Fort. The test was successful.

In February 1928, a committee from England came to India which was popularly known as the Simon Commission. The reason for its visit was to decide how much freedom and responsibilities could be passed on to the common people of India but no Indian was a part of this advisory group. This created intense anger among Indians. They chose to make it impossible for the Commission to work. They chose to drive it back to England.

Wherever the committee made a visit, people made an intense protest with black banners, yelling 'Simon, go back'. At the point when the Simon Commission visited Lahore in October, it faced a large procession of angry Indians confronting it. 'Naujavan Bharat Sabha' orchestrated the procession. A huge number of individuals participated in it. Its leader was the elderly loyalist, Lala Lajpat Ray. Problem got started near the railway station itself. The revolutionaries did not permit the Simon Commission to make a move. The police couldn't ensure the individuals. At that point, the Police Superintendent, one Scott by name, gave an order to lathi-charge.

The police started beating people with heavy sticks. People began to run and disperse. However, Lajpat Ray and his friends did not run away. A police officer by name Saunders hurried forward and hit Lajpat Ray on the chest. It was a very powerful blow. Since Lajpat Ray was old and was suffering from illness, the blow brought him demise. For over a month, he underwent painful trauma and finally died. Due to his demise, the revolutionaries met a heavy loss. They made a decision that they should take revenge for this dreadful act and that they should kill Scott who made an order for the lathi-charge. This is what was planned. A revolutionary by name Jayagopal was to keep a close watch on Scott's movements. Bhagat Singh and Rajguru were chosen to shoot him. Then, they also made a careful plan to escape from the spot after killing Scott.

A lot of planning was made under the initiative of Chandrasekhara Azad. But in the beginning itself, a little slip-up happened. Jayagopal mistook Saunders for Scott. The day of appointment approached. That night Saunders left the police headquarters and got on his motorbike. Jayagopal who was behind made an indication. Bhagat Singh and Rajguru who were waiting on the way shot at Saunders from his pistol as the motorbike approached Rajguru. A bullet struck the chest of the man who had hit Lajpat Ray's chest using a heavy stick; Saunders immediately tumbled down dead. Bhagat Singh and Rajguru fled away. The police ran behind them but the two hurried into a hotel close by. At that point they got away from the place. The entire city was loaded with the news of Saunders' murder. The police spies started a search for the killers everywhere throughout the city. Next day, posters showed up on the walls in all streets of Lahore which announced, 'Lala Lajpat Ray's death is avenged. Saunders has been murdered'. Besides, there were a few words of caution for the Government. The posters also included the name of The Hindustan Samajvadi Prajatantra Sena (The Indian Socialist Republican Army) in red letters.

This was done so that everybody could know who were behind the murder of Saunders, this generated a sense of great regards for the Kranti Dal among the common masses. The murder of Saunders shook the British Government. Bhagat Singh, Rajguru and Chandra Sekhara Azad all the three got away from Lahore. Bhagat Singh dressed himself as a foreign youth wearing a cap. Durga Bhabhi, the spouse of a revolutionary Bhagavaticharan, and their child accompanied Bhagat Singh so that people would think they were Bhagat Singh's family members. These three went via train in a first class compartment. Rajguru left the place masked as a conventional labourer. Azad went as a savant (researcher). The railroad station was loaded with eagle-eyed spies; however all the three left successfully.

A Bomb Bursts

The police looked and hunted for Bhagat Singh and Rajguru, yet couldn't discover them. Three months went by. In April 1929, the Central Legislative Assembly held a meeting in Delhi. The British Government desired to put before the Assembly two bills which were probably going to hurt the interests of the country. Regardless of the fact that the Assembly dismissed them, the Viceroy could utilize his special powers and endorse them, and would ultimately become laws. The Hindustan Samajvadi Prajatantra Sena (The Indian Socialist Republican Army) chose to oppose the move. Obviously, the revolutionaries got away after Saunders' murder but the common people of Lahore underwent torture by the police. The Sena chose that such a thing should not occur again. The revolutionaries must put opposition against the British and court arrest. They should see that the objects of the Prajatantra Sena were disclosed to the general population everywhere throughout the nation. With this object in view, the Sena made plans to send Bhagat Singh and

Batukeshwar Dutt to Delhi. Both of them were supposed to visit there, hurl a bomb in the Legislative Assembly and get arrested. For this reason two harmless bombs were designed. On the 8th of April 1929, the two men entered the Assembly Hall with the bombs. They sat in the guests' exhibition.

The session began. The government placed the bills before the Assembly. They were rejected by the members. At last, a member from the Government started a declaration that the Viceroy had practiced his special powers. Suddenly, a bomb tumbled from above and detonated causing a dreadful sound. Quickly another bomb fell. There were hints of shooting as well. The whole lobby was loaded with smoke. People started running here and there. Some were frightened that they tumbled down unconsciously. At that point, red leaflets tumbled from the visitors' exhibition. In them, particulars of Prajatantra Sena (the Republican Army) were given and the Government was denounced. The Hall echoed with the slogan, 'Long Live Revolution!' The police hurried to the spot. Just Bhagat Singh and Batukeshwar Dutt were there. They were holding guns. Scared of them, the police moved back. However, both tossed down their guns and got themselves handcuffed. The bombs tossed into the Assembly Hall did not hurt anyone except four or five people who got exceptionally minor wounds; that was all. The motto of revolutionaries was not to kill anyone. This event drew the attention of the whole world. The Kranti Dal's name became a popular word in every house.

The British Government was shaken. After the episode, the Government suspected the existence of factory at Lahore. The Government took into custody enough material to make almost seven thousand bombs. Another huge plant at Saharanpur too was found by the Government. Within a couple of days, a large number of the Kranti Dal leaders were captured. The Government lodged a case against them, blaming them for executing the Lahore plot. Bhagat Singh and his associates were put in jail in Lahore.

Gladly Receiving Death

The trial of the accused began. In those days, proper treatment was not offered to political detainees in the prison. Proper food was not given to them. They were made to undergo sufferings in every possible way. Bhagat Singh and his allies chose to battle against the pathetic conditions. Bhagat Singh was certain of getting hanged. But he thought at least other political detainees could profit. All the revolutionaries went on protest through fast. They underwent fasting for two months. At that point the Government accepted their demands. Some broke their fast but Jatin Das did not. He didn't pay heed to anyone.On the 64th day of his fast, he died. Bhagat Singh fasted for thirty-two days from there on. The trial of Bhagat Singh and his mates started; the attention of the entire world came to these events. The large number of police guarded the court. No common people were permitted inside the court. The detainees were brought to the court in chains. They used to yell 'Long Live Revolution' and then only used to go inside the court corridor. Bhagat Singh and BatukeshwarDutt expressed, 'If the deaf are to hear, the sound has to be very loud. When we dropped the bomb, it was not our intention to kill anybody. We have bombed the British Government. The British must quit India and make her free'.

They also clarified the objectives of their association. The entire world came to know about their objectives and activities on account of the press reports. At last judgment was announced. Bhagat Singh, Sukhdev and Rajguru were sentenced to death; some were to supposed to undergo life imprisonment; some were to be kept in prison for five years, some for seven, ten or for longer duration. Bhagat Singh was to be hanged! At the point when the news spread, the common people everywhere throughout the nation were red in anger. A number of appeals reached to the Government, arguing that he should be spared. A number of leaders of public life participated in making appeal. But, all endeavours fizzled. It was chosen to hang them on the 24th of March 1931. Not just that even the members from the detainees' families were not permitted to meet them. Besides, Bhagat Singh, Sukhdev and Rajguru were hanged a day prior to the designated day, that is, on March 23rd. Even upon the arrival of their hanging, they were less bothered.

That day no one in the jail touched food. Everyone was in tears. They were completely delightful. They competed with one other to get hanged first. It was chosen that first Sukhdev, then Bhagat Singh and lastly, Rajguru would be hanged. All the three climbed the stage. They kissed the rope and they themselves put the ropes round their neck. They left the world with the name of Bharat Mata on their lips. Such was the finish of the three fighters of India's independence. That day nobody in the jail took any food. Everybody was in pain and tears. The following day, not realizing that the three detainees had just been hanged, their relatives came to meet them. But it was done with them. The dead bodies of the martyrs had been burnt secretly on the bank of river Sutlej. As the news spread, a great number of people hustled to the spot, however just the fiery debris remained. The people cried with the ashes in their hold. Everywhere throughout the nation, tributes were paid to the legends who battled for freedom and made the ultimate sacrifice of their lives. Several compositions and songs were released highlighting the sufferings of Bhagat Singh. Indeed, even today, the gallant soul of Bhagat Singh is an unfailing source of inspiration to the youngsters of the country. His bravery, spirit of adventure and patriotism are examples for everyone to emulate.

INDIRA GANDHI

Indira Gandhi, prime minister of India (1966–77; 1980–84), whose disputable political career finished with her assassination by Sikh plotters. Following the passing away of her dad in May 1964, Gandhi moved towards becoming information and broadcasting minister in Lal Bahadur Shastri's cabinet. While holding this post she expanded telecom time, changed censorship policies and affirmed a TV education project in family planning. At the point when Shastri passed away all of a sudden in January 1966, Gandhi succeeded him as leader. The next year she was chosen to a 5-year term by the Parliament members of the overwhelming Congress party. She drove her party to a landslide triumph in the national elections of 1971. In 1975, Gandhi was found guilty of a minor infraction of the election laws amid the campaign of 1971. Maintaining guiltlessness, she charged the conviction was a piece of an endeavour to expel her from office and, rather than resigning, pronounced a national emergency on June 26. Despite the fact that her conviction was soon declined by the Indian Supreme Court, the crisis of emergency went on. Gandhi set numerous aspects of life in India under her strict control, and a great many protesters were detained. Many found in these activities the impact of her younger child, Sanjay Gandhi (1946–80), a political amateur on whom she depended increasingly for help. Wanting to exhibit well known help for her administration, which faultfinders contended was undermining India's democratic system, Gandhi called a general election in March 1977; she lost her seat in Parliament, and the Congress party was crushed. In the elections of January 1980, however, she made an astounding comeback and formed a majority government again. At a point when Sanjay died in a plane crash that June, she started preparing her older child, Rajiv Gandhi (1944–91), as her successor. On October 31, 1984, after she had moved energetically to stifle Sikh extremists, she was shot to death by Sikh member from her security guard. Rajiv at that point filled in as prime minister until 1989. He was killed in a bombarding at an election rally in Madras on May 21, 1991.

ALBERT EINSTEIN

Einstein was likewise an extraordinary thinker and ethical leader. A splendid man who was energetically inquisitive about the riddles of science, Albert Einstein changed the world as the most persuasive physicist of the twentieth century. He created the general hypothesis of relativity ($e = mc^2$), now considered the very basis of present day material science. Einstein got the Nobel Prize in Physics 'for his services to theoretical physics and especially for his discovery of the law of the photoelectric effect'.

Top Learning from his life

- ***Follow Your Inquisitiveness***: Inquisitiveness or curiosity helps boost our creativity. When we make inquiries of others, we can discover vital information to enable us to take care of problems, open new gateways and create associations. When we make inquiries of ourselves, we can shake up our convictions, uncover our deepest desires and roll out positive improvement. What unanswered inquiry is swimming around in your mind?
- ***Perseverance is Invaluable***: If you happen to have a dream, you'll be faced with impediments but by remaining with obstacles longer, as Einstein says, can mean the contrast between failure and achievement. Some approaches to start practising perseverance is by focusing on your dream, keeping up a positive attitude, remaining concentrated on what you need each day and bobbing once more from adversity.
- ***Concentrate on the Present***: What an extraordinary case Einstein uses to highlight the significance of concentrating on the present. We can miss the joys of the present by being excessively preoccupied with the past as well as future. Reminding ourselves daily to be available will bring us more peace and delight and in addition furnish us with a more noteworthy gratefulness for life.
- ***Creativity is Powerful***: Creativity is everything. It is the preview of life's coming events. Creativity is more imperative than information. A mere idea can help build an empire. Take for instance, Walt Disney, a genuine ace at creative energy. He got the

idea for Mickey Mouse from an old pet mouse that he used to keep on his farm. That highly black and white contrasting mouse turned into an animated legend. Creative energy opens the way to a Kingdom of possible outcomes!

- *Learning the Rules and afterwards Playing Better*: To gain expertise at something, study the success stories of others and try to do better than them. The stronger your dedication and energy to your undertaking, the more noteworthy your determination will be to succeed.

DR. A.P.J. ABDUL KALAM

A.P.J. Abdul Kalam was born to a poor Tamil Muslim family on 15 October 1931 at Rameswaram in the state of Tamil Nadu.

He was a well-known scientist and administrator by profession in India. He worked with Indian Space Research Organization (ISRO) and Defence Research and Development Organization (DRDO) as an aeronautical engineer before becoming the President of India. His work on developing launch vehicle and ballistic missile technology led him to be known by the name of the 'Missile Man of India'.

Important Lessons to Be Learnt from Dr. Kalam

- *Be Always Ready*: Life does not generally take the path we have set for it. At times, it takes its own particular course and influences us to follow it. And when that happens – an emergency, as would be called by some, we need to be better prepared. At least we should have the presence of mind to analyse what is the best course of action in that particular situation.
- *Have a Farsightedness*: This is single most powerful factor that drives our human civilization. Having a dream, supporting it, sitting tight for its realization, receiving its benefits—all offer importance to life. The human soul breaks down not when it is denied of food but when it is denied a dream. People with purpose advance far in life than those with none. The auto-pilot mode that functions admirably for an aircraft is lethal for a human. The youthful lament of 'getting bored' or the elderly hold back that all 'responsibilities are over' and there's nothing else left, does not look good for a country that still has far to go.
- *Making Connection with People*: In the frantic race for success, we frequently make distance among people and embrace numbers. If this event is accidental and not a planned one, the realization of the same comes as a surprise to even oneself. Gregarious that we are by nature, it is to our greatest advantage that we endeavour to know our neighbours and stay in contact with our family. Sound relations among individuals contribute extraordinarily to our joy and life span. Research demonstrates that individuals who are more connected with people are more delightful and undergo a better quality life.
- *Be Modest*: This should be in the priority list as all else may fail without this. Spiritual Masters have lauded the qualities like modesty and parents have shown us the path to be modest. The value education in schools aims to add this quality to our personality.

All achievement in life comes to nothing in the event that it is bound with vanity. Humility has, and will remain, a charming quality because where pride vacillates, modesty wins.

Important Values Possessed by Dr. Kalam

- Honesty
- Self-discipline
- Belief in goodness
- Deep compassion
- Teetotalism
- Patriotism
- Secularism

SOCIAL REFORMERS

Decades come and go but what remain are the impression and incredible works done by the social reformers. India has the advantage to have a number of incredible souls like Dayanand Saraswati and Raja Ram Mohan Roy. They figured out how to get revolution by rolling out radical improvements in the society. A number of the reformers took up the difficulties of breaking the jinx of existing caste system while some battled for the girls' education and widow remarriage. The role they played might appear simple yet highly extraordinary towards the service of humanity. Their activities and thoughts guided the country to a fresh start.

ACHARYA VINOBA BHAVE

Acharya Vinoba Bhave was a known freedom fighter and a teacher of spirituality. He is remembered as the founder of the 'Bhoodan Movement' (Gift of the Land). The reformer had a deep concern for the denied masses. According to Vinoba Bhave, 'All revolutions are spiritual at the source'.

BABA AMTE

From a child born with a silver spoon in his mouth, Baba Amte later changed his life into a social activist. He committed, as long as he could, to serve the downtrodden and deprived people of the society. He abandoned his highly lucrative profession to join India's battle for freedom.

DR. B. R. AMBEDKAR BIOGRAPHY

Dr. B. R. Ambedkar, prevalently known as Babasaheb Ambedkar, was one among the highly regarded architects and contributors of the Constitution of India. He was a notable politician and a famous law specialist. Ambedkar's endeavours to annihilate the social evils such as untouchability and caste barriers were highly noteworthy.

ISHWAR CHANDRA VIDYASAGAR

Ishwar Chandra Vidyasagar is regarded as one of the mainstays of Bengal renaissance. In a way, he figured out how to proceed with the reform movement that was initiated by Raja Rammohan Roy. Vidyasagar was a notable writer and scholar but above all an intense follower of humanity. He played an important role in the bringing necessary changes in the education system of Bengal.

JYOTIBA PHULE

In India, Jyotiba Phule was one of the most important social reformers of the nineteenth century. He led the movement against the existing caste barriers in India. He opposed the domination of the Brahmins and fought for the rights of labourers, peasants and other low-caste individuals.

MOTHER TERESA

Mother Teresa was a genuine supporter of humanity. Many individuals considered Mother as the 'reincarnated form of Lord Jesus'. Mother Teresa dedicated her whole life in the service of needy and abandoned people of Indian society. Despite the fact that her service activities began in India, she could bring people from different societies under one roof called humanity.

RAJA RAM MOHAN ROY

Raja Ram Mohan Roy is described as the pioneer of modern Indian Renaissance for the noteworthy changes he made in the eighteenth century India. Among his contributions, abolishing the sati-pratha: a practice in which the widow was forced to give up her life on the burial fire of her husband was very significant.

SRI RAMAKRISHNA PARAMHANSA

Sri Ramakrishna Paramhansa was a well-known holy soul of India. He had an intense faith in the presence of god. He respected each lady of the society, including his wife, Sarada as holy mother. Swami Vivekananda was one of the most important followers of Ramakrishna, who later established the Ramakrishna Mission.

SHAHU CHHATRAPATI

King Shahu Chhatrapati was regarded as a true democrat and social reformer. He was a priceless jewel in the history of Kolhapur. Shahu involved in a number of progressive activities in the society which also include women education. He was extraordinarily impacted by the contributions of social reformer Jyotiba Phule.

SWAMI DAYANAND SARASWATI

Dayanand Saraswati was a reformer and had a strong belief in pragmatic approach of life. He preached against a number of evil customs of the Hindu religion, for example, worship of idols, caste by birth, sacrificing animals and restricting women from perusing Vedas. He was an extraordinary researcher and rationalist as well as a social reformer and a political thinker.

SWAMI VIVEKANANDA

Swami Vivekananda is known for his inspirational discourse at the Parliament of the World's Religions at Chicago on 11 September, 1893, where he made the people of the west aware of the Hindu philosophy. But, this was not by any means the only contribution of this holy man. He discovered the true foundations of India's solidarity as a country. He showed how a country with such an immense variety can be kept together by a sentiment of mankind and fraternity.

Lessons to be Learnt from the Life of Great Social Reformers of India

India is known for a rich history of social reformers who have helped in establishing the foundation of modern India, and in some instances, have had a global effect through political activity and philosophic lessons. Particularly given India's inclination towards oral and mythical instead of a written custom throughout its history, it is practically difficult to assemble an exhaustive list of social reformers who have survived through the ages. The following are some of them.

BASAVESHWARA

Basava(1134–1196), otherwise called Bhakti Bhandari Basavanna or Basaveshwara, was a philosopher, Statesman and a social reformer from present day Karnataka, India. Basava battled against the barbaric practice of caste system, which made discrimination among people based on their birth and certain rituals in Hinduism. He spread social awareness by means of his verses, popularly known as Vachanaas. Basavanna utilized Ishtalinga to destroy untouchability, set up balance among every person and a way to accomplish spiritual enlightenment. These are sound and dynamic social thoughts combined with existing view about God in Hindu society. He was an incredible rationalist.

SRIMANTA SANKARDEV

Srimanta Sankardev (1449–1568), was a 15th-16th century Assamese polymath: a saint scholar, writer, dramatist, socio-religious reformer and a gigantic figure in the socio-cultural and religious history of Assam, India. He is credited with expanding on past social relics and formulating new types of music (Borgeet), plays (Ankia Naat), dramatic performance (Bhaona), dance (Sattriya), scholarly dialect (Brajavali). Additionally, he has left a concentrated scholarly ouvre of transcreated sacred writings (Bhagavat of Sankardev), verse and philosophical works written in Sanskrit, Assamese and Brajavali. The Bhagavatic religious movement he began, Ekasarana Dharma and furthermore called Neo-Vaishnavite movement, impacted two medieval kingdoms—Koch and the Ahom kingdoms—and the get together of devotees he started advanced into Sattras after some time, which continue to be vital socio-religious establishments in Assam and to a lesser reach in North Bengal. Sankardev inspired bhakti in Assam similarly as Guru Nanak, Ramananda, Kabir, Basava along with Chaitanya Mahaprabhu who inspired it somewhere else. His scholarly and imaginative commitments are living traditions in Assam today. The religion he preached is practised by a large number of people, and Sattras (cloisters) that he and his followers set up proceed to thrive and maintain his legacy.

RAJA RAM MOHAN ROY

'Raja Ram Mohan Roy' (May 22, 1772 – September 27, 1833) founded the Brahma Sabha in 1828 which caused the Brahmo Samaj, a well-known Indian socio-religious reform movement. He is best known for his endeavours to abrogate the act of 'sati'. It was he who initially presented the word 'Hinduism' into the English dialect in 1816. Raja Ram Mohan Roy is viewed as a noteworthy personality amongst the most important figures in the Indian Renaissance. Ram Mohan Roy's effect on current Indian history was a restoration of principles based on purity and morality.

MOHANDAS KARAMCHAND GANDHI

Mahatma Gandhi (2 October 1869 – 30 January 1948) (Father of the Nation, Rashtrapita), was one of the prominent political and spiritual leader of India at the time of Indian freedom movement. He was the leader of 'satyagraha'— a struggle against the oppression of the British through civil mass disobedience, solidly based upon ahimsa or complete non-violence which drove India to freedom and propelled developments for social equality and freedom all over the world. Gandhi drove countrywide struggle to ease poverty, extend women's rights, establish religious and ethnic harmony, remove untouchability and enhance economic confidence of the country.

KABIR

Kabîr (likewise Kabîra) (1440–1518) was a spiritual poet and holy man of India, whose works have significantly affected the Bhakti movement. The name Kabir originates from Arabic al-Kabîr which means 'The Great' – the 37th name of God in Islam. Kabir was affected by the overarching religious mind-set of his time, for example, old Brahmanic Hinduism, Tantrism, the lessons of Nath yogis and the individual devotionalism of South India blended with the imageless God of Islam. The impact of these different principles is completely apparent in Kabir's verses. Prominent history specialists like R.C. Majumdar, P.N. Chopra, B.N. Puri and M.N. Das have held that Kabir is the first Indian saint to have blended Hinduism and Islam by introducing a common path which both the Hindus and Muslims could accept and follow together.

VIRCHAND GANDHI

Virchand Gandhi was from Mahuva. He was a great supporter of women education. He is a nineteenth century Indian nationalist who was Mahatma Gandhi's friend and contemporary to Swami Vivekananda. In 1893, he and Swami Vivekananda brought about equal attention at the first World Parliament of Religions in Chicago. He received a silver award for the same. His statue still exists at the Jain sanctuary in Chicago. He was an important member from Indian National Congress and a reformer well-known.

1. Society for the Education of Women in India (SEWI). Under the name of SEWI, a number of Indian women came to USA to carry out their higher studies.
2. Gandhi Philosophical Society,
3. School of Oriental Philosophy,
4. Jain Literature Society in London. And he made a number of lectures, about 535 in the USA and Europe. Just like Swami Vivekananda, he also died at a young age. He died at the age of 37. Today Government of India has taken note of his service by issuing postal stamp in his memory.

SWAMI VIVEKANANDA

Swami Vivekananda (January 12, 1863 – July 4, 1902) was the founder of Ramakrishna Mission. Swami Vivekananda was also very popular as a great scholar. Narendra Nath Dutta was his real name. Vivekananda is thought to be a noteworthy contributor in reviving Hinduism in modern India. He was viewed as an important figure in introducing Vedanta and Yoga in Europe and America. He presented Hinduism at the Parliament of the World's Religions at Chicago in 1893.

JAMNALAL BAJAJ

Jamnalal Bajaj (4 November 1884 – 11 February 1942) was an industrialist, a philanthropist and Indian freedom fighter. Gandhi is believed to have embraced him as his child. He is well-known for his endeavours in advancing Khadi and village Industries in India. With the purpose of destroying untouchability, he battled the non-admission of Harijans into Hindu temples. He started a crusade by eating a supper with Harijans and opening public wells for them. He opened a number of wells in his fields and gardens. Jamanalal committed quite a bit of his wealth for the sake of poor people. He felt this acquired riches was a holy trust to be utilized for the advantage of the general population. To pay tribute to his social activities, a well-known national and universal honour called Jamnalal Bajaj Award has been initiated by the Jamnalal Bajaj Foundation.

VINOBA BHAVE

Vinoba Bhave (September 11, 1895 – November 15, 1982) was an Indian promoter of Nonviolence and human rights. He is regarded as the spiritual successor of Mahatma Gandhi. Vinoba Bhave was a researcher, thinker, author who delivered various books; interpreter who made Sanskrit writings available to normal man; speaker, linguist who had excellent command of a number of dialects (Marathi, Hindi, Urdu, English, Sanskrit) and was a well-known social reformer. He composed brief introductions to and criticisms of several religious and philosophical works like the Bhagavad Gita, works of Adi Shankaracharya, the Bible and Quran. His criticism of Dnyaneshwar's verse as likewise the output by other Marathi saints is very splendid and a declaration to the broadness of his mind. A college named after him Vinoba Bhave University is still there in the state of Jharkhand spreading learning even after his demise.

BABA AMTE

Baba Amte (December 26, 1914–February 9, 2008) was a well-known Indian social worker and social activist known especially for his work for the rehabilitation and strengthening of poor people experiencing leprosy. He invested some time at Sevagram ashram of Mahatma Gandhi, and turned into a supporter of Gandhism for the remaining part of his life. He had a great supporter of Gandhi's idea of a self-sufficient village industry that enables apparently vulnerable people, and effectively brought his thoughts into reality at Anandwan. He practised different aspects of Gandhism, including yarn spinning by making use of a charkha and wearing khadi. Amte established three ashrams for the treatment of patients and helped rehabilitate leprosy patients, disabled persons and marginalized people of society in the Indian state of Maharashtra.

SHRIRAM SHARMA ACHARYA

Shriram Sharma Acharya (September 20, 1911–June 2, 1990) was an Indian seer, sage, Indian social worker, a humanitarian, a visionary of the New Golden Era and the Founder of the All World Gayatri Pariwar. He committed his life to the welfare of individuals and the refinement of the moral and cultural aspects of society. He spearheaded the recovery of most profound sense of being, innovative coordination of the advanced and old sciences and religion relevant in the testing conditions of the present circumstances. To help individuals, his point was to analyse the main cause of the weak condition of the world today and empower the upliftment of society. Acharyaji identified some of the problems like the crisis of faith, individuals' ignorance of the power of inner-self and the absence of righteous attitude and conduct. During 1984–1986, he performed the special spiritual experiments of sukshmikaraña, which means sublimation of vital force and physical, mental and profound energies.

ISHWAR CHANDRA VIDYASAGAR

Ishwar Chandra Vidyasagar (1820–1891) was a scholar, academic, teacher, author, interpreter, printer, publisher, business person, reformer and philanthropist. His endeavours to simplify and modernize Bangla prose were highly beneficial. He was a Bengali polymath and an important figure of the Bengal Renaissance. Vidyasagar stressed on the need to uplift the status of women in India, especially in his local Bengal. Dissimilar to different reformers who looked to set up alternative social orders or frameworks, he looked for, in any case, to change customary Hindu society from inside. Vidyasagar presented the act of widow remarriages to mainstream Hindu society. In earlier times, remarriages of widows would happen sporadically just among progressive individuals from the Brahmo Samâj.

DHONDO KESHAV KARVE

Dhondo Keshav Karve (April 18, 1858 – November 9, 1962) was a social reformer of his time in India who worked for the welfare of women. Karve was one among the pioneers who promoted women's education and worked for the rights of widows to remarry in India. The Government of India took note of his reform works and granted him the highest civilian award, Bhârat Ratna, in 1958 (happened to be his centennial year). The designation Maharshi, which the Indian people frequently allocated to Karve, signifies 'a great sage'. The individuals who knew Karve tenderly called him as Annâ Karve. (In Marâthi-talking group, to which Karve belonged, the appellation Annâ is frequently used to address either one's father or an elder brother).

BALSHASTRI JAMBHEKAR

Balshastri Jambhekar (January 6, 1812–May 18, 1846) is regarded as Father of Marathi journalism for his endeavours in initiating journalism in Marathi dialect with the first daily paper in the dialect named 'Darpan' during the early period of British Rule in India. He founded Darpan as the first Marathi daily paper. He worked as an editor for this daily paper at the time of the British administration in India. This led to the start of Marathi journalism. He was well-versed in numerous dialects including Marathi, Sanskrit, English and Hindi. Aside from that he additionally had a decent hold of Greek, Latin, French, Gujarati and Bengali.

DR. B. R. AMBEDKAR

B. R. Ambedkar (14 April 1891 – 6 December 1956) was an Indian legal scholar, political leader, Buddhist activist, philosopher, thinker, anthropologist, historian, speaker, prolific writer, economic specialist, researcher, editor, revolutionary and the revivalist of Buddhism in India. He is also known as the main architect of the Indian Constitution. Ambedkar worked incessantly throughout his life against social discrimination, the arrangement of Chaturvarna—the Hindu classification of human society into four varnas—and the Hindu caste system. He is likewise credited with having started the bloodless revolution with his most amazing and inventive Buddhist movement. Dr. Baba Saheb Ambedkar has been honoured with the Bharat Ratna, which is India's highest civilian award.

ANNIE BESANT

Annie Besant (October 1, 1847 – September 20, 1933) was a conspicuous theosophist, women's rights activist, writer and speaker who supported the Irish and Indian self-rule. In 1908, Annie Besant got the responsibility of being the President of the Theosophical Society and started to lead the general public Hinduism away from Buddhism. She additionally ended up noticeably associated with politics in India when he joined the Indian National

Congress. At the point when war broke out in Europe in 1914 she assisted in launching the Home Rule League to battle for popular government in India and dominion status inside the Empire which ended up in her election as president of the India National Congress in late 1917. After the war she kept on battling for Indian freedom until her demise in 1933.

VITTHAL RAMJI SHINDE

Vitthal Ramji Shinde (April 23, 1873 – January 2, 1944) was a notable campaigner of the Dalit movement in Maharashtra and set up the Depressed Classes Mission to impart education to the Dalits in Maharashtra.

GOPAL HARI DESHMUKH

Gopala Krishnan (1823–1892) was a well-known social reformer in Maharashtra. Deshmukh began composing articles in the weekly Prabhakar under the pen name Lokhitwadi. This aimed to bring about desired social change in Maharashtra. In the initial two years, he penned 108 articles on social change. That gathering of articles has come to be referred to in Marathi writing as Lokhitwadinchi Shatapatre.

KANDUKURI VEERESALINGAM

On 16 April 1848, Kandukuri Veeresalingam was born who later became the first social reformer to achieve a renaissance in Telugu people and Telugu writing. He was impacted by the ideals of Brahmo Samaj especially those of Keshub Chunder Sen. He got associated with the cause for social changes. In 1876, he began a Telugu journal and composed the main writing for women. He stressed on the need for women education, and began a school in Dowlaishwaram in 1874. He began a social organization called Hitakarini (Benefactor). Unfortunately, he died on 27 May 1919.

JAWAHARLAL NEHRU

Jawaharlal Nehru (14 November 1889 – 27 May 1964) was an Indian statesman who was the first (and to date the longest-serving) PM of India, from 1947 until 1964. One of the main figures in the Indian freedom movement, Nehru was chosen by the Congress Party to assume office as free India's first Prime Minister, and re-chosen when the Congress Party won India's first general election in 1952. As one of the founders of the Non-aligned Movement, he was additionally a critical figure in the global governmental issues of the post-war period. He is often known as Pandit Nehru ('pandit' being a Sanskrit and Hindi honorific meaning 'scholar' or 'teacher') and, particularly in India, as Panditji (with -'ji' being an honorific suffix). His birthday is celebrated with lots of enthusiasm as children's day in India.

VIJAYPAL BAGHEL

Vijaypal Baghel (20 February 1967) is an environmental activist. He is known for his endeavours in securing environment at grass root level through customary strategies.

He is a noticeable campaigner in the interest of mission as Jhola Movement for battling against polythene across India, first planter of divine tree Kalpavriksha's (Adansonia digitata) at all popular pilgrims of around the globe, admirer of nature and lead promoter of spiritual/religious/herbal/therapeutic/ecological values having species of flora. He committed his life to preserve nature, save water, green resolution, decrease contamination and stop a global warming with the theme of 'Think globally Act locally'. He is popularly called as green man.

PERIYAR E. V. RAMASAMY

Periyar E. V. Ramasamy Thanthai Periyar or E. V. R., was a businessman, politician, Indian freedom and social activist, who began the Self-Respect Movement or the Dravidian Movement and supported the making of an autonomous state called Dravidasthan consisting of South India. He is also known for establishing the socio-cultural organization called Dravidar Kazhagam.

PANDURANG SHASTRI ATHAVLE

Pandurang Vaijnath Shastri Athavale (October 19, 1920 – October 25, 2003), also called Dada-ji, which actually means elder brother in Marathi, was an Indian philosopher, spiritual leader, social reformer and Hinduism reformist, who initiated the Swadhyay Movement and the Swadhyay Parivar organization (Swadhyay Family) in the year 1954, a self-information movement that takes its inspiration from the Bhagavad Gita, which has spread across almost 100,000 villages in India, with more than 5 million members. He was also known for his talks or 'pravachans' on Srimad Bhagawad Gita and Upanishads. He was born in the Konkan village of Roha in the Indian state of Maharashtra. He was one of five offspring of Sanskrit instructor Vaijanath Athavale and Parvati Athavale. At the point when Athavale was twelve years of age, his grandfather set up an autonomous course of study for the young man with individual tuition. Accordingly, Athavale was educated in a system fundamentally the same as that of the Tapovan arrangement of old India. In 1942, he began to give talks at the Srimad Bhagavad Gita Pathshala, a centre established by his dad in 1926. Athavale studied hard in the Royal Asiatic Library for a long time, perusing and assimilating each genuine writing (extending from Marx's theory to Whitehead's compositions to old Indian philosophy). In 1954, he went to the Second World Philosophers Conference, held in Japan. There, Athavale displayed the ideas of Vedic goals and the lessons of the Bhagavad Gita. All members were deeply influenced by his thoughts and wanted proof of such ideals being incorporated in different places across India. A Dr. Wilson Compton was so much inspired with Athavale's thoughts that he offered him a post in the US, where he could spread his thoughts. Athavale with all humility declined this post, saying that he had work to fulfil in the event that he needed to demonstrate the world a model group calmly practising and spreading the heavenly Vedic thoughts and the message of the Bhagavad Gita.

Lessons to Be Learnt from the Life of Great Leaders and Administrators from History

Leadership has been described as a process through which a person creates impacts and inspires others to get together to perform a specific task. This single definition, albeit generally acknowledged, neglects to characterize the specific ways and methods for individuals who are regarded as great leaders. Every single extraordinary leader had something one of a kind about them but then they were bound by enormity that helped them to lead masses to advancement and new belief systems. Since the most ancient times known to men, masses have been driven by leaders of high stature. Such men and women have been in charge of introducing individuals into a new and more modern world as we are aware of it now. In spite of the fact that circumstances are different, the contributions of these incredible leaders can't be overlooked and in spite of the fact that practices and methods for doing things have changed too, the methods for these extraordinary leaders can't be neglected. What made them extraordinary may in any case be appropriate in the present day as well. Here is a look at some of the greatest leaders of all time and what made them extraordinary.

MAHATMA GANDHI

Mohandas Karamchand Gandhi, otherwise called Mahatma Gandhi, was born as an ordinary child with a determination to excel in whatever is done. After finishing law from London, he turned into the most important personality of the Indian freedom struggle against the colonial rule. His non-violent policies and fight against the atrocities by involving the common masses inevitably succeeded when he drove his nation to freedom in 1947. His important attributes were resilience, knowledge, relationship building abilities, motivational approach and showing others how a work is done.

GEORGE WASHINGTON

George Washington, known as the founding father of the United States of America, was the pioneer of the American Revolution and the first president of the US. He was a genuine visionary whose vision has persisted for over 200 years. The reason behind making Washington great was his farsightedness, vision, strategic planning and his capacity to lead individuals to great success.

ABRAHAM LINCOLN

The sixteenth leader of the United States is likewise one amongst the most popular leaders of all time. He was in office amid the American Civil War when he kept the common people together because of which the country did not break into smaller parts. He also finished slavery in the US by signing the Emancipation Proclamation. His most noteworthy qualities were his determination, ability to work tirelessly, convictions and bravery.

ADOLF HITLER

Though hated across the world, Adolf Hitler was one of the great leaders of all time. Subsequent to turning into the chancellor of Germany in 1933, he was in charge of one of the best financial and military developments the world has ever observed. He effectively attacked more than 10 nations with his splendid strategy and meticulous planning. His speaking skills, purposeful publicity and planning made him a great leader second to none.

MUHAMMAD

One of the best leaders of all time, Muhammad played a crucial role in spreading Islam in and around Arabia. His contribution to Islam was so much that today Islam is considered to be the second largest and the quickest developing religion of the world. He helped unite a chaotic society on the basis of common values like ethics and morality and drove his people out of serious persecution and mistreatment. He helped his people migrate and mark victories in wars against armies much larger than theirs on many occasions. His most noteworthy leadership qualities were his own individual courage who believed in showing others how it's done, motivational approach, persistence along with right decision-making abilities.

MAO ZEDONG

Mao was the leader of the Chinese Revolution and the founding father of the People's Republic of China. He endured and repelled the invasion of Japan successfully amid the World War II and later changed the economy of China into one of the major industrialized economies of the world. As a result of him, China is a politically influential nation and a powerful opponent to the dominant United States of America.

NELSON MANDELA

Nelson Mandela was the first South African president who was chosen through fully democratic elections. Mandela role was also important in countering anti-apartheid movements in the nation for which he had to undergo a long jail sentence. This did not stop Mandela and in fact made him stronger to give his life in uniting his nation and he effectively figured out how to do this after his discharge from the jail sentence of about 30 years. His important qualities were his determination, industriousness, focus and a strong will-power.

JULIUS CAESAR

Effectively one of the best military leaders ever, Caesar was also one among the best political leaders the world has ever witnessed. He carried out many campaigns with various triumphs and was without any assistance accountable for expanding the Roman Empire. He was likewise in charge of improving the Roman government and in this way establishing the framework to a great empire. His most prominent characteristics were his decisiveness, bravery, inquisitiveness, inspiration, opportunism and strategic planning.

FIDEL CASTRO

Castro was one of the most prominent leaders of the Cuban Revolution who later became the Prime Minister of Cuba. He also took over the office of President of Cuba from 1976 to 2008. He persevered through numerous crises, attacks and assassination attempts and took them in the stride. His vision for Cuba still holds good and he has turned out to be a successful leader and commander. His attributes of bravery, right set of strategies, hiring the right individuals and spread of duties made him the leader he was.

WINSTON CHURCHILL

Leader of Britain from 1940 to 1945, Churchill drove Great Britain against the Nazi Germany amid the World War II. He collaborated with partners and subsequently prompted the thrashing and destruction of Hitler. His tenure as the British Prime Minister was in a period of dread and decimation caused by Hitler and his partners. Churchill was known for his fearlessness, determination, relentless steadiness and undying commitment to his objective.

WOODROW WILSON

Woodrow Wilson birthed the profession of public administration in the United States. He saw a requirement for individuals who might analyse what government can do and how it can be most potent, and he presented some key ideas that are vital to public administration even these days. He pushed a way to deal with public administration that included level of execution just as found in the private sector. He believed that personnel reform that did include evaluation based merit would at last prompt poor outcomes, and that it was to the greatest advantage of society as a group to push employees to improve their performance.

FREDRICK TAYLOR

The field of public administration is almost indistinguishable from organizational theory, and scientific management was one amongst the most conspicuous philosophies directing the improvement of business and governments amid the early twentieth century. Fredrick Taylor's approach underscored the requirement for objective measures of execution and cost controls. It was an ideal fit for the industrialized work environment, yet unfortunatelyworkers felt that it prompted workdays that were excessively ordinary and rigorous for normal individuals to meet the demands set upon them.

DOUGLAS MCGREGOR

Most organizational theories till the 1950s concentrated more on efficiency among many other components. This implied the human component of most associations turned out to be nothing more but another method for quantifying cogs inside a bigger machine. Douglas McGregor set out to change that by actualizing sociological examinations that would make it conceivable to discover individuals who fit well inside specific associations, and his thoughts likewise changed many organizations so that they could better fulfil the needs of the general population within them.

YEHEZKEL DROR

Public administrators worked resolutely during many years of time to discover better answers for actualizing public policy, and Yehezkel Dror's theories demonstrated incredibly effective when trying to anticipate the result of enactment before putting it in place. This is extremely significant in light of the fact that it enables public administrators to give input on enactment based on anticipated future results and ideally keep away legislators from causing unintended outcomes with well-intended, but not well-considered laws.

Attitude

10 CHAPTER

COMPREHENDING ATTITUDE

Renowned psychologist Gordon Allport in the past expressed attitude "the most distinctive and indispensable concept in contemporary social psychology." Attitude can be shaped from an individual's past and present events taking place in his life. In layman's term, attitude may imply the dissimilar perception of mood, or be specifically synonymous with adolescent agitation. An attitude can be described as a constructive or destructive analysis of individuals, objects, incident, actions, concepts, or roughly anything in their circumstances, but there is conflict about accurate descriptions. For example, Eagly and Chaiken describe an attitude "a psychological tendency that is expressed by evaluating a particular entity with some degree of favour or disfavour." While it is occasionally normal to express an attitude as affect toward an object, affect (i.e., discrete emotions or overall arousal) is usually considered to be different from attitude as an assessment of benevolence. This description of attitude permits for an individual's analysis of an attitude object to differ from exceedingly disapproving to exceedingly constructive, but also concedes that individuals can also be contradicting or uncertain towards an object implying that they might at various circumstances convey both constructive and destructive attitude towards the same object. This has initiated some talks about whether a person can hold numerous attitudes towards the same object.

Implicit and Explicit Attitudes

- Explicit attitudes are intentionally moulded.
- Implicit attitudes, usually unrecognized or outside of attentiveness, have effects that are gaugeable through advanced methods involving individual's reaction times to stimuli.
- Implicit and explicit attitudes appear to influence individual's behaviour, though in distinct manners. They tend not to have strong association with each other, even though in some instances they are. The association between them is inadequately comprehended.

Jung's Explanation

Jung described attitude as a "readiness of the psyche to act or react in a certain way". Attitudes very frequently come in sets, one conscious and the other unconscious. Within this comprehensive description, Jung characterized numerous attitudes.

Jung defined the following two key attitude dualities:

- ***Consciousness and the unconscious***: The "presence of two attitudes is extremely frequent, one conscious and the other unconscious. This means that consciousness has a constellation of contents different from that of the unconscious, a duality particularly evident in neurosis".
- ***Extraversion and introversion***: This set is so fundamental to Jung's theory of types that he named them the "attitude-types".
- ***Rational and irrational attitudes***: The reasonable attitude bifurcates into the thinking and feeling psychological capacities, everyone with its attitude. The irrational attitude bifurcates into the sensing and intuition psychological functions, everyone with its attitude. "There is thus a typical thinking, feeling, sensation, and intuitive attitude".
- ***Individual and social attitudes***: Hence, it can be deduced that "an attitude is an expression of favor or disfavor toward a person, place, thing, or event (the attitude object)."

Elements of Attitude/Cab Model

Every attitude is composed of three elements: cognitive, affective and behavioural. Inspite of each attitude having these three components, any specific attitude can be built on a particular component more in relation to another. It is also known as ABC model.

Components of Attitudes

- ***Cognitive***: This component consists of an individual's feelings, notions, and ideas about something. When an individual is the object of an attitude, the cognitive component is often a stereotype, for example,"welfare recipients are lazy".
- ***Affective***: This component consists of feelings or emotions aroused by something, such as, fear, sympathy and hate. Welfare recipients may be disliked under this component.
- ***Behavioural***: This component comprises propensity or temperament to behave in certain manners towards something. This component intends to keep welfare recipients away from neighbourhood. This component emphasizes on the propensity to act instead of genuine acting. Under this component, what individuals do could be quite different from what they desire.

Roles of Attitude

According to Daniel Katz, attitudes perform four main functions for a person:

1. The adjustments/utilitarian/adaptive (or instrumental) function
2. The ego defensive function

3. The value expressive (or ego-expressive) function
4. The knowledge function

1. ***Adjustment Function/Utilitarian Function***
    - The adjustment function guides individuals towards pleasing or remunerating objects and away from unlikeable, unwanted ones. It fulfils the utilitarian idea of extending reward and reducing punishment. People formulate favourable constructive attitudes towards things that support or remunerate them.
    - People approve political parties that will expand their economic lot—if they are in business, they prefer the party that will retain their taxes low, and if jobless they favour a particular party that will enhance social welfare benefits.
    - People are willing to adjust their attitudes in accordance with what suits the fulfilment of their goals or to escape unwanted consequences.
2. ***Ego-Defensive Function***
    - The ego-defensive function implies adhering to attitudes that safeguard people's self-pride or that rationalize activities that make us feel remorseful.
    - This function includes psychoanalytic standards where individuals utilize defence mechanisms to shield themselves from psychological injury. Methods of this function are listed as follows:
        - Denial
        - Repression
        - Projection
        - Rationalization
    - In case of a customer who has made a poor purchase choice or a poor investment, they may firmly endorse the decision to be right in those circumstances or to be the result of poor guidance from another person. This type of ego-defensive attitude enables people to protect their self-image and often they are ignorant of them.
3. ***Value expression function***
    - Although ego defensive attitudes are developed to safeguard an individual's self-image, value expressive attitudes empower the demonstration of the individual's central values. Central values have a tendency to set up people's identity and acquire them social approval thereby showing them who they are, and what they stand for.
    - Some attitudes are imperative to an individual because they convey values that are vital to that individual's self-impression, such that, their notions about who they are.
    - For instance if one views oneself as a Muslim, one can bolster that person by assuming Islamic beliefs and values.
4. ***Knowledge function***
    - Some attitudes are valuable because they enable people to understand the humankind in a much better way. They enable people attribute reasons to happenings and focus consideration towards characteristics of people or circumstances that are anticipated to be valuable in creating sense of them. As

a result, they enable to make the world more apprehensible, foreseeable and 'knowable'.

PSYCHOLOGICAL REQUIREMENT EXAMPLE

1. Utilitarian—People fond of their psychology degree because it will enable them secure employment in the future.
2. Knowledge—People fond of their psychology degree because it offers them with valuable knowledge in managing the individuals.
3. Ego defensive—People fond of their psychology degree since they actually desired to become a vet but were not good enough.
4. Value-expressive—People fond of their psychology degree because it demonstrates their commitment to facilitating people.

Attitude Building

In Doob's opinion, learning can answer for the majority of attitudes we embrace. The examination of attitude building is the analysis of how people make analysis of persons, places or things. Theories of traditional moulding, instrumental moulding and social wisdom are chiefly dependable for development of attitude.

In contrast to personality, attitudes are anticipated to vary as a component of experience. Moreover, disclosure to the 'attitude' objects may affect the way an individual builds his or her attitude. This notion was viewed as the "Mere-Exposure Effect".

Robert Zajonc demonstrated that there was more probability for individuals to have a positive attitude on 'attitude objects' when they were presented to it as regularly as possible than when they were not presented at all. Simply frequent introduction of the people to an impetus is an adequate condition for the augmentation of their attitude toward it.

Tesser has contended that inherited variables may influence attitudes—yet considers that they may do so in an indirect manner. For instance, consistency theories, which infer that people must be steady in their beliefs and values. Similar to any type of heritability, to find out whether a specific attribute has a root in people's genes, twin studies is used. The most prominent case of such a theory is Dissonance-reduction theory, related with Leon Festinger, which describes that when the elements of an attitude (including belief and behaviour) are contradictory, an individual may alter one to coordinate the other, for example, changing a belief to coordinate a behaviour. Different theories involve balance theory, initially suggested by Heider and the self-perception theory, initially suggested by Daryl Bem.

So we can say that

- Attitudes build exactly as a consequence of experience and learning. They may develop as a result of direct individual experience, or they may emerge from an outcome of an observation.

- Social responsibilities and social standards can strongly influence attitudes. Social responsibilities refers to the way people are expected to behave in a specific role or context. Social standards include society's rules for what demeanours are viewed suitable.

THEORIES OF ATTITUDE DEVELOPMENT

Attitudes concerning some issue, event, person or thing are generally formed in four different ways. In order of growing psychological complexity, the four ways leading to formation of attitudes are by mere exposure, by associative learning, by self-perception, and for functional reasons.

- ***Mere Exposure***: The mere exposure effect is the propensity of the people to grow more constructive viewpoints in relation to objects and individuals, the more they are exposed to them. No activity or communication with the object is required, and they do not need to have or even build any precise convictions about the object.
- ***Associative Learning***: People learn by association in two ways, either implicitly through classical conditioning, or explicitly through operant conditioning.
- ***Self-Perception***: According to Bem (1965), the concept behind self-perception theory is that people develop attitudes not because of exposure or associative learning, but by observing their own behaviour. In Bem's opinion, attitudes in people are built from observing their own behaviours, for example, the opinions we openly convey on specific issues, and then assigning them to either internal or external factors, with internal attributions (deduction that the behaviour is characteristic of an attitude) more probably when the behaviour was unreservedly opted.
- ***Functional Approach***: The three ways to form attitudes, which include exposure, learning and self-perception, all function clearly outside of an individual's understanding. Normally, individuals are not conscious of simple disclosure impacts (certainly, these impacts are powerful when individuals do not recognize of having seen something generally), nor moulding, nor the reality that their conducts can occasionally affect their attitudes. All of these hypotheses contend that attitude building is a passive method. Put differently, it does not require any self-examination, or conscious contemplation of concerns. Rather, attitudes are built through observation or relationship. In spite of this, it appears to be obvious that not all attitudes are shaped outside of our attentiveness asoccasionally we involve in measured thought about a problem with the intention of framing an opinion. The functional approach states that attitudes are occasionally framed grounded on the level to which they meet different psychological requirements, thus, this is considered to be an active rather than passive attitude theory. The four fundamental psychological requirements that could be dealt with by embracing diverse attitudes are utilitarian, knowledge, ego-defensive and value-expression.

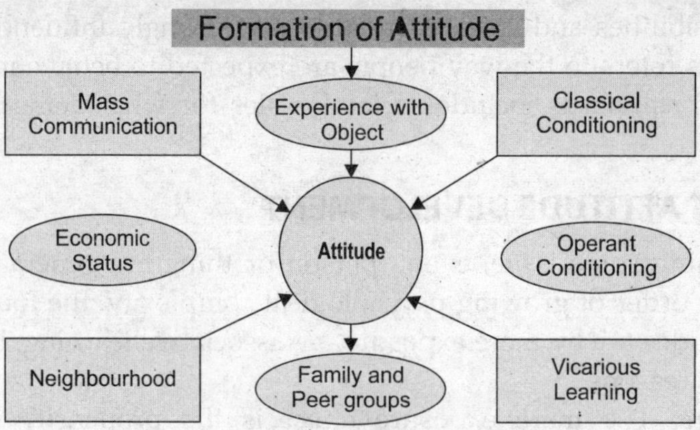

Figure showing formation of Attitude

Learning

Attitudes are the outcome of several dissimilar effects, yet the general feature is that it is formed through various types of learning.

THEORY OF CLASSICAL CONDITIONING OR RESPONDENT CONDITIONING

Classical conditioning theory includes acquiring a new behaviour through the method of relationship. Classical conditioning enables framing an attitude when an impartial impetus is combined with an impetus that naturally arouses an emotional reaction, that is, learning through association.

Example: A person is driving down a dark and curvy road when he misses by a whisker an accident with a heavy truck that has edged over into his path. He feels a speedy pulse, sweating palms, and a stomach-churning sensation. After this narrow escape, he keeps on driving down the road. After few days passed, while driving as he comes near the same curve, he begins to encounter the similar effects (his pulse rate starts to increase and his palms start to sweat) but he witnesses no vehicles around.

Pavlov and his experiments conducted with dogs made classical conditioning popular: Just before serving food to the dogs, a bell was rung. Food caused dogs to produce saliva. Thereafter, every time a bell was rung, dogs started to produce saliva even without the presence of food.

Another example is the use of classical conditioning by the advertisers to affect public attitude towards a specific product. In a television advertisement, showing a young, beautiful woman having entertainment on a tropical beach while relishing a sport drink. This beautiful and tempting imagery leads people to form a positive relationship with this specific beverage.

OPERANT CONDITIONING OR INSTRUMENTAL LEARNING

Operant conditioning is a process of acquiring knowledge that happens through encouraging and punishments for behaviour. Behaviours or attitudes that result in positive outcomes are strengthened and will more probably be recurrent than are behaviors and attitudes that result in negative outcomes.

Operant conditioning can be utilized in influencing the way attitudes develop. Consider the case of a young man who has taken to smoking quite recently. Every time that he illuminates a cigarette, people protest, rebukehim and request him to go away from their region. This negative reaction from people around him in the end results in framing ofa negative opinion about smoking in him favourable and he makes up his mind to relinquish the habit.

Operant conditioning is dissimilar from classical conditioning in that operant conditioning manages the encouragement and punishment to modify behaviour. Operant conditioning works on the surroundings and is conserved by its antecedents and outcomes, whereas classical conditioning is preserved by conditioning of reflexive behaviours, which are evoked by precedent circumstances.

OBSERVATIONAL LEARNING (OBSERVATION OF NEARBY INDIVIDUALS)

Individuals additionally learn attitudes by noticing the individuals around them. When a person admire somebody who significantly embraces a specific attitude, the chances for that person to develop the same beliefs are high. Take the case of children who spend a large amount of time noticing the attitudes of their parents and generally start to exhibit similar mindsets.

ATTITUDE CHANGE

Attitude change relies on the following components:

- ***Source***: The individual conveying the message is known as the communicator. The chances of changing the attitude of a person is greater if the message is conveyed by professionals believed to be trustworthy, appealing and akin to the individual receiving the message. Hence, an advertisement displaying the cricketer Sachin Tendukar saying that consuming a specific drink empowers him with vitality, the target audience is probably going to be young children who view him as a shining example to follow in the field of sports. The chances of their buying the drink are high because they presume that by consuming the drink they would be able to 'play like him'.
- ***Message***: The type of message is imperative since it conveys the data for attitude change. The message should be precise and well methodical. Messages that evoke worry and dread are more valuable. Hence, a commercial on soap may demonstrate that sweating from the body causes foul smell and turn the friends away from a person. Or, a person after having a shower with a specific soap have the probability of drawing in too many companions.
- ***Person***: The attribute of the individual whose attitude is to be modified plays a crucial role in attitude change. Attitudes that are resilient, individually significant, complicated and interrelated are hard to change. Hence, the attitudes of individuals towards their family would be hard to change instead of their liking towards a soap or drink.

Hence, 'who' (communicator) says 'what' (message) to 'whom' (person to be communicated the message) will ascertain whether attitude change will happen or not. What other individuals say and do has an impact on people. The advertising enterprise's objective is to alter attitudes towards a specific product or services. They utilize these three facets of attitude change in their commercials.

The Theories of Attitude Change

Cognitive Dissonance: Cognitive dissonance theory contends that conducting in a way that goes against the prevailing attitudes generates an emotion of discomfort. In other words, individuals feel unhappy when they execute a deedthat is conflictingwith their attitudes. Consider the example of an animal lover who may feel disturbed if they by coincidence run over a hedgehog; similarly, a pro-environmentalist may experience awful if they drink in excess and lob their chips on the ground towards the end of the night out.

In the opinion of Festinger, when individuals execute an activity that is inappropriate to their attitudes, this knowledge causes an internal disparity, or conflict. Festinger proposed that individuals will be inspired to try to resolve this disagreement. Individuals will search for approaches in an attempt to describe it and, if none are evident, they will turn to the only ways left to them to work out the discrepancy: they will alter their attitude so that it is compatible with the behaviour they have enacted. Similar to self-perception theory, cognitive dissonance theory envisions that behaviours make attitudes instead of the opposite way, but dissimilar to self-perception theory, a weak erstwhile attitude is not a precondition for the effect. In truth, disagreement will arise unless there is an erstwhile attitude that is reasonably robust; alternatively there will be no disagreement, and no hard feelings of uneasiness.

Factors Affecting Dissonance

There are three major aspects that ascertain whether cognitive discord happens when individuals execute a behaviour that is incompatible with their attitudes, and henceforth whether attitude change happens:

Justification, Choice, and Investment

The first is concerned with whether individuals believe they have explanation for having acted in a way that is in contradiction to their attitudes.

Freedom of choice is a second imperative aspect. If people are compelled to do something this is an explanation for why we did it in infringement of our attitudes, so again no disagreement should happen.

Finally, the third aspect in determining the attitude change is investment. The more invested somebody is in their viewpoint, the more significant it is for their self-notion, and so the greater will be any effects of discord. In total, when there is no explanation, we unreservedly select a behaviour, and the appropriate attitude is one that is crucial to us, cognitive dissonance is probable to happen, and people are more prone to change their attitudes to fit in with their behaviours.

PERSUASION

Although cognitive dissonance is attitude change through an internal error, persuasion is concerned with attitude change through an outer message. How do individuals contemplate about, and include, information they obtain that is contradictory to their present standpoint? What decides whether they are influenced by contentions or not? This is a question of evident significance to our comprehending of how individuals think, feel and act. Are TV commercials effective? When do individuals alter their brand of toothpaste? What affects individual's voting in political election campaigns? What causes individuals resolve to take on a healthier diet? How individuals respond to messages meant to influence their decisions is the centre of attention of this final section.

Dual Process Models of Persuasion

It is a dual-route approach that has turned out to be most effective in determining how, when and why people are or are not influenced by others. Two models illustrate this method, the elaboration-likelihood model and the heuristic-systematic model. While both the models are somewhat dissimilar in terms of importance both claim that there are two modes that a persuasive message can influence attitude change, each varying in the amount of cognitive effort or elaboration they require: the central (systematic) route and the peripheral (heuristic) route.

The central route is followed when individuals are stimulatedand are ready to ponder about the content of a message (implied as high elaboration conditions). Here individuals are persuaded by the strength and quality of the reasoning. In contradiction, the peripheral route is followed when people are reluctant or in ept to examine message content. Here individuals focus on prompts that are inappropriate to the content or quality of the communication (implied as low elaboration conditions), for example, the engaging qualityof the communicator or the quantity of information presented. It should be taken into consideration that attitudes can alter through both routes, but that the resulting attitudes may be qualitatively dissimilar as a consequence. Attitudes developed through the peripheral route do not require understanding of the message, are feeble, less resilient to counterclaim, and less predictive of behaviour than central route attitudes.

Numerous factors are there that specifically influence which route might be followed when people practice persuasive messages. Here we layout five of them: speed of speech, mood, involvement, individual differences and humour.

Rapid speech makes it difficult to manage the substance of an influential message, thus, people discard the central route in favour of the peripheral route, depending on merely the number of arguments as a heuristic for concluding whether to accept to message.

Mood can also influence the type of route taken. Generally, cheerful individuals use the peripheral route, whereas discontented people are inclined to use the central route. The justification for this is that negative moods can indicate that something is "wrong", which evoke an increase in attention to recognize the issue. The inference can be drawn that cheerful individuals are thus more vulnerable to feeble signals similar to source attractiveness.

The magnitude to which the issue is ***important to the self*** has an influence the type of route that is taken. If the result of the dispute or the issue at hand affects straightaway, and has important suggestions for the self then it is more probable that the perceiver will take a close watch and the central route will be followed. Martin and Hewstone performed an investigation which examined the way issue importance to the self, together with whether the message are derived from a numerical minority or majority, has an effect on whether the central or peripheral route is followed.

There are also ***individual differences*** that impact some individuals more probably than others to choose one route over another. Requirement for cognition is the level to which someone is focused to get involved in effortful however. People who are having higher requirement for cognition are thus more prone to take the central route whereas people with lesser requirement for cognition are more prone to choose the peripheral route. Comparable influences have been discovered using associated tendencies, for example, requirement for closure and the requirement to evaluate. Dissimilarities in self-observation can also have an effect. This is the extent to which somebody is apprehensive with what other people feel of them. Individuals who are higher in self-observation will more probably take the central route whereas people who are lower in self-observation will be more probably choose the peripheral route.

At last, utilizing the ***humour*** can impact the type of route taken. Appropriate humour prompts the central route being taken whereas inappropriate humour prompts the peripheral route being taken.

PERIPHERAL CUES

After taking a route, it may prove influential or not relying upon the attributes of the context. If the central route is chosen, the key determining factor of influence will be the quality of the argument (is it convincing or not). If the peripheral route is opted, then several attributes of the message source will be crucial.

First, peripheral route processing is more prone to result inchange of attitude if the source has physical appeal. For example, Chaiken discovered that experimenters attempting to influence undergraduates to sign a petition to bring an end to the practice of serving meat by the university were more successful if they were charming than if they were unappealing.

Second, resemblance to self is a crucialdetermining factor of attraction. Resemblance in relation to shared attitudes, appearance or social categories can all enhance the strength of a message.

Finally, source credibility is a principal peripheral cue that enhances the probability of change in attitude. A source is realized as reliable if they are considered to be a skilful, unbiased, and reliable.

MEASURING ATTITUDES

Numerous measurements and scales are utilized to analyse attitudes. Attitudes can be hard to determine because measurement is discretionary, which means individuals have to provide attitudes a scale to gauge it against, and attitudes are eventually a hypothetical construct that cannot be noticed directly.

In the wake of the explicit-implicit dichotomy, attitudes can be analysed through direct and indirect measures.

Explicit Measurements: Explicit measures are inclined to depend on self-reports or easily noticed behaviours. These have a tendency to include bipolar scales, such as, good-bad, favourable-unfavourable, support-oppose, etc. Explicit measures can also be utilized by measuring the direct attribution of features to choose groups, such as "I feel that Baptists are....?" or "I think that men are...?" Likert scales and other self-reports are also normally used.

Implicit Measurements: Implicit measures are not intentionally engaged and are considered to be spontaneous, which may render implicit measures more effective and dependable than explicit measures (such as self-reports). For instance, individuals can be encouraged such that they discover it socially appealing to seem to have certain attitudes. One illustrationof this is that individuals can hold inexplicit biased attitudes, but express explicit attitudes that convey little unfairness. Implicit measures help interpretations for these situations and consider attitudes that an individual may not know or want to demonstrate. Implicit measures thus generally depend on an implicit measure of attitude. For example, the Implicit Association Test (IAT) investigates the intensity between the target concept and an attribute element by considering the response time in which an individual can analyse two response keys when each has two meanings. With little time to precisely investigate what the memberis doing they react in relation to internal keys. This priming can displayattitudes the individual has about a specific object.

EFFECT OF ATTITUDE AND RELATION WITH THOUGHT AND BEHAVIOUR

Dissimilarity between Attitude and Behaviour

Attitude and behaviour are strongly related but they are two dissimilar concepts. Differences between the two can be explained as follows:

- Attitude is an inner state whereas behaviour is an outer state. In other words, behaviour can be very well observed by others as it is an outer state in contrast to attitude which is shelled inside the mind of the person and hence cannot be straightway observed by others.
- Attitude relates to what an individual thinks whereas behaviour relates to what an individual does. Attitude is concerned with the mind whereas behaviour relates to the actions performed by the individual.
- Attitude is thought-centred whereas behaviour is action-centred. Attitude can mould the behaviour of an individual. An individual with the upright attitude may be with upright behaviour also. However, occasionally individuals act in relation to their attitudes, and in different situations, they act in manners that are quite varying with their attitudes.

WHEN DO ATTITUDE AFFECT BEHAVIOUR?

The intensity of the attitude-behaviour relationship can be analysed through qualities of the behaviour, qualities of the person, qualities of the circumstances in which the behaviour is executed and qualities of the attitude itself.

1. *Qualities of the Behaviour*: A social psychologist might be interested in making predictions about the behaviours of a person on the basis of the knowledge of a person's attitudes. These can range from the very precise (e.g., will the individual attend church services this week?) to the very common (e.g., how many religious behaviours will the individual execute over the next month?).

   A particular behaviour is best anticipated by a question that is equally particular to the activity in question, the target of the activity, the context in which the activity is executed, and the time of the activity (e.g., "How do you think about attending church this Sunday?"). In an investigation conducted earlier to the prescribed utilization of lead-free gasoline, the real purchase of lead-free gas was better anticipated by questions asking particularly about purchasing lead-free gas than by questions measuring more common attitudes toward ecology.

   Contrarily, a general pattern of behaviour is best anticipated by a common attitude measure. In an investigation, participants' universal attitude towards "being religious" was made use of to predict the probability that they executed each of various particular religious behaviours (e.g., praying before or after meals, donating money to a religious institution) and a general measure of executing religious behaviours that was a composite measure of the numerous particular religious behaviours.

2. *Qualities of the Person*: Few individuals generally exhibit more attitude-behaviour consistency than do others. In common, two types of people have been considered: those who know about and directed by their inner notions and those having a tendency to depend greatly on signals in the circumstances to decide how to behave. As a whole, individuals who know about their feelings exhibit greater attitude-behaviour stability than do individuals who depend on circumstantial prompts.

   Any given conduct of a person can be directed both by the person's internal thoughts and by external prompts. However, numerous personality dimensions have been established and utilized effectively to evaluate whether a given individual tends to depend more profoundly on onc kind of prompt or the other.

Two Personality Dimensions are as Follows:

a. *Level of moral reasoning*: Degree of moral reasoning has been found to influence the connection between attitudes and behaviour.

   More advanced moral reasoning is portrayed by principled, ethically responsible thought based on an individual's own common principles of moral activity.

   Lower levels of reasoning are centred on the common positive or negative outcomes of a specific action or on an impression of being bound by social or legitimate regulations.

b. ***Self-monitoring***: People who score low on the self-monitoring scale assert to be directed by temperament, such that, their inner feelings. They concur with assertions such as "My behaviour is generally a manifestation of my true inner feelings, attitudes and beliefs."

Contrarily, people who score high on the self-monitoring scale consider their behaviour as originating generally from a reasonable concern with what is appropriate in each situation. They agree with statements such as "In different situations and with different people, I often act like very different persons". Hence, these people are said to control the impression that they make on other people and adapt that impression to fit with others' anticipations.

Low self-monitors act more steadily with their attitudes than do high self-monitors.

Individuals who concentrate on themselves have a tendency to act more reliably with their attitudes, for example, people with high moral reasoning and/or low self-monitoring.

In contrast, individuals who are directed more by the environment or other outer factors generally do not act in a way that is uniform with their attitudes, for example, people with low moral reasoning and/or high self-monitoring.

3. ***Qualities of the Situation***: Several circumstantial variables also influence the intensity of the attitude-behaviour relation. These incorporate normative factors and time strain to arrive at a decision.

   a. ***The Effect of Norms***: Norms, or notions about the way one should or is anticipated to behave in a given circumstance, can wield a strong impact on behaviour. People frequently behave as they consider others anticipate them to behave.

   A norm may be so powerful and so generally held that basically everybody in that circumstance behaves the same irrespective of his or her attitude. For instance, one might wish that someone were dead, yet one would hardly act on this attitude. Consequently, attitude-behaviour consistency is low.

   b. ***Time Pressure***: People are more prone to make choices based on their attitudes when they are short of time because their attitudes offer a heuristic for taking quick decisions. Time constraints push individuals away from a cautious analysis of the accessible information and towards a dependence on their pre-existing attitudes.

   For instance, in one investigation, participants were requested to consider job applications from both male and female job applicants. In case when there was no time pressure, and thus members could cautiously go through the entire details, their staff choices were dissimilar to their attitudes towards working women. In other words, members whose prior stated attitudes suggested some biasing against women were as prone to advocate hiring of a female candidate as were those who did not carry such biased attitudes. On the other hand, when participants were under time constraints to make a hiring suggestion, an attitude-behaviour relation was evident. Participants having a biased attitude against women were unlikely to suggest recruiting a female applicant.

The aforementioned example also indicates that, from a societal viewpoint, there are some instances when attitude-behaviour consistency is not appealing. In this case, acting in compliance with an attitude results in partiality against specific groups within our society.

4. ***Qualities of the Attitude***: Few types of attitudes seem to be stronger than other types. In this perspective, the word stronger is not utilized in the sense of the attitude being more intense. Rather, stronger refers to the obvious affect that the attitude has on a person's behaviour. In reality, in all of the investigation that is clarified before, groups of participants with various degrees of attitude strength were evaluated, yet the dissemination of attitude scores, for example, the extremity of attitudes, in the different groups were comparable to one another.

   a. ***The Role of Direct Experience***: One attitudinal feature is the way of attitude building. From one point of view is attitude building through direct behavioural experience with the attitude object, and from another point of view is attitude building through indirect non-behavioural experience with the attitude object. For instance, a child may develop an attitude towards a toy by playing with the toy, direct experience, or based on a friend's or a commercial's description of the toy, indirect experience.

   Attitudes formed on the basis of direct experience have been observed to be more prognostic of later behaviour than attitudes formed on the basis of indirect experience.

   b. ***Attitude Accessibility***: One thing that separates attitudes formed on the basis of direct experience from those formed on the basis of indirect experience is the accessibility of the attitudes from the memory. Accessibility in this regard relates to the ease with which attitudes come to mind. Few attitudes appear in the mind without any cognizant effort on individuals' part. In case ofindividuals seeing a cockroach, there are more chances of arousing a disgusting reaction, the "Yuck!"response, instantly in their mind. This attitude would be deeply accessible from memory. However, occasionally individuals have to ponderquite considerablyabout what their attitudes towards some object are. In case of individuals asked to choose the best restaurant out of several restaurants, they might have to think comprehensively to decide which one they consider the best. This attitude would not be at all available from memory.

   As these cases show, one way to gauge the accessibility of an attitude from memory is the time taken by people to answer whether they like or dislike something. Attitudes grounded on direct experience have a tendency to be more accessible from memory.

   There is also an operational usefulness of such attitudes. Accessible attitudes make it easy for a person to arrive at a decision. Visualize what would happen if every time a mangoes into an ice-cream parlour, he has to decide which flavour of ice cream he want by going through the entire list of offerings and in view of the relative merits of various types of ice creams. The person would take a long time to make a choice, and making the choice would probably be stressful. However, in case the fact that the person really likes two flavours promptly comes to his mind, it becomes easier for him to make a choice. Since accessible attitudes promptly strike the mind, it becomes easy for one to make the decision.

Examining the operational value of accessible attitudes suggests that accessible attitudes execute a number of valuable functions for people, and in fact they do. However, accessible attitudes also have a dark side. It may be highly difficult to change accessible attitudes, with the effect that people may be instead close-minded in relation to topics towards which they have accessible attitudes.

How do Attitude Influence Behaviour?

There are two distinct mechanisms by which attitudes can affect behaviour. The main difference between the two mechanisms rests on the extent to which the behaviour is carefully planned prior to its actual execution in opposition to being an impulsive reaction to an individual's perception of the instantaneous situation.

In ***first mechanism***, the person may reflect and contemplate about a behavioural strategy and may make a decision on how they intend to behave. In doing so, the person may intentionally consider the ramifications of their attitude. For instance, before purchasing a car or making a choice about which college to attend, a person will comprehensively contemplate about the decision and consider all the pros and cons before making a behavioural decision.

On the other hand, in the ***second mechanism***, the person might not actively contemplate on their attitude, but that attitude may affect the person's interpretation of the event that is taking place and, in that way, may impact their behaviour. When making a choice between a vanilla ice cream and a chocolate, an individual will hardly analyse the advantages and disadvantages of each flavour. Rather, the person's attitudes towards the various flavours ascertain which flavour seems better at that moment in time.

The previous kind of process is the core of Theory of reasoned action. The second kind of process is portrayed in Model of the attitude-to-behaviour process.

Theory of Reasoned Action

The theory of reasoned action considers that individuals contemplate about the prudence of a given course of activity.

As per this theory, a person's behavioural objective is the sole best indicator of his or her eventual behaviour. Every person takes into account certain factors in forming a behavioural objective. The individual considers, weighs and combines (a) his or her attitude towards the behaviour being referred to and (b) the subjective norms in relation to the behaviour.

The second aspect, subjective norms, incorporates both the individual's notions about what significant others consider he or she should do and the individual's stimulus to abide by the desires of these others. To arrive at a decision on whether to attend college, a person may consider what his or her friends and parents believe about attending college and how significant it is to abide by the desires of his or her friends and parents.

MORAL ATTITUDES

Moral attitudes provide a foundation to the entire moral life. Moral values come at the top of all natural values. Moral values are the criteria for good and evil, which defines a person's behaviour and choices.

Moral values exist as personal values at all times. They can only belong to man, and are attained by man. A material thing, similar to a stone or a house, cannot be ethically good or bad, just as moral excellence is not attainable to a tree or a dog. In the same way, works of the human mind, such as, discoveries, scientific books and works of art, cannot appropriately be said to be the possessors of moral values; they cannot be faithful, modest and loving. They can, at the most, indirectly mirror these qualities, as displaying the impression of the human mind.

A human being alone, as a free being, answerable for his activities and attitudes, for his resolve and endeavouring, his love and hatred, his happiness and distress and his core attitudes, can be morally good or bad. A person will have disposition transmitting moral values in case he is modest, pure, truthful, honest and loving.

So long as a human being recklessly disrespects the moral values of other people, so long as he does not differentiate the constructive value which belongs to truth, and the destructive value which is meant to error, so long as he does not realize the value which belongs to the life of an individual, and the destructive value linked to an injustice, he will be unqualified for moral goodness.

MERITS OF MORAL ATTITUDES

- Reverence
- Faithfulness
- Awareness of Responsibility
- Truthfulness
- Goodness

Reverence

The ability to hold moral values, to avow them, and to react to them, is the basis for understanding the moral values of human being. These characteristics can be discovered only in the person who possesses reverence.

Reverence is an impression or attitude of high regards towards others combined with awe and devotion.

Reverence is the attitude, which can be called as the mother of all moral life, for in it a man first takes a standpoint towards the world, which awakens his spiritual insight and empowers him to grasp values.

Faithfulness or Constancy

Among the demeanours of man, which are fundamental to his entire moral life, faithfulness is rated next to reverence. Faithfulness is the notion of consistently remaining faithful to someone or something and putting that allegiance into regular practice, irrespective of uncontrollable state of affairs.

One can make a viewpoint about faithfulness in a restricted sense and in an expanded sense. We have the restrictedvie wpoint in mind when we speak of loyalty towards human being, for example, fidelity to a friend, marital faithfulness and loyalty to one's country or to oneself.

The more loyal, the more consistent a human being is, the more considerable he will be, the more efficient of turning into a pitcher of moral values, an individual in whom chastity, justice, humbleness, affection and righteousness will lie permanently and will transmit from him to the world around him.

Awareness of Responsibility

A person is called a "morally conscious" man, and another person a "morally unconscious" one because of their different images in the mind of people decisive from their ethical point of view. The unconscious man conducts in accordance with the whims of his nature; he has not yet realized within himself the ability to guide himself uninhibitedly towards the objective requirements of the world of values exclusive of what is or is not compatible to his nature. Hence, they disregard the requirement for conscious endeavour to develop and enhance their moral stature. We do not discover any moral self-education in their lives. This moral apathy is a hindrance to the shaping of a moral personality.

Truthfulness

Truthfulness is another of the core presumptions for an individual's moral life. An untruthful or deceitful individual not only exemplifies a great moral harm, but he is disabled in his entire personality; his entire moral life; everything in him which is ethically positive is put at risk by his untruthfulness.

The dishonest man is devoid of any respect towards values. He believes in an imperious position over being, he treats with it the way he delights. This attitude indicates an element of haughtiness, of disrespect and impudence.

Goodness

Goodness is the very core of the entire rule of ethical values. It is by no mischance that the expression "good" implies moral value by itself, and also the particular ethical quality of goodness. Among the several ethical values, there is not a single one which represents more entirely the entire rule of ethical values than goodness.

It is the core of all morality, and simultaneously, it is the most sublime fruit of morality. Its fundamental significance in the moral scope is, thus, of an entirely distinct kind from that of the basic attitudes mentioned earlier: reverence, faithfulness or fidelity, awareness of responsibility and veracity. For, in addition to their own high ethical value, these virtues are acknowledged as a presumption for the ethical life. Goodness, on the other hand, is not an assumption, but the fruit of moral life. It concludes all morality and is considered the queen of all virtues.

POLITICAL ATTITUDES

Political attitudes are the attitudes of individuals to the spheres of public life enclosed by political psychology, such as, views on nationalism, political conservatism, political liberalism, political radicalism, etc.

Political attitude describes which party somebody should vote for, the type of political ideology somebody favours the most and the type of social, economic, cultural and international policy someone prefers, etc.

The expressions radical, liberal, moderate, conservative and reactionary are few of the terms most frequently employed in political discourse.

Radicals are individuals who discover themselves exceedingly dissatisfied with the state of affairs. Hence, they desire a prompt and intense variation in the existing order, encouraging something novel and dissimilar for society.

Liberals in comparison are substantially less discontented, but they still wish to alter the system significantly. All liberals share a trust in the equality, intellect and ability of people.

Moderates find little a miss with the present society, and their unwillingness to alter it is surpassed only by the conservatives.

Conservatives differ from liberals in most respects and are suspicious about valiant endeavours to amend the world for the apprehension that in ept intervention might, in reality, turn things worse.

Only the reactionaries discard present set-ups and contemporary values. They would envision society reiterate its steps and follow past political norms and policies.

Individuals on the privilege of the political range respect authority, tradition, elitism, and property rights, while those on the left lay emphasis on political freedom, social change, human equality and human rights.

Outside these philosophical beliefs, there are various other motives that cause people's inclination towards the left or right ideology. Mental aspects about the need for change are significant. Economic conditions also have a role to play. Age is another aspect. To end with, one's opinion about the state of human nature is likely to be the most important factor in deciding with which side of the spectrum one will distinguish. Each of these aspects influences individuals' political attitudes about specific policy alternatives.

Similarly to people's views that can amend over time, thus altering their position on the continuum, the spectrum can move to the left or right while an individual remains static.

It is also reasonable to draw attention to the fact that the political spectrum of one society assumes no specific resemblance to that of any other society unless the existing state of affairs is the same in each case. A specific strategy or protocol could be conservative in one society, liberal in another and radical in a third.

SOCIAL INFLUENCE

Social influence happens when the emotions, opinions, or behaviours of a person are influenced by others. Social influence assumes several forms and can be observed in conformity, socialization, peer pressure, compliance, control, influence, sales and marketing.

Three comprehensive types of social influence are as follows:

1. *Compliance* is a kind of social influence when people seem to be in agreement with others, but in reality keep their differing opinions private.
2. *Identification* is a kind of social influence where individuals are affected by somebody who is liked and respected, such as a well-known celebrity.
3. *Internalization* is a kind of social influence when individuals accept a belief or behaviour and are in agreement both publicly and privately.

Compliance

Compliance is the act of approving to a director indirect request offered by others. Technically, compliance is a variation in behaviour but not essentially attitude—one can comply due to mere conformity, or by otherwise choosing to suppress one's secretive thoughts due to social pressures.

The contentment gained from compliance is due to the social influence of the compliance affect, that is, individuals abide by an anticipated reward or punishment-antipathy.

Compliance implies a reaction—particularly, a submission—in response to a demand. The demand may be direct or indirect.

Identification

Identification is a cognitive method by which the subject imbibes a characteristic, property, or trait of the other and is transformed, completely or partially, by the model the other delivers.

Identification is the variation in attitudes or behaviours due to the effect of somebody that is liked. Advertisements that depend upon celebrities to advertise their products are benefiting from this phenomenon. The anticipated relationship that the identifier associates with the behaviour or attitude variation is the "reward".

Internalization

Internalization is the method of recognition of a set of standards formed by people or groups which are authoritative to a person. The person recognizes the effect because the subject matter of the influence accepted is inherently rewarding. It is compatible with the individual's value system, and the "reward" of internalization is "the content of the new behaviour".

ROLE OF BELIEFS, VALUES AND MORAL ATTITUDES

Beliefs and values are significant indicators of people's social and moral attitudes. Investigations on moral attitudes put up with two critical deficiencies:

1. A justifiable estimation of values is hard to obtain. Conceptions such as Inglehart's post-materialism have only feeble influence on moral attitudes. It appears that the

concept and its estimation need an exhaustive review. The theory of basic human values by Shalom Schwartz offers a further distinguished concept that executes well when clarifying social and moral attitudes (Beckers/Siegers/Kuntz 2012). In view of the intricacy of the measurement, it is much less regularly used for clarifying social and moral attitudes then post-materialism.

2. Religious beliefs are often utilized as an indicator for moral attitudes, specifically, in analyses of sexual morality. Present growth in sociology of religion has shown that novel types of beliefs surfaced in Europe, such as, alternative spiritualties, bricolage religiosity. Bruce and Voas (2007) opine that the varied character of novel convictions prohibit them from being socially noteworthy. Their line of reasoning has not been tried analytically yet.

Moreover, few preliminary investigations have revealed that beliefs and values are greatly correlated, both religious convictions and spirituality. The query is, whether beliefs still have an influence on attitudes when values are regulated. Some pattern in the data suggests that more intricate interrelationship between values and beliefs are realized with regard to the clarification of moral attitudes. The justification is that beliefs and values offer prescriptive norms for attitude building that might coincide but also diverge. The project will methodically examine interrelationships between beliefs and values. We will act with distinguishedvalue concepts and methodically take into account novel types of religious notions for theorizing and empirical analysis.

SERVICE MOTIVATION

Service motivation forms and maintains an organizational culture which allows others to offer the quality of service indispensable to great performance. It empowers others to attain the tools and assistancethey need to execute well. It displays an obligation to public service and influences people to acquire a spirit of service and make meaningful contributions to mission accomplishment. Service motivation is the basis of the expression "Public Servant" and exemplifies what the public anticipate from government personnel. It is exhibited in resolute integrity and honesty, remarkable consumer service that is provided to both internal and external associates, and in obligation to the mission and role of the Agency. An important component of service motivation is individual accountability with respect to all civil servants to improve credibility in the government. Civil servants need to offer exceptional service that is beyond ideological disagreements, exhibits continuity, rejects the unwarranted impact of special interests, and operates effectively regardless of the polarization of prejudiced politics.

ATTITUDE CHANGE: INDUCEMENT AND SOCIAL IMPACT

Motives for Agreeing with Others

A sign of social influence analysis is the description of the various intentions that stimulate conformityor discord with others. For more than 40 years, the central administrative viewpoint in this region has been a dual-motive scheme that distinguishes between informational influence, which involves acknowledging data received from others as testimony about actuality, and normative influence, which involves compliancewith the affirmative anticipations of "another," who could be "another person, a group, or one's self" (Deutsch & Gerard 1955:629).

However, present-day theories of motives for attitude change and resistance seem to be coinciding rather on a three-way distinction (e.g., Chaiken et al. 1996a, Cialdini & Trost 1998, Johnson & Eagly 1989, Wood 1999; for a prior exhibition of this type of framework, see Kelman 1958). While these classifications each have their own unique qualities, an ongoing idea is the realization that attitude change can be influenced by normative apprehensionsfor (a) assuring the consistent and preferable analysis of the self, and (b) assuring agreeable relations with others in view of the rewards/punishments they carry, along with an informational concern for (c) comprehending the entity or issue appeared in influence appeals. Hence, for example, Cialdini & Trost (1998) recognize the behavioural objectives of social influence recipients as administering the self-concept, building and sustaining associations, and acting efficiently. Similarly, Chaiken et al. (1996a) differentiated between individual's ego-defensive motives to acquire a valued, rational self-identity, impression-related motives to express a specific influence to others, and legitimacy-seeking motives to exactly evaluate external reality.

Social influence scholars conventionally considered that informational and normative motives are each related with unique procedures that produce attitude change and with unique kinds of change. The wish for a knowledgeable, exact position purportedly positions message recipients to handle the content of the request and results in withstanding individual change in judgments. The wish to fulfil normative expectations purportedly produces less informational analysis and public, context-dependent, transient judgment change. This perception has been questioned by dual-mode processing models of persuasion (Eagly & Chaiken 1993, Petty & Wegener 1998a), specifically by the manifestation that informational, precision-seeking motives can result in either extensive processing and persevering attitude change or to more cursory processing and transient variation. In the dual-mode context, motives for variation are not favourably associated to change procedures or outcomes.

Two contemporary investigations favour the persuasion analysis by providing testimony that normative and informational motives impact influence through a general set of information-processing procedures (Chen et al. 1996, Lundgren & Prislin 1998). Lundgren & Prislin (1998) discovered that, when contestants were inspired to be precise, they chose contentions to interpret on both sides (i.e., advantages and disadvantages) of the target issue, created thoughts that were comparatively poised in analysis of both sides, and suggested comparatively impartial attitudes. On the other hand, when members were inspired to suggest a preferential impression to a communication partner, they chose contentions to interpret that were compatible with the view presumably assumed by the partner and created thoughts and attitudes that were compatible with their partner's perspective. In the end, when members were inspired to safeguard their own status, they chose contentions to interpret that favoured their perspective, created thoughts favouring their position, and suggested comparatively polarized attitudes. Moreover, investigations to test mediation disclosed that the favourability of participants' thoughts (at least partially) arbitrated the impacts of motives on attitude change. Hence, it seems that the attitude impacts arose in part because accuracy motives produced a comparatively open-minded processing inclination, impression motives produced an agreeable inclination, and defense motives produced a protective inclination that preserved prevailing adjudications.

These two investigations also question the belief that recipients' motives are linked with unique types of attitude change. Irrespective of the primary motive guiding attitude judgments, the attitudes participants expressed to their apparent communication partners continued when participants later indicated their adjudications secretively (Chen et al 1996, Lundgren & Prislin 1998). Particularly impressive is the perseverance of attitudes designed to suggest an agreeable impression. In contradiction to classic theories of social influence, attitudes guided by impression-related normative motives were no more "elastic" than were attitudes guided by precision-seeking, informational motives. Rather, it appears that impression and defence motives, much similar to the accuracy motives analysed expansively in message-based persuasion research, can produce careful, methodical processing of appropriate information that results in steady adjudications. This discovery contends the outcomes of previous research in which impression motives were associated to cursory processing and transient judgment shifts (e.g., Cialdini et al. 1976). The elements that decide whether motives influence extensive or more cursory processing are explained as follows:

Public versus Private Influence

In social influence prototypes, scholars have frequently analysed the motive for attitude change from the persistence of recipients' adjudications throughout public and private contexts. In public settings, recipients trust that the source of the plea or members of their experimental group have close observation over their responses, whereas in private contexts, recipients consider that these others are ignorant of their adjudications. Purportedly, attitudes that sustain across public and private measures are internalized reactions that emerge from the thoughtful processing linked with precise motives, while attitudes that are demonstrated in public but not private reveal normative pressures such as approval from the source or group.

Latest empirical discoveries rather indicate that lack of persistence between public and private adjudications is not dependably indicative of recipients' motives. As aforementioned, undergoing attitude change is not the unique domain of educational motives, it also can arise from social motives such as the will to adjust with others (Chen et al 1996, Lundgren & Prislin 1998). Proof of judgment steadiness across public and private settings has risen also in influence in the Asch-type judgment model. In this investigation, participants are subjected to others' evidently wrong adjudications of line length and participants' concurrence with others typically is interpreted as public, shallow compliance to social pressure. Yet the meta-analytic composite by Bond & Smith (1996) of 97 studies using the Asch-type social influence prototype showed no greater concurrence in public than in private settings of attitude representation. It appears, then, that social motives for agreement influenced attitudes in public as well as private contexts.

The absence of methodical dissimilarities between public and private manifestations of judgment can be ascribed to various factors. One is that recipients' motives for conformity can have comparatively comprehensive impacts that simplify to new settings in which the original motives are no longer noticeable or applicable (e.g., Hardin & Higgins 1996, Higgins 1981, Ruscher& Duval 1998). Prolonged impacts can take place when the initial motivated judgment is regained in new contexts or when the data on which the adjudication was based is recovered, given that the motivated processing produced a prejudiced representation of the original data. Hence, since motives impact the judgments and the judgment-related information present in memory, initial motivations for processing may have impacts that exceed setting, and positions expressed in public settings may be retained in private. Kassin & Kiechel (1996) offer a striking example of the expanded outcomes of motivated processing. They replicated procedures occasionally used in the cross-examination of crime suspects by (falsely) indicating research participants of an act of neglect while entering data into a computer. When participants were individually doubtful about their innocence (since they were typing at a fast speed), they acknowledged a witness's account of their activities and (incorrectly) admitted to the accusation. For most of the participants, the concession was not simply agreement. Over half reported in a consequent discussion that they had executed the neglectful act, and over a third actually confabulated particulars in support of the false accusation.

Moreover, the difference between public and private settings indicates an excessively simplified perception of social impact, one that compares social presence with surveillance. Allport's (1985) well-known definition of social psychology offered a significantly more distinguished aspect of social impact, in which the influences of others emerge whether their existence is "actual, imagined, or implied." Since principal features of social impact may hold across public and private settings, attitudes that are influenced by these aspects may also hold across settings. For example, the manipulation by Baldwin & Holmes (1987) of social impact included merely asking female participants to mull over two of their older relatives. The ladies were later provided sexually explicit material to go through in a purportedly separate context, and they informed to have not liked it much. Probably, others' conservative moral values were actuated in the initial handling and proceeded to wield influence on consequent experiences.

Theoretical views need to evolve past the simple difference between open and secret attitude expression and take into consideration whether the characteristics of social pressure that are appropriate to attitude change are constant across settings. For example, in case of a meta-analytic synthesis of the minority-influence literature (Wood et al. 1994), the affect of opinion-minority, low-consensus sources was found equivalent in public and private contexts. Hence, it appeared that attitude change was not manipulated by surveillance and the apprehension that aligning with an abnormal minority source in public would result in social humiliation and rejection by others. Understanding differed, though, with another characteristic of the influence context; how instantly attitudes were assessed. "Direct" measures evaluate attitudes on the matter in the appeal, and recipients are conscious that their (public or private) judgment can adjust them with the source's standpoint. For example, "Indirect" measures might measure attitudes on matters vaguely associated to the appeal, and recipients are less mindful that their judgments can adjust them with the impact source. Minority influence was lesser on direct than on indirect measures. Wood et al (1994) deducedthat recipients' oppositionon direct measures is due to their particular individual learning that their judgments could adjust them with anabnormal minority source. It appears, then, that minority impact was impeded by recipients' apprehension for the favourability and honesty of their self-perception and their standing in their reference group, and that these motives applied in both public and private settings.

The present investigation of attitude expressions in public and private settings also questions the basic belief that when public and private judgments vary in correctness, privately stated ones are usually more reliable because public statements may be partial to attain social motives. While some aspects of public settings, for example, politeness norms, may adjust the correctness of attitude expressions, other aspects seem to boost thorough investigation and occasionally to increase correctness. Cowan & Hodge (1996) showed that to the magnitude public settings improve realizedresponsibility for judgements, individuals give specifically contemplative, logical responses in public. In the same way, Lambert et al. (1996) opined that the anticipation of public dialogue focuses individuals on their self-attitudes and inspires them to strengthen their beliefs; hence, attitudes were found to assume a greater part in managing idea and action in public than in private contexts.

In the end, provided that in social-influence standards respondents often pass their judgements first openly and then again secretly, continuity across judgment contexts can arise from the influences of initial judgements on consequent ones. Investigations on the influence of behaviour on attitudes has shown that individual's clarifications of their public statements and other attitude-related behaviours can incite change in secretly held attitudes to compare to public acts. This investigation also has shown that public-attitude expressions that are of questionable truthfulness, for example, when a public expression is made with low choice or high reward, do not influence the attitudes expressed in private contexts. However, Maio & Olson (1998) provide enthralling proof that even under low-option conditions, the act of delivering an attitude judgement can increase the accessibility of one's own attitude in memory; accessible attitudes then may influence consequent attitude-related judgements in apparently unrelated settings.

MOTIVES IN PERSUASION RESEARCH

Functional Theories

The motives triggering attitude change in message-based persuasion standards have been analysed chiefly in investigation on attitude functions. In addition to the common adaptive function of helping people to assess and review stimulants in their environment, attitudes are also considered to perform more precise functions. Functions recognized in previous work involve acquiring useful outcomes, ego defence, value expression and social adjustment (Katz 1960, Smith et al. 1956). These functions are mirrored in the tripartite motive scheme mentioned before: Accuracy motives relate normally to a utilitarian concern with expanding rewards and limiting punishments, self-concept motives relate to concerns for safeguarding the ego against impending threats and for communicating one's values, and social relation motives relate to apprehensions for social adjustment and for acquiring social rewards and keeping away from social punishments.

In a description of the purpose of attitude functions in influence, persuasive attempts are anticipated to be valuable to the degree that the function of, or argument for holding, the position delineated in the appeal corresponds to the function behind recipients' attitudes (Lavine & Snyder 1996, Murray et al 1996: Study 2). In one such case, Lavine & Snyder (1996) stated that for individuals who are normally receptive to the social outcomes of their behaviour, that is high self-monitors, appeals that put emphasis on the social-adjustive functions of voting, for example, increasing one's attractiveness to others, drew more favourable assessments and superiorattitude change than appeals that put emphasis on its value-expressive functions, for example, a way to express values. For individuals who depend on inner tendencies, that is, low self-monitors, appeals with value-expressive arguments resulted in more encouraging assessments and were more influential. Moreover, specific issues may be related tospecific attitude functions for most individuals. While not particularly formulated within a functional framework, the examination by Rothman & Salovey (1997) of health-related messages indicated that affect is highest when the inclination of an appeal corresponds to the inclination inherent to the health issue itself. Proposals to execute disease-detecting behaviours, such as, breast self-exams, potentially experience hazard and thus loss-framed appeals are probably, effective, whereas suggestions for deterrent behaviours, such as exercise, potentially experience positive consequences and thus gain-framed appeals are probably effective.

In another description, coordinating between attitude function and message orientation does not always increase influence but rather increases consideration about an appeal. Petty & Wegener (1998b) showed that coordinated messages enhanced inspection of message content but increased influence only when the message carried strong, cogent arguments and not when it carried weak contentions. However, because functionally coordinated messages possibly address major aspects of recipients' self-concepts, this thoughtful processing will not always be objective and impartial. This type of appeals may incite an attentive but defensive inclination, as recipients try to sustain valued expressions of the self. For example, Tykocinski et al. (1994) opined that messages composed to match individuals' present experiences and apprehensions can draw distress by finding out apparently appropriate goals that have not been followed. Hence, such messages have specifically high probability to yield counter arguing and resistance. Similarly, Marsh et al. (1997) stated that influencing messages that address a significant attitude function, that is, for college students, the value-relevant issue of sororities/fraternities on college campuses, are processed cautiously yet defensively and as a result are nominally influential.

Cognitive Dissonance Theory

This classic motivational theory of how attitudes vary to sustain cognitive consistency continues to generate interest. The primary notion of Festinger (1957) that dissonance results from psychological irregularity between related cognitions has been modified comprehensively in consequent research. In Cooper & Fazio's (1984) "new look" approach, dissonance emerges not from straightforward inconsistency but instead from freely opted behaviour that produces some anticipated negative outcome. A vital question for dissonance scholars has been the motivational grounds for dissonance and the reason for the aversive condition of dissonance emergence. In Aronson's (1992) self-concept analysis, dissonance emerges from unpredictable cognitions that endanger the consistency, stability, predictability, competence, or moral excellence of the self-concept. In Steele's (1988) self-affirmation theory, dissonance emerges from the intrusion of general self-integrity. From these self-related viewpoints, negative outcomes are formidable persuaders of dissonance because it is not in agreement with most people's self-views to perform in a way that results in predictable aversive outcomes. A substituting opinion on dissonance arousal, which has yet to be incorporated into conventional theorizing, is the contention by Joule & Beauvois (1998) that dissonance reduction is inclined towards justifying behaviour instead of attaining psychological consistency. In a fascinating integration that realizes that both self-concept threat and aversive outcomes can incite dissonance, Stone & Cooper suggested that dissonance emerges when individuals fail to act in a way coherent with some valued self-standard. The particular motivation behind dissonance purportedly relies on the kind of self-standard involved. Dissonance can arise from behaviour that is incoherent with individual self-standards and does not reveal the manner individuals want to be (ideal self) or believe they should be (ought self), or dissonance can arise from behaviour that produces aversive outcomes and does not reveal the way others want them to be (normative self-standards).

Numerous studies corroborate the inference that dissonance motivation can arise in situations be reft of negative outcomes. Participants in an investigation by Harmon-Jones et al. (1996) openly involved in the nonconsequential behaviour of confidentially acquiring a counter attitudinal stance, but they experienced enhanced arousal and attitude changes towards their stated position. Similarly, Prislin & Pool (1996) found slight proof that dissonance emerges only when behaviour has noticeably negative outcomes and rather determined that dissonance arises when behaviour and its outcomes challenge prevailing ideas about the individual. The hypocritical advocacy paradigm was established to study dissonance motivation in the absence of negative outcomes. In this investigation, participants support a proattitudinal stance, are made aware of their earlier failures to act with regards to this stance, and (in order to decrease dissonance) then involve in acts compatible with the position (e.g., Fried 1998, Stone et al 1997). While the absence of instant negative outcomes to this proattitudinal advocacy might seem to suggest that such outcomes are not grave for creating dissonance, advocates of the negative outcomes outlook can truly note that emphasizing earlier failures to sustain one's expressed beliefs recognizes aversive outcomes of earlier acts. However, Fried & Aronson (1995) opined for the significance of the self in stimulating dissonance by noting that dissonance in this prototype does not arise when individuals are only reminded of earlier transgressions,that is, negative consequences, and do not involve in proattitudinal advocacy and realize the self-relevant inferences of this conduct.

The second significant issue covered in dissonance analysis is the numerous routes or modes through which dissonance can be decreased. While self-affirming behaviour that restores individual integrity has been found to decrease dissonance (Steele 1988), self-affirmations are not every time the mode of selection. When several routes are existing, individuals obviously opt to reduce dissonance openly by varying attitudes and behaviours, that is, modifying the inconsistent cognitions, instead of alleviating it indirectly through self-assertions (Stone et al. 1997). Even individuals with high self-regard, who should own the resources to reduce dissonance by concentrating on positive features of the self-concept, have been discovered instead to transform cognitions (Gibbons et al. 1997). Other investigation has recognized boundary conditions for the utilityof self-affirmations. According to Blanton et al. (1997), affirmations do not reduce dissonance if they caution individuals of the offended self-standard, for example, reassurance of one's compassion when one has acted in a non-compassionate way, reasonably because such affirmations make it more challenging to substantiate the dissonance-inducing act and direct one to linger over the dissonant behaviour.

Other investigations on means of dissonance reduction has shown personal dissimilarities in the path of choice. Individuals who are high in attributional intricacy and typically look for abstract, complex clarifications seem to decrease the dissonance induced by counter attitudinal promotion by considering probable external explanations for the attitude-discrepant act rather than by changing attitudes (Stadler & Baron 1998). Moreover, indicating that investigation has only begun to draw from the range of means available, Burris et al. (1997) recorded the dissonance-reducing effects of transcendence, accommodating varying convictions under a broader principle, and reassertionof the attacked notion. An identification of the full range of paths existing for dissonance reduction can enable to explain some of the apparent discrepancies in the dissonance writing. For instance, when Fried (1998) upgraded the hypocrisy paradigm to make public participants' past disappointments to match their attitudes, participants did not enactattitude-congruent compensating behaviours to reduce dissonance. Rather, they reduced the dissonance caused by public misdemeanours by varying their attitudes to be congruent with the behavioural misdemeanours.

A novel viewpoint worth observing is the expansion of official mathematical models of dissonance-associated processes. Parallel constraint satisfaction systems exemplify dissonance as a dynamic, comprehensive process and offer a means to assess consistency and different features of the relation between beliefs (Read et al. 1997). In one application of this method, scholars determine a network of attitudes and various perceptions, simulate variations in the network (according to pre-specified rules of determining the relationship between the attitudes and cognitions) until it acquires a condition of overall consistency, and assess the results of the simulation to data from research participants. Shultz & Lepper (1996) were able to utilize this technique to effectively explain for judgment change in various classic dissonance paradigms.

MULTIPLE ATTITUDES

Sources of Multiple Attitudes

A chief presumption of much attitude theorizing is that individuals' analysis of a given object are consistent across time, setting, and method of assessment. Empirical proof of this consistency has arisen with rising precision in recent time, partly due to improved knowledge of the determining factors of coherence in attitudinal reactions, for example, strong attitudes (Petty & Krosnick 1995), and partly to upgraded methods to document coherence, for example, compatibility in measurement (Ajzen 1996). However, empirical proof that individuals can bear multiple attitudes towards a given object is arising as well, and this profile of dissociation has been clarified in numerous ways.

The proof for multiple attitudes has occasionally been discarded as revealingepiphenomena, such as context effects, "non-attitudes" or weakly held attitudes. However, multiple attitudes also can originate from more lastingeffects. For instance, attitudes that change with setting can denote transient constructions, for example, differential utilization of evaluation scales, anchoring, and adjustment effects, or more internalized propensities to react that are firmly connected to certain contextual characteristics (McConnell et al 1997). Moreover, various analysis of an attitude object can arise from attitude structure. They can reveal the shallow responses correlated with attitudes that have least cognitive and affective foundations or the more consistent reactions related with attitudes that have inconsistent elements, as when attitudes are structurally inconsistent (e.g., Chaiken et al 1995, Prislin et al. 1998), held with uncertainty (Priester & Petty 1996, Thompson et al 1995), or related with changing affective reactions, for example, immediate versus anticipated future affect (Richard et al 1996 a, b, Van der Pligt et al 1998).

In recent time, multiple attitudes have led to development of interest for their own right, as expanded theoretical knowledge presents a basis for forecasting both the consistency and the detachment that occurs in attitude assessments (e.g., Mackie & Smith 1998, Wilson & Hodges 1992). This is a still-developing investigation field that incorporatesa rather varied arrangement of impacts, including context-related attitudes, multiply categorizable attitude objects, explicit versus implicit attitudes, subjective construals and issue framing. The common theme relating these different research domains is that individual's reactions to a specific attitude object can reveal diverse analyses, cognitive representations and interpretations and affective reactions.

One source of detachments is the range of motivations that can govern attitudes. Dissociation is inferred in the assertion of social influence theorists that individuals are motivated to embrace attitudes of related reference groups to the magnitude that the group identity is noticeable and desirable (Kelman 1958, Turner 1991). That is, individuals may hold multiple cognitive demonstrations of attitudes on a matter that is significant to more than one of the groups with which they recognize. Introductory encouragement for this idea was presented in findings by Wood & Matz (unpublished data) that college students' attitudes towards social welfare programmes were more preferable when their social identities as devout individuals were noticeable (in comparison to a baseline attitude measure obtained with no noticeable group identity), while students' attitudes were less preferable when their identities as political fundamentalists were significant. Moreover, these attitude swings arose most strongly among individuals who believed religious or conservative social groups to be self-defining.

Dissociations also can emerge from cognitive methods. To the degree that an attitude object, such as yogurt, is related to a different set of issues and values, individuals can select from multiple categories, for example, dairy products, health foods, when interpreting the object. Numerous aspects decide the category chosen, including the ease of access of category attitudes (ER Smith et al. 1996). Moreover, a sole attitude object may produce several descriptions in memory when attitude-related information is saved distinctly from overall analysis of the object (Hastie & Park 1986). Indeed, McConnell et al. (1997) showed that various attitudes can be produced in diverse settings for a sole attitude object when perceivers do not try, online, to build an integrated attitude. Multiple cognitive demonstrations of a matter also can arise from knowledge processing in social influence contexts. After being subjected to the judgments of others in an influence appeal, recipients may later recover this data without identifying its source and, under some situations, unknowingly assume it as their own reaction (Betz et al. 1996).

Dissociations also can emerge as after-effects of the different sorts of processes through which attitude-related judgments are produced. Explicit, conscious judgments vary in numerous ways from judgements that are implicitly held, including the types of data considered (Ajzen 1996, Greenwald & Banaji 1995). For example, Wittenbrink et al. (1997) imply that explicit and implicit measures of ethnic partiality are only reasonably associated because people are more probable to build explicit judgments on an egalitarian ideology; hence, explicit attitudes towards racial minorities are more preferable than implicit ones.

Influence and Multiple Attitudes

Influence strategies have gained from multiple cognitive interpretations, affective reactions, and evaluations that individuals possess regarding a given object. Asch (1940) opined previously on that the primary process in influence is no variation in attitudes towards an object but instead variation in the interpretation and meaning of the object. When there is variation in meaning, attitudes vary accordingly. The relationship between meaning and evaluation is proposed in the result by Bosveld et al. (1997) that individuals are more biased towards "affirmative action" when others contend that it implies equal opportunity instead of, for example, reverse favouritism. Even fine facets of the manner an issue is framed or stand for in an appeal, such as the obviouslocation and time at which a proposal will come about, can influence recipients' attitudes (Liberman & Chaiken 1996). This latter discovery bring up difficult questions for persuasion research that has different individual importance through the assumed time or location of a message proposition, for example, introducing senior exhaustive exams at an individual's own university or another university. Usually, it has been considered that recipients are reacting to corresponding attitude objects irrespective of whether the time and location of the message proposition renders it individually relevant. Issue framing is an influence approach that benefits from multiple attitudes. In this methodology, the significance and relevance of certain outcomes or features of an issue are highlighted over other possible consequences (Ball-Rokeach & Loges 1996, Nelson & Kinder 1996, Nelson et al 1997, Price & Tewksbury 1997). For example, Eagly & Kulesa (1997) demonstrate the way persuasive appeals from both sides of environmental deliberations have set up desired positions as accomplishingvalues preferred by recipients, for example, a healthy economy grounded on tourism or logging and industry, and framed the non-anticipated position as acquiring values most recipients deny.

Readers may think how appeals that utilize framing vary from ones that utilize the conviction change approaches typical of message-based persuasion paradigms. Traditional persuasion appeals typically deal with intra-attitudinal relations and explain the particular attributes owned by an attitude object. In contradiction, as implied in the label, framing appeals generally deal with inter-attitudinal relations and put a matter or object in the context of different attitude issues, values and goals. Moreover, framing seems to emphasize the relevance or significance of prevailing knowledge structures and values. Nelson et al. (1997) described that framing effects are usually stronger for participants acquainted an issue, for example, holding the relevant knowledge structures, than for those unacquainted with it. Despite these exceptional characteristics of framing, instituted models of attitude change seem suitable for comprehending its effects. For instance, expectancy-value formulations can explain framing effects through disparities in the salience and likelihood of appropriategoals and values, as well as through dissimilarities in the assessment given to them (Ajzen 1996).

The processes fundamental to framing effects are likely to rely, as in standard persuasion paradigms, on the degree to which recipients are inspired and able to process message content and other appropriate data. For instance, the motivation to assume a novel construal or frame for a matter can emerge from motivational objectives such as denyingan intensely unpopular group identity. In a manifestation of this process, college students reported that their attitudes represent those of a detested group, the Ku Klux Klan, shifted their own explanations of the issue far from an apparently racist interpretation they then were able to change their attitudes away from those of the Klan (Wood et al 1996, Pool et al 1998).

DUAL-MODE PROCESSING MODELS OF PERSUASION

Persuasion research has persisted in the greatly effective ritual of the dual-mode processing theories, the heuristic/systematic model (Chaiken et al. 1996a) and the elaboration likelihood model (Petty & Wegener 1998a). The main principleof these theories is that the determining factor and practices of attitude change rely on individuals' motivation and ability to deal with issue-related information. When individuals are not highly inspired, for example, the issue is not individually involving, or they have low ability, for example, they are distracted, attitude assessments are grounded on easily accessible attributes of a source, message, or situation that are assessedvia effective processing strategies. For instance, they might utilize the heuristic rule, consensus denotes correctness, and thus is in accordance with a majority position. When individuals are both inspired and able to work on data carefully, then attitudes are founded on a more attentive, systematic analysis of appropriate information. As per the elaboration likelihood model, such high-elaboration methods include learning message content, creation of cognitive responses, and dissonance-induced reasoning (Petty & Wegener 1998a). For analyses of the resemblances and dissimilarities between the heuristic/systematic model and the elaboration likelihood model, see Chaiken et al. (1996a), Eagly & Chaiken (1993), and Petty & Wegener (1998a).

Research has proceeded swiftly recognizing the components that augmentsy stematic, thorough processing. As per the heuristic/systematic model, individuals are inspired to involve in methodical thought in order to acquire an adequate "desired level of confidence" in their judgments. Components that have been observed to enhance systematic processing (apparently by reducing actual confidence or improving desired confidence) include the following: framing of influential messages in an unanticipated manner (Smith & Petty 1996); self-relevance of messages, either because recipients self-reference or are made self-conscious (Turco 1996); and use in messages of token phrases that ambiguously signal broader values, such as, for Democrats, "family values" rhetoric (Garst & Bodenhausen 1996). Systematic processing also has been observed when recipients possess strong, accessible attitudes on the message theme (Fabrigar et al. 1998), possess uncertain attitudes (Maio et al. 1996), or relish exhausting cognitive activity (i.e. are high in requirement for cognition; for review, see Cacioppo et al. 1996). Moreover, recipients involve in methodological processing in situations in which vigilant thought is probable to produce judgment confidence, such as when recipients have faith in their own capacity and ability to analyse (Bohner et al. 1998b) and when the message is provided in accessible, not excessively complex language (Hafer et al. 1996). Systematic processing also may be associatedin opposition to influence. Pfau's (1997) intuitive review of resistance research concentrated specifically on inoculation methods, in which recipients acquire information that reinforcestheir attitudes before exposure to influentialattack. He opines that inoculation effects arise when expected threats,for example, cautioning of a possible attack to one's attitudes, motivate contemplative processing to promote one's own position or to resist opposing ones. Moreover, opposition to attitude change seems to enhance at midlife (Visser & Krosnick 1998). Middle-aged individuals seem to have specifically resilient attitudes that help them to tackle argue opposing positions.

Heuristic processing is utilized when a low-effort approachlead to attitudes with an adequate level of confidence (Chaiken et al. 1996a). Numerous heuristic prompts have been recognized in the latest research. For instance, known sayings can provide prompts to agreement (Howard 1997), and the subjective experience of visualizing about a matter can be a prompt, so that, for instance, individuals assume stances when they can easily produce supportive arguments and discard stances when they cannot (Rothman & Schwarz 1998). Moreover, pertinentto understanding the heuristic prompts utilized in day-to-day contexts are Dickerson's (1997) observations of politicians reinforcing their preferable positions with regard to unbiased, expert sources and sources with an obvious faithfulness to the opposition.

Cognitive Response Mediation of Attitude Change

Research has persisted to deal with the mechanics causing systematic, high-elaboration processing. One query is whether the valence of recipients' cognitive reactions mediates influence or whether valence characterizes either alternate substitutive estimation of attitude change or an after-the-fact explanation of change. To test causal priority, Romero et al. (1996) and Killeya & Johnson (1998) straightforwardly controlled considerations and analysed the influences on attitudes. Persistent with the viewpoint in which contemplations mediate change, acknowledgement of the position in the plea related to the degree and valence of the produced contemplations. Moreover, correlational analyses in these investigations, and in various investigations that analysed recipients' instinctively produced contemplations (e.g. Friedrich et al. 1996, Hafer et al. 1996), proved coherent with the mediational role of contemplations.

Conclusions regarding causal instructions arecomplex, however, by the few investigations that shuffledthe typical causal sequence tried in correlational designs and discovered that attitudes can effectively mediate the influence of independent variables on contemplations(Friedrich et al. 1996, Maio & Olson 1998). However, the proof of mutual mediation through attitudes as well as contemplations does not inevitably present a threat tothe cognitive response model. Mutual mediation could revealthe instantaneousutilization of dual processing modes. Individuals may involve instantly in effortful processing, in which a plea stimulates thoughts that then influence attitudes, along with less difficult processing, in which attitudes are at once influenced by a plea through, for example, heuristic analyses (Chaiken et al 1996a). When pleas have a straightforwardeffect on attitudes, then thoughts may revealan after-the-fact explanation for attitude judgments.

Another query is whether cognitive responses give an adequate prototype of mediation. Munro & Ditto (1997) and Zuwerink & Devine (1996) state that attitude change on preference-related issues is associated to message recipients' subjective experience of influence together with the favourability of their notions. While it is possible that the inadequacy of thoughts as an arbitrator originates from measurement constraints, for example, poor reliability or validity of coding of thought protocols, it also is probable that for prejudice and other attitudes with a resilient affective foundation, variations in affective reactions influence attitudes without depending upon cognitive responses.

Dual-Mode Processing Models and Social Influence

Dual-mode models too can give a model for comprehending attitude change in social influence context. For example, cautious analysis of other group members' responses to a judgment task seems to rest on members' motivation to execute well and their capability to perform their own assessments of the task. Baron et al. (1996) stated that highly motivated members trusted their own analyses barring when judgment impetuses were rendered too concisely to acknowledge the exact reply; then they seemed to assume the heuristic strategy of trusting on others' judgments. In contrary, members who were only reasonably motivated utilized the heuristic-like strategy of depending on others' estimates irrespective of whether they could decide upon the right answer themselves. The heuristic prompts crucial in social influence contexts involve not only others' judgments, but also facets of social communication and others' self-presentation. For instance, group members having more confidence in their judgements have been found to be more effective in arguments, irrespective of their real task accuracy (Zarnoth & Sniezek 1997).

The group discussion analysis by Kelly et al. (1997) also can be interpreted from a dual-mode viewpoint. When participants were motivated and able to accomplish accurate results, that is, the task had aapparently accurate result as the time was sufficient, group discussions involved extensive reasoning and argumentation. Moreover, systematic reasoning was obviously effective in producing reasonable solutions; more systematic consideration during discussion was linked to greater solution accuracy. In addition, explainable from this viewpoint is the finding by Shestowsky et al. (1998) that in dyadic conversations, members who were motivated to involve in cognitive activities, that is, were high in requirement for cognition, had the greatest influence on group decisions. While no direct proof was acquired that motivated members involved in thorough analysis during the discussion or that this is what made them effective, members' self-ratings proposed that those who regarded thinking activities produced many arguments, produced valid arguments, and tried intensely to be influential.

Motivated Processing and Bias Correction

Investigation has kept on documenting how recipients' motives, that is to defend self, sustain wanted relations with others and have correct judgements, provoke and guide systematic processing and produce more preferable analyses of objective-furthering than impeding information (Munro & Ditto 1997, Zuwerink & Devine 1996). Motives also can produce selective utilization of heuristic prompts, such as depending on social accord when it offers enough backing for one's wanted position (Giner-Sorolla & Chaiken 1997). Numerous elements seem to motivate biased processing, including recipients' comprehensive values (Eagly & Kulesa 1997, Maio & Olson 1998, Seligman et al 1996) and self-interests (Giner-Sorolla & Chaiken 1997), and attitude matters that are highly significant and engaging (Zuwerink & Devine 1996). However, the part of capacity in biased processing remains ill-defined. While some have theorized that bias surfaces when individuals depend on their (apparently primarily attitude-supportive) own beliefs and information to analyse an issue, Biek et al. (1996) found knowledge alone to be inadequate; considerate biased processing appeared only when well-informed individuals were also highly motivated, for example, by strong affect, to retain a specific position. Asymmetries too have been observed in motivated processing. Individuals occasionally react more forcefully to undermining information that weaken their wanted opinion than to compatible information that endorses it. Ditto et al. (1998) theorize that because intimidating inputs are probable to require an instantaneous behavioural reaction, it is versatile for individuals to perform an objective, crucial analysis of preference-inconsistent data while reacting more inertlyto amiable information. It appears probably, however, that individuals use different kind of processing strategies to achieve defensive objectives. For instance, an approach of defensive inattention to demanding information can justify the finding by Slater & Rouner (1996) that individuals more cautiously deal with congenial than intimidating health-related information. An interesting query that has aroused in the past few years is whether individuals are mindful of and can undermine prejudices and alternate ways in their information processing approaches. Wegener & Petty (1997) propose that individuals employ bias correction procedures to the level that they consider elements distinct from the exact qualities of the attitude issue have affected their judgments and to the degree that they are motivated and become capable to neutralize the bias. While an implicit assumption appears to be that rationality-seeking motives influence bias correction, other motives also are reasonable, for example, the self-related motive of being an objective, unprejudiced judge, the other-related motive of delivering this impression to others.

In a trial of bias correction, Petty et al. (1998) reproduced a context in which it would be unlawfulto trust on heuristic rules. Members were directed to abstain from letting their prejudices about an apparently affable or unlikable source impact their judgments of the source's proposition. The outcome was a noticeable over-correction in which the unpleasant source was more influential than the amiable one. Moreover, because the correction commands seemed to influence processing freely of members' motivation to examine the message, Petty et al. (1998) presumed that cautious message examination does not instantaneously involveefforts to neutralize possible prejudices. Bias correction also arises in jury ordeals when the evidence produced is consequently declared impermissible by the court. In experimental trial recreations, irrespective of whether such proof is disregarded seems to depend partially on the purpose for it being unacceptable. Evidence ruled out because it was untrustworthy or because it was produced for some individual motive had little impact on judgments, whereas evidence omitted for procedural causes continued to exert impact (Fein et al 1997, Kassin & Sommers 1997). Moreover, coherent with Wegener & Petty's (1997) model, individuals endeavouring to balance for impermissible proof have been discovered to both over- and under-correct, relying on whether they consider the evidence was probable to have a strong or a weak influence on their judgments (Schul & Goren 1997).

AFFECT AND INFLUENCE

Effects of Mood

Various models have been established to clarify the influence of mood on knowledge processing and attitude change. In the opinion of Wegener & Petty (1996), mood impacts alter with elaboration likelihood. Obvious impacts of mood on accord arise through low-elaboration methods, involving connection of an influential appeal with constructive or destructive thoughts, such as, classical conditioning, and use of heuristic rules depending on those thoughts, for example, "I feel bad so I must dislike it". When individuals are more comprehensively processing, the way an attitude object cause them think can act as a persuasive argument. It also can prejudice the information taken into account, such as when individuals attend more to messages that agree with their mood or when they recollect such data more precisely(Rusting 1998). The condition when the measure of elaboration isat some middle level, individuals react purposefully to "manage" moods. Happy individuals specifically process in view of maintaining their positive mood, for example, attending to data that cause them feel good, whereas unhappy individuals are less choosy because there is greater scope for any action to be mood boosting.

On the other hand, in the feelings-as-information account, moods indicatesuitable processing approaches (Bless et al 1996, Schwarz 1997, Schwarz & Clore 1996). In a similar way to the discussion carried out in the previous section in relation to asymmetrical impacts of motives on processing, positive moods propose a kind circumstance suitablefor heuristic approaches, whereas negative moods suggest a possible problem that may involve systematic evaluation. However, all negative feelings do not seem to have the same processing connotations. Ottati et al. (1997) discovered that anger (marginally) decreased systematic processing in relation to impartial moods, possibly because anger refers to agonistic settings requiring quick reaction.

Controversy has arisen regarding whether negative influence increases processing through mood administration, as proposed by the elaboration model of Wegener & Petty (1996), or through indicating a difficult situation, as indicated by the feelings-as-information account of Schwarz & Clore (1996). Presently, the accessible empirical data can be construed as supporting either viewpoints. Moreover, investigation findings have been taken to assist a third, affect-infusion model (Forgas 1995), in which affect instils thoughts and behaviours mainly when people involve in systematic, substantive processing. While Forgas (1998) opined that empirical tests promote affect infusion, the finding that moods prejudice and direct systematic processing of influence appeals also is coherent with the other two models studied here.

Fear Appeals

The impacts of fear-generating appeals have been of specific curiosity in the health domain. Various theories have delineated the proximal notions through which fear-stimulating appeals affect influence. The protection motivation theory (Rogers 1983) states that appeals that are intimidating and that suggest an effective way of dealing with the threat incite danger control methods, which include embracing the proposed coping strategy and alteringthe maladaptive behaviour (Prentice-Dunn et al. 1997, Sturges & Rogers 1996). Rogers & Prentice-Dunn (1997) inferred that about half of the studies to date that have executed suitable tests have backed the theory's anticipation of maximum acknowledgement when perceived threat and contending are both high.

The extended parallel process model (Witte 1992, 1998) has associated influence to fear-management as well as threat-control reactions. When threat is greater than coping, fear responses can initiate message refusal through defensive reactions (McMahan et al. 1998, Witte et al. 1998). In harmony with this view, Aspinwall & Brunhart (1996) presented that individual who are not very affirmative about their own health-coping approaches are less probable to join to intimidating health information than individuals who are more hopeful. Since fear-control reactions impede the acceptance implementation of self-protective acts proposed in the appeal, they can explain the occasionally obtained "boomerang" shifts in attitudes distant from messages when individuals do not consider they can manage effectively (Rogers & Prentice-Dunn 1997).

Investigation also has kept on examining the impacts of fear on message processing and to assimilatethe analysis of fear appeals into the comprehensive models of mood and influence discussed before. Fear, similar to other affective reactions, seems to influence extent of processing. At low-to-moderate stages, fear operates like individual participation and increases processing (Rogers & Prentice-Dunn 1997). Enhanced processing, at least of strong messages, may clarify the often-obtained finding that fear accelerates influence and acceptance of novel coping approaches(e.g., Dillard et al 1996, Millar & Millar 1996). However, fear also can prefer processing in a manner that clarifies existing coping (or non-coping) behaviours (Biek et al 1996). At high levels, fear seems to decrease systematic processing, for example, Jepson & Chaiken 1990. Normally, the nonlinear impacts of fear on processing are consistent with the notion that fear is multidimensional and involves both arousal and negative influence. Estimation scales that have been devisedto take advantage of the activation part have discovered that greater reported fear, such as arousal increases influence, while scales that have been devised to tap the negative tension component have discovered that greater fear, that is, negative affect, hinders influence or has minimal impact (Celuch et al. 1998, LaTour & Rotfeld 1997).

GROUP AND SELF-IDENTITY

Social identity theory (Tajfel 1981, 1982) has triggered great curiosity in group impact as well as in other components of group behaviour. From the social identity viewpoint, when individuals classify themselves as an in-group member, the in-group acts as an allusion for social assessment, and individuals embrace the prototypic in-group attitudes and convictions as their own. Extending on this analysis, Turner (1982, 1991) suggested that groups wield influence through a particular process, which he called referent informational influence. Following this viewpoint, agreement from people categorized as similar to self increses one's subjective certainty and indicates that the shared attitudes reveal external reality and the objective truth of the issue. Discord from similar`others produces subjective uncertainty and motivates individuals to tackle the disagreement through, for example, mutual social influence or attributional reasoning to clarify the discord.

Experiential data from different types of investigation paradigms are compatible with the social identity strategy. Content analyses by Reicher & Hopkins (1996a, b) of political and social speeches demonstrate the major purpose of in-group and out-group descriptions in day-to-day inducement. For instance, their analysis of a pro-life discourse conveyed to medical practitioners disclosed that it described doctors and pro-life activists as a regular in-group in their concern for others' wellbeing, described pro-life activity as in agreement with the medical identity, and described abortion-rights advocatesas a denigrated out-group. Other work has favoured the social identity assertion that influence originates from prototypic group attitudes. In the little group discussions examined by Kameda et al. (1997), concluding decisions were affected most strongly by "cognitively central" group participants, whose original convictions about the discussion topic coincided the most with other participants. The influence gain of prototypic participants was neutralof whether their preliminary judgment inclinations put them in the group majority or minority. Kameda et al. (1997) opined that the mutual convictions and knowledge offered social substantiation for other members' views and a foundation on which others could acknowledge prototypic members' know-how. The self-categorization analysis varies from customary persuasion models in tracing the elements of attitude change in individuals'creation of group identity instead of in their understanding of attitude issues. One sort of evidence produced in favour of this examination is that influence changes with group membership, for example, Haslam et. al. 1995. Other proof is that the influence of a group is not dependent on beneficiariesstudying the subject of the influence appeal (McGarty et al. 1994; see also Haslam et al. 1996). While some investigation has indicated that in-group influence is supplemented by acceptance and learning of the message (e.g. Mackie et al. 1992), Haslam et al. (1996) contend that such learning happens after embracing of the in-group position, as people endeavour to comprehend the group opinion with the intention of becoming an effective group participant.

The self-categorization theory assert that group identity can openly affect influence is consistent with a heuristic-like reasoning process in which individuals are influenced because of the apparent authenticity of in-group positions, for example, my kind of people believe X. However, proof also exists for various kinds of processing. Experimental analysis has recognized various conditions under which group identity inspires recipients to perform a systematic, thorough evaluation and explanation of the appeal, and attitude change or opposition depends on this analysis. Systematic processing has been discovered when the identification of the source group is appropriate to recipients' own self-definitions (Wood et al. 1996), when the matter is appropriate to recipients' association (Crano & Chen 1998, Mackie et al. 1990), when the message position is illustrative of in-group unanimity and thus is informative about the exact group rules(van Knippenberg & Wilke 1992), and when the influence appeal examines an in-group participant and thus has suggestions for recipients' self-evaluations (Budesheim et al. 1996). Systematic processing also arises when recipients are ineffective in processing heuristically, such as when the group position is specified after the message (Mackie et al. 1992), and when the context supports thorough examination, such as when individuals have adequate time to process a message from a noticeable, possibly significant in-group (Hogg 1996). Hence, the experimental data indicate that group influence does not function through a lone process. Individuals' motives to adjust with or distinguish from social groups can produce heuristic analyses and various kinds of comparatively shallow information processing, or they can produce meticulous, systematic processing of appropriate information.

Social Consensus and Validity of Information

Social identity and self-categorization theories provide a novel viewpoint on the issue of what makes information persuasive. In message-based persuasion paradigms, convincing, rational contentions normally have been characterized as ones that connect the attitude problem to highly esteemed outcomes and that produce encouraging responses from recipients, while frail contentions are ones that connect the issue to less-valued outcomes and that produce more negative responses (Eagly & Chaiken 1993). Contemporary effort within this tradition, for example, has been put to investigate how introducing weak arguments into an otherwise strong message can weaken persuasion or influence (Friedrich et al 1996, Friedrich & Smith 1998). Social identity outlook rather have concentrated on the social determining factors of information validity. This viewpoint was created in contradiction to Festinger's (1954) assertion that individuals favour objective reality testing and utilize social reality testing, for example comparison with others' views, mainlywhen objective norms are not accessible. In self-categorization theory, reality testing is a lone method in which individuals utilize the normative norms of appropriate reference groups to acquire a valid, unanimously shared knowledge of reality consistent with their social identity (Turner 1991). In a convincing declaration of the ramifications of this stance, Turner & Oakes opined that consensual judgments "are rationally more likely to reflect a deeper truth about the world, not because agreement always indicates accuracy, but because they have emerged from, and survived processes of discussion, argument, and collective testing" (1997:369).

Experimental information, however, indicate that the relation between social accord and the obvious exactness of data is dependent on various factors. Subjective validity arises from unanimitythat is accomplished through the confluence of independent instead of dependent opinions and through authentication by a person's own, personal cognitive processing (Levine 1996, Mackie & Skelly 1994). Moreover, social unanimity seems to generate more impact for some types of issues than for others, presumptively because in-group unanimity indicates subjective validity more convincingly for some problems than for others. For instance, majority consent has a particularly solid influence on judgments of individual favouritism, and less influence on judgments of objective impetuses, presumptively because consensus denotes favouritism probable to be shared with similar others (Crano & Hannula-Bral 1994, Wood et al. 1994).

Multiple Motives Instigated by Groups

In social identity and self-categorization theories, the motive for influence stems mostly from the will to accomplish and sustain a positive analysis of the self. In support of this viewpoint, Pool et al. (1998) showed that individuals uphold a favourable self-view by changing their attitudes to coordinate with positively esteemed groups and to differ from negatively esteeme dones. Attitude change inspired by social identity also can be determinedby various self-related concerns, for example, endeavouring to be genuine to oneself and to acquire a consistent, evident self-view (Abrams & Hogg 1988).

The tripartite investigation of motives provided in this chapter denotes extra motives for individuals to embrace or discard group positions. One engages the positive and negative consequences produced by others. For instance, cooperate with others with the intention of developing smooth relations with them, for example, receive social rewards and escape punishments, is probably going to be significant in close relationships and other in-group settings in which social accord is esteemed. Another possible motive for embracing or discarding group positions is to acquire an exact, valid knowledge of reality. This probability opposes viewpoints that have related group persuasion with preconceived notion. For instance, in an investigation of democratic involvement, Pratkanis & Turner (1996) suggested that active, contemplative discussion and examination of political problems happens when citizens observe problems as individually appropriate, while indiscriminating approval of political solutions and misinformationpresentedby a governing leader happens when people desire to undertakea specificsocial identity,such as party allegiance. Nevertheless, to the level that some social and group identities, for example, informed voter, responsible individuals, inspire individuals to assume valid, exact positions, then group-related motives are not essentially linkedwith biased processing.

OPINION MINORITY AND MAJORITY GROUPS

The seeming puzzlethat "few can influence many" has kept on triggering curiosity in minority influence. This work normally describes minorities as sources supporting occasional, low-consensus positions.

Contemporary investigations have advanced past the primary belief that minority sources are influential because they cause informational difference and test recipients' knowledge of issues (Moscovici 1985). Rather, the most reliable discovery seems to be that the social identity of minorities impedes influence. Minorities are extremely influential when their affect is evaluated on "indirect" judgment measures—ones on which recipients are comparatively uninformed that their judgments could adjust them with the aberrant minority source (Wood et al. 1994). However, even on indirect counts, proof of minority influence often fails to arise (Martin 1998). Minorities appear to confront two hindrances to wielding influence. By definition, they are not significant reference groups. Hence, source group identity is improbable to inspire individuals to attend to and assess an appeal (De Vries et al. 1996). Moreover, even when individuals process the appeal, the source's low consensus, aberrant stance is probably going to produce a negatively prejudiced processing orientation. Accordingly, recipients oppose influence (Mugny 1980, Erb et al. 1998) or reveal"boomerang" movesaway from the minority viewpoint (Pool et al. 1998, Wood et al. 1996).

In a sequence of sophisticated experiments, Crano and his colleagues (Alvaro & Crano 1996, 1997; Crano & Alvaro 1998; Crano &Chen 1998) showed that these hindrances to minority influence can be overcome by in-group minority sources. It seems that the uniqueness of in-group minority stances inspires cautious message processing, however, with the compassionate, open-minded inclination normally concurred to in-group members. The aberrationof the minority view reduces acknowledgment on direct attitude measures but the disparity in attitude formation that arises from message processing produces attitude change towards the minority viewpoint on measures indirectly associated to the appeal.

Various lines of investigation have recorded the types of thought recipients produce to minority appeals. Specifically in analytical contexts in which new solutions are esteemed(Nemeth 1986), minorities promote recipients to ponder about problems in a deviating way and to consider new ideas and solution approaches (Butera et al. 1996, Erb et al. 1998, Gruenfeld et al. 1998, Nemeth & Rogers 1996, Peterson & Nemeth 1996). Attributional reasoning is also going to arbitrate influence, given that minority positions are often unanticipated and need clarification. Investigation findings normally aid the analysis by Eagly et al. (1981) that influence is reduced when the supported position can be ascribed to a conceivably biasing characteristic of the source or situation, such as the source's individual self-interest (Moskowitz 1996). In a similar way, influence is increased when the supported stance can be ascribed to external reality or the truth about the issue (Bohner et al. 1996, 1998a). Similarly, proposing attributional reasoning is the finding that minorities are influential when they offer their opinions in situations, for example, face-to-face interaction, in which aberration can bring about costs (McLeod et al. 1997). Advocacy then proposes a source who is adequately dedicatedand sure to stakesocial disapproval.

A valuable objective for upcom inginvestigation will be to recognize the particular facet(s) of minority identity that motivate accord or opposition. Going by the three-motive scheme of this chapter, it might be the case that the minority source has applicability for recipients' individual identities and characterizes, for example, an aberrant other from whom they desire to distinguish or an esteemed pioneer they desire to follow (Wood et al. 1996). Another motive involves recipients' association with others, for example, the wish to be compassionate with in-group minority sources (Crano & Chen 1998). In the end, recipients could acquire a perfect knowledge of an issue by coming to an agreement with minorities whose positions seem to reveal external reality (Bohner et al. 1996).

11 CHAPTER

Emotional Intelligence

EMOTIONAL INTELLIGENCE AND ITS HISTORY

For the last twenty years, 'emotional intelligence' and 'emotional literacy' have leapt to paramount importance in the spheres of education and business.

Leuner, a German psychiatrist hypothesized some reasons in his article, 'Emotional Intelligence and emancipation' in 1966 that a few women intentionally turned down the social roles and responsibilities expected of them and they did it owing to their 'low Emotional Intelligence'.

Howard Gardner's Frames of Mind: the Theory of Multiple Intelligences, in 1983, presented the idea that traditional intelligences like IQ have proved its failure to explain the cognitive ability completely. The idea of multiple intelligences which he introduced comprised interpersonal intelligence i.e. the ability to make out the intentions, motivations and desires of other people and intrapersonal intelligence i.e. the ability to make out oneself, to praise one's feelings, fears and motivations.

Wayne Leon Payne, a graduate student in 1985 at an alternative liberal arts college in the USA, used the term, 'emotional intelligence' in the title of his doctoral dissertation and it is possibly the first academic use of the said term. It seems that none used the term in their any academic papers in the next five years. The researchers Peter Salovey, Jack Mayer and their colleagues brought out two articles in 1990 with the introduction of term 'Emotional Intelligence' in the mainstream of the American psychology.

However, Daniel Goleman, the psychologist and New York Times science writer, popularized the idea of 'emotional intelligence' in his book, ***Emotional Intelligence: Why It Can Matter More Than IQ*** in 1995.

DEFINITIONS

The ability to observe one's own as well as other people's emotions, to differentiate between emotions and label them accurately and to utilize emotional information in order to guide the process of thinking and behaviour is emotional intelligence.

- People, who have high Emotional Quotient (EQ), show a high level of self-awareness, empathy, motivation and social skills.
- In the opinion of Daniel Goleman, IQ is the prime quality that helps entering the high-level management jobs, but it is of no use to the leaders as most of them have a high IQ already. However, the effective leaders distinguish themselves from ineffective ones by their ability to control their own emotions and understand the emotions, internal motivation, and social skills of other people.

Definition of Emotional Intelligence by Daniel Goleman

"The capacity for recognizing our own feelings and those in others, for motivating ourselves, for managing emotions well in ourselves and in our relationships."

Emotional Intelligence (EI) is the ability to reason about emotions, and to boost the thinking of emotions. The abilities to appropriately conceive emotions, to access and create emotions in order to assist thought, to make out emotions as well as emotional knowledge, and reflective regulation of emotions are included with a view to promoting emotional as well as intellectual growth.

EMOTIONAL INTELLIGENCE AND EMOTIONAL LITERACY

In the United Kingdom, the term, 'emotional literacy', has wide use, sometimes with the preference to 'Emotional Intelligence'. This was possibly because of those who felt the use of the word 'intelligence' undermining rather than buttressing to their concerns. However, for some people, 'literacy' implies the importance of being able to utter feelings and besides 'teaching' or 'training' young people the objective of empowering them emotionally associating with the phrases like 'critical literacy'.

Practically, when the terms are simplified conceptually there remains little difference between emotional literacy and Emotional Intelligence in spite of people's strong feeling attached to one or the disagreement to other. The high degree of overlap is interpreted comparing the Goleman's unpacking of Emotional Intelligence with the definition of emotional literacy by Katherine Weare in her *Developing the Emotionally Literate School* published in 2004. It is as follows: The ability to understand ourselves and other people, and being aware of particularly understanding and using information about the emotional conditions of ourselves and others competently is emotional intelligence which including the ability to understand, express and manage our own emotions, and react to the emotions of others, in the manners that are helpful to ourselves as well as others.

MAJOR COMPETENCIES OF EMOTIONAL INTELLIGENCE

There live eight special, learnable, measurable competencies under the three pursuits measured through the *Six Seconds Emotional Intelligence Assessment* (SEI). The competencies with definitions are given below:

1. ***Enhancing Emotional Literacy***: It implies the appropriate identification and interpretation of the simple as well as compound feelings. Its pursuit is to know oneself.

2. *Recognising Patterns*: It denotes the acknowledgement of recurring reactions and behaviours frequently. It intends to know oneself.
3. *Applying Consequential Thinking*: It means estimating the costs and benefits of your choices. Its pursuit is to choose oneself.
4. *Navigating Emotions*: It refers to the Assessment, harness, and transformation of emotions as a strategic resource. It includes the pursuit of choosing oneself.
5. *Engaging Intrinsic Motivation*: It means the gaining of vitality from personal values and commitments being run by external forces. It is in the pursuit of choosing oneself.
6. *Exercising Optimism*: It defines the undertaking of a proactive viewpoint of hope and possibility. It includes the pursuit of choosing oneself.
7. *Increasing Empathy*: This competency refers to the ways of recognizing and reacting to the emotions of others. Its pursuit is to give oneself.
8. *Pursuing Noble Goals*: This competency refers to the ways of connecting one's daily likes with one's overarching intentional sense. It is the pursuit of giving oneself.

The Fact of Six Seconds: Six Seconds is an international non-profit organization set up in 1997 and based in California contributed to the awareness of 'emotional intelligence' or 'emotional quotient'. It brings out EQ tests. Particularly, the SEI test has been used in many peer-reviewed studies regarding emotional intelligence.

MODELS OF EMOTIONAL INTELLIGENCE

These are ability, mixed and trait models.

Ability Model

Emotions are taken in as useful sources of information helping one to make sense of and deal with the complicated social environment. The ability to process information relating to an emotional nature and the ability to touch emotional processing to a wider cognition is indicated by this model. It is considered as the mode of manifesting itself in specific adaptive behaviours.

This model again has four kinds of abilities. They are as follows:

1. *Perceiving emotions*: This type includes the ability to detect and decipher emotions in faces, voices, pictures and cultural artefacts along with the ability of identifying one's own emotions. It presents the fundamental aspect of emotional intelligence with the feasible involvement of all other processing of emotional information.
2. *Using or facilitating emotions*: This process implies the ability to control and use emotions in order to simplify several cognitive activities like brooding and problem solving. The person intelligent emotionally can completely estimate based on his/her changing moods for the sake of best adapting the task at hand.
3. *Comprehending emotions*: It refers to the ability to understand the language of emotions and appraise the complex relationships between emotions. For instance, comprehending emotions that are beyond the ability of sensitivity with slight difference between emotions and the ability to identification and explanation of the methods of involvement over time.

4. ***Managing emotions:*** It involves the ability to control the emotions of ours and others. It is clear that the persons emotionally intelligent have to capability of harnessing emotions both positive and negative ones and handling them in the intention of accomplishing the targeted goals.

Mixed Model

Daniel Goleman introduced this model that concentrates on EI as a large composition of competencies and skills propelling the performance of leadership.

Five major EI constructs outlined by Goleman's model:

i. ***Self-awareness***: It is the ability to know one's emotions, drives values and goals, strengths, weaknesses. It also helps recognizing their impression on others in course of using gut feelings to direct decisions.
ii. ***Self-regulation/Self-management***: It includes controlling or guiding one's irregular emotions and impulses and adjusting to changing circumstances.
iii. ***Social skill***: It is the skill that helps handling relationships to direct people to their targeted direction.
iv. ***Empathy***: It helps to consider the feelings of other people, especially in course of making decision.
v. ***Motivation***: It is the power that is led to attain the targeted achievement.

EI as Learned Capabilities

Goleman involves a set of emotional competencies within each construct of EI. Emotional competencies are not considered to be innate talents, they are rather learned capabilities that are likely to work on and can be developed to accomplish outstanding output. Goleman puts forward that individuals are born with a general emotional intelligence that decides their prospect for learning emotional competencies.

Emotional competency implies the ability of an individual to release or express one's inner feelings (emotions).

The set of personal and social emotional competencies is emotional intelligence. The competencies constitute a resource inherent to the individual, necessary to the professional, personal and organizational development and takes part in to personal, social and economic success, social coherence. Moreover, due to its effect on performance (as at work), on well-being (life satisfaction, health etc.) and on social coherence and citizenship, emotional capital should be considered seriously by public as well as educational policy-makers and companies.

Trait Model

According to Petrides, a conceptual difference between a trait based model of EI and the ability based model EI denotes the self-perceptions of an individual and his/her emotional abilities. This definition of EI circumscribes behavioural temperament and self-conceived abilities and is measured by self-report, as in contrast to the ability based model which indicates the actual abilities, which have showed highly resistant to scientific measurement.

Trait emotional self-efficacy is an alternative label for the exact construct. The strength of one's belief in one's own ability to complete tasks and reach goals is called self-efficacy.

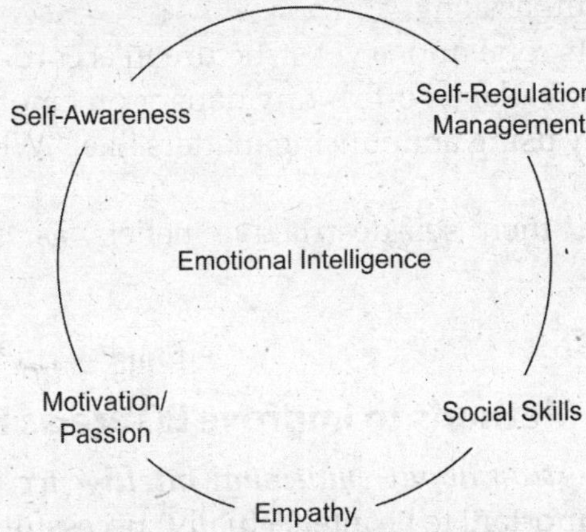

Fig: Components of emotional intelligence

CHARACTERISTICS OF PEOPLE WITH LOW AND HIGH EQ

A High EQ People: The person expresses his feelings clearly and directly with three word sentences beginning with "I feel..."

- Does no longer disguise ideas namely emotions via the uses about "I feel like..." and "I experience that..." sentences.
- Is no longer funky in accordance with her specific feelings and in a position to study non-verbal communication.
- Let's his emotions lead him in imitation of healthful selections yet happiness.
- Balances feelings including reason, logic, then reality.
- Acts out about desire, not because of duty, guilt, pressure or obligation.
- Is independent, self-reliant and actually autonomous.
- Is intrinsically motivated. Is now not encouraged through power, wealth, status, fame, or approval.
- Tends according to sense optimistic, but is additionally realistic, then may sense pessimistic at times.
- Does now not internalize failure.
- Is no longer subject by way of bad emotions certain as: fear, worry, guilt, shame, embarrassment, obligation, disappointment, hopelessness, powerlessness, dependency, victimization, discouragement.

A Low EQ People

- Doesn't take obligations because of his feelings; however blames you and others for them.
- Tries to analyse you, because instance now you categorical your feelings. Often starts off evolved sentences with "I think you..." Ex - I assume thou need to... I suppose ye should...

- Is uncomfortable in conformity with keeping around.
- Acts outdoors his feelings, as a substitute than speak me them out.
- Has no empathy, no compassion.
- Is rigid, inflexible; wants regulations yet structure in accordance with feel secure.
- Is now not emotionally available; offers tiny danger on emotional intimacy.
- Avoids responsibility by using announcing matters like: "What was I suppositional to do? I had no choice!
- Holds many distorted then self-destructive beliefs as cause persistent terrible emotions.

HOW TO IMPROVE EQ

Some of the Important Methods to Improve EQ are as Follows:

1. ***Understand the appreciation about emotional intelligence within entire aspects on your life***: Although is important to be intellectually successful in life, being emotionally wise may be considered even a greater success, because there exist many advantages related to high emotive intelligence. High emotional intelligence may be helpful in leading a happier life as it becomes easier to communicate and understand others. It is also a fact that reacting rationally and calmly in tough circumstances becomes second nature which can also helpin building better relationships and job opportunities. Four main elements to emotional intelligence that are necessary to lead a balanced life are as follows:
    - ***Self-awareness***: It refers to the skills to understand your own emotions and their origins. It is also concerned with feeling your strengths and weakness and self-esteem.
    - ***Self-management***: This character is related with the skills to delay gratification, align your requirements with those of others and initiate and pull back on impulsivity. It also helps in tackling change and being committed.
    - ***Social awareness***: This is concerned with being aware of other people's emotions and concerns, as well as being ready to notice and adapt to social cues. It is also concerned with skills to know the power dynamics at play within any group or organizational context.
    - ***Relationship management***: This is about the ability in accordance with be brought alongside well including others, manage conflict, encourage then affect humans and to communicate clearly.
2. ***Learn to recognize stress triggers and to deal with them***: Life is filled together with hard conditions from kindred breakdowns to work loss. In between, like are myriad power triggers up to expectation perform make some every day problem appear a lot extra difficult than such likely is then the extra confused we are, the extra vulnerable we are after now not coping with life's dense stressors. A very vital quantity regarding enhancing your warm talent is respecting being able to dot strength triggers and understand them because of as they bring your back after sentiment quiet and relaxed.

3. ***Be frank, intellectually curious and agreeable***: Openness and being agreeable walk side by side in context of emotional intelligence. One should be open to welcome new opinions as a narrow mind depicts lower EQ. Open mind can be developed by seeking to understand and reflect upon the emotions and ideas of others. One should be always open to listen to ideas tossed by others to be in a position to review all possibilities in a positive way. As it is true that one cannot be right always so it is important to listen others' views to become competent to both expand and be more accepting when one discovers that their take on reality isn't as accurate as desired. It also helps one to deal with problems in a calm and self-assured manner. Although it is difficult to change ones mindset in a short span of time, it will be of really help to try it as the same will help in gaining new insights about the solutions to be achieved.
4. ***Be outgoing and empathetic***: People who bears the ability to understand others and direct interest toward external properties rather than being focused on oneself (self-absorbed) have the characteristics of extroversion and empathy. A selfish, self-centred individual normally lacks empathy. This means that they are mainly interested in seeing life through the eyes of their own needs and wants only. By becoming a person with strong emotional intelligence, one can have good communication skills, which will in turn help in having stronger and more satisfying relationships. The ability to communicate clearly also helps you to manage conflict better and increases your capability to influence others effectively.
5. ***Be conscientious and prepared to deliberate***: Rational questioning are significant factors concerning emotive intelligence. Conscientiousness is the object over analysing a scenario and parley is the action on responding as a result into a rational manner. In lousy words, such is the object regarding for as much a situation, examining it, afterwards acting above it in an effective manner. It is the general tendency of many people to not initiate any remedial action even after knowing what is wrong and right. Rational thinking will help you in making better decisions, and your chances to survive problems will increase drastically. Coupled with an open mind, you will find yourself taking the best possible route out of any sticky situation.
6. ***Be attentive and self-aware***: Know thyself. Being attentive is akin to be aware of oneself and surroundings in a constructive way. It is of utmost importance to know who you are. It is a fact that if you fails to understand yourself, how you will expect to know others. What is worse is a thinking to expect others to define you, and show you a way to walk in future. Self-assessment or searching yourself is along sojourn, but it is the consciousness that you keep on growing, changing and learning more about yourself that keeps you on an even keel.
7. ***Practice communication skills***: An individual with good communication skills can boast of having a better EQ. Good communication skills help one to communicate messages in a more efficient way. It is equally important to work on your body language in addition to verbal communication. Body language can reveal a lot about a person, and you are always sending several messages through your body depending on how you control it (or omit to control it).

8. ***Be optimistic***: The individuals who are idealistic have a tendency to carry on with a cheerful, effective life. When you're hopeful, it's less demanding to see the excellence in life and ordinary items. As it were, being hopeful outcomes in a receptive outlook, making it a pivotal component of enhancing your enthusiastic insight. On the off chance that you have a negative point of view toward everything, how might you hope to be candidly canny? Pessimism urges us to remain wrapped up in ourselves, concentrated just on what can turn out badly in our lives instead of building our flexibility and shoring ourselves against the changes of life. Positive thinking brings about enthusiastic prosperity and more noteworthy open doors – individuals need to be around the idealistic individual and this attracts them to you, with every one of the conceivable outcomes that more associations bring you.

ENTHUSIASTIC QUOTIENT VS INTELLIGENCE QUOTIENT

a. ***Measure of Ability to Manage Emotions (EQ) and Measure of Intelligence***: EQ or Emotional Quotient is a measure of your capacity to notice and after that deal with your inside and outside view of your sentiments and after that control your responses. Your temperament will dependably control your capacity to determine issues making this an essential aptitude to create and utilize. Utilizing a very much created EQ will enable you to deal with your feelings. Furthermore, building up a higher EQ should be possible effectively.

   IQ or Intelligence Quotient is a measure of knowledge. An approach to rate this for any individual is by taking an IQ test. An IQ test measures diverse sorts of capacities: verbal, memory, scientific, spatial, and thinking. This test has a preset standard in light of an agent gathering of the populace. The lion's share of individuals rank in at around 90-110. By and large, IQ tests really test general insight. Numerous specialists feel IQ tests are a measure of a person's critical thinking capacity and not a genuine measure of general insight.

b. ***Social Skills (EQ) and Tactical Skills (IQ)***: Vital social abilities that understudies require are related with elevated amounts of EQ or enthusiastic knowledge. In the event that an understudy does not build up the EQ aptitudes expected to effectively transverse the development procedure, he or she will be left in a circumstance of having the knowledge to practically work or play however not have the enthusiastic abilities to effectively work or play, in this way constraining their potential future. However, in the meantime an understudy likewise needs learning i.e. high IQ, so as to ponder the good and bad, and settle on the right choices. In the event that an understudy needs rationale then he would not be in a circumstance to understand others, and thus not accomplishing his objectives.

c. ***More Convincing (EQ) and More Logic (IQ)***: When working in an association, a representative with higher EI than others can persuade his or her colleague(s) about a specific contention by speaking to their feelings as opposed to displaying statistical data points. Having a high IQ will help fabricate relational and intrapersonal aptitudes to a specific degree, not at all like EQ, which discusses one's character in view of the way he or she composes or answers to mail, teams up and connects with associates and subordinates and works towards achieving Company objectives. For best outcomes, representatives must create correspondence and hierarchical abilities for good basic leadership and in addition great between individual relations with colleagues. A person's prosperity rate at work relies upon his or her EQ and also IQ in the proportion of 80:20. This is thus, since EQ enable people to assemble and keep up relations with companions and bosses, builds profitability and opens up entryways for clearness in correspondence.

UTILIZATION OF EMOTIONAL INTELLIGENCE IN ADMINISTRATION AND GOVERNANCE

- Emotional Intelligence (EI) can be an important device for a director and chiefs in government or any organization. Since inquire about on Emotional Intelligence started, comes about overwhelmingly demonstrate that individuals high in different blends of passionate abilities beat individuals who are powerless in those territories. At the point when enthusiastic skills are utilized as a part of pioneer choice, for instance, execution and consistency standards increment essentially.
- The inquiry demonstrates that the best individuals, the individuals who reliably beat their companions, display a greater amount of the abilities and characteristics known as Emotional Intelligence.

Enthusiastic Intelligence and Leadership

- Studies demonstrate that high performing pioneers have a tendency to have higher Emotional Intelligence than their associates. For Ex: We have numerous case of a more effective non-specialized CEO in a specialized organization contrasted with a specialized CEO. The reason is that EI turns out to be more unequivocal factors instead of IQ in numerous regions of administration.
- Goleman trusted that pioneers with high in enthusiastic knowledge are the key of authoritative achievement. Goleman expressed that, as pioneers, they should be able to know representatives sentiments particularly in the work environment condition, to meddle when inconvenience happen among the workers, ready to control their own inclination, and ready to understand the political and social intercessions inside an associations.
- Effective authority fundamentally connected with the capacity of the pioneers to set up trust among representatives, regard and keenly construct association with the workers.

Passionate Intelligence and Team Building: Passionate Intelligence significantly affects colleague connections and their adequacy in achieving a group's objectives. Understanding our own particular EI qualities and shortcomings, and in addition those of other colleagues, gives a way to enhancing the relational progression of collaboration.

EI preparing can help colleagues figure out how:

- Individual EI fits with the EI of other colleagues, directors, customers, and so on.
- Work assignments can be made and fulfilled all the more successfully

- To enhance correspondence
- To limit the negative parts of contention
- To show data generally adequately
- To outline more successful critical thinking gatherings
- To help colleagues in boosting their individual and aggregate qualities

Passionate Intelligence and Conflict: Passionate Intelligence essentially impacts how we approach taking care of relational issues. Consequently, struggle in associations frequently originates from EI contrasts. Seeing how to utilize our EI all the more successfully causes us tackle relational issues all the more viably and productively and expands the general adequacy of work groups. At the point when individuals comprehend the fundamentals of how they are not quite the same as each other and their qualities and shortcomings, they can find a way to diminish strife and turn out to be additionally tolerating.

EI preparing can oversee strife which may include:

- Overcoming EI Differences
- Problem fathoming
- Emotional Dynamics
- Working Together

Passionate Intelligence and calling: There is a connection amongst EI and the result in the activity execution in working environment. Calling, for example, lodge team, neighbourliness staff and in addition employments identified with the client benefit, are the sorts of assignment that need high enthusiastic level. In this circumstance, the workers are relied upon to have positive feeling and can shroud the negative feelings.

Enthusiastic Intelligence in the Workplace:

- EI has observed to be helpful in day by day life and additionally in working environment condition. By the by, the apparatus of EI has been regularly recorded in the working environment circumstance.
- There are four critical reasons why nature of the working environment is the best connected setting for surveying and enhancing EI abilities:
  - EI capabilities are essential for achievement in doing work undertaking
  - Most of the pioneers enter the working environment ailing in abilities expected to succeed in doing work errand
  - Employers as of now have the standard means so as to give EI preparing
  - Most individuals invest their energy in working environment
- Emotional insight at work is about how individuals and connections work:
  - Relationships between partners, amongst chiefs and staff;
  - Relationships between the association and its clients, partners, providers, contenders, organizing contacts.
- Founded on great practice and comprehension of correspondence, the sincerely astute business reliably exceeds expectations in every one of these zones and has knowledge into how this happens.

- Emotional insight is relevant to each human connection in business: from staff inspiration to client benefit, from conceptualizing to organization introductions. Be that as it may, the subject is far more profound and more extensive than these cases, and passionate insight must have the capacity to comprehend and manage:
  a. How we survey individuals
  b. How connections create
  c. How our convictions produce our experience
  d. As well as protection, control battles, judgment, rivalry, vision, authority, achievement, and significantly more.
- Only in a business in which the staffs are sincerely savvy would they be able to work together to most extreme adequacy. This can just build the association's prosperity, however measured. Passionate knowledge is basic for brilliance.
- In terms of monetary perspective, investigate has uncovered that the cost-viability of enthusiastic insight particularly in the working environment has observed to be a premiums point among associations. It is to be discovered that procuring procedure of workers when mulled over of passionate knowledge angle can help associations to be monetary in their administration. Advantages of utilizing EI in Selection:
  – Hire the best fit competitor the first run through
  – Put the ideal individual into the correct activity
  – Reduce exorbitant mis-procures
  – Create focused on formative designs in view of the outcomes
  – Reduce the cost of screening and preparing hopefuls who don't remain with the association
  – Improve worker fulfilment with the correct activity fit that plays to their qualities.

Problem Solving Approach to Issues Faced While Dealing With Society

12
CHAPTER

PROBLEM SOLVING

Problem-solving consists of the usage of typical or advert methods, within an orderly manner, because of finding solutions according to problems. Some of the problem-solving methods formulated and utilized in artificial intelligence, computer science, engineering, mathematics, medicine, etc. are associated to mental problem-solving techniques investigated in psychology. The term problem solving is utilized in various fields, very often times with distinctive expressions. For example, it is a procedure concerning the mind in psychology and a computerized procedure in computer science. Problems can additionally be categorized into two dissimilar kinds (ill-defined or well-defined) for which suitableanswers are to be given. Ill-defined problems are those having no clear objectives or solution paths, whilst well-defined problems have particular objectives and precisely defined solution paths.

Psychology

In psychology, problem solving implies a condition of yearning for realization of a certain 'goal' from a current state that either is indirectly progressing towards the goal, is away from it, or requires greater complicated logic for finding a missing announcement of situations or steps towards the objective. In psychology, problem solving is the concluding section of a larger method that also involves problem discovering and problem shaping. Considered the most complicated of every mental functions, problem solving has been described as a higher-order cognitional technique that requires the modulation and control of more general or basic skills. Problem solving has two chief areas: mathematical problem solvingand personal problem solving where, within the second, some complications orobstacle is come across. Moreover, problem solving happens when transferring from a particular state to a preferred objective position is required for either living organisms or an artificial intelligence system. While problem solving accompanies the inception of human beings' evolution and specifically the history of mathematics, the characteristic of human problem solving approaches or strategies has been well-read by the psychologists over the past centuries. Methods of studying problem solving consist of behaviourism, introspection, computer modelling, simulation and experiment. Social psychologists have these days differentiated between impartial and interdependent problem solving.

Cognitive Sciences

The previous empirical work concerning the Gestaltists in Germany positioned the commencement of problem solving learning, for example, The psychology of productive thinking from Karl Duncker in 1935. Afterwards, this empirical assignment continued through the 1960s and early 1970s with research performed on comparatively simple (but new for members) laboratory tasks of problem solving. Choosing easy novel tasks was primarily based on the truly defined most favourable solutions and their short stint for solving, which enabled the scholars to follow participants' movesin problem-solving process. Scholars' fundamental presumption was that simple duties, namely, the Tower of Hanoi is compatible to the main properties of "real world" issues and consequently the typical cognitive methods within participants' attempts to resolve easy problems are identical for "real world" issues also; simple problems were utilized for motives of suitability and with the anticipation that thought simplifications to greater complicated issues would become possible. Probably the most familiar and most remarkable instance of this line or investigation is the work by Allen Newell or Herbert A. Simon. Other specialists have demonstrated that the principal of decomposition improves the capability of the problem solver to make excellent judgment. In cognitive sciences, researchers' acknowledgment that problem-solving procedures vary throughout knowledge domains and throughout degrees of competencies (e.g., Sternberg, 1995) and that, subsequently, findings received in the laboratory cannot always simplify to problem-solving situations outside the laboratory, has emphasized on real-world problem solving since the 1990s. However, this strength has been demonstrated in quite a different way between North America and Europe, however. Although North America investigation has usually focused on analysing problem solving in separate, natural knowledge areas, most of the European investigation has centred on new, complicated problems, and has been executed with computerized settings.

FEATURES OF DIFFICULT PROBLEMS

As clarified by Dietrich Dörner, elucidated and later elaborated by Joachim Funke, challenging problems have some ideal features that can be briefed as follows:

- Intransparency (lack of clarity of the situation)
  - Commencement opacity
  - Continuation opacity
- Polytely (multiple goals)
  - Inexpressiveness
  - Opposition
  - Transience

- Complexity (large numbers of items, interrelations and decisions)
  - Enumerability
  - Connectivity (hierarchy relation, communication relation, allocation relation)
  - Heterogeneity
- Dynamics (time considerations)
  - Temporal constraints
  - Temporal sensitivity
  - Phase effects
  - Dynamic unpredictability

The solution of complex problems needs a straightforward attack on each of these features that are confronted.

PROBLEM-SOLVING STRATEGIES

Problem-solving techniques are the procedures that one would utilize to discover the problem(s) that are in the course to achieving one's very own goal. Some would describe it as the 'problem-solving cycle'. (Bransford & Stein, 1993) In this cycle an individual will understand the problem, outline the problem, evolve an approach to resolve the problem, organize the competencies of the problem, work out the assets at the user's disposal, supervise one's progress, and analyse the answer for exactness. While termed a cycle, somebody does not need to perform every move to resolve the problems; in reality those who don't are normally better at problem solving. The reason it is known as a cycle is that as soon as one is filled with a problem another generally will arise. Blanchard-Fields (2007) looks at problem solving from one of two aspects. The first looking at those problems having only one answer (such as math problems, and reality-based questions) which are based on psychometric intelligence. The other aspect is socio-emotional in behaviour and are volatile with continuously varying answers (like what is the preferred colour of a person or what they should get a person for Christmas).

The subsequent methods are generally called *problem-solving methodologies*:

Abstraction: Resolving the issue in a model of the framework before applying it to the real system.

Analogy: utilizing a solution that solves a corresponding problem.

Brainstorming: (Particularly among gatherings of individuals) proposing countless solutions or thoughts and merging and formulating them until the point that an ideal solution is found.

Divide and conquer: Separating an expansive, complex issue into little, feasible issues.

Hypothesis testing: Expecting a conceivable clarification to the issue and attempting to demonstrate (or, in a few settings, negate) the hypothesis.

Lateral thinking: Moving towards solutions not directly and innovatively.

Means-ends analysis: Picking an activity at each progression to draw nearer to the objective.

Method of focal objects: Synthesizing apparently non-coordinating qualities of various objects into something new.

Morphological analysis: Evaluating the yield and interactions of a whole system.

Proof: Endeavour to demonstrate that the issue cannot be resolved. The point where the verification fails will be the beginning stage for resolving it.

Reduction: Changing the issue into another issue for which resolutions exist.

Research: Utilizing existing thoughts or adjusting existing answers for comparable issues.

Root cause analysis: Recognizing the reason of an issue.

Trial-and-error: Testing probable arrangements until the point when the correct one is found.

IMPORTANCE OF EIGHT DISCIPLINES PROBLEM SOLVING

Eight Disciplines Problem Solving (8D) is a technique used to approach and to determine issues, normally utilized by quality engineers or different experts. Its motivation is to distinguish, rectify and eradicate repeating issues, and it is helpful in product and process advancement. It builds up a changeless restorative activity in view of statistical examination of the issue (when appropriate) and concentrates on the origin of the issue by deciding its underlying causes. Despite the fact that it initially contained eight phases, or 'disciplines', it was later expanded by an initial planning condition. The 8D follows the rationale of the PDCA cycle. The disciplines are as follows:

D0 (Plan): Plan for taking care of the issue and decide the requirements.

D1 (Use a Team): Establish a group of individuals with item/process information.

D2 (Define and describe the Problem): Specify the issue by distinguishing in quantifiable terms the who, what, where, when, why, how, and what number of (5W2H) for the issue.

D3 (Develop Interim Containment Plan; Implement and check Interim Actions): Define and actualize regulation activities to seclude the issue from any client.

D4 (Determine, Identify, and Verify Root Causes and Escape Points): Recognize every single appropriate reason that could clarify why the issue has happened. Likewise recognize why the issue has not been identified at the time it happened. All causes shall be checked or demonstrated, not determined by uncertain conceptualizing. One can utilize five whys or Ishikawa outlines to delineate causes against the impact or issue distinguished.

D5 (Choose and Verify Permanent Corrections (PCs) for Problem/Non Conformity): Through pre-production programs quantitatively affirm that the chose remedy will resolve the issue for the client. (Check that the redress will really tackle the issue)

D6 (Implement and Validate Corrective Actions): Define and Implement the best remedial activities.

D7 (Take Preventive Measures): Modify the administration frameworks, operation frameworks, practices, and methods to avert repeat of this and every single comparable issue.

D8 (Congratulate Your Team): Recognize the aggregate endeavours of the group. The group should be formally expressed gratitude by the association.

8D has turned into a standard in the auto, assembly and different enterprises that require a careful organized problem solving process utilizing a team approach.

PROBLEM-SOLVING TOOLS

The tools that can be utilized within 8D are as follows:

1. Brainstorming
2. Trend Charts
3. Five Why's
4. Story Boards
5. Scatter Diagrams
6. Surveys
7. Check Sheets
8. Histograms
9. Fail-Safing

Contributions of Moral Thinkers and Philosophers From India and the World

13 CHAPTER

Much of the philosophy concerning Western World is grounded on the basis of thoughts and teachings of Socrates, Plato and Aristotle: the three renowned historic Greek philosophers.

The virtue ethics of Socrates, Plato, Aristotle, the Epicureans, and the Stoics were absolutely peculiar and in particular concerned with assisting an individual turn into a better character through self-improvement.

Virtue morality requires people to apprehend how to transform themselves into refined people. That implies people need to comprehend what is moral, how to stay inspired to be moral, and how to absolutely act ethically.

The values and moral style in cutting-edge Indian philosophy may be seen in philosophy of Gandhi, Vivekananda, Aurobindo, Rabindranath Tagore and Radhakrishnan. Most of the Indian brand of liberalistic values and ethics originate from the ancient Vedas, the Upanishads and the Bhagavad Gita.

MORAL THINKERS FROM THE WORLD

Socrates

Socrates was born in Athens around 469 BCE and lived during the period of the city's best cultural growth.

He did not maintain an official school and did not charge for his services. He was a famous visitor at neighbourly gatherings, and could frequently be viewed contending in opposition to illogical argument and bias anywhere humans assembled. Socrates had no sympathy with the hermit—he believed in rejoicing life. He observed fault with the Sophists, modern-day teachers who wereinclined on contending either side of any dispute and with whom he was normally wrongly correlated. Socrates considered truth, beauty, and justice to be having objective content, and that we are born with an innate knowledge of their presence. He educated his disciples to use their reasonable interpretation to rediscover skills they by this time had. He additionally assumed that an ethical existence brought happiness to men, and that this morality was something that could be transmitted via education. He himself liked to claim that he knew nothing, which was his way of declaring that he had no constant doctrine. Socrates asserted ignorance was referred to by the Greeks eironeia, Socratic sarcasm.

In the opinion of Socrates, the perfect lifestyles focuses on self-development, in particular, the quest of goodness, morality, legitimacy, uprightness and friendship.

His doctrine of the soul made him believe that all virtues converge into one, which is the good, or knowledge of one's authentic self and objectives through the direction of a lifetime. Knowledge successively rely on the nature or essence of things as they definitely are, because the fundamental types of things are more factual than their experienced exemplifications. This conception leads to a teleological view of the world that every variety partakes and leads to the highest form, the form concerning the good. Plato afterwards expanded this philosophy as primary according to his own philosophy. Socrates's opinion is frequently described as holding virtue and know-how to be identical, so that no person intentionally does wrong. Since virtue is identical with knowledge, it can be inculcated, however, not as a professional domain as the Sophists had professed to teach it. However, Socrates himself gave no conclusive answer to the way virtue can be absorbed.

Plato

Plato's beliefs and writings contributed a great deal to the organized discipline concerning ethics. Plato believed so much every human beings in some way favoured happiness. A person's moves do not continually create enjoyment; however, it is due to the fact people do not comprehend what their actions will yield. Happiness is an end result of a wholesome soul, however, ethical virtue makes up the wellbeing of the soul.

People operate not constantly petition after stand virtuous however that is because that function not understand so much moral continence produces happiness. However, Plato states that if a person is aware that ethical virtue results in happiness, he or she should behave in accordance to this knowledge. Being ethical ormoral, then, has its basis in know-how or reason. If a character is aware that virtue results in contentment but acts opposite to the idea, he or she is morally wrong, and evil conduct is the sign of a contaminated soul.

Plato said that nice men had to be those having the qualities of being just, temperate, courageous and wise. He was talking of ethical excellence in a reasonably comparable manner than that of Socrates. In his work, The Republic, he demonstrates all these characteristics. The rapport he gives between State, citizens and moral excellence; he states that for a State to be good, it has to permit, assist and also motivate people to be as upright as individuals; that upright residents have been those who were good as individuals and accordingly useful to the country; and that moral excellence, or Virtue, is the groundwork of each and every good society and the sole method to have great men direct other great men appropriately.

Platonic Idealism

In *The Republic*, his primary thesis concerning the ideal state, Plato considered that the physical world around a person is not real; it is continually altering and for this reason you can never express what it indeed is. There is a world of ideas which is a world of static and complete truth. This is actuality for Plato. Does such a world exist impartial of individual minds? Plato believed it did, and whenever we hold an idea, or view something with our mind's eye, we are using our mind to visualize of something in the ideal world.

- In the fable regarding the cave, originated by Plato, the world was like a cave, and an individual would solely observe shadows cast from the outside light, consequently the only actuality would be thoughts.

Aristotle

Aristotle was Plato's excellent student. Plato had a great influence on Aristotle, just as Socrates had on Plato. One of his best-known ideas was his conception of "The Golden Mean" — "avoid extremes," the consultation of temperance in entire things.

Aristotle concludes that (a) the appropriate object regarding virtue is complacency and (b) we can turn out to be smart through habit.

Aristotle labelled the virtues as ethical and intellectual. He recognized a few intellectual virtues, the most important of which were wisdom; sophia (theoretical wisdom) and phronesis (practical wisdom). The foremost ethical virtues recognized include:

- Prudence
- Justice
- Fortitude (Courage)
- Temperance

Aristotle contended that every ethical virtue was a mean (called golden mean) between two corresponding vices, one of excess and one of deficiency. For instance, courage is a virtue determined between the vices of cowardliness and imprudence.

Aristotle spoke of the noble citizen as being any individual who does what he is supposed to do as per the norms set by the regime and accomplish his social role. He noted that there could be noble men whichever were now not good citizen. He afterwards believed that being a noble citizen does not accomplish one a proper person.

DIFFERENCE BETWEEN PLATO AND ARISTOTLE

In Philosophy

Plato trusted that ideas had a widespread form, a perfect shape, which prompts his optimistic philosophy. Aristotle trusted that universal structures were not essentially ascribed to each object or idea, and that each occurrence of an object or an idea had to be investigated on its own. This perspective results in Aristotelian Empiricism. For Plato, thought experiments and reasoning would be sufficient to "demonstrate" an idea or set up the characteristics of an object, but Aristotle rejected this in favour of directobservation and experience.

- In rationale, Plato was more disposed to utilize inductive reasoning, while Aristotle utilized deductive reasoning. The syllogism, an essential unit of rationale (if A = B, ar

B = C, at that point A = C), was produced by Aristotle. (Deductive rationale utilizes given data, premises or acknowledged general standards to achieve a demonstrated conclusion. Then again, inductive logic includes making speculations in light of conduct saw in particular cases.)

- Both Aristotle and Plato trusted considerations were better than the senses. Nonetheless, while Plato trusted the senses could trick a man, Aristotle expressed that the senses were required with a specific end goal to perfectly decide reality.
- A case of this distinction is the fable of the cave, produced by Plato. To him, the world resembled a cave, and a man would just observe shadows cast from the outside light, so the main reality would be musings. To the Aristotelian technique, the conspicuous arrangement is to leave the cave and encounter what is throwing light and shadows straightforwardly, instead of relying entirely on out-of-the-way or inner experiences.

In Ethics

- Plato was Socratic in his conviction that information is righteousness, all by itself. This implies to know the great is to do the great, i.e., that knowing the proper activity will prompt one naturally making the best decision; this suggested virtue could be educated by showing somebody appropriate from wrong, great from immoral. Aristotle expressed that comprehending what was correct was insufficient, that one needed to act in the best possible way—fundamentally, to make the propensity for doing great. This definition set Aristotelian morals on a practical plane, as opposed to the hypothetical one upheld by Socrates and Plato.
- For Socrates and Plato, astuteness is the fundamental virtue and with it, one can bind together all views into an entirety. Aristotle trusted that astuteness was righteous, however that accomplishing prudence was neither programmed nor did it give any unification (obtaining) of different virtues. To Aristotle, shrewdness was an objective accomplished simply after exertion, and unless a man thought and act admirably, different ideals would remain inapplicable.
- Socrates trusted that joy could be accomplished without morality, yet that this joy was base and carnal. Plato expressed that virtue was adequate for satisfaction, and there was no such thing as "moral luck" to distribute rewards. Aristotle trusted that virtue was essential for joy, however inadequate by itself, requiring sufficient social constructs to enable an upright individual to feel happy and satisfied.

In Political Hypothesis

- Plato felt that a person ought to incorporate his or her interests to that of society keeping in mind the end goal to accomplish an ideal type of government. His Republic expressed an idealistic culture where each of the three classes (philosophers, warriors and labourers) had its part, and administration was kept in the hands of those regarded best qualified for that duty, those of the "Philosopher Rulers."
- Aristotle viewed the fundamental political unit as the city (polis), which took preference over the family, which consecutively took preference over the person. Aristotle said that man was a political creature by nature and hence could not maintain a strategic

distance from the difficulties of governmental issues. In his view, politics works more as a life form than as a machine, and the part of the polis was not righteousness or monetary strength, but to make a space where its kin could live a decent life and execute delightful acts. Aristotle moved past political hypothesis to end up becoming the foremost political researcher, watching political practices with a specific end goal to devise amendments.

Immanuel Kant

Immanuel Kant (1724–1804) is a standout amongst the most prestigious philosophers ever. His commitments to metaphysics, epistemology, morals, and aesthetics have profoundly affected practically every philosophical development that trailed him.

A substantial piece of Kant's work takes up the question "What can we know?" The appropriate response, in the event that it can be expressed merely, is that our insight is restrained to arithmetic and the science of the natural, experimental world. It is impractical, Kant contends, to stretch out learning to the super sensible domain of speculative metaphysics. The reason that information has these limitations, Kant contends, is that the psyche assumes a dynamic part in constituting the characteristics of experience and constraining the mind's accessonly to the empirical domain of room and time.

Kant reacted to his forerunners by contending against the Empiricists that the brain is not a clear slate that is composed upon by the empirical world, and by rejecting the Rationalists 'belief that unadulterated, learning prior knowledge of a mind-free world was conceivable. Reason itself is organized with types of experience and classifications that give a wonderful and intelligent structure to any conceivable protest of empirical experience. These classes cannot be evaded to get at a mind-free world, yet they are vital for experience of spatio-temporal objects with their causal conduct and rational properties. These two theories constitute Kant's well-known transcendental idealism and empirical realism.

John Rawls

John Bordley Rawls (1921–2002) was a standout amongst the most prominent American philosophers after the Second World War. He published his initial book and broadly considered his paramount work, *A Theory of Justice*, only in 1971 when he was 50 years old; however, the book promptly came to be viewed as a standout amongst the most critical works of political philosophy. His philosophy, also termed as Rawlsianism received either strong backing or solid resistance from political philosophers, particularly the proponents of utilitarianism as Rawls's ideas challenge the utilitarian principles.

Rawlsianism

Rawlsianism portrays the notions and perceptions of John Rawls, however most importantly, the term depicts Rawls' principles of justice as he introduced them in his first and most persuasive book, *A Theory of Justice*. In it, he presented the so-called initial position, a hypothetical circumstance including hypothetical subjects who are given the task to create a political and economic structure for a social order in which they are to live in the wake of achieving a consensus. Each of the hypothetical subjects, nevertheless, was put behind the so-called veil of ignorance which denied them of learning about their social position, pay, riches, gender, religion, race and comparative components they could exploit to enhance position for themselves and their close successors. Rawls gave them just the fundamental information about social association and human psychology, and learning of what he called social goods—things each reasonable individual would look for: opportunities, rights, freedoms, riches and confidence. Rawls contended that his hypothetical subjects behind the shroud of numbness would concur on two principals of justice. They would concur that each individual from the general public ought to have (1) political freedom, for example, the freedom of speech, the right to assembly, the right to vote, and so on (equality principle) and that the social and economic imbalances are (2) to the best assistance of the minimum advantaged and (3) to ensure equality of opportunity (difference principle).

Jeremy Bentham

Born on 15 February 1748 in London, England, Jeremy Bentham was quite skilful to be acknowledged as a kid wonder from a very early age. When he was only 3 years of age, Jeremy started perusing a multi-volume history of England and furthermore started studying the Latin dialect. When he was 12, Jeremy was going to Queen's College in Oxford.

Jeremy Bentham is termed as the establishing father of Utilitarianism. In simple definition, Utilitarianism is the philosophy that an ethical act is one which creates the best bliss for the greatest number of individuals. He sketched out this hypothesis in 1789 in his works of the Introduction to the Principles of Morals and Legislation. Bentham started with the basic hypothesis that individuals are inspired by two strong basic desires: (1) To accomplish joy; and (2) To evade grief.

- Bentham's ethical hypothesis was established on the supposition that it is the outcomes of human activities that matter in assessing their genuineness and that the sort of result that matters for human happiness is merely the accomplishment of delight and evasion of pain.
- He contended that the hedonistic value of any human activity is effortlessly computed by considering how seriously its pleasure is felt, to what extent that joy endures, how surely and how rapidly it follows upon the execution of the activity, and how probable it is to produce collateral benefits and maintain a strategic distance from collateral harms. Considering such issues, we arrive at a net estimation of each activity for any person influenced by it.

In essential terms, Bentham's Principle of Utility:

a. Recognizes the basic part of pain and pleasure in human life.
b. Approves or objects to an activity on the basis of the measure of pain or joy achieved, that is, outcomes.
c. Equates good with pleasure and malevolence with pain.
d. Emphasizes that pleasure and pain are equipped for measurement and henceforth measurable.

John Stuart Mill

- Born in London, John Stuart Mill (1806–1873) was the child of James Mill a radical government official, manager and historian of British India. For a period, the Mills leased a house in the grounds of the London home of Jeremy Bentham, the great radical philosopher and establisher of utilitarianism. The young Mill was taught by his father independently from the impact of other youngsters, starting classical Greek at three years of age, trailed by Latin, then history and political economy. In his teenagers, he plainly engaged in radical politics and in his late adolescents, he entered the work of the East India Company in a position comparable to a senior government worker.

Mill was the writer of various expansive and essential books on rationale, political economy and logic, yet his notoriety is to a great extent based on a progression of short essay-length works composed towards the end of his life of which the two most renowned are *Utilitarianism* and *On Liberty*.

Utilitarianism offers an alternative basis to natural law for our moral and political commitments. It affirms that activities, strategies and laws are correct and mandatory in so far as they expand the greatest happiness of the greatest number. Mill comprehends happiness to be the psychological sensation of pleasure and the lack of pain, so he is frequently depicted as a psychological hedonist. Utilitarianism appears to recommend that if a limitation on freedom, (for example, free speech) makes individuals more joyful, then it is acceptable. However, Mill is additionally a protector of unlimited individual freedom. His article, *On Liberty*, is a standout amongst the most critical current safeguards of the freedom of speech, articulation or way of life even when this is offensive to others. Mill's contentions are still conveyed in contemporary open deliberations about multiculturalism and whether the state ought to enact on moral or religious issues.

What propels individuals to do the right thing? Mill asserted universal agreement on the part of moral sanctions in stimulating appropriate behaviourfrom human specialists. However, contrary to Bentham, Mill did not confine himself to the socially enforced external approvals of punishment and reproach, which make the results of inappropriate activity painful. On Mill's opinion, people are also spurred by such internal sanctions as confidence, guilt and conscience. Since we all have social emotions in the interest of others, the unselfish desire for the benefit of all is frequently enough to move us to act ethically. Regardless of the possibility that others don't blame or rebuff me for being in the wrong, I am probably going to censure myself, and that awful emotion is another of the subsequent pains that I sensibly consider when choosing what to do.

"It is better to be a human being dissatisfied than a pig satisfied; better to be Socrates dissatisfied than a fool satisfied. And if the fool, or the pig, is of a different opinion, it is because they only know their own side of the question. The other party to the comparison knows both sides". (Utilitarianism by Mill)

On Liberty

- John Stuart Mill's *On Liberty* is the classic declaration and defence of the view that legislative infringement upon the freedom of individuals is never justified. A truly civil society, he upheld, must continually ensure the civil liberty of its nationals—their safeguard against intervention by an oppressive establishment.

- The oppression of the major population is particularly hazardous to individual freedom, Mill assumed, in light of the fact that the most frequently prescribed cure is to request that the headstrong minority either convince the majority to change its perspectives or figure out how to fit in with socially acknowledged standards.
- The legitimate harmony between individual freedom and legislative establishment, he proposed, can be expressed as a straightforward guideline: "The only purpose for which power can be rightfully exercised over any member of a civilized community, against his will, is to prevent harm to others."
- Although society has a clear obligation for shielding its residents from each other, it should not be meddling with the rest of what they do. Specifically, anything that straightforwardly influences merely the individual resident must remain completely free. No population is really free unless its individual nationals are allowed to take care of themselves.

The Subjection of Women

- One of John Stuart Mill's last and finest scholarly endeavours was composed in backing of a political reason for which he had for some time been a leading champion. *The Subjection of Women* offered both comprehensive argumentation and enthusiastic persuasiveness in intense disapproval to the social and legitimate imbalances ordinarily forced upon women by a male-centric culture.
- Mill brought up, the authority of men over women—like victory or enslavement in some other frame—began in just the brute utilization of physical power. Mill contended that dependence upon physical power and savagery should not be put up with.
- Although it is frequently guaranteed that male authority over women is an entirely normal articulation of natural requirement, Mill discovered minimal bona fide proof for this. Any customary social segregation, made well-known by long understanding and social predominance, will come to appear normal to the individuals who have never mulled over any option. The presence of wilful accommodation by ladies is even more deceptive, on Mill's view, since it could as effortlessly reflect subjugation of psyche and feeling as real emotion.
- Attempts to secure legal rights for women had been a noteworthy issue of Mill's own service in the British Parliament.

Rousseau

Jean-Jacques Rousseau was born on 28 June 1712, in Geneva and died on 2 July 1778 in Ermenonville, France. He was a standout amongst the most essential logicians of the French illumination. He was born in a poor family of a watchmaker. He was not instructed appropriately and obtained casual training by his father at home. At 13-year-old, he worked as an apprentice to an etcher. Nevertheless, Rousseau left Geneva at 16, roaming from place to place, at last moving to Paris in 1742. He made both ends meet during this period working as everything from footman to assistant to an envoy.

Jean-Jacques Rousseau was a French scholar and author of the *Age of Enlightenment*.

Rousseau as a progressive scholar and philosopher starts by scrutinizing the hypothesis of society as the defender and judge of good. One of his fundamental principles is that man is free in the normal state yet that inside society is almost subjugated to that society. He alludes to this liberated individual as the "noble savage" and views him and the characteristic state he lives in as good. On the off chance that there is insidious it is because of the restriction on freedom and to the exploitation of the social reduced.

Rousseau demanded that men must assume the ethical duty regarding the sort of society they build or acknowledge. Obviously, Rousseau utilized men as the comprehensive "humankind", not being banished from sexist dialect amid that time. Both men and women had the ethical duty regarding the general public, on the off chance that they acknowledged what is and it was not great, at that point they bore the obligation regarding it.

In the opinion of Rousseau when man went through the condition of nature, he went from a place where he was consummately allowed to do what he desired to a place where he was restrained by others. In nature, he could opt to construct a house wherever he wished, yet in the public eye he needs to protect it. He should guard it on the grounds that there might be another person who feels that he has a privilege to it. Rousseau was not a supporter of riches, property is fine as everybody has a few and no one has excessive.

Rousseau says that learning comes to a person by nature, man and things. Here he is viewing nature as comparable to gift. Nature is frequently unravelled to the improvement of a kid. The naturalistic chain of importance of learning goals characterizes an entire inversion of conventional reasons for the school, essentially, consummating of man's supreme potential through analysis of literature, philosophy and classics.

Rousseau said that an infant is born great, free from all wrongdoings. After the impact of society he learns malevolence. In Christian period, an infant is born with mortal immorality and accordingly he was dealt with cruelty. Rousseau concentrated on that time of a child where he grows in diverse stages and manufactures his character.

As per Rousseau "Childhood has its place in the sequence of human life; the man must be treated as man and the child as a child". He stressed that a youngster has distinctive limit of learning and he develops his character continuously. He ought to be dealt with otherwise, unlike grown-up people and being a learner he ought to be given sufficient space to learn and develop unaccompanied by others in light of the fact that at last he is the consequence of the social order. Individuals are continually searching for a grown-up in the general public without realizing what a youngster is.

Rousseau was the first to give youth its legitimate place. He felt the need of instruction as indicated by the requests of a kid.

Dalai Lama

The fourteenth Dalai Lama, Tenzin Gyatso, is the other worldly pioneer of Tibet. He was born to a cultivating family on 6 July 1935, in a little village situated in Taktser, Amdo and northeastern Tibet.

Apart from being the profound pioneer of Tibetan Buddhism, His Holiness the fourteenth Dalai Lama has devoted his life to proffering introspective exchanges on the topics of Science and Buddhism, Education and Secular Ethics, Compassion and Universal Responsibility, and in addition Ethics in the fields of Environmental Sustainability, Global Warming and Leadership. He has fairly grasped the quintessence of all religions, as adoring generosity and minding which our twenty-first century society is in much need of. What is more, he has incorporated in his message the importance of all religions, that is, the acknowledgment of the importance of cherishing graciousness and minding, as an advantage to all humankind. In each of these domains, he views people as having basic fundamental esteems, and therefore, he supports that we should cooperate in peace for a superior world. His work in each one of these territories has made him a standout amongst the most powerful figures of the twentieth and twenty-first Centuries.

He has shaped the belief that religion solely is never again satisfactory as a reason for the encouragement of morals, and has turned into a solid voice for the advancement of Secular Ethics, as indicated by the Indian meaning of the words, which is characterized in a more extensive sense as a component of fundamental human moral philosophy, attach importance to all the people including non-devotees, and regarding all religions through veritable and impartial benevolence.

He is a man who lives what he instructs, and his lessons on universal responsibility, morals, sympathy, environmental issues and science of the psyche have turned out to be extraordinary motivation and consolation to a huge number of individuals around the globe. He continually advises us that we are for the most part participating in an extraordinary voyage, so every individual has the ethical duty to make the biological community that is our planet a superior place. Together we bring awesome changes into our reality.

He Advocated the Following Ideals

1. Universal compassion is fundamental to take care of worldwide issues;
2. Compassion is the mainstay of world peace;
3. All world religions are as of now for world peace along these lines, just like all helpful people of whatever belief system;
4. Each individual has an universal obligation to shape organizations to serve human needs.

MORAL THINKERS FROM INDIA

Gautam Buddha

Gautama Buddha, the establisher of Buddhism, was born in an imperial family. He lived for a long time, passing on in 487 B.C. He accomplished edification (i.e., he turned into the Buddha) at the age of thirty-five. Amid the years 532-487 B.C., he systematized the major standards of his idea, which came to be known as Buddhism.

The term Buddha signifies 'illuminated', one who has achieved the information of life. Buddhism originates from the lessons of Siddhartha Gautama, a Hindu sovereign in a little kingdom in South Nepal in the sixth century B.C.

The focal rule of Buddhism is that a specific lifestyle would prompt salvation (nirvana), that is, freedom from the life cycle. Buddhism perceives the four 'noble truths':

1. Life is enduring.
2. The reason for sufferings rests in wants (trishna, lobha), the feelings of connection (moha), and unawareness (avidya).
3. As the wants cause envy, outrage, and disdain, in this manner yielding distress, their disposal is a vital condition for salvation.
4. Therefore, one ought to take after the way prompting the condition of desirelessness, on the grounds that it is the best way to joy (sukh), which is freedom.

Since individuals have wants, they are bound to the wheel of predetermination, and go starting with one body then onto the next, agonizingeach time. Toward the finish of their lives, a great many people have such a large amount of desires left with them that they are born again in another body. They begin the cycle of want and distress afresh.

Keeping in mind the end goal to begin one's excursion along the way of liberation, one ought to follow the Eightfold Path (asthapatha). It comprises right views, right attitude, right speech, right conduct, right means of livelihood, right effort or purpose, right mind control, and right meditation. This way will lead one from the condition of selfishness (ahamkara) to that of compassion (karma). It is by following a path of moral living that one will have the capability to part from the chain of re-birth, adulthood and demise.

Other than the Eightfold Path, one must hold to the accompanying standards:

- Abstain from harming living things.
- Abstain from taking what is not given.
- Abstain from all types of sexual wants (Kama).
- Abstain from all types of lies, that is, lies, in word and deed. Shun common pleasures: no medications, no drink, and no lethargy.

The Buddhist should attempt to raise himself to a condition of brahmavihara, that is, where his body is possessed by divine element. For this he ought to take after four tenets:

- ***Loving kindness (melta)***: A Buddhist secures a total comprehension of his kindred creatures. He sees them as his own particular relatives, whose sufferings he knows.
- ***Compassion (karma)***: Once the Buddhist realizes that he is one of the components in the whole existence, he tries to help other people in their sufferings. He tries to enable them come out of agony.
- ***Joy (mudita)***: The Buddhist shares the delight he gets with each one of the individuals who need it. The Buddha is said to have said over and again: 'Let all be happy.
- ***The condition of being tranquil in mind and temper (upekkha, upeksha)***: Nothing must be permitted to disrupt the clearness of the Buddhist personality. Every robustfeeling is unsafe. Demise does not terrify the individuals who are not attached to life. As such, one who is edified does not fear anybody.

Vardhmana Mahavira

Vardhmana Mahavira, normally viewed as the establisher of Jainism, was born in Vaishali. He achieved pre-eminent learning at the age of forty-two. The valuable period of his religious life might be set in the vicinity of 497 and 467 B.C. However, Jainism asserts to be substantially more ancient than this period. Jains trust that there were twenty-three 'instructors' (tirthankara) before Mahavira, and Mahavira was the last tirthankara.

Buddhism does not recognize the existence of any incomparable god. The notions, in this way, formed around god have no place in it. Neither does it have the possibility of an individual god, one with whom one has relations of adoration and love. In Buddhism, the best way to accomplish salvation (nirvana, i.e., forever liberation from the cycle of birth and demise) is by following an arrangement of ethical and moral principles. It declines to acknowledge the principles of the Hindu social request, that is, the Varna and Jati framework. It does not encourage the arrangement of animal sacrifice.

Jainism likewise comprises of huge numbers of the components that describe Buddhism. It championed the act of 'non-violence' (ahimsa), which is vital to its beliefs.

Swami Vivekananda

Swami Vivekananda is one of the best masterminds of Indian Renaissance. Vivekananda felt sorry on observing the ruined condition of the people.

In the opinion of Swami Vivekananda, social, financial and political recreation of the nation is a pre-essential for the spiritual boost of the people. At the point when the general population request sustenance, to offer religion to a starving people is to affront him. To show religious standards to a starving man is an attack against his confidence. He reprimands unequivocally the failings and shortcomings of the general population, the malicious routine with regards to untouchability, the sentiment of rank predominance, cleric specialty and religious oppression. He wishes to see the general population as affirmed agnostics as opposed to superstitious simpletons, for the sceptics might be of some utilization. In any case, with respect to superstitions it holds away, the cerebrum is bread, the brain is immobilized and debasement immerses life. So it holds good if the humanity ends up plainly agnostic by depending on reason as opposed to aimlessly trusting in two hundred millions of Gods on the influence of anyone.

He has explained dynamic thoughts and intensely contradicted idealist beliefs like supernatural quality. He keeps up that occultism and mysticism have obliterated the general population.

Vivekananda contradicted child marriage, persecution of lower standings, and enslavement of ladies. He focused on the requirement for administration to poor people, ignorant, and the unwell. He trusted that no religion or law was higher than 'service to mankind'. He called his religion '*practical Vedanta*', in light of the fact that for him, religion must be practiced only. Vivekananda's main goal was to make a 'European society' with India's religion, that is, a religious society where the requirements of all were met. In other words, Vivekananda attempted to consolidate in his contemplations both the spiritual and material perspectives.

Contribution of Swami Vivekananda to India

In many ways, the life and work of Swami Vivekananda denote the ancient procedure of India rediscovering herself in present day times. These are also typical of the courses in which a custom renovates or develops alternative forms of innovation.

As a rule, his commitment to India and to the bigger world might be summed up in four ways:

1. First, in present day India, it was Vivekananda who initially accentuated that our regular day-to-day existences would turn out to be more significant just when spiritualized. It was in this other worldliness that he re-found, in a manner of speaking, India's message to herself and to the world. For Vivekananda, this otherworldly self-acknowledgment prompted individuals to completely understand their own possibilities. Particularly, with regards to a colonized society like that of nineteenth century India, this was commensurate to men and ladies finding more noteworthy self-belief in themselves.
2. Second, despite the fact that the Swami rejected political praxis and West motivated social and religious amendments, his basic message was the strengthening of the general population: through education, aggregate idea and activity yet most importantly, acknowledging the fundamental solidarity of all human presence. In the Hindu convention, austere separation from the world had been disapproved even before Vivekananda. However, it was he who first effectively joined the possibility of individual renunciation to submit social administration. In this sense, he gave new importance or implication to the general thought and establishment of sanyas.

   The Ramakrishna Math and Mission is presently, a working manifestation of this heritage.
3. Third, there is the adoration that Vivekananda reliably showed for the socially underestimated and abused. He could be equally at home in poor homes and royal quarters, be lavishly facilitated by the rich and the influential and furthermore share the coarse chapatti of a scrounger or share the hookah with a shoemaker. It is he, who even before Gandhi, recreated and adequately utilized the more established religious figure of speech of God particularly dwelling in the humble and poor people (daridra narayan).
4. Fourth, it was the Swami's persistent wish to bring back India's pride of place in the gathering of countries, as a civilization which, despite significant historical highs and lows, had yet held hidden strings of commonness and solidarity. In the meantime, similar to his master, Sri Ramakrishna, Vivekananda had complete faith in universality, cosmopolitanism and benevolence. As he saw it, mutual consideration and sympathy amongst human beings was more essential than that originating from a far-off God.

Notwithstanding above, he additionally took religion not to be some private inclination or eccentricity but rather that which was socially dedicated and accountable. self-determination for him was truly a bigger idea; it had more to do with the liberating of the psyche than the body. The Swami stuck his confidence in people, not establishments and thus picked a way that was noiseless, indirect and natural. One can dare to dream that the all the more persevering facets of his life and work keep on inspiring us in the days to come.

Raja Ram Mohan Roy

The Indian Renaissance of the nineteenth century lays more emphasis basically at restoration of the Indian soul, with the splendour of ancient history and immaculateness significantly influencing religion, society and culture. National arousing has conveyed itself as an impression of religious arousing. In the underlying stages, religious cognizance is observed to be an impression of political awareness. Social and political beliefs, democratic and patriotic yearnings that seek after a superior life have been communicated as religion. The Indian Renaissance started in the nineteenth century by the social reformers does not point towards a total break with religion. It is against the outdated religious traditions and practices from one perspective and reinterpretation and renewal of religion to suit the new conditions on the other.

Macnicol says: "*Raja Ram Mohan Roy is the spiritual father of this Renaissance who appears to be the herald of a new age.*"

He is against numerous traditions and convictions of the debauched social framework. He has completely dismissed the code of belief predominant in Hindu society as to their various Gods, ceremonies, the principle of rebirth; embodiments, their routine with regards to idol worship, animal sacrifices and most importantly the detestable routine with regards to sati pervasive in those days which cruelly suppresses.

Keeping in mind the final goal to advance the human uniformity, the expulsion of the handicaps of ladies in social life is another vital issue. He supported the conceding of equal property rights to men and ladies. He battles in help of widow remarriage and against youngster marriages. He promotes education for women. He looks to embrace the new esteems introduced by Western science to merge them with the conventional estimations of India to address the difficulty of the new age.

Hinduism as he comprehends is established in a wide humanistic standpoint. In this way, he has set himself the undertaking of cleaning Hinduism and clearing the sluggishness of superstitions which have built upthrough the ages. He is of the sentiment that the renaissance of Hinduism as a genuine national religion would suit to the new states of social life. His humanism can be called as universal humanism for his accentuation on world cooperation with a liberal soul, and for his laying emphasis on warm relationship among the different countries of the world.

Mohandas Karamchand Gandhi

Mohandas Karamchand Gandhi was one of the not very many individuals who presented a thought for a historic period. That thought was practice of non-violence. Gandhi's ideology of non-violence demanded that individuals' battle for their rights ought to never defy their fundamental commitment to regard life.

Gandhi was both religious and liberal, and saw all religions as ways to achieve a similar objective. He was enlivened by the lessons of Jesus, specifically, the accentuation on affection for everybody, even one's adversaries, and the need to exert oneself for justice. He likewise took from Hinduism the significance of activity in one's life, without worry for progress. The Hindu content Bhagavad-Gita expresses:

"On action alone be thy interest/Never on its fruits/Abiding in discipline perform actions/ Abandoning attachment/Being indifferent to success or failure".

Gandhi's way to deal with the truth is religious as opposed to philosophical. He moved toward reality through non-violence.

Non-violence is a vital fragment of each religion. He says that: 'Non-violence is in Hinduism, it is in Christianity as well as in Islam. If non-violence disappears, Hindu Dharma disappears. Islam does not forbid its followers from following non-violence as a policy.'

In the wake of having examined the Bhagavad-Gita against the foundation of Indian culture and convention, he has arrived at the conclusion that the crucial teaching of the Gita is to take after truth and non-violence.

Gandhi's commitment to the human development lies in his showing truth and peacefulness in each stroll of life for people or countries.

As indicated by him peacefulness is the kingdom of heaven. It guarantees peace and euphoria, amicability and harmony, sensitivity and co-operation, in human issues. These are its natural products. As the competitor looks for the kingdom of paradise as the most astounding objective, so peacefulness is the Heaven, it is a flawless state.

Gandhi as a Practical Idealist

Gandhi was not a visionary but rather he guaranteed to be a pragmatic dreamer. He was a man of activity. It was the optimist that influenced him to work as a useful man. He was additionally an irrepressible positive thinker. His idealism depended on the conviction that man is enriched with unending conceivable outcomes of improvement. His faith in the law as the perfect is undisputable. It makes a difference whether people miss the mark regarding the perfect. In spite of the fact that he knew about the truth, his endeavouring was continuously to conform to the belief.

It is a wayof centring his devotion to the definitive objective. He needs to tread the correct way without diversion. This is the benchmark by which man's advance is measured. Gandhi's theory was the immediate aftereffect of human relations and it was in the circle of human collaboration that his policy took solid shape. His methodology was progressive and human. The world is there for every realistic reason. It is the field of most noteworthy action.

Gandhi has confidence in the imperfect man who can enhance his condition by developing an impeccably blameless heart unequipped for malevolence. Subsequently, the error-prone man, being an obstruction to his own self-improvement, can be redressed to take after the way of advance in good spirit. It can just occur through life-lessons. Gandhi states that: "It is not literacy or learning which makes a man but education for real life."

Sarvepalli Radhakrishnan

Among present-day Indian scholars, Radhakrishnan was an extraordinary mastermind who was a professor in Eastern and Western colleges and furthermore as a Vice-Chancellor. As the leader of the University Education Commission he had an event to test profound into the issues of advanced education in India. Alongside his varied experience of the field of education, Radhakrishnan had wide learning and profound knowledge into Indian and Western, old and contemporary way of life. He was without a doubt a standout amongst the most qualified people to talk about Indian philosophy of education with the administration. His perspectives are discovered scattered in his different books, for example, *An Idealist View of Life, The Philosophy of Rabindranath Tagore, The Brahma Sutra, The Bhagavad-Gita, The Hindu View of Life, Eastern Religion and Western Thought*.

Radhakrishnan was a promoter of antiquated Indian Vedanta philosophy. He was a perfectionist scholar. He characterized philosophy as a mix of reflection and instinct. Radhakrishnan's objective of philosophy is to explore that amalgamation which may incorporate every facets of creation. Philosophy in his opinion: *"Is an attempt of human being to know the problems of creation and the nature of ultimate reality."*

Radhakrishnan conceded the value of reason and confidence, rationale and encounter and the value of perceptual, theoretical and instinctive knowledge in education. As per him, instinctive knowledge is the most elevated learning and is an indispensable experience. He clarified spiritualist experience as a piece of instinctive experience. Overall experience is picked up by total self and it is substantially higher than some other experience picked up by add up to self and it is considerably higher than some other experience gained by total self and innovative understanding has an imperative place in all-out information. His reasoning has been properly translated as essential experience, and this experience discovers place for each other kind of experience in it.

As indicated by Radhakrishnan, human identity is not controlled by monetary or physical condition. So far as physical changes are concerned they might be by and large dictated by the environment by the human will which is allowed to choose to win or lose. The genuine human liberty is the liberty of wish. In the custom of antiquated Indian scholars Radhakrishnan had conceded the principle of Karma. As indicated by this standard our present is controlled by our past and future relies on the present. In the expressions of Radhakrishnan:

"Karma or relationships with the past does not mean that man cannot do anything freely but free action is involved in it."

The law of Karma is not fatalism "An individual will gain according to the use of his energy. The world will respond to the individual Jivatma's demand. The nature will reply the insistent call of the man."

Similar to Karl Marx, Radhakrishnan trusted that man can transform the world. On the premise of his determination he can build his future. The standards of Nature are the standards of impartiality. In nature and in human world, all over, one all-inclusive celestial law functions. Along these lines, the law of Karma is not an outer yet an inner determinant of human life. In the line of assessment, man is differentiated by self-awareness which is not discovered either in plants or in creatures. The mental procedures cannot be translated with regard to physical changes. The physical developments do not clarify total conduct.

14 CHAPTER

Corporate Governance

ETHICAL LEADERSHIP

In the present times, business is mainly dependent on new and greater obstacle and external factors such as regulatory amendments. Globalization also poses a great challenge. It is experienced that organizations face various standards of values and practices.

With business world facing new challenges and faulty business ethics by each passing day, business leadership around the world is feeling the need of ethical leadership. Nonetheless, ethical leadership is not only a requirement, but also a chance to bring changes into the faulty business system to enable good management of business.

Any institution's legitimacy gets a jerk if it is found to have supported corrupt practices. As a result of declining legitimacy, business world will see more supporters of regulations. This may result in introduction of more complex laws those will make business even more difficult. The result is that, in a framework when one company undermines the law, it proves more difficult for other organizations to operate cleanly.

This scenario gives rise to the demand of Ethical Leadership. It has become evident that it is only through clear, unequivocal policies and controls stipulating zero tolerance that the companies ensure good practice.

By ensuring that Ethical Leadership is practiced in the company, a manager could actually bring positive change to his or her reputation and inspire and motivate others to work ethically at all levels of the firm.

Gaining consumer trust and confidence has always been the main aim of industry. Because of the ever-increasing competition in the present market, Ethics has always played a big role in crafting, shielding and enhancing 'Reputation' and 'Confidence of a brand', via transparency, free flow of information and good governance.

Ethical Governance provides us a good chance to differentiate from the competition in the market, that is, to add value. An organization running as per the ethical principles will be more trustworthy by customers, shareholders and investors, and it will come out as more successful than those less ethical companies.

In short, by working with a social conscience, the ethical leader not only builds confidence and loyalty with staff, but also builds goodwill in the market, community and society at a wide scale.

Ethical Leadership poses its own types of challenges. For example, ethics are often highly personal. It is also true that Ethical Leadership cannot be instilled in any company or firm overnight.

Ethical Leadership can become truth by making it a habit and by implementing proper regulations. Education and communication must be further encouraged, Ethical subjects must find and gain support in the workplace and also in the society and finally there must be proper motivation and recognitions awarded to those wishing to pursue Ethics.

ETHICS, TRANSPARENCY AND ACCOUNTABILITY

The conclusion of the cold war; scattering democratization; a swing in balance among the state, the market and civil society; globalization; and fluctuating social mores—among other factors—are responsible for changing the environment in which governments are functioning. The emergence of new ICT is also providing a rapid, global spreading of ideas and practices, encouraging the public to seek higher standards of ethics, transparency and liability in the public sector. These essential values of good governance and justifiable development not only prop responsive public policy and high levels of public sector performance but also play an important role in curtailing systemic corruption. It is now internationally recognized that corruption hinders economic development, weakens stability and erodes faith in public institutions. The evil effects of corruption such as the lack or poor quality of essential public infrastructure and services are felt by those the least able to do so: the poor.

Given its decision of encouraging good governance and sound public administration in development, the Division for Public Administration and Development Management (DPADM) backs framing out of international standards, carries out comparative policy research and analysis, and helps in building capacity in organizations safeguarding public sector ethics, transparency and liability. The Division's actions are based on the scrutiny that corruption is one symptom of poor administration and mismanagement. These conditions let corrupt public officials to grab chances for putting self above public interest, in contrast to the spirit of public service. Furthermore, the Division's actions also try to preserve the honour of other 'honest' public officials by framing an 'ethics infrastructure' that not only offers guidance for good conduct but also administratively and legally penalizes misconduct. The 'ethics infrastructure' consists of measures to boost and preserve organizational integrity, reach to material that promotes transparency and accountability, and lapse by independent institutions and the public at large. In performing its actions in this area, the Division has sought to best leverage the United Nations' uniquely global membership, by nurturing international dialogue and the exchange of experiences.

BACKGROUND OF CORPORATE GOVERNANCE

The financial lapses of Enron, WorldCom and Parmalat have given a momentum to the discussion about the proper governance of companies. Corporate governance includes a lot of issues borne by the separation of ownership and control. Interest in the corporate governance practices of modern organizations, particularly regarding accountability, increased after the high-profile collapses of a number of large corporations during 2001–2002, many of which involved accounting scam; and then again after the recent financial crisis in 2008.

In 1997, the East Asian Financial Crisis severely caused a major setback to the economies of Thailand, Indonesia, South Korea, Malaysia and the Philippines by the exit of foreign capital after property assets bowed. The dearth of corporate governance frameworks in these countries presented the weaknesses of the institutions in their economies.

WHAT IS CORPORATE GOVERNANCE?

- Corporate Governance can be stated as a framework of systems, processes and principles which confirm that an organization is governed in the best interest of all stakeholders. It is the framework that directs and manages companies. It is related to endorsing corporate fairness, transparency and liability. In other words, 'good corporate governance' is simply 'good business'. It guarantees:
  - Acceptable disclosures and effective decision making to attain corporate objectives;
  - Transparency in business dealings;
  - Statutory and legal agreements;
  - Protection of shareholder interests;
  - Commitment to values and ethical conduct of business.
- In other words, corporate governance is the approval by management of the absolute rights of shareholders as the true owners of the company and of their own role as trustees on behalf of the shareholders. It relates to performing the affairs of an organization such that there is fairness to all stakeholders and that its activities prove beneficial for the greatest number of stakeholders. In relation to this, the management requires to avoid unevenness of benefits between various sections of shareholders, specifically between the owner-managers and the remaining shareholders.
- It is related to obligation to values, ethical business conduct and making a division between personal and corporate funds while managing an organization. Ethical impasses arise as a result of conflicting interests of the parties involved. In this context, managers decideon the basis of a set of values affected by the values, context and culture of the company. Ethical leadership is considered important for the running of successful business as the institutionis expected to perform as per the expectations of all stakeholders.
- It states the procedures by which organizations' aims are set and executed keeping in mind the social, regulatory and market environment. Governance system consists of observing the actions, policies and decisions of organizations and their agents.

N.R. Narayana Murthy Committee on Corporate Governance formed by SEBI defines corporate governance as the 'acceptance by management of the inalienable rights of shareholders as the true owners of the corporation and of their own role as trustees on behalf of the shareholders. It is about commitment to values, about ethical business conduct and about making a distinction between personal & corporate funds in the management of a company'.

The Kumar Mangalam Birla Committee formed by SEBI has stated that 'Strong corporate governance is indispensable to resilient and vibrant capital markets and is an important instrument of investor protection. It is the blood that fills the veins of transparent corporate disclosure and high quality accounting practices. It is the muscle that moves a viable and accessible financial reporting structure'.

IMPORTANCE OF CORPORATE GOVERNANCE

Basically, level of confidence fluctuates as per the company's corporate governance performance. A proactive team of independent directors on the board helps a company to grow its confidence in the market.

Corporate governance has come out as main criterion for foreign institutional investors to decide company to invest.

It also leaves a good impact on the share price of the company. It is beneficial for company to have a clean image on the corporate governance front as it makes it simpler for organizations to source funds at more reasonable costs. Regrettably, corporate governance comes to limelight only after the exposure of a large scam.

FOUR PILLARS OF CORPORATE GOVERNANCE

a. **Accountability**: It confirms that management is accountable to the Board and the Board to shareholders.
b. **Fairness**: It safeguards shareholders rights; treats all shareholders including minorities, equitably, and offers effective redress for violations.
c. **Transparency**: It confirms timely, accurate release on all material matters, including the financial situation, performance, ownership and corporate governance.
d. **Independence**: Process and frameworks are there to minimize or prevent completely conflicts of interest; Independent Directors and Advisers free from the influence of others.

OBJECTIVES OF CORPORATE GOVERNANCE

The goal of '*Good Corporate Governance*' is to make sure that pledge of the board in operating the organization in a transparent manner for maximizing long-term value of the company for its shareholders and all other partners is achieved. It unites all the actors involved in a process, which is economic, and at the same time social.

The main aim of corporate governance is to boost shareholders' value and guard the interests of other stakeholders by improving the corporate performance and liability. Hence, it corresponds the requirement for an organization to maintain a balance at all times between the need to boost shareholders' wealth whilst not in any way being detrimental to the interests of the other stakeholders in the company.

Further, its aim is to make an environment of trust and confidence amongst the actors sharing competing and conflicting interests. It is vital to the very existence of an organization and builds up investor's confidence by safeguarding company's commitment to higher growth and profits.

Largely, Corporate Governance Strives to Attain the Following Aims:

- A well-structured board proficient of taking sovereign and objective decisions is in place at the helm of affairs;
- The board is balance as regards the representation of adequate number of non-executive and independent directors who will take care of their interests and well-being of all the stakeholders;
- The board embraces transparent processes and practices and arrives at decisions on the strength of adequate information;
- The board has an effective framework to subserve the concerns of stakeholders;
- The board keeps the shareholders informed of relevant advances affecting the company;
- The board effectively and regularly observes the working of the management team;
- The board remains in effective control of the affairs of the company at all times.
- The overall effort of the board should be to take the company forward so as to get the most out of long-term value and shareholders' wealth.

STAKEHOLDER BENEFITS AND PRINCIPAL-AGENT ISSUE

In organizations, the central external stakeholders are shareholders, debt holders, trade creditors and suppliers, clients and communities impacted by the corporation's actions. Internal stakeholders include the board of directors, executives and other personnel.

All parties have some interest in corporate governance, regardless of whether direct or indirect, in the financial activities of the corporation. Directors, employees as well as management get compensations, facilities and name, while investors hope to get returns in terms of money. For loan specialists, it is specified interest payments, while returns to equity investors emerge from dividend distributions or capital gains on their stock. Customers are worried about the assurance of the arrangement of goods and services of a right quality; suppliers are worried about pay for their products or services.

A great part of the contemporary interest in corporate governance is associated with reducing the conflicts of interests between business partners. In vast firms where there occurs a separation of ownership and management and no controlling shareholder, the principal-agent issue emerges between upper-administration (the 'agent') which may have altogether different interests, and by definition significantly more (information asymmetry), than shareholders (the 'principals'). The shareholder abandon decision rights (control) and depends on the manager to act in the best (joint) interests of the shareholders.

The risk emerges that, as opposed to regulating management from shareholders' side, the board of directors may move towards becoming insulated from shareholders and indebted to management. This perspective is especially seen in contemporary public debates and advancements in administrative policy.

Partially because of this separation between the shareholders and managers, mechanisms of corporate governance incorporate an arrangement of controls planned to assist align managers' incentives with those of shareholders.

Methods for moderating or keeping these conflicts of interests or irreconcilable situations incorporate the procedures, traditions, regulatory mechanisms, laws and organizations which affect the way an organization is regulated. A significant topic of governance is the nature and degree of corporate responsibility.

An important factor in a party's decision to take an interest in or draw in with a company is their certainty that the enterprise will bring the results as per party's expectations. At the point when categories of parties (stakeholders) don't have adequate confidence that an organization is being controlled and directed in a way consistent with their expected results, they are less inclined to draw in with the company. At the point when this turns into an endemic system feature, the loss of certainty and interest in business sectors may influence numerous other stakeholders.

PRECONDITIONS AND COMPONENTS OF CORPORATE GOVERNANCE

Today selection of good Corporate Governance practices has developed as a fundamental component for working together. It isn't just a pre-essential for confronting extraordinary rivalry for economic development in the rising worldwide market situation but on the other hand is an encapsulation of the parameters of fairness, responsibility, disclosures and transparencyto enhance value for the stakeholdersor partners.

Corporate administration can't be managed by enactment alone. Enactment can just set out a typical system – the 'form' to guarantee benchmarks. The 'substance' will at last decide the believability and uprightness of the whole process. Substance is unyieldingly connected to the attitude and moral standards of management.

Investigations of corporate administration practices carried out in a number of countries directed by the Asian Development Bank, International Monetary Fund, Organization for Economic Cooperation and Development and the World Bank uncover that there is no single model of good corporate administration.

The OECD Code additionally perceives that diverse lawful frameworks, institutional systems and conventions in countries have prompted the advancement of a range of various ways to deal with corporate administration. But, a high level of priority has been put on the interests of investors or shareholders.

Independent of the model, there are three unique types of corporate obligations which all models do regard:

- ***Political Responsibilities***: The fundamental political commitments are following authentic law; regard for the arrangement of rights and the doctrines of constitutional state.
- ***Social Responsibilities***: The corporate moral obligations, which the organization comprehends and advances either as a community with shared values or as a part of bigger community group with shared values.
- ***Economic Responsibilities***: Acting as per the rationale of competitive markets to ensure benefits on the premise of advancement and regard for the rights/popular government of the shareholders which can be communicated as administrations' commitment as 'maximizing shareholders value'.

Moreover, business morals and corporate consciousness of the ecological and societal interest of the community, inside which they work, can affect the notoriety and performance of organizations in the long-term.

The three important components of corporate administration are:

1. The Board of Directors
2. The Shareholders and
3. The Management

Board of Directors

A board of directors or board of governors refers to a collection of chosen or appointed individuals who together supervise the exercises of an organization or association. The vital role in any arrangement of corporate administration is performed by the governing body. It is responsible to the shareholders and guides and controls the administration. It stewards the organization, sets its key goals including financial goals and regulates their implementation, sets up required internalregulations and intermittently reports the activities and development of the organization in a transparent way to every partners or stakeholders.

The OECD Principles of Corporate Governance (2004) depict the duties of the board; some of these are summed up below:

- Members of the Board ought to be informed and act morally and in compliance with common decency, with due constancy and care, to the greatest advantage of the organization and the shareholders.
- Review and guide corporate system, target setting, significant plans of activity, riskpolicy, capital designs and yearly spending plans.
- Keep a watch on significant acquisitions and divestitures.
- Choose, compensate, keep a watch and replace important executives and keep an eye on succession planning.
- Align important executives and board compensation pay with the longer-term interests of the organization and its investors or shareholders.
- Ensure a formal and transparent nomination of board member and election process.
- Ensuring the integrity of the companies accounting and budgetary reporting frameworks, including their autonomous review.
- To ensure the establishment of suitable frameworks of internal control.
- Oversee the procedures like exposure and interchanges.
- Where committees of the board are set up, their mandate, formation and working strategies ought to be well-defined and disclosed.

The Shareholders

The shareholders' contribution in corporate administration is to make an appointment of the directors and the auditors and to make the board responsible for the best possible administration of the organization by requiring the board to furnish them intermittently with the required data in a transparent manner, of the activities and growth of the organization.

The Management

The administration's obligation is to embrace the administration of the organization as far as the direction given by the board, to set up desired control frameworks and to guarantee their operation and to give information to the board on a timely basis and in a transparent way to empower the board to keep a watch on the accountability of management to it.

The basic standards of corporate governance or administration spin around three essential inter-related components. These are:

- Integrity and Fairness
- Transparency and Disclosures
- Accountability and Responsibility

PRINCIPAL CONSTITUENTS OF GOOD CORPORATE GOVERNANCE

i. ***Functions and Powers of Board:*** The chief prerequisite of good corporate administration is the clear recognizable proof of powers, functions, duties and accountability of the Board, CEO and the Chairman of the board.

ii. ***Legislation:*** A clear and unambiguous legislative and administrative structure is central to viable corporate governance.

iii. ***Code of Conduct:*** It is necessary that an association's unequivocally recommended sets of conducts are conveyed to all partners or stakeholders and are unmistakably comprehended by them. There ought to be some framework set up to periodically quantify and assess the adherence to such set of conduct by every individual from the association.

iv. ***Independence of the Board*:** An autonomous board is necessary for sound corporate governance. It implies that the board is fit for evaluating the performance of managersobjectively. Subsequently, the larger part of board members ought to be autonomous of both the management group and any business dealings with the organization. Such autonomy guarantees the adequacy of the board in regulating the exercises of management and also ensures that there are no real or perceived conflicts of interests.

v. ***Skills of the Board*:** To have the capacity to embrace its functions successfully, the board must have the important mix of characteristics, abilities, knowledge and experience to make quality contribution. It incorporates operational or specialized mastery, financial skills, lawful skills and additionally learning of government and administrative prerequisites.

vi. ***Environment of the Management:*** Incorporates setting up of clear targets and fitting moral structure, building up due procedures, ensuring transparency and clear articulation of duty and responsibility, actualizing sound business planning, urging business risk evaluation, having right individuals and right aptitude for occupations, building up clear limits for satisfactory conduct, setting up performance assessment measures and assessing performance and adequately perceiving contributions of individual and group.

vii. ***Appointments of Members in the Board:*** To guarantee that the most equipped individuals are appointed in the board, the board positions must be filled by means of in-depth inquiry. A well-defined and open process must be set up for reappointments and for appointing new directors.

viii. ***Board Induction and Training:*** It is fundamental to guarantee that directors be a part of all development, which are or may affect corporate administration and other related issues.

ix. ***Meetings of Board:*** Board Meetings are the forums for taking important decisions. These meetings allow directors to perform their duties. The viability of board meetings is subject to precisely arranged plans and giving pertinent papers and materials to directors adequately before the meetings of the board.

x. ***Forming Strategy:*** The goal of the organization must be plainly documented in a long-term corporate strategy which may include an annual plan for business success together with achievable and quantifiable performance targets and breakthroughs.

xi. ***Obligations associated with Business and Community:***.Though the fundamental role of a business entity is characteristically business yet it should likewise deal with the obligations of community. The partners or stakeholders must be informed about the endorsement by the proposed and initiatives taken continuously to meet the obligations of the community.

xii. ***Report on Financial and Operational Processes:*** The board requires extensive, consistent, dependable, timely, right and applicable data in a form and of a quality that is fitting to perform its function of checking the corporate performance.

xiii. ***Keeping a watch on the Performance of the Board:*** The board must keep a watch and assess its consolidated performance and furthermore that of individual directors at periodic intervals.

xiv. ***Audit Committee*:** It is inter alia in charge of contact with management, internal and statutory examiners, inspecting the ampleness of internal control and consistence with noteworthy approaches and systems, reporting to the board on the key issues.

xv. ***Management of Risk*:** The board has the ultimate responsibility for identifying major risks to the organization, setting acceptable levels of risks and ensuring that senior management takes steps to detect, monitor and control these risks. Risk is an essential component of corporate working and administration. There ought to be an evidently established procedure of distinguishing, assessing and treating risks, which could keep the organization away from viably accomplishing its targets. The board has a definitive obligation regarding distinguishing important risks to the association, establishing adequate levels of risks and guaranteeing that senior management finds a way to identify, screen and control these risks.

Transparency in Corporate Sector

Corporate transparency portrays the degree to which a company's activities are noticeable by outsiders. This is a result of regulatory mechanism, local standards and the set of data, privacy and business approaches concerning corporate decision-making and operations receptiveness to workers, partners, investors and the public in general. Standard & Poor's has incorporated an explanation of corporate governance in its GAMMA Methodology with an aim to analyse and evaluate corporate governance. As a part of this work, Standard & Poor's Governance Services transparency depicts the degree to which a company's activities are recognizable by outsiders. This is an outcome of control, local norms and the arrangement of data, privacy and business policies concerning corporate decision-making and operations receptiveness to employees, partners, investors and the public in general. Standard & Poor's has incorporated an explanation of corporate transparency in its GAMMA Methodology with an aim to analyse and examine corporate administration. As an important part of this work, Standard & Poor's Governance Services distributes the Transparency Index computed as the average score for the biggest public organizations in different nations. Transparency International distributes a record of corporate transparency in view of public disclosure of anti-corruption programmes and country-wise reporting. Corporate transparency is additionally used to denote radical transparency in corporate administration.

CODES AND GUIDELINES

Corporate governance doctrines and codes have been created in various nations and issued from stock exchanges, corporations, institutional investors or affiliations (foundations) of directors and managers with the help of governments and global associations. Generally speaking, consistence with these governance recommendations isn't mandated by law, in spite of the fact that the codes connected to stock exchange listing prerequisites may have a coercive impact.

One among the most compelling guidelines has been the Organization for Economic Co-operation and Development (OECD) Principles of Corporate Governance. Its guidelines are frequently referenced by nations creating local codes or guidelines.

Building on the work by the OECD, other international associations, private sector affiliations and over 20 national corporate governance codes framed the UN Intergovernmental Working Group of Experts on International Standards of Accounting and Reporting (ISAR) to deliver their Guidance on Good Practices in Corporate Governance Disclosure. This globally concurred benchmark comprises of over fifty different disclosure items crosswise over five broad categories:

1. Auditing
2. Structure and process associated with Board and management
3. Corporate responsibility and compliance in organization
4. Transparency in Financial processes and disclosure of information
5. Ownership structure and implementation of control rights

INTERNAL & EXTERNAL CORPORATE GOVERNANCE CONTROLS

Internal

- Monitoring by means of the board of directors
- ***Internal control methodology and internal evaluators*:** Internal control systems are strategies actualized by an entity's governing body, review advisory group,

administration and other faculty to give sensible assurance of the entity accomplishing its goals identified with solid financial reporting, working productivity and consistence with laws and directions. Internal auditors are employees inside an establishment who test the plan and execution of the entity's internal control methods and the reliability of its financial detailing.

- ***Balance of power***: The least complex balance of power is really very common; require that the President be some other individual from the Treasurer. This utilization of partition of power is additionally created in organizations where separate divisions check and balance each other's activities. One group may put forth expansive managerial changes, another group audit and can veto the progressions and a third groupkeep a watch on the interests of individuals (customers, shareholders, employees).
- ***Remuneration***: Performance-based compensation. It might be payments as cash or non-cash, for example, shares and share choices, superannuation or other facilities.
- Regulating by extensive investors or shareholders and/or additionally regulating by banks and other big loan creditors.

External

External corporate governance controls incorporate the controls external stakeholders have over the establishment, organization or association. Examples are:

- Competition
- Debt covenants
- Demand for and evaluation of performance information (particularly financial statements)
- Regulations by the government
- Managerial labour market
- Pressure of media
- Takeovers

BENEFITS OF CORPORATE GOVERNANCE

The model of corporate governance has been garnering public attention for quite some time. It is being accepted by large number of people due to its relevance and importance to the industry and economy. It helps not only to make business enterprise efficient, but also to grow and develop country's economy.

In a welcome step, many companies have willingly implemented systems of good corporate governance for the following reasons:

As per the findings in India and abroad, it has been seen that well-managed organizations are more likely to attract the attention of investors. The presence of good governance system in such organizations helps the top brass to work for the progress of their companies while being within the framework of effective accountability.

In is the need of today's globalized world that organizations take steps to attract and retain the best human capital from various parts of the world. In this scenario, an organization will fail to achieve the desired position unless it embraces and demonstrates ethical conduct.

The promise presented by good corporate governance norms also helps boosts confidence of investors, both foreign and domestic, to draw more long-term capital. This will ultimately induce more stable sources of financing.

An organization includes stakeholders, like customers, employees, investors, vendor partners, government and society. And cooperation of all is important for the growth. Hence, it is important for an organization to be fair and transparent to all its stakeholders in all its transactions by following the best corporate governance practices.

Good Corporate Governance ethics improve company's value by:

- Encouraging strategic thinking at the top through appointment of independent directors who bring in experience and new ideas;
- Rationalizing the management and constant reviewing of risk that a company faces globally;
- Restraining the accountability of top management and directors by carefully articulating the decision-making process;
- Promising the integrity of financial reports, etc.

It also leaves a long term reputational effects among key stakeholders, both internally and externally.

Also, the cases of financial crisis have brought the subject of corporate governance to the fore. They have moved the stress on compliance with substance, rather than form, and got to sharper focus the necessity for intellectual honesty and integrity. This occurs as financial and non-financial disclosures done by any firm are only as good and honest as the people behind them.

Good governance system, presented by adoption of good corporate governance practices, helps in inducing confidence amongst stakeholders as well as prospective stakeholders. Corporates practicing strict ethical norms are more likely to get higher prices by investors.

Impactful governance cuts perceived risks, consequently lessens cost of capital and permits board of directors to take swift and improved decisions.

Adopting good corporate governance procedures helps in long-term sustenance and fortifies stakeholders' relationship and provides stability and growth to the enterprise.

A good corporate citizen is respected and enjoys the position of icon.

No legislation can measure effectiveness of corporate governance system, and neither can any system of corporate governance be static. As competition surges, the environment in which companies work also alters, and in such a competitive environment, the systems of corporate governance also need to evolve. Those who fail to implement good governance procedures pays by losing investors who have big amount of money to invest in the market.

RESTRICTIONS AND FUTURE PROJECTIONS OF CORPORATE GOVERNANCE

The concerns relating to the governance, liability and transparency in the functioning of the firm, as well as regarding the rights of shareholders and role of Board of Directors have gained much prominence in today's time.

India emerged as one of the nations to have adopted new and happening global trends in Corporate Governance. This has enabled Indian organizations to align themselves with the needs of newer and larger markets around the world and to procure more businesses. The Indian government has also responded positively and quickly to meet the challenges of corporate delinquency. Due to the constant changing of business environment, it is important to adopt and sustain good governance to reap maximum benefit and set the positive tone for the future.

It is true that the 'corporate governance' has no distinctive arrangement or strategy and is largely considered unclear. Awareness related to various matters such as quality and frequency of financial and managerial disclosure, compliance with the moral of best practice, roles and duties of Board of Directories, shareholders rights, etc. Due to the unearthing of many failures and scams in corporate world such as conspiracy between companies and their accounting firms, existence of weak or ineffective internal audits, dearth of required skills by managers, deficiency of proper disclosures, non-compliance with standards, both management and auditors have come under greater scrutiny.

As Indian economy now is working with global markets, it is important for corporate houses to increasingly adopt better and transparent corporate practices. In the present times, investment decisions in the company depend largely on the extent to which organizations practice basic principles of good corporate governance. If organizations desire to extract the maximum benefit from the global capital market, corporate governance standards must be observed in a credible, consistent, coherent and inspiring way.

The success of corporate governance mainly depends on matters such as integrity of the management; capability of the Board; competence of the processes; commitment level of individual Board members; quality of corporate reporting; contribution of stakeholders in the management. This being an essential factor impacting the long-term financial health of organizations, the model of good governance also seeks effective legal and institutional environment, business ethics and alertness of the environmental and societal interests.

Hence, the model of corporate governance will attain more prominence worldwide in the years to come. This can be experienced byseveral events undertaken by many organizations in devising and implementing codes of conduct and honest business rules; practicing more strict standards for financial and non-financial disclosures, as per the law; accepting higher and appropriate accounting standards; introducing tax modifications coupled with deregulation and competition; etc.

Nevertheless, faulty implementation of corporate governance requirements can badlyimpact the rapport amongst participants of the governance system. As proprietors of equity, institutional investors are increasingly seeking a key role in corporate governance. Individual shareholders, who usually do not practice governance rights, are very concerned regarding getting fair treatment from controlling shareholders and management. Creditors, mainly banks, play animportant role in governance systems, and also play the role of external monitors over corporate functioning. Personnel and other stakeholders also contribute to the long-term achievement and performance of the firm.

Thus, it is important to implement governance practices in a right way for better growth of a company.

It is also important to make entrepreneurs aware about the various factors of corporate governance. Some areas that need special attention are as follows:-

- Quality of audit, which is most important for effective corporate governance;
- Role of Board of Directors as well as liability of the CEOs and CFOs;
- Quality and efficacy of the legal, administrative and regulatory system, etc.

LEGAL OUTLINE FOR CORPORATE GOVERNANCE

In fast-changing domestic and international business setting, it is important to regulate corporate entities as per the emerging economic trends, inspire good corporate governance and assist safety of the interests of the investors and other stakeholders.

Moreover, because of the constant increase in the complications of business operation, the faces of corporate organizations are continuously changing. This has presented a scenario where it is needed to devise a common law as per the needs of different organizations to which all types of organizations may refer while framing their corporate governance structure.

The significant legislations for regulating the entire corporate framework and for tackling various aspects of governance in companies are Companies Act, 1956(Now Companies Act, 2013). These laws have been framed and revised, from time to time, to bring more clarity and answerability in the rules of corporate governance. To bring more clarity and provide a system that would provide faster economic growth, these laws have been simplified.

Secondly, the Securities Contracts (Regulation) Act, 1956, Securities and Exchange Board of India Act, 1992, and Depositories Act, 1996, safeguard the interests of investors in the securities markets and maintain the standards of corporate governance in the nation.

COMPANIES ACT, 2013

Companies Act, 2013 replaces old Companies Act 1956.

Main Characteristics of Companies Act, 2013

- ***One Person Company:*** This Act offers new type of private company, i.e., one Person Company. It may consist of only one director and one shareholder. The earlier act of 1956 needs minimum two shareholders and two directors in case of a private company.
- ***Financial Statements:*** There was no information about Financial Statements in the Companies Act, 1956. The New Companies Act has given the term Financial Statements. The Financial Statements consist the following:
  - Balance Sheet
  - Profit and Loss Account
  - Cash Flow Statement

- Statement of Changes in Equity
- Explanatory Note

Four New Statutory Bodies

1. *NFRA (National Financial Reporting Authority):*

This body was constituted to replace National Advisory Committee on Accounting Standards (which was toothless). The NFRA was formed to perform the following functions:

- Suggest recommendations to Central Government for framing of Accounting and Auditing policies and Standards
- Review and enforce the compliance with accounting standards
- Monitor the quality of service given by professionals, specially of Chartered Accountants
- Frame accounting standards for firms
- Will have powers of civil court.
- Has the authority to debar CA and accountants for professional misconduct.
- Aggrieved person can appeal at NFRAA (National Financial Reporting APPELATE Authority).

2. ***National Company Law Tribunal:***

The new Companies Act enacted in 2013 formed National Company Law Tribunal and the National Company Law Appellate Tribunal to replace the Company Law Board and Board for Industrial and Financial Reconstruction.

They would take the burden of the Courts while simultaneously delivering specialized justice.

Following are the matters or disputes where NCLT will adjudicate:

- Organization fails to obey any provisions of the act (e.g., quorum not maintained, auditors not changed after deadline, etc.)
- Merger and acquisition disputes
- Converting public ltd. to private ltd.
- Filing class action suits

3. ***Investor and Education Protection Fund Authority:***

This fund is constituted to make investors aware about the traps of wrongdoers. Companies are liable to pay dividend, interest and principal to their investors. But if any money remains unclaimed (death, disappearance of investor, etc.), then that money goes to corporate affairs ministry and then into this fund.

This provision already existed, but ***2013 Act provided it statutory status***, with following provisions:

- Headquarter at New Delhi
- Regional offices across India
- Chairman: Secretary of Corporate Affairs Ministry
- Membership: executive directors from RBI, SEBI; experts from legal and financial sector

4. *Serious Fraud Investigation Office (SFIO):*

It was constituted in 2003 under corporate affairs ministry (based on Naresh Chandra report).

Changes Executed in SFIO Under Companies Act, 2013

- SFIO is made a statutory body.
- It was conferred with the power to search, seize and arrest (earlier, it could only scrutinize documents)
- SFIO investigators to possess same powers under CrPC, like a police officer.
- Once case is under SFIO, other agencies can't proceed.
- State police, ED, CBI, etc. will be liable to handover documents, witness and cooperate in further investigation.

AUDIT-RELATED PROVISIONS

1. *Audit Committee:*
   - An audit Committee has to be formed from board of directors.
   - Its chairman must be an independent director.
   - Provision for internal audit by CA, Accountants, even other (non-CA) persons.
   - Organizations will have to form whistleblower mechanism.
2. *External Auditors terms and responsibility:*
   - Individual auditor can inspect maximum of 20 organizations.
   - If he discovers any loopholes, he has to report to both Union Government (ministry of corporate affairs) and during the AGM (Annual General Meeting).
   - The term of auditor is 5 years and has to be approved every year. If a Firm of Auditor has been formed, then the period is 10 years.
   - Act forbids Auditors from carrying out non-audit services to the company where they are auditor to guarantee independence and accountability of auditor.
   - The new Act also levies Penalties of Auditor. They can be imposed by NFRA. Supplying any misleading information could mean an imprisonment up to one year.
3. *Company Secretary:*
   - Company Secretary acts as a bridge between board of directors and shareholders.
   - He manages BoD meetings, AGM, ensure quorum, minutes of the meeting, etc.
   - Organizations above certain share capital are liable to compulsorily hire company Secretary.
4. *Company's Loans:*
   - Firm is not authorized to give loan to director/related persons.
   - If organization provides loan to anyone, then its minimum interest rate should be more than that of Government securities (G-sec).
   - Firms hould get Credit rating before accepting public deposit (in collective investment schemes)
   - Firms need to hire a chief finance officer to look after audit and account.

BOARD OF DIRECTORS, BOARD MEETING, BOD COMMITTEES AND AGM MEETING

1. *General Provisions:*
   - There should be 1, 2 or 3 directors in One member company, Pvt Ltd. Company and Public Ltd. Company, respectively.
   - There should be maximum 15 directors.
   - More directors could be added by resolution in AGM (Annual general meeting of shareholders).
   - One person can be a director in maximum 20 firms.
   - One director must be Indian resident (i.e., staying in India for 182 days or more).
   - There should be one women director in the board.
   - If director remains absent from his office for 12 months, consider his position vacant, and a new guy should be appointed.
   - The Companies Act 2013 does not confine an Indian company from indemnifying (compensate for harm or loss) its directors and officers like the Companies Act, 1956.
   - The new Act has given new responsibility to Directors about declaration in the Directors Responsibility Statement. The Act also lays down the type of punishment if the information is not furnished.
2. *Independent Directors:*
   - This Act states that all listed firms must have at least one-third of the Board as independent directors. Such other class or classes of public firms as may be prescribed by the Central Government shall also be needed to anoint independent directors.
   - Performance of these directors will be scrutinized in shareholders' Annual General Meeting (AGM).
   - It is stated that no independent director can hold office for more than two consecutive terms of five years.
   - After 10 years of service, if they want to join same company as ID again, they will have to wait for 3 years cooling period.

   Independent director is responsible to safeguard the interests of shareholders, mainly the minority shareholders. He has to fulfil following criteria:
   - He is not a Promoter of the company, NOT nominated by the Chairman.
   - He has no monetary interest in the company, except salary as director.
   - He is not a worker of the company.
3. *Board Meetings:*
   - It doesn't apply to one person companies.
   - Organization must hold minimum 4 meetings per year.
   - Gap between two meetings should not be more than 120 days.
   - Quorum: 1/3rd strength or two directors, whichever is maximum.
   - If directors fail to appear physically, videoconferencing is permitted.

- Directors must be given 7 days prior notice. (So they can make prior travel arrangements.) The notice may be sent by electronic means to every director.

4. *Committee*
   - Firms will be needed to form following Committees out of their board members:
     - Audit Committee
     - Stakeholder Relationship Committee (SRC)
     - CSR Committee (CSRC)
   - Nomination and Remuneration Committee (NRC) will observe following:
     - MD/Directors' salary doesn't exceed 11% of firm's profit
     - Pay rise of CEO, directors, etc. versus company performance
     - This data will be presented in AGM.
5. *Annual General Meeting (AGM):*
   - Not liable for one person company
   - Public & Private Ltd. firms both have to hold AGM.
   - General notice can be sent by letter/email to shareholders.
   - Proxy voting is permitted.
   - Electronic voting is also permitted.
   - Quorum depends on number of shareholders.

OTHER PROVISIONS IN THE ACT

Dividend

The earlier Companies Act needed that a certain amount of profits has to be deposited to Reserve before declaring Dividend, the maximum being 10%. The 2013 Act has done away with the provision and now the firm does not have to mandatorily transfer to reserve. It may as per the convenience transfer any amount of profit to Reserve.

Private Placement

This Act offers Private Placement. It is related to issue of shares to private person, i.e., apart from public. If shares are issued to 50 persons or less, then it is called a private placement.

Electronic Medium

This act has allowed to carry out meetings through videoconferencing and other audio means.

This Act also proposed to implement e-Governance in various company processes like upkeep and audit of documents in electronic form, decision of keeping of books of accounts in electronic form, financial statements to be placed on company's website, etc.

Registered Valuers

Only registered Valuers are authorized as per this act to value any stocks, shares, etc. The Act states the eligibility to become Registered Valuer and the functions to be performed by it.

Class Action Suits for Shareholders

A new concept of class action suits was introduced by this act with an aim of making shareholders and other stakeholders more informed and knowledgeable about their rights.

More Power for Shareholders

The 2013 Act enables approvals from shareholders on various significant transactions.

Fast Track Mergers

This Act offers a fast track and simplified process for mergers and amalgamations of certain class of companies such as holding and subsidiary, and small organizations after getting approval of the Indian government.

Cross Border Mergers

This Act allows cross border mergers, both ways, that is, a foreign firm merging with an India firm and vice versa but with prior permission of RBI.

Prohibition on Forward Dealings and Insider Trading

This Act bars directors and key managerial personnel from purchasing call and put options of shares of the firm, if such person is reasonably likely to have access to price-sensitive information.

Increase in Number of Shareholders

This Act has provided to increase the number of maximum shareholders in a private company from 50 to 200.

Limit on Maximum Partners

The maximum number of persons/partners in any association/partnership may be up to such number as may be prescribed but not exceeding 100. This limit will not apply to an association or partnership by professionals like lawyer, chartered accountants, company secretaries, etc. who are legislated by their special laws.

The Companies Act, 1956 stated that, there was a limit of maximum 20 persons/partners, and there was no exemption granted to the professionals.

CORPORATE SOCIAL RESPONSIBILITY

- As per this new act, firms are liable to spend 2% of their last three years' average profit on CSR activities (e.g., schools, slum redevelopment, etc.).
- Firms with net worth of ₹ 500 crore or more or turnover of ₹ 1000 crore or net profit of more than ₹ 5 crore during a financial year have to spend at least 2% of its average net profits earned during last 3 years in pursuance of CSR activities.
- This 2% rule doesn't apply to income earned from foreign branches of the above companies.
- Above companies have to setup CSR Committee made up of 3 board of directors.

- Committee will frame and manage CSR policy.
- If firms do not spend, they need to have proper reason for the same.

UNDERSTANDING CORPORATE SOCIAL RESPONSIBILITY (CSR)

While there might be no single all around acknowledged meaning of CSR, every definition that right now exists supports the effect that organizations have on society everywhere and the societal desires of them. Despite the fact that the underlying foundations of CSR lie in altruistic exercises, (for example, gifts, philanthropy, alleviation work, and so forth.) of organizations, internationally, the idea of CSR has advanced and now includes every single related idea, for example, triple primary concern, corporate citizenship, magnanimity, key charity, shared esteem, corporate maintainability and business obligation.

As indicated by United Nations Industrial Development Organization (UNIDO), Corporate Social Responsibility is an administration idea whereby organizations unite social and ecological concerns in their business operations and collaborations with their partners. CSR is for the most part comprehended just like the route through which an organization accomplishes an adjust of monetary, natural and social objectives ('Triple-Bottom-Line-Approach'), while in the meantime tending to the desires of investors and partners. In this sense, it is critical to draw a distinction between CSR, which can be a vital business administration idea, and philanthropy, sponsorships or magnanimity. Despite the fact that the latter can likewise influence a profitable commitment to poverty eradication will specifically upgrade the notoriety of an organization and reinforce its image, the idea of CSR plainly goes past that.

The TBL approach is utilized as a structure for measuring and revealing corporate performance against financial, social and ecological execution. It is an endeavour to align private ventures to the objective of sustainable worldwide development by giving them a more extensive arrangement of working destinations than simply benefit alone. The point of view taken is that for an association to be sustainable, it must be monetarily secure, limit (or preferably dispose of) its negative ecological effects and act in similarity with societal desires.

The LBG model

Organizations over the world adopt LBG's estimation model keeping in mind the end goal and the impact of their investment to both, the business and society. This model encourages organizations to comprehend the aggregate sum of money, time and in-kind contributed inside the group, and empowers them to comprehend the geographic spread of their group support and the sort of subjects helped, for example, training, wellbeing and expressions and culture. Through this model, organizations can track the way in which their group program underpins more extensive business objectives, for example, building worker assurance or making reputational focal points.

Likewise, it aidsto evaluate the distinction their projects make to the group in the wider sense. Under this model, member organizations share information and best practices which thusly help in the benchmarking procedure.

OECD CSR Policy Tool

The OECD CSR policy enables organizations to pick up understanding into their current CSR exercises, survey its value and decide other CSR exercises that can be utilized. This arrangement depends on the OECD Guidelines and the ISO26000 usage rules. The aftereffect of this policy is a total CSR policy, incorporating an activity design with errands, duties and a correspondence system design.

International Compact Self-Assessment Tool

The Global Compact Self-Assessment Tool is a simple-to-utilize guide intended for use by organizations of all sizes and across sectors focused on maintaining the social and ecological guidelines inside their individual operations.

- The tool comprises 45 inquiries with an arrangement of three to nine pointers for each inquiry.
- It includes an 'administration area' and four different areas, including human rights, labour, environment and anti-corruption that identify with the standards of the UN Global Compact.
- The tool is in accordance with the UN Guiding Principles on Business and Human Rights.
- For a little organization, this tool acts as a measure of the organization's performance in every aspect of the UN Global Compact and how well these issues are overseen.
- For a big association, this device serves to constantly enhance existing strategies and frameworks, connect with auxiliaries, providers or different partners, and enhances inside and outer announcing.

The SROI Network

The SROI Network is a structure related to social generally accepted accounting principles (SGAAP) that can be utilized to help oversee and comprehend the social, financial and natural results made by an association or a man.

Keeping in mind the positive impact of the task, SROI helps in understanding, overseeing and imparting the social esteem that a specific errand makes in a reasonable and reliable path with clients, recipients and funders.

It also aids in overseeing risks and tracking chances and raise finances. It flags potential upgrades to administrations, data frameworks and the best approach to represent the organizations.

By determining the value, an organization hopes to make utilizing SROI, one can recognize the regions where changes are needed and a correlation of performance against estimates will help make extra esteem.

Key CSR issues: Environmental management, eco-efficiency, responsible sourcing, stakeholder engagement, labour standards and working conditions, employee and community relations, social equity, gender balance, human rights, good governance, and anti-corruption measures.

From the Above, it can be Understood that

- The CSR model is universal and combined with the core business strategy for tackling social and environmental impacts of businesses.
- CSR needs to address the prosperity of all partners and not only the organization's investors.
- Philanthropic actions are just a part of CSR, which generally consists of a much larger set of actions important for strategic business benefits.

ISO 26000: Social Responsibility

This is a guidance device facilitated by the ISO which empowers firms to comprehend the importance and criticalness of social duty.

It is necessary to know that this is not a certification but only a guiding device. Subsequently, associations which consent to these models are self-guaranteed. It covers six fundamental areas of social responsibility, including:

(i) Human rights
(ii) Labour practices
(iii) Environment
(iv) Fair operating practices
(v) Consumer issues
(vi) Community involvement and development.

This guarantees an all-inclusive methodology to the concept of social responsibility and sustainable development.

Training and Advisory Services in Corporate Social Responsibility (CSR)

'Corporate Social Responsibility' (CSR) is related with treating the partners of an organization or foundation morally or in a dependable way. 'Morally or dependable' mean treating key partners in a way regarded acceptable as per the standards. Social incorporates monetary and ecological obligation. Partners exist both inside a firm and outside. The extensive aim of social duty is to make high standards of life, while protecting the gainfulness of the organization or the honesty of the foundation, for people groups both inside and outside these elements. CSR is a procedure to accomplish sustainable development in social orders. CSR is an administration idea whereby organizations incorporate social and natural concerns in their business operations and communications with their partners. CSR is by and large comprehended similar to the route through which an organization accomplishes a balance between financial, ecological and social objectives (Triple-Bottom-Line-Approach), and keeping in mind that in the meantime tending to the desires of investors. In this sense, it is essential to draw a distinction between CSR (which can be a key business administration idea) and philanthropy, sponsorships or generosity. Advancing the process of practicing CSR among SMEs requires approaches that fit the individual needs and limits of these organizations, and don't unfavourably influence their financial feasibility.

For example, UNIDO constructed its CSR programme in light of the Triple Bottom Line (TBL) Approach, which has turned out to be a fruitful tool for SMEs in the developing nations to help them in meeting social and natural measures without compromising their intensity. The TBL approach is utilized as a system for measuring and announcing corporate performance against financial, social and natural performance. It is an endeavour to align private ventures to the objective of sustainable global development by giving them a more far-reaching set of working targets than just benefit alone. The viewpoint taken is that for an association to be supportive, it must be monetarily secure, limit (or preferably take out) its negative ecological effects and act in congruity with societal desires.

Key CSR factors consist of environmental management; eco-efficiency; responsible sourcing; stakeholder engagement; labour standards and working conditions; employee and community relations; social equity; gender balance; human rights; good governance and anti-corruption measures. An appropriately actualized CSR idea can bring along ample of advantages, for example, upgraded access to capital and markets, expanded deals and benefits, operational cost reserve funds, enhanced profitability and quality, effective human asset base, enhanced brand picture and notoriety, improved client reliability, decision making and risk management procedures. As of late, expanding consideration has been given to the idea of Corporate Social Responsibility (CSR), characterized as far as the responsiveness of organizations to partners' legal, moral, social and environmental desires. CSR has by and large been a sober minded reaction to consumer and civil society pressures. These have chiefly been centred on trans-national partnerships (TNCs) serving markets in the North, however regularly working in nations in the South. Allegations by governments and common society of ecological contamination, human rights violation and abuse of worker in supply chains have constrained organizations to become more environmentally and socially responsible. Be that as it may, the business group has immediately perceived the strategic value of being more capable and is starting to adjust items and business connections, specifically through their supply chains, in like manner. Guaranteeing that CSR underpins, and does not undermine, the advancement of small and medium-sized enterprises (SMEs) in developing nations is vital to meeting the objective of enhancing the effect of business on society. SMEs make up over 90% of all organizations worldwide and are fundamental to the 'way out of destitution' for some developing nations. If CSR demands are protective, socially wrong or absurdly bureaucratic, the net impact will be to undermine occupations in the South. On the contrary, the small and medium enterprises (SME) segment must not be permitted to become a gap in which polluting, exploitative industries thrive. Help for SME advancement can be a critical part of the CSR duty of large organizations with regard to responsible supply chain management, and developments in social and environmental effects can go simultaneously with better quality and management.

Indian CSR Situation

The advancement of CSR in India implies modifications over time in India of the cultural standards of enterprises' involvement of CSR, with CSR alluding to the manner that businesses are administered to cause a general positive effect on the groups, cultures, societies and environments in which they function. The basis of CSR rely on the reality that apart from public policy corporates should also be accountable enough to address social concerns. Hence,enterprises should manage the difficulties and issues taken care of to a specific degree by the states. Among different nations, India has one of the wealthiest conventions of CSR. A lot has been done as of late to make Indian Entrepreneurs mindful of social obligation as an imperative fragment of their business activity yet CSR in India still doesn't seem to receive broad acknowledgment. To realize this objective the CSR approach of corporates must be in accordance with their attitudes towards conventional business—organizations setting clear targets, undertaking potential investments, measuring and reporting performance publicly.

The historical backdrop of CSR in India has its four stages which run parallel to India's historical development and has brought about various methodologies towards CSR. However, the stages are not static and the highlights of each stage may cover different stages. In the primary stage, philanthropy and generosity were the fundamental drivers of CSR. Culture, religion, family esteems and custom and industrialization influentially affected CSR. In the pre-industrialization period, which continued till 1850, affluent merchants shared a piece of their riches with the more extensive society by means of establishing temples for a religious purpose. In addition, these traders helped the general public in getting over periods of famine and epidemics by offering nourishment from their godowns and cash and in this manner securing fundamental status in the general public. The entry of colonial rule in India from 1850s onwards changed the approach towards CSR. The industrial dynastiesof the nineteenth century for example, Tata, Godrej, Bajaj, Modi, Birla, Singhania, and so on, were strongly disposed towards economic and social contemplations. Nevertheless, it has been found that their endeavours towards social and industrial development were not only the result of their selfless and religious motives but also determined under the influence of caste groups and political objectives. In the second stage, amid the independence movement, there was added emphasis on Indian Industrialists to exhibit their devotion towards the advance of the general public. This was when Mahatma Gandhi presented the idea of "trusteeship", as indicated by which the business pioneers needed to deal with their riches in order to profit the common man. "I desire to end capitalism almost, if not quite, as much as the most advanced socialist. But our methods differ. My theory of trusteeship is no make-shift, certainly no camouflage. I am confident that it will survive all other theories." This was Gandhi's statement which emphasizes his contention towards his idea of "trusteeship". Gandhi's impact put weighton different Entrepreneurs to work towards building the country and its socio-economic progress. In the opinion of Gandhi, Indian organizations were assumed to be the "temples of modern India". Under his impact organizations built up trusts for schools and universities and furthermore enabled in setting up training and scientific institutions. The operations of the trusts were to a great extent in accordance with Gandhi's reforms which looked to abolish untouchability, promote empowerment of women and rural development. The third period of CSR (1960–1980) had its connection to the component of "mixed economy", arrival of Public Sector Undertakings (PSUs) and laws pertaining to labour and environmental norms. During this phase, the private sector was compelled to assume a lower priority. The public sector was viewed as the prime mover of advancement. In light of the stringent legitimate rules and regulations encompassing the actions of the private sector, the phase was termed as an "era of command and control". The policy of industrial licensing, high taxes and confinements on the private sector promoted corporate misconducts. This resulted inpassing of legislation in relation to corporate administration, labour and environmental concerns. PSUs were established by the state to guarantee appropriate allocation of assets (wealth, food and so on) to the deprived. Nevertheless, the public sector was successful only to a specific limited degree. This prompted expectation to shift from the public to the private sector and their effective engagement in the socio-economic progress of the nation turned out to be totally significant. In 1965, Indian academicians, politicians and entrepreneurs established a national workshop on CSR intended for settlement. They stressed upon transparency, social responsibility and regular stakeholder negotiations. Despite such endeavours, the CSR failed to influence entrepreneurs. In the fourth stage (1980 until the present) Indian organizations began to abandon their conventional commitment with CSR and incorporated it into a sustainable business approach. In 1990s, the initial steps towards globalization and monetary liberalization were undertaken. Controls and licensing system were partiallyabolished which provided a thrust to the economy the marks of which are very clear in the present day. Enhanced growth momentum of the economy enabled Indian organizations to contribute quickly and this made them additionally eager and capable to play a part towards social cause. Globalization has resulted in transforming India into a significant destination with regard to production and manufacturing bases of transnational corporations (TNCs) concerned. As Western markets are growing increasingly worried about labour and environmental norms in the developing nations, Indian organizations who manufacture and export items for the developed world need to give careful consideration to comply with the international standards.

As mentioned earlier, CSR is not a novel idea in India. Ever since their establishment, organizations, such as Tata Group, the Aditya Birla Group and Indian Oil Corporation, to give some examples, have been engaged in serving the group. Several other corporations, through donations and charity event shave been contributing to the wellbeing of the society. The fundamental goal of CSR nowadays is to expand the organization's general influence on the society and stakeholders. CSR policies, practices and programs are being integrated at length by an ever-increasing number of organizations throughout their business operations and procedures. An increasing number of organizations believe that CSR is not merely another type of indirect expense but is critical for safeguarding the goodwill and reputation, protecting from attacks and expanding business competitiveness. Organizations have dedicated CSR teams that devise policies, strategies and objectives for their CSR programs and allocate budgets to fund them. These programs are frequently dictated by social attitude which have clear goals and are well characterized and are aligned with the standard business. These programs are put to use by the employees who are significant to this procedure. CSR programs ranges from group advancement to upgradation of education, environment, healthcare and so on.

For instance, a more thorough procedure of expansion is embraced by some organizations such as Bharat Petroleum Corporation Limited, Maruti Suzuki India Limited and Hindustan Unilever Limited. Supply of enhanced medical and sanitation amenities, building schools and houses, and enabling the villagers to be self-sufficient and in process turning them more independent by imparting vocational training and a know-how of business operations are the amenities that these organizations concentrateupon. Several corporations are helping different people by offering them good level of comfort. On the contrary, the CSR procedures of organizations like Glaxo SmithKline Pharmaceuticals' emphasize on the health aspect of the group. They establish health camps in tribal towns which provide medical inspections and therapy and take on health awareness programs. A section of non-profit corporations which conduct health and education programs in regressive areas are to a specific degree funded by such organizations. Moreover, organizations progressively join hands with Non-governmental organizations (NGOs) and utilize their know-how in formulating programs to deal with extensive social issues. For instance, a considerable measure of work is being carried out to reconstruct the lives of the tsunami-affected victims. This is absolutely carried out by SAP India in association with Hope Foundation, an NGO that concentrates mostlyon carrying out development in the lives of the deprived and needy. The SAP Labs Center of HOPE in Bangalore was launched by this enterprise which take care of the food, clothing, shelter and medical care of street children.

CSR has experienced various stages in India. The capability to leave a mark in the society and enhance the general standard of life has undoubtedly been substantiated by the organizations. Not one but all organizations should endeavour tocause a variation in the present social circumstances in India with the intention to have an efficient and long-term solution to the social issues. Collaboration between organizations, NGOs and the legislature should be simplified so that a combination of their competences such as expertise, strategic thinking, manpower and money to bring widespread social transformation will put the socio-economic advancement of the nation on a fast track.

The enactment of the new company law from 1 April 2014 has made India the only nation in the globe with legislated CSR and an expenditure threshold of up to $2.5 billion (₹ 15,000 crore). The new law dictates that all organizations, involving foreign corporations, with a minimum net worth of ₹ 500 crore, turnover of ₹ 1,000 crore and net profit of at least ₹ 5 crore, expend at least two percent (2%) of their profit on CSR. As per the industry estimations, around 8,000 organizations will fall under the scope of the CSR provisions in the country and this would translate into an estimated CSR expenditure of $1.95 billion to $2.44 billion. With higher economic development and rise in companies' incomes, this compulsory spending will go up. The new law would result in a remarkable increase in expenditure by organizations on CSR activities. Several big companies have been effectively involved in the CSR activities, yet the number is low. The new law will result in a remarkable increase in the numbers. Presently, the instructed expenditure would be in the range of ₹ 10, 000 crore to ₹ 15, 000 crore annually. The industries, in general, hail the new guidelines. Nevertheless, since CSR is a transformative concept, it will progressively advance over a period of time. Industry is thus restless on the enactment of this new provision. The new Companies Act 2013 that came into operation from 1 April 2014, substituted six-decade old legislation Companies Act 1956. CSR has been made obligatory under the new directive and there are terms of penalizations, in of the event of insolvency. Beyond doubt, the industries'apprehensions about the new legislation are mostly related to taxation and limit on actions that fall under the scope of CSR. The biggest worry of corporates is with regard to the effect of CSR contribution from a tax deductibility position. The Industry anticipates that the ministry of finance will find it appropriate to confirm CSR expenditure remains tax-deductible, more so since this expenditure is an essential cost of accountable business. Under the present income tax regulation, the CSR expenditure cannot be treated as expenditure. It will be a portion of profit and attract taxes. According to the present law, unless expenditure is in the course of the business of the organization, the same is rejected and the query may be raised as to whether CSR costis incurred in the course of the business of the organization or not. Hence, the CSR Rules could result in significant expenses being refused in course of tax evaluation. Therefore, unless the Income Tax law is also altered concurrently, this could result in years of extended proceedings and arguments.

NATIONAL VOLUNTARY GUIDELINES ON SOCIAL, ENVIRONMENTAL AND ECONOMIC RESPONSIBILITIES OF BUSINESS

These rules enacted by the Ministry of Corporate Affairs in India, were created through a broad consultative process with the goal of giving a particular India-driven approach for Indian organizations to comprehend the subtleties of capable business, pertinent to extensive and private companies alike. They are easy to fathom and execute, and urge organizations to receive the triple bottom line approach. These rules comprises nine principles which identify with ethics and transparency, product life cycle sustainability, employee well-being, stakeholder engagement, human rights, environmental stewardship, responsible policy advocacy, inclusive development and consumer well-being. Every guideline comprises of centre components that further express the reason and feeling of every principle.

It likewise gives a way to embrace these rules.

Clause 135, Companies Act 2013: In India, the idea of CSR is represented by clause 135 of the Companies Act, 2013, which was passed by the two Houses of the Parliament, and had obtained the consent of the President of India on 29 August 2013. The CSR provisions inside the Act is appropriate to organizations with a yearly turnover of minimum amount of 1,000 crore INR or a networth of minimum amount of 500 crore INR, or a net benefit of minimum five crore INR. The new guidelines, which will be applicable from the financial year 2014–2015 onwards, additionally anticipate organizations to set-up a CSR council comprising of their board individuals, including no less than one independent director.

The Act urges organizations to spend no less than 2% of their average net profit in the past three years on CSR exercises. The ministry's draft instructions, that have been set up for open remark, characterize net profit as the profit before tax according to the books of accounts, barring profits emerging from branches outside India.

The Act lists out an arrangement of exercises suitable under CSR. Organizations may execute these exercises considering the local conditions after pursuing for board endorsement.

The characteristic activities which can be attempted by an organization under CSR have been indicated under Schedule VII of the Act.

The draft rules (as of September 2013) give various elucidations and keeping in mind that these are anticipating open remark before notification, some features are as per the following:

- Surplus emerging out of CSR exercises should be reinvested into CSR activities, and this will be far beyond the 2% figure

The organization can execute its CSR exercises through the following strategies:

- Directly all alone
- Through its own non-profit establishment set-up in order to encourage this activity
- Through freely enlisted non-benefit associations that have a record of no less than three years in similar such related exercises
- Collaborating or pooling their assets with different organizations
- Only CSR exercises embraced in India will be thought about
- Activities implied solely for workers and their families will not be eligible
- A layout for the board presentation CSR has been producedwhich incorporates among others, activity-wise, explanations behind expenditure under 2% of the average net profits of the past three years and an accountability statement that the CSR policy, implementation and monitoring process is in conformity with the CSR targets, in letter and in soul. This must be signed by either the CEO, or the MD or a director of the organization.

RUNDOWN OF ACTIVITIES UNDER SCHEDULE VII

- Promotion of Education
- Eradication of extreme hunger and poverty
- Gender equity and women empowerment
- Reducing child mortality and improving maternal health
- Combating HIV-AIDS, malaria and other diseases
- Environment supportability
- Social Business projects
- Contribution to Prime Minister's relief fund and other such state and central funds
- Employment enhancing vocational skills Governance

Clause 135 of the Act sets out the rules to be followed by organizations while building up their CSR program. The CSR committee will be in charge of setting up a comprehensive plan on CSR exercises, including the expenses, the sort of activities, roles and duties of different partners and a monitoring component for such exercises. The CSR committee can likewise guarantee that all sorts of salary accumulated to the organization by means of CSR activities ought to be credited back to the group or CSR corpus.

REPORTING

The new Act requires that the leading body of the organization might, in the wake of the suggestions made by the CSR advisory group, affirm the CSR approach for the organization and reveal its substance in their report and furthermore publish the particulars on the organization's official website, assuming any, in such way as might be endorsed. In the event that the organization fails to spend the proposed sum, the board, in its report, might indicate the reasons.

BUSINESS RESPONSIBILITY REPORTING

The other reporting prerequisite ordered by the legislature of India, including CSR is by the SEBI which issued a circular on 13 August 2012 directing the leading 100 listed organizations to report their ESG activities. These activities need to be reported in form of a BRR as a piece of the yearly report. SEBI has given a template to file the BRR. Business responsibility reporting is in accordance with the NVG published by the Ministry of Corporate Affairs in July 2011.

Arrangements have likewise been made in the listing agreement to incorporate the accommodation of BRR by the applicable organizations. The listing agreement also gives the format of the BRR. The BRR expects organizations to report their functioning on the nine NVG principals. Other listed organizations have also been urged by SEBI to intentionally reveal data on their ESG execution in the BRR format.

CSR: Planning and Strategizing

The initial move towards enacting CSR projects in an industrial set up is the constitution of a CSR committee according to the provisions in the Companies Act, 2013, clause 135. Clause 135 of the Companies Act, 2013 demands a CSR committee to be established by the board of directors. They will be in charge of setting up a comprehensive plan of the CSR activities including, choices with respect to the expenditure, the sort of activities to be attempted, roles and obligations of the concerned people and a monitoring and reporting system. The CSR advisory group will likewise be required to guarantee that all the income accumulated to the organization by means of CSR activities is credited back to the CSR corpus.

Companies Act, 2013, Clause 135: CSR Committee Requirements

- A CSR advisory group of the board ought to be constituted. It should comprise of no less than three directors out of whom no less than one is an independent director. This composition will be revealed in the board's report according to sub-section (3) of section 134.

- The CSR committee shall:
  - Formulate and prescribe a CSR approach to the board, showing the activities as indicated in Schedule VII of the Act
  - Endorse the measure of expenses to be incurred on the activities demonstrated in the policy
  - Monitor the CSR policy on regular basis

This is a phenomenal beginning stage for any organization new to CSR. In the event that an organization as of now practice CSR,, this council ought to be set up at the earliest so that it can direct the alignment of the organization's activities with the necessities of the Act.

A set of such empowering processes, their inter-connections and the sequence in which they should be established have been described as follows:

CSR Processes

While building up these procedures, no standard set of suggestions exist for all organizations. Nevertheless, an outlineof the required particulars, the activities required to be finished for each of these procedures along with some additional guidance on important issues has been provided further as follows:

STEP ONE: DEVELOPING A CSR STRATEGY AND POLICY

Purpose

The Companies Act, 2013 requires each organization to put out its CSR policy in the public space. The direction proposed in the Act and the draft regulations on what constitutes a CSR strategy are that it should:

- Exclude typical business exercises of the organization
- Include a list of the CSR projects or activities which the organization intends to embrace amid the implementation year
- While determining the yearly report prerequisites, the draft rules go on to state that the organization must givea brief blueprint of its CSR strategy, including 'the statement of intent reflecting the ethos of the company, broad areas of CSR interest and an overview of activities to be undertaken'
- A web link to the CSR strategy that provide the full list of projects, activities and programmes proposed to be undertaken by the company

Since a large portion of the advancement requires long-term commitments and their effect frequently requires a long time to accrue, a good CSR practice requires that an organization that is serious about its CSR ought tobuild up a long-term (three to five years) vision and policywhich is assessed every year and the activities and budgets are planned on yearly basis. The latter will conform to the CSR policy requirements of the Companies Act, 2013.

To preventconfusion in relation to terms like policy, strategy, project and programme, a short clarification has been provided here:

- CSR strategy alludes to what the organization hopes accomplish in the following three to five years and incorporates the vision, mission and objectives on more extensive level. It likewise implies how it intends to accomplish these in terms of organization and approach.
- CSR policy alludes to what the organization hopes to accomplish throughout the following year. This is aligned with the prerequisites of the Companies Act, 2013.
- Programme alludes to a sector or a problem that the organization recommends to address through its CSR. This can, for example, be 'education of the girl child' or 'agriculture development'. Programmes will be plainly delineated in the organization's CSR strategy.
- Programme objectives will be accomplished through a sequence of distinctive projects and, a project refers to an array of interventions, normally in a particular geography and attend to a particular stakeholder community, with a well-definedset of objectives, beginning and end and a budget allocated for it.
- Each project in succession will comprise a number of events. All of which play a part in achieving the project goals.

CSR AND SMEs

What are SMEs?

Small and medium enterprises (SMEs) remarkably play a partin achieving India's economic development. These serve autonomously and furthermore as subordinate to bigger units and help produce employment and industrialize the rural and backward regions of the nation. They utilizeabout 40% of India's labour force and contribute about 45% to India's manufacturing output.

WHAT DO THEY DO?

The business deedsof SMEs are executed in proximity to the local people. This empowers them to know about community needs, manage expectations and create CSR programmes suitably.

Now that the CSR clause in the Companies Act, 2013 encompasses organizations having a minimum net profit of five crore INR, it is anticipated that while smaller scale enterprises will not qualify, numerous small and medium enterprises (SMEs) will.

SMEs are being dealt with independently in this handbook on account of their individual characteristics.

The CSR exercises of these organizations are impelled by the individual interests of supporters who hold a note worthy financial stake in the business. They have a tendency to be in groups and engage in comparable business activities. While the quantum of income accessible for CSR with specific SMEs is anticipated to be small, all authorized organizations in a particulargeological group, who solitaryandcooperativelyaffect the same group, can pool their assets to form a sizeable CSR fund.

HOW CAN SMEs CONTRIBUTE TO CSR INITIATIVES?

This section analyses the choice of taking on combined CSR activities by SMEs. This association can likewise be utilized by different organizations to maximize the impact of their CSR activities while decreasing the operational expenditure for fund management.

WHY COLLABORATE FOR CSR INITIATIVES?

CSR is for all organizations. SMEs in India have taken partin CSR actions yet these attempts have not been optimally delivered. One probable motive can be the reality that CSR activities rely on the benefits of a SME and any fluctuations in benefits can negatively impact their capacity to proceed with their commitment for CSR. Another reason can be the restricted human resources accessible to SMEs which may similarly bring about the absence of an expert approach.

SMEs tend to concentrate on short-term activities that include lesser operational expenses. A survey organizedby UNIDO in 2008 on five SME groups in India, found that 31% to 79% of the SMEs in these groups, favoured charity donations as opposed to long-term programmes for local groups.

With the presentation of the new Companies Act, 2013, the SME's methodology to deal with CSR must be adjusted while keeping operational costs low. One reasonable option is to pool assets with different SMEs in the group and make joint CSR programmes administered by a sole entity. This associationcan be framed within the units in a bunch as they communicate with the same groups and have already formed associations that oblige the business needs of the units.

Collaboration has the following benefits:

- ***Decreases operational cost***: Individual CSR endeavours by an organization comprise setting up a CSR division, evaluating the necessities of local groups, undertaking programmes straightforwardly or through an NGO and performingregular impact assessment analyses. A typical corporation taking into account various organizations will perform these activities as a group and thus reduce the operational cost of administration.
- ***Undertake long-term projects***: A noteworthy obstacle in building up long-term projects is the uncertainty in the CSR budget.

This is subject to the economic performance of the organization.

A varying performance infers that the CSR budget allocations can be untrustworthy and can risk a programmeintroduced before. Pooling assets addresses this issue to a specific degree as the other stakeholders can increase their share in the event that there is fluctuation in assignment from a specific segment of the bunch. The long-term programmes also have noteworthy effect than the short-term assignments.

Communities are progressively acknowledging the significance of the assistance provided by these programmes in improving their lives. Long-term programmes additionallybring aboutbetter community relations and this guarantees averting circumstances of community restlessness that impede business activities.

- ***Learning from experiences***: A typical entity with numerous participants from the bunch will help evaluate community requirements, take on appropriate programmes in light of past experiences and address a more noteworthy number of community issues.

Coordinated effort among the SMEs in a group gives a chance to oversee social and environmental issues and react better to the demands from buyers, who are attempting to build up ethical supply chains and gain acknowledgement from the worldwide community. Collaborations can likewise be fashioned among bigger organizations, potentially through industry relationship, to empower them to address basic issues plaguing a topographical region or a corporation.

THE PROCEDURE FOR AN SME

The initial step taken in collaborating is to create a partnership between interested SMEs. This might be started by the group relationship in of the event of large-scale participation from the group. On the other hand, it can be started by an individual SME on the off chance that there are just a couple of units interested in embracing CSR activities in collaboration. Participation of the cluster alliance will guarantee that the local precedencies are given due consideration while building up CSR programmes. In the event ofan adequate number of SMEs in a cluster notwilling to participate or are not needed under the Companies Act, 2013 to spend on CSR activities, the limit might be extended to other groups, though this expands complexity.

The association should then frame a directing committee with the officials from each SME in order to democratically settle the issues. The guiding advisory group should examine the institutional method of execution, that is, taking on activities through an established trust, society, and a Section 8 company or establishing a new entity or straightforwardly administering the funds.

The means other than the rules specified by the guiding committee in the section "CSR: Planning and strategizing", incorporate the following:

- Deciding the thematic areas from Schedule VII of the Companies Act, 2013, beneficiary groups and topographies that it will target in light of the contributions from members.
- Developing internal procedures to track specific contribution by participants and their use in CSR activities, finalizing long-term assignments based on projected contributions by participants and addressing non-payment by participants.

The CSR strategy of specific SMEs ought to be designed to permit for flexibility in the event of a combinedeffort to embrace CSR. This infers that the policy, on top of the rulesdescribed in the section "Step one: Develop CSR strategy and policy", should permit the following:

- Flexibility in choosing thematic fields from Schedule VII of Companies Act, 2013, beneficiary groups and topographies according to the needs of the whole association.
- Support to start CSR programmes to the degree conceivable, on the off chance that the association is abandoned.

The subsequent stages associated in the due diligence of execution or the concept development partner are as follows:

1. Project development
2. Operationalizing institutional mechanism
3. Contracting
4. Budgeting and payments
5. Monitoring
6. Impact measurement

In situations where the aggregate CSR funds are inadequate to take care of the expense of collaboration, SMEs can likewise add to the Prime Minister's National Relief Fund or some other fund established by the central government or the state governments according to activity IX of the Schedule VII of the Companies Act, 2013.

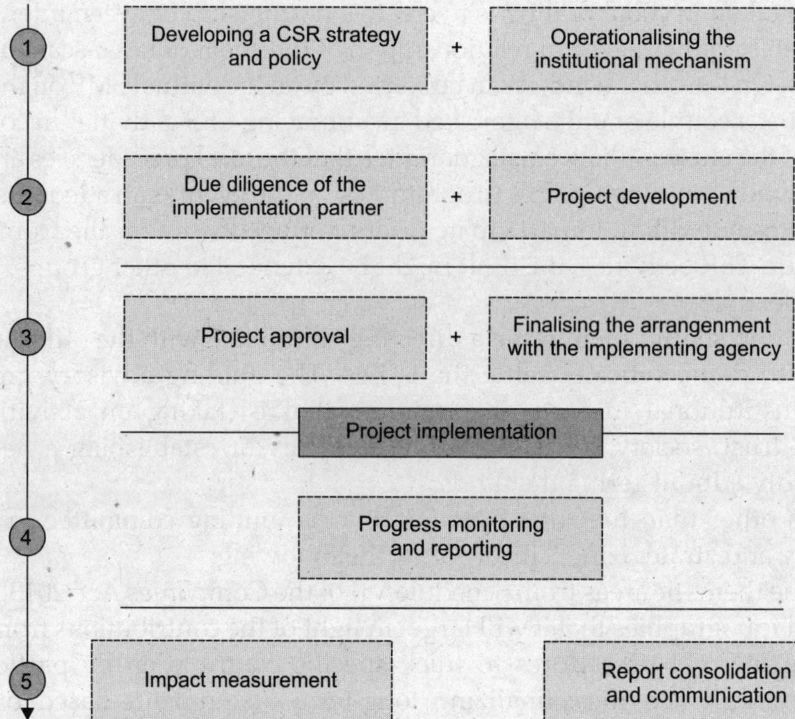

CSR and Sustainability

Sustainability (corporate sustainability) is taken from the idea of sustainable development which is characterized by the Brundtland Commission as "development that meets the needs of the present without compromising the ability of future generations to meet their own needs". Corporate sustainability basically alludes to the part that organizations can play in meeting the plan of sustainable development and involves a balanced way to economic advancement, social advancement and environmental stewardship.

CSR in India tends to concentrate on what is finished with benefits after they are made. On the contrary, sustainability is about factoring the social and environmental effects of directing business, that is, the manner by which profits are made. Therefore, a significant part of the Indian practice of CSR is a significant segment of sustainability or responsible business, which is a bigger thought, a reality that is apparent from different sustainability systems. An interesting case in consideration is the NVGs for social, environmental and economic obligations of business issued by the Ministry of Corporate Affairs in June 2011. Principle 8 identifying with comprehensive advancement covers most of the aspects encompassed by the CSR clause of the Companies Act, 2013. Nevertheless, the remaining eight principles associate with other facets of the business. The UN Global Compact, a broadly utilized sustainability structure has 10 principles encompassing social, environmental, human rights and governance issues, and what is portrayed as CSR is implicit instead of explicit in these principles.

Worldwide, the idea of CSR and sustainability appears to be converging, as is apparent from the different definitions of CSR set forth by worldwide associations. The origin of this convergence can be seen from the preamble to the freshly released draft norms pertaining to the CSR clause within the Companies Act, 2013 which discuss about partners or stakeholders and incorporating it with the social, environmental and monetary goals, all of which constitute the concept of a triple bottom line methodology. It is also recognized in the Guidelines on Corporate Social Responsibility and Sustainability for Central Public Sector Enterprises issued by the DPE in April 2013. Two existing separate guidelines on CSR and sustainable development, issued in 2010 and 2011, respectively, have been replaced with the new guidelines that mention the following:

"Since corporate social responsibility and sustainability are so closely entwined, it can be said that corporate social responsibility and sustainability is a company's commitment to its stakeholders to conduct business in an economically, socially and environmentally sustainable manner that is transparent and ethical."

15 CHAPTER

Ethics of Administration

With the passage of time, the concept of civil service has been reformed as well as ideas of its role and responsibilities. The comprehensive civil service structure and established practices of Independent India came down from the administration system of the British India. Its usefulness for confirming national unity as well as better administration in the country was marked by Sardar Vallabhbhai Patel and granted by the Constituent Assembly and incorporated in the Constitution. ***It is appropriate currently to recollect the Sardar's insight and his vision:***

'I need hardly emphasize that an efficient, disciplined and contented service, assured of its prospects as a result of diligent and honest work, and is sine qua non of sound administration under a democratic regime even more than under an authoritarian rule. The service must be above party and we should ensure that political considerations either in its recruitment or in its discipline and control are reduced to the minimum, if not eliminated altogether'.

ADMINISTRATIVE ETHICS

A set of principles, norms and rules of behaviour, moral values and moral requirements are called administrative ethics. In the domain of public administration, these are applicable to persons who act as professional managers. Ethics is a branch of philosophy which seeks to address morality. In the public sector, ethics addresses the fundamental premise of a public administrator's duty as a "steward" to the public. Ethics is the moral consideration and justification for decisions made and actions taken in time for completion of daily responsibilities while working to provide the general services of government and non-profit organizations.

It is generally emphasized that the employees of the government establish ethical standards for managerial decisions, analyse these standards and bear personal and professional accountability for the decisions made. **"A set of moral norms and requirements for those in public administration targeting their professional activity at attainment of common wealth and effective use of moral values" is considered Civil service ethics.**

The objective of civil service ethics is keeping the essence and content of professional activities approved socially and to regulate employee relations by dint of norms, behaviour and actions, and to form an ethical ingredient element in the consciousness of public administration employees.

The moral norms are the basis of Civil service ethics. The Latin word 'norm' implies rule and pattern. This being one of the easiest types of ethical requirement and is utilized as an element of ethical relations and as a type of ethical consciousness.

THE ETHICS OF ADMINISTRATION CONSIST OF THREE BASIC COMPONENTS

1. ***Standards and norms:*** The actions of people and employees are guided by certain principles which help in leading and controlling their behaviour, fore example, formulation of laws, codes and rules.
2. ***Values:*** These are the individuals, group and social statements, opinions and attitudes towards concepts such as justice, freedom, responsibility, loyalty, neutrality, honesty, etc.
3. ***Behaviour:*** It depends on the different kinds of employee actions limited by particular standards and norms relating to social values.

SPECIFIC ETHICAL REQUIREMENTS FOR THE CIVIL SERVICE

Ethical requirements for civil servants are determined by various methods described as follows:

1. They reflect the ideas and objectives of the civil service and certain tasks of different governmental institutions.
2. The conception of an ideal or targeted public administration model adopted in society influence these principles. A civil society is the source of administrative ethics, as its requirements, concerns and expectations are highlighted in ethical norms and requirements.

Administrative ethics should perform the following fundamental tasks:

- Taking part in the regulation of the relationship between government and citizens
- Promoting public and state concerns in government activities in the maximum possible manner
- Providing public administration staff with certain behavioural standards on the basis of morality.

REQUIREMENT FOR ADMINISTRATIVE ETHICS

The civil service of the nation was regarded as the chief agent of socio-economic change. It has brought about a notable shift after independence in mid-sixties. The administrators were demonstrating disinterest and lack of promise to the socio-economic initiatives of the legislature. In this regard, the remark of the Prime Minister Rajiv Gandhi on the administrative culture are as follows:

"......and what of the iron frame of system, the administrative services.....and the myriad functionaries of the state...but as the proverb says there can be no protection if the fence starts eating the crop. This is what has happened. The fence has started eating grass... we have government servants who do not serve but oppress the poor and the helpless....who don't uphold the law...but connive with those who cheat the state....they have no work ethic, no feeling for the public cause, no involvement in the future of the nation. They have only a grasping mercenary outlook, devoid of competence, integrity and commitment..."

The Indian government held a conference of chief secretaries in 1996 with a view to developing an agenda for fruitful and responsive administration to ensure responsive, responsible, transparent, decentralized and public-friendly administration from top to bottom. An action plan of Effective and Accountable Administration was put before the Conference of Chief Ministers held in 1997. Three major areas of action plan discussed in the conference were as follows:

1. Making administration accountable and citizen friendly;
2. Confirming transparency and right to information and
3. Motivating civil services.

The Fourth Report of Second Administrative Reform Commission on Ethics in Governance emphasized on the need of developing special set of values for public service. The commission observed:

"Public Service Values' towards which all public servants should aspire, should be defined and made applicable to all tiers of Government and parastatal organizations. Any transgression of these values should be treated as misconduct, inviting punishment."

Concerns and Dilemmas Related to Ethics in Government Institutions

16

CHAPTER

DEFINITION AND SIGNIFICANCE OF ETHICS

Ethics has been recognized as the 'Science of morals; the rules of conduct, the science of human duty' since the seventeenth century. Hence, in common terms, ethics can be defined as the principles that influence a person's or a group's behaviour according to both the science of the good and the nature of the right. Mention of the ethical concerns of governance can be abundantly found in Indian scriptures and other treatises such as *Ramayana, Mahabharata, Bhagvad Gita, Buddha Charita, Arthashastra, Panchatantra, Manusmriti, Kural, Shukra Niti, Kadambari, Raja Tarangani* and *Hitopadesh*. At the same time, one can also refer to the views provided by the Chinese philosophers such as Lao Tse, Confucius and Mencius related to ethical governance. Western philosophy refers to three eminent schools of ethics. The first, motivated by Aristotle, states that qualities (such as justice, charity and generosity) are dispositions to act in ways that turn out to be beneficial for the one who holds these virtues and the society of which he is a part. The second, inspired by Immanuel Kant, holds that the concept of duty is important for morality: human beings are destined, as per the knowledge of their duty as rational beings, to follow the categorical rule to respect others with whom they interact. The third includes the Utilitarian viewpoint that states that the guiding principle of conduct should make large number of people happier. There are ample of ethical guidelines for rulers as per western thoughts, whether in a monarchy or a democracy. Mention of these guidelines can be traced in the works of Plato, Aristotle, Thomas Jefferson, Alexander Hamilton, Thomas Penn, John Stuart Mill, Edmund Burke and others.

The theory of justice given by Rawls deals with the adaptation of two fundamental principles of justice, which will guarantee a just and morally acceptable society in return.

- The former principle assures each person a right to have the most extensive basic liberty compatible with liberty of others.
- The latter principle holds that social and economic positions should be open for all and advantageous to everyone.

The aim of Rawls here is to make sure to depict how such principles would be globally accepted. Here, his composition states only general ethical issues. He presents a hypothetical 'veil of ignorance', where all 'players' in the social game would be positioned in a situation called the 'original position'. With only a general knowledge about the realities of 'life and society', 'rationally' sensible choice should be made by each player regarding the type of social institution they would enter into contract with. Denying the players any specific information about themselves compels them to embrace a generalized point of view that that is similar to the moral point of view to a great extent. This viewpoint, which is mainly related to moral conclusions, can be formed without rejecting the prudential viewpoint and posting a moral outlook just by following one's own prudential reasoning under any procedural bargaining.

Wisdom on administrative ethics means that in Administrative State, the public administrators are regarded as the 'guardians'. Hence, it is expected that they should respect public trust and not violate it. Two crucial questions that emerged in this context are 'why guardians should be guarded?' and 'Who guards the guardian?' It is important to guard administrators against their bent to misinterpret public interest, encourage self-interest, practice corruption and cause subversion of national interest. They are also required to be guarded by the external establishments such as the judiciary, legislature, political executive, media and civil society establishments. These different ways of control turn out to be instruments of accountability.

EVOLUTION OF ETHICAL CONCERNS IN ADMINISTRATION

It is of utmost importance to acknowledge that Political Science and the science of Management have largely influenced the discipline of Public Administration in the initial years of its growth. On the one hand, the philosophical ideals of Public Administration were influenced primarily by Political Science. On the other hand, Management Sciences designed its technological aspect. The early Political Science was a mix of Moral Philosophy and Political Economy, whereas its current curriculum includes secular, practical, empirical and scientific aspects relate to the past century. During the initial years of the last century, Political Science students in the USA were discouraged due to lack of the ethical approach in the Gilded Age. Influenced by the interaction with the German universities and by the thinking of scholars such as J.N. Burgess, E.J. James, A.B Hart, A.L Lovell and F.J Goodnow, they thought of recreate Political Science as a true science. They increasing started to observe and analyse 'actual governments'. Natural and Social Sciences have had a great influence on their ideas and approaches.

Later, scholars such as Herbert Simon were influenced by the logical positivism of the Austrian School, resulting in the increase in followers with the common aim of developing a Science of Politics and a Science of Administration that will likely `predict and control' political and administrative life. As Dwight Waldo comments, there was a shift from the old faith that good government was the government of moral men to a morality that was unrelated and that suitable institutions and expert personnel were the deciding factors in shaping good government. `The new amorality became almost a request for professional respect'.

Due to the prominence of behaviouralism until the mid-1960s, the ethical issues in the study of Political Science and Public Administration were marginalized further. Beginning of Post-behaviouralism in Political Science and of the accent on New Public Administration in Public Administration helped scientific methods of Behaviouralim and humanistic (read `ethical') values to strike a balance with administration, resulting in resolving the dispute between facts and values.

The present form of public administration focuses mainly on the `values' of equity, justice, humanism, human rights, gender equality and compassion. The movement of Good Governance, started by the World Bank in 1992, emphasizes, *inter alia*, on the ethical and moral conduct of administrators. Although the New Public Management movement focuses on administrative effectiveness, administrative ethics in its broader manifestation take the centre stage in the New Public Administration. Both the movements are complementary to each other.

The ideal-type structure of bureaucracy, coined by Max Weber, also stated on an ethical imperative of bureaucratic behaviour. Weber (1947) observed:

'In the rational type, it is a matter of principle that the members of the administrative staff should be completely separated from ownership of the means of production and administration. Officials, employees and workers attached to the administrative staff do not themselves own the non-human means of production and administration.... These exist, furthermore, in principle complete separation of property belonging to the organization, which is controlled within the sphere of office and the personal property of the official, which is available for his own private uses'.

Weber's study reveals that there is a need to avoid misuse of an official position for personal gains. While his ideal-type structure related to bureaucracy is not empirical, yet it has an empirical flavour, because it seems to have considered the existential reality of bureaucratic behaviour. Message, donot misuse official property for personal benefit, is also clear from a normative angle even after knowing that Weber was not normative in his ideal-type constructs.

Bureaucrats have been criticized by most of the critics of real-world bureaucracies, including Harold Laski, Carl Friedrich, Victor Thompson and Warren Bennis, for flouting the specified rules of moral conduct. Fred Riggs, while debating the qualities of a prismatic society like **`formalism'** and **'nepotism'**, highlights the wide gap between the **`ideal'** and the **`real'** in administrative behaviour. It is difficult to let these deviations go as they are too glaring. Immoral behaviour thus came out as an integral element of **`bureau pathology'**.

CONTEXT OF ETHICS AND ITS SIGNIFICANCE FOR PUBLIC ADMINISTRATION

Ethics, keeping in view an entire society or a social sub-system, develops over a long period of time and is affected, while nurturing and growing, by various environmental factors. Administrative ethics is no way different. It is the creation of several contextual structures and always keeps on growing and changing. Some of these contextual factors that affect ethics in the public administrative systems are as follows:

The Historical Context

The history of a country greatly shapes the ethical character of the governance system. During the early phase of the America, the ethical setting of the American Public Administration was destroyed by the Spoils System in the USA. The then American President Jackson asserted 'To victor belong the spoils'. If President Garfield was not assassinated by a disgruntled job seeker in 1881, things would have continued the same way. It is only after Garfield's assassination that civil service reforms took place in the USA. The constitution of Civil Service Commission in 1883 was the first important step in this direction.

Indian governance system has long been plagued with unethical practices. Some of the corrupt practices practised by the administrators of those times are mentioned in Kautilya's *Arthashastra*. Corruption also existed in the Mughal Empire and the Indian princely states, where courtiers and administrative functionaries used 'bakashish' for selling and buying favours. Even the East India Company was not immune to corruption and corrupt people who were criticized even by the British parliamentarians.

The existence of forces of probity and immorality together can be traced back to ancient times. The intensity of these forces depends upon the support these attain from the main actors of politico-administrative system. More worrisome aspect of it is that a long heritage of immoral practices in governance is likely to grow the tolerance level for administrative immorality. In most developing countries with a colonial history, the gap between the people and the government continues to be wide. During the colonial era, a majority of people do not happily accept the lawfulness of governance and hence true devotion to the rulers was a rare phenomenon. As the differences between the governing elite and the citizens have been reduced significantly in the new democratic regimes, affinity and trust between them has not achieved the desired result. Regrettably, the rulers do not seem to have embraced the essence of emotional unity with the citizens. The heritage of competitive collaboration between the people and the administrators remains. This relationship adversely affected 'administrative ethics'.

The Socio-cultural Context

The nature of governance system is determined by values that infuse the social order in a society determine. The Indian society today had more love for wealth compared to any other value. The means-ends debate has been put on the backseat while busy in generating wealth. Unfortunately, ends have gained supremacy over means. Hunt for wealth in itself is not bad. In fact, it is a mark of civilizational progress. What is more important is the means used while being engaged in this hunt.

We appear to be living in an economic or commercial society, where unit-dimensional growth of individuals is preferred and valued, where ends have been overshadowed by means, and ideals have been inundated under the weight of more practical concerns of economic progress. Can we change this social order? Mahatma Gandhi was very much eager to transform the priority-order of the Indian society, but rarely anyone supported his radical thinking that was immersed in a strong moral order. This is a fact that after

Gandhi, no one has ever matched his persona and there has been not a single strong voice in independent India challenging the authority of 'teleology and unidimensionalism'. It is sad that our families and educational system have failed as a whole as no one has questioned this unilinear growth of society and no serious steps have been initiated to inject morality into the impressionable minds of our youth. We have baldly failed on these fronts. There is a need to devise new viewpoints on what kind of the Indians we wish to evolve and how? Till then, it is important to focus on the non-social fronts.

It is not confirmed whether the matters of morality are embedded in the religious ethos of a society. Wealth earned through illegal or wrong means is not taken in a good taste as per the Indian religious scriptures. Amusingly, Thiru Valluvar's *Kural*, written two thousand years ago in Tamil Nadu, states that although wealth is akin to fame, respect and a chance to aid and serve others, but the same should be attained by right means only. Is this dictum capable to form the basis of our socio-moral orientation?

A class of people believes that integrity among Protestants and Parsees is relatively higher in contrast to other religions, and one can easily trace the roots of such integrity in the well-ingrained customs of these religions. However, this view does not fit for all, as there exist other religious and secular groups eminent for their high moral conduct. The cultural system of any nation, with its religious orientation, plays a big part in framing the work ethics of its people. For example, it is only because of importance given to hard work, feature of the Protestant ethics, that several Christian societies have been able to boost their per capita productivity. Although physical labour is considered good by Judaism, the Hindu and Islamic societies consider physical labour to be inferior to the mental work.

It is not sure whether work ethics are linked with religious moorings. Although subjective aspects, they make for an exciting study. The family system and the educational system make powerful tools of socialization and training of the mind in its early years. It is evident that if good values are inculcated in schools in early years, it will likely have a good and positive impact on society.

Legal-judicial Context

Nation's legal system is credited with the responsibility to ensure the effectiveness of the ethical concerns in governance system. It is very important to frame efficient and well-formulate laws, keeping in mind fair and honest conduct, to distinguish chaff from grain in the ethical universe. Conversely, nebulous laws, which are not formulated in an efficient manner and have vague explanations about corruption, will only help violators to conduct more of these acts as it would not be able to instil the fear of God or fear of law among them. Therefore, efficient judiciary with fast-tract justice system is necessary to curtail immorality in public affairs. In contrast, a slow-moving judiciary will only help perpetrators of crimes to remain fearless by giving them freedom through prolonged trials and benefits of doubt.

In the same way, the anti-corruption wing of the government, through its complex procedures, unintentionally provide relief to the accused who are indirectly helped by slow and tricky procedures. In India, there is a dearth of effective anti-corruption institution. As already read in Unit 7 earlier on in this Course, the Lok Pal is still in the process of finalization, Lok Ayuktas are weak and ineffective agencies, while the state vigilance bodies are low-key actors. The concerns are too obvious to give any explanation.

The Political Context

The political leadership, either in power or outside power, leaves significant impact on the customs and values of citizens. The rulers do rule the minds, but in particularly a democratic setup, all political parties, pressure groups and the media play a big role in moulding attitudes on moral questions. If politicians act with full ethics and morality, as can be seen in the Scandinavian countries and in most South Asian countries, political morality can be attained by the administrative system very easily.

The Indian election system is regarded to be the biggest catalyst for political corruption. Elected candidates likely earn money spent during elections through fair or foul means. Although fair has limits, foul has none. As it is evident that the administrative class–civil servants at higher, middle as well as lower levels – belongs to society itself, they are likely to work as keeping in mind the customs, values and behavioural patterns predominant in the society. It is impractical to think that the administrators will be insulated from the orientations and norms present in the society.

Although the argument, presented here, has a valid point, there can be a disagreement that the rulers are expected to have stronger moral fibre than the subjects. Due to the lack of any means to protect and nurture administrative morality vis-à-vis the general social morality, such a belief remains an elusive ideal. Hence, it is of utmost importance to mine the problem further.

In India, the actions of civil servants are largely influenced by the politicians. Political class has an upper hand over civil servants. It is sad that moral codes in a nation like India are influenced more by its politicians as compared to any other social group. Objective and honest media can play a good role in curtailing the evil of corruption. It may also encourage administrators to embrace ethical behaviour. Hence, those who control the media should act with responsibility to curtail evil practices. The efforts in this direction are underway as many channels have been regularly airing their 'expose' on malpractices in the system. This role of the media, sans sensationalism, will play a great role in making India a better place to live.

The Economic Context

There exists a positive correlation between level of economic development of a nation and the level of ethics in the governance system. Even when there is no causal relation between the two, a correlation cannot be ruled out. Low level of economic development along with inequalities in the economic order is expected to form a gap among social classes and groups. Class belonging to deprived society will likely be attracted to indulge in unfair means to fulfil their needs. It is evident that rich will mainly be more honest (though they can afford to be so) as compared to the poor who are more likely to compromise with the principles of integrity.

After the introduction of liberalized economic regime in developing nations, the WTO regime stressed on following the rules of integrity in industry, trade, management and the governance system. This is what Fred Riggs would call `exogenous' inducements to administrative change.

ISSUE OF ETHICS: FOCI AND CONCERNS

Now, the moral obligation of an administrative system gives rise to an important question. Is the administrative system restricted to acting morally in its conduct or does it also share the duty of shielding and encouraging an ethical order in the larger society? Although there is a focus on the aspect of probity within the administrative system under the administrative morality, for nurturing and protecting the basic moral values, it is important to keep in mind the aspect of the responsibility of the governance system (of which the administrative system is an integral part) to frame and sustain an ethical atmosphere in the socio-economic system. As per the moral political philosophy, the rulers will not only be moral themselves, but would also be the protectors of morality in a society. Truly, it is required by a person to be moral for being a guardian of wider morality. Both the obligations are knotted.

It is known that ethical decision-making is the main step in attaining administrative morality. It is almost impossible to separate ethical decision-making from the questions of facts and values, resulting in integrating the science of administration with the ethics of administration. In this integrated system, empirical concern that values the normative concerns in the distribution of administrative services is valued.

Which are the important apprehensions related to administrative ethics? There are a number of values regarded necessary in an administrative action. Nevertheless, one has to pick most important values in being selective. It is now time to focus on values of justice, fairness and objectivity. Woodrow Wilson, 'The Study of Administration' (1887), in his first speech stated that justice was more important than sympathy, thus putting justice at the first position in value-hierarchy in a governance system. Paradoxically, despite discussing the formal-legal aspects of administrative law since then, very little analysis has been done on the philosophical dimension of administrative justice.

Other integral parts of administrative justice include fairness and objectivity, i.e., other two issues of ethical decision-making. When administrators act wisely and honestly, they are thought of as impartial and fair and not get attracted by nepotism, favouritism and greed while making decisions of governance. Objectivity should not be misinterpreted as a mechanical and firm adherence to laws and rules. When seen from the point of view related to decision-making, it has certainly broader consequences surrounding a set of positive orientations.

In the present times, the scope of ethics has expanded itself to involve all major realms of human existence. Here are certain salient aspects of ethics in public administration. Largely, they could be defined as following maxims:

- ***Maxim of Legality and Rationality***: An administrator will abide by the codes and conduct devised to administer and direct several categories of policies and decisions.

- ***Maxim of Responsibility and Accountability***: An administrator would not think twice in taking responsibility for his judgement and actions. Moreover, he would be eager to be held responsible to superior authorities of governance and even to the people who are the real beneficiaries of his decisions and actions.
- ***Maxim of Work Commitment***: An administrator would be dedicated to his obligations and accomplish his duties with involvement, intelligence and dexterity. As Swami Vivekananda observed: 'Every duty is holy and devotion to duty is the highest form of worship'. This would also let them learn respect for time, punctuality and fulfilment of promises made. Work is regarded not as a burden but as a chance to serve and fruitfully contribute to society.
- ***Maxim of Excellence***: An administrator would work to maintain the highest level of quality in administrative judgements and action and would not side line standards because of convenience or complacency. In a competitive international environment, an administrative system should devotedly follow the fundamentals of Total Quality Management.
- ***Maxim of Fusion***: An administrator would wisely bring together individual, organizational and social goals to devise unison of ideals and inculcate commitment in his behaviour for such a fusion. Concerning conflicting aims, a concern for ethics should decide the choices made.
- ***Maxim of Responsiveness and Resilience***: An administrator will react successfully to the appeals and challenges from the external and internal environment. By adapting to environmental transformation, he keeps the ethical norms of conduct. When deviation from the set ethical norms is noticed, the administrative system would show flexibility and bounce back into the established ethical mould at the earliest chance.
- ***Maxim of Utilitarianism***: While framing and executing policies and judgements, an administrator will make it a point that the benefits lead to the greatest good (happiness, benefits) of the greatest number.
- ***Maxim of Compassion***: Without flouting the prescribed codes and conduct, an administrator would show compassion for the poor, the disabled and the weak while making judgements. At least, it is important for him to be impartial and not shown any favouritism to any section of the society.
- ***Maxim of Transparency***: An administrator will decide on and execute policies in a transparent way so that those influenced by the decisions and who wish to estimate their rationale, will be able to recognize the reasons for such decisions and the sources of information on which these decisions were made.

There are still many doctrines those could be added to the above list of maxims of morality in administration. However, the overall goal is to guarantee 'Good Governance' keeping in mind ethical principles, practices, orientations and behaviour. There are no doctrines involved in the process of describing administrative ethics. It is important to keep in mind the positive significance of administrative action and not just seemingly normal modes of administrative processes. Some of the important concerns and foci of ethics are described as follows.

ETHICAL DILEMMAS

The new century appears to have started with the pressure regarding ethical and philosophical dilemmas which leave experts and academics of public administration alike in a fix. Only answers and convictions were predominant at the dawn of the 20th century, this century is facing new questions, uncertainties and doubts arising as a result of the overarching procedure of the globalization of market economies and IT as well as the localization of political struggle, authority systems and culture. The process called the institutionalization of doubt (Giddens, 1990) then has a wider significance.

Dealing with Ethical Dilemmas in Public Administration

In a situation full of uncertainties and faced with the fundamental question what to do and how to act in difficult times, and to the level that contrasted values or decisional premises could be used in the situation, one is standing in front of the world of ethical dilemmas or that of 'hard choices'.

Dilemma has a wider scope as compared to a problem, irrespective of the difficulty or complexity of the latter (Rapoport, 1960). It is because of the reason that it is almost impossible to solve dilemma, unlike problem, in the terms in which they are firstly catered to decision-maker. When facing a dilemma, the decision-makers are not only tackling opposed and perhaps equally unwelcome options. They are facing a challenge in which one can only be satisfied by sacrificing other. It can then be said that deciphering a dilemma is akin to a zero sum game, in which the choice of one value alternative is certainly followed by the annulment of the other. Therefore, this way of solving the dilemma would be an ambiguity in terms and a misnomer as the resolution reached likewise would appear to be only a scission and a dichotomic split of the intertwined aspects of the issue at hand.

A more effective and efficient way of dealing with the dilemma is by altering the terms of reference and reframing the whole situation, which will then be considered and arranged among themselves in a more systematic and coherent manner. Naturally, dilemmas are seen to be thriving in complex establishments, which lack the expertise to tackle them effectively. As a result, state officials and civil servants facing serious dilemmas find it difficult to find any solution and slip into the state of confusion and embarrassment. These situations force public administration into a state of confusion and indeterminacyinstead of working as a well-organized state of legitimate purposes. In hard case, ethical ambiguity and dearth of clarity about overall values to act may come close to set free a spirit of unbound relativism if not cynicism whereby everything stands. In a situation where everything stands and anything goes, there is nothing left that can be taken seriously, neither ethics and values nor rights and responsibilities of public servants and citizens alike.

In order to understand the host of norms that enter and frequent the organizational landscape of public administration in different ways, a number of ground rules have been recognized which, first, define basic administrative dilemmas in an organized form, and second, are needed to be kept in mind while being engaged in the business of dealing with them. It is likely that the host of guiding ethical doctrines, heuristic in nature, is built based on an ideal type (after Max Weber, 1964, 1978). To make sequential mode of their application in concrete cases manifest, the values have also been set in the form of a lexical ordering and a kind of scalar logic (after John Rawls, 1971).

The advanced list of fundamental principles or criteria that helps in integrating and rearranging the procedure of tackling ethical dilemmas in public administration includes following: (1) democratic liability of administration, (2) the rule of law and the law of legality, (3) professional reliability and (4) openness to civil society.

TOWARDS NEW DIMENSIONS OF ETHICS

The best way to ensure best standards of administrative ethics includes promoting 'sunshine' in public administration. Openness is seen as the foe of corruption. Freedom of Information or Right to Information Acts have been practised in almost all countries of the world. Freedom of information and open hearing provisions have been a vital part of the Administrative Procedure Act at the federal level in the USA. Indian government amended the Freedom of Information Act of 2002 as Right to Information Act, enacted in 2005. In addition, lots of states like Goa, Rajasthan, Tamil Nadu and Maharashtra have framed and implemented laws that help in setting accountability of public employees through this device.

It is to be understood that just framing of legislation alone is not enough, its implementation would need a will of the State, willingness of administrators and an initiative along with courage on the part of citizens themselves. The State machinery should always be upfront in dealing with the officials obstructing the smooth execution of Right to Information Act. The contemporary views of regarding every information as `secret' must be shunned and all should strive for greater openness and transparency. This effort will only be successful if change of mind-set happens of administrators to change the thinking of administration at all levels, more particularly at the cutting-edge level.

The movement to seek transparency will fail without the active participation and demand for the fructification of this Right. Although enactment of this act has given some hope for the bright future, there are still serious efforts to be made for ensuring its effective implementation. People's groups, such as the one led by Aruna Roy, will have to continue to take initiative on a massive scale. Even the educational system and the media will need to play a purposive role in this realm.

In the USA, 'whistle blowing' is a way to lodge their (public employees) protest against any activity that is illegal or immoral. This is considered as moral and appropriate, and legitimate and statutorily protected. They can even resign from their post to give more fire to their actions.

The USA has a hotline, called `Fraud Net', for reporting any case of fraud, waste and abuse. This paves the way for any employee, who witnessed any act of misconduct, anonymously report such instances for investigation to the General Accounting Office. In addition, the American public employees have Constitutional protection on addressing matters of public concern like dangers to public health or safety.

Britain also took some steps to ensure control of illegal activities by enacting a new appeals procedure for civil servants. This procedure lets a civil servant to raise concerns, confidentially, with an individual outside his normal hierarchy. If he thinks response as unsatisfactory or unreasonable, he has the right to report the matter to the Civil Service Commissioner. The Constitutional Review Commission in India discussed the viability of whistleblowing, but the same was not accepted as a viable choice. This is the right time to have a fresh perspective on this issue.

Laws, Codes, Conducts and Conscience as Sources of Ethical Guidance

17 CHAPTER

POLITICS AND ETHICS

Man is both a social being and a political being. The individual and the state depend on each other. Political science defines the duty of the individual and the state towards each other. As rights and duties are managed by the state, moral life is intimately related to the political life.

Both ethics and politics are normative sciences and strongly inter-related. Ethics works for the supreme good of the individual, whereas politics works for public good. It is possible to achieve public good through individual good; therefore politics aims at the building of an ideal welfare state where more perfection of the citizens can be realized.

In the same way, individual good can be attained via public good. Although politics can be regarded as a practical science, ethics is not. However, it is difficult to ignore the effect of ethics on the practical life.

When looking back in the history of politics and ethics, we can see that in Plato's time ethics and politics were intimately related to each other.

In contrast, Aristotle gave two separate theories on politics and ethics, differentiating the scope of the subjects. There had always been a difference of opinion among the experts regarding the relation between ethics and politics.

For instance, Gandhiji stated that a happy marriage should be instituted between politics and morality. A moral base should exist in high politics.

On the other hand, Machiavelli and Lather stated that politics and ethics have no connection with each other. The will of the sovereign is law. For the protection of people, it is important to exercise power efficiently.

Hence, it need not have any connection with morality. Hobbes and his supporters state that good conduct is enforced by the state and therefore ethics is only a part of politics.

The relation between ethics and politics is still argued. There exists a mutual dependence of ethics and politics irrespective of these differences of opinion. Moral philosophers have tried to influence state politics.

Politicians at their times have played avital part in changing the moral outlook of the state.

The study of the various forms of government and their operations is included in political philosophy. Politics differentiates various forms of government and evaluates its constitutions to draw the picture of the best form of a government.

On the other side, ethics includes study of a man, his character, intention, desire, etc. to evaluate his conduct. In this sense, the scope of ethics is wider and altruistic.

Both ethics and politics are related to the values of duty, responsibility, etc. The moral thinker undertakes a theoretical and analytical study to recognize what responsibility is and what is not.

The duty of politician is also the same, but the extra effort that he puts in is to determine responsibility and recommend the quantum of penalty on the wrong door. He executes his duty for the smooth running of the government.

The person who teaches moral values administer a sense of discrimination between right and wrong but cannot endorse anything. It is well known that laws formulated by the state are externally levied upon the people, but moral laws are self-imposed.

Politics can be commonly understood as an expressive and realistic science as it studies working of government at the time of peace and war. In contrast, ethics determines the conduct of any person in relation to a particular norm. Thus, it is a normative science. It determines what ought to be, not what really happens or what is the case.

ETHICS IN PUBLIC LIFE

Ethics is mainly related to the idea of responsibility and accountability. In a democratic setup, each and every public official is accountable ultimately to the people. This accountability is ensured by enforcing laws and rules that were framed by the elected representatives in their legislatures. Ethics offers the platform for the formation of such laws and rules. Moral views of people are responsible for shaping the character of laws and rules. Our legal system is shaped on the basis of common vision of what is good and just. The fundamental principle in a democracy is that all public officials derive their powers from the people; in other words, all public representatives are trustees of the people. As the role of the government is getting wider, public officials are bound to have significant impact over the lives of people. The relationship between the public and the officials should be such that the responsibility entrusted to the officials be performed in the best interest of the people.

Ethics plays diversified roles in the lives of people. In the one hand is the expression of high moral values. On the other hand is the specifics of action for which a public official can be held legally liable.

Following elements are important for any framework of ethical behaviour:

- Organizing ethical norms and practices.
- Unveiling personal interest to evade clash between public interest and personal gain.
- Crafting a machinery for imposing the appropriate codes.
- Providing standards for qualifying and disqualifying a public official from office.

It is very tough even for extensive framework laws and rules to satisfy all conditions. It is without any uncertainty desirable, and perhaps possible, to direct the behaviour of those who are posted in the lower echelons and exercise limited or no discretion. It is to be noted that with the higher echelon in public service increases the ambit of discretion. It proves to be very difficult to offer a framework of laws and rules that can efficiently cover and control the exercise of discretion in high positions. The Committee on Standards in Public Life in the United Kingdom, known as the Nolan Committee, provided the following seven principles of public life related to ethical standards for holders of public office:

1. ***Selflessness***: Public officials should take judgments keeping in view public interest. They should not act to attain financial or other material perks for themselves, their family or their friends.
2. ***Integrity***: Public employees should not come under any financial or other obligation to outsiders or any external organizations that might affect their performance in performing official duties.
3. ***Objectivity***: Public officials should always make wise decisions based on merit while doing public business, including making public appointments, awarding contracts or recommending individuals for rewards and benefits.
4. ***Accountability***: Public officials should be liable to public for taking any decisions and actions and must submit themselves to whatever scrutiny is suitable to their office.
5. ***Openness***: Public employees should be transparent and open regarding taking any decision for public interest. They should provide explanations for their decisions and confine information only when the wider public interest clearly demands.
6. ***Honesty***: Public representatives should be honest with their duty keeping in mind the public interest and should take steps to resolve any conflicts.
7. ***Leadership***: Public officials should lead from the front for the public interest issues.

INTERNATIONAL APPROACHES

Public Service

A service or facility that people get from the government within its ambit, either directly (through the public sector) or by funding private provision of services, is called public service. The term relates to a social consent (usually expressed through democratic elections) that certain services should be accessible to all, irrespective of income. At instances where public services are neither publicly provided nor publicly funded, for social and political reasons, they are normally based on regulation going beyond that applying to most economic sectors. Public service is also a discipline that can be included in the curriculum at a college and/or university.

Public services seem to be regarded so important for modern life that for moral reasons their global provision should be assured. They may be related to fundamental human rights (such as the right to water). Institutions such as Volunteer Fire Dept. and Ambulance Corps. aim for servicing the community. A service means supporting others with a specific need or want. Types of service include doctor treating an illness, person repairing something or food pantry. A public service may occasionally have the features of a public good (being non-rivalrous and non-excludable), but most are services which may (as per the prevailing social standards) not be provided in good quantity by the market. In maximum cases, public services are only services, and they do not include goods production. They may be offered by local or national monopolies, specifically in segments which are natural monopolies. They may include outputs that are tough to attribute to definite individual effort and/or tough to evaluate in terms of key characteristics such as quality. They, many a times, need high levels of training and education. They may fascinate people with a bent towards public service ethos who wish to support community via their work.

PUBLIC SERVICES VERSUS SERVICES OF GENERAL INTEREST

In Europe, some nations use the term service of general interest instead of public services. It has been a debatable issue, for example, while writing of the European Constitution (the term services of general interest has been used). ETUC termed its petition 'for high quality public services' but explains 'Public services are known as Services of General Interest (SGI) and Services of General Economic Interest (SGEIs) in European Union terminology'.

Public Sector

As per the InvestorWords, the public sector refers to 'the part of the economy concerned with providing basic government services. The composition of the public sector varies by country, but in most countries the public sector includes such services as the police, military, public roads, public transit, primary education and healthcare for the poor. The public sector might provide services that non-payer cannot be excluded from (such as street lighting), services which benefit all of society rather than just the individual who uses the service (such as public education), and services that encourage equal opportunity'.

ORGANIZATION

Different forms of the organization of the public sector (public ownership) are as follows:

- Direct administration financed by taxation; the delivering institution usually is not bounded to achieve commercial success criteria, and verdicts related to production are decided by government.
- Public organizations (in some perspectives, specifically manufacturing, 'state-owned enterprises') are different from direct administration as they enjoy greater commercial freedoms and are thought to act as per the commercial criteria, and decisions regarding production are not usually taken by government (though goals may be framed for them by government).
- Partial outsourcing (of the scale many businesses do, e.g., for IT services) is regarded as a public sector model.

  A borderline form can be seen as follows:
- Total outsourcing, with a private organization providing the complete service in the name of government. This may be seen as a combination of private sector operations

with public ownership of assets. However in some forms, the control or risk of private sector is such that the service may no longer be regarded the part of the public sector (Barlow et al., 2010).

Conduct Guide

It is necessary to frame, execute and encourage a code of conduct by all the public sector agencies covered by the *Public Sector Management Act 1994*. These codes of conduct must comply with the Code of Ethics. The Conduct Guide helps these institutions to efficiently implement the Code of Ethics within their workplace. The Conduct Guide by PSC offers these agencies a system to frame their own codes of conduct. It provided the accountability system derived by legislation and across-government requirements such as Premier's Circulars, Commissioner's Instructions and Treasurer's Instructions. This guide also highlights common conduct segments where a public official needs to portray the most suitable conduct. It is necessary for public officials to obey with the said framework framed by law and by Government. These conduct categories areas need to be reflected in your agency's code of conduct.

CONDUCT GUIDE FOR BOARDS AND COMMITTEES

Government values and seeks high standards of all its officials, which are clearly codified by the Western Australian Public Sector Code of Ethics. Boards and committees that are formed keeping in mind public interest must observe and follow the WA Public Sector Code of Ethics.

United Nations Public Service Awards

The excellence in public service is internationally recognized by conferring the United Nations Public Service Award. It determines the creative accomplishments and aids of public service organizations that paves a way for a more effective and responsive public administration in nations worldwide. The UN Public Service Awards with the help of an annual competition encourages the role, professionalism and visibility of public service. In 2003, to 'celebrate the value and virtue of public service to the community', the United Nations General Assembly, in its resolution A/RES/57/277, elected June 23 as the United Nations Public Service Day. To acknowledge the roles played for promoting the role, prestige and visibility of public service, the UN Economic and Social Council decided that the United Nations Public Service Awards be awarded on Public Service Day.

The United Nations Millennium Declaration stressed the role played by democratic and participatory governance in guaranteeing the privileges of all to 'live their lives and raise their children in dignity, free from hunger and from the fear of violence, oppression, or injustice'. It also considered that good governance within each nation is a necessity to 'making development a reality for everyone and to freeing the entire human race from want'.

It is experienced that good governance, locally or globally, and an efficient, competent, professional, responsive and highly dedicated public service are important to ensure sustainable development and livelihood. The ex UN Secretary-General, in his discourse at the World Youth Forum in 1998, reiterated the significance of public service by inspiring the world's youth to look towards this field. He said, 'In this changing world of new challenges, we need, more than ever before, dedicated and talented individuals to enter public service. More than ever before, we need people like you sitting here today, to make the choice of service to humankind'.

PURPOSE OF THE AWARDS

The aim of the United Nations Public Service Awards is to recognize the institutional role played by public officials to widen the role, professionalism, image and visibility of the public service (Economic and Social Council decision 2000/231). This can be more clearly understood by following objectives:

(a) To recognize service to citizens and promote public officials globally to maintain the drive of innovation and the improvement of the delivery of public services;
(b) To accumulate and spread fruitful practices and skills in public administration to help efforts for developments in nation-level public service delivery;
(c) To decrease the impact of any negative perception of public administration, raise the image and prestige of public officials and rejuvenate public administration as a noble discipline on which development greatly depends with the help of success stories;
(d) To promote, encourage and expedite communication among organizations important to public administration and support the networks of the United Nations programme on public administration and development; and
(e) To encourage professionalism in the public service in pleasing the successful experiences in innovations and excellence in the public service.

ELIGIBILITY

All public institutions/agencies at national and sub-national levels, as well as public/private companies carrying out outsourced public service functions, are eligible for nomination. The United Nations Public Service Awards considers geographical distribution of five regions while scrutinizing the nominations. In order to make the process of selecting nominations easy, the following five regions have been established:

(a) Africa
(b) Asia and the Pacific
(c) Europe and North America
(d) Latin America and the Caribbean
(e) Western Asia

It is important to note that self-nomination is not accepted, that is, nomination has to be done by a different entity than the institution being nominated. Eligible nominators consist of government departments and agencies; universities, non-governmental organizations, professional associations, etc. Complete scientific discoveries, e.g., in medical or environmental science, do not qualify for the United Nations Public Service Awards.

UNPSA CATEGORIES AND CRITERIA

In 2011, the United Nations Public Service Awards were facilitated in the following five categories:

Category 1 : Preventing and combating corruption in the Public Service.
Category 2 : Improving the delivery of services
Category 3 : Fostering participation in policy-making decisions through innovative mechanisms
Category 4 : Advancing knowledge management in government
Category 5 : Promoting gender responsive delivery of public services

Refer to UPAN Public Service Awards 565 for more information on the categories and application criteria.

ASPA Code of Ethics, USA

The American Society for Public Administration (ASPA) promotes the science, art and discipline of public administration. The society upholds its efforts to advance the spirit of responsible professionalism within its membership and to spread awareness and commitment to ethical principles and standards among all public officials in all sectors.

ASPA Commits to Uphold the Following Principles

1. ***Advance the Public Interest:*** Promote the interests of the public and put service to the public above service to oneself.
2. ***Uphold the Constitution and the Law:*** Respect and support government constitutions and laws, while seeking to improve laws and policies to promote the public good.
3. ***Promote Democratic Participation:*** Inform the public and encourage active engagement in governance. Be open, transparent and responsive, and respect and assist all persons in their dealings with public organizations.
4. ***Strengthen Social Equity:*** Treat all persons with fairness, justice, and equality and respect individual differences, rights, and freedoms. Promote affirmative action and other initiatives to reduce unfairness, injustice, and inequality in society.
5. ***Fully Inform and Advise:*** Provide accurate, honest, comprehensive, and timely information and advice to elected and appointed officials and governing board members, and to staff members in your organization.
6. ***Demonstrate Personal Integrity:*** Adhere to the highest standards of conduct to inspire public confidence and trust in public service.
7. ***Promote Ethical Organizations:*** Strive to attain the highest standards of ethics, stewardship, and public service in organizations that serve the public.
8. ***Advance Professional Excellence:*** Strengthen personal capabilities to act competently and ethically and encourage the professional development of others.

A separate document contains practices that serve as a guide to behaviour for members of ASPA in carrying out its principles.

- **ASPA Code Revision Process:** In March 2011, ASPA initiated an interesting discussion about ethics, particularly its Code of Ethics. It is believed by most that ethical behaviour should have particular standards. Being a professional member association, ASPA is committed to promoting ethics within the profession.

Various Legal Provisions to Guide Ethical Behaviour of Civil Servants (International Scenario)

For the smooth functioning of democratic setup, it is important for civil service to maintain the same standards of professionalism, responsiveness and impartiality while working for successive political governments. An efficient civil service is expected to attain a set of values and standards that differentiate it from other occupations. The features of an effective civil service include integrity, devotion to public service, impartiality, political neutrality, anonymity, etc. Some nations have these values embodied in laws, e.g., Australia,and some have these enshrined in the respective Constitutions.

Article 153 of the Polish Constitution

It states that:

(1) A corps of civil servants shall operate in the organs of government administration in order to ensure a professional, diligent, impartial and politically neutral discharge of the State's obligations.

(2) The Prime Minister shall be the superior of such corps of civil servants.

Civil Service Values in the United Kingdom are as Follows as per the *www.gov.uk*:

1. The Civil Service is an integral and key part of the government of the United Kingdom. It supports the government of the day in developing and implementing its policies, and in delivering public services. Civil servants are accountable to Ministers, who in turn are accountable to Parliament.
2. As a civil servant, you are appointed on merit on the basis of fair and open competition and are expected to carry out your role with dedication and a commitment to the Civil Service and its core values: integrity, honesty, objectivity and impartiality. In this Code: 'integrity' is putting the obligations of public service above your own personal interests; 'honesty' is being truthful and open; 'objectivity' is basing your advice and decisions on rigorous analysis of the evidence; and 'impartiality' is acting solely according to the merits of the case and serving equally well governments of different political persuasions.
3. These core values support good government and ensure the achievement of the highest possible standards in all that the Civil Service does. This in turn helps the Civil Service to gain and retain the respect of Ministers, Parliament, the public and its customers.

Countries, such as New Zealand, Australia and the UK, where civil services have undergone reforms have framed a set of guidelines to guide civil service behaviour in the form of values and a legally enforceable code of conduct.

In the UK, as per the recommendations of the Nolan Committee on standards in public service, the Civil Service Code was made into a law that came into effect on 1 January 1996. The Code is a clear and concise guideline to be followed by the civil officials, and is a part of the civil servants' terms and conditions of employment. Apart from defining the integrity and loyalty required by civil officials, the Code makes it illegal to deceive Parliament or the public, misuse of official positions and unauthorized disclosure of confidential information. If any problem fails to be solved within the department, this code gives a right of appeal to independent Civil Service Commissioners on subjects of propriety and conscience.

In New Zealand, keeping in mind ethics and public service ethos, the State Services Act was enacted while carrying reforms. This was needed because civil servants were loyal to his/her department or agency instead of the public service as a whole. So, it was of utmost importance to promote the values and public service ethos. Leading from the front, the State Services Commission issued the Code of Conduct for civil servants besides setting up Standards and Ethics Board.

Australia has done a significant effort for bringing reforms in this respect. Section 10 of the Public Service Act, 1999, reveals a declaration of 15 values, which describe that the Australian Public Service:

- Is apolitical, carrying out its functions in an neutral and professional way.
- Is openly liable for its actions, under the system of Ministerial responsibility to the Government, the Parliament and the Australian public.
- Is open to the Government in offering frank, honest, comprehensive, accurate and timely advice and in executing the Government's policies and programs.
- Provides services honestly, effectively, impartially and politely to the Australian public and is delicate to the diversity of the Australian public.
- Offers a reasonable opportunity to all eligible members of the community to apply for APS employment.
- Is a public service in which employment decisions are taken on merit.
- Offers a workplace without discrimination and identifies and uses the range of the Australian community it caters to.
- Forms workplace relations that consider communication, consultation, cooperation and suggestions from employees on subjects that affect their workplace.
- Offers an impartial, bendable, safe and rewarding workplace.
- Emphasizes on attaining results and managing performance.
- Encourages equity in employment.
- Offers a fair guideline of review of decisions taken in view of APS employees.
- Enjoys the highest ethical standards.
- Boasts of the highest quality of leadership.
- Is a career-based service to widen the scope of effectiveness and cohesion of Australia's democratic system of government.

Section 13 of Australia's Public Service Act states the guidelines for Australia's civil service. It states that an employee during the course of APS employment must:

- Work fairly and with truthfulness
- Perform with care and attentiveness
- Have to be impartial to everyone.

UNDERSTANDING CIVIL SERVICE

The concept of civil service can be understood either as (a) a branch of governmental service in which individuals are selected based on the performance in competitive examinations, or (b) an organization of employees in any government agency other than the military. A civil official or public servant is an individual working in the public sector for any government department or agency. The degree of civil servants of a state as part of the 'Civil Service' differs on the basis of various nation's preferences. In the UK, for example, only employees directly under the Crown are considered as civil servants, whereas county or city officials are not. The study of civil service is also considered to be a fragment of the discipline of public administration. Employees in 'non-departmental public bodies' (sometimes called 'QUANGOs') may also be considered and treated as civil servants keeping in view statistics and their terms and conditions. State's civil servants together constitute its Civil Service or Public Service. An international civil servant or international staff member is a civilian worker employed by an international company. These international civil officials do not obey any national legislation (from which they have immunity of jurisdiction) but work as per an internal staff regulation. In case of any disputes, the case is brought before special tribunals formed by these international institutions like the Administrative Tribunal of the ILO. Any specific or special case may be referred to the International Civil Service Commission (ICSC) of the United Nations, a sovereign expert body under the United Nations General Assembly. It plays the role of regulating and coordinating the circumstances of service of staff in the United Nations common system, while keeping in mind high standards in the international civil service.

Early History

Administrative institutions derived their powers from the personal servants of high officials, just as in the Roman Empire. This created a complex administrative arrangement, mentioned the Notitia Dignitatum and the creations of John Lydus. However, it is known that appointments to it were entirely on the basis of inheritance or patronage and not on merit. Officers also have the power to get their work carried out by others while getting salary for the same work themselves. There are obvious similarities here with the early bureaucratic organizations in modern states, such as the Office of Works or the Navy in 18th century England, where again it is told that appointments were on the basis of patronage and not on merit.

Modern Meritocratic Civil Service

The modern meritocratic civil service has its origin from Imperial examination traced in Imperial China. The Imperial exam was devised to appoint the best administrative officials for the state's bureaucracy on the basis of merit. As both society and culture were largely influenced by this system, this framework was directly responsible for the creating a class of scholar-bureaucrats regardless of their family pedigree. During the period starting from the rule of the Han Dynasty (206 BC to 220 AD) to the introduction of the imperial examination system, most selections in the imperial bureaucracy were on the basis of recommendations from influential aristocrats and local servants and recommended officials were mainly of aristocratic rank. Laying the foundation stone for a change to make appointments on the basis of merit, emperor Wu of Han initiated an early form of the imperial examinations, in which local employees would select candidates to take part in an examination of the Confucian classics. The system attained its maturity during the Song dynasty. The Chinese civil-service system has played a great role in providing stability for more than 2,000 years and provided one of the major outlets for social mobility in Chinese society.

It is the imperial system that has played a part in devising the modern examination system for selecting civil service staff. Impressed with its results, this system was and then adopted by European nations from the 16th century onward, and is now predominant in most countries around the world. The first European power to efficiently execute the meritocratic civil service was the British Empire, while the rule of India: 'company managers hired and promoted employees based on competitive examinations in order to prevent corruption and favouritism'. British colonial administrators, such as Thomas Taylor Meadows, Britain's consul in Guangzhou, China, based in China suggested the spread of the system to the rest of the Commonwealth countries. Meadows successfully stated in his *Desultory Notes on the Government and People of China*, published in 1847, that 'the long duration of the Chinese empire is solely and altogether owing to the good government which consists in the advancement of men of talent and merit only', and that the British must reform their civil service by making the institution meritocratic. The report was significant. The British implemented a meritocratic civil service after the Northcote-Trevelyan Report in 1853, and the Americans followed the track in 1883, with the Pendleton Civil Service Reform Act.

In India, the Civil Service can be understood as 'appointive positions by the Government in connection with the affairs of the Union and includes a civilian in a Defence Service, except positions in the Indian Armed Forces'. The civil servants act at the pleasure of the President of India, and Article 311 of the constitution guards them against any politically motivated or vindictive action. There are two types of Civil Services of India: the All India Services and the Central Civil Services (Groups A and B). The civil servants who are all university graduates (or above) are selected via a rigorous system of examinations, known as the Civil Services Examination (CSE) and its technical part known as the Engineering Services Examination (ESE), both of which are held by the Union Public Service Commission (UPSC). State Civil Services gets talent via a competitive examination conducted every year by state public service commission. Almost 3.5 lakhs candidates apply every year for the 400 to 500 vacancies that may arise.

Civil Services of India

The Civil Services of India include the civil service and the permanent bureaucracy of the Government of India. The administrative system works as per the civil service system. In India, the vital responsibility for running the administration is conferred to the elected representatives of the people which are the ministers. The ministers, which are elected by the people through elections, are liable to the legislature. Therefore, ministers are indirectly responsible to the people. However, limited numbers of ministers are not competent to deal personally with the manifold problems of modern administration. Thus, it is the responsibility of civil servants to implement policies laid down by these ministers for the proper functioning of democracy. Indian civil officials are held liable to implement the executive decisions. A civil servant is any individual, a citizen of India, employed by the Government to any civil service or post in relation to the functioning of the Union and includes a civilian in a Defence Service. Although civil servants are employees of the Government of India, not all officials of the Government are civil servants. As per the data till 2010, the number of civil servants in India stood at 6.4 million. Civil servants in a personal capacity are paid from the Civil List. Senior civil servants may be called to account by Parliament. The present setup of modern civil services of India is mostly akin to system of the Imperial Civil Service of the British India. It was framed after India attained independence from the rule of British government in 1947. It was the vision of Sardar Patel that the Civil Service will strengthen cohesion and national integrity. He was in favour of a solid and energetic federal administrative system, which will only be achieved by All India Services. Considering today's scenario, it is true to say that the Civil Services have provided the setup for the administration of the country. The values of unity, impartiality and merit are the main guiding principles of Indian civil services.

Constitution

In case the government feels the need for more All India Civil Services branches for proper functioning, as per the constitution, the Rajya Sabha (upper house of the Parliament of India) has the power to set up more of these with a two-thirds majority. The Indian Forest Service, Indian Administrative Service and Indian Police Service were set up by this constitutional provision only.

Power, Purpose and Responsibilities

The civil services is bestowed with the responsibility to run the administration of India effectively and efficiently. It is no doubt that efficient and effective management of its natural, economic and human resources is needed to administer a vast and diverse country like India. The country manages its functions via a number of Central Government organizations as per the policy directions given by the ministries. The members of the civil services have diversified roles depending on the nature of organizations: they act as administrators in the central and state governments; ambassadors in the foreign missions/ embassies; as tax collectors and revenue commissioners; as civil service commissioned police officers; as permanent representative(s) and officials in the UN and its agencies and as Chairman, Managing Director, full-time functional Director/Member of the Board of Management of various Public Sector Undertakings/Enterprises, Corporations, Banks and financial organizations. They may also be appointed to different agencies of India and can also be employed as advisors or special duty officers or private secretaries to ministers of the Union and the State Government. The Appointments Committee of the Cabinet plays an important role in all the appointments in the rank of Joint Secretary to Government of India and above, other major appointments, empanelment and extension of tenure. In contrast, all appointments to the rank below Joint Secretary in the federal government are handled by the Civil Services Board.

GOVERNANCE

Head of the Civil Service

The highest-ranking civil servant serves as the Chief of the Cabinet Secretariat of Republic of India who is also the Cabinet Secretary. In addition, he is ex-officio Chairman of the Civil Services Board; the head of the Indian Administrative Service and chief of all civil services under the ambit of business of the Indian Government. He even enjoys the 11th spot in the Order of Precedence of India. He is liable to oversee and ensure that the Civil Service is armed with the skills and ability to conquer the everyday challenges it faces and that civil servants work in a fair and decent environment.

VALUES AND CODES

Values

A civil service position holder while serving the nation should maintain complete integrity, loyalty to the constitution and the law of the nation, patriotism, national pride, devotion to duty, honesty, impartiality and transparency.

Codes

The Government of India encourages certain values and code of ethics:

- To conduct his/her duty responsibly, honestly and impartially.
- To provide effective management, leadership development and personal growth.
- To not practice misuse of official position or information.
- To act as catalyst to attain good governance and foster social economic development.

CONSTRUCTION

The Civil Services of India can be divided into two types as follows:.

All India Civil Services (AIS)

The President of India is responsible for all appointments to All India Civil Services.

- Indian Administrative Service
- Indian Forest Service
- Indian Police Service

Central Civil Services (CCS)

The Central Civil Services are mainly related to the administration of the Union Government.

Group A

All appointments to Civil Services, Group A are made by the President of India.

- Armed Forces Headquarters Civil Services, Group A
- Archaeological Service, Group A
- Botanical Survey of India, Group A
- Central Engineering (Civil) Service, Group A
- Geological Survey of India, Group A
- Central Engineering (Electrical and Mechanical) Service, Group A
- Central Engineering Service (Roads), Group A
- Central Health Service, Group A
- Central Information Service
- Central Legal Service (Grades I)
- Central Power Engineering Service, Group A
- Central Revenues Chemical Service, Group A
- Central Secretariat Service, Group A
- Central Secretariat Official Language Service, Group A
- Central Trade Service, Group A
- Central Water Engineering Service, Group A
- Company Law Board Service, Group A
- Directorate General of Civil Aviation DGCA, Group A
- Directorate General of Mines Safety, Group A
- Delhi and Andaman and Nicobar Islands Civil Service, Grade I.
- General Central Service, Group A
- Indian Audits and Accounts Service, Group A
- Indian Corporate Law Service, Group A
- Indian Civil Accounts Service, Group A
- Indian Cost Accounts Service, Group A
- Indian Defence Accounts Service, Group A
- Indian Defence Estates Service, Group A
- Indian Economic Service, Group A
- Indian Engineering Services, Group A
- Indian Foreign Service
- Indian Frontier Administrative Service, Group A
- Indian Information Service, Group A
- Indian Meteorological Service, Group A
- Indian Ordnance Factories Service, Group A
- Indian Postal Service, Group A
- Indian Posts and Telegraphs Accounts and Finance Service, Group A

- Indian Railway Service of Engineers, Group A
- Indian Railway Service of Mechanical Engineers, Group A
- Indian Railway Service of Electrical Engineers, Group A
- Indian Railway Service of Signal Engineers, Group A
- Indian Railway Stores Service, Group A
- Indian Railway Accounts Service, Group A
- Indian Railway Personnel Service, Group A
- Indian Railway Traffic Service, Group A
- Indian Revenue Service
- Indian Salt Service, Group A
- Indian Statistical Service, Group A
- Indian Telecommunication Service, Group A
- Indian Trade Service, Group A
- Mercantile Marine Training Ship Service, Group A
- Railway Inspectorate Service, Group A
- Survey of India, Group A
- Telegraph Traffic Service, Group A
- Zoological Survey of India, Group A

Group B

All appointments to Group B are made by the authorities specified by a general or special order of the President.

- Income Tax Service, Group 'B'
- Indian Foreign Service, Group 'B' - (General Cadre, Grade I and General Cadre, Grade II only)
- Central Secretariat Service, Group 'B' (Section and Assistants' Grade officers only)
- Indian Posts and Telegraphs Accounts and Finance Service, Group 'B' Telecommunication Wing.
- Indian Posts & Telegraphs Accounts & Finance Service, Postal Wing, Group 'B'
- Indian Salt Service, Group 'B'
- India Meteorological Service, Group 'B'
- Central Secretariat Official Language Service, Group 'B'
- Central Secretariat Stenographers' Service, (Grade I, Grade II and Selection Grade officers only)
- Central Health Service, Group 'B'
- Botanical Survey of India, Group 'B'
- Geological Survey of India, Group 'B'
- Geological Survey of India, Group 'B'
- Survey of India, Group 'B'
- Zoological Survey of India, Group 'B'
- Central Electrical Engineering Service, Group 'B'
- Central Engineering Service, Group 'B'
- Central Power Engineering Service, Group 'B'

- Postal Superintendents' Service, Group 'B'
- Postmasters' Service, Group 'B'
- Telecommunication Engineering Service, Group 'B'
- Telegraphs Traffic Service, Group 'B'
- Central Excise Service, Group 'B'
- Customs Appraisers Service, Group 'B'- (Principal Appraisers and Head Appraisers)
- Customs Preventive Service, Group 'B' – (Chief Inspectors)
- Defence Secretariat Service
- Union Territories Administrative Service
- Union Territories Police Service

State Civil Services (SCS/PCS)

Examinations and recruitments to the State Civil Services, also known as Provincial Civil Services, are held by the individual states of India. The state civil services handles the subjects like land revenue, agriculture, forests, education, etc. The state civil services officials are selected by different States via the State Public Service Commissions. The categories of services to which candidates are selected through the state civil services (SCS) examination are as follows:

- State Civil Services, Class-II (SCS)
- State Police Service, Class-II (SPS).
- State Forest Service, Class-II (SFS).
- Block Development Officer.
- Tehsildar/Talukadar/Assistant Collector.
- Excise and Taxation Officer.
- District Employment Officer.
- District Treasury Officer.
- District Welfare Officer.
- Assistant Registrar Cooperative Societies.
- District Food and Supplies Controller/Officer.
- Any other Class-I/Class-II service notified as per rules by the concerned State i.e. officers/lecturers/ assistant/associate professors/principals of Government Degree Colleges, Class I.

EMPLOYMENT BY AGENCY

Federal Government Executive Branch Civilian Employment

- Ministry of Defence
- Ministry of Finance
- Ministry of External Affairs
- Ministry of Home Affairs
- Ministry of Agriculture
- Ministry of Tribal Affairs

- Ministry of Panchayati Raj
- Ministry of Micro, Small and Medium Enterprises
- Ministry of Science and Technology
- Ministry of Earth Sciences
- Ministry of Health and Family Welfare
- Ministry of Power
- Ministry of Corporate Affairs
- Ministry of New and Renewable Energy
- Ministry of Petroleum and Natural Gas
- Ministry of Urban Development
- Ministry of Overseas Indian Affairs
- Ministry of Civil Aviation
- Ministry of Communications and Information Technology
- Ministry of Urban Development
- Ministry of Human Resource Development
- Ministry of Information and Broadcasting
- Ministry of Law and Justice
- Ministry of Minority Affairs
- Ministry of Labour and Employment
- Ministry of Road Transport and Highways
- Ministry of Commerce and Industry
- Ministry of Textiles
- Ministry of Heavy Industries and Public Enterprises
- Ministry of Culture
- Ministry of Housing and Urban Poverty Alleviation
- Ministry of Tourism
- Ministry of Steel
- Ministry of Shipping
- Ministry of Parliamentary Affairs
- Ministry of Social Justice and Empowerment
- Ministry of Railways
- Ministry of Rural Development
- Ministry of Chemicals and Fertilizers
- Ministry of Coal
- Ministry of Statistics and Programme Implementation
- Ministry of Mines
- Ministry of Women and Child Development
- Ministry of Environment and Forests
- Ministry of Development of North Eastern Region
- Ministry of Youth Affairs and Sports
- Ministry of Consumer Affairs, Food and Public Distribution
- Ministry of Food Processing Industries

- Ministry of Civil Aviation
- Ministry of Culture
- Ministry of Drinking Water and Sanitation
- Ministry of Minority Affairs
- Ministry of Water Resources
- Ministry of Petroleum and Natural Gas

Independent Agencies

- Reserve Bank of India
- Securities and Exchange Board of India
- Department of Space
- Department of Atomic Energy
- Planning Commission
- Directorate General of Economic Enforcement
- Directorate General of Income Tax Investigation
- Directorate of Income Tax Intelligence and Criminal Investigation
- Directorate General of Anti-Evasion
- Directorate of Revenue Intelligence
- Employees' Provident Fund Organization
- National Advisory Council
- Central Bureau of Investigation
- Intelligence Bureau
- Central Vigilance Commission
- National Security Guards

REFORMS AND CHANGES

As per the report revealed in 2011, regarding the civil service reforms in developing countries and India As of 2011, over 450 charge sheets were filed and approximately 943 cases are under investigation by CBI against civil servants from 2009 to 2011. A Hong Kong-based corporate consultancy company, in his 2012 report, ranked Indian bureaucracy as the worst in Asia, with a rating of 9.21 out of 10. Another research conducted in 2012 by the Ministry of Personnel, Public Grievances and Pensions revealed that corruption is institutionalized and rooted at all levels in civil services. In a welcome step, the Department of Personnel and Training (DOPT) of the Ministry of Personnel, Public Grievances and Pensions on 28 November 2011 proposed to retire and expel incompetent, inefficient and unproductive AIS officials just after 15 years of service, instead of bearing them to the age of 60. This move got support from former Cabinet Secretary TSR Subramanian who said, '*Periodical weeding out is very good. But the process to determine who needs to be prematurely retired should be fair and transparent. There is a possibility that even good IAS and IPS officers may be targeted because of political reasons*'. Even former UPSC chairman PC Hota expressed his concern, '*We need drastic remedies. The situation has become terrible. The other day an IAS officer in Delhi was arrested for disproportionate assets of ₹ 31.5 million. She is just a 2000-batch*

IAS officer with 11 years of service. But at same time, the officers' service records should be analysed before a decision against him was taken'. The proposal was accepted and rule 16(3) of the All India Services (death-cum-retirement benefits) Rules of 1958 was revised on 31 January 2012.

In a bid to induct better candidates in these services, UPSC introduced changes in the Prelims stage of the Civil Services Examination in 2011 by eliminating the optional subject paper and introducing Civil Services Aptitude Test (CSAT). Changes to the Mains stage of the exam were implemented 2013 onwards.

Civil Service Day

The Civil Service Day is marked on 21 April every year. The aim to celebrate this day is to rededicate and recommit themselves to the cause of the people. It is observed by all Civil Services. This day provides civil servants a chance for self-examination and thinking about future plans to deal with the situations being faced by them with each passing day. To mark this day as one that is remembered by all officers, the Prime Minister of India honours all officers of Central and State Governments for excellence in public administration. The 'Prime Minister Award for Excellence in Public Administration' is presented in three segments. As per this scheme of awards introduced in 2006, all the officers individually or as group or as organization are eligible. This prize consists of a medal, scroll and a cash amount of 100,000 (US$1,700). Regarding a group award, the total prize money is 500,000 (US$8,600) subject to a maximum of 100,000 (US$1,700) per person. Regarding award for an organization, the cash amount is limited to 500,000 (US$8,600).

ADMINISTRATIVE REFORMS COMMISSION OF INDIA

The Indian government has constituted Administrative Reforms Commission or ARC for suggesting recommendations for revising the public administration system of India. The very first ARC was set up on 5 January 1966. It was first chaired by Morarji Desai, MP, and then by K. Hanumanthaiah, MP, when Desai became the Deputy Prime Minister of India. Named Commission of Inquiry, the second ARC led by Veerappa Moily was formed on 31 August 2005 for formulating a comprehensive design for overhauling the public administrative system.

First Administrative Reforms Commission

The first ARC was formed by the Ministry of Home Affairs under Government of India by resolution no. 40/3/65-AR (P) dated 5 January 1966. Resolution defines the structure of the ARC, the mandate of the commission and the processes to be followed.

Mandate

The Commission was tasked with the responsibility to provide best suggestions for achieving the highest standards of efficiency and integrity in the public services, for making public administration an apt instrument for implementing and achieving the social and economic policies and goals of the Government, as also one which is responsive to the people. The Commission specifically was set up to consider the following:

1. The mechanism of the Government of India and its procedures of work;
2. The mechanism for planning at all levels;
3. Centre-State associations;
4. Financial administration;
5. Personnel administration;
6. Economic administration;
7. Administration at the state level;
8. District administration;
9. Agricultural administration; and
10. Problems of redress of citizen's grievances.

Exclusions

As the subjects of defence, railways, external affairs, security and intelligence work were already being examined by various committees, the commission was given a signal to exclude these from the purview of the commission. However, the commission was free to review the problems of above-mentioned sectors and recommend reorganization of the machinery of the Government as a whole or of any of its common service agencies.

Recommendation Reports

The following 20 reports were submitted by the commission before winding up in mid-1970s:

1. Problems of Redress of Citizens Grievances (Interim)
2. Machinery for Planning
3. Public Sector Undertakings
4. Finance, Accounts & Audit
5. Machinery for Planning (Final)
6. Economic Administration
7. The Machinery of GOI and its procedures of work
8. Life Insurance Administration
9. Central Direct Taxes Administration
10. Administration of UTs & NEFA
11. Personnel Administration
12. Delegation of Financial & Administrative Powers
13. Centre-State Relationships
14. State Administration
15. Small Scale Sector
16. Railways
17. Treasuries
18. Reserve Bank of India
19. Posts and Telegraphs
20. Scientific Departments

The above-mentioned 20 reports included 537 major recommendations. On the basis of inputs from various administrative ministries, a report, which was indicating implementation position, was placed before the Parliament in November 1977.

Second Administrative Reforms Commission

The Second ARC with a resolution no. K-11022/9/2004-RC was set up as a committee of inquiry of the Government of India to formulate a detailed blueprint to renovate the public administration system.

Mandate

A mandate was given to the Commission to recommend measures to attain a responsive, proactive, efficient, accountable and, sustainable administration for the country at all the stages of the government. The Commission was asked to, *inter alia*, consider the following: (i) Organizational structure of the Government of India (ii) Ethics in governance (iii) Refurbishing of Personnel Administration (iv) Strengthening of Financial Management Systems (v) Steps to ensure effective administration at the State level (vi) Steps to ensure effective District Administration (vii) Local Self-Government/ Panchayati Raj Institutions (viii) Social Capital, Trust and Participative public service delivery (ix) Citizen-centric administration (x) Promoting e-governance (xi) Issues of Federal Polity (xii) Crisis Management (xiii) Public Order.

Exclusions

As the detailed examination of administration of defence, railways, external affairs, security and intelligence was already being done by other sources, the Commission was to exclude these subjects from its purview. However, the Commission was given a nod to take the problems of these sectors into account in recommending re-organization of the machinery of the Government or of any of its service agencies.

Working of Second ARC

The Commission was expected to formulate its own procedures (including for discussions with the State Government as may be thought suitable by the Commission) and appoint committees and consultants/advisers to for assistance. The Commission was free to consider old reports and build on those instead of attempting to address all the issues *ab initio*. The government ministries and departments were directed to provide necessary information and documents as required by the Commission. The Government of India commended the State Governments and all others concerned to fully support the Commission.

Recommendation Reports

The 15 reports have been presented by the commission to the Government for consideration, which are as follows:

1. Right to Information: Master Key to Good Governance (9 June 2006)
2. Unlocking Human Capital: Entitlements and Governance-a Case Study (31 July 2006)
3. Crisis Management: From Despair to Hope (31 October 2006)
4. Ethics in Governance (12 February 2007)
5. Public Order-Justice for each: Peace for all. (25 June 2007)
6. Local Governance (27 November 2007)
7. Capacity Building for Conflict Resolution: Friction to Fusion (17 March 2008)
8. Combating Terrorism (17 September 2008)

9. Social Capital: A Shared Destiny (8 October 2008)
10. Refurbishing of Personnel Administration: Scaling New Heights (27 November 2008)
11. Promoting e-Governance: The Smart Way Forward (20 January 2009)
12. Citizen Centric Administration: The Heart of Governance (30 March 2009)
13. Organizational Structure of Government of India (19 May 2009)
14. Strengthening Financial Management Systems (26 May 2009)
15. State & District Administration (29 May 2009)

Implementation of Recommendations

A group of ministers (GoM) was constituted by the Government on 30 March 2007 under the Chairmanship of the External Affairs Minister to consider the endorsements of the Second ARC and to review the pace of implementation of the endorsements as well as to provide assistance to the concerned Ministries/Departments in implementation. It has since been reconstituted on 21 August 2009 under the Chairmanship of Union Finance Minister. Core Group has completed the examination of all the 15 reports on Administrative Reforms under the Chairmanship of Cabinet Secretary. Eleven reports have been considered by this Group of Ministers, which are as follows:

1. Right to Information: Master Key to Good Governance (First report)
2. Unlocking human capital: Entitlements and Governance: a Case Study relating to NREGA (Second Report)
3. Crisis Management From Despair to Hope (Third report)
4. Ethics in Governance (Fourth Report)
5. Local Governance (Sixth Report)
6. Capacity Building for Conflict Resolution (Seventh Report)
7. Citizen Centric Administration: The Heart of Governance (Twelfth Report)
8. Social Capital:A Shared Destiny (Ninth Report)
9. Organizational Structure of Government of India (Thirteenth Report)
10. Promoting e-Governance: The Smart Way Forward (Eleventh Report)
11. State and District Administration (Fifteenth Report)

The decisions on these reports by GoM are at various stages of implementation. The Ministry of Home Affairs handled the report on 'Combating Terrorism (Eighth Report)', and it is well understood that necessary action has already been taken on this report. Thus, 12 Reports have been considered in all, so far. The remaining three reports (Report Nos. V, X and XIV) are also soon being put up for consideration by GoM. On 3 December 2009, the Cabinet in its meeting had taken note on the progress of action taken in respect of second report (Unlocking human capital) related to NREGA and on 29 December 2009, in its meeting, cabinet has taken note on the progress of action taken in respect of the first report (Right to Information) and third report (Crisis Management).

18 CHAPTER

Code of Ethics for Civil Servants in India

In 1964, 'Santhanam Committee', The Committee on Prevention of Corruption had mentioned:

'For a country like India, development of her material resources and raising the standards of life of all classes are, indeed imperative. At the same time, the deterioration in the standards of public life has to be arrested. Ways and means have to be found to ensure that idealism and patriotism have the proper place in the ambition of our youth. The lack of moral earnestness, which has been a conspicuous feature of recent years, is perhaps the greatest single factor which hampers the growth of strong traditions of integrity and efficiency'.

Conduct rules and analogous rules are current set of ethical norms in India. Conduct rules are contained in the Central Services (Conduct) Rules, 1964 and analogous rules are applicable to members of the All India Services or employees of various State Governments. The code of behaviour as articulatedin the conduct rules, while containing some general norms like 'maintaining integrity and absolute devotion to duty' and not indulging in 'conduct unbecoming of a government servant', is usually directed towards itemizing specific activities which is considered as unfavourable for government servants. A code of ethics is not framed by conduct rules.

Code of ethics is prescribed in other nations but it is not recommended for civil servants in India. In India, several conduct rules exist, which forbid some common activities or behaviours. There is a need to add more 'generic norms' in the list of accepted conduct. In the code; conflict of interest is an important topic, which should be focused and should be addressed properly. It is necessary to build safeguards to prevent conflict of interest, it is necessary to take safety measures. A draft 'Public Service Bill' now under the table of Ministry of Personnel, Public Grievances and Pensions looks to form various basic demands from government employees, which are alluded to as 'values'. The prominent'values' imagined in the Bill are:

- Allegiance to the various ideals enshrined in the preamble to the Constitution
- A political functioning
- Good governance for betterment of the people to be the primary goal of civil service

- Duty to act objectively and impartially
- Accountability and transparency in decision-making
- Maintenance of highest ethical standards
- Merit to be the criteria in selection of civil servants consistent, however, with the cultural, ethnic and other diversities of the nation
- Ensuring economy and avoidance of wastage in expenditure
- Provision of healthy and congenial work environment
- Communication, consultation and cooperation in performance of functions, i.e., participation of all levels of personnel in management.

The second Administrative Reforms Commission has considered the issue of morals in the public life in different nations and in its report on 'Morals in Governance', it has featured the seven standards of public life articulated by the Nolan Committee in the United Kingdom. The commission would propose the consideration of the accompanying standards in the code of ethics for government employees in India:

- ***Integrity***: Civil servants ought to be guided exclusively by public interest for their official basic leadership and not by any money related or other thought either in regard of themselves, their families or their companions.
- ***Impartiality***: Civil servants should take decisions based on merit alone in execution of their official work, including functions such as procurement, recruitment and delivery of services etc.
- ***Commitment to public service***: Civil servants should give services in a fair, effective, impartial and well-mannered behaviour.
- ***Open accountability***: Civil servants are responsible for their decisions and actions, and should be capable to subject themselves to appropriate examination for this objective.
- ***Devotion to duty***: Civil servants should be dedicated towards their duties and responsibilities at all times.
- ***Exemplary behaviour***: It is the responsibility of civil servants to treat all public members with respect and politeness, and they should behave in a manner that supports the rich traditions of the civil services.

ETHICS COMMITTEE

Since ancient times, Ethics and morality have been the characteristicof public life in India. Rulers were required to observe stricter moral esteems and an unscrupulous king was demonstrated no leniency. In other words, ethics and politics were inseparable. This moral and good heritage was acquired by its national pioneers, who exhibited a high level of integrity and genuineness in the public life amid the flexibility battle drove by Mahatma Gandhi, who was the identity of this convention. He not only brings morality in public life but also practiced it. He believed that politics without morality is a thing to be avoided. According to his belief, morality is important in politics and in its functioning.

It is true that in recent times, it can be seen clearly that Indian system is functioning under huge strain, as not everything is well. The values in public life are decreasing which is a matter of concern. Also, recent trends in governmental issues seem to have made an impression as the limit of our popularity-based framework, to guarantee honour in the public life, is progressively going down. Such a circumstance does not foreshadow well for the eventual fate of majority rules system and should be captured promptly.

The Vohra Committee

There has been general disintegration of good esteems in all kinds of different backgrounds. Role of people's representatives, who are responsible for directing the framework in such a circumstance, becomes very critical. Members from Parliament as individuals' agents are taken a gander at by the general population as their good examples and the ones, who are conducting their fate, have, therefore, to be past the domain of any sort of doubt. Generally, the ideological base and the soul of administration which ought to actuate the vast majority of them is getting disintegrated and the sort of components who are endeavouring to impact the political gatherings and the political framework everywhere, influence everyone to think as to how integrity in the whole framework could be guaranteed. There might be numerous routes for guaranteeing honour in public life, yet a self-training system, seems, by all accounts, to be the best in an institution like Parliament.

It was in this background and in the midst of claimed charges of defilement including legislators and general view of criminalization of governmental issues, that the legislature of the day delegated on 9 July 1993, a Committee headed by Shri N.N. Vohra, the then Home Secretary, Government of India, to check out all accessible data about the activities of wrongdoing syndicates/mafia associations who professedly had developed links with and were being secured by some Government functionaries and political identities. The Committee, after analysing the issue, presented its report to the Government of India, which put it before both Houses of Parliament on 1 August 1995. On 8, 23 and 24 August 1995, the report was discussed in the Houses of Parliament.

The Committee, in its report, mentioned that 'the nexus between the criminal gangs, police, bureaucracy and politicians' had become visible clearly in different parts of the nation. The existing criminal justice system was definitely planned to deal with the individual offences/crimes, but was not enough capable to deal with the actions of the mafia. The provisions of law related to economic offences were found weak, and there were insuperable legal struggles in attaching/removing the properties acquired through mafia actions.

The report proposed setting up of a nodal office under the Ministry of Home Affairs, Government of India, to be dealt with straightforwardly by the Union Home Secretary, who would be assisted by at least one chosen officers of the Ministry for the gathering of all information got from various intelligence agencies. Consequently, an All-Party Meeting was held on 15 September 1995, under the Chairmanship of the then Union Home Minister, Shri S.B. Chavan, to investigate the entire range of criminal-legislator nexus and the related issue of affirmation of benefits and liabilities by the members of Parliament and ministers. The points, which constituted the agenda were:

1. Establishment of a Parliamentary Committee on Ethics as separate from the Committee of Privileges which would function as a guardian on the activities of members of Parliament.

2. Implementation of a code of conduct at the level of political parties to ensure a cleaner public life, e.g., not to provide party tickets to persons having criminal record.
3. All political parties must have open audited accounts which must be published yearly.
4. Giving more teeth to the Nodal Group set up as a result of the suggestions of the Vohra Committee Report.
5. Modifications in the legal system, simplification of the process and privilege of quick justice.

Birth of Ethics Committee

Also, the Second Chamber of Indian Parliament, Rajya Sabha, was seized of the matter for a long while. In 1966, the Business Advisory Committee of Rajya Sabha had decided that this issue ought to be considered by leaders of parties and groups in the House. After the efforts of the previous Prime Minister of India, Shri I.K. Gujral, former External Affairs minister, a meeting was held in 1996, with the leaders of parties and groups in Rajya Sabha to examine the issue. From that point, the issue was set before the General Purposes Committee of Rajya Sabha in 1997. After analysing the matter critically, the committee decided to have an interior component of the House itself, which would function as a self-administrative body for the individuals from Rajya Sabha. The committee approved the Chairman, Rajya Sabha to constitute an ethics committee with an order to supervise the ethical and moral direct of its individuals.

Thus, on 4 March 1997, the Chairman, Rajya Sabha had constituted the ethics committee, Rajya Sabha, the first such committee by any legislature in India to supervise the moral and ethical conduct of the members and to examine the cases referred to it with reference to ethical and other misconduct of individuals. It was provided that in all respects of procedure and other matters, the rules applicable to the Committee of Privileges shall apply to the ethics committee with such variations and modifications as the Chairman, Rajya Sabha may, from time to time, make. It was given that in all regards of procedures and other matters, the principles pertinent to the Committee of Privileges might apply to the ethics committee with such varieties and changes as the Chairman, Rajya Sabha may, occasionally, make. On 30 May 1997, the former Vice-President of India and the Chairman of Rajya Sabha, Shri K.R. Narayanan inaugurated the committee.

With the consolidation of tenets relating with the committee on ethics in the Rules of Procedure and Conduct of Business in the Council of States from July 20 2004, the order of the committee was enlarged to, aside from administering the good and moral lead of members, setting up a code of conduct for members and to propose corrections or increases in that from time to time in the forms of reports to the council; looking at cases concerning the alleged breach of code of conduct by members as likewise cases concerning claims of some other moral wrongdoing of member; and offering counsel to members from time to time on questions including moral guidelines either *suo motu* or on accepting particular solicitations. The committee was additionally gave with the ability to prescribe imposition of approvals, for example, blame, revile, suspension from the council for a particular period and some other sanction for demonstrated untrustworthy conduct or other unfortunate behaviour and contradiction of the code of conduct/rules with respect to the members.

The committee comprises of 10 members and according to hone, the leaders of best ten parties, according to their numerical quality in the House, are usually designated to be the individuals from the committee, and in case, the leaders happen to be ministers then the decision is lengthened to the Deputy Leaders of the parties. Amongst the members of the committee, the Chairman is appointed. The Chairman of the committee presented the reports to the House from time to time or, in his absence, any other member of the committee authorized by the committee is allowed to present the report.

The Committee on Ethics of the Lok Sabha

To regulate the good and moral lead of Members of that House, there is a Committee on Ethics of the Lok Sabha. The Committee on Ethics (Thirteenth Lok Sabha) in its first report viewed that standards of moral conduct for members have been sufficiently provided in the Rules of Procedure and Conduct of Business in the Lok Sabha, headings by the Speaker and in the traditions which have developed over the years on the basis of suggestions made by different Parliamentary Committees. Apart from the existing norms, the Committee suggested that the members ought to stand by the general ethical principles as mentioned below:

- Individuals must use their position to propel general prosperity of the general population.
- In the situation of conflict between their personal benefits and public welfare, they must solve the conflict so individual interests are subordinate to the obligation of public office.
- Conflict between private financial/family interests ought to be settled in a way that the public interest is not risked.
- Members holding public offices should utilize public resources that may lead to public welfare.
- Members should keep in their mind the essentialand duties listed in Part-IV of the Constitution.
- It is expected from members that they would maintain morality, dignity, decency and values in public life.

Challenges before the Ethics Committees in India

India has seen a great growth in the number of clinical trials conducted in the recent few years. This is creditedto the vast patient population, genetic diversity and rich technical pool in our nation. However, the economical upsurge in the clinical trial industry has also caused concerns pertaining to the efficiency of the Regulatory Agencies and Ethics Committees (EC). Additionally, the economical upsurge in the clinical trial industry has additionally caused concerns relating to the productivity of the Regulatory Agencies and Ethics Committees (EC). In the regulation of clinical research at the local level, the EC has played an important role. It is stated that ECs need standard working methodology, do not have an adequate representation, subsequently influencing their capacities in directing clinical research. Further, ECs seem to work in isolation, as self-sufficient bodies, having no interaction with the regulatory agency or other ECs. This delivers the requirement for ECs to meet up and share their experiences and perceptions, with the point of refreshing themselves and refining their capacities. Endeavours also required to be aimed on capacity building, centralized registration of ECs and getting an oversight mechanism in place. In India, in an effort towards encouraging themselves, it is important for the Ethics Committees to function in close association with forums like the Forum for Ethics Review Committees in India and the Forum for Ethical Review Committees in Asia Pacific.

In people, Clinical Research is a methodical investigation that is intended to find or add to a group of generalizable information. As clinical research includes human members, scientists are morally committed to secure them. The two vital securities offered to an individual taking part in clinical research are Written Informed Consent and Ethics Committee (EC) review. The reason for an EC survey of biomedical research is to defend the nobility, rights, well-being, and prosperity of the research participants. The EC audit contains moral standards and basic leadership to illuminate real or expected issues in the direct of human research.

In February 1980, the first official guidelines for the formation of ECs were issued by the Indian Council for Medical Research (ICMR). These rules included proposals for enrolment criteria and ethical standards for review, which set out the establishment for the foundation of ECs in India. This was trailed by announcement of the ICMR rules in bioethics, which was a direction record for look into in medical, epidemiology and public health, in the year 2000, which was additionally updated in 2006.

But, in spite of the foundation of moral rules since quite a while, the ECs in our nation are still struggling with fundamental issues such as, lacking or no standard working techniques (SOPs) and rebelliousness with the Schedule Y proposals. The EC has the prime obligation of controlling clinical research and defending the rights and security of research members, however, the organizations and hospital that focus on upgrading their research facilities have a tendency to overlook the EC, which supports their research. ECs need to manage fundamental issues, for example, absence of prepared labour, substantial workload, deficient space allotted for EC operations, absence of regulatory help and lacking compensation offered to individuals serving on EC boards. These issues come full circle into hesitance of trained people to fill in as individuals from the EC.

ECs also have to deal with issues like insufficient space allotted to them for operations and archival of records etc. ICMR conducted a study in which it was observed that there were no legal specialistson most of the ECs and there was a obscurity in the appointment processes of EC members. In addition, it was also observed that record keeping was poor, and the independence and ability of EC was doubtful.

The shortage of legitimate specialists and lay people on the EC majority, which is required according to Schedule Y details, also makes arrangement of regular occasional gatherings with the nearness of these individuals a troublesome errand. Generally, it is seen that the Head of the Institution's function as director of its EC, thus negotiating its free status.

According to another survey did by ICMR, there are over 200 institutions with working ECs in India. But, many of the existing ECs do not have their standard functional procedures in place, and are not formed as per Schedule Y recommendations. In fact, ECs do not have sufficient representation of members during their conferences, which is about to make a unfairbelief.

Added to this is the sporadic timetable of gatherings, with no procedure set up for sped up audit. According to the Bulletin report of the World Health Organization (WHO), there are below 40 ECs in our nation, which are appropriately constituted and working.

This report, too, raises worries about the autonomy of ECs referring to that there is no lawful prerequisite for individuals declaring Conflict of Interest (COI). This is an essential issue given the expanding number of private hospitals partaking in clinical research. The presence of individuals with conflicting interests is probably going to confine the capacity of a fair-minded audit by the EC.

During the review process, it is also seen that a lot of EC members are confusing about their roles and responsibilities. It is true that EC members consist of highly knowledgeable and experienced representatives from non-scientific communities, but most of them are silent viewers during meeting procedures and even unable to take part in scientific or ethical discussions in the review processes.

Similarly, insufficiency of formal training in bioethics, directs to an incomplete knowledge of difficult ethical problems like diminished independence, distributive equity, subject powerlessness and subject remuneration. EC individuals see their obligations restricted to giving endorsement to inquire about proposal submitted for survey and are neglectful of the requirement for a persistent audit. Rarely, ECs attempt point by point observing of studies and examine the educated assent process.

This, additionally, advocates the requirement for an oversight system to be set up amid the operations of the EC. So far, there is no focal registration system for ECs working in our nation, raising worries about responsibility. Because of absence of noticeable oversight by the administrative specialists, there is rebelliousness with the prescribed moral guidelines noted among ECs.

In India, the presentation of the Clinical Trial Registry India (CTRI) is considered as a moral basic for research done in India, however, this should be combined with a focal oversight for ECs supporting research studies. Even though, clinical research in India has expanded immensely in the previous years, administrative changes and moral practices have been not able keep pace with it. The Drug Controller General of India (DCGI) has discharged rules for review of investigator sites, however, there are no proposals for administrative assessments to be led on ECs. Centralized registration of ECs is a long-time strategy, yet to be executed.

Government Initiatives

Albeit, marked by a moderate pace, government bodies have taken activities toward controlling Indian ECs pertinent to Indian ethos. The moral rules discharged by the ICMR are detailed, and give a complete direction to biomedical research led in the nation.

To create SOPs for ECs, the ICMR has worked together with the Forum for Ethics Review Committees of Asia Pacific (FERCAP), which are accessible on their official site. FERCAP is a medium of bioethicists and restorative specialists who have met up with the goal of cultivating an enhanced understanding and better execution of the moral audit of biomedical research in Asia and the western Pacific district. It is an undertaking of the World Health Organization (WHO) Special Training and Research Program in Tropical Diseases (TDR), and is a forum under the umbrella of the Strategic Initiative for Developing Capacity in Ethical Review (SIDCER). All the diverse territorial forum for ethics committees from different nations are being brought under a solitary head of SIDCER, of which ICMR is an establishing part. FERCAP works towards encouraging research and education opportunities by functioning as a provincial collaborator for ECs and different partners in health research.

In November 2011, the First National Conference on Research Ethics was organized at the Tata Memorial Hospital by FERCI. In India, the national conference was considered as an innovative step towards bettering the working of ECs. Also, along with WHO and SIDCER, FERCI decides to hone the capacity building of ECs and add authorizations to them.

The DCGI has discharged the updated rendition of Schedule Y, which portrays the parts and obligations of EC individuals according to the ICMR rules and gives clearness on the administrative duties of EC capacities. However, these activities should be combined with solid usage designs, to guarantee stringent administrative controls to defend subject rights.

The DCGI assigns the EC as a vital controller of moral research, nonetheless, both the bodies appear to work in separation. There is no appropriate contact between the ECs functional in the nation and the DCGI. Both the ICMR, which has issued guidelines in Bioethics for research led in our nation and DCGI, which is the essential specialist for inquire about in India, do not have any independence over the research viewed and endorsed by the ECs in our nation. There is no focal public authority that is in charge of managing the proper and skilful working of ECs. Consequently, ECs working as independent bodies worried about endorsement of research conducted in their institutes, with no responsibility at all. The ramifications of absence of focal self-governance are apparent in the findings of a current report, locating the ethical concerns in India. The study highlighted moral issues saw amid the direct of clinical trials, for example, infringement of ICMR rules, inability to answer to administrative expert/EC, if an investigation is dismissed by some other EC, and absence of training procedures for EC individuals.

Moreover, the ICMR rules are not administered, hence, the ECs cannot act against the individuals who disregard the recommended rules. The part of the EC is only confined to being an admonitory or to encourage inquire about. The DCGI has given ECs the ability to dismiss trials not confirming to the suggested moral models. Also, the DCGI gives clearance just to those trials that have been looked into and approved by the concerned EC. Therefore, aside from governing the moral parts of research, the EC also plays a significant role of a moral controller for the DCGI. However, the absence of a national ethics body, with a solid administrative control, has additionally hampered the foundation of a legitimate ethics policy.

Ethics Committees: Facing the Challenges

The survey considered 11 ECs in India for their insight into the moral rules, and the demeanours and practices took after by them. The outcomes revealed absence of learning of Schedule Y standards among the EC individuals, combined with insufficient training in Good Clinical Practice (GCP), inability to enlist the basic archives for EC review, and inability to understand the critical part of EC approval in clinical research. The study too had few promising discoveries, as all the ECs had created SOPs and one-third of them had directed inner reviews, to guarantee the quality of their operations. Despite the fact that the outcomes were empowering, when contrasted with ICMR-WHO surveys held in 2003 and 2007. The investigation proposed that ECs in India has a challenging task in the future.

In 2009, another study conducted to study the profile and roles of EC members in Pune, stated similar results. It was observed in study that most EC members were senior in age, highly educated, and well experienced in research, but, very few of them had actual knowledge of the ethical principles. In fact, with a suitable EC constitution, the individuals had imperfect comprehension of the moral issues and standards. The study also mentioned that a dominant part of them felt that a formal training in morals was important and that there ought to organize among different ECs, to share considerations and experiences.

An updated survey held on the compliance of issued EC approval letters to the Schedule Y/ICMR rules found visible non-compliance in the EC audit procedure to prescribed administrative rules. The study stated lack of legal specialistsand social scientists in the EC approval meetings, absence of minimum requirement as per Schedule Y and failure to go through essential documents like the clinical trial agreement and the insurance policy.

Capacity Building for Ethics Committees

In our nation, the actual need for ECs is to emphasis on capacity building and members of ECs should be experienced in the principles of bioethics, local regulatory guidelines and Good Clinical Practices (GCP). Preparing projects ought to be directed keeping the social and social situation in context and aim at community welfare and security. In organizing training programmes for EC members, government agencies such as the ICMR along with the FERCI need to take vanguard initiatives. Being the actual partners in clinical research, sponsors need to put resources into EC training, a zone that has lamentably being overlooked by them.

As EC members belong from different academic and research backgrounds and may not be aware of the ethical principles and technical requirements of the EC evaluation process, so, training is essential for these members.

A national training program in bioethics should be presented and made compulsory for each utilitarian EC part. This ought to be combined with strategic workshops, organized by the local ethics committees and research institutes. Training programmes ought to underline on the codes ethical conduct, principles of GCP, compliance with applicable regulatory guidelines, developing SOPs, composition of ECs, roles and responsibilities of the members, and review procedures. The EC individuals ought to be trained on difficult, yet, essential points in clinical research, for example, vulnerable populations, therapeutic misconception, informed consent process, and issues identified with subject remuneration and protection.

The substance of the projects ought to be planned keeping the non-scientific EC individuals in context, and thus, prepare them to release their duties proficiently. Bioethics ought to be presented as a subject in medical, life sciences, drug store and other significant educational programmes to sharpen our future scientists to this point. The ICMR and FERCI ought to unequivocally attempt the way towards granting approvals to the ECs accomplishing competency in their methods, thus promising and spurring their endeavours. There appears to be no disputeon the strong focus required on capacity building to empower ECs, the imperative controllers of research.

Need for Central Registration of Ethics Committees

The decentralization of independence over research directed in our nation is extremely important, as it unfavourably influences the commitments of both the EC and the DCGI towards the control of ethics in research. A critical step that should be taken towards this way is the foundation of a Central Registration System for ECs in India at standard with the CTRI. This ought to be a critical advance towards presenting administrative control in the procedures of the ECs. The DCGI should make it obligatory for all ECs working in our nation to be enrolled, without which an EC approval ought not to be viewed as substantial. The focal registry ought to keep up record of the EC points of interest such as the associated organizations, member details along with their qualifications, training records, registered personal account number (PAN) details, official address and data about EC reviewed trial approval status. Foundation of a central registry ought to realize the truly necessary straightforwardness and responsibility in the direction of clinical research in India. This would also help fortify the endeavours to control events of any misconduct in EC operations. These means, in expanding responsibility of ECs, would additionally empower them to refine their systems.

A turning point in this way is the planned Bill to the Health Ministry on Biomedical Research on Human subjects (Regulation, Control and safeguard). The bill visualizes foundation of National Biomedical Research Authority along with creation of National Ethics committee on Human Research. The bill also comprises of central registration of institutional ethics committees. Once set up, the bill will guarantee regulation of biomedical research on human subjects, confine corrupt clinical trials and give legislative powers to the ICMR moral rules.

Oversight Mechanisms

A fundamental assignment that requires to run close by with building up the central registry for ECs is acquiring a proficient oversight methodin place. It is fundamental that administrative and moral developments are presented in pace with the regularly expanding clinical research exercises in India. DCGI has issued the trial assessment rules for investigator sites, however, have not disclosed any inspection plans for ECs. The DCGI should conduct casual inspections and also ensure that ECs must fulfil with the recommended standards. ECs, by themselves, should take actions in guaranteeing the competency of their methodology. To ensure that SOPs and review-related documents are in place, independent auditors can do periodic internal audits.

To guaranteean oversight mechanism for clinical studies, the ECs need to adapt innovative procedures. It is important for ECs to realize that ensuring the rights and well-being of trial members does not end with giving trial approval, but rather needs to proceed all through the conduct of the study.

Need for a National Forum

The confined presence of the ECs and the absence of correspondence system between the ECs and the administrative bodies make it fundamental for ECs in our nation to meet up and work in a cooperative way to build up a uniform set of principles. The members of various ethics committees need to considertheir roles and responsibilities and come up with solutions for problems faced during the EC review procedure. It is essential for Ethics committees to communicate with each other and share their experiences and opinions with the purpose to update themselves and improve their functions. Also, it is important to understand for the EC members that their responsibilities are not simply limited to the ethical review of research, but towards the welfare of the community they represent. This encouragesthe need for ECs to come together and form a cooperative network, firstly, at a local level, and then expand to the regional and national levels. There is a necessity to shape joint forums of ECs, which can serve as platforms to address the issues and issues looked by them.

Focusing the aforementioned need, an experimental initiative, Pune Model, was taken by the Independent Ethics Committee (IEC) associated with the Chest Research Foundation (CRF) Pune, in which a Scientific Meeting in Human Ethics was organized. The motive of the meeting was to unite all the ECs functional in Pune, and form a joint forum to interact and communicate with each other. The meeting included a conversation by Dr. Urmila Thatte regarding the 'Challenges faced by Ethics Committees' followed by a discussion, in which all the present EC members asked their questions on EC operations and shared their experiences. The idea of having a joint forum of ECs in Pune was also proposed by Dr. S. M. Karandikar, Chairperson IEC-CRF. This meeting gave clearness on the moral issues experienced by EC individuals identified with subject compensation, trial protection and educated assent.

The Pune Model was an innovative action towards forming a cooperative link of ECs across India. This was the initial step taken in making a stage for considering moral and operational issues looked by the morals councils at a local level. The local forum will also work as a basis for key designs in capacity building, a basic requirement for EC individuals today. The forum can sporadically organize workshops for training in bioethical issues, in a joint effort with FERCI and ICMR. Similarly, it can be used as a channel for updating members about new controls and rules issued by the administrative experts.

Sustainability will be a challenging task for the Pune Model. This meeting was organized by the EC associated with Lupin Research Center (Pune) and more than 50 EC members had attended this meeting in Pune. The focuses of this meeting were article presentations by authorized members of ECs on subject compensation and trial insurance. The ECs in Pune forum have commonly decided to host periodic meetings among themselves. Given the expanding mindfulness among EC individuals to prepare themselves, and late reviews directed by DCGI at a few ECs, sustainability of the Pune Model is essential.

A proposal was given to expand the joint local forum of ECs, The Pune Model, to the regional level, Maharashtra, and then to a national level, India. The aim of the Pune Model is closely related with the ICMR and FERCI in their efforts towards encouragement of ECs in India.

STRENGTHENING OF ETHICAL AND MORAL VALUES IN GOVERNANCE

Case Study: Governance in India (Vision 2020)

Over five decades after autonomy and foundation of the Republic, there is a broadly shared need, in the nation, to assess the achievements made as also to evaluate our future. Without a doubt, the general population of the nation and the administrators of society can be saluted on many reasons for India's accomplishments since autonomy which include independence in self-sufficiency grains, a solid mechanical base, a rising expectancy of life, a higher level of education, a unified and better coordinated India and a developing acknowledgment by the world of our capabilities and potential on the negative side, one could tally the bothering issues of joblessness, ignorance and destitution emphasized by a consistently expanding population. Moreover, low per capita income, insufficient infrastructure and feudalistic inclinations and most noticeably awful is a terrible scorn of rule of law and morals in the public life and at last, an organization which is seen as selfish and native hostile.

Governance is affected by all the above-mentioned factors. For the unity of nation, in strengthening public administration, in realizing social and economic goals and in the improvement of the conditions of the people, the policy rules, public investment and approach to governance have contributed a lot. Lamentably, in the meantime, the real areas of administration, particularly the political executives, the council, the legal, the common administrations and the common society need to assume the fault for a large number of the ills of society and the unfulfilled promises that we made to ourselves in November 1949, when we accepted the Constitution. It is useful to recall the Preamble to the Indian Constitution in its original form:

'WE, THE PEOPLE OF INDIA, having solemnly resolved to constitute India into a SOVEREIGN DEMOCRATIC REPUBLIC, and to secure to all its citizens:

JUSTICE, social, economic and political;

LIBERTY of thought, expression, belief, faith and worship;

EQUALITY of status and of opportunity; and to promote among them all;

FRATERNITY assuring the dignity of the individual and the unity of the Nation:

IN OUR CONSTITUENT ASSEMBLY this twenty-sixth day of November, 1949, do HEREBY ADOPT, ENACT AND GIVE TO OURSELVES

THIS CONSTITUTION'.

In this manner, a few words were added to the Preamble, which scarcely add to its loftiness or substance. These could even be overlooked for our present talk. The quintessence of our responsibility regarding the country stands embodied in the first Preamble to which one reverts repeatedly.

A typical desist, especially when the general population investigate the situation in the nation, has been that the nature of administration needs much to be desired. Those in the administration, keep on feeling that they are fulfilling their duties and nothing could be better. The national plainly feels otherwise. This disparity in the perceptions of the general population and the legislature is reflected in the believability gap, which exists between the public and the administration. At this point, the general feeling outside the administration is that the legislature is enormous, it needs course, it is unmanageable, is inefficient and it is uncaring of the citizen. The administration, on its part, continues reasserting itself with new policy perceptions from time to time in an offer to 'win friends and influence people'. A phase has been achieved when the general population bring with a squeeze of salt whatever the government says or guarantees.

The entire scenario is changing rapidly. In this context, it would be interesting to know that what would be the shape of governance in India after twenty or twenty-five years from now: governance in its broad form comprising the transnational and national, the state level and at the cutting edge, i.e., the district and below. As the timeclock is moving speedily and we have already moved into the third millennium, so it is important and appropriate to put such questions to ourselves. The procedure of globalization too demands that we have a brisk investigate the future and assess where one ideally would be say in 2020 or 2025. In the life of a nation, 50 years is not a huge period, yet for an individual, even 10 years have any kind of effect. Thus, let us take a gander at the feasible situation of administration in India in 2020.

In the way of shaping our future, it is important to consider the major factors, which can affect the Indian society and the governance in the coming times. These can be specified below:

Indian population has already crossed the 1.25 billion mark. It is a possibility that by the end of the year, another few millions would be added to our population. If we compare this with the total population of a country like Switzerland having less than 7 million people. An yearly accumulation of 15 million plus would be comparable to the total population of a nation like Australia and many others. Growing population brings up new challenges and issues of its own. Some prudent individuals express that: "People are an asset". Certainly, they are. However, it rests on the quality of the asset, the feature and traits they possess and the capability of the society to keep them productively employed. However, it appears highly difficult for the administration to effectively utilize, properly educate and train, and actually turn such ever-increasing population into an asset. The social pressures brought about by the ever-increasing population are huge and thus it causes an immense burden on civic facilities and the socio-economic infrastructure.

According to the current literacy levels, we still have more than 350 million illiterates in India. The percentage is excluding greater than the total population of any other nation in the world, except China. Illiteracy is the sole reason of several problems.

Poverty and unemployment are the other two serious inter-related issues. In fact, if we consider that the number of people below poverty line has reduced to 27% or so, according to the latest Sample Survey, or even to 25%, 250 million people or a quarter of population is still living below poverty line or say 50 million families are surviving in miserable poverty. Unemployment also continues to be high or more specifically, the underemployment, low wage employment and the poorly waged self-employment. The reality is that literacy, poverty and idleness are an inter-related disease which is disappointing and troublesome.

The life expectancy may rise between 70 and 75 by 2020 as the health care facilities are expanding with better income levels and access to medicare. There are the chances that if India's population reaches 1.3 billion by 2020, the number of people over 60 years of age, which is standard age for retirement, would be a few hundred million. An immense armed force of old and resigned individuals will have its effect in social, monetary and budgetary terms. Annuity obligation would increase, especially when we do not have the way of life of keeping up separate pension funds. Security of the older folks and their leisure utilization will be basic issues.

The present pattern of GDP development of 6% is looked to be raised to 7% for each annum or considerably more. Indeed, even with the present levels of residential reserve funds, it can be raised to at least 8% if the productivity of speculation enhances and the incremental capital output ratio (ICOR) turn out to be more positive. We should work for in perfect ICOR for 3:1 and if that happens, even by 2020, we will be successful. The last decade has seen another wonder which, without a superior term, could be called 'mandalization of governmental issues and society'. The essential target in giving extraordinary advantages to specific areas of society was unexceptionable, however, its aftermath in the shape of social strains and conflicts between various positions has been somewhat irritating. While unique advantages to the socially disabled would prompt social consideration, yet, the negative effect of these new strategy bundles must be viewed and precisely balanced. There are the chances that the Indian culture would be more broken in 2020 unless we are careful. The procedure of social stirring is continuing throwing its shadow over administration.

The last 15 years have seen a continuous, however, sharp decrease in the strength of public finance at all levels, i.e., the Union Govt., the states and the neighbourhood bodies both urban and rural. Monetary shortfall has been running into twofold digit as a percentage of GDP. The state is injured by reimbursement liability and interest payment liability. Nearby bodies, especially PRIs, are usually unequipped for raising sufficient assets. Over it, public fundscontinue to be misused. In 1999–2000, alone the states acquired a net extra obligation of ₹ 67,000 crores rising it to ₹ 4,01,570 crores.

There is a kind of obligation on the head of the Central Government. This thoughtless overspending is bamboozling our future generations of their genuine assets and opportunities, since it will be their obligation to reimburse tomorrow what we are obtaining today.

In the last few years, world has viewed a huge explosion in information technology sector. The heavyweight PCs have given way to smooth gadgets and the laptops. The intersection of hardware and broadcast communications has opened new vistas of transmission, stockpiling and recovery of data as never before. These are in effect progressively utilized for decision-making in the Corporate World as well as in public organization. Nowadays, e-commerce and e-governance is boom in IT sector. This trend will turn out to be considerably more critical as years pass.

Globalization is considered as an important factor in trade and commerce, in financial services, in entertainment electronics and in cultural exchanges as well as in various serious areas of public administration. It is not possible to for any nation to remain isolated from the outside world. In fact, if we are unable to fight with them, we need to go along with them. The importance of globalization is being felt in India as never before and with the progression of time, it will increase. Indian society is affected by all the above-mentioned factors, creating serious challenges but providing new opportunities to those who are linked with the governance of the nation. In the matter of interface with the resident, there is an increased emphasis on clarity and right to information. It is in this perspective that one needs to consider India's administration in the current state and the eventual fate of the administration in our nation in the year 2020. Obviously, it is not possible to 'predict' the future as unexpected advancements do happen both in technology and human activities. Once the former Prime Minister of Japan stated: 'Life is like a rugby ball: You do not know which way it will bounce'. It is very difficult to visualize the actual picture of 2020, yet, it is possible to imagine the expected picture two decades from now. As mentioned in Article 1 of the Constitution, India might keep on being a union of States. On the other hand, as the present trends propose our quasi-federal structure is very close to become even more centralizedin character suggesting that the States and the constituent units of the Union may acquire greater powers. The need for independence may not be consented to in the way it is caught on. But, of the three ideas — 'autonomy', 'devolution' and 'decentralization' — the last two will turn out to be more articulated.

One noteworthy accomplishment of the most recent 50 years is a superior incorporation of the constituent units of India and this procedure of combination is probably become more effective. With more prominent development in the political administration of the nation, with a more creative administration, with a more intelligent judiciary and with a powerful affable society, the fundamental structure ought to remain un-influenced. NGOs will have a more prominent part in self-administration. It is another issue that there will be an increment in the number of states of the Indian Union. Besides 28 States, we may have 35 to 40 States by 2020, thanks to the process of breaking down of larger States. This may happen despite lack of economic feasibilitysince the political ambitions of individuals and the social strains would lead to the creation of new States. Moreover, the number of districts, which currently is close to 600, is bound to increase. Generally, the factors that lead to the formation of new states will support the requirement for the creation of new districts and lower administrative establishments. So, there is no matter of surprising if the total number of districts in the nation touches a figure of 800 by 2020. Other than 28 States as of now excluding Delhi, we may have 35 to 40 States by 2020, this is all because of the way towards division of bigger States. This may happen regardless of absence of financial practicality since the political desires of the general population and the social weights would lead the formation of new states. Additionally, the number of districts, which is approximately 600, will undoubtedly increase. Generally, the factors that lead to the formation of new states will support the requirement for the creation of new districts and lower administrative developments. So, there is no surprise, if the total number of districts in the nation touches a figure of 800 by 2020. Then, with smaller states and smaller districts, the administration is obligedto be better networked. Identity cards, information technology hook-up, a nationwide computerized driving license storage system and similar other devices and facilities would positively prompt a greatly improved networking everywhere. At the pinnacle national level, amidthe departments and the divisions of government and the units of civil society; alsoat the state level and at the district level, and vertically as between the Central government, the states and the district level including Panchayati Raj Institutions and urban local bodies, there would be substantially more prominent and faster trade of thoughts and information.. It should causegreater efficiency in administration.

Thirdly, the span of government and the recurrence and power of its intercession in the life of the citizen might radically reduce with a more prominent attestation of the common society and with more noteworthy decentralization and devolution. Government should be thinner and smaller. Currently, 19 to 20 million people are actively working in the government at the national level, at the state level and at the local level, which covers almost 2% of India's population. Due to greater efficiency and pressures of financial limitations, the number of employees should decrease both in minimal terms and surely as a percentage of India's population. I do not imagine government having the strength of more than 15 million by 2020 or something like that, and unquestionably not over 1.5% of India's populace. It ought to occur through divestment of public sector undertakings, through decelerated enrolment in government and by exchanging a considerable lot of the state duties to the common society. The effect of such diminishment will be remarkable: government will be more slender and more streamlined, public expenditure as a percentage of GDP will decrease and basic leadership will turn out to be speedier.

This conveys me to the next issue, that is, the assertion of the civil society. The recent years have seen an increasing demand for strengthening of the civil society. This accentuation radiates from various factors and is worldwide in its appearance. The some factors that support the civil society include the disappointment of the legislature to convey productively, satisfactorily and in time, the slow fortifying of the segments of common society, simple access to data and close difficulty of the State to manage its activities in all circles. The policy functions of the State might stay with it, yet, in a large number of areas especially training, wellbeing, transport and correspondences, human asset advancement, and so on, the operational perspective will pass on to the civil society.

Indeed, one can imagine a greater interface between the civil society and the government in the future. The citizen must influence decision-making as therein lies the spirit of democracy. Another conclusion of the downsizing of the administration will be the concurrent decentralization of specialist and devolution of forces and the expulsion of the present uncertainty of the State Governments in empowering the urban neighbourhood bodies and the Panchayati Raj Institutions. The constitutional revisions for this behalf were made numerous years back.

After the acceptation of the 73rd and 74th amendments to the Constitution, the states have sanctioned follow up enactments for the setting up and working of the Panchayati Raj Institutions and the urban local bodies, the setting up of the State Finance Commissions and of the District Planning Committees. Albeit, almost a decade has gone since this state supported development started, it has not assembled full momentum and is simply shuffling along. Generally, the state governments have been unwilling in granting monetary and functional authorities to these local bodies which is very disastrous. The 11th and the 12th Schedules of the Constitution contain 29 and 18 items correspondingly for the Panchayati Raj Institutions and the Urban Local Bodies, however, without the authoritative powers, money-related powers and official powers not much has really happened. The issue is gettingattention of the Constitution Review Commission, and positively some effective guidelines would be suggested. One thing, in any case, looks likely and that will be that certainly before 2020, say by 2010 or something like that, the Panchayati Raj Institutions and the Urban Local Bodies would have been assigned with sufficient powers and duties to release their functions successfully in the territories endowed to them such as civic amenities, health, education and local area development. At the same time, with the authorization of the Urban Local Bodies and the Panchayati Raj Institutions and the strengthening of the civil society, the empowerment in the people would be a key factor in the governance of the nation.

Few steps in this direction are effort for clear administration, accountability and citizens'contracts. All divisions of governance for example the political masters, the judiciary, the permanent civil service and the legislatures should regard the right of the citizen to deal with his undertakings. Aversely but definitely, by 2020, people's empowerment would come and will be one of the strengths for self-governance.

Seen in this situation, I do anticipate that the civil services should in any case be there: in the present form or in a modified form is the question. The real obligations of the civil services are not liable to change much in the following couple of decades. In any case, what will undoubtedly change is their inner synthesis, the destinations set for them, their orientation and their interface with the civil society. The intonation on their aptitude development and skill upgradation will turn out to be considerably sharper. As regards the staffing to the administrations, the underlying training and the requirements for entry into services are being taken a gander at nearly by a powerful Committee set up by UPSC. Regardless of whether the IAS itself holds its pre-distinction, could be discussed but there should be a most optimized plan of service which has its effect on the administration of the nation.

The rapport between the civil servants and the political masters, be at the local level, state level or national level, needs an extremely careful relook. It is proposed that as in the case of members from the judicial services, the perspectives of the government employees should also be openly known and should extend afar the perspectives of the political ace. It would, initially, appear to be a noteworthy variation from the present practice, however if we are searching for a strong, brave, productive and devoted civil service, some such idea should be advanced. That will guarantee better responsibility and straightforwardness.

If public servants are expected to act as public servants, and this includes all of them specifically the political administrators, the civil servants, members of judiciary and the elected representatives of the people, they should be subjected to full responsibility for their misfeasance as well as for nonfeasance. In fact, this will have to be ensured seriously and purely. Few supporters of democracy lack responsibility while they look for responsibility of others, and this will have to be restructured. Undoubtedly, the next 20 years will see the reinforcing of the process of accountability not only of the distinct wings of governance but also of the Press and the Media, the Controller and Auditor General, members of the judiciary and the elements of civil society. In the vast majority of these cases, the idea of responsibility should be informalized.

The coming 20 years will see a time of smoothening and restructuring of tax administration which would get more citizen-friendly. The harsh methodologies of tax collection, which we acquired from the pioneer aces 54 years prior is gradually changing in character. The Income-tax department and the States Sales-tax departments have taken some initiatives. In respect of indirect taxes, a widespread VAT system has been applied in 2010, which had included the central excise duty and sales-tax, etc. Before introducing a wide-ranging VAT, some important constitutional, legal and administrative issues, for instance, which agency would collect the tax, whether there would be a tax sharing between the States and the Union and who will have the power to allow exemptions, have been sorted out. For the smooth transition to a comprehensive VAT, government has decided to set up a commission.

While discussing duties and public finance management, one is suitable to think towards the present dispensation, which acknowledges both the Planning Commission and the Finance Commission. With the progression of time, the Planning Commission itself has lost a lot of its significance and there is not really requirement for two separate organizations settling on the vertical stream of assets to the States and down beneath. Taking a gander at 2020, one would state that by then there ought to be an incorporated body, which could carry out some essential planning functions and give the formulae to devolution of funds to states. I do imagine that by 2020, the inclination, which has been seen in the last 10–15 years of doles being offered by the Prime Minister and other senior functionaries in government, would have decreased.

As a result of the IT revolution and other emotionally supportive networks, running government workplaces in the conventional way would experience a change. May be, the representatives should observe certain core hours, say from 10.00 am to 4.00 pm what's more, what's more, they could either come early in the morning or stay in the office at night making a total of no less than 8 hours every day. Display day gatherings would likewise experience a change. Teleconferencing and videoconferencing at all levels ought to be conceivable. It would spare part of time and cash as well as prompt faster basic leadership.

As an expansion of the previous specified aspect, it is important to minimize the holidays in government. There would be not more than six or seven more holidays in the year, which would incorporate three National holidays, apart from Saturday and Sunday as holidays. The remaining could be considered as 'Confined Holidays' of which each representative could take three or four in the year. There ought to be no common holiday for any religious or denominational holiday. The various leaves getting now days are a relic of the past. A thorough leave system, say 30 days in a year would be set up. Obviously, moreover, the times of hospitalization in view of ailment or mischance and so forth and on account of female workers for their confinement and delivery would be allowable. It is important for us to move towards an advanced system of administration.

As we know in the next two decades, the public sector will experience a radical change. Not just the majority of the business endeavours of the legislature at the national and state level known as Public Sector Undertakings would have been disinvested, however even the functions at present released by some public authorities could be transferred to the private part. The process of disinvestment is already happening. The economic, political and social compulsions would result in a thinner and more adaptable public sector, which should not demand monetary help. Mostly services currently delivered by the public service agencies would be transferred to private enterprises. There are already important changes have been done to privatize power and water supply. Transport and health services are also in for important changes and education should transfer to private parts. Only the essential responsibilities should remain with the government and the public sector. There is a requirement to justify the public services at the grass root level especially at the village level. The present course of action by which different departments of the State governments, e.g., development and *panchayats*, social welfare, revenue, agriculture, and so forth have their different authorities at the town level is a chronological error and a misuse of assets. One single functionary representing the government and encouraging the life of the general population in the town would be a vastly improved substitute. Actually, this ought to happen certainly before 2020.

One noteworthy viewpoint on which so much will depend, the extent that the nation's administration is concerned, relates with the political changes for running the political government. The last few years have witnessed continuing weakening of the Congress party and the arrival of the BJP and some of the regional parties. This has prompted many variations of coalition politics. History advises us that a strong Central Government, which has its effect felt in various parts of the nation has performed superior to the weak administrations in Delhi. In the situation of decentralization and transference of powers, development of the civil society and people's empowerment, one does not search for an despotic focal government. Meanwhile, a national government, which is helpless before constituent units of a democratic alliance subject to the impulses of local gathering pioneers, does not improve the nation's picture nor does it give effective administration. Also, individuals see the negative ramifications of a frail coalition. That's why, it isnot questionable that certainly before 2020 there is a noteworthy political stirring bringing about the rise of two or three in number political gatherings either of whom will summon a dominant part in the Lok Sabha. New political connections are probably going to rise.

Aside from the above-mentioned, more prominent homogeneity and cohesiveness in the system of administration is called for, and should be guaranteed certainly before 2020. The political executive, the civil services, the legislature and the judiciary donot appear to bring an impression of homogeneity shared understanding and regular offer assistance. Obviously, on occasions, there are assertions of some accursed conspiracies or else, there is a quality of conflict and argumentative relationship. Behaviours, which harm the harmony among the participants, should be removed. Ideally, by 2020, actually a long time before that, a smoother and stronger prototype of administration ought to rise.

As a feature of the procedure of de-bureaucratization and de-centralization of specialist, the way towards entrusting decision-making duty of Government to Regulatory Commissions is evidently clear. It is very likely that such Commissions should be set up in several zones of administration. For the staffing of civil servants, we already have the Public Service Commissions. Also, we have the Insurance Regulatory Authority, the Telecom Regulatory Authority and the Power Regulatory Authorities at the Centre and in the States. Similarly, by 2020, the procedureof decision-making and implementation of such decisions in many sectors will be in the partsof Regulatory Commissions and the government will have little control over that. Regardless of whether this would be to improve things or it will have unfavourable ramifications for administration, will rely upon how these commissions work and are permitted to behave. As much asthe performanceof the civil services is involved, it is possible that by 2020 they will secure a more keen edge in their delivery. This would be possible through gaining of improveds kills, greater professionalism, better networking and greater opportunity for functioning. The idea of worldwide administration will undoubtedly turn into a reality in the following 20 years if not prior and the administration of the nation will be incredibly impacted by global phenomena. Not that India would lose its power or that our laws will become out of order in the land. Regardless, the global order would reduce the impact of a portion of the national arrangement bundles and certain laws and techniques. Worldwide policing will be a more grounded plausibility as one does not see a conclusion to trans-border terrorism and other trans-border exchanges. However, the police organization itself would require a noteworthy change to have the capacity to address the difficulties of policing and support of law and order.

The fundamental structure of the Constitution and the basic aspects of the Constitution, vertically and horizontally, should be integral. Certainly, the civil society will have an important contribution in the management of the matters of the society. Though, the market will not be capable to overcome the state and nor it should. In other words, by 2020, the state, the market and the civil society should exist together in a more firm way. Also, the national and worldwide powers should find an adequate wavelength for concurrence.

In India, while one perceives several positive aspects in the scenario of governance in 2020, few major issues that government faces nowadays may remain. One of the issuesis corruption, which has seriously weakened the system. It can be dealt but the only condition is if we take key actions for removing corruption, including clearness and accountability. Unemployment, poverty and illiteracy are the other issues superimposed by the increasing populace. It would be easy to handle these issues if we follow a transparent policy on family planning and family interests. The benefits of socio-economic development would happen in a considerable measure when numbers are contained. Other issues, which will turn out to be much severer are those relating to accessibility of energy and drinking water. Indiscriminate utilize, non-monetary taxes and wastage are intensifying the issue. If the present tendency continues, drinking water would run in short supply while milk and liquor may be available in abundance. Transport could be the source of major risk, especially road transport. Air traffic and rail transport may be better systematized. Broadcast communications will be one of the brighter prospects. The Public Administration in the nation will still be perplexed by some bothering issues, and loads of pulls and counter pulls will be applied on it. However, it would be better prepared to address the difficulties of administration than it is today.

Corruption in India and International Cooperation

19 CHAPTER

The term corruption can be understood as misuse of public resources or position in public life for private benefits. The possibility for corruption increases when command on the public administrators become delicate and the division of power between political, executive and bureaucracy is uncertain and confusing. Political defilement, which is sometimes indistinguishable from bureaucratic debasement, has a tendency to be more extensive in authoritarian regimes where the public views and the Press cannot criticize corruption. However, in India, despite an attentive and aware press and public view, the intensity of corruption is extremely high. This might be credited to the articulate insensitivity, absence of disgrace and the nonappearance of any feeling of open ethical quality among the bribe-takers. In fact, they wear their identification of defilement and shamelessness with equal confidence and boldness. The expansion of chances in state intervention in financial and social life has immeasurably expanded the open door for political and bureaucratic corruption, more specifically since politics has too progressed towards becoming professionalized. We have proficient government officials who are politicians on a full-time basis, in fact, out of office also. In the corruption perception index prepared by a non-governmental Organization, Transparency International, India is ranked at 73 out of 99 nations. Presently, corruption is considered as a threat not only to the quality of governance but also for the every base of our society and the state. Corruption in defence purchases, in other purchases and contracts have a tendency to weaken the security of the state. Few power contracts are creating such financial load upon some of the states that the financial capabilityof those states has fallen into question. There appears a connection between terrorism, drugs, smuggling, and politicians, which was highlighted in the Vohra Committee Report.

Corruption has grown because one is unable to see successful examples of successfully prosecuted cases of corruption. Cases, inadequately established upon, weak and fragmented investigation, trailed by a slow and delayed trial confluence an ethically ill-deserved but a lawfully unavoidable exoneration. The acknowledgment of corruption as an inflexible reality has prompted quiet compromise and acquiescence to such wrongs.

Truly, the present procedure of pulling back the State from different parts in which it have never entered or in which it is not fit for performing productively, may decrease the scope of corruption to some degree, in fact, if we move to a free market economy, there must be control of economy as distinct from controls upon the industrial activity. The necessities of administration would yet call for going into contracts, purchases etc.

MENACE OF CORRUPTION IN PUBLIC LIFE

The Scandinavian economist-sociologist, Gunnyar Myrdal, had portrayed the Indian society as a 'soft society'. He also clarified the meaning of 'soft society'. According to Gunnyar Myrdal, a ***soft society*** is:

(a) one, which does not have the political force to authorize the laws fundamental for its growth and advancement as well as does not have the political will to apply the laws, even when formulated, and

(b) Wherever there is lack of discipline, even, he has emphasized the second aspect greater than the first. He told, due to the lack of discipline in the society, no genuine or meaningful growth is possible. Lack of discipline in the society has caused corruption. Corruption and indiscipline support each other very much. One method of encouragingthe discipline among the society is by reducing the scope of corruption, and handling it strictly, wherever it is noticed. Due to this, the faults in the criminal judicial system have to be rectified. Corruption is also anti-poor, such as, the Public Distribution System (PDS) and the welfare schemes for the underprivileged including Scheduled Castes (SCs) and Scheduled Tribes (STs). Everyone is aware from the fact that a large fraction of grain, sugar and kerosene oil intended for PDS, goes into black market and that only just 16% of the funds intended for STs and SCs reach them, remaining all are misused by few members of the political, official class and dishonest dealers and businessmen. The well-known economist, Mehbub-Ul-Haq, briefly and piercingly set out the evil impacts of corruption in the South-Asian nation like our own. According to him:

'Corruption happens everywhere. It has been at the center of election campaigns in Italy and the United Kingdom, led to the fall of governments in Japan and Indonesia, and resulted in legislative action in Russia and the United States. But, if corruption exists in rich, economically successful countries, why should South Asia be worried about it? The answer is simple: South Asian corruption has four key characteristics that make it far more damaging than corruption in any other parts of the world.

First, corruption in South Asia occurs upstream, not downstream. Corruption at the top distorts fundamental decisions about development priorities, policies, and projects. In industrial countries, these core decisions are taken through transparent competition and on merit, even though petty corruption may occur downstream.

Second, corruption money in South Asia has wings, not wheels. Most of the corrupt gains made in the region are immediately smuggled out to safe havens abroad. Whereas there is some capital flight in other countries as well, a greater proportion goes into investment. In other words, it is more likely that corruption money in the North Asia is used to finance business than to fill foreign accounts.

Third, corruption in South Asia often leads to promotion, not prison. The big fish – unless they belong to the opposition – rarely fry. In contrast, industrialized countries often have a process of accountability where even top leaders are investigated and prosecuted. For instance, former Italian Prime Minister Bettino Craxi was forced to live in exile in Tunisia to escape extradition on corruption charges in Rome. The most frustrating aspect of corruption in South Asia is that the corrupt are often too powerful to go through such an honest process of accountability.

Fourth, corruption in South Asia occurs with 515 million people in poverty, not with per capita incomes above twenty thousand dollars. While corruption in rich rapidly growing countries may be tolerable, though reprehensible, in poverty stricken South Asia, it is political dynamite when the majority of the population cannot, but to massive human deprivation and even more extreme income meet their basic needs while a few make fortunes through corruption. Thus corruption in South Asia does not lead to simply Cabinet portfolio shifts or newspaper headlines inequalities. Combating corruption in the region is not just about punishing corrupt politicians and bureaucrats but about saving human lives. There are two dimensions of corruption. One is the exploitative corruption where the public servant exploits the helpless poor citizen. The other is collusive corruption where the citizen corrupts the public servant by a bribe because he gets financially better benefits. Collusive corruption depends on black money'.

The Uniform Framework has occurred with the definitions as mentioned below:

- A corrupt practice can be explained as 'the offering, giving, receiving, or soliciting, directly or indirectly, of anything of value to influence improperly the actions of another party'.
- A fraudulent practice can be explained as 'any act or omission, including a misrepresentation that knowingly or recklessly misleads, or attempts to mislead, a party to obtain a financial or other benefit or to avoid an obligation'.
- A coercive practice can be explained as 'impairing or harming, or threatening to impair or harm, directly or indirectly, any party or the property of the party to influence improperly the actions of a party'.
- A collusive practice can be explained as an 'arrangement between two or more parties designed to achieve an improper purpose including influencing improperly the actions of another party'.

CORRUPTION IN INDIA

In our developing nation, India, corruption is a main issue and negatively affects its economy. According to study conducted by Transparency International in India, 2005, it was observed that greater than 62% of Indians was involved in giving bribes or influence peddling to get jobs in public offices successfully. Another study done in 2008, Transparency International stated that approximately 40% of Indians had direct involvement of paying bribes or using a referenceto get a job in public office. In 2012, India has graded 94th out of 176 nations in Transparency International's Corruption Perceptions Index, joined with Benin, Colombia, Djibouti, Greece, Moldova, Mongolia and Senegal. Entitlement programmes and social spending schemes passed by the Indian government are the largest sources of corruption in India, for examples, Mahatma Gandhi National Rural Employment Guarantee Act and National Rural Health Mission. Other regular sources of corruption involve India's trucking industry, which is forced to give billions in bribes to several regulatory and police stops on its regional highways. Indian media has published cases of corrupt Indian citizens hiding trillions of dollars in Swiss banks, however, Swiss authorities refuse these claims.

Excessive regulations, complicated taxes and licensing systems, various government divisions each with dark administration and flexible powers, monopoly by government controlled institutions on some goods and services delivery and the lack of transparent laws and processes are some causes of corruption in India. There are huge varieties in level of corruption and in state government endeavours to decrease corruption throughout India.

History

From the 1950s until the late 1980s, the economy of India was under socialist-inspired policies for the whole generation. The economy was described by extensive regulation, protectionism and public ownership, policies weak to pervasive corruption and slow development. In 1960s, it was recommended by Chakravarthi Rajagopalachari that License Raj was regularly at the core of corruption. In 1993, the former Indian Union Home Secretary, N. N. Vohra, submitted the Vohra report and stated the issue of the criminalization of politics and of the connection amid criminals, politicians and administrators in India. The report contained many studies made by official agencies on the criminal network, which was nearly running a parallel government. In addition, the report has also highlighted about criminal gangs who benefited from the support of politicians and the protection of government bodies. Jitendra Singh said that, 'in the bad old days, particularly pre-1991, when the License Raj held sway, and by design, all kinds of free market mechanisms were hobbled or stymied, and corruption emerged almost as an illegitimate price mechanism, a shadowy quasi-market, such that scarce resources could still be allocated within the economy, and decisions could get made.... These were largely distortions created by the politico-economic regime. While a sea change has occurred in the years following 1991, some of the distorted cultural norms that took hold during the earlier period are slowly being repaired by the sheer forces of competition. The process will be long and slow, however. It will not change overnight'. One of the key issues and barriers in the development of India has been widespread corruption and political disinterest to change.

Politics

According to India's First Information Report procedure, December 2008, where anybody can affirm another of perpetrating a crime, out of 523 parliament members in India, 120 were blamed for crimes. If we look behind, since 2008, then it can be clearly seen that in mostly biggest scandals like Cabinet Ministers and Chief Ministers, such as in the 2G spectrum scam, the 2010 Commonwealth Games scam and the Adarsh Housing Society scam, Coal Mining Scam, mining scandal in Karnataka and cash for vote scam, very high levels of government were involved.

Bureaucracy

According to 2005 study conducted by Transparency International in India, greater than 62% of the people had direct experience of paying bribe to get a job in a public organization. Taxes and bribes are usual between state borders. Transparency International approximates that truckers pay annually 22,200 crores in bribes. Government regulators and police are also involved in sharing of the bribe money, 43% and 45% individually. The stoppages, en route, including those at checkpoints and entry-points take up to 11 hours in a day, and about 60% of forced stoppages on road by concerned authorities like government regulators, police, forest, sales and excise, weighing and measuring department are for coercing money. The loss in efficiency due to these stoppages is a notable national issue. If forced delays are avoided, the number of truck trips could increase by 40%. According to World Bank published report in 2007, the travel time for a Delhi-Mumbai trip can be decreased by approximately 2 days per trip, if the corruption and associated regulatory stoppages, to extort bribes, was removed. A 2009 review of the leading economies of Asia, disclosed Indian administration to be not least efficient out of Singapore, Hong Kong, Thailand, South Korea, Japan, Malaysia, Taiwan, Vietnam, China, Philippines and Indonesia; in fact it was also mentioned that working with India's government workers was a 'slow and painful' procedure.

Land and Property

Authorities are suspected to take state property. In India, urban areas and villages, comprising of municipal and other government officials, elected lawmakers, legal officers, real estate developers and law enforcement officials, get, develop and offer land in unlawful ways.

Tendering Processes and Awarding Contracts

According to 2006 report, state-funded construction activities in Uttar Pradesh, like road building, were controlled by construction mafias, which are groupings of dishonest public works servants, materials suppliers, politicians and construction contractors. Corruption not only affects government-funded projects that are limited to the state of Uttar Pradesh. The World Bank stated that assistance programmes are affected by corruption, poor administration etc. The World Bank study stated that the public distribution programmes and social spending contracts have been proved as waste due to corruption.

For example, on 25 August 2005, the government implemented the Mahatma Gandhi National Rural Employment Guarantee Act (MGNREGA). The Central government expenditure for this welfare scheme is 40,000 crores in FY 2010–2011. In 2011, the programme was broadly criticized as no more effective than other poverty reduction programmes in India. In spite ofits best purposes and intents, MGNREGA faces the troubles of corrupt officials, supposedly taking money for the advantage of fake rural labourers, low nature of the programme's infrastructure and unintended unsafe effect on poverty.

Medicine

In case of government hospitals, corruption is linked with non-availability/duplication of medicines, getting admission, meetings with doctors and profiting diagnostic facilities. One more health care-related government programme, National Rural Health Mission (NRHM) is another example of large-scale corruption accusations. It is expected that this social expenditure and entitlement programme would improve and benefit health care services across rural India. The programme was launched on 12 April 2005 by the former Indian Prime Minister, Manmohan Singh. The NRHM was initially started in 18 states that had been found as having weak public health indicators. The Indian government instructed an expenditure of INR 277 billion in 2004–05, and increased it yearly about 1% of India's gross domestic product. The NRHM programme has been faced by a large-scale corruption scandal in which high-level government appointed officials were caught, many of whom died under secretive conditions including one in jail. Corruption, waste and extortion-related losses from this government programme have been charged approximately 100 billion.

Science and Technology

The Council of Scientific and Industrial Research (CSIR) has been weakened in constant efforts to eliminate corruption in India. It was established with the purpose to do translational research and make genuine advancements, but CSIR has been blamed of transforming into a formal, excessively bureaucratic association that does minimal more than produce papers. Indian scientists are facing many issues like, requirement for transparency, a meritocratic system and an overhaul of the bureaucratic agencies that supervise science and technology. Sumit Bhaduri said, 'the challenges of turning Indian science into part of an innovation process are many .... Many competent Indian scientists aspire to be ineffectual administrators [due to administrative power and political patronage], rather than do the kind of science that makes a difference'. The former Prime Minister, Manmohan Singh, spoke at the 99th Indian Science Congress and stated on the condition of sciences in India, after an advisory council updated him regarding problems with 'the overall environment for innovation and creative work' and a 'warlike' approach was required.

Income Tax Department

In India, there have been numerous instances of secret agreement of officials of the income tax department for special tax treatment and relaxed prosecutions in return for bribes.

Preferential Award of Mineral Resources

In India, corruption is a major issue and negatively affects its economy. In the beginning of August 2011, in India, an iron ore mining scam turned into a media focus. In September 2011, Janardhana Reddy, a selected member from Karnataka's administrative assembly, was captured on charges of defilement and unlawful mining of iron ore in his home province of Karnataka. It was affirmed that his organization got special share of resources, organized and exported billions of dollars of iron mineral to China in recent years, without paying any payment to the state government exchequer of Karnataka or the Central government of India. In fact, these Chinese companies had paid to shell organizations controlled by Reddy and enrolled in Caribbean and north Atlantic tax asylums.

Also, it was suspected that dishonest or corrupt government authorities coordinated with Reddy, beginning from government authorities responsible for controlling mining to government officials accountable for directing port offices and shipping. In exchange for allowing the illegal export of illegally mined iron ore to China, these officials got monthly bribes. Such outrages have prompted a requirement in India for consensually driven action plan to destroy the piracy of India's mineral assets by an unlawful political-corrupt government officials-business link, expulsion of motivating forces for illicit mining, formation of motivators for legitimate mining and local utilization of iron metal and steel manufacturing.

Driver Licensing

According to a study conducted between 2004 and 2005, it was observed that India's driver licensing process was a tremendously contorted bureaucratic process, and permits drivers to be licensed in spite of their low driving skill. People with high readiness to pay make a noteworthy payment over the official expense, and the greater part of these additional payments is made to agents, whose role is an intermediary between administrators and applicants. The standard licensee paid is ₹ 1080, around 2.5 times the official expense of ₹ 450, keeping in mind to get a license. The individuals who hired agents had a lower driving skill. With the help of agents, unskilled drivers got licenses and avoided the legally required driving examination. According to the survey done among individuals, it was found that around 60% of the license holders did not take the licensing exam and 54% of those license holders failed an independent driving test.

In the bureaucratic driver licensing system, agents are the means of corruption who provides easy access to licenses among unqualified people to drive. One of the main reasons for the failures of this licensing system is caused by corrupt officials who work together with agents by creating other barriers within the process against those who avoids hiring of agents.

Claimed Trends

In the book *Corruption in India: the DNA and RNA*, Professor Bibek Debroy and Laveesh Bhandari claimed that the public officials in India may be earning as much as ₹ 921.22 billion ($18.42 billion), or 1.26 per cent of the GDP, through corruption. In addition, it also claims that a large part of bribery exists in the transport industry, real estate and government delivered services. According to KPMG study reports, 2011, it was stated that India's real estate, telecommunications and government-run social development projects are the three top most corruption-affected areas. It was also found in the study that Defence system of India, information technology industry and energy sectors are the greatest competitive and minimum corruption prone sectors. In 2010 India Corruption

Study report, CMS India claims that government corruption has very much negatively affected the socio-economically weaker section of the Indian society, which includes the rural as well as urban underprivileged. The study also states that the level of corruption countrywide has reduced in 2005–2010. Over the 5-year period, many people from the middle class as well as the poorest sections of Indian society, in all parts of the India, claimed that government corruption had reduced over time.

Index trends in major states by respective anti-corruption effort

State	1990–95	1996–00	2001–05	2006–10
Bihar	0.41	0.30	0.43	0.88
Gujarat	0.48	0.57	0.64	0.69
Andhra Pradesh	0.53	0.73	0.55	0.61
Punjab	0.32	0.46	0.46	0.60
Jammu & Kashmir	0.13	0.32	0.17	0.40
Haryana	0.33	0.60	0.31	0.37
Himachal Pradesh	0.26	0.14	0.23	0.35
Tamil Nadu	0.19	0.20	0.24	0.29
Madhya Pradesh	0.23	0.22	0.31	0.29
Karnataka	0.24	0.19	0.20	0.29
Rajasthan	0.27	0.23	0.26	0.27
Kerala	0.16	0.20	0.22	0.27
Maharashtra	0.45	0.29	0.27	0.26
U.P.	0.11	0.11	0.16	0.21
Odisha	0.22	0.16	0.15	0.19
Assam	0.21	0.02	0.14	0.17
West Bengal	0.11	0.08	0.03	0.01

The table shown above compares the perceived anti-corruption effort within some of the most important states in India. A rising index indicates higher anti-corruption effort and decreasing corruption. From the table, it can be observed that the states of Bihar and Gujarat have seen noteworthy improvements in their anti-corruption efforts. In contrast, the conditions have worsened in the state of Assam and West Bengal. In 2012, a BBC News report claimed that the state of Bihar has improved in recent years to convert into the least corrupt state in India.

Black Money

Black money is defined as money that is not completely authentically the property of the 'owner'. A white paper on black money in India by the Indian government proposes two probable sources of black money in India. Firstly, the activities that are not permitted by the law, for example crime, drug trade, terrorism and corruption, all of which are illegal.

Secondly, the wealth may have been produced through a legal activity but collected by not declaring income and paying taxes. A part of this black money ends up in unlawful financial transactions across international borders, like deposits in tax haven nations. According to Washington-based Global Financial Integrity report, November 2010, it was estimated that over a 60-year period, India lost US $213 billion in illegal financial flows starting in 1948; keeping in view the inflation rates, this is approximated to be 462 billion in 2010, or about $8 billion per year. The report also revealed the size of India's underground economy to be around US$640 billion at the end of 2008.

Black Money in Switzerland

According to *The Hindu* article, 2010, it was unofficial estimated that Indians had more than US$ 1456 billion in black money, which were deposited in Swiss banks. But, some news reports claimed that figures provided by the Swiss Banking Association (SBA) Report, 2006, showed that India has more black money than the combined rest of the world. A recent report quoted the SBA's Head of International Communications as stating that no such official Swiss Banking Association statistics exist. Another report stated that Indian-owned Swiss bank account deposits are worth 13 times the nation's national debt. These claims have been refused by the Swiss Bankers Association. In an interview about alleged black money from India, James Nason of Swiss Bankers Association holds that 'The (black money) figures were rapidly picked up in the Indian media and in Indian opposition circles, and circulated as gospel truth. However, this story was a complete fabrication. The Swiss Bankers Association never published such a report. Anyone claiming to have such figures (for India) should be forced to identify their source and explain the methodology used to produce them'. Dev Kar of Global Financial Integrity, in a separate study, concludes that 'media reports circulating in India that Indian nationals held around US$ 1.4 trillion in illicit external assets are widely off the mark compared to the estimates found by his study'. Dev Kar states that the amounts are considerably lesser, only about 1.5% of India's GDP on average per annum basis, between 1948 and 2008. This includes corruption, inducement, criminal activities, trade mispricing and endeavours to protect wealth by Indians from India's tax authorities. According to a third report, published in May 2012, Swiss National Bank stated that at the end of 2010, the total amount of deposits in all Swiss banks, by Indian citizens were CHF 1.95 billion (INR 92.95 billion, US$ 2.1 billion). The Swiss Ministry of External Affairs has affirmed these data upon ask forinformation by the Indian Ministry of External Affairs. The report has also given detail of the comparison of the deposits held by Indians and by citizens of other countries in Swiss banks, which constitutes only 0.13% of the total bank deposits of citizens of all nations. Additional, the share of Indians in the total bank deposits of citizens of all countries in Swiss banks has decreased from 0.29% in 2006 to 0.13% in 2010.

Judiciary

According to Transparency International, in India, judicial corruption is because of issues like 'delays in the disposal of cases, shortage of judges and complex procedures, all of which are exacerbated by a preponderance of new laws'.

Armed Forces

The Indian Armed Forces have seen corruption by senior armed forces officers from the Indian Army, Indian Navy and Indian Air Force. Numerous scandals, in the 2000–2010, have spoiled the military's status. These scandals involved stealing of armed forces money, re-selling of government assets and faking battle missions.

Right to Information Act

The Right to Information Act (2005) and similar acts in the states, which require government authorities to give data asked for by citizens, computerization of services and different Central and state government acts that built up vigilance commissions have extensively lessened corruption or at least have opened up possibilities to rectify injustices.

Anti-Corruption Laws in India

In India, public servants can be punished for corruption under the

- Indian Penal Code, 1860
- Prosecution Section of Income Tax Act, 1961
- The Prevention of Corruption Act, 1988
- The Benami Transactions (Prohibition) Act, 1988, to prohibit benami transactions.
- Prevention of Money Laundering Act, 2002

Since 2005 (ratified 2011), India is a signatory to the UN Convention against Corruption. The agreement covers wide-ranging acts of corruption, and also suggests some preventive policies. The Lokpal Bill, 2011, is a bill which is still in the waiting list before the Rajya Sabha. India's lower house of parliament, the Lok Sabha voted to pass The Whistle Blowers Protection Bill, 2011 which is pending in the Rajya Sabha, the upper house.

Anti-Corruption Police and Courts

The Directorate General of Income Tax Investigation, Central Vigilance Commission and Central Bureau of Investigation all manage anti-corruption activities. Some states like Andhra Pradesh (Andhra Pradesh Anti-corruption Bureau) and Karnataka (Lokayukta) too have their own anti-corruption agencies and courts. Andhra Pradesh's Anti-Corruption Bureau (ABC) has propelled a vast scale investigation in the 'cash-for-bail' scam. On 19 June 2012, CBI court judge, Talluri Pattabhirama Rao was arrested for accepting bribe to permit bail to former Karnataka Minister, Gali Janardhan Reddy, who was supposedly increasing properties which is inconsistent to his known sources of income. Investigation disclosed that India Cements, one of India's largest cement, had been investing in Reddy's businesses as an end-result of government contracts. Under the Indian Penal Code and the Prevention of Corruption Act, a case has also been opened against seven other individuals.

Anti-Corruption Organizations

To fight against corrupt government and business practices, many organizations have been founded in India. Important organizations include:

- Bharat Swabhiman Trust, established by famous Yog Guru Swami Ramdev, and leading a large campaign against black money and corruption since last 10 years.

- 5th Support is well-known for the creation of the zero rupee note, a valueless note designed to be given to corrupt officials when they request bribes.
- India Against Corruption, is a movement started by the citizens from various professions and statuses to work against corruption in India and it is currently lead by Anna Hazare.
- Jaago Re! One Billion Votes, to increase youth voter registration, this organization was originally founded by Tata Tea and Janaagraha. Since then, they have expanded their function to include other social issues, including corruption.
- Association for Social Transparency, Rights and Action (ASTRA) is an NGO focused on fundamental work to fight corruption in Karnataka.

The organization, the Lok Satta Movement, has changed itself from a civil organization to a developed political party, the Lok Satta Party. The party has handled candidates in Andhra Pradesh, Tamil Nadu, and Bangalore. It obtained its first elected post in 2009, when Jayaprakash Narayan won the election for the Kukatpally Assembly Constituency in Andhra Pradesh.

Roots of Corruption in India

According to 2011 report on Corruption in India, KPMG, who is one of the world's largest audit and compliance firms, reports numerous sources that encourage corruption in India. The report suggests one of the major sources of corruption is high taxes and excessive regulation bureaucracy. India has high marginal tax rates and numerous regulatory bodies with the ability to prevent any citizen or business from approaching their day-to-dayactivities. This power to search and question open doors for dishonest and immoral public officials to extract bribes; each individual or business decides if the effort required in due process and the cost of delay is worth not paying the bribe demanded. In instances of high taxes, paying off the corrupt official is less expensive in compare to the tax. As per report, this is one of the major causes of corruption in India and 150 other nations across the world. In real estate industry, large-scale corruption is hugely encouraged by the high capital gains tax in India. The KPMG report claims that the relationship between high real estate taxes and corruption is high in India as well as other nations including the developed economies. This relationship has been true in nowadays as well as for centuries of human history in many civilizations.

The want to give lower taxes than those required by the state describes the demand side of corruption. Consequently, the corrupt officials collect bribes and state fails to collect taxes for its own finances, further corruption increases. The report proposes regulatory reforms, process simplification and lower taxes as ways to increase tax receipts and decrease sources of corruption. Additionally, the KPMG report claims that corruption is due to the unclear process and official procedure on the part of the government. Absence of clarity permits space for move for both the demanders and suppliers of corruption. Corruption grows in that condition when objective standards and transparent processes are lost, and subjective opinion driven regulators and hidden processes exist. Vito Tanzi in an International Monetary Fund study proposes that in India, like other nations in the world, excessive regulations and authorization requirements, complicated taxes and licensing systems, lack of competitive free markets, monopoly of some goods and service providers by government controlled institutions, bureaucracy, lack of penalties for corruption of public officials and absence of transparent laws and procedures cause corruption.

Effects of Corruption

As indicated by a report by KPMG, 'high-level corruption and scams are now threatening to derail the country's credibility and [its] economic boom'.

Economic Concerns

Corruption may cause additional bureaucratic delay and ineffectiveness, as in order to extort more bribes, corrupted bureaucrats may introduce rules and regulations. Such insufficiencies in institutional efficiency could influence development indirectly by reducing the private marginal product of capital and investment rate. Levine and Renelt revealed that investment rate is a strong factor of economic development. As indicated by the neoclassical growth model, institutional variables contribute in deciding steady state per capital income levels and speed of convergence to its steady state, hence influencing its growth rate. Bureaucratic inefficiency also influences development directly, like through misallocation of investments in the economy. In addition, corruption brings lower financial development for a given level of earnings.

Lower Corruption, Higher Growth Rates

There is the chance that India's GDP growth rate could increase at a higher rate annually, if corruption levels in India decreases to levels in developed economies like Singapore or the United Kingdom. C. K. Prahalad revealed the lost opportunity due to corruption, in terms of investment, development and jobs for India is more than US$50 billion annually. The level of corruption is not consistent in India, it varies in various parts of India. According to the July 2011 report, *The Economist* for instance refers to the state government of Gujarat, which has kept paperwork to a minimum, does not demand bribes, and does not interfere with entrepreneurial firms. The article claims that the state has less corruption, less difficult labour laws and effective bureaucracy. With development rates matching few fastest developing economic zones of China, Gujarat continues to outstrip development in other Indian states.

Increasing Development through Better Utilization of Public Resources

The battle against worldwide poverty might be going to get an essential boost from a surprising quarter. All frequently, well-meaning advancement programmes have been weakened in the past by inefficiency, wrong-headed needs and outright graft. It is essential to improve the effectiveness of developing nations' public spending on social purposes. However, in general, the public sector cannot be depended upon to change itself in segregation. Vital stimulus includes the pressure of informed domestic public opinion. An important missing element is a strengthened role for independent supervisory body, grown within developing nations, and savagely dedicated to opening up government finances and policies for public review and discussion. An emerging new kind of non-governmental organizations, free from special interests, Part think tank and part advocacy war-room has the ability to promote greater transparency and accountability in how developing nations operate, share information, and communicate with their citizenry, in the future.

These groups, in coordination with governments and development assistance channels to clean up their own performances, could result in better performing governments and better informed citizens who are more able to utilize their voices and vote to publicize, and mitigate public sector missteps. Though for making this happen, will require support, financial and other, from key players in the international community, motivated by leaders among the donors and foundations, to help supervisory body to build up their capacity from the delicate state that most of them are in now. Promising pilots have demonstrated that quick' scaling up' is the right next priority. The groups' needs contain not just more fundamental support to build and support stronger teams, but also needs training and technical assistance, and cross-country networking so they can gain from each other.

Significance of Efficient Utilization of Public Resources

For the achievement of development objective, it is important to utilize the public resources effectively. Within the public sector, essential programmes in education and health are overwhelmingly conducted. Although, private provision of infrastructure has developed in regions such as telecommunications and energy, private investors remain careful of socially-oriented areas like water and sanitation, and furthermore show little inclination to invest in the poorest nations. Recent research shows that in most developing nations, increases in public expenditure are feebly associated with the achievement of development outcomes. And, the government ineffectiveness, in the form of waste, inefficiency and corruption, is mostly accountable for this.

The fact that public spending is a typical, multidimensional procedure, which lacks natural transparency, proves to be the main factor for poor resource. Generally, budgets pass through a series of levels that includes formulation by ministries, scrutiny by legislative committees, approval by the legislature, distribution of funds to ministries, after that distribution to state and local authorities, and end-point distribution. Deficiencies like closed-door discussions, limited documentation and poor data reliability are the some unavoidable reasons, which hamper the accountability.

In the absence of external pressure, weakly performing public institutions can rarely be expected to improve themselves in the lack of external force. Public sectors face no direct competitive pressures, and political systems, particularly in developing nations, are insufficientat increasing public pressure for specific institutional improvement. Faults in public finance management can cause ineffective resource use through various channels. Often, corruption takes a significant toll, but even in nations where government personnel are mostly honest and sincere, there are the chances that they can be tottered by poor systems, insufficient training or due to other weaknesses. Wherever allotment decisions are taken outside informed independent scrutiny, society's strong and fluent groups tend to influence those decisions to favour urban areas over rural, middle-class subsidies over pro-poor programmes and certain ethnic/cultural groups over others. Case studies demonstrate additional ways that inadequate governance hinders use of resource effectively.

Various studies in Bangladesh and India have showed that generally, underprivileged class do not gain the expected level of public services. Heavy absentee rates are an important part of the problem among service providers, who usually lack adequate incentives to perform their assigned functions successfully. And, a latest study proposes that lowering average corruption levels in infrastructure projects in Latin America to the level of its best performer, Costa Rica, could decrease the average nation's operating costs in electricity by 23%. The quantitative impact from major improvements in public budget performance could be noteworthy. In 2003, government consumption expenditures, in low- and middle-income nations, have achieved around $1,017 billion. While quantitative appraisals of overall waste, inadequacy, and corruption are hypothetical, even if 5% of public funds constituted a recoverable loss, the following $50 billion savings could greatly increase resources in regions such as education, health and infrastructure.

Assessing Fiscal Transparency

Studies affirm that the public availability of precise, timely information on public sector expenditure fluctuates tremendously across nations. Latest work at the IMF has created operational measures of economic/fiscal transparency, drawing on information from nation-level studies known as Reports on Observation of Standards and Codes (ROSCs). The table of fiscal transparency has been created based on evaluations of nation adherence to best-practice in four fields:

- ***Data assurance***: i.e., safeguards to ensure credible and reliable published data;
- ***Medium-term budgeting framework***: efforts to place annual data in a multi-year context;
- ***Budget execution***: e.g., the quality of accounting and auditing safeguards; and,
- The public disclosure of fiscal risks.

Putting Accountability to Work

Micro-level case studies fortify comprehension of the advantages that collect when citizens have the opportunity to hold the public sector responsible:

Public expenditure tracking: In 1995, official Ugandan statistics showed that a three-fold increment in financing for primary education appeared to have produced no increment in enrolments. Advanced tracking shown that local governments were able to divert allowances planned for schools to other purposes (up to 98% of the total in 1991). The Central government reacted by: publishing amounts moved to the districts in newspapers and radio broadcasts; schools are required to maintain public noticeboards on monthly transfers of funds; and for accountability and transparency, legal provision should be strengthen. By 1999, schools were getting almost 100% of the grant funds.

Community control of programme implementation: After the civil war in El Salvador, the EDUCO school programme was set up initially with an objective to provide local communities unprecedented responsibility for managing local primary schools, including authority to appoint and dismiss teachers. The consequences of this empowerment of the communities are major improvements in teacher performance as well as in their attendance and student achievement that the programme has been made permanent within El Salvador, and also implemented by other Central American nations.

Citizen report cards: In various parts of India, offering bribes can be a usual way of obtaining public services. Once Civil society organization (CSO) created a 'Citizen Report Card' on public service delivery across various agencies and locations. A 2003 study indicated that bribery had decreased greatly and satisfaction with public services had increased.

Benchmarking: It is a method, which gathers comparable data on performance and costs of relatively standardized tasks across various local government jurisdictions, such as, the cost of building one kilometre of a standard design of road or a standardized design of primary school. With the help of press and other channels, by making this data accessible, effective public pressure is mounted on jurisdictions that seemclearly deviated in their performance.

Shortcomings and Requirements

Developing nation governments have to do a lot to increase clarity and accountability of public expenditure, including publishing detailed budgets, sharing data on actual financial flows, strengthening the transparency of public procurement etc.

However, political leaders and civil servants do not work in void. In fact, the strongest and most public-spirited leadership needs the political support that comes from public involvement in the growth of national priorities. In nations, where clarity and responsibility are intense, residents usually work in public policy-making not by engaging themselves in raw data, but by drawing on the outputs of 'interpreters', like think tanks and academics, whose own detailed work gets filtered to the public via intermediates in the media, politics. For example, the Brookings Institution, which initially issued its 'Setting National Priorities' series, an independent assessment of key US national budget choices, around 35 years prior.

On the other side, the translators of policy information to the public in low- and middle-income nations are usually few and weak also. In most developing nations, there is a need of stronger domestic non-government groups to monitor, analyse and publicize findings on public expenditure, and support press governments for greater transparency and accountability. On the practical side, serious independent work on public expenditure will need developing CSOs' capacity to focus on at least four areas of interest:

- Aggregate fiscal discipline;
- Allocative efficiency of budget funds;
- Transparent allocationof budget spending; and,
- Efficient service delivery.

In terms of staffing profile, CSOs will require to activate several key capabilities:

- Devotedpolicy professionals to conduct the necessary underlying analysis;
- Skilled, respected interpreters and communicators; and,
- Accessibility to international network resources that can provide benchmarking data and best practice standards.

Some of these are specified functions, which do not easily grow naturally. However, the determinations of pioneering organizations recommend that it is possible to build capacity relatively quickly with the support of well-targeted intercessions.

Building on Existing Efforts

Some existing international efforts endeavour to help improve budgetary quality and transparency. According to independent evaluations, the incentives established by the EU accession process have encouraged states in Central and Eastern Europe to develop and apply anti-corruption policies and improve transparency in the usage of public assets. Multilateral organizations, such as the IMF and World Bank, carry out periodic analytical study on national budget issues within member nations. Many international organizations actively encourage work on general governance issues, including CSOs such as Transparency International, though to date the main international CSOs have undertaken only limited work specifically on improving transparency and accountability in public expenditure.

Revolutionary efforts by some players show the ability of focused externally assisted interventions. Two programmes are of specific importance:

- In 1997, the International Budget Project was started with an objective to support and assist CSOs in new democracies and low- and middle-income nations to conduct analytical and advocacy work on promoting budget transparency and accountability. The project has included training, diagnostic tools and small allowances, up to $40,000 each, to groups in more than 60 nations.
- To enhance accountability in natural resource-rich nations by strengthening the ability of citizens, governments and other interested parties, the Open Society Institute's Revenue Watch Initiative has worked since 2002. Revenue Watch is functioning in more than 20 resource-rich nations, and conducts and publicizes research, supports transparency and accountability and civil society capacity building, including functioningwith the media, local NGOs etc.

In spite of these innovative basic programmes, there are clear limits for the current efforts on economictransparency in developing nations. Firstly, gaps remain in nation coverage. Secondly, coverage within nations requires greater depth, and more budget components need appraisal. Essentially, investigation by outside agencies such as the World Bank and IMF, however technically modern, cannot completely substitute in a political sense for domestic 'owned' capacity. With the possible exceptions, most national governments have not given high priority to financing public institutions, who are willing to fulfil their own tasks for crucial public scrutiny. As such, strengthening of independent capacity to estimate public expenditure will require support from the sympathetic sources of funding other than native national governments. This may involve private foundations, bilateral government programmes and multilateral organizations.

Support should include funds that support the planning and implementation of institutional development ideas to deal with critical CSO's functions, including research, analysis, communications, advocacy and networking, as well as important administrative tasks like personnel and economic management.

Learning-by-doing exercises should also be funded, which include assigning specific analytical work. This methodology has been followed by the World Bank Institute, United Nations Development Programme and the Consultative Group on International Agricultural Research, and permits more effective integration of external experts, delivery of technical assistance better targeted to an organization's genuine requirements, and a chance to supervise the effectof intervention.

Also, support should be provided for a range of networking and knowledge-sharing activities. These include: workshops in few cross-country to share lessons learned and best practices and work together on new plans; competitive scholarships for individual researchers to perform advanced studies; development of publications to publicize work among the audience; a network internship programme; 'twinning' arrangements that match-up individuals or teams working on similar subjects in different nations and spreadingof benchmarking data and best practices of the public sector. For the improvement of developing nations' effectiveness in utilizing scarce public funds, efforts must be strengthened to achieve transparency and accountability in budget processes. This brief argues particularly for expanded initiatives to strengthen domestic civil society capacity to provide practical analysis of budget choices and the sharing and effectiveness of public expenditure, and to make the results accessible to the citizen both directly and via intermediaries like media. This proposal works on the basis that domestic citizens and NGOs already have relevant resources, including local knowledge and credibility, which can play an important role in improving the transparency and quality of public expenditure. Based on promising experimental programmes that are underway, the proposal supports improving international efforts to support appropriate local actors with training, technical support and facilitated access to the stock of international knowledge on public expenditure review. Advancing the procedure of setting budgetary priorities, ensuring that public funds are spent according to plan and raising the effectiveness of publicly financed services will need constant determinations by dedicated personnel with local trustworthiness. Effectively managed, such endeavours possess the abilityto improve current development efforts and play a key role in achieving development goals, including the internationally agreed Millennium Development Goals.

INTERNATIONAL COOPERATION

Corruption has exceeded the national boundaries. So, national anti-corruption actions need strengtheningat the international level with mutual assistance and cooperative law enforcement initiatives against corruption in various regions like bribing of and by foreign nationals, mutual legal assistance, gathering and transferring evidence, money legalizing, technical assistance and information exchange, extradition, tracing, freezing etc. For the prevention of corruption, strengthening of provisions related to the prevention of laundering of the proceeds of corruption and safety measures to stop offshore financial centres from sheltering the proceeds of widespread corruption are essential steps.

INTERNATIONAL MEASURES TO COMBAT CORRUPTION

- In 1996, the United Nations Declaration against corruption and bribery in international commercial transactions accepted by the General Assembly is an important landmark and it deals with public as well as private sectors. The Declaration is in the nature of political obligation supported by actions to be taken through institutions at national, regional and international levels dependent on each nation's Constitution, basic legal principles, laws and procedures. The Declaration demands for legislation and implementation of laws, disallowing bribery in international transactions, laws banning the bribery of foreign public officials and laws ensuring that bribes are not tax deductible. It also demands for international cooperation in disciplinary measures regardinginvestigation, trial and extradition.
- International Code of Conduct for public officials is another UN initiative, adopted in December 1996 to direct the member-states in their struggles against corruption through guiding principles that public servants should obey and follow in the functioning of their duties, and the principles are loyalty, integrity, efficiency, effectiveness, fairness, impartiality, prevention of conflict of interest, disclosure norms, receiving of gifts and favours etc.
- Also, the UN has created a guide on anti-corruption policy, and an anti-corruption tool kit as a policy guide and an operational tool. The United Nations has also created a model law on money laundering and proceeds of crime.
- In October 2003, the UN General Assembly adopted the United Nations Convention against Corruption, which provides an effective international legal method against corruption which has been signed by India but is yet to be approved. The Convention binds the signatories to provide particular forms of mutual legal assistance in collecting and transferring evidence for use in court to send back the offenders and to carry out measures to support tracing, freezing, seizure and confiscation of proceeds of corruption. Asset recovery is an important principle of the Convention, although the needs of the nation looking for illegal assets have to be accommodated with the legal and procedural safeguards of the nations whose assistance is sought. The UN Office of Drugs and Crime (UNODC) has been organizing meetings of specialists to identify the main challenges in the field of repatriation of illegally transferred amounts, the findingand identification of such funds and the endeavours and procedures required for the return of such amounts to their nations of origin. Nations, in quest of the return of looted assets, often face severe issues in recovery because of the issues taking place from diversity of legal systems, strugglesin meeting the evidentiary and procedural requirements of developed nations, intermingling of such proceeds with other assets and so on. Further, developing nations are obliged in these efforts due to the shortageof financial resources and expertise to effectively investigate and prosecute these kinds of

cases to a logical end. Capacity building natively merged with effective coordination at the international level, particularly in the field of technical assistance, coordination and communication will be essentialfor making progressin this crucial zone.

- The ADB/OECD Anti-Corruption Action Plan for Asia Pacific, which has been signed by the Government of India, is not a binding agreement but a wide understanding to the reason of inter-regional cooperation in the prevention of corruption.
  In a Joint Statement as agreed upon by a number of international regional groups at Singapore the signatory institutions 'recognize that corruption undermines sustainable economic growth and is a major obstacle to the reduction of poverty'. Development is affected due to corruption by increasing prices at a given level of efficiency of operations or by decrease in efficiency. In case of poverty, the most direct unpleasant impact will be visible if capitals meant to fight against poverty are misused and stolen.
- International cooperation is not simply limited between governments, but also among international private sector business and professional groupsand the national parts; and international networking and mutual assistance between civil societies in the jobof prevention of corruption in the public and private sectors. Private and public sector can have commonly cleansing or corrupting relationships. Initiatives should also be taken on the part of Indian private sector, professional groups and civil societies.

LEGAL FRAMEWORK FOR FIGHTING CORRUPTION IN INDIA

Evolution of the Anti-Corruption Laws in India

To fight with corruption in the pre-independence period, the Indian Penal Code (IPC) was the main tool. The Code includes a chapter on 'Offences by Public Servants'. Sections 161 to 165 give the detail of legal structure to prosecute corrupt public employees. At that time, no one felt the requirement of any special law to deal with corruption.

The Second World War made scarcities, which gave chance to corrupt groups or individuals to misuse the situation directing to wide-ranging corruption in public life. Even, after the war, situation remained the same. The legislators were worried about this threat, and also sensed that there is a need of strong legislative actions. As a result, to fight the evils of bribery and corruption, the Prevention of Corruption Act, 1947 was passed.

The Prevention of Corruption Act, 1947

Under this Act, the definition of offences related to corruption was not redefined or expanded, as already existing in the IPC. Also, the definition of 'Public Servant' is same as in the IPC. Nonetheless, the law defined a new offence—'Criminal misconduct in discharge of official duty'—for which enhanced punishment, minimum 1 year to maximum 7 years, was specified. With the intention to remove the burden of proof in certain cases to the accused, it was stipulated that whenever the charge on a public servant of accepting the gratification will be proved, it would be believe that the public servant had accepted such gratification as a motive or reward under Section 161 of IPC. For the prevention of harassment to honest officers, it was mandated that no court shall consider offences punishable under Sections 161,164 and 165 without the permission of the authority able to remove the accused public servant. The Act also specified that the statement given by bribe-giver would not subject him to prosecution. Granting such protection to the bribe-giver was considered necessary, as the person might have been forced by situations into giving a bribe.

The Criminal Law (Amendment) Act, 1952

This act has brought some modifications in laws related to corruption. The punishment stated under Section 165 of IPC was increased to three years. If this liberty were not provided, all complainants would become accountable for punishment, which would discouragethem from giving complaints against any public servant who accepted a bribe. Also, a new Section 165A was added in the IPC, which considered abetting of offences, defined in Sections 161 and 165 of IPC, as an offence. It was also specified that all offences related to corruption should be heard only by special judges.

Amendments in 1964

In 1964, some modifications were done in the anti-corruption laws. Under IPC, the definition of 'Public Servant' was expanded. The Santhanam Committee had also suggested an expanded definition of the term 'Public Servant'. The CrPC was revised to help precede camera trial if any party or the court wants. The presumption, which was existing under Section 4 of The Prevention of Corruption Act, was revised to include offences defined under Sections 5(1) and 5(2). The definition of 'criminal misconduct' was revised and ownership of assets disproportionate to the known sources of income of a public servant was considered as an offence. To empower the State Governments to authorize officers of the rank of Inspectors of Police to investigate cases (previously, this could be done only with the approval of the Magistrate), Section 5(A) was amended. Police officers, ableto investigate cases under the Act, were authorized to inspect bankers' records, if they had explanations to suspect commission of an offence under the Act.

The Prevention of Corruption Act, 1988

On 9 September 1988, this Act received Presidential approval. It strengthens the provisions of the Prevention of Corruption Act, 1947, the Criminal Law Amendment Act, 1952 and some provisions of IPC. Also, it has certain provisions expected to effectively fight against corruption among public servants. The salient characteristics of the Act are mentioned below:

- The term 'Public Servant' is defined in the Act. The definition is broader than what existed in the IPC.
- A new concept—'Public Duty' is introduced in the Act.
- Offences relating to corrupti on in the IPC have been brought in Chapter 3 of the Act, and they have been deleted from the Indian Penal Code.
- All cases under the Act are to be tried only by Special Judges.
- Proceedings of the court have to be held on a day-to-day basis.
- Penalties prescribed for various offences are enhanced.
- CrPC is amended to provide for expeditious trial {Section 22 of the Act provides for amended Sections 243, 309, 317 and 397 of CrPC}.

- It has been stipulated that no court shall stay the proceedings under the Act on the grounds of any error or irregularity in the sanction granted, unless in the opinion of the court it has led to failure of justice.
- Other existing provisions regarding presumptions, immunity to bribe-giver, investigation by an officer of the rank of Deputy SP, access to bank records etc. have been retained.

TRAINING FOR INDIAN OFFICIALS ON ETHICS, VALUES IN PUBLIC GOVERNANCE

After recent cases of corruption in which departments were involved, the Central government has decided to train its officials on 'ethics and values in public governance' to ensure transparency and to prevent bribery. Officials in the Ministry of Personnel, Public grievances and Pensions, nodal ministry of the government told they were working on a training module to teach integrity and ethics for its officials at all levels.

An official said, 'The Department of Personnel and Training (DoPT) is working on a module to train officials on ethics in public governance. All the officials working in different central controlled departments and ministries will be imparted training on it'. He told that the government will set up a detailed plan on providing phase-wise training to all the employees. He also said, 'The aim behind conducting such a training is to sensitize the government employees on the ill-effects of corruption in governance and in ensuring an efficient public delivery system'.

It was said by officials that private experts in the field and the Central Vigilance Commission were asked on the matter. This step is significant following exposure of various multi-crore scams, involving the allocation of second generation (2G) spectrum to certain telecom firms and in the conduct of Commonwealth Games in the national capital. The official said, 'The eradication of corruption is a very gigantic task and needs involvement of each and every official involved in governance. Hence, all the personnel will be made aware on anti-corruption measures and the importance of ethics and values. The training module is likely to be prepared by September this year'. He stated that firstly the project would be started for Central Government ministries, departments and public sector undertakings. Then, the government will evaluate the result of the training module and after that, it can be proposed to all state governments and union territory administrations.

In addition, the official said, 'The government needs help of all stake holders from the common man to central and state government employees. The government will consult states and recommend the module to them after seeing the outcome here in the national capital'. Recently, the Central government has also decided to review its combat against corruption by individual experts. Recently, the DoPT had invited Expression of Interest (EoI) from registered Indian law schools, law firms, academic or research organizations to commence the study, which is a mandatory duty of the nation under the United Nations Convention Against Corruption (UNCAC). On 9 May 2011, UNCAC was ratified by India, who functionsas a universal legal instrument to deal with the corruption worldwide.

The report of the Second Administrative Reforms Commission (ARC) on Ethics in Governance begins with a well-known quote from Mahatma Gandhi—'You must be the change you wish to see in this world. As human beings, our greatness lies not so much in being able to remake the world – that is the myth of the atomic age – as in being able to remake ourselves'. At first sight, this quote seems as a routine cut and paste job by a hack who is loaded with the task of churning out a commission report. But, those who will deeply think the hidden meaning of the quote will definitely realize the effort that was put into the writing of this report. Among the 14 reports submitted by this commission to the government, which was headed by current Law Minister, the report on Ethics in Governance should be of particular note to all those who demand for an ethical model for politics in the nation. The commission has made many recommendations to usher in stability and accountability in the field of politics, while taking cognizance of the beneficial measures introduced in recent years at the prompting of the Supreme Court and a pro-active Election Commission. While supporting measures such as disclosure of backgrounds of candidates in elections and strict supervision of electioneering, it has advised partial state funding of political parties, amendment of the Representation of the People Act, 1951, to disqualify candidates facing charges related to serious and morally very bad offences and corruption, appointment of a collegium to select election commissioners and a constitutional amendment to provide stability to coalition governments. When the ruling United Progressive Alliance (UPA) entered office in 2004, it felt need of administrative reforms. Some recent statements by the government raise the hope that few of the commission's recommendations will be implemented soon, if not all. The Prime Minister, who has regularly highlighted the necessity for administrative reform, made it a point to refer to the reports of the Second ARC in his Independence Day speech last year. He stated to the country that his government has plannedto 'act with speed' on the suggestions of the commission. Soon after, the government informed the Rajya Sabha that the suggestions of the commission were 'under active consideration' of the government. Similar tothe first ARC that looked at the complete range of administration four decades ago, the second ARC too has done a comprehensive analysis of the strengths and weaknesses of the political system and its impact on governance. In addition, unlike other commissions of inquiry whose reports reek of officials, the ARC has implemented a fresh, reader friendly approach to report writing, summary of recommendations and pagination that is worthy of simulation in every department of government. The commission's recommendations regarding the political defections are important.

By the mid-1960s, the problem of defections was huge in many states due to the absence of a law forbidding defections of legislators from one political party to another. As the Congress Party's vote share in elections started to decline and regional parties emerged, political horse-trading became the order of the day. Any party, which lacking majority in a legislature got down to purchase the allegiance of legislators of opposing parties. The union government took the initiative to end the menace two decades ago during the Prime ministership of Rajiv Gandhi. Parliament revised the Constitution and includedan anti-defection law as the Tenth Schedule, which has forbiddendefection of individual legislators but legitimized splits divisions in political parties, provided one-third of the members of a political party in a legislative chamber broke away from the main party to form a separate group. Even, it allowed merger of political parties, whenever two-third of the members of a party in a legislative chamber permitted its merger to another party. These provisions had prevented defection of individual legislators, but did not make political stability because of the cleverness of politicians to outsmart legal draftsmen. Since the anti-defection law has forbidden'retail trade', every political party began splitting rival parties and encouraging wholesale defections in want of extra support in legislatures. Parliament blocked this gap with the passage of the Constitution, 91 Amendment. On July 2004, these changes came into effect and forbade party splits, banned defections and prevented defectors from being rewarded with ministerial berths or other remunerative political posts. It met the extensive demand for implementing a limit on the size of ministries both at the Centre and in the states. In 1960's, the limit on the size of ministries was advised by the first Administrative Reforms Commission. This amendment has forbidden party splits but it has not focused the issue of unstable coalitions because the law does not take awareness of coalitions and pre-poll electoral adjustments among political parties. For the integrity of coalitions, the Second Administrative Reforms Commission has advised that something more needs to be done. It states that the ethics of coalition government is 'seriously strained' when parties in a coalition, 'primarily driven by opportunism and craving for power in utter disregard of the common minimum programme' abandon the coalition midstream. Therefore, it wants the opportunistic redrawing of coalitions between elections to be legally banned. This prohibition can be enforced through a constitution amendment which states that 'if one of more parties in a coalition with a common programme mandated by the electorate either explicitly before the elections or implicitly while forming the government, realign midstream with one or more parties outside the coalition, then members of that party or parties shall have to seek a fresh mandate from the electorate'. Further, this proposal takes the anti-defection law, as it takes into account the issue of mid-stream instability of coalitions when a coalition partner decides to join other sides. Since Mr. Veerappa Moily, the Chairman of the commission, hails from Karnataka, he unquestionably has direct learning of the threat that precarious coalitions can posture to the democratic process and to governance. Some years ago, the Congress Party collaborated with the Janata Dal (S) to form a coalition government in that state. The Janata Dal(S) suddenly ended this coalition after 20 months and collaborated with the Congress Party's arch-rival—the Bharatiya Janata Party (BJP)—to form another unprincipled partnership. The BJP, which is the main opposition party in Parliament, has had its share of issues with dishonest coalition partners. The recentis the tenserelationship that this party has with the Jharkhand Mukti Morcha (JMM) in Jharkhand. Nonetheless, the two main communist parties have succeeded in shaping more ideologically compatible and practicalcoalitions in West Bengal, Kerala and Tripura, they are not likely to oppose the measures which give stability to coalitions at the national and regional level. And so, the government should be able to summon the support of major political parties, if it were to decide to implement the ARC's suggestion in this regard. Many other suggestions of this commission relating to ethics in politics should elicit support over the political range.

The appointment of the commission by the United Progressive Alliance (UPA) and the terms of reference given to it talke dabout the government's good goals. As the commission has finalized its duties, now, these intentions need to be converted into action. In order to bring transparency and accountability, the Prime minister has himself showed interest in reforming the system. It seems like at least someone is paying attention to the quote of Mahatma Gandhi that is printed on the cover page of its report.

CORRUPTION IN INDIA: AN OUTLINE

There is no requirement to comment on the issue of corruption in India as it is extensive and infecting every nerve and cell of the administrative system. It is important to destroy it from its root.

Roots

The issue is general. After involving into it once, the person usually ends up practicing it not because others are doing the same, but because he might have involved into the system through a corrupt method of bribery on one hand. Secondly, it may also mean that there are people who are ready to maintain the mechanism going for their own advantage, meeting injustice to the poor and, perhaps, ignoring it would cause a loss of job etc.

Challenges

There are many still in the structure, which are correct, while the judicial system that depends mainly on proofs would fail to find some to prove the corrupt. There is also the threat that some are mistakenly condemned in place of or with the corrupt. The challenge is for corrective justice, not mainly for retributive justice.

SOLUTIONS

Plato has related the State to the human body. Administration of proper drugs can get rid of ailments and let natural remedial to take place. Truth is the best medicine. The result of it is justice. Mostly, entertainment media and traditional cultures encourage false world views and expectations that give actual space for corruption as a quick substitute. These must be effectively and correctly countered by truth.

Since the ailment is dense, so, the doses should be accordingly it. Hitler knew that Information has power, and the Nazi government flourished on a system of heavy propaganda. The propaganda was incorrect, thus, the consequences were devastating. For the truth, the modern world does not have enough time. It desires anything that could create fast wealth, success and materialist meaning in life. This is considered as surrender of spirit to brute forces. It happens when people fail to realize they need to halt and search for spiritual wisdom. We are required more representatives of truth who will stand for it, in their own little corners, bringing light to the darkest sections of our society in order to bring healing to the nation.

Truth is champion and truth exists. But, it is not possible without its ambassadors. Candles should be burnt and lanterns should be taken out in the open. But the question arises—who will do it? The answer is—not those who are confined but only those who are open and unrestricted.

Corruption and Government

The origin of corruption is government and it is a governmental issue. No government means no corruption. But, it is not possible to vanish the government and it is not the solution. It has been well said, 'That government is best that governs the least'. There are more cases of corruption in states under dictatorship than under any other form of government. Wherever, governmental power exists, corruption exists but in weakness. The government is not universal and omniscient, and so problems start up and increase, allowing injustice, disorder and desire to corrupt the governmental regulation. There is always a possibility if the ship has not breached the law of buoyancy. Nonetheless, once the wreckage has occurred, the only salvation remains in deserting the ship and getting into some safe place (if it exists…). But, there is always hope if there is life. The body will only survive if the members do not attack each other to destroy them; but, will work in harmony and mutual construction. Those who are in authority have to remember that authority or power is a vast responsibility. It is the responsibility of the 'rulers' to keep the head in its proper place. The wise man should keep his eyes on his head. Any person who is not able to see cannot supervise. The sort of leadership and the choice of the right leadership is essentialto the health and life of the country.

Becoming Corruption-Free

A corruption-free government is like the law of gravity or the law of aerodynamics. It is the way it works. The functioning creates the knowledge of justice, liberty and equality. The letter of the law is not the main point of focus. The spirit of the law is vital; and, justice, liberty and equality are the spirit of law.

A corrupt government helps in reducing moral justice, moral liberty and moral equality. It is immoral in core. It is immoral because it is principally outside the law. It may have written and verbal laws. But, it does not have the spirit of the law of human community function. Even, a corrupt government is also a law: a law of ailment and end.

The Essence of a Healthy Nation

Love is the core of morality. The sum of all law is 'Love your neighbour as yourself. Love is something that incorporates a person or any nation into a healthy living. Thus, any law that demoralizes the rule of 'Love your neighbour as yourself' is immoral and without the soul of justice, liberty, and equality.

Love cannot be considered as an emotional game. It is the act that emerges from recognition of the dignity of the human individual. Love is not simply idealistic. It is individual.

A corrupt government directs the country into

1. Disbelieve of governmental justice
2. Aristocracy, bribery and marginalization
3. The government is looked at as a monster. It has weapons, forces and power. It rules by force and not by honour and devotion.

Citizen's Responsibility in Creating Corrupt Government

1. Want to avoid justice and personal responsibilities.
2. Desire to create money and wealth to the level that the respectability of a human as human loses value.
3. *Selfishness*. Absence of love for one's partner man/woman, whoever it is, is the first act of murder.
4. Valuing inequality by permitting religion, anti-religion, communalism, cultural nationalism, sexism, racism, etc. to influence the feelings of inequality.
5. *Pride*. Desire for power through despotic thinking: desiring everyone to believe in you. In reality, such things are not possible, even in families. Disagreements will definitely occur, as diversity is the rule of community.
6. Rational blindness and non-scientific temper, in the name of science.
7. Tolerating injustice and allowing violence to reduce the voice of reason and fact.
8. Lastly, fake hope that without doing anything, at last everything will be all right.

Citizen's Responsibility in Creating Corruption-free Government

1. Verbalize absolute dislike to corruption.
2. Unite against all practices of corruption.
3. Instil hatred in children against bribery and immoral practices.
4. Be an example to children and youth of true nationalism, integrity of character, pureness in love for fellow-citizens and moral responsibility.
5. Deny the esteem of money-mongering culture; deny greediness; promote the virtue of social responsibility.
6. Inform NGOs, Media workers, etc. regarding any case of corruption, who are committed to a corruption-free government.
7. Faith in God, the True Judge of the Universe, that he will give justice.

20 CHAPTER

Probity in Governance

Probity in governance is a very important necessity for governance's system to work in a phased manner for socio-economic development. Eradication of corruption is the topmost condition for guaranteeing probity in governance. Other important requisites include operational laws, rules and regulations governing every aspect of public life and an effective and rational execution of those laws. Indeed, implementation of law in an appropriate, reasonable and effective way is a facet of discipline. Regrettably, public life is rapidly becoming devoid of in India, and sans discipline, as per the Scandinavian economist-sociologist Gunnyar Myrdal, real progress is just a dream. Public-private morality and a sense of honesty compose discipline in a real sense. In western nations, the higher position a person holds, the more respect he has for laws. In contrast, in India, holding higher position means a person can break laws and regulations easily without any scrutiny. Indiscipline and untruth have affected our nation really bad; morality, both public and private, is at a premium.

People, over the period, have lost their trust on governance system owing to issues like corruption, insensitivity, red tapism, irresponsibility and disrespect to office and law.

It is the high time to work for restoring people's confidence in the government machinery. Some necessary measures that can be taken are as follows:

- For making civil servant more people oriented, they should undergo sensitivity training.
- Strong anti-corruption machinery is important to probe government officials and influential politicians instead of investigative body with limited power.
- Strict assessment of government servant's behaviour and attitude. A performance appraisal is also necessary to evaluate their duty towards public.
- IPC and ICPC should have strict and clear law against corrupt officers.
- Establishment of a high-level intellectual and independent body to look after the issue of transfer and promotion of government servants.
- Insertion of ethical code from the first day of selection process to retirement day.
- To motivate morality and spirit of honest servants, there should be a provision of reward.

Before the year 325 B.C., Socrates said "Knowledge is virtue; knowledge is that promotes virtue and knowledge is something which inform not only the mind but also the soul. It influences the human character and conduct as a matter of fact one cannot be virtuous without knowledge but today in our society knowledge is a rare commodity and the knowledgeable person is few and far between". Regarding Socratarian tradition, Aristotle said in similar vein, "It is better for a city to be governed by a good man than even by good laws". Later, British PM had once said, 'When men are pure, laws are useless, when men are corrupt, laws are broken'. The British Education System played a significant role in harming people of India, and the same pattern has been following since independence to a great extent. Sir Wavell admitted the fact when he said, 'We have done worse in the field of education, because we have given Indians the education of letter and not of character'. It is not possible for law to eradicate crimes overnight, but it is evident that it can prevent more blatant abuses over a period of time. As corruption has rooted itself firmly in our character, it is very difficult to eradicate the same. But, serious efforts are needed to contain it.

To find out the system of diseases in our governance system, analysing, examining and scrutinizing the power and composition of the three wings of the state, legislature, executive and judiciary, is important.

- ***Legislature***: It is normal to feel frustrated after knowing the composition of parliament as out of 500 members, only 10% are able and competent. Another 10% are doubtful and dubious characters. The rest of them come from illiterate and criminal backgrounds. As the constitution doesn't prescribe any minimum qualification for parliamentarians, one can think of the contribution they give in the making of laws. I still remember the day when due to lack of quorum, an important bill related to Shah Bano case could not be passed in one city. However, the bill had to be passed by whip.
- ***Executive***: Although the executive power is exercised by the electorate body, civil servants, also called 'departmental experts', have the real power. These experts come from IAS. Three types of IAS are as follows:
  - Who are recruited by merit by conducting competitive examination
  - The second class IAS belong to the SC/ST and
  - Third category belongs to nominated IAS.

Diverse composition enables them to come from all these categories. Conflicts of interest remain among themselves, the purpose of the legislation is lost in tiff between real and unreal and the act takes place in the backburner. Because the same was not implemented properly for the above reasons, further amendment of the act is recommended. Our constitution has gone through 53 amendments in 36 years, and that of the USA only 26 amendments in 198 years.

- ***Judiciary***: As per the SC Advocate On Record VS. Union Of India and others (AIR 1994 SC 268), the judges were appointed on merit which should be the predominant: this decision further been supported by a verdict on presidential reference case reported in AIR 1999 SC1, wherein it was ruled that the Chief Justice of India's viewpoint so given has privacy in the matter of all appointments, but it is not clear whether those decisions are followed in practice or not. Because of the constant interventions by the political leaders, the merit takes backseat. For example, I know about an able lawyer whose name was put forward by the Chief Justice of the High Court plus two senior judges on the basis of the provision of the decision of the Hon'ble Supreme Court. However, just because of political interference, he could not be appointed as the judge even after all the initial formalities. This means that merit is not the first criteria for making appointments. The condition is worse in the lower judiciary where 90% of the presiding officers are corrupt and loyal to their political masters. A famous journalist once said that 'The law is up for grabs and justice knocked down to the highest bidder'.

The lawyer, being an integral part of the judiciary, plays an important role. According to Shakespeare, most of the lawyers are 'leeches' who are only busy fathering their own nest. At present, contribution of lawyers towards society is negligible. For example, the free legal aid Scheme is of no great use for society as good lawyers hardly engage in these free legal aid cases.

In connection with the executive malpractices, in a case between P.V. Narasimha Rao Vs State (CBI reported in AIR 1998 SC 2120), the Supreme Court held that 'a member of parliament against whom there is a prima facie case of corruption should be immune from prosecution in the court of law is to my mind an unacceptable proposition at the present time. I do not believe it to be the law The corrupt public servant should be dealt with severely so that they cannot escape punishment'. It is told that property earned by illegal means should be seized and the related individuals concerned should be expelled from service through due process of law. The existing laws like IPC and the Prevention of Corruption Act can successfully tackle corruption cases.

GOOD GOVERNANCE AND e-GOVERNANCE

According to Kofi Annan: 'Good governance is perhaps the single most important factor in eradicating poverty and promoting development'.

- **Good governance** is the essence of Democratic country. Probity in governance is important for people to understand the Democratic principles that are necessary to generate in citizens the feeling of respect and patriotism for the state.
- **Good governance** is fundamental and **e-governance** is instrumental.
- **e-Governance** is a tool.
- For attaining good governance, it is important that e-Governance tool is able to focus on reforms that will help in the process.
- Good governance decides the strategy and outline of e-tools for better governance outcomes and processes.
- **e-Governance** can prove to be an important tool if the process of reforms is carried out properly. Automation of complex government procedures will generate more complications than it can resolve. In e-Governance, the letter 'e' is small and the letter 'G' is big.
- With the help of **re-engineering process,** proper execution of e-Governance can make IT available to the common man, helping the government to devise services as per the varying needs of both citizens and other stakeholders.

TOOLS FOR GOOD GOVERNANCE

Participation of Civil Society

Corruption can be restrained if citizens raise their voice to bring a change in the process of governance. This can only be attained by if civil society and the media together work to educate citizens about the harms of corruption and giving them a 'voice' by letting them participate after making them aware of the process. This brings a new aspect to the idea of **accountability of government to the people** in contrast to the traditional horizontal mechanisms of legislative and legal accountability of the executive and internal vertical accountability. Civil society here denotes formal as well as informal entities and consists of the private sector, the media, NGOs, professional associations and informal groups of people from various genres.

Citizens' Charters

Citizens' Charters play an important role in making administration both accountable and citizen-friendly. Almost every government department and organization revealed its Citizens' Charter a few years back. The Charter is a list of duties a public service organization provides for the citizens, to ensure a high level of service while working as per the standards notified in the declaration. Over a period, these Citizens' Charters have become a burden rather than a responsibility. The undertakings made in the charters have taken a back seat with no machinery to execute them. For desired results, it is important that these Citizens' Charters should have specific provisions and set out specific obligations for the public services, the time within which the department would have to provide a service or to respond to a query or complaint. As per the Commission, it is important for these charters to have specified remedy/penalty/compensation in case of default for the proper functioning of these tools.. It is good to have a few promises which can be kept rather than a long list of supercilious declarations which are impractical.

Right to Information (RTI)

According to Henry David Thoreau, 'That Government Is Best Which Governs Least'.

Right to information is one of the fundamental rights and is an important requisite for the survival of participatory democracy. As per Article 19(1) of the Constitution, each and every citizen has freedom of speech and expression. The Universal Declaration of Human Rights under Article 19, the Right to information is treated as human right. What is good in this act that it gives every individual the same powers as that of an elected representative.

The law regarding the right to freedom of information was enacted by Sweden for the first time more than 200 years ago in Sweden, which resulted in the publication of the Freedom of Press Law in 1776.

The fact that we can express our opinions regarding functions of Government and Public Institutions only if we are aware of them has been recognized by the Supreme Court many times since 1977.

The Right to Information Act (RTI) was passed by Indian Parliament in 2005, enabling common citizen to seek information regarding government projects, schemes and other activities. It was regarded as a landmark Act that has the potential to change the very idea of governance and the power equation between common people and the government.

The RTI act helped in democratizing the information and decentralizing the power. This made sure that information can be accessed by all.

Transparency

Transparency is a tool that can make government work efficiently by winning people's faith. In Indian bureaucratic system and government functionaries, transparency was an exception rather than being a norm.

India holds the 94th position out of 176 nations as per the 2013 ranking of Transparency International ranking. This study even reported that 54% Indians indulged in the act of corruption, at least once, to get things done. The RTI act has the potential restrain this evil practice both at grass root level and at power corridors of high and mighty. Post implementation, many cases of corruption have come to fore. As per the 2014 index, India held 85th position, showing some improvement in addressing corruption.

Importance of Systemic Reforms

Combination of mix of punitive and preventive steps is very important to combat this evil of corruption. Punitive procedures act as a deterrent, whereas preventive procedures decrease chances for corruption by making systems transparent, increasing accountability, decreasing discretion, rationalizing procedures etc. Better preventive procedures act as 'Systemic Reforms' as they tend to make better systems and processes.

Some of the Initiatives taken Recently in this Direction are as Follows

- *Railway Passenger Bookings (Indian Railways)*: The step to computerize railway passenger bookings, including 'online' booking and e-ticketing, helped in restraining the middlemen, decongesting booking offices and attaining significant transparency to the Railway reservations process.
- *Common Entrance Test (Karnataka)*: This helped in ensuring merit-based selection to professional colleges in a timely and transparent manner.
- *Teachers Appointment Scheme (Karnataka)*: This presented a complete, objective and a transparent system for the appointment of teachers.
- *Registration & Stamps (Maharashtra)*: The motive of this process is to frame more transparent property valuation tables, computerization of records, fixing time limits for the return of registered documents, using of digital cameras for photos and finger-printing, etc. The introduction of 'valuation tables' has almost side lined arbitrary assessment of stamp duty and attained the manifold purposes of curtailing of harassment of immoveable property's purchasers, enhancing tax collection and decreasing corruption.

- ***Unit Area Scheme (Delhi)***: This has devised a process or system for payment of property tax and registration of property along with self-assessment and normative basis of calculation.
- ***e-Cops (Punjab)***: This is a platform to register online complaints so as to keep a 'real time' watch over the manner the 'cutting edge' level officials take action on complaints.
- ***e-Governance in Andhra Pradesh (e-Seva), and Kerala (FRIENDS standing for Fast, Reliable, Instant, Effective Network for Distribution of Services)***: These ensure an efficient and fast service delivery by streamlining transactions between government and citizens by introducing the use of IT for paying various bills or seeking different services on a single platform.
- ***'e-Choupals' in Madhya Pradesh***: This platform is of great benefit for farmers for selling their products.
- ***Rural Kiosks, known as RSDP (Rural Service Delivery Points) in Andhra Pradesh***: This helps people to access e-Seva via internet for paying bills, surfing information, downloading of forms, etc., making the life easy for public and giving employees time to perform other more 'substantive' public duties.
- ***Parishkaram (Andhra Pradesh)***: 'Parishkaram', a call centre, is an initiative taken by Andhra Pradesh government to satisfy citizens of their query about government services or for redressal of grievances. Parishkaram means rectifying complaints and problems. Any citizen in need can dial a toll-free number '1100' to seek information on different departments of state or register grievance. The service was initially meant to cater to services regarding the agriculture department but later covered 13 other departments. If the query is regarding information, operator answers the call and give the necessary information, with the details of the call are being recorded into the specified system. If the operator fails to satisfy the query, the same is forwarded to the concerned department official. A Management Information 13 System (MIS) helps the operator to direct the calls to the officials of concerned departments and convey the obtained response back to the citizen. The good thing about the system is that if operator fails to attend the call, it automatically gets escalated to higher level.

PROBITY IN GOVERNANCE: SLEW OF MEASURES IN INDIA

With a view to better the image of government, marred by recent scams, the Government of India recently took some steps to bring reforms in the functioning of government for greater transparency, probity and accountability in governance and to restrain bribery by domestic and foreign public officials. In his first address to the joint sitting of Parliament, former President Pranab Mukherjee also expressed his views on various issues like economy's slow growth and efforts to tackle aspects responsible for the slowdown. Concerned with the insensitivity among people and increasing graph of crimes like rape and assault of women, he proposed to frame an ordinance providing for stringent punishment in such cases.

'My government remains committed to ushering in reforms for greater transparency, probity, integrity and accountability in governance', said Mukherjee, just after ₹ 3,600 crore Augusta Westland scam came to fore to make situation difficult for the government.

'To this end, my government attaches priority to the enactment of legislation proposed in the Whistle Blowers' Protection Bill, the Prevention of Bribery of Foreign Public Officials and Officials of Public International Organizations Bill, Citizens' Right to Grievance Redress Bill, and The Lokpal and Lokayukta Bill, which already stand introduced in the Parliament', he said.

The President also reiterated that the government is planning amendments to the Prevention of Corruption Act to penalize the guilty and shield the honest public servants 'more effectively'.

The address by President, a constitutional requirement, begins the Budget session of Parliament.

Keeping in view the judicial reforms, Mukherjee also declared that government will introduce the Judicial Standards and Accountability Bill in this session.

The issues of economic situation, job securities, slowdown and employment opportunities were mainly addressed in the speech by the President.

'People are concerned about the security of our women and children. They are also anxious about timely delivery of their entitlements and about persisting social and economic inequality', he said.

Citing the Europe's recession, Mukherjee said the global economy has gone through many ups and downs in the past year. He added that it has been a tough year for India as well owing to both global and domestic factors that have affected our growth.

'We need to address the impact of both. My government has responded to the situation by taking several measures to revive investment activity and investor sentiment', he said.

Mukherjee, who held finance ministry before his election as President, acknowledged that the Indian economy was growing slowly.

'Real GDP grew by 5.4% in the first half of the current fiscal year. This is significantly lower than the average of around 8% in the last decade. Our slower growth is the consequence of a combination of global and domestic factors', he said.

Assuring nation of better future, Mukherjee said that government was taking steps to tackle factors responsible for the slowdown.

'Inflation is easing gradually but is still a problem. In recent months, there have been positive developments too. There has been a moderation in core inflation and recovery in growth is likely. Policy measures announced during the year have also restored optimism at home and abroad', he said.

'My government has announced a road map for fiscal consolidation by containing the current year's fiscal deficit at 5.3 per cent of the GDP. The Government is also working with State Governments to reach a consensus on the Goods and Services Tax', he said.

Concerned with the crimes against children, he signalled the enactment of a 'path-breaking' (the Protection of Children from Sexual Offences Act) act, which will be responsible for tackling accused with the best punishment possible. The Sexual Harassment of Women at Workplace (Prevention, Prohibition and Redressal) Bill was cleared by Lok Sabha for safeguarding women from any harassment in workplaces.

'My government is also deeply concerned about incidents of sexual offences against women. After considering the recommendations of the Justice JS Verma Committee, the Government has promulgated an ordinance, amending the criminal law to provide for stringent punishment for heinous sexual offences against women'.

'The government has also begun to implement a series of administrative measures to improve the safety and security of women in the country', the President said.

Major Points

- Last year was like a bumpy road Indian economy. The government has taken measures to tackle the situation in best possible manner.
- Women's security and persisting economic issues were main concerns among people.
- With the rise in sexual harassment crimes, the government is determined to pass strict laws to tackle sexual crimes.
- Youth energy and enterprise will take India to greater heights.
- Although the government has managed to control inflation, it is still posing a problem for nation.
- Government will take action on food bill.
- Budget session will be productive.
- The government will take all necessary steps to control the slowdown in an efficient manner. MGNREGA provided employment to 5 crore families.
- The menace of polio has been eradicated to a minimum.
- Indian telecom network is the second largest network in world.

While delivering former Kerala Chief Minister, C Achutha Menon's birth centenary memorial lecture on the topic 'Accountability and Transparency in Governance', the then Comptroller and Auditor General of India (CAG) Vinod Rai said that the organization work is not only to prepare reports but also to hold the government financially accountable to the legislature. He reiterated that audit helped in attaining greater probity, transparency and accountability in governance and warned that desired results of reforms cannot be attained if these issues are not tacked properly.

Rai said that the Constitution has given CAG the responsibility of keeping a tab on government's account to hold it financially accountable to the legislature as 'it is totally independent of the Government'.

The UPA government has accused CAG of breaching its jurisdiction after its reports on spectrum allocation and coal blocks allocation mired Congress in a great political mess.

'If the general levels of probity, transparency and accountability do not improve in our governance set up, the desired results of reforms cannot be attained', Rai said.

He cited a few cases of dearth of probity, transparency and accountability at several stages of governance, including corporate governance.

'To make public opinion, CAG initiated to spread audit findings to citizens groups, non-governmental bodies, educational institutions,media and so on', Rai said.

He said, 'Corruption in society had led to skewed allocation of incomes and allowed domestic elites and large corporate a supercilious hold over policies and laws'.

It is also acknowledged that corruption, if not tackled on time, can make even the finest of system collapse. It makes the system hollow by contaminating the thoughts and ideals starting from the lowest level, resulting in a bad relations between citizens and government or state. As common people feel lack of transparency and accountability as the main hurdle in the path of good governance, criminalization and 'compulsions' of coalition politics, and loopholes in corruption/grievance redressal machinery are the most significant reasons for bad governance and sustaining corruption in the country. Further, this weird scenario is a result of attitudes of corrupt officials and a weak, apathetic and unaccountable government machinery. The state of anti-corruption institutions remains bad as they are mostly controlled by the corrupt politicians, and these lack real teeth and powers. These institutions face problems such as lack of staff, non-filling up of the vacancies and so on.

Service Delivery Excellence

The first step in the process of development is improving governance. It is debated that the menace of corruption can be tackled only if strategic changes are introduced in governance by bringing in participation, transparency, accountability and probity in administration. The right to good governance can be considered as an important part of the citizen's rights. Accordingly, citizen's concerns have also been kept in mind while formulating a policy for better quality and reliability of services. Tools such as the Citizens' Charters, Right to Information, e-Governance, Report Cards and Social Audits can help in attaining the desired result. In addition to this, each department now has a public grievance redress mechanism chaired by a senior officer as Director of Grievances', who holds the power to call for files/papers relating to grievance. The public can use him/her help for redressal of their grievances. It is mandatory for him to be available on every Wednesday between 10:00 and 13:00 hours. The Right to Information Act, 2005 bestows the common man to know his right to avail a particular public service, and redress the grievance, if any. The system also includes the 'Right to be Heard and Consumer Education', that is, informing the consumers about their rights. It is based on the rationale of 'participatory, transparent and accountable governance'. The Right to Information Act made public servants accountable to any delays in the process as they can also be questioned on their conduct. Electronic governance or e-Governance is an efficient tool to introduce transparency to the services by ensuring easy and speedy access to the information with the help of public and other agencies. Following steps could help in effectively introducing e-Governance:

1. Computerize all the public dealing departments, including the Police, Judiciary, transportation, and registration of properties.
2. Advent of e-Procurement (preferably on the lines of KONEPS) in all public procurements and contracts.
3. Starting 'Touch Screen System' which shows pictures to avail particular service.
4. Introduction of software like 'Lok Vani' for attending public grievances.
5. Solidifying the infrastructure of e-Governance and spreading awareness about e-Governance.

Thus, e-Governance is stated as one of the best tools in a process to improve governance.

21 CHAPTER

Concluding Review of Ethics, Integrity and Aptitude

ETHICS

Ethics, otherwise called moral theory, is a branch of philosophy that includes systematizing, protecting and suggesting ideas of good and bad behaviour. The term originates from the Greek word ethos, which refers to 'character'. Ethics complements aesthetics in the philosophy field of Axiology. In theory, ethics examines the ethical conduct in people and how one needs to act. Ethics might be classified into four prominent areas of study:

- Meta-ethics, about the hypothetical meaning and reference of ethical propositions and how their truth values (if any) may be ascertained;
- Normative ethics, about the practical methods for deciding an ethical strategy;
- Applied ethics, about how moral results can be accomplished in particular circumstances;
- Descriptive ethics, also called comparative ethics, refers to studying people's convictions about ethics;

Ethics aims to determine questions associated with human morality—concepts like good and evil, right and wrong, good and bad habit, justice and crime. As indicated by Tomas Paul and Linda Elder of the Foundation for Critical Thinking, 'most people confuse ethics with behaving in accordance with social conventions, religious beliefs and the law', and don't regard ethics as a stand-alone idea. Paul and Elder describe ethics as 'a set of concepts and principles that guide us in determining what behaviour helps or harms sentient creatures'. The Cambridge Dictionary of Philosophy expresses that the word ethics is 'commonly used interchangeably with "morality" and sometimes it is used more narrowly to mean the moral principles of a particular tradition, group or individual'. The general meaning of ethics: rational, optimal (viewed as the best arrangement of the given alternatives) and right decision made based on commonsense. This includes the probability of destruction if it is required and if it does not take place because of intentional ill will. If, for instance, there is a danger of physical clash and one seems to have no other option, it is all right to cause the required injury so as to ensure self-defence. Thus, ethics does not provide rules like morals but rather it can be utilized as a way to decide moral values (states of mind or practices offering need to social values, e.g., morals or ethics).

META-ETHICS

Meta-ethics is a field inside philosophy that tries to comprehend the idea of normative ethics. The study of meta-ethics stresses on how we comprehend, think about and what is the meaning of what is correct and what isn't. Meta-ethics has constantly gone well with philosophical ethics, yet in this unequivocal sense it came to the fore with G.E. Moore's *Principia Ethica* from 1903. In it, he initially expounded on what he called *the naturalistic error*. Moore apparently rejected naturalism in morals, in his Open Question Argument. This influenced scholars to take a look again at second order inquiries concerning ethics. Previously, the Scottish thinker David Hume had advanced a similar view on the contrast between facts and values. Investigations of how we know in ethics partition into cognitivism and non-cognitivism; this is like the differences between descriptivists and non-descriptivists. Non-cognitivism is the claim that when something is judged as right or wrong, this is neither genuine nor false. We may for instance be just communicating our passionate emotions about these things. Cognitivism would then be able to be viewed as the claim that when we discuss good and bad, we are discussing matters of certainty. The philosophy of ethics relates to value-bearing things or properties, i.e. the type of things or stuff denoted by moral suggestions. Non-descriptivists and non-cognitivists are of the belief that ethics does not require a particular ontology, since ethical propositions don't allude. This is known to be against pragmatist position. Pragmatists should then clarify what sort of entities, properties or states are important for ethics, how they have esteem, and why they control and spur our activities.

NORMATIVE ETHICS

Normative ethics refers to studying moral activities. It is the branch of philosophical ethics that researches certain queries that emerge while considering how one should act, ethically. Normative ethics is different from meta-ethics since it inspects measures for the rightness and wrongness of activities, while meta-ethics considers the importance of good language and the metaphysics of moral facts. Normative ethics is also different from descriptive ethics, as the latter is an empirical examination of individuals' ethical convictions. In other words, descriptive ethics would be concerned about figuring out what extent of individuals trust that killing is never right, while normative ethics is worried about whether it is right to hold such a conviction. Subsequently, normative ethics is once in a while called prescriptive, instead of descriptive. Notwithstanding, on specific renditions of the meta-ethical view called moral realism, moral realities are both descriptive and prescriptive at the same time.

HISTORICAL THEORIES ASSOCIATED WITH ETHICS

Virtue Ethics

Socrates

Virtue ethics portrays the character of an ethical specialist as a main force for moral conduct, and is utilized to depict the ethics of Socrates, Aristotle and other early Greek scholars. Socrates (469 BC–399 BC) was one of the first Greek thinkers to energize both the scholars and the common citizen to turn their focus from the outside world to the state of mankind. In this regard, knowledge having an effect on human life was placed most noteworthy while all other learning to be secondary. Self-information was viewed as vital for progress and inherently a necessary good. A mindful individual will act totally within his abilities to his zenith, while an oblivious individual will fumble and experience trouble. To Socrates, a person must be mindful of each reality (and its specific situation) relevant to his experience in the event that he wishes to achieve self-knowledge. He set that individuals will normally do what is great, if they recognize what is correct. Malicious or awful activities are the aftereffect of ignorance. If a criminal was genuinely mindful of the mental and spiritual outcome of his activities, he would neither carry out nor even think to indulge in such activities. Any individual who recognizes what is really right will naturally do it, as indicated by Socrates. While he related learning with goodness, he similarly made comparison between virtue and happiness. The really insightful man will comprehend what is correct, do what is great and thus be cheerful.

Aristotle (384 BC–322 BC) placed a moral framework that might be named 'self-realizationism'. In view of Aristotle, when a man acts as per his inclination or interest and understands his maximum capacity, he will do great and be content. During childbirth, an infant isn't a person, however a potential individual. In order to become a 'real' individual, the youngster's characteristic potential must be figured out. Despondency and dissatisfaction are caused by the undiscovered capability of a person, prompting fizzled objectives and a poor life. Aristotle stated, 'Nature does nothing in vain'. Therefore, it is necessary for people to act as per their inclination and build up their hidden abilities with a specific end goal to be content and satisfied. Joy was described to be a definitive goal. All other things, for example, civic life or wealth, are simply means to the end. Self-acknowledgment, the consciousness of one's tendency and the improvement of one's abilities, is the definite path to satisfaction.

Aristotle affirmed that man had three natures: vegetable (physical/metabolism), creature (sentiments/hunger) and logical (mental/theoretical). Physical nature can be mitigated through exercise and care, tender compassion through indulgence of impulse and inclinations, and mental through human reason and created potential. Rational advancement was viewed as the most imperative, as fundamental to philosophical mindfulness and as interestingly human. Balance was supported, with the extremes seen as corrupted and unethical. For instance, boldness is the moderate virtue between the extremes of cowardice and heedlessness. Man ought not just live, but rather live well with conduct administered by moderate virtue. This is viewed as troublesome, as goodness signifies making the best choice, to the ideal individual, at the ideal time, to the best possible degree, in the right form, for the correct cause.

Stoicism

The Stoic logician Epictetus placed that the greatest good was happiness and tranquillity. Mental serenity or Apatheia was of the most noteworthy value; self-authority over one's wants and feelings prompts spiritual peace. The "unconquerable will" is fundamental to this philosophy. The person's will ought to be free and untouched. Enabling a man to aggravate the mental harmony is generally offering yourself in slavery. In the event that a man is allowed to outrage you voluntarily, you have no influence over your inward world and in this way no liberty. Freedom from material connections is equally important. When a thing breaks, the individual ought not be upset, but rather acknowledge it was a thing that could break. Likewise, if somebody should die, those near them should hold to their tranquillity in light of the fact that the loved one was made of flesh and blood bound to death. Stoic theory says to acknowledge things that can't be altered, leaving oneself to presence and continuing in a rational manner. Demise isn't dreaded. Individuals don't 'lose' their life, yet 'return', for they are going back to God (who at first gave what the individual is as a person). According to Epictetus, troublesome issues in life should not be neglected, but instead accepted. They are spiritual activities required for the strength of the soul, as similar to physical exercise required for the soundness of the body. He additionally expressed that sex and sexual want are to be avoided as the greatest risk to the uprightness and balance of a man's mind. Restraint is very alluring. Epictetus opined that staying abstinent even with enticement was a triumph for which a man could feel proud of.

Hedonism

Hedonism sets that the essential ethic is amplifying delight and limiting torment. A number of schools of Hedonist thought exist which may range from those supporting the indulgence of even transient desires to those educating a quest for spiritual joy. In their thought of outcomes, they vary from those supporting self-satisfaction irrespective of the torment and cost to others, to those expressing that the most ethical pursuit augments delight and joy for the vast majority of people.

Cyrenaic Hedonism

Established by Aristippus of Cyrene, Cyrenaics supported quick satisfaction or delight. 'Eat, drink and be merry, for tomorrow we die'. Even fleeting desires should be indulged, for fear the opportunity should be forever lost. There was next to zero worry with the future, the present ruling in the interest for quick joy. Cyrenaic gratification energized the quest for delight and liberality decisively, trusting joy to be the only good.

Epicureanism

Epicurus ethics is a pleasure seeker type of virtue ethics. Epicurus 'presented a sustained argument that pleasure, correctly understood, will coincide with virtue'. He dismissed the fanaticism of the Cyrenaics, trusting some delights and indulgences to be damaging to individuals. Epicureans made an observation that aimless indulgence at times brought about negative outcomes. A few experiences were accordingly dismissed out of hand, and some unpleasant experiences persisted in the present to guarantee a superior life later on. To Epicurus the *summum bonum*, or most noteworthy good, was reasonability, practiced through balance and alert. Too much of indulgence can be ruinous to delight and can even prompt agony. For instance, eating one food over and over again will make a man lose taste for it. Eating excessive food without a moment's delay will prompt uneasiness and bad health. Pain and fear were to be kept away. Living was basically great, barring pain and ailment. Death was not something to be dreaded. Fear was viewed as the source of most despondency. Vanquishing the fear of death would normally prompt a more joyful life. Epicurus contemplated if there was an existence of immortality after death, the fear of death was irrational. In case there was no life after death, at that point the individual would not be alive to undergo suffering, dread or stress; he would be non-existent in death. It is irrational to worry over conditions that don't exist, for example, one's state in death without an afterlife.

State Consequentialism

State consequentialism, also referred to as Mohist consequentialism, is an ethical theory that assesses the ethical worth of an activity based on how much contribution it makes to the basic goods of a state. The *Stanford Encyclopedia of Philosophy* depicts Mohist consequentialism, going back to the fifth century BC, as 'a remarkably sophisticated version based on a plurality of intrinsic goods taken as constitutive of human welfare'. Unlike utilitarianism, which sees joy as a moral good, 'the basic goods in Mohist consequentialist thinking are—order, material wealth, and increase in population'. At the time of Mozi's period, war and starvations were normal, and population growth was viewed as an ethical need for a harmonious society. The 'material wealth' of Mohist consequentialism means fundamental needs like shelter and clothing, and the 'order' of Mohist consequentialism means Mozi's position against fighting and violence, which he saw as useless and a danger to social stability. Stanford sinologist David Shepherd Nivison, in the *Cambridge History of Ancient China*, composes that the moral goods of Mohism 'are interrelated: more basic wealth, then more reproduction; more people, then more production and wealth—if people have plenty, they would be good, filial, kind, and so on unproblematically'. The Mohists trusted that morality depends on 'promoting the benefit of all under heaven and eliminating harm to all under heaven'. As opposed to Bentham's perspectives, state consequentialism isn't utilitarian since it isn't hedonistic or individualistic. The significance of results that are useful for the community exceeds the significance of individual joy and agony.

Normative Elhics in Modern Era

Customarily, normative ethics referred to the study of what influences activities to good and bad. These theories provided an all-encompassing moral principle one could interest in settling troublesome moral decisions.

By the twentieth century, moral theories turned out to be more complicated and are never again concerned exclusively with rightness and wrongness, but are occupied with a wide range of moral status. Amid the century, the study of normative ethics declined as meta-ethics developed in noticeable quality. This attention on meta-ethics was to a limited extent caused due to an intense linguistic concentration in analytic philosophy and due to the popularity of logical positivism. In the year 1971, John Rawls brought out *A Theory of Justice*, essentially in its quest for moral contentions and shunning of meta-ethics. This issue set the pattern for re-established interest for normative ethics.

Virtue Ethics in Contemporary world

Modern virtue ethics was advanced amid the late 1900s in large part as a reaction to G.E.M. Anscombe's *Modern Moral Philosophy*. Anscombe contends that Consequentialist and Deontological ethics are just possible as universal theories if the two schools ground themselves in divine law. As a profoundly committed Christian herself, Anscombe recommended that either the individuals who don't give moral confidence to thoughts of divine law take up virtue ethics, which does not necessitate universal laws as agents themselves are researched for virtue or bad habit and held up to 'universal standards', or that the individuals who desire to be utilitarian or consequentialist ground their theories in religious conviction. Alasdair MacIntyre, who composed the book *After Virtue*, was an important person who greatly contributed and proposed modern virtue ethics, despite the fact that MacIntyre supports a relativistic record of virtue in light of cultural standards, not objective standards. Martha Nussbaum, a contemporary virtue ethicist, objects to MacIntyre's relativism, among that of others, and reacts to relativist complaints to frame an objective account in her work 'Non-Relative Virtues: An Aristotelian Approach'. *Complete Conduct Principles for the 21st Century* mixed the Eastern virtue ethics and the Western virtue ethics, with a few alterations to suit the 21st Century, and shaped a piece of contemporary virtue ethics.

Consequentialism

Consequentialism means moral theories according to which the results of a specific action form the foundation for any substantial moral judgment about that activity (or make a structure for judgment, see rule consequentialism). In this way, from a consequentialist stance, an ethically right activity is one that delivers a good result or outcome. This view is frequently communicated as the saying *'The ends justify the means'*. In 1958, the word 'consequentialism' was introduced by G.E.M. Anscombe in her essay 'Modern Moral Philosophy', to depict what she saw as the focal mistake of some moral theories, for example, those proposed by Mill and Sidgwick. From that point onwards, the term has turned out to be regular in English-dialect ethical theories. The defining characteristic of consequentialist moral theories is the weight given to the outcomes in assessing the rightness and wrongness of acts. In consequentialist theories, the outcomes of an activity or rule by and large exceed different considerations. Besides this fundamental outline, little else is there that can be unequivocally stated with regard to consequentialism. One approach to partition different consequentialisms is based on the types of results that are taken to account the most, that is, which outcomes consider good states of affairs. As indicated by epicurean utilitarianism, a good activity is one that outcomes in an expansion in joy, and the best activity is one that outcomes in the most delight for the greatest number.

Closely associated is eudaimonic consequentialism which emphasizes on a full, thriving life, which might possibly be the same as enjoying a lot of joy is the endpoint. Likewise, one may receive an aesthetic consequentialism, in which a final goal is to create beauty. Nonetheless, one may settle on non-psychological goods as the important impact. In this way, one may seek after an expansion in material equality or political freedom as opposed to something like the more transient 'pleasure'. Different theories receive a bundle of many goods, all to be advanced equally. Regardless of whether a specific consequentialist theory concentrates on a single good or many, clashes and strains between various good states of affairs are to be expected and should compulsorily be adjudicated.

Utilitarianism

Utilitarianism refers to a hedonistic ethical theory that contends the best possible course of action is one that augments complete 'happiness'. Jeremy Bentham and John Stuart Mill are dominant advocates of this school of thought. In *A Fragment on Government*, Bentham opines 'it is the greatest happiness of the greatest number that is the measure of right and wrong' and portrays this as a central axiom. In *An Introduction to the Principles of Morals and Legislation* he discusses 'the principle of utility' but later leans towards 'the greatest happiness principle'. Hedonistic utilitarianism is the paradigmatic case of a consequentialist moral theory. This type of utilitarianism holds that what makes a difference is the total bliss, the joy of everybody and not the happiness of a specific individual.. John Stuart Mill, in his composition of hedonistic utilitarianism, proposed a progressive system of delights, implying that the quest for specific types of joy is more highly valued than the quest for other joys.

Deontology

Deontological ethics or deontology is an approach to deal with ethics that decides goodness or rightness from inspecting acts, or the rules and obligations that the individual doing the act endeavoured to fulfil. This is as opposed to consequentialism, in which rightness depends on the results of an act, and not simply the act by itself. In deontology, an act might be viewed as right regardless of the possibility that the act delivers a bad outcome, in the event that it follows the *rule* that 'one should do unto others as they would have done unto them', and even if the individual who does the act lacks virtue and had a bad intention in doing the act. As indicated by deontology, we have an obligation to act in a way that does those things that are intrinsically great as acts ('truth-telling' for instance), or follow an unbiasedly obligatory rule (as in rule utilitarianism). For deontologists, the ends or outcomes of our activities are not vital all by themselves, and our intentions are not vital all by themselves. Immanuel Kant's theory of ethics is regarded as deontological for a number of reasons. In the first place, Kant contends that to act in the ethically-right way, individuals must act from obligation (deon). Second, Kant contended that it was not the outcomes of activities that influence them to right or wrong but the intentions of the individual who performs the activity.

Kant's contention that to act in the ethically right way, one must act from obligation, starts with a contention that the most astounding good must be both good in itself and good without qualification. Something is good in itself' when it is good from within, and good without qualification when the expansion of that thing never creates an ethically worse circumstance. Kant at that point contends that those things that are typically thought to be good, for example, intelligence, perseverance and delight, neglect to be either inherently good or good without qualification. Joy, for instance, seems not be good without qualification, as people have a tendency to enjoy watching somebody suffering, this appears to create a situation ethically worse. He infers that there is just a single thing that is genuinely good:

Nothing on the planet—in fact nothing even beyond the world—can be imagined which could be called good without qualification with the exception of a *good will*.

Pragmatic Ethics

Related with the practical people, Charles Sanders Peirce, William James, and particularly John Dewey, pragmatic ethics means that ethical accuracy evolves similarly to scientific information: socially over the course of numerous lifetimes. Therefore, we ought to make preferences among social reforms over endeavours to represent outcomes, individual virtue or obligation (despite the fact that these might be beneficial endeavours, if social change is accommodated).

Role Ethics

Role ethics is an ethical theory in view of roles of family. Not at all like virtue ethics, role ethics isn't individualistic. Morality is something that is obtained from a man's association with their community. The example of this is Confucian ethics. Confucian roles base on the idea of dutiful devotion or xiao, a regard for the members of a family. As indicated by Roger Ames and Henry Rosemont, 'Confucian normativity is defined by living one's family roles to maximum effect'. The determination of morality is done through a man's satisfaction of a role, for example, that of a parent or a child. Confucian roles are not reasonable, and find their origin through the xin, or human feelings.

Ethics in Postmodern Era

The twentieth century witnessed a wonderful advancement and evolution of critical theory, following on prior Marxist Theory endeavours to find people inside bigger structural arrangements of philosophy and activity.

Antihumanists, for example, Louis Althusser and Michel Foucault and structuralists, for example, Roland Barthes objected the potential outcomes of individual organization and the cognizance of the idea of the 'individual' itself. As crucial theory created in the later twentieth century, post-structuralism looked for problematizing human connections to knowledge and 'objective' reality. Jacques Derrida contended that access to meaning and the 'real' was constantly set aside, and tried to exhibit through plan of action to the linguistic domain that 'there is nothing outside context' (tragically, 'il n'y a pas de hors-texte' is frequently wrongly translated as 'there is nothing outside the text'); in the meantime, Jean Baudrillard formulated a theory that signs and images or simulacra mask reality (and in the end the nonattendance of reality itself), especially in the customer world.

Post-structuralism and postmodernism contend that ethics must investigate the complicated and relational states of activities. A straightforward arrangement of thoughts of right and specific acts isn't conceivable. An ethical remainder will always occur that can't be considered or regularly even perceived. Such scholars discover story (or, following Nietzsche and Foucault, family history) to be a useful instrument for comprehending ethics as narrative is constantly about specific lived experiences in all their complications as opposed to the task of a thought or standard to separate and individuated activities. Zygmunt Bauman is of the opinion that Postmodernity is best portrayed as Modernity without illusion. The illusion being the conviction that mankind can undergo improvement by some ethic doctrines. Postmodernity can be found in this light as accepting the messy nature of mankind as unchangeable. David Couzens Hoy expresses that Emmanuel Levinas' works on the face of the Other and Derrida's meditations on the significance of death to ethics are indications of the 'ethical turn' in Continental theory that happened in the 1980s and 90s. According to Hoy, post-critique ethics can be described as the 'obligations that present themselves as necessarily to be fulfilled but are neither forced on one or are enforceable' (2004). Hoy's post-critique model makes use of the word *ethical resistance* whose examples would be a person's protection from consumerism in a retreat to an easier yet maybe harder way of life, or a person's protection from a terminal disease. Hoy depicts Levinas' record as 'not the attempt to use power against itself, or to mobilize sectors of the population to exert their political power; the ethical resistance is instead the resistance of the powerless' (2004). The ethical resistance of the weak others to our ability to apply force over them is in this manner what forces unenforceable commitments on us. The commitments are unenforceable decisively as a result of the other's absence of power. That actions are at once obligatory and simultaneously unenforceable is the thing that places them in the classification of the ethical. Commitments that were implemented would, by the virtue of the power behind them, not be freely embraced and would not be in the domain of the ethical. (2004).

In present day times, the weak may incorporate the unborn, the terminally ill, the aged, the mad and non-human creatures. It is in these areas that ethical activity in Hoy's sense will apply. Until the point when enactment or the state apparatus implements an ethical order that tends to be the reasons of resistance these issues will stay in the moral domain. For instance, should experiments on animals become unlawful in a society, it will never again be a moral issue on Hoy's definition. In this manner one hundred and fifty years back, not having a dark slave in America would have been a moral choice. This later issue has been consumed into the texture of an enforceable social order and is hence no longer a moral issue in Hoy's sense.

APPLIED ETHICS

Applied ethics is a discipline of philosophy that endeavours to apply moral theory to real-life circumstances. The discipline has many areas of specialization, for example, Engineering Ethics, bioethics, geoethics, public administration ethics and business morals.

Specific Questions

The sort of questions that applied ethics addresses include: 'Is getting an abortion immoral'? 'Is euthanasia immoral'? 'Is affirmative action right or wrong'? 'What are human rights, and how do we determine them'? 'Do animals have rights as well'? And 'Do individuals have the right of self-determination'? A more particular query could be: 'If someone else can make better out of his/her life than I can, is it then moral to sacrifice myself for them if needed'? Without these inquiries, there is no visible support on which law, politics and the practice of arbitration are balanced — in reality, no common assumptions of all members—so the capacity to formulate the queries are prior to adjusting rights. In any case, not all inquiries considered in applied ethics relate to public strategy. For instance, making moral judgments associated with inquiries, for example, 'Is lying always wrong'? And, 'If not, when is it permissible'? is preceding any etiquette. Usually people are more comfortable with dichotomies (two contrary components). However, in ethics the issues are usually multifaceted and the best-proposed activities address a wide range of territories simultaneously. In ethical decisions, the appropriate response is never a 'yes or no', 'right or wrong' statement. Many buttons are pushed with the goal that there is overall improvement and not to the advantage of a specific group.

Public Sector Ethics

Public sector ethics is an arrangement of rules that guides public authorities in their support of their constituents, including their decision-making for their constituents. Core to the idea of public sector ethics is the thought that decisions and activities depend on what best serves the interests of common people rather than the official's individual interests (including monetary interests) or self-serving political interests.

MORAL PSYCHOLOGY

Moral psychology is a branch of study that started as a topic in philosophy and that is presently formally considered part of psychology subject. Some make use of the word 'moral psychology' generally to describe the study of the development of morality. However, others tend to make use of the term all the more extensively to incorporate any topics at the convergence of ethics and psychology (and philosophy of mind). Such issues are ones that include the mind and are of high significance to moral issues. Some of the principal topics of the field are moral duty, moral development, moral character (particularly as identified with virtue ethics), altruism, psychological selfishness, moral luck and moral contradiction.

Evolutionary Ethics

Evolutionary ethics is related to methods to deal with ethics (ethical quality) in light of the role of evolution in forming human psychology and conduct. Such methodologies might be situated in the fields of science, for example, evolutionary psychology or socio-biology, with an emphasis on comprehension and clarifying watched moral inclinations and options.

DESCRIPTIVE ETHICS

Descriptive ethics is a value-free approach to deal with ethics, which characterizes it as a social science instead of a mankind. Its examination of ethics doesn't begin with a biased theory, but rather researches observations of real choices made by moral operators in reality. A few philosophers depend on descriptive ethics and choices made and unchallenged by a society or culture to infer classes, which commonly shift by setting. This can prompt situational ethics and situated ethics. These thinkers regularly see aesthetics, manners and arbitration as more basic, permeating 'bottom up' to suggest the presence of, as opposed to explicitly prescribe, theories of significant value or of conduct. The study of descriptive ethics may incorporate examinations of the following:

- Application of ethical codes by different groups. There are some who believe aesthetics itself to be the foundation of ethics—and an individual moral core created through craftsmanship and narrating stories as extremely compelling in one's later ethical choices.
- Informal theories of etiquette that have a tendency to be less rigorous but rather more situational. Some look at behaviour as a basic negative morals, i.e., where would one be able to dodge an awkward truth without fouling up? One eminent promoter of this view is Judith Martin ('Miss Manners'). As per this view, ethics is increasingly an outline of social decisions based on common sense.
- Practices in arbitration and law, for instance, the claim that ethics itself involves adjusting 'right versus right', i.e. putting preferences on two things that are both right, yet that must be traded off with care in every circumstance.
- Observed choices made by common people, without the help or advice of experts, who vote, purchase and choose what is worth valuing. This is a noteworthy concern of sociology, political science and economics matters.

PRINCIPLES ASSOCIATED WITH SOCIOLOGY AND ETHICS

Following a general rule, in any society at any specific time, more humiliation and wretchedness happen as against what a society takes note of, much more than what it concedes and considerably much more than what it makes plans to reduce or correct. This is the main cause behind why justice is always an inaccessible cry, a much ahead and away from all that we perform to ensure human prosperity and honour. However, we can't trust the humiliated unless we at least go after magnificence. Social idea tends to improve the situation for the advantage of mankind when it demonstrates to us how we can decline to act in methodically hurtful ways even while living under conditions that influence the savage treatment of others to appear to be easy but difficult to acknowledge. As comparatively free creatures, there is possibility to decide to care somewhat more. In that case lies our human honour and ethical feelings. The role of critical sociology is to settle on these decisions more available by showing that our present socially worthy methods of thinking and acting depend on historically detached and likely imperfect arrangements of social ethics. Sociologists are realistic utopians who think they know how to set the world right at last to protect that all individuals live everlastingly in peace and concordance. This can be dismissed in light of the fact that the practice of sociology is purely associated with the estimations of the specific culture that encompasses it—those which similarly tie all men and ladies in the group of social scholars. However, sociology is a critical operator in rethinking and re-trying the present world. It is likely that this denies the prevailing establishments of the day the air of safety they frantically need to keep on operating unopposed. What humanism gravely needs to satisfy its mandate is a developed open forum in which individuals can meet up to reproduce their world first in thoughts, without the fear that every one of our expectations and aspirations will be dominated by people's desire to influence a scene out of private lives. It is this forum that our society prominently and shockingly lacks and needs to revive politics, particularly in this time of most prominent need.

The push to give some social choices over other options is the thing that we call 'ethics'. Society is a progressing push towards building the likelihood of some choices happening over others. In this manner, sociology can't however be investigated into the routes in which moral guidelines are built. Societies are frameworks of facilitated decisions and any society you contemplate is however one reality picked among numerous. Society might be 'good' or bad' based on various convictions, yet for each situation it might be superior to anything it is. Being moral means making an acceptance of new choices that might be good or bad, yet it doesn't mean knowing, let alone knowing for sure which are good and which are bad. Being moral refers to being committed to make such new choices under states of intense and difficult vulnerability. To be moral means never to feel good about our choices or about the present condition of our world—this is the anxiety related with being human. Other ethics proves to be useful as a tranquilizer, as a medication to moderate strings of soul. However, getting to be plainly reliant on the same tired old ethics of legitimization may over the long haul wreck our ethical immune framework and deny the self of the little capacity it may have had in looking up to intense moral dilemmas and pursuing the good on its own volition. This anxious and relentless effort to find methods to get rid of the wrongs of our world never runs a straight line since new activities carry with them new shades of evils. History has been more similar to a pendulum that a straight edge ruler. To protect ourselves from the shades of evils executed previously, we walk with our backs moved in the direction of future times, but no sooner do we swing to investigate the future than it progresses towards becoming in its turn a past with ugliness presenting again.

Modernity has frequently been tied in with making the world a 'clean' and unsurprising spot. Ordering the world in such a preplanned design implies making reality tremendously not the same as it right now is by disposing of the elements of reality which are considered to be in charge of the contamination of the specific human conditions. On this way, we may rapidly reach at a decision that a few people should be denied assistance, tossed out or crushed for the sake of a more prominent good and other person's more noteworthy joy. Would we be better or more awful off in the absence of modern ethos? Nobody truly knows we still have to wait for full stock to be made of the atrocities which it might have blinded us to so far. Modernity's forte is the power of its devices. What reckons in the estimations of its success include efficiency, speed and the scale of execution. Its shortcoming is the unclearness and vulnerability about the ends to which these devices might be connected. There is a quickly developing irregularity between the methods we (as individuals from the special lot of mankind) have available to us and the ends which we by and large can concede to as deserving of our attention and endeavour. If you think you know precisely what the good society resembles, at that point any cruelty you commit in its name is advocated and absolved. We can refuse confident demonstrations of mercilessness just when we are uncertain of our shrewdness and concede the likelihood of our own ideological unsteadiness. The horrible disappointment of our utopias has turned people's thoughts away from what a superior life would require to be done in the here and now. It appears that societies manipulate morality instead of producing it. Powerful groups implement the types of ethics that propel their own particular interests. It is this socially produced reality which needs to legitimize itself, to be attempted and judged at the tribunal of ethics.

Freedom might be the characteristic state of mankind, but a large portion of mankind's history has been devoted to repression. Securing minimum necessities for all people is the key to discharging mankind's stunning inventive potential. In this period of 'liquid modernity', the hoops one must hop through to accomplish security are infamous for being liquefied when they are moulded. For too many, only motel beds and bags meant for sleeping are accessible for readjustment. We are told day by day that our conceivable outcomes are boundless and that we require just pick and select those that fit us best. We then get punishment for not able to locate the best of these promoted options, as though what we had been told of their accessibility had some guarantee secured. This myth can't turn out to be valid for more individuals as long as the present-day decoupling of freedom and security holds on. These two values can't be engaged independently. We are urged to trust that security is in disabling facts, in charge of rearing the type of reliance that is considered to constrain human freedom. In any case, acrobatics and tight rope strolling without a [social] security net is a craftsmanship few individuals can master and recipe for debacle for all the rest. The first loss is taking away of security and freedom. Most barbarities in modern times have been the results of a desperate search for security. As more established and self-reproducing orders got fallen under the progressions of innovation, subduing the feelings of trepidation expedited by this unsettling influence was brought to obsessive extremes by means of modernity, which always permitted urgent and damaging reactions. Freedom is the highest among human values but as a matter of first importance it is a destiny. Free creatures, in they are really free, may grasp that destiny or make efforts to escape it, make it into their employment or battle against it: this is additionally the ability to which they owe their freedom. Usually, freedom is by all accounts an ambivalent value as it draws in and repulses simultaneously. It is vexing and alarming to represent one's activities utilizing the words 'I had to' in place of 'I wanted to'. Thus the misleading appeal of 'there is no alternative' philosophies and in addition a lot of marvellous tempting forces of totalitarian regimes. Keep in mind, there is never a lack of offers to clear us of our freedoms.

By itself, the idea of justice has no particular significance. It just bodes well as a challenge against injustice. A fair society is a society which sees itself as not simply enough, which addresses the adequacy of any accomplished level of justice and considers justice to be a step forward. A fair society is one which responds angrily to any instance of injustice and speedily starts rectifying it. While modernity has obscured numerous conventional differentiations between amongst fair and unfair acts, its guarantee is providing so much information on which judgements are based. Today, the idea of injustice or unfairness is more fervently debated as opposed to some other time before. However, quick-paced change in the structure and substance of our lives has made the idea of justice hazier than at any other time. Since justice can just be portrayed as a consistently evolving ideal, the fair society must look for it through continuous contention, not majority rule consensus. Like modernity, justice isn't only an incomplete venture, it is an unfinishable task with just an exceptionally constrained conception of future headings. What is more detectable nowadays is the propensity to overlook or dismiss a portion of the world's most severe and additional contrasts in ways of life (caused both by particularities in the history of mankind and by the current financial administration) as 'facts of nature' about which we unitedly can do nothing but politely acknowledge and comply. This happens while the ethical readiness of the common people is diverted to concentrate on the demands for acknowledgment from small groups and classes of individuals adequately free and sufficiently clever to pick another way of life and demanded its acknowledgment. The expanding worldwide impacts of our local activities require obligation on a scale which has never been confronted before. A global responsibility is warranted by global power. The global obligation has been much slower to arrive even as it gets itself progressively inept in the light of united transnational corporate power. The portion of our pay or gross domestic product we are set to distribute with faraway impoverished individuals who are denied of livelihood partly because of our economy's worldwide search for wealth is sadly modest. Investing resources for the poor people might be an ethically right form of act, however it doesn't any economic meaning under capitalism – less cash in affluent buyers' pockets just raises costs. The issue of discovering approaches to catch up with quickly globalizing financial powers through our local and national organizations of democracy may currently constitute the main challenge to our benchmarks of justice and ethics.

A contemporary feeling among people can be observed even in the most free and prosperous social orders that some of the most fundamental and vital patterns of their lives can't be changed easily and concern with these issues may be an exercise in futility. This is on the grounds that generally the foundations of whatever inconveniences us most and obstructs a noble and ethically fulfilled life are stuck well past the scope of our individual activity. These roots are socially planted and developed and only collectively would they be able to be uncovered and detoxified. Once set in action, individualization is a self-moving and self-increasing phenomenon. One of its first impacts is the undermining of the likelihood to act socially to ask society and after that following this critique with a common methodology. It is the duty of sociology to reconstitute society as the common property and obligation of free people going for a noble life.

With the world undergoing quick changes on a daily basis, levels of uneasiness and segregation keep on rising as people and families try to adapt alone—bringing about extremely contrary results for a few. With the practically overlooked ties of the extended family distant during need and insecurity, many individuals aspire for a social group they can never again find. We can't help missing the missing community but the community we miss can't be found. Most perturbing to the present consumer masses is that it can't be commissioned or made on demand. A genuine community must have the capacity to address genuine crises as a whole, but additionally secure stable and productive lives for its individual members. Like cultures, genuine communities are not as much impositions of fixed identities as they are processes of making sense with and through others.

CONTRIBUTION OF SOCIAL PSYCHOLOGY

Within the setting of psychology, social psychology is the scientific investigation of how individuals' thinking, emotions and behaviours are impacted by the real, envisioned or inferred presence of others. With this definition, *scientific* relates to the empirical method of investigation. The terms *thoughts, feelings* and *behaviours* incorporate all psychological variable that are quantifiable in a human being. The statement that others' presence might be *imagined* or *implied* shows that we are inclined to social impact even when no other individuals are available, for example, when sitting in front of the TV, or following internalized cultural standards. Social psychologists usually describe human conduct because of the connection between mental states and immediate social circumstances. In general, social psychologists have an inclination for laboratory-based observational discoveries. Social psychology theories have a tendency to be specific and focused, as opposed to global and general.

Social psychologists in this manner manage the variables that lead us to act in a particular way in the presence of others, and observe the conditions under which certain conduct/actions and emotions exist. Social psychology talks about the way these sentiments, considerations, convictions, expectations and objectives are built and how such psychological components, in turn, impact our interactions with others. Social psychology is an interdisciplinary space that crosses over any barrier between psychology and sociology. Amid the years quickly following World War II, there was frequent coordinated effort between psychologists and sociologists. In any case, the two disciplines have turned out to be progressively specialized and segregated from each other lately, with sociologists concentrating on 'macro variables' (e.g., social structure) to a considerably more noteworthy degree. However, sociological ways to deal with social psychology remain an imperative partner to psychological research here. Besides the split between psychology and sociology, there has been a somewhat less degree of articulated distinction in emphasis between American social psychologists and European social analysts. Broadly, American specialists generally have concentrated more on the person, while Europeans have given more consideration to group level phenomena.

Ethics

The objective of social psychology is to comprehend cognition and conduct as they normally happen in a social setting, however the very act of watching people can impact and change their conduct. Therefore, numerous social psychology tests use deception to hide or twist certain parts of the study. Deception may incorporate false cover stories, false participants (known as confederates or stooges), false input given to the members, etc. The act of misdirection has been challenged by a few psychologists who view that duplicity under any conditions is untrustworthy, and that other research procedures (e.g. playing a role) ought to be utilized instead. Shockingly, research has demonstrated that role-playing studies don't bring the same outcomes as from the studies of deception causing ambiguity about their validity. Besides deception, experimenters have now and then placed individuals into possibly awkward or humiliating circumstances (e.g. the Milgram experiment and Stanford jail experiment), and this has additionally been criticized for ethical reasons. To secure the rights and well-being of research members, and in the meantime find significant outcomes and knowledge into human conduct, virtually all social psychology research must pass a process of moral review. This is led by an ethics committee or Institutional Review Board at most schools and colleges. This group looks at the proposed research to ensure that no mischief is probably going to be done to the members, and that the advantages of the study exceed any conceivable dangers or discomforts to individuals participating in the study. Moreover, a process of informed consent is regularly used to ensure that volunteers comprehend what will occur in the experiment and comprehend that they are permitted to stop the trial at any moment. A questioning is commonly done at the conclusion of experiment so as to bring forth any deceptions used and for the most part ensure that the members are unharmed by the process. Today, most research in psychology includes no more danger of harm than can be expected from routine psychological testing or ordinary every day chores.

SOCIAL PSYCHOLOGICAL METHODS TO COMPREHEND THE WORLD

Social psychology thinks about how circumstances influence our conduct and the way in which we see ourselves/others. Our patterns of interaction in particular circumstances situate us to each other, our way of life and ideas associated with 'human nature'. Social psychology is not the same as sociology in that it situates for the most part to interaction of small group. Likewise, it tends to utilize lab trial strategies, while sociology utilizes more naturalistic perception, studies/interviews and statistical control of extensive informational data. They need to utilize 'average people' to get deterministic theories.

CONSTRUCTING THE SELF IN A SOCIAL WORLD

- Socially shared convictions (belief systems) enable us to understand the world, however thwart the search for better explanations.
- **Hindsight partiality:** Propensity to overstate the degree in the wake of learning a result that 'I knew it all along'.

- **Impact of self-reference:** Data significant to our conception of our identity (self-schemas) is remembered well.
- **Spotlight impact:** Inclination of individuals to irrationally imagine that others will see their each act and emotion.
- **Looking-glass self:** We utilize what we believe others consider us to assemble impression of ourselves in comparing.
- **Mis-desires, distortion as well as dual attitudes:** Individuals overestimate the connections of joy and acquisitions will bring them, think little of their capacity of psychological immune system to rationalize, discount/excuse emotional injury and our automatic implicit attitudes about a man or thing vary from our reasoned attitudes.
- **Self-Serving Bias:** Propensity to credit accomplishment to individual qualities but inability to uncontrollable externalities.
- **Optimism of unrealistic nature:** Propensity to think we are superior to the normal individual and generally safe to adversity.
- **Wrong consensus:** Propensity to overestimate the quantity of individuals who agree with us on issues of fact/opinion.
- **Wrong uniqueness:** Propensity to serve self-portrait by trusting our abilities and ethical judgments uniquely superior.
- **Self-Esteem Maintenance:** Confronting disappointment, we have a tendency to see others as failing and put down weak others.
- **Self-Handicapping:** The propensity to ensure self-portrait with conduct that make valuable excuses for future failure.

SOCIAL CONVICTIONS AND JUDGMENTS

- **The Fundamental Attribution Partiality:** Propensity to think little of situational impacts and overestimate individual character/disposition/capacities while clarifying the conduct of an individual or a gathering of individuals in a social setting.
- **Confirmation partiality:** We are probably going to utilize blended evidence on any point to strengthen our current convictions on the idea of a phenomenon. The solution for this predisposition is to effectively attempt to clarify why the contrary might be right.
- **Recreating convictions and recollections:** We reproduce the past by joining pieces of memory with our present information, sentiments and desires. Memory is regularly amended to legitimize basic change in convictions that may appear to be hypocritical—states of mind appear to be steady and somewhat pleasant events are more rosy in photographs.
- **Effect of misinformation:** We review subtle details and relationship from memory erroneously, but with extraordinary certainty.
- **Heuristic:** A dependable guideline of mental methodology that enables us to make fast/productive judgments (not all that exact)
- **Availability Heuristic:** Inclination to judge the legitimacy or probability of a contention in light of occurrences of proof that come most promptly to mind.

- **Representativeness Heuristic:** Propensity to assume, against the odds, that somebody or something has a place with a particular group since they by some means show similarity with an ordinary member.
- **Illusory Correlation:** Inclination to see connections between events or conditions where none really exists.
- **Deception of Control:** The possibility that chance events are subject to our impact, and positive results are proofs.
- **Behavioural Confirmation:** A kind of self-fulfilling prophesy whereby individuals' social desires lead them to act in ways that makes others confirm such desires.

CONNECTION BETWEEN ATTITUDES AND BEHAVIOURS

The proof doesn't bolster the idea that changing attitude will undergo change in conduct, in reality, the contrasting pattern is substantially more typical—under which conditions might attitude have the capacity to impact conduct? (significance of policy).

- Limit different effects on assumed attitude convictions and on related conduct.
- Make the attitude particularly important to the activity you are planning to deliver.
- Make attitude as powerful as could be expected under the circumstances.
  - **Cognitive Dissonance:** Pressure emerging when somebody has irregularity between convictions and/or activities.
  - **Insufficient Justification Effect:** Diminishing dissonance by defending conduct from inside when outside legitimization is deficient.
  - **Over Justification Impact:** In the event that you pay somebody to accomplish something they effectively like, they may start to credit that conduct to the cash rather than inherent inner inspirations.

OTHER CONCEPTS ASSOCIATED WITH ASSORTED SOCIAL PSYCHOLOGY

- **Outgroup Homogeneity Effect:** Observation that individuals in groups not quite the same as one's own are fundamentally very similar.
- **Just World Phenomena:** Individuals have a tendency to trust that the world is fair and individuals in turn get what they actually deserve.
- **Displacement:** Redirection of aggression to an objective other than the source of the disappointment; one that is safe and can be accepted.
- **Proximity and Interaction Effect:** Just vicinity and positive conduct towards people brings about affection.
- **Bystander Effect:** Probability that somebody will give assistance to another is decreased when more individuals are around.
- **Adaptation Level Phenomena:** The inclination to adjust to a given level of incitement, then only respond to that level.
- **Depressive Realism:** Inclination of somewhat discouraged individuals to make more precise (less self-serving) attributions.
- **Sleeper Effect:** Late effect of a message; successful later after we overlook early causes behind reducing it.

- **Mere Exposure Effect:** Novel stimuli liked more after one is over and over presented to them; paying little attention to quality.
- **Moral Inclusion/Exclusion:** View of specific individuals as inside/outside our limits of ethics or ethical concern.

CONSIDERING ETHICS IN SOCIOLOGICAL RESEARCH

Ethics are self-regulatory rules for settling on choices and defining professions. By setting up moral codes, professional associations keep up the honesty of the profession, characterize the expected behaviour of individuals, and secure the well-being of subjects and clients. Moreover, ethical codes give direction to the professionals while standing up to moral dilemmas or perplexed circumstances. A case in point is a decision of scientist whether to purposefully trick subjects or inform them about the genuine dangers or objectives of a questionable yet truly necessary experiment. A number of associations, for example, the American Sociological Association, formulated moral doctrines and rules. Most of the present day social scientists submit to their individual associations' moral doctrines. The American Sociological Association's (ASA's) Code of Ethics puts forward the doctrines and moral measures that underlie sociologists' expert obligations and behaviour. These principles and standards ought to be utilized as guidelines while looking at professional activities on daily basis. They constitute normative statements for sociologists and give direction on issues that sociologists may experience in their professional work. The ASA's code of ethics contains five general principles and clarifications:

1. ***Proficient skill***: Sociologists endeavour to keep up the most elevated levels of ability in their work; they perceive the limitations of their proficiency; and they embrace just those assignments for which they are educationally qualified, trained or experienced. They perceive the requirement for continuous education keeping in mind the end goal to remain professionally skilled; and they use the suitable scientific, professional, technical and administrative assets required to guarantee competence in their professional exercises. They counsel with different experts when important for the advantage of their students, research participants and clients.
2. ***Honesty***: Sociologists show honesty, fairness and respect for others in their professional exercises—in research, educating, practice and service. Sociologists don't intentionally act in ways that imperil either their own or others' professional welfare. Sociologists carry out their activities in ways that encourage trust and confidence; they don't purposely make articulations that are false, deceptive or tricky.
3. ***Professional and scientific obligations***: Sociologists stick to the most advanced scientific and professional norms and acknowledge duty regarding their work. Sociologists comprehend that they make a group and show regard for different sociologists even when they differ on theoretical, methodological or individual ways to deal with professional exercises. Sociologists give importance to people's trust in sociology and are always careful about their moral conduct as some other sociologists may compromise on that trust. While attempting always to be collegial, sociologists should never give the desire to be collegial outweigh their common obligation

regarding moral conduct. Whenever suitable, they counsel with partners keeping in mind the end goal to prevent or overcome an unethical behaviour.

4. ***Regard for individuals' rights, pride and variety***: Sociologists regard the rights, dignity and value of every person. They endeavour to remove partiality in their professional exercises, and they don't endure any types of ill-treatment due to age, sex, race, ethnicity, nationality, religion, sexual orientation, inability, health conditions or marital, local or parental status. They are sensitive to cultural, individual and role contrasts in serving, educating and studying groups of individuals with distinctive qualities. In the greater part of their business related exercises, sociologists recognize the privileges of others to hold values, attitudes and opinions that differ from their own.
5. ***Social obligation***: Sociologists know about their professional and scientific duty to the communities and societies in which they live and work. They apply and make public their knowledge for good of common people. When undertaking research, they endeavour to propel the science of sociology and to serve people for public good.

MORALITY

Morality is associated with good and evil. Each human relationship is governed by two important things what in fact exists and what in fact should be. Each group recommends for its individuals certain rule of conduct which should be seen by them. The family recommends that the children should always obey their parents. Married couples should be faithful to each other. The school recommends that the students should show respect to their teachers.

There are certain guidelines of social conduct in every community group which ought to and should be seen by its members. These guidelines and doctrines talk about good and evil as shown to us by inner conscience constitute morality. These guidelines are conceded everywhere by the group. Genuineness, honesty, steadfastness and virtue are part of ethics.

SOCIAL CODE AND MORALITY

A number of writers recognize ethics with social code. Remarkable among them are Durkheim and Sumner who are of the belief that things are good or bad in case they are so considered by society or popular opinion. Durkheim expressed that we don't object to an activity as it is a crime and it is considered so as we oppose it. As indicated by Sumner mores having the authority of fact is the only criterion for the consideration of right and wrong. It implies that there is no good or bad intrinsically but is made so by society and that ethics relies on the feeling or opinion of society. People do make distinction between the breach of moral code and that of social traditions. In the event that one doesn't keep up silence in a social gathering, he would not feel disgraced of a similar kind. The breaking of social code may at times bring fulfilment and respect. Should the specialist come clean to a patient that he won't survive? In such instance, one would be fulfilled in not following the ethical code. The distinguishing proof of the ethics with the society would prompt the conclusion that all the sacrifices of mankind for equity, peace and love are disastrous delusions for which no genuine support can be held. It would prompt circumstances in which neither the ethical nor the social have clear meaning. In such an instance of distinguishing proof, there would be no ethics in society. In spite of the fact that social code manages outer and shallow issues, it doesn't imply that there is no need of it in society and that ethical code alone is fair and adequate. Without it the burden of decision would be unbearable and vagaries of conduct absolutely diverting. The social code bears a strong foundation on which man can deal man. They uncover to him both his similarity to and his solidarity with his colleagues. They carry home to him his enrolment in the group, his present hour of participation in the progression of the past and future of mankind and his unit of commitment to the life of the entire society.

INTEGRITY

Integrity is an idea associated with consistency of activities, values, methods, measures, principles, desires and results. In ethics, integrity is viewed as the honesty and genuineness or exactness of one's activities. Honesty can be viewed as the inverse of hypocrisy, in that integrity sees inner consistency as a quality, and proposes that groups holding evidently clashing values should account for the inconsistency or adjust their convictions. The term 'Integrity' originates from the Latin descriptive word *integer* (entire, complete). In this specific situation, integrity is the internal feeling of 'wholeness' emerging from qualities, for example, honesty and consistency of character. As such, one may judge that others 'have integrity' to the degree that they act as per the values, convictions and principles they claim to hold A value system's abstraction depth and range of applicable interaction may likewise work as important factors in recognizing integrity because of their coinciding or absence of consistency with perception. A value system may evolve with time while holding integrity if the individuals who espouse the values account for and resolve irregularities.

Evaluation of Integrity

One can test a value system's integrity to be either:

- Subjective — by human constructs of responsibility and inner consistency, or
- Objective —by means of the scientific technique.

Where the measures of the test are consensual just to the group being measured, the test is made by a similar value system as the activity being referred to and can come about just in a positive evidence.

Hence, an impartial perspective requires testing measures consensual to anybody expected to rely the outcomes. This counterintuitive procedure is uneventful in a normal way. Honesty can likewise be referred to as having honour, being honest, being dependable and doing the correct things.

EVALUATING INTEGRITY BY MEANS OF THE SCIENTIFIC METHOD

The scientific technique expects that a framework with perfect honesty yields a solitary extrapolation inside its area that one can test against perceived outcomes. Where the aftereffects of the test match the desires of the scientific hypothesis, integrity exists between the cause and end results of the hypothesis by means of its strategies and measures. Where the aftereffects of the test don't match, the correct causal relationship outlined in the hypothesis does not exist. Keeping up an unbiased perspective requires scientific testing to be presentable by autonomous parties. For instance, Newtonian physics, general relativity and quantum mechanics are three different systems, each scientifically demonstrated to have integrity as indicated by their base presumptions and measures, however every one of the three of which deliver distinctive extrapolated values on applying to true world circumstances. None of them claim to be absolute truth, but simply best value systems for specific situations. Newtonian physics shows adequacy for a number of activities on Earth, but delivered a calculation more than ten feet in error on applying to landing on NASA's moon, while calculations of general relativity were correct for that application. General relativity, in any case, inaccurately predicts the aftereffects of an expansive group of scientific trials where quantum mechanics demonstrates its adequacy. Therefore integrity of every one of the three types is pertinent just to its domain.

Integrity Associated with Ethics

In consultations on conduct and ethics, an individual is considered to have the quality of integrity if the person's activities depend on an internally reliable structure of doctrines. These doctrines ought to consistently hold fast to sound sensible axioms or hypotheses. One can depict a man as having moral respectability to the degree that the person's activities, convictions, strategies, measures and doctrines all arise out of a solitary core collection of values. An individual should thus be adaptable and willing to modify these values so as to keep up consistency in case these values are challenged, for example, when a desired test outcome neglects to be compatible with every watched result. Since such adaptability is a type of responsibility, it is viewed as an ethical obligation and a virtue. A person's value system offers a system inside which the individual acts in ways which are steady and anticipated. Integrity can be viewed as the state or state of having such a system, and acting compatibly inside the given structure. The idea of integrity refers to a wholeness, an extensive corpus of convictions, usually denoted as a worldview. This idea of wholeness underlines honesty and credibility, requiring that one performs an activity as per the person's picked perspective. Ayn Rand was of the view that integrity 'does not consist of loyalty to one's subjective whims, but of loyalty to rational principles'.

Subjective Interpretations

In common public usage, individuals some of the time utilize the term 'integrity' in reference to a single 'absolute' ethics instead of in reference to the presumptions of the value system in question. In an absolute reference, the term 'integrity' refers to no meaning between individuals with varying definitions of absolute ethics and turns out to be just an ambiguous declaration of perceived political accuracy or fame, like utilizing terms like 'good' or 'ethical' in a moralistic setting. One can likewise discuss 'integrity' outside of its prescriptive importance, in reference to a man or group of individuals of which the speaker subjectively approves or disapproves. In this manner a favoured individual can be portrayed as 'having integrity', while a foe can be viewed as 'completely lacking in integrity'. Such marking, without measures of free testing, renders the allegation itself unjustifiable and (unexpectedly) others may call the integrity of the statement into question.

TESTS ASSOCIATED WITH PSYCHOLOGICAL/WORK-SELECTION

The processes called as 'integrity tests' or (more fiercely) as 'honesty tests' plan to recognize forthcoming employees who may hide perceived negative or derogatory parts of their past, for example, a criminal conviction, psychiatric treatment or misuse of drugs. Distinguishing unacceptable applicants can spare the business from issues that may otherwise emerge amid their term of work.

Other Integrities

Subjects and fields with an inclination for integrity incorporate philosophy of activity, rationality of pharmaceutical products, arithmetic, the brain, cognition, consciousness, materials science, structural engineering as well as political issues. Famous psychology distinguishes individual integrity, integrity in profession, creative honesty and scholarly integrity. The idea of integrity may likewise include in business settings beyond the issues of employee/boss honesty and moral conduct, remarkably in advertising or marking settings. The 'integrity' of a brand is viewed by some as a desired result for organizations trying to keep up a predictable, unambiguous position in the psyche of their group of people. This respectability of brand incorporates reliable informing and usually incorporates utilizing an arrangement of graphics standards to keep up visual integrity in the field of marketing communications. Another utilization of the word, 'integrity' is found in Michael Jensen's and Werner Erhard's works in their scholarly paper, 'Integrity: A Positive Model that Incorporates the Normative Phenomenon of Morality, Ethics, and Legality'. In this paper, the authors investigate another model of integrity as the condition of being complete and whole, unbroken, unimpaired, stable and in a condition of perfection. They set another model of integrity that gives access to expanded execution to people, groups, associations and communities. Their model 'reveals the causal link between integrity and increased performance, quality of life, and value-creation for all entities, and provides access to that causal link'. Electronic signs are believed to possess integrity in case of no corruption of data between one area and another, for example, from a disk drive to a display of PC. Such integrity is a key doctrine of data affirmation. Corrupted data cannot be trusted, yet uncorrupted data is of some use.

FAIRNESS

Unprejudiced nature (additionally called fairness or reasonableness) is a doctrine of justice ensuring that decisions have to be based on objective criteria, as opposed to on the premise of partiality, preference or leaning towards the advantage to one individual over another for uncalled reasons.

CONCEPTS OF RELIGION

Buddhism

- Enlightenment has seven components: clear memory, the correct examination of things, vitality and sensitivity, serenity, unbiasedness and a disposition for focus. The last four factors include the 'four sublime states,' and are accepted to be pre-condition for avoiding cyclic presence (Occhiogrosso 96).

Christianity

- 'For there is no respect of persons with God'. —Romans 2:11, KJV.
- 'But he that doeth wrong shall receive for the wrong which he hath done: and there is no respect of persons'. —Colossians 3:25, KJV'.
- 'My dear brothers and sisters, how can you claim that you have faith in our glorious Lord Jesus Christ if you favour some people more than others? For instance, suppose someone comes into your meeting dressed in fancy clothes and expensive jewellery, and another comes in who is poor and dressed in shabby clothes. If you give special attention and a good seat to the rich person, but you say to the poor one, 'You can stand over there, or else sit on the floor'—well, doesn't this bias show that you are governed by false intentions? Hear me out, dear brothers and sisters. Hasn't God picked the poor in this world to be rich in faith? Aren't they the ones who will acquire the Kingdom he guaranteed to the individuals who love him? Yet you insult the poor man! Is it safe to say that it isn't the wealthy who mistreat you and drag you into court? Aren't they the ones who defame Jesus Christ, whose respectable name you bear? Truly for sure, it is great when you really comply with our Lord's regal summon found in the sacred writings: "Love your neighbour as yourself". But in the event that you give careful consideration to the rich, you are committing a sin, for you are liable of overstepping that law'. — Epistle of James 2:1-9, NLT.
- 'But the wisdom that comes from heaven is first of all pure; then peace-loving, considerate, submissive, full of mercy and good fruit, impartial and sincere'.—Epistle of James 3:17, NIV.

Hinduism

'Truth, O Bharata, as it exists in all the world, is of thirteen kinds. The forms that Truth assumes are impartiality, self-control, forgiveness, modesty, endurance, goodness, renunciation, contemplation, dignity, fortitude, compassion and abstention from injury'.—Truth, The Mahabharata, Santi Parva, Section CLXII.

Islam

- 'The Absolute Criterion of Justice and Equity, was sent down by Allah so that people may conduct themselves with equity'. Quran, 52:25.
- 'Establish weight with justice and fall not short in the balance. Maintain the balance with fairness and justice, without differentiating anybody's rights and obligations'. Quran 55:9.

Judaism

- 'You shall do no injustice in court. You shall not be partial to the poor or defer to the great, but in righteousness shall you judge your neighbour'. —Leviticus 19:15, English Standard Version.
- 'You shall not be partial in judgment. You shall hear the small and the great alike'. —Deuteronomy 1:17, ESV.
- 'These things also belong to the wise. It is not good to have respect of persons in judgment'. —Book of Proverbs 24:23, KJV.

NONPARTISAN

In political science, nonpartisan signifies an election, occasion, association or individual in which there is no formally announced relationship with a political party. The Merriam-Webster lexicon's meaning of 'nonpartisan' is:

'Not partisan; free from party affiliation, bias, or designation'.

A number of associations guaranteeing to be unprejudiced are really such; others, especially in the USA, are ostensibly neutral (for reasons of law or public recognition) yet in reality nearly take after the policies of a political party. While the meaning of the word 'partisan' incorporates followers of a party, cause, individual, and so on., in many instances nonpartisan denotes a particular reference to political party associations as opposed to being the strict antonym of 'partisan', and an association depicted as unprejudiced can have numerous emphatically disputable policies. In the Republic of India, the Jaago Re! One Billion Votes crusade is a non-factional battle started by Tata Tea, and Janaagraha to urge nationals to vote in the Indian general election, 2009.

No Party Democracy

Nonpartisan democracy system (additionally no-party democracy) is an arrangement of representative government or association to such an extent that all universal and periodic elections happen without reference to political parties. On some occasion, electioneering and even talking about candidates might be disheartened, so as not to bias others' decisions or make a contentious environment. Nonpartisan democratic rule may have indirect elections whereby an electorate are picked who thusly vote in favour of the representative(s). (This is on some occasions called as a 2-tier election, for example, an electoral college). The framework can work with a first past the post electoral system but is incompatible with (divided) proportional representation systems apart from Single Transferable Vote.

A nonpartisan framework varies from a single party system in that the governing group in a solitary party framework distinguishes itself as a party, where membership may give benefits not accessible to those who are not members. One party system regularly requires government authorities to be individuals from the party, includes a complicated hierarchy of party as a key organization of government, compels people to accept a partisan ideology, and may implement its control over the administration by making every other parties unlawful. Individuals from a nonpartisan government may not share any philosophies (however in voluntary associations, they obviously may). Different socialist countries, for example, China or Cuba are single-party countries despite the fact that the Members of Parliament are not chosen as the candidates of the party. A direct democracy system can be viewed as nonpartisan since people vote on laws themselves as opposed to choosing representatives. Direct democracy can be partisan, in any case, if groups are given rights or privileges that non-members don't have.

In numerous countries, the head of state is nonpartisan, regardless of the possibility that the PM and parliament are picked in partisan elections. The heads of state are relied upon to stay impartial with respect to partisan politics. There are two essential forms of nonpartisan governments – de facto and de jure. De facto nonpartisan governments are such systems where no laws inhibit the making of political parties, however no parties exist. The vast majority of the de facto nonpartisan governments have very small representation of the population as seen in Niue, Tuvalu and Palau. On the contrary, governments that outlaw political parties but do have decisions are referred to as de jure nonpartisan systems. A number of de jure nonpartisan national governments are Persian Gulf states, for example, Oman and Kuwait. The law making bodies in these Gulf state nonpartisan governments ordinarily have only advisory capacity (i.e. They may give comments on laws initiated by the executive branch, however can't make real laws themselves.), but are partially or totally chosen by subjects. Unless there are legitimate confinements on political parties, groups inside nonpartisan governments may develop into political parties. The United States of America at first did not have enfranchised political parties, but rather these advanced not long after independence.

Protecting Non-Partisanship in the Public Service

Non-partisanship is a fundamental component of both a professional public service and capable democratic government. A non-partisan public service is one where appointments depend on merit and free of political impact and where public servants carry out their obligations, and are believed to carry out their obligations, in a politically impartial way. I In Canada, the Public Service Commission (PSC) has ensured the non-partisanship of people in general administration since 1908, when the merit principle was first embraced with an end goal to wipe out political support. In a 1991 historic case of Supreme Court of Canada perceived the need to adjust the significance of the political unbiasedness of people in general administration and the constitutional right of all Canadians, including public servants, to take part in political exercises. The PSC has a unique part to play in relation to this. It secures the non-partisanship of the public service through emphasizing on three areas: The reflection of this was seen in the new *Public Service Employment Act* (2003). Maintaining the non-partisan character of people in general administration is the obligation of every single public servant, including deputy heads and senior managers. The PSC has an extraordinary part to play in such cases. It protects the non-partisanship of the public service through an attention on three regions:

- Non-partisanship Associated with staffing; and Non-partisanship in staffing; and
- Political activities by public servants. Political exercises by public servants.

Non-partisanship is firmly identified with the democratic and professional values of people in general administration, which are addressed in the Values and Ethics Code for the Public Sector.

Non-Partisanship Associated with Staffing

As the guardian of merit and non-partisanship in the government public administration, the Public Service Commission (PSC) is in charge of guaranteeing that staffing choices are free of political impact. The PSC completes this part by exploring appointment processes (internal or external) where there is a reason to trust that an appointment or proposed appointment was free from political impact. Thorough checks are directed in light of the standards of procedural decency. In situations where allegations or concerns are established, restorative activities might be justified, up to and including the denial of the appointment.

OBJECTIVITY

Objectivity is a focal philosophical idea, identified with reality and truth, which has been differently characterized by sources. By and large, objectivity implies the state or nature of being genuine even outside of a subject's individual sentiments, imaginings or understandings. A proposition is by and large thought to be dispassionately valid (to have objective truth) when its truth conditions are met and are 'mind-independent'—that is, existing unreservedly or freely from a mind (from the considerations, sentiments, thoughts and so on of a sentient subject). In a more vivid explanation of the term, objectivity denotes the capacity to judge fairly, without partiality or outside impact, which additionally happen as phenomenological way. 'Objectivism' is a word that depicts a branch of philosophy that finds its origin in the early part of nineteenth century. Gottlob Frege was the first to apply it, when he elucidated an epistemological and metaphysical theory against that of Immanuel Kant. Kant's rationalism endeavoured to accommodate the disappointments he saw in philosophical realism. Much stronger versions of this claim hold that there is just a single right portrayal of this reality. In case this is right that reality is not dependent on mind, at that point reality may incorporate items that are unknown to consciousness and accordingly may incorporate objects not the subject of intentionality. Objectivity in referring needs a meaning of truth. As per metaphysical objectivists, an object may honestly be said to have either this or that attribute, as in the statement 'This question exists', while the statement 'This object is true' or 'false' is good for nothing. For them, just propositions are known to have truth values. The words 'objectivity' and 'objectivism' are not identical, with objectivism being an ontological theory that consists of a commitment to the objectivity of objects.

Plato's realism was a type of metaphysical objectivism, believes that the Ideas exist unbiasedly and autonomously. Berkeley's empiricist optimism, on the contrary, could be known as a subjectivism: he opined that things just exist to the degree that they are experienced. The two theories claim techniques of objectivity. The definition of objectivity as per Plato can be found in his epistemology, which takes as a model mathematics, and his metaphysics, where knowledge of the ontological status of objects and thoughts is impervious to change. Plato believed information of geometry as a condition of philosophical learning, both being associated with eternal truths. Plato's resistance between objective knowledge and *doxa* (feelings) would form the basis for later philosophies expectation on settling the issue of reality, learning and human presence. Individual beliefs have a place with the changing sphere of the sensible, opposed to a settled and universal ethereal domain which is mutually comprehensible. Where Plato recognizes what and how we know things (epistemology) and their ontological status as things (metaphysics), subjectivism, for example, Berkeley's and a mind depending on knowledge and reality fails to distinguish between what one knows and what is to be known, or in the least describes the distinction in a superficial way. In Platonic terms, a criticism of subjectivism is that it is hard to make distinction between knowledge, doxa and subjective knowledge (genuine conviction), distinction which Plato puts forth. The significance of perception in assessing and understanding objective reality is debated. Pragmatists contend that perception is important in straightforwardly observing target reality, while instrumentalists believe that perception isn't really of use in specifically observing objective reality, however is helpful in deciphering and anticipating reality. The ideas that envelop these thoughts are significant in the philosophy of science.

OBJECTIVITY ASSOCIATED WITH ETHICS

Ethical Subjectivism

The word 'ethical subjectivism' consists of two different theories in ethics. As indicated by cognitive versions of ethical subjectivism, reality of moral statements relies on individuals' values, attitudes, emotions or convictions. A few types of cognitivist ethical subjectivism can be considered as types of realism, others are types of anti-realism. David Hume put forth the concept of cognitive ethical subjectivism. The standard understanding of his theory says that a characteristic of character considers an ethical virtue when it incites a feeling of approbation in a thoughtful, educated and rational human observer. So also, as per Roderick Firth's ideal observer theory, correct acts are those that an unbiased, rational observer would endorse of. As per William James, another ethical subjectivist, an end is good (to or for a man) just in the situation it is wanted by that individual. As per non-intellectual forms of ethical subjectivism, for example, emotivism, prescriptivism and expressivism, ethical explanations can't be valid or false, at all: in fact, they are articulations of individual sentiments or commands. For instance, on A. J. Ayer's emotivism, the statement, 'Murder is wrong' is having similar significance as that of the meaning to the emotive, 'Murder, Boo'!

Ethical Objectivism

As indicated by the ethical objectivist, reality or deception of typical moral judgments does not rely on the convictions or sentiments of any individual or gathering of people. As per this view ethical propositions closely resemble propositions associated with chemistry, biology or history: they depict (or fail to portray) a reality independent of mind. When they portray it precisely, they are valid—regardless of what anybody trusts, expects, desires or perceives. When they are unsuccessful to portray this mind-independent moral reality, they are false—regardless of what anybody trusts, expects, desires or experiences. There are numerous variants of ethical objectivism, including different religious perspectives of morality, Platonistic intuitionism, Kantianism, utilitarianism, and certain types of ethical egoism and contractualism. Note that Platonists characterize ethical objectivism in a considerably more restricted way, with the goal that it requires the presence of intrinsic value. Thusly, they dismiss the possibility that contractualists or egoists could be ethical objectivists. Objectivism thusly gives importance to the origin of the frame of reference and in that capacity considers any arbitrary frame of reference to be eventually a type of ethical subjectivism by a transitive property, even when the frame by chance harmonizes with reality and can be utilized for measurements.

APTITUDE

An aptitude is a part of a competency to do a specific type of work at a specific level, which can likewise be considered 'talent'. Aptitudes might occur in two forms: physical or mental. It isn't knowledge, understanding, learned or acquired capacities (skills) or attitude. Its intrinsic idea is opposed to accomplishment, which denotes knowledge or capacity that is acquired.

Intelligence

Aptitude and intelligence quotient are connected, and in some courses inverse perspectives of human mental capacity. Though intelligence quotient considers intelligence to be a solitary quantifiable characteristic influencing all mental capacity, aptitude denotes one of various qualities which can be autonomous of each other, for example, aptitude for military flight, air traffic regulation or PC programming. This is more like the theory of various intelligences. Concerning a solitary quantifiable characteristic influencing all mental capacity, investigation of any group of intelligence test scores will almost dependably indicate them to be profoundly associated. The U.S. Department of Labour's General Learning Ability, for example, is dictated by consolidating Verbal, Numerical and Spatial aptitude subtests. In a particular individual, some are low and others high. With regards to an aptitude test, the 'high' and 'low' scores are normally not far separated, on the grounds that all capacity test scores have a tendency to be related. The application of aptitude is better done intra-independently to figure out what tasks a particular individual is more skilled at doing. The differences of inter-individual aptitude are usually not extremely huge because of IQ contrasts. Obviously this considers people have not as of now been pre-screened for aptitude through some different procedure, for example, SAT scores, GRE scores or completing medical school.

Combined Aptitude and Knowledge Tests

Tests that evaluate learned abilities or information are very often called accomplishment tests. However, certain tests can survey the two kinds of constructs. A case that inclines both ways is the Armed Services Vocational Aptitude Battery (ASVAB), which is given to recruits entering the military of the United States. Another is the SAT, which is composed to evaluate aptitude for college in the United States, but has accomplishment components. For instance, it tests numerical thinking, which depends both on intrinsic numerical capacity and arithmetic knowledge gained. Aptitude tests can usually be classified as per the kind of cognitive capacity they measure:

1. ***Fluid intelligence***: The capacity to think and reason conceptually, successfully take care of issues and think strategically. It's all the more generally known as 'street smarts' or the capacity to 'quickly think on your feet'. Cases of what employers can gain from your fluid intelligence about your suitability for the role for which you are applying.
2. ***Crystallized intelligence***: The capacity to gain from the experiences of the past and pertinent learning, and applying this learning to situations associated with work. Work circumstances that require crystallized intelligence incorporate delivering and analysing composed reports, grasping work guidelines, utilizing numbers as an apparatus to make right decisions and so on.

Aptitude and Basic Values for Civil Service

Core Values *Include Self-belief*

Core values are attributes or qualities that you consider not simply beneficial, they denote a person's or association's most astounding needs, profoundly held convictions, and core, principal driving forces. Core values characterize what your association accepts and how you need your association resounding with and appealing to representatives and the outside world. Core values are likewise called guiding doctrines because they make a strong core of your identity, what your beliefs are and what you think about your identity and desire to keep moving ahead. Values create the base for everything that occurs in your work environment. The principal values of the employees in your working environment, alongside their experiences, upbringings, etc. combine together to shape your corporate culture. The main values of the founder of an association penetrate the working environment. His or her primary values are effective shapers of the association's way of life. The main values of your senior leaders are likewise significant in the advancement of your way of life. The reason? These executive leaders have a great deal of power in your association to set the course and define day by day activities. The executive leaders and the manager who answer to them set the tone in building up the quality of the workplace for individuals. This work environment mirrors the main values of all employees, however the primary values of executive leaders who walk their discussion, are overreaching. Furthermore, your leaders and managers have chosen employees who they believe have harmonious primary values and fit your work environment culture.

Your objective, when you recognize the primary values of your association, is to distinguish the key values, not a laundry list of cookie cutter values that you replicated off of another association's list of primary values. An association's workers would experience serious difficulties living any more than 10–12 key values (at a maximum). Primary values are made approachable by transforming them into value proclamations. Value propositions are grounded in values and describe how individuals need to act with each other in the association. They are explanations about how the association will give importance to customers, suppliers as well as the internal community. Value proclamations portray activities that are the living institution of the basic primary values held by most people in an association.

ATTITUDE

An attitude is an outflow of favour or disapproval towards a man, place, thing or occasion (the attitude object). Noticeable psychologist Gordon Allport once portrayed attitudes 'the most distinctive and indispensable concept in contemporary social psychology'. Attitude can be created based on a man's past and present. In layman's words, attitude may denote the distinct idea of mood, or be particularly synonymous with teenage rebellion. An attitude can be characterized as a constructive or antagonistic assessment of individuals, objects, occasion, actions, thoughts or pretty much anything in your environment, however discussions are still on about its exact definitions. Eagly and Chaiken, for instance, characterize an attitude 'a psychological tendency that is expressed by evaluating a particular entity with some degree of favour or disfavour'. Though it is now and then usual to characterize an attitude as influence towards an object, influence (i.e., discrete feelings or overall excitement) is by and large comprehended to be distinct from attitude as a measure of favourability. This meaning of attitude takes into account one's assessment of an attitude object to vary from to a great degree of antagonistic to a great degree of constructive, yet in addition concedes that individuals can likewise be at odds or undecided towards an object implying that they may at various times express both positive and negative attitude towards a similar object. This has prompted some discussion of whether individual can possess different attitudes towards a similar object. Regardless of whether attitudes are explicit (i.e. intentionally shaped) versus implicit (i.e. subconscious) has been a theme of impressive research. Research on implicit attitudes, which are by and large unacknowledged or outside of awareness, utilizes advanced strategies that involve individuals' reaction times to stimuli to demonstrate that implicit attitudes exist (probably in tandem with explicit attitudes of the same object). Implicit and explicit attitudes appear to influence individuals' conduct, though in multiple ways. They tend not to be firmly connected with each other, in spite of the fact that in some instances they are. The connection between them is ineffectively comprehended.

Definition by Jung

Attitude refers to one of Jung's 57 definitions in Chapter XI of *Psychological Types*. Jung's meaning of attitude is a 'readiness of the psyche to act or react in a certain way'.

Attitudes very often come in pairs, one conscious and the other unconscious. Within this broad definition Jung defines several attitudes. The main (but not only) attitude dualities that Jung defines are the following. Attitudes all the time come in sets, one conscious and the other unconscious. Within this broad range of definition, Jung characterizes a number of attitudes. The primary (yet not just) attitude dualities that Jung defines are as follows:

- **Consciousness as well as the unconscious:** The "presence of two attitudes is extremely frequent, one conscious and the other unconscious. This means that consciousness has a constellation of contents different from that of the unconscious, a duality particularly evident in neurosis".
- **Extraversion as well as introversion:** This pair is so basic to Jung's theory of types that he regarded them the 'attitude-types'.
- **Rational as well as irrational attitudes:** 'I conceive reason as an attitude'.
- The rational attitude can be subdivided into the thinking and perceiving psychological functions, each with its attitude.
- The unreasonable attitude can be subdivided into the detecting and instinctive psychological capacities, each with its attitude. 'There is thus a typical thinking, feeling, sensation, and intuitive attitude.
- **Individual as well as social attitudes:** A considerable lot of the last are 'isms'.

Besides, Jung talks about the abstract attitude. 'When I take an abstract attitude...' Abstraction is differentiated with creationism. 'CREATIONISM. By this I mean a peculiarity of thinking and feeling which is the antithesis of abstraction'. For example: 'I hate his attitude for being Sarcastic'.

Measuring Attitudes

Numerous measurements and scales are utilized to evaluate attitudes. Attitudes can be hard to quantify on the grounds that measurement is arbitrary, which means individuals need to give attitudes a scale to measure it against, and attitudes are at last a speculative construct that can't be observed in a direct way. Following the explicit-implicit dichotomy, attitudes can be inspected by means of direct and indirect methods. Explicit Measurements have a tendency to depend on self-reports or easily watched behaviours. These have a tendency to include bipolar scales (e.g., good-bad, favourable-unfavourable, support-oppose and so on). Explicit measures can likewise be utilized by measuring the direct attribution of qualities to designate groups, for example, 'I feel that Baptists are....'? or 'I think that men are...'? Liker scales and other self-reports are usually in application. Implicit Measurements – Implicit measures are not intentionally directed and are thought to be automatic, which may make implicit measures more substantial and dependable than explicit measures, (for example, self-reports). For instance, individuals can be propelled with the end goal that they discover it socially desirable to seem to have certain attitudes. An instance of this is that individuals can hold implicit biased attitudes, but express explicit attitudes that report little bias. Implicit measures help represent these circumstances and take a look at attitudes that a man may not know about or wish to show. Implicit measures in this manner as a rule depend on an indirect measure of attitude.

For instance, the Implicit Association Test (IAT) analyses the strength between the target concept and an attribute component by considering the inactivity in which a man can look at two reaction keys when each has two implications. With little time to cautiously inspect what the member is doing, they react as indicated by interior keys. This priming can indicate attitudes the individual has about a specific object.

Structure of Attitude

The classic, tripartite view put forth by William J. McGuire is that an attitude contains cognitive, affective and behavioural aspects. Observational research, however, fails to assist with clear differentiation between thoughts, feelings and behavioural intents related with a specific attitude. A criticism of the tripartite perspective of attitudes is that it requires intellectual, full of feeling and behavioural relationship of an attitude to be steady, however this might be farfetched. Consequently, a few perspectives of the structure of attitude see the cognitive and behavioural aspects as subsidiary of effect or influence and conduct as being derivatives of inherent convictions. In spite of open deliberation about the specific structure of attitudes, there is substantial proof that attitudes reflect more than assessments of a specific object that fluctuate from positive to negative. Attitudes likewise have different qualities, for example, significance, conviction or accessibility (measures of the strength of attitude) and related learning. There is additionally significant enthusiasm in inter-attitudinal structure, which links distinctive attitudes to one other and to all the more basic psychological structures like values or belief system.

Attitude Function

Another great perspective of attitudes is that they serve specific functions for people. That is, specialists have attempted to comprehend why people hold specific attitudes or why they hold attitudes in general by examining how attitudes influence people who hold them. Daniel Katz, for instance, writes that attitudes can serve 'instrumental, adjustive or utilitarian', 'ego-defensive,' 'value-expressive' or 'knowledge' functions. The functional perspective of attitudes recommends that with the goal for attitudes to change (e.g. through influence), appeals must be made to the function(s) that a specific attitude serves for the person. For instance, the 'ego-defensive' function may be utilized to impact the racially biased attitudes of a person who considers themself to be receptive and tolerant. By speaking to that person's picture of themselves as tolerant and liberal, it might be conceivable to change their biased attitudes to be more reliable with their self-idea. Correspondingly, a persuasive message that puts self-image in danger is substantially more prone to be rejected. Daniel Katz categorized attitudes into four distinct groups keeping in view their functions.

1. ***Utilitarian***: Gives us general approach or evasion propensities.
2. ***Knowledge***: Enable individuals to sort out and decipher fresh inputs or information.
3. ***Ego-guarding***: Attitudes can enable individuals to secure their morale.
4. ***Value-expressive***: Used to express focal values or convictions.

Utilitarian People receive attitudes that are fulfilling and that assist them stay away from punishment. As such any attitude that is embraced in a man's own particular self-interest is viewed to serve a utilitarian function. Think as if you have a condo, individuals with condos pay property cess and accordingly you would prefer not to pay more duties. In the event that those variables prompt your attitude that 'Increases in property taxes are bad,' your attitude is serving a utilitarian function.

Formation of Attitude

As indicated by Doob (1947), learning can create the majority of the attitudes we possess. Studying the formation of attitude is referred to as the study of how individuals make assessments of people, spots or things. Theories of traditional conditioning, instrumental conditioning and social learning primarily form the attitude. Not at all like personality, attitudes are believed to change as a component of experience. What's more, presentation to the 'attitude' objects may affect how a man creates his or her attitude. This idea was viewed as the 'Mere-Exposure Effect'. Robert Zajonc demonstrated that individuals will probably have an uplifting attitude on 'attitude objects' if they were presented to it every now and then than if they were most certainly not. Only repeated introduction of the person to a stimulus is an adequate condition for the upgradation of his attitude towards it. In 1993, Tesser has contended that hereditary factors may influence attitudes – however notes that they may do so in an indirect manner. For instance, consistency theories, which infer that we should be steady in our convictions and values. Similarly as with a heritability, to decide whether a specific attribute has a premise in our genes, twin examinations are carried out. The most popular case of such a theory is reduction theory, related with Leon Festinger, which clarifies that when the parts of an attitude (counting conviction and conduct) are inconsistent an individual may adjust one to match the other (for instance, changing a conviction to match a conduct). Other theories incorporate balance theory, initially put forth by Heider (1958), and the self- perception theory, initially put forth by Daryl Bem.

Change in Attitude

Attitudes can be altered through influence and a significant area of investigation on attitude change concentrates on reactions to communication. Empirical investigation into the components that can influence the persuasiveness of a message include the following:

1. *Target Characteristics*: These are attributes that describe the individual who obtains and processes a message. One such quality is intelligence—it appears that more judicious individual are less effortlessly influenced by one-sided messages. Another variable that has been analysed in this classification is self-esteem. While it is occasionally believed that those having superior self-esteem are less easily influenced, there is some proof that the association between self-esteem and persuasibility is in reality curvilinear, with individuals of mild self-esteem being more easily influenced than both those of high and low self-esteem levels (Rhodes & Woods, 1992). The mindset and temperament of the target also plays a part in this process.

2. *Source Characteristics*: The chief source features are know-how, credibility and interpersonal appeal or attractiveness. The trustworthiness of an anticipated message has been noticed to be a crucial variable here; if one go through a report about health and considers it came from a professional medical journal, one may be more effortlessly influenced than if one trusts it to be from a popular newspaper. Few psychologists have argued whether this is a long-lasting impact and Hovland and Weiss (1951) discovered the effect of conveying individuals that a message coming from a trustworthy source vanished after several weeks (the so-called "sleeper effect"). The existence of a sleeper effect is disputable. Perceived intelligence is that if people are made aware of the source of a message before listening to it, there is less probability of a sleeper effect than if they are conveyed a message and then conveyed its source.
3. *Message Characteristics*: The character of the message plays a part in persuasion. Occasionally offering both sides of a narrative is of use to enable change of attitudes. When individuals are not inspired to process the message, merely the number of arguments provided in a persuasive message will affect attitude change, such that a larger number of contentions will cause greater attitude change.
4. *Cognitive Routes*: A message can influence a person's cognitive analysis to enable change in an attitude. In the *central route* to persuasion, the person is provided with the data and inspired to analyse the data and reach an attitude-changing conclusion. In the *peripheral route* to attitude change, the person is persuaded to not give attention to the content but to the source. This is generally witnessed in contemporary advertisements that highlight celebrities. In various cases, physician, doctors or experts are employed for promoting the change in attitude. In other instances, film stars are employed for their appeal.

Emotion and Attitude Change

Emotion is a basic component in persuasion, social impact, and attitude change. Much of attitude exploration underscored the significance of emotive or emotion components. Emotion goes together with the cognitive process, or the way we contemplate, about a problem or situation. Emotional appeals are generally obtained in commercials, health campaigns and political messages. Latest instances include no-smoking health drives and political campaign commercials highlighting the fear of terrorism. Attitudes and attitude objects are works of cognitive, affective and conative elements. Attitudes are segment of the associative networks of human brain, the spider-like structures inhabiting in long term memory that comprises affective and cognitive nodes. By triggering an affective or emotion node, attitude change is likely to take place, though affective and cognitive elements have a tendency to be interlinked. In fundamentally affective networks, it is more challenging to present cognitive counterarguments in opposition to persuasion and attitude change. Affective forecasting, also called as intuition or the prediction of emotion, also influences attitude change. Investigations proposes that envisaging emotions is a crucial element of decision making together with the cognitive processes. How we think about outcome result may supersede solely cognitive rationales. In connection with the research methodology, the task for scholars is measuring emotion and consequent effects on attitude. Since we cannot check inside the brain, different models and measurement instruments have been developed to access emotion and attitude data. Measures may involve the utilization of physiological signals such as facial expressions, vocal variations, and different body rate measures. For example, fear is linked with raised eyebrows, accelerated heartbeat and enhanced body strain (Dillard, 1994). Various processes involve concept or network mapping, and utilizing primes or word signals in the era.

Attitude-Behaviour Relationship

The impacts of attitudes on behaviours signifies an important investigation initiative within psychology. Two hypothetical methodologies have dictated this investigation: the theory of reasoned action and, its theoretical descendant, the theory of planned behaviour, both of which are associated with Icek Ajzen. Both of these theories describe the link between attitude and behaviour as a contemplative process, with a person actively opting to involve in an attitude-related behaviour. A substituting model, called MODE for "Motivation and Opportunity as Determinants" was suggested by Russell H. Fazio, which concentrates on motivations and scope for contemplative attitude-related behaviour to occur. MODE is a Dual process theory that anticipates that contemplative attitude-behaviour linkages—similar to those modelled by the theory of planned behaviour—only happen when people have impetus to reveal upon their own attitudes. The theory of reasoned action (TRA) is a model for the forecast of behavioural objective, encompassing forecast of attitude and behaviour. The consequent parting of behavioural intention from behaviour provides clarification of constraining components on attitudinal affect (Ajzen, 1980). The Theory of Reasoned Action was proposed by Martin Fishbein and Icek Ajzen (1975, 1980), inferred from earlier investigation that commenced as the theory of attitude, which resulted in the investigation of attitude and behaviour. The hypothesis was "born largely out of frustration with traditional attitude-behaviour research, much of which found weak correlations between attitude measures and performance of volitional behaviours" (Hale, Householder & Greene, 2003).

The theory of planned behaviour was suggested by Icek Ajzen in 1985 through his article "From intentions to actions: A theory of planned behaviour." The theory was built from the theory of reasoned action, which was suggested by Martin Fishbein along with Icek Ajzen in 1975. The theory of reasoned action was successively established in different theories of attitude, for example, learning theories, expectancy-value theories, consistency theories and attribution theory. As per the theory of reasoned action, in case of individuals who evaluate the proposed conduct as positive (attitude), and think that their significant others want them to execute the conduct (subjective norm), this leads to a higher level of intention (motivation) and there are more chances of them doing so. A high relationship of attitudes and subjective norms to behavioural objective, and consequently to behaviour, has been substantiated in many investigations.

An opposing contention against the high correlation between behavioural intention and actual behaviour has also been propositioned, as the consequences of some investigations demonstrate that, because of circumstantial restrictions, behavioural objective does not always result in actual conduct. Specifically, since behavioural objective cannot be the sole determinant of behaviour where a person's influence over the conduct is incomplete, Ajzen proposed the theory of planned behaviour by including a fresh component, "perceived behavioural control." Hence, he expanded the theory of reasoned action to deal with non-volitional behaviours for forecasting behavioural intention and actual behaviour.

WAY TO TACKLE ISSUES CONCERNED WITH ATTITUDE, INTEGRITY AND PROBITY IN PUBLIC LIFE

Attribute of Attitude

The analysis of attitudes has been at the cutting edge of social psychology for several years. Attitude domain is huge and varied accruing over 80-plus years. The investigation of attitudes has been a basic topic in social psychology. Attitudes are engaged in practically every different field of discipline, incorporating social perception, interpersonal attraction, prejudice and discrimination, conformity, compliance, and so on. The main idea behind assuming why the concept of attitude is so fundamental to psychology is because the objective of psychology is to investigate conduct, and attitudes are *supposed to* affect behaviour. For this, one should first try to comprehend what exactly an attitude is. In the beginning, attitudes were described very broadly. Allport (1935) expressed attitude as with such a wide characterization it can be easily realized why attitudes were considered as the main construct of social psychology.

"A mental and neural state of readiness, organized through experience, and exerting a directive or dynamic influence upon the individual's response to all objects and situations with which it is related".

Since defined by Allport, the definition of attitude has further evolved substantially and become limited. Attitudes are now considered as evaluative proclamations — either ideal or disapproving—relating to various facets of the social world. For example, Fishbein and Ajzen (1975) provide a definition of attitude as "Object" and incorporates individuals, things, events and issues. When people make use of words such as like, dislike, love, hate, good, bad, yuck, and so on, they are describing attitudes of another person. From this perspective, attitudes are analyses of a specific individual, group, activity, or thing.

"A learned predisposition to respond in a consistently favourable or unfavourable manner with respect to a given object".

A similar definition was provided by Eagly and Chaiken (1993), in the opinion of whom, an attitude is centred on a specific entity or object, instead of all objects and situation with which it is associated.

"Attitude is a psychological tendency that is expressed by evaluating a particular entity with some degree of favour or disfavour".

Psychologists utilize particular terms to define certain categories of attitudes. For instance, an attitude towards the self is called *self-esteem*, negative attitudes towards particular classes are called *prejudice*, attitudes towards people are called *interpersonal attraction*, and attitude of people towards their own job is called *job satisfaction*. In basic terms, attitudes are normally positive or negative opinions of an individual (including oneself) place, thing or event (the attitude object).

ATTITUDES, VALUES AND BELIEFS

There are two psychological concepts narrowly correlated with attitudes: values and beliefs.

Attitudes and Values

The most often cited description of what forms a human value is offered by Rokeach (1973) as an "enduring belief that a specific mode of conduct or end-state of existence is personally or socially preferable to an opposite or converse mode of conduct or end-state of existence". Values form a significant facet of self-concept and act as guiding standards for a person. Rokeach opined that, taken into account together, values constitute values systems where a value system is "an enduring organization of beliefs concerning preferable modes of conduct or end-states of existence along a continuum of importance" (1973). Hence, the significance of various values should alter in correlation with the significance of others in the value system. For instance, one may value 'honesty' over 'success'. Human values are intensely prescriptive in nature and build the base around which other less persisting beliefs are arranged. Intrinsically, they are significant in a range of other processes, like attitudes. It is asserted that the establishment of individual attitudes is grounded upon more common values. Values indirectly affect behaviour through their effects on attitudes. Attitudes and Behaviour: While values *can* mould attitudes, it does not however imply that values mould *all* attitudes. For instance, peoples' attitude in regard to love versus arranged marriage is likely to be shaped by their values, but their inclination for one brand of toothpaste over another is less probable to be affected by crucial life objectives. It is certain that some attitudes are developed through the impact of long-standing values adopted in the childhood. These are termed as symbolic attitudes, on the basis that the attitude object is a sign of something else. In contradiction, there are some attitudes that are founded on utility, an immediate benefits and costs of the attitude object. These are called instrumental attitudes, since they are instrumental to accomplish those objectives. Curiously, the same attitude object could act as an emblematic or an influential requirement. For instance, individuals' decision to have only vegetarian food could depend on utility (if they stay in a place like Europe or America, where it is more challenging to get vegetarian food) or taste—instrumentally grounded attitudes— versus contemplations of animal privileges and right to live—emblematically founded values. Values are comparatively more steady and long lasting than attitudes, because they are fundamental beliefs about what is correct and incorrect. Attitudes are less steady than values. Moreover, in case of us being aware of an individual's values, we are better able to judge his behaviour in a specific situation.

Attitudes and Beliefs

Beliefs are perceptions about the possibility of an object or event being correlated with a given attribute. Few theorists consider belief as an element of an attitude. However, there are dissimilarities between attitude and belief. Attitude can be regarded as a total of beliefs. An individual can have several beliefs about an occurrence, constructive and destructive. This individual will have an attitude with regard to that phenomenon founded on the overall analysis of his or her beliefs. For instance, a person may consider that Pepsi is sweet, which contains preservatives. Here, it is high on calories is a belief and I like Pepsi implies attitude. In the opinion of Eagly and Chaiken (1993), it is likely to authenticate or misrepresent some beliefs (at least) using external standards. For instance, the belief that water freezes at 0 degree Celsius can be substantiated either realistically or even by accord among various people; however, few attitudes can be 'tested' using such interim consensus. Several social attitudes, for example, political, aesthetic or customer preferences are mainly unpredictable across individuals. While one person may like Pepsi, other person may not like it at all. Both beliefs and values are key to the dynamic influences that create and transform existing attitudes.

Role of Attitude

The aforementioned facts throw light on the fact that people hold several attitudes about almost all facets of the world around us. One may wonder over the concern shown by people about forming the several attitudes that each one of them have. In this segment, we will discuss some functions served by attitudes. The operational utility of attitudes was brought up by Allport (1935) in his classic discussion of attitudes. In his opinion, attitude was social psychology's most essential concept. He expressed, "Without guiding attitudes the individual is confused and baffled. Attitudes determine for each individual what he will see and hear, what he will think and what he will do; they 'engender meaning upon the world'; they draw lines about and segregate an otherwise chaotic environment; they are our methods for finding our way about in an ambiguous universe".

This has been labelled as the object appraisal function by Fazio (2000). In his view, the mere possession of any attitude is convenient to the person in terms of positioning him to the attitudinal object. This object appraisal function can be considered as the principal value of having an attitude. Fazio further opines, "*Every* attitude, regardless of any other functional benefits that it may also provide, serves this object appraisal function". In the same way, both Katz (1960) and Smith, Bruner and White (1956) expressed their opinion on this object—appraisal function in their functional theory of attitudes. One of the basic postulates of functional theory is that we often contain or convey our attitudes and prejudices in order to interact something about ourselves to other individuals. This denotes that attitudes with regard to particular issues, products or notions aid to express wider information about us to people who are interested. For instance, Smith et al. (1956) stated, *"Attitudes aid us in classifying for action the objects of the environment, and they make appropriate response tendencies available for coping with these objects"*. Katz (1960) holds the opinion that attitudes are decided by the functions they perform for us. Individuals contain given attitudes since these attitudes enable them realize their basic objectives. Katz differentiates four kinds of psychological functions that attitudes perform. Let us investigate these four functions now. Attitudes are constituted by various mechanisms.

In classical conditioning, attitudes are built when an earlier impartial attitude object comes to induce an attitude reaction by being paired with some other object that normally arouses the attitude response. Another strong manner in which attitudes are constituted is through influential conditioning, using reward and punishment eventualities. Few attitudes are also constituted via observational learning by indirectly experiencing rewards and punishments given to others. In the end, genetic factors are also significant in moulding some attitudes. The functional approach considers that people hold attitudes that fit their requirements. All attitudes, irrespective of any other requirements that they satisfy, also carry out an object appraisal function. Initial functional theorists suggested four psychological functions that attitudes may carry out: utilitarian, knowledge, ego defensive and value-expressive. Later, a social-identity function of attitude was included.

ETHICAL CONDUCT IN GOVERNANCE

All over the globe, solid accord is building in public on the ethical conduct of politicians or pioneers in public life. There have been a growing number of instances where leaders have been grilled over their behaviours including the countries like Egypt and Syria. Many rulers have become the object of public wrath and outrage for their unethical behaviour. Comparable allegations have been levelled against prominent leaders in France and Italy. In India, over the previous decade, conduct of politicians or leaders has come under the watchful eyes of public and courts. Apparently, individuals all over the world anticipate the leadership to agree to moral norms and their behaviour to be completely straightforward and ethical in public and personal scenario. Moreover, they anticipate the leader to emulate the character of Caesar's wife and behaviour of Plato's "philosopher king", completely devoted to the public, directing faithfully and generously the society to accomplish its potential and goals.

Ethics: Implications for Governance

Ethics implies adhering to the ethos and values that are considered sacred in the society and operating in congruity with the belief held in the Constitution. It also suggests firm devotion to the laws in effect and not demanding any individual exemption from the writ of laws. Hence, moral conduct demands the leader to adhere to law and the law enforcing agencies should be unbiased in law implementation, booking any violation of protocols with liberty. Hence, even the Prime Minister in case of crossing red light should not be spared under the law, and the traffic constable on duty should have the nerve to issue the ticket and the Prime Minister should have the level-headedness to abide by the law. The Prime Minister has as much the privilege to use road securely as any other inhabitant and the traffic constable is obliged to book anybody who endangers safety of others by breaking the traffic rules. Governance is administration of socio-economic structure of the society. It is the directive of authority to make certain that the social and ethical values, as treasured in the laws, are objectively, transparently and efficiently enforced. Hence, governance is a system that controls social conduct and relations as also insures peace in the society. Concurrently, the institutional mechanism so established provides services to the individuals with impartiality. Governance, in actuality, is required to ascertain that every person enjoys his privileges with freedom and is able to access the service and opportunities that are offered to the individuals by the state.

Governance, therefore, is essential for the welfare of the society and welfare can be assured if individuals at large have trust in the organization produced by law for administering economic, social and political issues of body politic. Faith of the individuals can be gained by the administration if it is honest, transparent, responsive and sensitive. Like law, governance has to be completely unbiased in implementation and unbiased in the delivery of services. Reliable governance is conceivable if the conduct of government representatives is ethical and guaranteeing ethical behaviour is the foremost challenge before the management. Since leaders are a public figure, their behaviour is under consistent public scrutiny and those working with them. In case the leaders themselves fail to follow ethical norms, they would not be having the ethical privilege to insist on others to be trustworthy. Moreover, an untruthful leader's preaching on ethics are constantly jeered at by the followers. Ethics in governance is of paramount importance because evil conduct based on unethical practices compromises the image and integrity of system among the general public. Corruption allows the superior and the powerful to violate the privileges of the poor and widens the gap between the rich and the poor. Those lacking wealth, who normally make up the majority, become resentful with the system and express their wrath either by rebelling against the structure or by waging war against the instituted establishment. The rising cases of insurgency in the nation are, among other things, a response of the individuals who are dissatisfied with the administration authorities. Corruption in the system of governance consistently creates 'toutism'. Time and again people find it highly difficult to get a driving licence without hiring the services of a "facilitator". This expediter has secret relationships with the authorities and work for a predetermined issue. In the same way, a booking in train can be secured straightaway by making contact with the correct facilitator. Proliferation of 'toutism' in the systems of governance has not only tainted the image of government but has substantially impacted its trustworthiness in a negative manner.

TRANSPARENCY AND CREDIBILITY

The structure of a reliable arrangement of administration can be produced only when the top governance is totally honest and public oriented. It should demonstrate its example of honesty, transparency and sensitivity for the lower officials to follow. When top management itself is confronting allegations, demoralization permeates into the entire system. There are various occasions where wealth has played a significant part in postings, transfers and even in seeking employments. States where such unethical practices are widespread have poor administration while states having merit as the guiding norm for public appointments, administration is appreciated and it builds people's belief in the system. Moreover, in states with objectivity and clarity in enactment of development policies, the administrative system is rated well. In these states, invariably, the governance has set a case for the lower officials to follow, resulting in alleviation of corruption and surge in sensitivity and reactions to public demands. Ethics also refers to paying due respect to the ethos and sensitivities of the individuals. This envisions that those in charge of affairs pay due respect to the traditions of the individuals and should not, in any case, jeer at their values or customs, even if they fail to adjust the contemporary way of life. One of the reasons behind the British strengthening their position was their persistent efforts to recognize themselves with the public. It was their forbearance and regards for the local societies and their values that enabled not only alliance but also integration of the huge Indian empire. Prior to the British, Emperor Akbar had exhibited exceptional tolerance that which encouraged brotherhood in the Indian community, leading to unity of the Indian nation. The advantages gained by Akbar were consequently reduced by orthodox social policies of Shahjahan and Aurangazeb. The excessive fundamentalist strategies of Aurangzeb resulted in disintegration of the intimidating Mughal Empire, with the summons of the empire restricted to the walls of the Red Fort in Delhi. In this situation, ethics in public life undertakes a wider implication as it holds onto individual morality as well as a strict code of behaviour in inter-personal associations. Hence, in the moral composition, not only formal statutes but also conventions are composed. Conventions, though not enforceable in the courts of justice have authorization of the public and their breach deteriorates public confidence.

In the Indian setting, the doctrine of public sector was principally to upgrade the national foundation, provide stimulus to the development to less developed areas and also offer jobs to the jobless. Nevertheless, with a surge in population density, land possession itself has become a grave issue, because in the wake of land ceiling, the properties have become small. Hence, every acre of possession impacts many families. The problem before the authority is how to boost industrialization and mining without triggering large scale dislodgment of the individuals. Territories that have low population density are precious forest regions and the Forest Act disallows any fiddling with these lands. Over the recent decade, the matter of an agreeable relief and rehabilitation policy has been standing up to the administration with no feasible solution. Industrial development and mining of necessary minerals has encountered unpleasant climate due to lack of a plausible relief and rehabilitation policy. The cases of Posco in Odisha and Nandigram in West Bengal are some examples of such division. There is significant merit in the argument that individuals cannot be denied of their assets and livelihood unless they are reasonably rehabilitated. Since, even small land possessions involve dislodgment of a vast number of individuals, it is impossible for the industries to offer employment to amateur workers, because the numbers engaged are much more than the capability of the industry to gainfully deploy them. Macro-economic deliberations and international commitment to be consistent with the management of General Agreement on Tariffs and Trade and the World Trade Organization has led to the globalization of Indian economy which, in turn, has resulted in a modular shift from the prior controlling regime to a regime that is principally free of controls. This shift in policy has though created considerable flexibility for private enterprises to function yet at the same time, it has pulled out the protection that was experienced by comparatively weaker businesspersons who continued to depend on old-fashioned production technologies that were labour centric. Competition arising from open markets and removal of tariff barriers compelled these industries to close down their units, leading to large-scale unemployment. A nation where the Constitution decrees that the legislature should work for the wellbeing of the individuals, ethics in governance authorizes the administration to interpose efficiently to safeguard these displaced groups from adversity. Economic ethics at the macro level, thus, indicates that the modifications should be made bearing humanity in mind. These adaptations require a virtual redefinition of the part, objectives and operations of the legislature and consequently, rearrangement of the administration within the recently defined role. Novel social preventive measures have to be formed to save individuals from simulated famishment. In monetary terms, it refers to an allocation of more capitals fór social sector agendas. There is a growing inclination of legislature to shed its capacities to the private segments with little respect for well-judged control on their capacities. Generally, these accomplices in legislature are blamed of immoral conduct. It is frequently stated that the employees involved in outsourced activities are poorly paid and are deprived of social security or health coverage. In several public sector enterprises contract employees engaged for carrying out outsourced activities are not provided the benefits of provident fund and insurance coverage. This goes against the ethical norms within the legislature and it is an antagonistic reflection on ethics in governance.

INTEGRITY IN PUBLIC SERVICE

Gunnyar Myrdal, a well-known Scandinavian economist-sociologist, had termed the Indian society as a 'soft society'. He also described what is meant by the expression 'soft society'. He described a soft society as (a) one that lacks the political determination to enact the laws needed for its growth and expansion and/or lack the political determination to execute the codes and conduct, even when made, and (b) where there is a lack of discipline. In reality, he stressed on the latter aspect more than the former. He reiterated that sans discipline in the society, it is almost impossible to attain real or meaningful development or progress. He further stressed that the root cause of corruption at all levels is the lack of discipline in the society. Corruption and indiscipline go hand in hand. The best way of inducing discipline in the society is to try and mitigate corruption and to take strict actions against those found engaged in it. To make it reality, the loopholes in the criminal judicial system have to be redressed.

In relation to the same, Lord Acton's insightful observation "Power corrupts and absolute power tends to corrupt absolutely" seems to have global validity. Corruption has always proved to be a main issue, if not a problem, affecting all systems of governance at all times. It can be regarded as a multiheaded hydra, with no Hercules insight to kill it. Corruption is so evident and yet so secretive. It is not a big surprise to know that efforts to capture it in a systematic definition have not met with total success. Even after so many studies, only some magnitudes of corruption are traced, and the remaining are still hiding from the most perceptive eyes. Corruption has been understood as 'the use of public power for private profit in a way that constitutes breach of law and as dishonesty and illegal behaviour in position of authority and power'. In different words, it refers to the misuse of one's official position for one's own interest at the cost of public good. Joseph Nye observes corruption as a conduct that diverges from the formal duties of a public role because of influence form some outer or private elements.

Similarly, Carl J Friedrich states that: Corruption is a kind of behaviour which deviates from the norm actually prevalent or believed to prevail in a given context, such as the political. It is deviant behaviour associated with a particular motivation, namely that of private gain at public expenses. Such private gain may be monetary one, and in the minds of the general public it usually is, but it takes many other forms.The Santhanam Committee defines corruption in public systems with a different angle as follows: 'Any action *or failure to take action* in the performance of duty by a Government servant for some advantage is corruption'. Therefore, the possibility of a corrupt act is increased by including within its realm action as well as non-action, with the same level of motivation in both cases. Krishna K. Tumniala states that dimensions of behavioural patterns should be kept in mind while defining the content and scope of corruption. A clear picture regarding this will be helpful in in confronting the menace of corruption.

Tumniala also states that if corruption is interpreted in wider sense, even incompetence in performance would be regarded as corruption, whereas the prime view is that corruption refers to money-changing hands either in hope of favours or in return to those already rendered. Second, corruption can also be understood as situational, that is, what amounts to corruption in one sense may not be so in other. Third, in developing nations, one's personal and official life may be judged as per different norms. Fourth, there should be distinction between corruption and scandal as both of them may be independent of each other. Fifth, distinctions in the extent of corruption and the rate of its occurrence should be made. Sixth, corruption may be of different types, with the diversified impact of each form. Seventh, extreme indulgence in corruption might avert attention from the more important evolving aspects of governance. Eighth, political and administrative corrupt element, though interrelated, should be distinguished analytically and, if possible, operationally.

It is generally regarded that corruption is dysfunctional to the system of governance and to society as a whole. It is seen to stimulate illegality, unethicalism, subjectivity, inequity, injustice, waste, inefficiency and inconsistency in administrative conduct and behaviour. Besides, it shakes the trust of the common man in the lawfulness of the politico-administrative system and eventually saps the idealism of those in public service and terminates the moral fabric of society.

There seem to be a different view that corruption may in fact be functional in specific circumstances. Samuel Huntington states that corruption may help in integrating new gatherings into the framework and in this way fill in as a substitute for reform. Myron Weiner observes that corruption is weakening the rigidities of bureaucracy and making it moderately adaptable. There obviously exists a view that the beneficiary of a corrupt practice would find it 'useful'. In contrast, these opinions have only restricted currency and acceptance. Even after the presence of their situational validity, it is nearly impossible to undervalue the harmful effects of corruption on individuals, communities and nations. Corruption is mainly considered to be a regular, repetitive and integral part of an organizational society, with universal pervasiveness. According to Ralph Braibanti, 'government corruption is found in all forms of bureaucracies, in all periods of time.' Further, corruption is a phenomenon that is present in both democratic and non-democratic regimes. The great historian of the Roman Empire, Edward Gibbon, said: 'Corruption is the most infallible symptom of constitutional liberty'. On the contrary, one comes around several accounts of corruption prevalent in the erstwhile Soviet Union and other totalitarian regimes. A totalitarian government, by nature and necessity, cannot but be irremediably corrupt.

Indira Gandhi had once said that 'corruption is a global phenomenon'. Although she was right, its global existence cannot be taken as an excuse for complacency in combating it. Whether Louis XV, Cesare Borgia or Nero from the past or Spiro Agnew (USA), Roh Tae Woo (Korea), Carlos Salinas de Gortari (Mexico) or many former Japanese Prime Ministers of present times, a corrupt public servant can breed anywhere at any time. In condition of extreme concentration of power and too little liability, immorality and payoffs rule the roost. Even as corruption has no boundaries, it seems that it mostly prevalent in poverty-stricken areas. The Transparency International states that graft and poverty go side by side. Nonetheless, irrespective of their developing economies, Thailand and China have a significantly high level of official corruption. It is obvious that they would still come within the *zone* of developing countries. A survey conducted in 1995 of 10,000 people in 23 Latin American nations revealed that corruption is the top most problem faced by all. The same apprehension is prevailing in the thought process of the people of most developing nations even about two decades later.

ETHICS AND HUMAN INTERFACE

Etymologically, 'ethics' is derived from the Greek word *'ethos'* which refers to character, habit, customs, ways of behaviour and so forth. It is also termed as 'moral philosophy'. The term 'moral' has its origin from Latin word *'mores'* which refer to customs, character, behaviour and so forth. Hence, ethics may be defined as, *the systematic study of human actions from the point of view of their rightfulness or wrongfulness, as means for the attainment of the ultimate happiness.* It can be understood as the insightful study of what is good or bad in that segment of human conduct for which one has some personal obligation. In simple terms, ethics alludes to what is good and the best approach to get it, and what is terrible and how to stay away from it. It alludes to what should be done to accomplish what is great and what should not to be done to maintain a strategic distance from what is malicious. Ethics, in any case, is said to be the end product of all sciences since it at last perfects human individual, by requesting all other sciences and all aspects else related to an extreme end that is totally free. Ethics, being considered as a philosophical subject, is the study of the codes and conducts by which we live. It additionally includes the explanation of these codes and conducts. Ethics doesn't plainly follow a convention or custom. Rather it needs examination and assessment of these rules in light of global standards. Considered in the context of moral philosophy, ethics is the philosophical consideration regarding values, moral issues and moral judgements. Morality is akin to nutrition. The greater number of us have never had a course in nutrition or even read much about it. However, a significant number of us do have some general information of the segment, of what we have to eat and what not. Be that as it may, we likewise commit errors about these things. Constantly thinking about the good a specific eating regimen can do over a long run to our wellbeing, we may let it all out despite the fact that it might bring no quick satisfaction. The same goes with our moral life. Nutrition centres on our physical health, whereas morality is mainly related to our moral health. It tries to enable us to figure out what will sustain our ethical life and what will harm it. It tries to improve our lives, to aid us to live better lives. Morality intends to give us a common perspective from which we can come to understanding about what every one of us should do. It seeks to find a more objective stand of assessment than that of simply individual inclination.

ETHICS IN HUMAN ACTIONS

Ethics is mainly related to right or wrong conduct defined with regard to moral choices. Ethics is related to guidelines by which to assess conduct as right or wrong, good or bad. Aristotle considers ethics to incorporate the good life which implied a life worth living or life that is fulfilling. Ethics is speculating about right behaviour and great life, whereas morals are the real practice with regards to right behaviour and great life. For instance, theft, lying, cheating, murdering and indifference to the welfare of others are regarded to be unethical, whereas conserving human life, concerns for others, trustworthiness and truthfulness are regarded to be ethical. Ethics can be categorized in two types—descriptive and normative ethics. Normative ethics refers to the guidelines for the rightness and wrongness of actions, whereas descriptive ethics refers to an experimental examination of people's moral beliefs. There are three main normative ethics theories:

Modern Moral Philosophy

With the advent of the 20th century, moral philosophies have attained a more complex form and are no longer related with rightness and wrongness, although they are concerned with many different types of moral status. W.D. Ross states that moral philosophies cannot tell normally whether an act is right or wrong, but only whether it inclines to be right or wrong as per certain type of moral duty such as beneficence, fidelity or justice. A number of philosophers have puzzled whether or not these codes or conducts can be framed at all at a theoretical stage; a few have moved away from the theories and standards of normative ethics closer to descriptive morality and meta-ethics. Other theorists are still shielding moral theory on the basis that it is not required to be flawless to include essential moral insight.

Current moral idea is mainly concerned with claims-based or rights-based ethics, which are ethical philosophies on the basis of fundamental code of human rights and other rights or claims of the individual. Rights-based philosophies state that citizens have several freedoms and rights, like liberal theories which emphasize on people's claim to freedoms like the freedom of speech, association, religion, etc. These recent philosophies are emphasizing on people's claim to rights like human rights, civil rights, political rights and social/economic rights. The Universal Declaration of Human Rights of the United Nations is an example of the same scenario. Another specimen of rights-based theories is 'welfareism', which states that citizens have a right to a welfare state that can offer them security, basic health services, education, jobs, housing, etc.

SOCIAL AND ETHICAL SUITABILITY OF NBICs FOR PURPOSES OF HUMAN ENHANCEMENT

The advent of high-tech technologies for the help of humankind such as nanotechnology, biotechnology, information sciences and cognitive science (NBICs) has opened the gate for debates and moral opinions that must be involved by theorists who think to take seriously the question of the ethical and social adequacy of these technologies. The philosophical argument between humanism and transhumanism revolving around the subject of the social adequacy of NBICs for catering to humans has so far been mired in stalemate due to a number of argument-based complications that we have just analysed, which can be described as follows:

- The uncertainty of the kinds of moral argument used: nature and human nature; dignity-autonomy; the good life. The uncertainty occurs due to the fact that a single name for a model is not enough to express the accurate meaning of the moral utterance being deployed. This is the reason for its role in both positive and negative assessments of the development of NBICs. This trouble does not constitute a stalemate if humanists and transhumanists will decide to describe the sense given to the main concepts (nature, dignity, the good life). A clear utterance of the moral argument, coupled with specific explanations regarding the validations for these utterances, will aid in tackling the problem related to meaning and will help to more clearly recognizing the problem related to justification.
- Every moral dispute contains its personal justification. In the reviewed texts, there is very little mention of the justification for these disputes. Furthermore, no argument was discovered regarding the supremacy of a given justification for an argument. No one can offer details that make it likely to say that the moral responsibility they are evolving based on nature, dignity or the good life is related to reason. The absenteeism of discussion regarding the rationality of the reasons for supporting a moral debate appears to confirm that morality is nothing much than a matter of beliefs and lies outside any type of rationality. The lack of decision on how to settle these irreconcilable arguments is clear.
- What the discussion about the application of a moral utterance to a specific case shows? Both transhumanists and humanists have the same notion of practical reason, seeking that several divisions be made clear and precise a priori to align a given debate to a condition. Instead, this stance should be re-evaluated in view of the dialogue of a priori and a posteriori. Is it required, for practical reasoning, to attain a priori divisions or a posteriori ones? Must we discard all divisions that are a priori? The truth that

divisions made a priori are unclear does not essentially mean they should be written off. As effectively given by 'the paradox of the heap', the proposed tactic to a solution includes saying that it is only case-by-case that the senses of the divisions will become clear a posteriori.

- The final stalemate is a bit complex as it is twofold. In this paper, we are mainly reviewing the stalemate concerned with moral debate. The matter of how we can fix a place for moral argument in a democratic setup is another thing. In the clash between the debates of humanists and those of transhumanists, moral restrictions on autonomy are contrasting to democratic social restrictions on sovereignty (rights). This dialogue on moral and legal restrictions to nanotechnology appears to reconsider the basic supposition that positive law symbolizes the separation of law and morals.

There exist a number of dialogical standoffs identified under the above text behind the imprint of routine recourse to moral debated in nanoethics. Theorists face many debates and standoffs while taking part in an interdisciplinary dialogical course of ethical, economic, environmental, legal and social assessment of nanotechnology.

PROFESSIONAL RESPONSIBILITY AND CODES OF CONDUCT

Professional responsibility and codes of conduct give a summary of main issues related to professionalism as they are connected with the Responsible Conduct of Research (RCR). Joe Herkert describes both the micro (between individuals) and macro (between professionals and society) ethical magnitudes of professional responsibility and codes of conduct. Any person can compare ethical values with facets of moral theory, intensifying the dialogue with some of the significant readings for this topic.

Although codes of conduct differ as per different professional societies, they normally also have common characteristics in defining the duties of engineers to the public, their employers and clients and their colleagues. All current engineering values describe that the most important duty of engineers is to guard the public safety, health and welfare. Values often also underline such features as competence, trustworthiness, honesty and fairness.

One way to understand professional values is to look them as a structured tactic to umpiring the conflicts that can happen when an individual, acting in their professional capacity, performs several tasks. The other opinion is that formal codes of conduct are a reflection of the association between society and trained experts.

PROBITY IN GOVERNANCE

Probity in governance is a very important necessity for governance's system to work in a phased manner for socio-economic development. Eradication of corruption is the topmost condition for guaranteeing probity in governance. Other important requisites include operational laws, rules and regulations governing every aspect of public life and an effective and rational execution of those laws. Indeed, implementation of law in an appropriate, reasonable and effective way is a facet of discipline. Regrettably, public life is rapidly becoming devoid of in India, and sans discipline, as per the Scandinavian economist-sociologist Gunnyar Myrdal, real progress is just a dream. Public-private morality and a sense of honesty compose discipline in a real sense. In western nations, the higher position a person holds, the more respect he has for laws. In contrast, in India, holding higher position means a person can break laws and regulations easily without any scrutiny. Indiscipline and untruth have affected our nation really bad; morality, both public and private, is at a premium.

MENACE OF CORRUPTION IN PUBLIC LIFE

The term corruption can be understood as misuse of public resources or position in public life for private benefits. The possibility for corruption increases when command on the public administrators become delicate and the division of power between political, executive and bureaucracy is uncertain and confusing. Political defilement, which is sometimes indistinguishable from bureaucratic debasement, has a tendency to be more extensive in authoritarian regimes where the public views and the Press cannot criticize corruption. However, in India, despite an attentive and aware press and public view, the intensity of corruption is extremely high. This might be credited to the articulate insensitivity, absence of disgrace and the nonappearance of any feeling of open ethical quality among the bribe-takers. In fact, they wear their identification of defilement and shamelessness with equal confidence and boldness. The expansion of chances in state intervention in financial and social life has immeasurably expanded the open door for political and bureaucratic corruption, more specifically since politics has too progressed towards becoming professionalized. We have proficient government officials who are politicians on a full-time basis, in fact, out of office also. There appears a connection between terrorism, drugs, smuggling, and politicians, which was highlighted in the Vohra Committee Report. Corruption has grown because one is unable to see successful examples of successfully prosecuted cases of corruption. Cases, inadequately established upon, weak and fragmented investigation, trailed by a slow and delayed trial confluence an ethically ill-deserved but a lawfully unavoidable exoneration. The acknowledgment of corruption as an inflexible reality has prompted quiet compromise and acquiescence to such wrongs. Truly, the present procedure of pulling back the State from different parts in which it have never entered or in which it is not fit for performing productively, may decrease the scope of corruption to some degree, in fact, if we move to a free market economy, there must be control of economy as distinct from controls upon the industrial activity. The necessities of administration would yet call for going into contracts, purchases etc.

The Scandinavian economist-sociologist, Gunnyar Myrdal, had portrayed the Indian society as a 'soft society'. He also clarified the meaning of 'soft society'. According to Gunnyar Myrdal, a ***soft society*** is:

(a) One, which does not have the political force to authorize the laws fundamental for its growth and advancement as well as does not have the political will to apply the laws, even when formulated, and

(b) Wherever there is lack of discipline. Even, he has emphasized the second aspect greater than the first. He told, due to the lack of discipline in the society, no genuine or meaningful growth is possible. Lack of discipline in the society has caused corruption. Corruption and indiscipline support each other very much. One method of encouraging the discipline among the society is by reducing the scope of corruption, and handling it strictly, wherever it is noticed. Due to this, the faults in the criminal judicial system have to be rectified. Corruption is also anti-poor, such as, the Public Distribution System (PDS) and the welfare schemes for the underprivileged including Scheduled Castes (SCs) and Scheduled Tribes (STs). Everyone is aware from the fact that a large fraction of grain, sugar and kerosene oil intended for PDS, goes into black market and that only just 16% of the funds intended for STs and SCs reach them, remaining all are misused by few members of the political, official class and dishonest dealers and businessmen. The well-known economist, Mehbub-Ul-Haq, briefly and piercingly set out the evil impacts of corruption in the South-Asian nation like our own. According to him:

Corruption happens everywhere. It has been at the center of election campaigns in Italy and the United Kingdom, led to the fall of governments in Japan and Indonesia, and resulted in legislative action in Russia and the United States. But, if corruption exists in rich, economically successful countries, why should South Asia be worried about it? The answer is simple: South Asian corruption has four key characteristics that make it far more damaging than corruption in any other parts of the world.

First, corruption in South Asia occurs upstream, not down-stream. Corruption at the top distorts fundamental decisions about development priorities, policies, and projects. In industrial countries, these core decisions are taken through transparent competition and on merit, even though petty corruption may occur downstream.

Second, corruption money in South Asia has wings, not wheels. Most of the corrupt gains made in the region are immediately smuggled out to safe havens abroad.

Third, corruption in South Asia often leads to promotion, not prison. The big fish—unless they belong to the opposition—rarely fry.

Fourth, corruption in South Asia occurs with 515 million people in poverty, not with per capita incomes above twenty thousand dollars.

The apex court, in the case of Vineet Narain vs. Union of India (AIR 1998), stated with consent the references of Lord Nolan Committees on Standards in Public Life in the United Kingdom. The principles of public life, of general application, were stated by the court as follows:

'***Principles of public life***: The general principles of conduct which underpin public life need to be restated. We have done this. The seven principles of selflessness, integrity, objectivity, accountability, openness, honesty and leadership are set out (later on).

Codes of conduct: All public bodies should draw up codes of conduct incorporating these principles.

Independent scrutiny: Internal systems for maintaining standards should be supported by independent scrutiny.

Education: More needs to be done to promote and reinforce standards of conduct in public bodies, in particular through guidance and training, including induction training'.

The Nolan Committee Report recommended following seven Principles of Public Life:

- Selflessness
- Integrity
- Objectivity
- Accountability
- Openness
- Honesty
- Leadership'

Certain actions needed to be taken for ensuring probity in governance:

- Requirement for enforcing section 5 of the Benami Transactions (Prohibition) Act, 1988
- Misfeasance in Public Office—A Remedy
- Need for a law offering for seizure of illegally attained assets of public servants
- Enactment of a Public Interest Disclosure Act
- Enactment of a Freedom of Information Act
- Need for enacting a Lok Pal Bill plus the Central Vigilance Commission Act
- Strengthening of the Criminal Judicial System'.

INTEGRITY IN PUBLIC LIFE

In summary, integrity comprises honesty, sincerity, truthfulness and so forth. Integrity in public life seeks seamless coordination, harmonization in thoughts, acts and deeds. An individual should practice the same values that he believes. In the present scenario, human aspirations are spiralling vertically as they all want to accumulate wealth. Greed rules all other deeds. Public Life is full of private needs and wishes. People who attain power are hungry for more power. As someone aptly said:

"Power Corrupts—Absolute Power Corrupts absolutely".

There is a small proportion of people left who are honest in public life. It is important for all in public life to follow the values given below:

- **Integrity:** Ethics, fairness in all their dealings.
- **Selflessness:** Decisions in public life should only be taken on merit and public interest. There should not be any want for getting material benefits for themselves.
- **Accountability:** They should willingly submit themselves to inspection.
- **Fairness/Openness:** All pronouncements should be fair and open and transparent.
- **Honesty:** The general population places substantial significance on 'Honesty' in its widest logic as an expected behaviour by public-office holders.

Contradictory interest in any actions should be publicly stated. All judgements taken by individuals in public life should be for the common good of the people. Individual enrichment is unjustified. 'Integrity in Public Life' is a lifetime threefold pledge to reflecting extremely on the following:

- What is correct
- Performing on what we have discerned

- Ethical principles to be followed even at personal cost and inconvenience,
- Supporting moral codes and conducts publicly.

What then is expected from us during the period of transition from private life into the arena of public leadership? A pessimist may have a view that there is no place for ethics in politics. For others, it may be an excuse. But I am not a pessimist. I say that, in reality, the calls of integrity in public life as compared to those that you and I may face not that these are ever easy, but public life seeks far, far more. Integrity for all refers to voting, writing, taking a public opinion, maybe shaping, even shifting the way we live. For the politician it means all this and more. For them, it is also akin to being successful and powerful. But in the context of political leadership, we are referring to responsibility for results, responsibility to God, to our eventual principles, and even to the state and its people. In the context of honesty and integrity in public life, we in India refers to the period of our struggle for independence. Post-independence, the whole world was of the opinion that India would be split into many small independent states. The situation at that time was controlled by "the Iron Man of India" Mr. Sardar Patel by integrating the nation. A selfless man whose only goal was public good and public welfare. Integrity in Public Life also refers to

- Steadfast adherence to a strict Moral Code
- Steadfast adherence to a strict Ethical Code
- Quality of being perfect and pure.

Integrity also refers to:

- Honesty
- Uprightness
- Purity
- Probity
- Sincerity
- Decency

But there exists one other desirable thing for all of us in public life: Humility. It is not serious, you may think. A politician humble? But I mean by that more than being humble. I mean being motivated by something more than ego, more than power. I mainly mean to say respect for individuals, caring about our common life and realizing that all of us have something to give. Triumph in public life calls for results, and results seek that we take the public with us, identify that we lead not only a faction or party but a city, state or country. It seeks esteem for those we disagree with not only for their voting rights, but also for the likelihood that they might, at least in part, be right. It also seeks an inclination to listen, and occasionally to let go of our predetermined notions, and toughest of all to look beyond the immediate calls of our constituencies and take a longer, wider view. Therefore, humility refers to such love for the larger community that we are up to take the risk of losing office. With any of the system, those finally appointed face judgements that, for an individual of integrity and conviction, can be unbearable. You possess a boundless reserve of ethical morals, but only a restricted store of political chips. What will you do if you are John Kennedy, and you seek civil rights but rest on conservative southern whites for your backing? That's a different form of stating that it isn't sufficient, if we're to live with honesty, to be authentic to just one moral in life. The most challenging choices in life ascend when our values contrast even such broad values as fairness and mercy. There also are struggles within a single moral, such as the holiness of human life. Whose lives count the most?

- American soldiers lives versus Iraqi personnel lives
- Lives of Poor or those of Rich and Powerful
- Lives of Politicians or the common man

All human beings should calmly co-exist. We living creatures must negotiate on what shall be appropriate to whom. We should allow everyone to live a worthy life.

PROBITY IN PUBLIC LIFE

The term 'probity in public life' would have meant brazen when I was elected in the Indian Police Service, for in the words of Charles Dickens 'it was the best of times'. In the present times, we have stooped to such a pity level of moral that relating probity in public life is pure stupid. Panditji had just infused us of our encounter with destiny, and we were hoping that India would leave behind its immediate past and become a role model in public life. As far as we young men from the universities were concerned, it was 'blessed to be alive, to be young was very heaven'. Since then we have caused much harm to the institutions that were so carefully crafted, and serious doubts are now cast on whether the threats closing in on us can be effectively warded off. We have substantiated Gibbon right when in his Decline and Fall of the Roman Empire he stated, 'corruption is the infallible symptom of liberty'.

Not that graft is a new disorder in India. When the English agents in quest to making an easy money were also our rulers, corruption governed the roost. The positive aspect, sadly lacking now, was that the Directors of the East India Company Board acknowledged the forthcoming hazard and tried to discontinue the rot before it presumed greater magnitudes. It is exciting to acknowledge that Robert Clive was sent to India a second time not to enhance new areas to the Empire but with a strong directive to clean up the Writer's Building in Calcutta with the help of military. The astute hero of Plassey quickly learned that winning a combat was not tough but tackling the unethical writers under him was a much tougher proposition. He devised an easy strategy—relocate the entire lot to Fort St. George in Madras and swap them with the Madrasis with whom he had worked and whom he knew. That proved to be a national adversity—the Bengali was not corrected, the Madrasis soon became corrupt and it spread all over India. Ladies and Gentlemen, the people from Bengal and Madras were not the native Indians but white writers from UK. The thing to reminisce is that the powers that be took mindful steps to clean the administration of the dangerous stuff of corruption. Then the Indian Civil Service and the Indian Police Service were born boasting of high standard of integrity. Today we transfer employees from one end to the other. This mechanism is employed to penalize upright officials who do not bend low enough. The axe falls on the Chief Secretary and the Police Chief as the power in government changes!

Until the 1960s, things were all okay though cracks started appearing here and there. The disturbing issue was that political corruption became more prominent than the same among government officials. To tackle the growing menace, Lal Bahadur Shastri formed a committee under K. Santhanam to review the menace of corruption in public services and recommend remedial measures. The committee thought that political corruption was only infiltrating into public life at a slower rate, and the general gossips and reports were inflated. In reality, they were unknown of a cultural change conquering the country in which citizens were slowly losing faith in public institutions. Rajaji had invented a term for that—permit licence raj. What was more dangerous was the bureaucracy transforming into a hybrid traditional civil servant and the modern Indian politician. Not all civil servants or ministers were culpable, but very few senior civil servants complained or made a public opinion emphasizing cleanliness in the government service. Their fight was supressed, and they voiced their views in hush and whispers or 'they sighed like a lover but obeyed like a son'. What is worse that even the judiciary is maligned in corruption. One recalls what Walt Whitman, the radical American poet, wrote of circumstances in the United States nearly 150 years ago: 'the official services of the state, national and municipal, in all their branches and departments, except the judiciary, are saturated in corruption, bribery, falsehood, maladministration; and the judiciary is tainted'.

The Santhnam Committee's statement and the subsequent action with a Central Vigilance Commission at the top and a consolidated Central Bureau of Investigation to examine cases proved to be more an eyewash. Serious political will was missing. One is retold a delightful story told by Professor Galbraith. Once in Cambridge, he was having breakfast with a Professor of Sociology from Soviet Russia. They were talking about a report in the New York Times about the conviction of a Senator for fraud of some public funds. Galbraith questioned the Russian Professor whether they had comparable instance of misconduct by public workers, specifically with the state having almost total control over all public actions. The Soviet Professor vociferously dissented and said that dishonesty was opposed to Marxist-Leninist doctrine. When Galbraith still insisted and wished to know if any investigation was made, the Russian answered that there was an investigation by the Russian Institute of Social Sciences and they found that in a city a few miles far from Moscow, practically every commanding public official was corrupt. Galbraith questioned the government about the action taken by it. The answer was that the state administration took a very serious notice and the Social Sciences branch of the Institute was straightaway dissolved. We have attained the same outcomes without awkwardly liquidating the CBI or the CVC. We have just reduced them completely weak—our ahimsa insurgence in public administration. Desire and gold have been our Gods. In this novel religion, there is an interconnection between criminals and politicians with administration playing a less important role. These are not careless observations of reviewers of the legislature but discoveries of the high-power Vohra Committee. Gold, Columbus affirmed hundreds of years before, is a magnificent thing. He who owns it can accomplish anything, why he can even purchase a place in Paradise. Also for avarice, our companions in public workplaces are more than divine. The divine beings are contented with 'leaves, fruit, flowers and water' as offerings to satisfy them. However, the ministers and their followers do not like anything except dollars and the solid yellow metal. Gandhiji's land cannot meet the expense of this lavishness.

Indira Gandhi made an amazing statement that corruption was no longer a problem in India for the straightforward argument that it was a worldwide phenomenon. Not a single person had the guts to counter her that small pox was widespread at one time, AIDS is intimidating to render the whole planet dangerous to live, but that does not imply that all the public health units need to be shut down. The fact of the matter is that if we see corruption as an evil, it needs to be tackled in a strict manner. The fact of the matter is we do not have anyone who is without guilt to deal with it. Our public officials who should lead the example are the worst reprobates. The evil has expanded even to jurisdictive establishments. The CBI, which is the foremost body to deal with these cases, is itself completely controlled by and subservient to the Ministry. In spite of the Supreme Court restating what Lord Denning announced in England, that the police officer is accountable to the law and no Minister shall influence him which case to probe and whom to take into custody, the condition in this country has not changed. Morality in public life does not seem to be a grave concern of anybody in India.

History educates us that no nation has been devastated by external invasion but several countries have been destroyed by internal debauchery. We can still retrieve the circumstances if we keep this lesson in mind. We do not appear to take pleasure in the rule of law in this nation. That will happen only in case of absolute transparency in government administration. Glasnost is necessary for India to survive. The common man has been misled by governments both at the Centre and in the States that they are resolved to open government. A few bills have surfaced here and there. However, public administration is close to public examination. Tolstoy composed, "Slavery has been abolished in Rome, it has been abolished in America which provoked even a civil war, and it has been abolished in Russia—the word has been abolished but the fact remains." This has been achieved with clarity and the rule of law. One cannot bargain on lack of uprightness in public organizations or even corporate organizations barring at our own risk. It is not hard to accomplish a sensibly honest social order if there is greater education and some amount of coercion from the voters. The American system, with all its shortcomings, has its administration and judiciary operating openly and free of party influences. The judges and several public administrators are selected in the United States among those belonging to the party in power. President Truman once experienced that the best way to transform a fast friend into an adversary was to choose him to a public office specifically the Supreme Court. Eisenhower professed that one of his extremely foolish faults was employing Earl Warren as Chief Justice of the United States. Nixon lost his case in a court headed by his own candidate, Warren Burger. In England, conventionally, the civil services and the judiciary refuse to abide by the party's rule. There is some unusual transformation in them, which we have missed.

In India, unless we build up this approach, and our officials in all the units of the state demonstrate a measure of autonomy and stop to be boneless miracles, the future is miserable. During the Falkland war, when an Exocet missile submerged an Argentinian ship transporting civilians, the Defence Minister cooked-up the story in Parliament as a military assault. However, once the war finished, a Deputy Secretary in the Ministry disclosed the fact in a letter to the MP who had raised some questions in Parliament over the matter. The official was impeached for breach of the Official Secrets Act. The pleasant succession was that in England, they could not discover a jury to convict this upright guilty person who believed that his accountability was to the public and not to the Minister. The lessons are evident since we have in common several characteristics of British Parliamentary procedure and civil services.

Transparency in public services was the reason which Rajaji waged war all through his life. It was Gandhiji's chief principle of faith. Men of prominence such as Nanda, Radhakrishnan, Morarji, Charan Singh and Kamaraj, to refer some of our leaders, were representatives of absolute uprightness. In the same manner, we had administrators such as H. V. R. Iyengar, L. P. Singh, Rustomji, Parthasarathy Iyengar, Arul and Kohli barely to cite a few. They were the example for others to follow. Presently, even after searching all over the land, one may yet not find an administrator of their like. However, our Secretaries and Chief Secretaries and some senior police officers are observed not in government workplaces but in penal institution for some or other conviction. When Prime Minister and the entire Cabinet are found guilty for corruption, the scenarios is not a pleasant one. When judges are prosecuted for serious dereliction of duty, management of law and justice becomes a travesty.

A learned and watchful public is the only solution to the issue and as discussed before we should persist on ingenuousness in government if we want to safeguard our existence. Globalization should not be restricted to trade and commerce. We should also have in us some of the organizational qualities of other democracies. Ombudsmen, autonomous police forces and unbiased civil servants are essential requirements. The commotions in Southeast Asia and Latin American nations, Africa and Russia hold serious lessons in regard to this. Sarvepalli Radhakrishnan alerted the people when he cautioned that when aspiration and power overtake a nation's capabilities and sense of values, disaster is the surest end. Answerability is the core of a democratic structure. In the end analysis, all of us are answerable to that "little man with a little pencil making a little mark on a little piece of paper. All the rhetoric cannot diminish a bit of its importance." That was Churchill addressing the House of Commons on disclosing with the public the war stratagem. It is time that rather than general indifference and a sarcastic sense, we bustle ourselves to our obligations and maintained our significance in the affairs of state. The excerpt taken from Shakespeare's Julius Caesar 'Let us remind ourselves that the fault, dear Brutus, is not in our stars but in ourselves that we are underlings' holds true in the present scenarios as well.

CULPABILITY

Culpability derives from the Latin idea of fault (*culpa*). The idea of culpability is closely bound to concepts of agency, freedom and free will. All are generally considered to be necessary, yet not adequate, conditions for culpability. In clarifications and forecasts of human action and inaction, culpability is a measure of the extent to which an agent, such as an individual, can be held ethically or legally accountable. Culpability indicates the separating line between ethical vice, such as murder, for which somebody may be held accountable and natural disaster, such as earthquakes, for which nobody can be held accountable.

From a legal point of view, culpability expresses the amount of one's *blameworthiness* in the commitment of a crime or offense. Barring strict liability crimes, the kind and gravity of penalty often is a consequence of the degree of culpability.

Contemporary criminal codes in the United States generally make different four degrees of culpability. Legal descriptions are as follows:

1. A person acts purposely with respect to a material element of an offence when:
   (i) If the element involves the nature of his conduct or a result thereof, it is his conscious object to engage in conduct of that nature or to cause such a result; and
   (ii) If the element involves the attendant circumstances, he is aware of the existence of such circumstances or he believes or hopes that they exist.
2. A person acts knowingly with respect to a material element of an offense when:
   (i) If the element involves the nature of his conduct or the attendant circumstances, he is aware that his conduct is of that nature or that such circumstances exist; and
   (ii) If the element involves a result of his conduct, he is aware that it is practically certain that his conduct will cause such a result.
3. A person acts recklessly with respect to a material element of an offense when he consciously disregards a substantial and unjustifiable risk that the material element exists or will result from his conduct. The risk must be of such a nature and degree that, considering the nature and intent of the actor's conduct and the circumstances known to him, its disregard involves a gross deviation from the standard of conduct that a reasonable person would observe in the actor's situation.
4. A person acts negligently with respect to a material element of an offense when he should be aware of a substantial and unjustifiable risk that the material element exists or will result from his conduct. The risk must be of such a nature and degree that the actor's failure to perceive it, considering the nature and intent of his conduct and the circumstances known to him, involves a gross deviation from the standard of care that a reasonable person would observe in the actor's situation.

(The above excerpt has been quoted precisely from the Pennsylvania Crimes Code. That in succession arises from the American Law Institute's Model Penal Code, which is the origin for large segments of the criminal codes in most states. The only dissimilarity is that the MPC uses "purposely" rather than "intentionally".)

In brief:

- An individual produces a result intentionally if the outcome is his/her objective in doing the action that triggers it,
- An individual produces a result intentionally if he/she is aware that the outcome is almost certain to happen from the action he/she assumes,

- An individual produces an outcome irresponsibly if he/she is mindful of and disrespects a substantial and inexcusable risk of the result triggering from the action, and
- An individual produces an outcome inattentively if there is a substantial and indefensible risk he/she is unmindful of but should be aware of.

The initial two kinds of culpability are each a subdivision of the following. Hence, if somebody acts intentionally, they also act knowingly. When somebody acts knowingly, they also act irresponsibly. The descriptions of particular crimes allude to these extents to establish the mens rea (mental state) essential for an individual to be culpable of a crime. The severer the culpability requirements, the more difficult it is for the tribunal to prove its case. For example, the first degree murder (again in PA) is expressed as "A criminal homicide constitutes murder of the first degree when it is committed by an intentional killing." Thus to be held blameworthy of murder in the first degree, one need to have an obvious objective in one's mind to trigger the death of another. On the contrary, irresponsible endangerment has a much extensive necessity: "A person commits a misdemeanour of the second degree if he recklessly engages in conduct which places or may place another person in danger of death or serious bodily injury." Hence, to be held culpable of this an individual only needs to be aware of a considerable risk he is putting others in danger of; it does not have to be one's obvious goal to put people in danger. (But, if one's objective *is* to put others in considerable risk of death or grave bodily injury, this is, obviously, sufficient.) There is another type of culpability, and that is *strict liability*. In strict liability crimes, the actor is accountable whatever his mental state is; in case the result occurs, the actor is accountable. An instance of this is the felony murder rule: if the prosecution establishes beyond sensible doubt that a person commits a qualifying crime during which death occurs, that person is held stringently accountable for murder and the prosecution need not prove any of the general culpability conditions for murder.

SCAPEGOATING

Scapegoating (from the verb "to scapegoat") is the process of discriminating any party for unjustified negative treatment or accusing as a scapegoat. Scapegoating might be directed by people against people (e.g., "Hattie Francis did it, not me!"), people against communities (e.g., "I failed because our school favours boys"), communities against people (e.g., "Jane was the reason our team didn't win"), and communities against communities (e.g., "Immigrants are taking all of the jobs"). A scapegoat might be a grown person, relative, child, worker, contemporary, ethnic or religious group, or country. A whipping boy, recognized patient or "fall guy" are kinds of scapegoat.

A medical description of scapegoating is as follows:

"Process in which the mechanisms of projection or displacement are utilized in focusing feelings of aggression, hostility, frustration, etc., upon another individual or group; the amount of blame being unwarranted."

Scapegoating is a strategy frequently utilized to describe a whole community of people as per the unethical or immoral behaviour of a small number of people pertaining to that group. Scapegoating correlates to guilt by connection and typecasting. Scapegoated communities throughout history have comprised almost every conceivable group of individuals: genders, religions, individuals of various races or countries, individuals with various political notions, or individual disagreeing in conduct from the majority. Nevertheless, scapegoating might also be utilized to establishments, such as governments, corporations, or different political communities. Projection: Undesirable views and feelings can be unintentionally projected onto another who becomes a victim for one's own issues. This idea can be expanded to projection by communities. In this case, the preferred person, or communities, becomes the scapegoat for the communities' issues. "Political agitation in all countries is full of such projections, just as much as the backyard gossip of little groups and individuals." Swiss psychiatrist Carl Jung believed in reality that "there must be some people who behave in the wrong way; they act as scapegoats and objects of interest for the normal ones".

In psychopathology, projection is a particularly regularly utilized defence system in individuals with the following personality disorders:

- Antisocial personality disorder
- Borderline personality disorder
- Narcissistic personality disorder
- Paranoid personality disorder
- Psychopathy

The scapegoat theory of intergroup argument offers clarification for the association between times of comparative economic despondency and increases in predisposition and aggression towards outgroups. For instance, analyses of anti-black hostility in the southern United States between 1882 and 1930 show a relationship between inferior economic conditions and outbreaks of hostility, for example, lynching, against blacks. The relationship between the value of cotton (the primary product of the region at that time) and the number of killing of black men by whites ranged from –0.63 to –0.72, indicating that a deprived economy provoked white individuals to take out their disappointments by assaulting an outgroup. Scapegoating as a community nevertheless, demands that in-group members settle on a particular target to hold accountable for their troubles. Scapegoating is also more probable to emerge when a group has come across difficult, prolonged negative experiences, as in opposition to minor annoyances.

When negative circumstances discourage a community's efforts at successful attainment of its most necessary requirements, for example, food, shelter, communities may develop a persuasive, shared belief that—when combined with social and political tensions—may result in the most extreme kind of scapegoating: genocide. Scapegoating can also instigate oppressed communities to assault on other oppressed communities. Even when discriminations are executed against a minority community by the majority community, minorities sometimes assault against another minority group to make up for antagonizing the more powerful majority. In administration: Scapegoating is an acknowledged practice in management where a subordinate staff worker is held responsible for the faults of senior executives. This is mostly due to lack of answerability in upper management. For instance, a teacher who consistently gets blamed or accused of misdeeds could be a scapegoat if said teacher is only embarrassed for doing her job so well that in comparison her colleagues and supervisory administration look bad. This could lead to letters being kept in permanent files, demeaning remarks from colleagues and consistent accusations from management.

BRIBE PAYERS INDEX

Bribe Payers Index (BPI) is a measure of willingness of a country to conform to the demands for corrupt business practices. The first BPI was issued by Transparency International on 26 October 1999.

METHODOLOGY

The BPI 2011 positioned 22 of the prominent exporting nations on the possibility that their multinational businesses will make use of bribery when functioning abroad. The ranking is computed from reactions by industrialists to a couple of queries on the World Economic Forum's Executive Opinion Survey. The first query asks for the nation of starting point of foreign-owned organizations doing the most business in their nation. The second query is: "In your experience, to what extent do firms from the countries you have selected make undocumented extra payments or bribes?" Answers should be provided on a scale of 1 (bribes are common or even necessary) to 10 (bribes are unheard of). The BPI rating is the mean score, with higher scores indicating a lower probability of using bribery. These countries were chosen as the prominent international or regional exporting nations. Their collective global exports constituted 75 per cent of the world total in 2006.

CORRUPTION PERCEPTIONS INDEX

Since 1995, Transparency International (TI) issues the Corruption Perceptions Index (CPI) per annum rating countries "by their perceived levels of corruption, as determined by expert assessments and opinion surveys." The CPI usually states corruption as "the misuse of public power for private benefit." Since 2012, the CPI has rated 176 nations "on a scale from 100 (very clean) to 0 (highly corrupt)." In previous years, the scale vary from 10 to 0.

METHODS

Transparency International appointed Johann Graf Lambsdorff of the University of Passau to create the Corruption Perceptions Index (CPI). The 2012 CPI draws on 13 diverse surveys and assessments from 12 diverse establishments. The organizations are the African Development Bank, the Bertelsmann Foundation, the Economist Intelligence Unit, Freedom House, Global Insight, International Institute for Management Development, Political and Economic Risk Consultancy, Political Risk Services, the World Bank, the World Economic Forum and the World Justice Project. Many of these private establishments have formidable connections to specific governments or countries, such as the World Bank which is financed by particular nations. The 13 surveys/assessments are either industrialist opinion surveys or performance analyses from a group of analysts. Early CPIs utilized public opinion surveys. Countries must be evaluated by at least three bases to figure in the CPI. The CPI determines perception of corruption because of the complexity in measuring absolute levels of corruption.

Validity

A report issued in 2002 discovered a "very strong significant correlation" between the Corruption Perceptions Index and two other substitutes for corruption: Black Market operations and excess of regulation. All three systems of measurement also possess a highly noteworthy relationship with real gross domestic product per capita (RGDP/Cap). The Corruption Perceptions Index relationship with RGDP/Cap was the most formidable.

Year-to-Year Comparisons

Since the set of sources varies, matching corruption scores and ranking over time is unsuitable. Moreover, the practice of this index changed in 2012. Nevertheless, with the novel practice, it will be conceivable to make year-to-year correlation after 2013.

2012 REPORT

For the 2012 study, the countries that were rated as having the lowest perceived stages of corruption were Australia, Canada, Denmark, Finland, Luxembourg, New Zealand, Sweden, Singapore, Switzerland, Norway, Netherlands and Iceland.

RELATION TO GDP GROWTH AND FOREIGN INVESTMENT

Research papers issued in 2007 and 2008 studied the economic outcomes of corruption perception, as described by the CPI. The researchers discovered a relationship between a higher CPI and higher long-term economic development, and a rise in GDP growth of 1.7% for every unit rise in a country's CPI score. Also revealed was a power-law dependence connecting higher CPI score to higher rates of foreign investment in a nation.

WHISTLEBLOWER

A whistleblower (whistle-blower or whistle blower) is an individual who reveals wrongdoing, asserted deceitful or unlawful movement happening in a corporation. The asserted misbehaviour might be categorized in several ways; for instance, a breach of a legislation, rule, regulation and/or a direct menace to people's interest, such asdeception, health and safety breaches and corruption. Whistleblowers might make their accusations internally (e.g., to other individuals within the accused corporation) or externally (to regulators, law enforcement agencies, to the media or to groups pertaining to the issues). One of the foremost laws that shielded whistleblowers was the 1863 United States False Claims Act (revised in 1986), which attempted to contend fraud by providers of the United States government amid the Civil War. The act emboldens whistleblowers by assuring them a percentage of the wealth recovered or recompenses won by the government and shields them from unlawful dismissal. Whistleblowers often face retaliation, occasionally at the hands of the corporation or community which they have indicted, occasionally from associated corporations, and occasionally under law. Queries about the legality of whistle blowing, the ethical accountability of whistle blowing, and the assessment of the institutions of whistle blowing are part of the domain of political ethics.

OVERVIEW

Origin of Term

The term *whistle-blower* originates from the whistle a referee uses to signal an unlawful or foul act. US civic activist Ralph Nader introduced the expression in the early 1970s to steer clear of the negative implications found in other words such as "informers" and "snitches".

Definition

Most whistleblowers are *internal whistleblowers*, who describe misbehaviour on an associate worker or higher-ranking official within their organization. One of the most noteworthy queries with regards to internal whistleblowers is why and under what situations individuals will either work on the spot to stop illegal and otherwise intolerable conduct or report it. There is some motivation to trust that individuals are more prone to take action with regards to intolerable conduct, within an establishment, if there are complaint systems that provide not merely choices ordered by the planning and control establishment, but a *choice* of options for total confidentiality.

External whistleblowers, nevertheless, give an account of misconduct to external individuals or entities. In such instances, relying on the information's harshness and nature, whistleblowers might report the wrongdoing to lawyers, the media, law enforcement or ombudsman agencies, or other local, state, or federal agencies. In some instances, external whistleblowing is emboldened by proposing monetary remuneration. Under most US federal whistleblower rulings, in order to be considered a whistleblower, the federal employee must have motive to trust his or her employer has broken some law, rule or regulation; testify or start a legal proceeding on the legally protected matter; or refuse to break the law. In the event where whistleblowing on a particular topic is secured by law, US courts have normally held that such whistleblowers are shielded from retribution. Nevertheless, a firmly isolated US Supreme Court decision, Garcetti v. Ceballos (2006) held that the First Amendment free discourse ensure for government workers do not shield revelations made within the scale of the employees' duties.

Common Reactions

Notions about whistleblowing shift extensively. Whistleblowers are occasionally assumed as selfless martyrs for society's interest and administrative accountability; others perceive them as "traitors" or "defectors," merely following individual glory and fame. Some scholars (such as Thomas Alured Faunce) believe that whistleblowers should at least be authorized to a rebuttable hypothesis that they are endeavouring to put into operation ethical principles in the face of problems and that whistleblowing would be more regarded in governance mechanisms if it had a stronger academic base in virtue ethics. It is likely that many individuals do not even think about blowing the whistle, not only because of fear of reprisal, but also due to apprehension of losing their connections at work and outside work.

Harassment of whistleblowers has become a grave concern in several parts of the world (as mentioned in the excerpt taken from Whistleblowing, Project Gutenberg Self-Publishing—eBooks)

Employees in academia, business or government might become aware of serious risks to health and the environment, but internal policies might pose threats of retaliation to those who report these early warnings. Private company employees in particular might be at risk of being fired, demoted, denied raises and so on for bringing environmental risks to the attention of appropriate authorities. Government employees could be at a similar risk for bringing threats to health or the environment to public attention, although perhaps this is less likely. There are examples of "early warning scientists" being harassed for bringing inconvenient truths about impending harm to the notice of the public and authorities. There have also been cases of young scientists being discouraged from entering controversial scientific fields for fear of harassment.

Although whistleblowers are frequently shielded under legislation from employer retribution, there have been numerous instances where penalty for whistleblowing has occurred, such as termination, suspension, demotion, wage garnishment, and/or harsh mistreatment by other workers. For instance, in the United States, most whistleblower protection laws offer for limited "make whole" cures or compensations for employment losses if whistleblower retribution is proven. Nevertheless, numerous whistleblowers state that there exists an extensive "shoot the messenger" state of mind by establishments or government agencies alleged of wrongdoing and in some instances whistleblowers have been exposed to criminal trial in retaliation for reporting misconduct. As a response to this, many private corporations have established whistleblower legal defence funds or support groups to help whistleblowers; two such examples are the *National Whistleblowers Center* in the United States and *Public Concern at Work* in the UK.

LEGAL PROTECTION

Legal protection for whistleblowing changes from nation to nation and might rely on any of the nation of the primary activity, where and how confidential facts were uncovered, and how they ultimately became published or publicized. More than a dozen nations have now embraced all-inclusive whistleblower protection laws which form procedures for reporting, investigate reports and offer legal securities to the individuals who informed them. More than 50 countries have embraced more constrained safety rules as part of their anti-corruption, freedom of information, or employment laws. *For objectives of the English Wikipedia, this section put emphasis on the English-speaking world and encompasses other authorities only insofar as they denote remarkably greater or lesser protections.*

The Government of India has been contemplating embracing a whistleblower protection law for many years. In 2003, the Law Commission of India proposed the embracing of the Public Interest Disclosure (Protection of Informers) Act, 2002. In August 2010, the Public Interest Disclosure and Protection of Persons Making the Disclosures Bill, 2010 was presented before the Lok Sabha, lower house of the Parliament of India. The Bill was endorsed by the cabinet in June, 2011. The Public Interest Disclosure and Protection of Persons Making the Disclosures Bill, 2010 was given a new name as The Whistleblowers' Protection Bill, 2011 by the Standing Committee on Personnel, Public Grievances, Law and Justice. On 28 December 2011, the Whistleblowers' Protection Bill, 2011 was approved by the Lok Sabha. The Bill was presented before Rajya Sabha on 29 March 2012 by V. Narayanasamy, Minister of State for Parliamentary Affairs. On 21 February 2014, the Bill was passed by the Rajya Sabha and the President gave his approval on 9 May 2014. All establishments, whether public, private, or non-profit (including governmental) should, as a best mechanism, embrace a solid whistleblower mechanism to encourage its workers to internally report unlawful or extremely risky activity straightforwardly to its board of directors or trustees. Without a strong whistleblower mechanism, directors/trustees of the corporation may fail in their oversight obligations. A strong whistleblower mechanism promotes internal reporting of wrongdoing so as to allow it to be rectified. It is specifically significant in nations, such as the United States, which offer significant monetary rewards to whistleblowers who externally report unlawful conduct to government units. There have been various instances of boards of directors/trustees who have been ignorant as to issues in the corporations, even though lower level employees were aware of these issues. These boards were misinformed because they depended chiefly on top administration and the auditors for their communication or knowledge.

Protection of Whistleblower in India

The process of safeguarding whistleblower in India is related to procedures implemented to shield someone who plays a role in unearthing alleged wrongdoing. The act of wrongdoing might include fraud, corruption or mismanagement. India did not have any law to safeguard whistleblowers until 2012 even as the Public Interest Disclosure and Protection to Persons Making the Disclosure Bill, 2010, was already passed by the Cabinet of India as part of an effort to eradicate corruption in the country's bureaucracy.

NEED OF LEGISLATION

Whistleblowers have been facing threat to their life as can be seen from the instances of threatening, harassment and even murder of few of those. An engineer, Satyendra Dubey, who busted a scam in the National Highways Authority of India's Golden Quadrilateral project, was killed in November 2003. Following the suit two years later, an Indian Oil Corporation official, Shanmughan Manjunath, was killed mercilessly for closing a petrol pump that was selling adulterated fuel. A Karnataka employee SP Mahantesh, allegedly a whistleblower in debated land allotments by societies, was killed in May 2012. Mahantesh was deputed as Deputy Director of the audit wing in the state's Cooperative department and reported loopholes in different societies involving some officials and political people. In another instance, when a senior police officer reported that Mayawati's government was corrupt and had misappropriated large amounts of funds, he was admitted to a psychiatric hospital. Social activists and concerned figures were demanding a quick passage of the Whistleblowers Protection Bill in Parliament. There were demands for a law to safeguard whistleblowers, provide the disclosure of information and uncover corruption in government organizations. In June 2011, there was a recommendation from parliamentary panel that ministers, the higher judiciary, security organizations, defence and intelligence forces and regulatory authorities should be brought under the whistleblowers' protection bill to monitor and control corruption and the wilful misuse of power.

ANALYSIS OF THE LEGISLATION

As per the Indian law reports, the bill has been criticized at many fronts for its limited access or jurisdiction which is only for the government sector and those who are working for the Government of India or its agencies and not for the state-government employees. Although the bill for guarding whistleblowers is considered a positive move, the absence of public debate and discussion on the bill brings to the fore the danger of it becoming another 'paper tiger'. Usually, ministries recommending draft legislation follow a stage of public consultation so that public opinion can be inculcated in the proposed act. This stage was given a miss during the planning of this very act, which has not gone unnoticed. Law neither includes provisions to encourage whistleblowing (financial incentives), nor provides any help for corporate whistleblowers; it fails to extend its jurisdiction to the private sector (a strange omission, after the fraud at Satyam). The Directorate of Income Tax Intelligence and Criminal Investigation is one of the only departments sanctioned for the safeguarding of whistleblowers. The principle of the bill is to bring equilibrium to the need to protect honest officials from harassment with safeguarding people making a public-interest disclosure. It also has guidelines for those who file false complaints. In contrast, it does not offer a penalty for attacking a complainant. The Central Vigilance Commission (CVC) was elected in 2004 to accept public-interest revelations via government resolution; A few hundred complaints are being registered every year since then. The provisions of the bill are akin to that of the resolution. Therefore, it is not possible that the number of complaints will differ significantly. The CVC only has the power to make recommendations. It doesn't have the authority to impose penalties, as compared to the influences of the Karnataka and Delhi Lokayukta. The bill fails to define disclosure and victimization in a wider sense in contrast to other nations such as the USA, the UK and Canada. It differs to a great length when compared with the proposed Bill of the Law Commission and the Second Administrative Reform Commission's report. Discrepancies include non-admission of anonymous complaints and absence of punishments for officials who abuse whistleblowers. It was thought that after its implementation, the law to safeguard whistleblowers would help in identifying corruption, confirming better information flow and making the way for successful trial of corrupt individuals through clear and protected procedures. It is evident from hostilities against whistleblowers that people in India have lack of determination in fighting the evil of corruption as they fear for unwanted intimidation by the accused. Another loophole is the lack of any specified time period for disposing of these cases. The bill sans public debate makes it difficult for people to understand its core values and functions.

CENTRAL VIGILANCE COMMISSION INITIATIVE: BLOW YOUR WHISTLE

In a bid to make people aware over the issue of corruption in the system and empowerment of the citizens in their struggle against corruption, the CVC has set up Blow your whistle technology. It was devised to tackle all issues of Corruption in the Central Government.

CLASSIFIED INFORMATION

Classified information refers to sensitive and secret information or material of government that requires secrecy based on national or regional security needs. Access to this information is restricted by law or regulation to particular groups of people, and mishandling can attract criminal punishments. It can only be accessed after attaining formal security clearance from the concerned authorities. The stage of clearance usually needs a detailed background investigation. There exist typically different hierarchical levels of sensitivity (e.g. restricted, confidential, secret and top secret), with variations in clearance requirements. The process involves the formal categorization and marking of information (material) by level of sensitivity, but it has given rise to a sense in line with 'censored' in US English. The stage of assigning the level of sensitivity to data is known as data classification. A comparison is usually done between formal security classification and privacy markings such as 'commercial in confidence'. Particular practices and jargon undergo variations by country and language. Some companies and non-government establishments make multiple levels of protection for sensitive information, either via a wish to guard trade secrets, or due to codes and conducts governing various matters such as personal privacy, sealed legal proceedings and the timing of financial information releases.

GOVERNMENT CLASSIFICATION

Classification of data is performed to safeguard information from being used to tarnish or jeopardize national security. Classification ratifies what forms a 'state secret' and assigns different levels of protection on the basis of the probable harm any breach would cause. In contrast, the secret data are usually 'leaked' to correspondents secretly by officials for political motives. Several US presidents have revealed sensitive data to fulfil their political motives.

Classification Levels

Although every nation has its own classification systems, most of them have levels relating to the following British definitions (from the highest level to lowest)

Top Secret (TS)

Being the highest level on a national level assigned to information, apart from items of 'Cosmic TS' or 'Code word TS', such data would cause 'exceptionally grave damage' to national security if made publicly available.

Secret

Such information would pose 'serious damage' to national security if it were available to public.

Confidential

This type of information would pose 'damage' or be 'prejudicial' to national security if made available to all; in several nations like Taiwan, this level is also known as 'Classified'.

Restricted

If this material is leaked, it would cause 'undesirable effects'. Some nations lack such a classification; in public sectors, such as commercial industries, this level is also known as 'Private Information'.

Unclassified

Although not a classification level, it is assigned to government documents that do not have a classification listed above. Such materials can sometimes be accessed by those without security clearance.

There are a excess of pseudo classifications in this level. For more information, refer to the articles on Sensitive but Unclassified and Controlled Unclassified Information.

Clearance

There exist various rules regarding attaining the clearance to access such documents based on the level of classification. These rules also states how documents must be stored, transmitted, and destroyed. Besides, access is not granted on a 'need to know' basis. These documents cannot be viewed just by getting clearance, but an individual must also present a legitimate 'need to know'.

Compartmented Information

To make the breach almost impossible to occur, there are often additional limitations on access, such as (in the U.S.) Special Intelligence (SI), which safeguards intelligence sources and methods, No Foreign dissemination (NOFORN), which confines spreading to U.S. nationals, and Originator Controlled dissemination (ORCON), which guarantees that the creator can track bearers of the information. Documents in several compartments are marked with specific 'code words' in addition to the classification level.

Nuclear Information

Information with the government regarding nuclear weapons such as nuclear warheads often has a supplementary marking to show it contains such information.

Sharing Classified Information between Countries

Information sharing among countries happens on a different classification scheme that both parties have previously agreed to honour. For instance, the marking ATOMAL is marked to U.S. RESTRICTED DATA or FORMERLY RESTRICTED DATA and United Kingdom ATOMIC information that has been released to NATO. ATOMAL documents are assigned COSMIC TOP SECRET ATOMAL (CTSA), NATO SECRET ATOMAL (NSAT) or NATO CONFIDENTIAL ATOMAL (NCA). In cases where any nation desires to share classified documents bilaterally (or multilaterally) with a nation that has a sharing agreement, the information is with the nations it can be shared with. Those nations are required to uphold the classification of the information at the level initially classified (TOP-SECRET, SECRET, etc.) with the suitable caveat (USNZ, AUSGE, CANUK, etc.).

NATO Classifications

For instance, sensitive documents shared amongst NATO nations have four levels of security classification; from most to least classified:

1. COSMIC TOP SECRET (CTS),
2. NATO SECRET (NS),
3. NATO CONFIDENTIAL (NC), and
4. NATO RESTRICTED (NR).

There are some exceptions related to NATO UNCLASSIFIED (NU) information. Documents with this marking are the sole NATO property (copyright) and must not be made public sans the nod of NATO. Unless marked as RELEASABLE FOR INTERNET TRANSMISSION, these types of documents cannot be cleared for internet-transmission either. Information that can be made public, however, should be clearly mentioned with NON SENSITIVE INFORMATION RELEASABLE TO THE PUBLIC.

Besides the above classification levels, NATO operates with the following:

COSMIC TOP SECRET - A

This level is granted to those who require to have access to the joint Atomic programme of NATO. This level is never granted permanently to anyone, irrespective of job title, for example, President of the U.S.A. etc. It is granted only for a given or short period, when needed.

International Organizations

- European Commission holds five levels as follows: EU TOP SECRET, EU SECRET, EU CONFIDENTIAL, EU RESTRICTED and EU COUNCIL/COMMISSION. (Note that usually the French term is used.)
- OCCAR, a European defence organization, defines three levels of classification as follows: OCCAR SECRET, OCCAR CONFIDENTIAL and OCCAR RESTRICTED.

CITIZEN'S CHARTER

Citizen's Charter states a concerted effort to emphasize on the promise of the Organization towards its Citizens regarding Standard of Services, Information, Choice and Consultation, Non-discrimination and Accessibility, Grievance Redress, Courtesy and Value for Money. This also highlights hopes of the Organization from the Citizen for achieving the commitment of the Organization. The term 'Citizen' in the Citizen's Charter refers to the clients or customers whose interests and benefits are addressed by the Citizen's Charter and, therefore, consists of not only the citizens but also all the stakeholders, i.e., citizens, customers, clients, users, beneficiaries, other Ministries/Departments/Organizations, State Governments, UT Administrations etc. It includes not only the Central Government Ministries/Departments/Organizations but also the Departments/Agencies of State Governments and UT Administrations. Many Departments/Agencies of several State Governments and UT Administrations have framed their Charters. More than 600 of these types of Charters have so far been framed by Agencies/Organizations of 24 States/Union Territories. These are not legally enforceable and, hence, are non-justiciable. However, it is a framework to ensure the delivery of services to citizens with specified standards, quality and time frame, etc. with promises from the Organization and its clients. The Department of Administrative Reforms and Public Grievances in Ministry of Personnel, Public Grievances and Pensions, Government of India, for providing more responsive and citizen-friendly governance, manages the efforts to frame and implement Citizen's Charters in Central Government, State Governments and UT Administrations. It also highlights guidelines for framing and executing the Charters as well as their review.

Following features are a must for a good Citizen's Charter:

(i) Vision and Mission Statement of the institution

(ii) Information of business transacted by the institution

(iii) Information of 'Citizens' or 'Clients'

(iv) Statement of services, including standards, quality, time frame, etc., offered to each Citizen/Client group separately and how/where to get the services

(v) Information of Grievance Redress Mechanism and how to access it

(vi) Anticipations from the 'Citizens' or 'Clients'

(vii) Added promises such as compensation in the event of failure of service delivery.

The following road map can be used to frame the Citizen's Charter in your institution:-

(i) Constituting a Task Force in the Organization to frame the Citizen's Charter

(ii) Mark all partners in the Organization and major services provided by Organization;

(iii) Constituting a Core Group in the Organization having representatives from all stakeholders which may consist of Top Management, Middle Management, cutting-edge level, staff representatives, strategic partners, Customers/Clients, etc.; This Group shall manage the formation of the Citizen's Charter and accept it. Later, its implementation is also monitored.

(iv) Discussions with Clients/Stakeholders Staff (Primarily at cutting-edge level) and their representative associations;

(v) Formation of Draft Citizen's Charter;

   (a) Circulation for comments/suggestions

   (b) Adjustment of Charter to include suggestions.

(vi) Submission of draft Charter to Department of Administrative Reforms and Public Grievances

(vii) Consideration of the Charter by Core Group

(viii) Alteration of Charter by the Ministry/Department as per suggestions/observations by the Core Group
(ix) Agreement by Minister-in-charge
(x) Formal issue/release of Charter and putting up on website
(xi) Distributing copies to People's Representatives and all stakeholders
(xii) Nomination of a Nodal Officer to ensure effective implementation.

THE CITIZENS' CHARTER: INDIAN EXPERIENCE

Basic Concept, Origin and Principles

It has been experienced that sustainable development, both economic and social, can become a reality only after having good governance. The three important features related to good governance are transparency, liability and openness of the administration. 'Citizens' Charters' initiative is a solution to the problems citizen faces, day in and day out, while tackling with the organizations providing public services.

The idea of Citizens' Charter protects the faith between the service provider and its users. The concept was initially proposed and executed in the United Kingdom by the Conservative Government of John Major in 1991 as a nation-wide programme with a simple goal to constantly improve the quality of public services for the people of the nation so that these services react to the requirements and desires of the users. The programme was reintroduced in 1998 by the Labour Government of Tony Blair which named it 'Services First'.

The main aim of it is includes empowering the citizen with respect to public service delivery. Six principles that were firstly constituted regarding the Citizens' Charter movement were as follows: (i) Quality: Improving the quality of services; (ii) Choice: Wherever possible; (iii) Standards: Specify what to expect and how to act if standards are not met; (iv) Value: For the taxpayers' money; (v) Accountability: Individuals and Organizations; and (vi) Transparency: Rules/Procedures/Schemes/Grievances. Later, these were expanded by the Labour Government as following nine principles of Service Delivery (1998):-

- Set standards of service
- Be open and offer full information
- Consult and involve
- Encourage access and the promotion of choice
- Treat all fairly
- Put things right when they go wrong
- Use resources effectively
- Innovate and improve
- Work with other providers.

THE INTERNATIONAL SCENE

The Citizens' Charter introduced by the UK impressed many nations around the world, resulting in several countries executing similar programmes, for instance, Australia

(Service Charter, 1997), Belgium (Public Service Users' Charter 1992), Canada (Service Standards Initiative, 1995), France (Service Charter, 1992), India (Citizens' Charter, 1997), Jamaica (Citizens' Charter 1994), Malaysia (Client Charter, 1993), Portugal (The Quality Charter in Public Services, 1993) and Spain (The Quality Observatory, 1992) (OECD, 1996). Some of these newly framed charters have great similarity to the UK model, whereas others opted for new ground by leaning on the service quality model of the Total Quality Management (TQM) movement. Other modes are pitched somewhere in between. Even in the UK, concerning the Next Steps/Modernizing Government Initiatives, Citizens' Charters have adopted a service quality face for delivery of public services. The quality tools used for improving public services comprise the Business Excellence Model, Investors in People, Charter Mark, ISO 9000 and Best Value (Government of UK, 1999).

The Malaysian Government proposed Guidelines on the Client's Charter in 1993 to help governmental organizations to frame and execute Client's Charter, which is 'a written commitment by an agency to deliver outputs or services according to specified standards of quality' (Government of Malaysia, 1998). To boost the process, a Best Client's Charter Award was presented in 1993. The Client's Charter introduced in Malaysia closely relates to the UK Model. A difference was kept between agency-wide and unit charters. The model of 'service recovery' aims to restore the trust and confidence of the client in a positive way when things go wrong. In 1997, in a bid to improve the quality of service offered by governmental organization to ensure customer-focussed outcomes, the Service Charter initiative was launched by the Commonwealth Government of Australia. Service Charters are thought of as a powerful tool for bringing change and require the agencies to emphasize on services delivered, to measure and assess performance and to start performance improvement. This Charter has an upper hand in bringing change as they have no competitor (Department of Finance and Administration, 1999). Centrelink is a one-stop platform that grants entry to Australian government services for over six million customers. Centrelink has accepted one-to-one service as an innovative and personalized method to service delivery. One-to-one service treats clients respectfully and consistently and makes the process of dealing with the government easy.

A Service Standard Initiative, being impressed by Citizens' Charters of the United Kingdom, with a wide scope has enlarged its scope considerably. This Initiative in Canada was initiated because of the citizen expectations relating to friendly, respectful and courteous service; faster reaction times; longer hours at government offices; and 'one-stop-shopping'. It is also needed that deficit should be reduced and value for money should be provided by efficiently using resources (Treasury Board of Canada, 1995). A comparison of these four major Citizens' Charter initiatives highlights that the service quality model is rooted in them at various degrees. Once the intention is clear to make public services citizen-centric, the customer focus of the Total Quality Management (TQM) variety cannot be far behind. In fact, the Citizens' Charter model has some similarities with TQM. Both start by concentrating on satisfying customer/citizen requirements. Other important common elements are conformance to standards, stakeholder involvement and constant improvement.

The Indian Scene

In India, over the course of time, there is a significant progress in the field of economic development. This has substantially increased in the literacy rate (from 51.63% to 65.38% in the last decade)as well as made Indian citizens increasingly aware of their rights. Citizens are now becoming more articulate, and they expect the administration to not only respond to their demands but also anticipate them. It was in this climate that since 1996 a consent had evolved in the Government on responsive and effective administration.

A conference of Chief Ministers of various States and Union Territories was held at New Delhi on 24 May, 1997 presided over by the Prime Minister of India in which an "Action Plan for Effective and Responsive Government" at the centre and state levels was used.

One major conclusion at the conference was that the Central and State Governments would formulate Citizens' Charters, initiating with those zones that have a large public interface, which can include Railways, Telecom, Posts, Public Distribution Systems.

These Charters were needed to incorporate benchmarks of service and time limits that the people can rationally anticipate, avenues of complaint redress and a facility for autonomous scrutiny with the engagement of citizen and consumer groups.

Department of Administrative Reforms and Public Grievances in Government of India (DARPG) commenced the job of synchronizing, planning and operationalizing Citizens' Charters. Guidelines for devising the Charters as well as a list of do's and don'ts were corresponded to different government divisions/organizations to empower them to bring out focused and effectual charters. To formulate the Charters, the government organizations at the Centre and State levels were encouraged to constitute a team with representation from users, senior administration and the advanced staff. A Handbook on Citizen's Charter has been brought out by the Department and forwarded to all the State Governments/UT Administrations. The Charters are anticipated to include the following components:-(i) Vision and Mission Statement; (ii) Details of business transacted by the organization; (iii) Details of clients; (iv) Details of services provided to each client group; (v) Details of grievance redress mechanism and how to access it; and (vi) Expectations from the clients. Mainly a modification of the UK model, the Indian Citizens' Charter has an added element of 'expectations from the clients' or put differently 'obligations of the users'. Engagement of consumer institutions, citizen groups, and other participants in the formulation of the Citizens' Charter is highlighted to make certain that the Citizens' Charter meets the requirements of the users. Consistent monitoring, review and analysis of the Charters, both inside and through external groups are enjoined. Till April 2006, 111 Citizens' Charters had been figured by the Central Government ministries/departments/institutions and 668 Charters by different departments of state governments and administrations of union territories. Most of the national Charters are displayed on the government's websites and are accessible for public scrutiny. The institutions with Citizens' Charters are instructed to utilize mediums such as print/electronic media and awareness campaigns to give publicity to their Charters.

COMPREHENSIVE WEBSITE ON CITIZENS' CHARTERS

An all-inclusive website of Citizens' Charters in Government of India (www.goicharters.nic.in) has been formulated and was commenced by the Department of Administrative Reforms and Public Grievances on 31 May 2002. This includes the Citizens' Charters released by different central government ministries/departments/organizations. The website presents valuable information, data and links.

EXEMPLARY IMPLEMENTATION OF THE CITIZENS' CHARTER

While the general endeavours and activities of the government on Citizens' Charter were enduring, it was comprehended that commendable enactment of the Charter in a key public interface area of government would not only bring about the novel idea in the inertia-prone administration but also work as a role model for replication in other segments/domains. The banking sector was recognized for this purpose taking into consideration the second stage of economic reforms and the reality that this sector was reasonably progressive with regards to customer service and was also exploiting the use of information technology to accelerate different processes. The main goal of this activity was to build the Banking Sector as a model of perfection in the enactment of the Citizens' Charter. In the initial stage, three major national level banks, namely, Punjab National Bank, Punjab and Sind Bank and Oriental Bank of Commerce, exercise by the DARPG in the year 2000. The following major issues were emphasized for commendable enactment of the Citizens' Charter:- (i) stakeholder engagement in the formulation of Citizens' Charters; (ii) deployment of the Citizens' Charters in the banks by full engagement of the staff, particularly the employees at the advanced level; (iii) creation of consciousness about the Charter amongst the clients of the banks; and (iv) exceptional training for employees at every stage about the concept and implementation of Citizens' Charter.

After an analysis of the present standing of the Charters by the recognized banks through autonomous organizations, Action Plans were drawn up to correct deficiencies. The Charters were, consequently, amended and institutionalized on the basis of the model/mother Charter developed by the Indian Banks Association (IBA). Training for workers of chosen branches through master trainers, trained by the National Institute of Bank Management utilizing a module created in consultation with Department of ARPG were conducted. A number of measures to give wide exposure to Citizens' Charter were also adopted. An external agency was involved once again to assess and analyse the enactment of Citizens' Charter of these banks at the end of this activity and also to record the hand-holding activity. National Institute of Bank Management was allocated this task which had since been implemented and a documentation was disclosed in the Year 2003.

EVALUATION OF CITIZENS' CHARTERS

An analysis of the Citizens' Charters of several government organizations was executed by DARPG and Consumer Coordination Council, New Delhi, an NGO, in October 1998. The results were quite positive given the budding phase of this proposal in India. A concise questionnaire has been distributed to all ministries/departments and state governments/union territories to empower them to carry out an in-house analysis of their Citizens' Charters. Organizations have also been instructed to carry out external analysis, rather through NGOs. During the Year 2002–2003, DARPG involved a professional organization to create a systematized model for internal and external analysis of Citizens' Charters in a more efficient, quantitative and objective manner. This agency also realized analysis of enactment of Charters in 5 central government organizations and 15 departments/organizations of states of Andhra Pradesh, Maharashtra and Uttar Pradesh. This organization was also needed to propose methods for enhancing awareness, both within the agency and among the users, and to recommend possible procedures for acclimatization of management and the employees in the assignment of formulating and implementing Charters.

According to the report of analysis undertaken by the organization, key findings were as follows:-

(i) In most of the cases Charters were not planned through a consultative approach;
(ii) Generally, service providers are not accustomed to philosophy, objectives and main characteristics of the Charter;
(iii) Sufficient promotional campaign to the Charters had not been carried out in any of the divisions analysed. In maximum divisions, the Charters are only in the nascent or middle phase of enactment;
(iv) No funds have been particularly allotted for awareness creation of Citizens' Charter or for orientation of employees on several elements of the Charter;

Key suggestions, among others, include:- (i) requirement for citizens and employees to be referred to at every phase of planning of the Charter, (ii) acclimatization of employees about the noticeable characteristics and aims/objectives of the Charter; vision and mission statement of the division; and expertise such as team formation, problem solving, management of complaints and communication skills, (iii) requirement for development of database on consumer complaints and remediation, (iv) requirement for widespread promotion of the Charter through print media, posters, banners, leaflets, handbills, brochures, local newspapers, etc., and also through electronic media, (v) allocation of exclusive budgets for awareness creation and acclimatization of employees and (vi) replication of best operations in this domain.

The Department of Administrative Reforms and Public Grievances has created a model for conceptualizing and enacting a Scheme for acknowledging distinction in service distribution by government agencies. The Scheme has been customized for government agencies with exclusive focus on citizen interface and expectations and is scheduled for enactment in the ministries in a phased manner. The model combines the ground actualities in India with International Best Practices and is grounded on appropriate enactment of citizen charters, efficiency of public grievance redress system and condition of service delivery enablers from the citizen's point of view and endeavours made by the departments in enhancing their own potential to deliver. The model had been tried among various institutions and was introduced before Workshops of NGOs, citizen groups and government agencies. These discourses have ultimately ended in enactment of the certification requirements. Utilizing the tools offered by this model, government organizations can self-evaluate and enhance quality of their service delivery, and over a time period advance to a level where an objective analysis can be done and excellence can be openly acknowledged.

INFORMATION AND FACILITATION COUNTERS (IFCs)

Information and Facilitation Counter (IFC) is a service established by chosen central government organizations to offer information to general population about their programmes/schemes, rules and processes, etc., as well as condition of cases/applications. An IFC also operates as a nodal point for indemnification of public grievances. The IFC, thus, is a physical demonstration of Citizens' Charter. Hence, a decision has been made at present to establish IFCs in all government ministries/divisions having Citizens' Charters. A total of 105 Information and Facilitation Counters/May I Help You/Inquiry Counters have been established as yet. Analysis of the working of the IFCs was executed by the DARPG and the Consumer Coordination Council. The establishments involved have acted on inadequacies mentioned in these analyses. This Department also frequently scrutinizes the functioning of the IFCs through a half-yearly return recommended for all the establishments that have set up IFCs.

PROBLEMS FACED IN IMPLEMENTING THE CHARTERS

As remarked, the Citizens' Charters programme in India had begun in 1997 and the Charters planned are in a budding phase of enactment. Initiation of a novel idea is always challenging in any institution. Initiation and enactment of the concept of Citizens' Charter in the Government of India was much more challenging because of the old bureaucratic establishment/procedures and the inflexible approaches of the manpower. The key challenges came across in this initiative were as follows:-

1. The general point of view of corporations which planned Citizens' Charters was that the activity was to be accomplished because there was an instruction from the top. The consultation procedure was nominal or largely absent. It thus became one of the everyday happenings of the institution and had no focus.
2. For any Charter to succeed, the workforce accountable for its implementation should have adequate training and acclimatization, as obligations of the Charter cannot be anticipated to be rendered by the employees that are uninformed of the essence and content of the Charter. Nevertheless, in several instances, the concerned staff were not properly trained and sensitized.
3. Occasionally, transfers and rearrangements of related officers at the critical phases of planning/implementation of a Citizens' Charter in an institution harshly destabilized the strategic methods which were put in place and hindered the progress of the initiative.
4. Awareness movements to teach clients about the Charter were not conducted systematically.

5. In some instances, the standards/time rules of services mentioned in Citizens' Charter were either too relaxed or too tight and were, thus, impractical and produced an disapproving impression on the clients of the Charter.
6. The idea behind the Citizens' Charter was not correctly understood. Information brochures, publicity materials, pamphlets created previously by the institutions were misconstrued as Citizens' Charters.

LESSONS LEARNT

The following lessons have been learnt from the experience up to now of executing Citizens' Charter initiative:

1. As with any novel endeavour, the Citizens' Charter initiative is bound to be viewed initially with scepticism by both administrators and general population. An effective awareness campaign amongst all the participants at the opening level is indispensable to overcome this scepticism. These awareness drives should be planned and delivered in a novel and efficient manner.
2. The issuance of Citizens' Charter will not transform instantaneously the mindset of the workforce and the consumers, build up over a period of time. Hence, regular, tireless and persistent endeavours are needed to produce the attitudinal changes.
3. A novel proposal always come across barriers and apprehensions from the workforce. There is an inherent opposition to change, specifically among the pioneering workforce. Engaging and consulting them at all the stages of conceptualization and execution of Citizens' Charter will go afar in surmounting this opposition and will make them an equal companion in this activity.
4. Rather than trying to modify all the procedures at once and come across massive opposition, it is sensible to split it into small elements and confront them one at a time.
5. The charter initiative should have an in-built procedure for monitoring, analysing and reviewing the working of the Charters, rather through an outside agency.

FUTURE VISION: DEVELOPMENT OF CHARTER MARK

In 1992, the UK Government initiated Charter Mark, a scheme for identifying and promoting merit in public service. To claim a Charter Mark the institution has to display excellence against the following nine Charter Mark standards which correspond to the standards of public service delivery, that is, (1) Performance standards; (2) Information and openness; (3) Choice and consultation; (4) Courtesy and helpfulness; (5) Putting things right; (6) Value for money; (7) Use satisfaction; (8) Improvements in service quality; and (9) Planned improvements and innovations. The Government of Malaysia also introduced a "Best Client's Charter Award" in 1993 grounded on the UK model. In India, the DARPG has recognized a specialized organization to create a suitable Charter Mark scheme. This scheme will promote and reward amendment in public service delivery with regard to the commitments and criteria reported in the Charter. The 'Charter Mark' is recommended to be granted after evaluation by an autonomous panel of judges. This would not only impart a sense of accomplishment to the institution bestowed the Charter

Mark but also boost a spirit of competitiveness amongst different institutions that have released Citizens' Charter and creating awareness among general public. A prototype has been formulated by the professional institution and is in the process of substantiation in recognized departments/institutions.

The execution of Citizens' Charter is a continuing activity because it has to reflect the widespread and frequent changes happening in the field of public services. Indian Government consistently endeavours to work for the citizens in an effectual and well-organized way so as not only to meet but to surpass their expectations. The Citizens' Charter scheme is a key step in this direction.

WORK CULTURE

An institution is established to realize specific goals and objectives by bringing people simultaneously on a general platform and inspiring them to offer their best services. It is necessary for the workforce to revel in the workplace for them to foster a sense of allegiance towards it.

Work culture holds a significant importance in extracting the best out of workforce and enabling their long-term association with the organization. The institution must provide a constructive environment to the workforce for them to focus effectively on their work instead of meddling in each other's work.

Work culture is an idea which deals in the study of the following:

1. Beliefs, thought processes, attitudes of the workforce.
2. Ideologies and principles of the institution.

The work culture decides the way workers interact with each other and determines the way an institution functions. In layman's term work culture implies the state of mind of the workforce which further determines the environment of the institution. An institution is said to have a robust work culture when the workforce abide by the institution's rules and regulations and stick to the existing guidelines. Nevertheless there are specific institutions where workforce are unwilling to abide by the directives and are made to work only by stringent processes. Such institutions have a weak culture.

FEATURES OF A HEALTHY WORK CULTURE

- A healthy work culture results in contented workforce and an enhanced output.
- Workers must be friendly with each other. They must have mutual respect for each other. Backbiting is regarded as stringently amateurish and must be shunned for a healthy work culture. One achieves nothing out of disputes and malicious politics at work.
- The behaviour towards each employee should be open-minded and unbiased. Favouritism leads to demoralized workforce and ultimately a negative work culture. Staffs should be assessed only by their work and nothing else. Individual relationships should be given a secondary status at the workplace. An employee should not be favoured just because of having blood relationship with the administrator.

- Acknowledging the top performers is of great consequence. Appreciate the staffs to anticipate good work from them on every occasion. Encourage and praise them to do well. They should be made to feel imperative for their institution. The administration should not find fault with those who have not performed well, rather ask them to make efforts to further improve their performance up to the mark for the next time. Provide them one more opportunity instead of terminating them instantaneously.
- Promote discourses at the workplace. Staffs must engage in discussion to sort out issues among themselves to arrive at better conclusions. Each employee should be given the liberty to express his own opinion. The group leaders and administrators must communicate with the subordinates regularly. Clarity is required at every stage for better coordination among staffs and a healthy work culture. Controlling information and data manipulating is strictly prohibited at the workplace. Information should be allowed to flow in its desired form.
- Institutions must have staff friendly procedures and workable guidelines. Anticipating a worker to work till late night on his birthday is just not viable. Rules and regulations should be formed for the benefit of the employees. Staff need to behave appropriately in order to maintain the decorum of the institution. Maintaining discipline is a must at the workplace.
- The "Hitler approach" does not work in the present circumstances. The superiors should behave more like mentors to the staff. The group leaders should set examples for the subordinates to get inspired from. The superiors are anticipated to offer a sense of direction to the staff and mentor them whenever required. The team members should be permitted a trouble-free access to their superior's cabin.
- Encourage team-formation activities to connect the staff together. Conduct training schedules, workshops, seminars and presentations to enhance the prevailing expertise of the staff. Keep them ready for the difficult times. They should be prepared to deal with any unfavourable situations or change in the work culture.

22 CHAPTER

Case Studies

UNDERSTANDING CASE STUDY

A case study is the explanation of an administrative circumstance or a typical life situation that involves decision making or problem solving. It could be an actual scenario that really happened just as mentioned, or a hypothetical scenario. Most case studies are composed in such a manner that the reader acts as administrator whose duty is to decide to help solve the problem. The case study model as a learning mechanism has seen a surge in its use in recent times globally. The Harvard Business School is credited with developing the case-study approach. It is thought of as a better form of elucidating the concepts to students. Mainly concerned with the administrator and the business managers, the case-study model is of great help as the administrator/manager often finds himself in dilemma conditions while tackling day-to-day management issues. The case studies let an individual to comprehend the condition better and put himself in the shoe of the person who has to take the decision. Hence, it prepares the candidate for various decision-making circumstances in the career. In reality, case study examination lets candidates to attain following two skills:

- *Applying theories to real situations*
- *Generating solutions to real problems*

The UPSC has also recently included in its curriculum the case-study model in scrutinizing the civil service aspirants.

TACTICS TO ANSWER CASE-STUDY QUESTIONS

UPSC had given three model case studies for the Main Examination 2013. These studies were analysed as below:

- *Real-life situations*
- *Administrative situations*

Principally, the UPSC desires to scan the aspirants on the following qualities:

- *Ability to deal with the ethical dilemmas in real life situations.*
- *Ability to deal with the ethical dilemmas in administrative situations.*
- *Administrative aptitude to deal with complex management issues.*

These problems are subjective, and there is no 'One-Best-Answer'. In particularly the mains examination, the way we take a decision making stage is more important. These case study problems can be solved in the following four steps. It is okay to use concepts or theory or quotes, but be careful not to overemphasize on this aspect.

The Four Step Process

- Identify the problem/issue
- Analyse the problem/dilemmas
- Identify the decision choices available
- Make the decision with reason

Starting with the Main Examination 2013, the UPSC started supplying Question-cum-Answer sheets. The space for answers has been fixed, and the aspirants are bound to answer within the space. So it becomes essential for all to decide what to write and till what extent. The four-step process helps in analysing and taking a decision. The definite solution in the examination need not be the whole analysis, it can just be the decision and the reasons.

SAMPLE CASE STUDY

You have been working with your team for almost a year. One of your subordinates Mr. A is very effective and hardworking; he takes responsibility and gets things done. However, you have heard that, that Mr. A makes loose comments about women. Mrs. X who is working under Mr. A comes to you, she is visibly disturbed. She tells you that Mr. A has been making undue advances towards her and had even asked her to go out for dinner with him. She wants to give a written complaint seeking action against Mr. A. What would you do and why?

Step-1: *Issue—Sexual harassment in office.*

Step-2: *Dilemma—The sexual harassment complaint is against a 'very effective and hardworking' subordinate. Should you take strict action or lenient view? You have already heard about such behaviour of this subordinate. So there must be some background to the allegations being made by Mrs. X.*

Step-3: *Taking action against Mr. A means demotivation of Mr. A due to disciplinary action, leading to problems in executing the projects in the office.*

1. *Not taking action leads to more such cases, indiscipline and other serious administrative issues.*
2. *What is more important—moral stand or administrative expediency?*

Step-4: *Sexual harassment in office is an unacceptable behaviour and has to be punished. Mrs. X wants to give the complaint in writing. The procedures have to be followed in such cases. The Supreme Court in Visakha case (1997) has given guidelines for action in case of sexual harassment at work places.*

- *The written complaint of Mrs. X will be sent to the Complaint Committee (Every office is supposed to have a committee to deal with such sexual harassment complaints).*
- *On the basis of the enquiry report of the Complaints Committee, criminal proceedings will be initiated in case of violations of any provisions of the Indian Penal Code.*

The answer need not be in the step process. The above four steps are to be used to take a decision. The solution should just explain—'What would you do and why?'—The decision/course of action and reasons. Since the question is 'What would you do....', so write the answer in first person. 'I will send the complaint to Complaints Committee...'.

SAMPLE CASE STUDY

You have grown up with X, who has been your best friend since childhood. You have shared your joys and sorrows and have been each other's confidante. Both of you are in your final year graduation and writing your final exams. In the exam, you notice that your friend is copying and cheating a lot. What would you do and why?

Step-1: *Issue—Cheating in exam.*

Step-2: *Dilemma—The person cheating is your best friend.*

It is immoral to cheat in exam. But complaining to the examiner will destroy the career of your friend.

Step-3: *The options before you are*

1. *Be silent—which is immoral on your part.*
2. *Complaint to the examiner—Your friend might get debarred from examination and his entire career is at stake. After complaining, you might get disturbed yourself and hence, you might spoil your performance in the exam.*
3. *Tell friend not to copy.*

Step-4: *Will adopt the following course of action:-*

- *Indicate to the friend not to copy otherwise you will complain to the examiner.*
- *If he stills copies, tell loudly to the examiner that someone in the room is copying but you can't name them. (This will make the friend alert and knows that you are serious about it).*
- *Still continues copying, complain to the examiner.*
- *The above course will take care of your moral conscience and the fact that you have given a chance to your friend to reform without causing irreparable damages. However, if situation compels, you will take the necessary strong action.*
- *(There are no correct answers in such questions. You may or may not agree with the answer given above).*

SAMPLE CASE STUDY

You are posted as the Medical Superintendent of a District level Govt. Hospital which caters to the need of poor patients from surrounding rural areas along with the local people from the district town. As such the hospital has very good infrastructure and adequate equipment to cater to this need. It also receives sufficient funds to meet the recurring expenditure. In spite of this, there have been repeated complaints particularly from the patients which include the following

(i) Very poor maintenance and unhygienic conditions in hospital premises.

(ii) The hospital staff frequently demanding bribes from the patients for the services rendered.

(iii) The negligent attitude of the Doctors resulting in times of causalities.
(iv) Siphoning of a substantial stock of medicine by the staff and selling it out.
(v) Strong nexus between the senior Doctors of the hospital and the owners of the local private nursing homes and testing labs as a result of which the patients are strongly misled and dissuaded from availing the hospital facilities and rather compelled to purchase costly medicine from market and get medical tests and even operations done from private medical houses.
(vi) There also exist a notorious employee union which puts undue pressure and resents any reformative step by the administration.

Ponder over the situation and suggest effective ways to tackle each of the above mentioned problems.

Step-1: *Issues—Negligence, dereliction of duty, corruption, indiscipline.*

Step-2: *Dilemma—The administrative situation requires urgent strong action to maintain quality health service delivery, but it might lead to friction with the staff and union and may affect the health services due to strikes.*

Step-3: *Take a head-on collision course with the doctors, staff and enforce discipline.*

1. *Take a practical approach to dealing with the complex administrative situation.*

Step-4: *This is a typical situation in government set-up. In the case of a hospital, it is very difficult to deal with the strike of the employees as the health services will be affected leading to many casualties and immense public pressure. Therefore, a balanced long-term strategy should be adopted.*

The primary stakeholders in this case are the patients and local citizens. Involving the stakeholders will ensure a strong constituency for the reforms to improve the health service delivery. Secondly, the support of the top officials in the district is essential to tackle any untoward situations arising out of strong action against the staff. Therefore, the starting point to initiate the reforms is the Rogi Kalyan Samiti. Every district hospital has a Rogi Kalyan Samiti, normally headed by the District Collector. The strategy should be to take the Collector into confidence, ensure participation of the eminent citizens of the town and the civil society in the Rogi Kalyan Samiti meetings. Then tackle the issues in the hospital management one by one through discussion and passing resolution in the Rogi Kalyan Samiti meetings.

1. Hygiene and housekeeping activities are better managed through outsourcing. Take measure to outsource following all transparent procedures.
2. Put up boards at all the important locations in the campus asking patients not to pay bribe and mobile numbers of Medical Superintendent/District Collector be displayed to inform in case of any harassment. Then based on the reports and complaints, trap some staff red-handedly, with the help of the District Collector and Superintendent of Police. This should be followed up by strict disciplinary action. And ensure vigilance regularly. This will instil fear in the minds of the staff.
3. Medical negligence cannot be tolerated as it leads to loss of valuable life. This should be made clear in all meetings repeatedly. At the first instance of any case of medical negligence leading to a casualty, a criminal liability case along with disciplinary

proceedings should be initiated. The message has to be loud and clear that medical negligence will not be tolerated.

4. Proper accountability system with check and balances should be put in place to account for every medicine in the hospital stock. Computerization along with regular inspection mechanism should be ensured. A vigilance squad can be formed along with the Rogi Kalyan Samiti members to make surprise checking. Action should be initiated on the staff involved.
5. The issue should be discussed in Rogi Kalyan Samiti meetings and resolution passed against such practices and expressing a will to take strong action against the doctors deviating from the service norms. Since the senior doctors attend the Samiti meetings, the message will be clear to them. A vigilance team should be formed to collect evidences against the main doctors who indulge in this practice and show-cause notices should be issued.

   If still the practice continues, the disciplinary proceedings should be initiated against the errant doctors. Simultaneously, with the help of District Collector, the private nursing homes should be sent notices for harassment of the poor patients and indulging in unethical medical practices. A general atmosphere of fear will be created both in the doctors and the nursing homes. This should be followed up regular vigilance and also an inspection mechanism to check the performance of every doctor like say how many patients were attended to operate etc. An MIS will be helpful in tracking the doctors' performance.
6. The Union will no doubt try to create obstacles and resist any reform measure. You should have an emergency plan in case of strike by the staff and doctors. It included requisition of doctors and staff from neighbouring districts. The pressure of Rogi Kalyan Samiti and the District administration will ensure implementation of the above measures. In the worst case scenario, the Essential Services Maintenance Act (ESMA) can be imposed to check breakdown in health services due to a strike.

So, please note that given the time and space constraint in Examination, it is impossible to allot lot of time for a single question, and it is not feasible to write the lengthy answers as above. The points in earlier paragraphs are given only to understand the practical administrative issues. A short and clear answer is always appreciated.

CASE STUDY: 1

Mr. X works as an auto-rickshaw driver in Delhi. Recently, the Delhi government has mandated that no auto-rickshaw shall deny service to any commuter, and that anyone doing so would lose his/her commercial driving license and would also have to pay a heavy fine. One night, Mr. X got a phone call from his wife that their son is critically ill and he must reach home immediately. As Mr. X prepares to rush for home, a young woman asks him to drop her to the airport. The airport is about 30 km in exactly opposite direction to Mr. X's home, and if he chooses to go to the airport, he would not be able to attend to his son in time, and the delay can be fatal for his son. The lady is repeatedly requesting him to help her because it is very late in the night and she is not feeling safe.

She says that if he refuses to drop her to the airport, she will complain to the police and Mr. X's driving license may be suspended.

Questions

1. Identify the ethical and moral dilemma in this case.
2. What are the options available before Mr. X?
3. Which option should he choose and why?
4. In such cases where one has to choose between private and professional life, what should be the objective criteria for taking a decision?

CASE STUDY: 2

You are the District Magistrate of a town, which has seen communal clashes in recent past. Though the clashes are in control right now, the situation is still tense. In the meantime, 'Ramnavami'—a festival of Hindus—is coming up, where the devotees take out loud processions on foot, through the streets of the city. In normal years, the procession takes a route that passes through a Muslim-majority area. But this year, you are conscious that in a communally charged atmosphere, such a route may fuel further tension between the two communities. However, when you sit down with the district administration team to prepare an alternate route for the procession, you realize that the shortest alternate route is at least 15 kilometres longer than the traditional route. Such a long route would not be practical for the devotees and is bound to face strong opposition from the Hindu group.

Questions

1. What would you do? Evaluate the below options:
   a. Insist on the longer route and try to convince the Hindu groups.
   b. Continue with the traditional route, with enhanced security measures.
   c. Cancel the procession ritual for this year's Ramnavami.
2. Any other option(s) you may suggest. Which one would you choose and why? Give reasons.

CASE STUDY: 3

You are the Superintendent of Police of a backward tribal district, which is infamous for child labour. Ever since you joined office, you have taken strict action against hotels and restaurants employing children. One day, the Police Commissioner invites you for a dinner at his residence, and there, you are shocked to see that a 12-year-old tribal girl is employed as a domestic help at your boss's house. You object about this to the Commissioner, but he takes it very lightly and says that he treats her like his own daughter, ensures education at home for her and his wife delegates very 'light' tasks to the girl. You, however, insist that this is against the law—to which the Commissioner threatens you with dire consequences, including suspension from service. When you enquire about this incident from your colleagues, they advise you to keep away from this case as it involves a senior officer, and its pursuit will ultimately hit a dead-end since the Commissioner can easily manipulate the evidences against him.

Questions

1. What are the options available to you? Identify the merits and demerits of each.
2. Choose the best option and justify your answer.
3. Why do you think senior officers, such as the Commissioner of Police in this case, are often able to defy the law with impunity? Suggest measures to overcome such a situation.
4. In the absence of proper rehabilitation schemes for the rescued child labourers, how justified is it to deprive them of their source of livelihood?

CASE STUDY: 4

You are the Chairman of the Municipal Corporation of a city. Of late, the city has seen a steep rise in the number of dog-bite cases, with more than 5 children succumbing to injuries caused due to biting of street dogs in the last week. The Resident Welfare Associations' (RWAs) representatives meet you and urge you to take action urgently. You have tried to control the menace by sterilizing the dogs, but this has not helped to contain the situation. Moreover, the Municipal Corporation is severely short-staffed and inadequately funded—because of which you are unable to take any long-term measures. The district administration and RWAs have suggested you to consider the option of culling the street dogs. But the animal welfare groups are strictly opposed to such a move, as it is against the nature's laws and infringes upon the rights of animals. They have threatened to launch a citywide strike if the street dogs are culled. Local MLA is also a dog-lover and is totally against culling.

Questions

1. Is this case really a trade-off between human rights and animal rights? Examine.
2. How can this situation be handled peacefully and effectively? Give pragmatic solutions.

CASE STUDY: 5

You are the Executive Engineer in a State Electricity Board (SEB). The SEB is suffering heavy financial losses due to theft of electricity and you have decided to act to curb this menace. In the meanwhile, you come to know about rampant electricity theft in the outskirts of the town. You take a team of law-enforcement officials to that area and notice that indeed, ten to fifteen families are blatantly flouting rules by engaging in electricity theft. When you question these people, you are told that they had applied for a metered electricity connection about 8 months ago. They also show a valid receipt of the application. They, however, allege that the junior engineer in the electricity department is asking for a bribe of ten thousand rupees per house to sanction the metered connection. Since these families are poor, they cannot pay such a hefty bribe. As a result, even after 8 months, they have still not got the connection—while the normal timeframe for issuing fresh connection is 15 days. Moreover, these people have school-going children, and without electricity they cannot study at night. Hence, they say that they have no option but to steal electricity till they get a metered connection.

Questions

1. What would you do in this situation? Evaluate each of the below options with merits and demerits, and suggest the best one with justification –
   (a) Ask the law-enforcement officers to book the people engaged in electricity theft.
   (b) Dismiss the Junior Engineer accused of asking for a bribe.
   (c) Waive the electricity charge for the poor families.
2. How can the SEBs reduce the problem of electricity theft? Suggest one innovative solution.

CASE STUDY: 6

You are posted as the District Officer of a temple town, which holds a Kumbh Mela every 12 years. Pilgrims from all over the country come to the fair—making it one of the largest religious gatherings in Asia. Unfortunately, due to the large volume of the crowd, almost every Kumbh Mela in the past has seen some major or minor incident of stampede and subsequent loss of lives. This year, however, you have resolved to ensure that there are no such incidents and have asked the police, NGOs and religious associations for active cooperation in this regard. You have conducted mock drills, demarcated the slots and areas for different sections of the crowd, and the sequence in which they will take ritualistic 'holy bath' on the final day of the fair.

However, on the final day, you get a phone call from the Chief Minister's Office (CMO) that the CM and his family want to perform the holy bath at the fair. You are asked to ensure that the VIP family gets quick and adequate space for the same. You are in a fix because the request has come too late for you to make proper arrangements. Any alteration in the arrangements now may lead to haphazard crowd movement and a sudden rush among the crowd for the rituals—which has all the possibilities for a catastrophic stampede. You attempt to reason with the CMO, but they are not willing to listen.

Questions

1. Do you think VIPs and their families should get preferential treatment at such fairs? Why or why not?
2. As the District Officer, what are the options before you? Identify the merits and demerits of each. Which option will you choose and why? Give justifications.

CASE STUDY: 7

You are posted as a District Magistrate in a town, which often sees communal clashes. Recently, a movie, based on a sensitive religious issue, was released in the country after getting requisite Censor Board certification. However, after the release of the movie, there has been anger among the minorities who claim blasphemous content in the movie and demand a nationwide ban. The Supreme Court, however, has refused to allow such a pan-India ban. In the meanwhile, minority groups approach you, requesting that the movie not be allowed in the sensitive town. After seeing the movie yourself, you are also convinced that it is derogatory to the minority community. Also, being in-charge of the communally sensitive district, you are concerned about the law and order scenario on the day these movies release.

Questions

1. What would you do? Some of the options to deal with the issue are mentioned below. Evaluate these options and suggest the best course of action, giving your reasons for it.
   (a) Do not allow the release of movie in your district as you feel that it hurts the religious sentiments.
   (b) Make sure the movie is released, but provide additional security forces to prevent any untoward incident.
   (c) Ask for guidance from the superiors.
2. Do you think that the Freedom of Expression should be allowed to be held hostage to religious groups? Justify your answer.

CASE STUDY: 8

Mr. X has recently started working as a cyber-security analyst at a government intelligence organization. During the course of his work, he stumbles upon documents, which reveal that the government is spying on leaders of opposition parties with alleged Maoist links. He discusses this matter with his superior officer who tells him that though the spying was illegal, it was essential for national security. He also tells Mr. X that sanction for the spying came from the highest echelons of the government. He further warns him not to divulge facts of the case to anyone else in the organization and especially no one on the outside as it may lead to his dismissal from the organization or even his arrest for treason. However, Mr. X being an honest person finds himself in a deep conflict. He feels that the spying, apart from being illegal, could also be misused by the government for settling political scores with its opponents.

Questions

1. The following are some options that Mr. X has. Evaluate the merits and demerits of each of these:
   (a) Do nothing, as he does not want to risk losing his job or end up in jail for treason.
   (b) Talk to the head of the organization to get his opinion on the matter and then do as he says.

(c) Send an anonymous letter to the press leaking the details of the case.
(d) Go to the press directly with the details of the case.

2. Also indicate (without necessarily restricting to the above options) what you would like to advise, giving proper reasons.

CASE STUDY: 9

You have recently been voted as the President of the Resident Welfare Association (RWA) of your locality, which is near a prominent coaching hub of the town. Hundreds of students from all over the country come to this region to enrol in the coaching institutes and stay as tenants in the nearby areas. During the weekly meetings with the residents of the colony, you notice that there is a strong anti-minority feeling amongst them. They have in fact given you a written memorandum to ensure that no Muslim tenant is allowed in their colony. Even though you have explained to the residents that such an act is inappropriate both on social and legal grounds, they are adamant. In the meanwhile, you hear about many cases in the neighbourhood where Muslim students are being denied rented accommodation.

Questions

In the above context, answer the following:

1. What can be the reasons for even well-educated people often having such a communally-biased attitude? Can their attitude be justified based on a history of communal violence in their families?
2. How can the values of compassion and empathy be inculcated in such people? Give one pragmatic solution.
3. How can you effectively handle the above situation?

CASE STUDY: 10

You have recently joined as the District Magistrate (DM) of a city. This is your first posting as a DM and you are eagerly looking forward to the experience. However, few months into the job, you start feeling frustrated with the overall inefficiency of the staff and their lack of commitment for public service. In your routine surveys to other government offices of the city, you notice a similarly dull work culture—with problems like non-punctuality, absenteeism, lack of cleanliness, improper handling of files and records and so on. You are also aware that this kind of work culture is resulting in inefficient delivery of services to the people. When you take up this matter with your senior officer, he says that as a young officer, you have a great opportunity to improve the condition and develop your city as a 'model city'—which can be emulated by others.

Questions

Answer the following questions:

1. In the above case, what steps would you take to improve the work culture in the government offices of your city?

2. Suppose that while you are implementing your steps with great zeal and sincerity, you are abruptly transferred to a different city. You also come to know that your successor would not be interested in carrying forward your measures and in fact may not be bothered at all about work culture.
   (a) What would you do in this situation?
   (b) Will it lead to loss of motivation in you? How will you maintain your motivation level?

CASE STUDY: 11

You are collector of a district. One day, you come to hear the shocking news that in a village, within the legal jurisdiction, 5 people were killed and 25 arrested for a crime. The situation is tense in that village. There is a possibility of counter retaliation and the murders could continue unabated unless a solution to the problem is found. On visiting the spot of the crime, located in the fields almost at the village boundary, you discover further that the cattle of one party would go along the field bunds of the other parties' land in order to reach the pasture land at the village boundary. The field owners objected to this because they felt that the cattle have caused damage to their crops. The record of customary rights of the villagers permitted people to use bunds to move their cattle around. Therefore, when the field owners stopped the movement of cattle, the cattle owners became annoyed. As a result, the fracas developed and 5 of the field owners were killed. In turn, 25 of the cattle owners were in custody on a murder charge.

Questions

1. How will you solve the case and what steps will you take to ensure that the root cause of the problem is addressed and there is no more violence on this issue?

CASE STUDY: 12

The Minor Irrigation Department of a State Government sanctions huge funds to the District Rural Development Agency (DRDA), of which the District Collector is the Chairman. The District Collector provides irrigation tubewells to small and medium farmers at a time of unprecedented droughts.

The scheme is to give 1/3rd subsidy from the fund, get 2/3rd from the individual farmer and sink the tubewell in the particular farmer's land under District Collector's general supervision. The Collector has to ensure timely action and good quality tube wells.

The Managing Director of DRDA and the Executive Engineer of Minor Irrigation Department in the district are not in good terms and are labelling charges of incompetence and previous malpractices against each other. Each approaches you (as if you are the Collector) to allocate the entire funds exclusively at his disposal for implementing the scheme.

Your number two, the District Development Officer (who is on verge of retirement), who is also the Vice-Chairman of DRDA, is non-committal and leaves it to you to decide how to implement the scheme. Time is running out due to the extreme drought conditions.

Question

1. How will you proceed to implement the scheme?

CASE STUDY: 13

More than a dozen PILs (Public Interest Litigations) are filed in High Court of a State by few people and NGOs alleging large-scale irregularities, malpractices, abuse of authority and misappropriation of huge public funds for private gains by organized groups in Government with close nexus with political executives of the State Government. All PILs are praying for CBI inquiry, as The State Police and Vigilance Department will not conduct fair enquiry against big wigs in the state government, who are themselves involved in the huge scandal.

As senior civil servant of the State Government, you are directed by the State Government to sign statement of facts of the cases as drafted by senior officers (including your service colleagues) of various Departments and file affidavit in the High Court, informing the High Court about the facts of the cases and opposing CBI inquiry, as the State Government is competent and sincere to punish the guilty without any favour or fear.

Question

1. What will you do in such situation?

CASE STUDY: 14

You are head of an organization engaged in research and development of cutting-edge technologies in electronics, essential for economic and security needs of our country. You have a dedicated team which is highly motivated also and has been giving desired outcomes. Your quality control unit's head is Mr. Sharma, a very competent person and honest to his job.

One day, a junior lady scientist working under Mr. Sharma came to you and wanted to lodge the complaint against him. She told you that for last few days Mr. Sharma has been making undue advances towards her, and when she expressed her opposition to such a behaviour, he is threatening her to keep quiet or he will ruin her career. She also told you that if the problem is not shorted out, she will formally lodge a complaint to the police in this regard.

Questions

1. What options you are left with?
2. Which option will you consider as solution and why?

CASE STUDY: 15

Recently you have taken charge as the head of a government organization. On the first day in your office, you observed that the organization is facing irregularities, such as:

i. The staff is not punctual.
ii. The staff waste their time in gossips.
iii. There is no prompt action on public grievances.
iv. The corruption in office is rampart at all levels.
v. The quality of service provided by the organization is low.

Questions

1. What actions would you take to resolve above problems?
2. What will you do to ethically motivate your staff?

CASE STUDY: 16

You are head of an organization. Your junior officer working just below you is arrogant, ill-tempered and poor manager. His levels of achievements are low.

You have to write his ANNUAL CONFIDENTIAL REPORT (ACR) at the end of the financial year. You are aware that he will come to know about your written comments. He will continue to work in your team for indefinite time, over which you have no control. A bad ACR is bound to weaken his future promotion and annoy him against you.

Question

1. What kind of ACR you will write?

CASE STUDY: 17

You are a doctor in the night shift looking after the emergency unit of a hospital. A female patient is rushed into the emergency ward while you are in charge of the ward. You are a conscientious doctor recognized for saving lives in this unit, and your reputation is built on the foundation of several years of service you have provided to those who faced life and death situations under your care. The patient is a victim of a traumatic accident and needs immediate blood transfusion to save her life. However, she belongs to a Christian community whose religion forbids her from taking blood into her body from outside. She is represented by her relatives and priests of her denomination, who do not permit blood transfusion.

Question

1. What will you do and why?

CASE STUDY: 18

Mr. Pandey is working as a jailor of a jail. As part of his duty, he gets the opportunity to interact with the inmates. In course of his interaction with the inmates, he is especially impressed by one of the inmates. It is revealed to him that the prisoner is not a hard-core criminal. A minor incident leading to accidental murder led to his incarceration. He has a family to look after with minor kids. Without Mr. Singh's realization, he ends up developing emotional attachment with the prisoners as between an elder brother and his younger brother. One day, he notices that he has indulged in a violent fight with other prisoners. The jailor thinks, the prisoner is innocent and wants to help. Mr. Singh also wants to help him fight his case further so as to minimize his punishment.

Questions

1. What should Mr. Pandey do and why?
2. Should he help him or not to prove his innocence in the crime for which he is being punished and why?

CASE STUDY: 19

Your friend is an editor of a newspaper. He is free, fair and impartial in his opinions. He is independent minded and writes independently free of fear and favour on any issue. Due to his independent nature, he has landed into controversy several times earlier. He wants to write an editorial piece on Kashmir. In his writing, he wants to take the position that the fate of Kashmir should be left upon the people of Kashmir. His arguments are that referendum is the best democratic way to decide upon the fate of people. The democratic aspiration of the people can no longer be suppressed as was evident in Soviet Russia and many other Eastern European nations. However, he is also aware that this kind of argument can raise controversies and could possibly threaten his life. Yet he is independent minded and does not fear personal harm coming as a consequence of speaking up the truth.

Questions

1. Advise your friend on the possible course of action for him. Should or shouldn't he write the article?
2. Is it unethical to speak up one's mind? Is his opinion on Kashmir morally correct?

CASE STUDY: 20

AIDS (Acquired Immunodeficiency Syndrome) afflicts 38 million people worldwide. Almost 3 million people died from AIDS in 2003 alone, and over 20 million have died since the epidemic began. A vaccine that could prevent or slow down the spread of this deadly disease would be a boon to the world. However, since 1981 when the first cases of AIDS were diagnosed, researchers have been unsuccessful in their attempts to develop such a vaccine. The efforts of a company called VaxGen illustrate the complexity of this task.

VaxGen, which is located in Brisbane, California, developed a vaccine called AIDSVAX. The vaccine contained synthetic proteins of recombinant gp120, a protein normally found on the surface of HIV, the virus that causes AIDS. The vaccine was designed to induce the immune system to respond to this non-infectious protein and to produce antibodies that could protect the recipient from an actual HIV infection. In phase I clinical trials, the vaccine was tested for safety. Phase II clinical trials included a larger-scale test for safety as well as a test for the production of antibodies against gp120. As a result of these trials, AIDSVAX was shown to be safe, and patients receiving the vaccine did develop antibodies against gp120.

Phase III clinical trials involved large-scale, placebo-controlled, double-blind tests of the vaccine's effectiveness. The first trial began in June of 1998 and involved 5,100 gay men and 300 women, all volunteers, from the United States, Puerto Rico, Canada and the Netherlands. The second trial began in March of 1999 and involved 2,500 IV drug abusers from Bangkok, Thailand. Both trials were completed in 2003. Unfortunately, these trials revealed no difference in the overall rate of HIV infection between the vaccinated and the unvaccinated participants. The data indicate that recipients of the vaccine did produce antibodies against gp120, but that those antibodies were not adequate to protect against HIV infection. (It did appear that certain subgroups—ethnic minorities other than Hispanic—exhibited a small but statistically significant lowering of the infection rate, but these results are still being examined.)

Questions

1. Why do you think a person would volunteer to test an AIDS vaccine?
2. In the AIDSVAX trials, some people were given a placebo instead of the vaccine. All the recipients had been told of this possibility ahead of time, but they did not know which substance they were receiving. Is it ethical to give some of the trial participants only a placebo?

CASE STUDY: 21

You have recently joined as the head of a district-level government office, which registers the unemployed people of the district and provides necessary help and guidance so that they can get gainful employment. When you join, you find that the office keeps its resources in a very poorly organized manner. Many rooms of the office are full of dirt, files and records are randomly stacked and many files are virtually thrown across the Record Room, roof of which also leaks in rains. The subordinate officials are very rude to the visitors and ask money for providing various services to the youth who come for seeking information and assistance. As head of the organization, what will be your specific response to the following? Also, provide answers with proper justifications.

Questions

1. What step will you take for keeping the files and records in proper order?
2. What will be your specific action for creating a suitable grievance redressal mechanism?
3. How will you try to improve the work culture of your office?

CASE STUDY: 22

Rajiv is newly posted as secretary in a Panchayat. Within few days he got a circular which said that he should soon conduct Grama Sabha to finalize the action plan of MGNREGA. Action plan contains the list of works to be undertaken in the villages and their estimated expenditures. This should be decided in the Grama Sabha, and the decision of Gram Sabha is immutable.

The Gram Sabha was held and chairman, all elected members, officer in-charge, engineer and people from villages debated and finally listed important works to be undertaken, and the estimated expenditure was decided there itself.

Next, this plan had to be approved in the Panchayat meeting and sent to Tehsil for further approval for sanction of funds. The chairman of Panchayat, who was also a class-I contractor, met Rajiv and asked him to manipulate the funds estimates. Even few members who themselves were small-time contractors and who had previously used machines in MGNREGA scheme to finish works and draw money joined Chairman in demanding manipulation of the action plan.

Rajiv strongly objected to this. On the day of meeting, which was a close-door meeting inside the Panchayat office, he was manhandled by some members in the office after he resisted their attempt to snatch the action plan and manipulate it, and was threatened that if he didn't act according to their orders, he would be thrashed again and again. Someone outside called the police. But when police arrived, the chairman alleged that Panchayat secretary behaved in an indecent manner with female members and hence he was thrashed. Female members seconded this allegation.

Rajiv was taken to police station. Police refused to accept his version of the incident, which was true. He was helpless at the moment.

Question

1. You are his superior officer i.e. BDO. Rajiv contacts you and tells you his part of the story. At the same time, Panchayat members narrate their version. How will you proceed from here?

CASE STUDY: 23

Your close friend, Asit, successfully cleared the prestigious civil service examination and was excited about the opportunity that he would get through the civil services to serve the country. However, soon after joining the services, he realized that things are not as rosy as he had imagined.

He found a number of malpractices prevailing in the department assigned to him. For example, funds under various schemes and grants were being misappropriated. The official facilities were frequently being used for personal needs by the officers and staffs. After some time, he noticed that the process of recruiting staffs was also not up to the mark. Prospective candidates were required to write an examination in which a lot of cheating was going on. Some candidates were provided external help in the examination. Asit brought these incidents to the notice of his seniors. However, he was advised to keep his eyes, ears and mouth shut and ignore all these things which were taking place with the connivance of the seniors. Asit felt highly disillusioned and uncomfortable. He comes to you seeking your advice.

Question

1. Indicate various options that you think are available in this situation. How would you help him to evaluate these options and choose the most appropriate path to be adopted?

CASE STUDY: 24

You are an honest and sincere officer. You have been transferred to a remote district to head a Department that is notorious for its inefficiency and callousness. You find that the main cause of the poor state of affairs is the indiscipline of a section of employees. They do not work themselves and also disrupt the working of others. You first warned the troublemakers to mend their ways or else face disciplinary action. When the warning had little effect, you issued a show cause notice to the ring leaders. As a retaliatory measure, these troublemakers instigated a women employee amongst them to file a complaint of sexual harassment against you with the Women Commission. The Commission promptly sought your explanation. The matter is also publicized in the media to embarrass you further. Some of the options to handle this situation could be as follows:

i. Give your explanation to the Commission and go soft on the disciplinary action.
ii. Ignore the Commission and proceed firmly with the disciplinary action.
iii. Brief your seniors, seek directions from them and act accordingly.

Question

1. Suggest other possible option(s). Evaluate all of them and suggest the best course of action, giving your reasons for the same.

CASE STUDY: 25

Suppose you are the CEO of a company that manufactures specialized electronic equipment used by a Government Department. You have submitted your bid for the supply of this equipment to the Department. Both the quality and cost of your offer are better than those of the competitors. Yet the concerned officer is demanding a hefty bribe for approving the tender. Getting the order is important both for you and your company. Not getting the order would mean closing a production line. It may also affect your own career. However, as a value conscious person, you do not want to give any bribe.

Question

1. Valid arguments can be advanced both for giving the bribe and getting the order, and for refusing to pay bribe and risking the loss of the order. What could be those arguments? Could there be any better way to get out of this dilemma? If so, outline the main elements of this third way, pointing out its merits.

CASE STUDY: 26

You are head of an organization in Central Government. 'A', an IAS Officer, is reporting to you and 'B', an IRTS Officer on deputation to your department, is reporting to 'A' in the same organization. 'B' complains to you repeatedly that 'A' is in the habit of harassing him and is also threatening him that 'A' will ruin his records by writing adverse remarks. 'B' pleads before you to shift him out of 'A's' control and let him work under another officer, or he will go back to his parent cadre prematurely, even before his deputation tenure ends.

You know that 'B' is a good officer. You would like to keep him in your department. But allowing the request of 'B' and transferring 'B' out of the control of 'A' and placing him, i.e. 'B' under another senior officer in your department is sure to annoy 'A', who will continue to work under you.

Question

1. In such a scenario, how will you act to the plea of 'B'?

CASE STUDY: 27

A person has taken charge as an Additional District Magistrate (ADM). He realizes that there is huge corruption in the Public Distribution System (PDS). He also watched that corruption is also widespread in various schemes of development, such as rural roads, bridges and clearing silt from the ponds. Due to widespread corruption, people of the District find themselves hopeless and feel insecure.

This Additional District Magistrate decided to act firmly against aforementioned malpractices. He raided the PDS shops to expose the corrupt dealers and take action by cancelling the quota itself wherever he finds abnormalities. He has also taken stern actions against corrupt contractors who were responsible for not executing properly the development schemes. He has also enforced the rule of law in the district under his proper supervision.

As a result of appropriate actions taken by the A.D.M., the P.D.S. began to work properly and the people got their fair share of ration from P.D.S. outlets. Also, they got better quality of roads and improved law and order conditions in the district. All these actions resulted in an improved quality of governance and re-established public faith in the administration.

Questions

In the context of above case study, answer the questions given below:
1. Which type of Administrative and moral value you see in the above administrator?
2. What was the basic problem of that District?
3. If you were on the same post, what type of actions would you have taken?

CASE STUDY: 28

You have just taken charge as the Director in an important Ministry of Government of India which is responsible for carrying out development schemes worth the value of thousands of crores of rupees. On the very first day of joining as the Director of the Department, you called a meeting of all your subordinate officers and staffs. You found out that two of your subordinate officers of the rank of Deputy Director, Mr. 'A' and Mr. 'B', are absent. You also noticed that Section Officers, Mr. 'C' and Mr. 'D', are not at good terms with one another. The other staffs also seemed to be demotivated.

At the afternoon of the same day, your superior officer of the level of Joint Secretary called you in his office. He discussed with you a very important new project (of thousands of crores rupees) that must be launched as soon as possible in your supervision. He also asked you to insure its effective and speedy implementation.

You have doubts whether the present team will be able to properly handle the project.

Question

1. What would you do in the present situation and why?

CASE STUDY: 29

Suppose one of your close friends, who is aspiring for Civil Services, comes to you for discussing some of the issues related to ethical conduct in public service. He raises the following points:

i. In present time, when unethical environment is quite prevalent, individual attempts to stick to the ethical principles may cause a lot of problems in one's career. It may also cause hardships to the family members as well as risks to one's life. Why should not we be pragmatic and follow the path of least resistance and be happy by doing whatever good we can?
ii. When so many people are adopting wrong means and are grossly harming the system, what difference would it make, if only a very small minority tries to be ethical? The fact remains that they are going to be rather ineffective and are bound to get frustrated in long run.

iii. If we become very fussy about the ethical considerations, will it not hamper the economic progress of our country? After all, in the present age of high competition, we cannot afford to be left behind in the race for further development.

iv. It is understandable that we should not get involved into the grossly unethical practices. But giving and accepting small gratifications and doing small favours increase every body's motivation. It also makes the system more efficient. Then the issue remains that what is wrong in adopting such practices?

Question

1. Critically analyse the above viewpoints. On the basis of such analysis, what will be your advice to your friend?

CASE STUDY: 30

You are placed as 'Qualify Control Officer' in the Ministry of Defence, Government of India. In a recently organized defence expo, you happen to meet your college day friend. He is currently working as 'Marketing Executive' with a well-known company which supplies important defence instruments and components. Your friend invites you for a dinner which you accept. During the dinner, your friend makes a good offer to you. But you humbly deny the offer and tell him that you are not going to quit the job. After a pause, he tells you that it was not his intention that you should quit the job. But he only wants that in near future, when there is going to be huge defence procurement deal, you should help him so that his company successfully gets major chunk of that deal. He also offers you a 10% cut of the deal amount to you as incentive. And he also tells you that being an old friend, he will keep everything secret in future.

Questions

1. What option will you choose from the options given below? And why?
   (i) You are not in hurry to make money. So, you will tell about this lucrative under the table offer to your colleagues.
   (ii) You are an honest person and you feel badly hurt by this offer of your friend. You also know that you have to face this type of situation again and again in this job. So, you try to find another good job and quit this one.
   (iii) You will make a complaint to the police about this incidence involving such a bribe.
2. Suggest any other option you may have.

CASE STUDY: 31

You are appointed as Medical Superintendent at a district-level hospital which provides medical aid and healthcare facilities to the people of the town as well as those of rural areas of the District. The hospital has good infrastructure and is properly equipped with medical instruments required to effectively conduct medical surgical operations. Also, there exists appropriate fund for general and recurring expenditures. However, you find that patients are regularly complaining about the following in that hospital:

i. Housekeeping of the hospital premises is very poor and unhygienic.
ii. The hospital personnel often demand bribe to provide facilities.
iii. On many occasions, the grave carelessness by the Doctors causes death of the patients.
iv. Huge amount of the hospital medicine is sold out by the hospital staff illegally to private medical stores.
v. There is a nexus between doctors and private nursing homes and testing labs, due to which patients are forced to buy costly medicines and undertake costly and often unrequired medical tests.
vi. There exists a defamed workers' union which opposes all the efforts of positive reforms.

Question

After properly assessing the above situations, what measures will you take to improve the overall condition of hospital?

CASE STUDY: 32

You are working as an Executive Engineer in the construction cell of a Municipal Corporation. You are presently in-charge of the construction of a flyover. There are two Junior Engineers under you who have the responsibility of day-to-day inspection of the site and are reporting to you, while you are finally reporting to the Chief Engineer who heads the cell. While the construction is heading towards completion, the Junior Engineers have been regularly reporting that all constructions are taking place exactly as per the design specifications. However, in one of your surprise inspections, you noticed some serious deviations and lacunae, which in your opinion are likely to affect the safety of the flyover. Rectification of these lacunae at this stage would require a substantial amount of demolition and rework which will cause a tangible loss to the contractor and will also delay completion. There is a lot of public pressure on the Corporation to get this construction completed because of heavy traffic congestion in the area. When you brought this matter to the notice of the Chief Engineer, he advised you that in his opinion it is not a very serious lapse and may be ignored. He advised for further expediting the project for completion in time. However, you are convinced that this was a serious matter which might affect public safety and should not be left unaddressed.

Question

What will you do in such a situation? Some of the options are given below. Evaluate the merits and demerits of each of these options and finally suggest what course of action you would like to take? Give reasons.

i. Follow the advice of the Chief Engineer and go ahead.
ii. Make an exhaustive report of the situation, bringing out all facts and analysis along with your own viewpoints stated clearly, and then seek written orders from the Chief Engineer in this regard.
iii. Seek explanations from the Junior Engineers and issue orders to the contractor for necessary correction within targeted time.
iv. Highlight the issue to an extent so that it reaches superiors to the Chief Engineer.
v. Considering the rigid attitude of the Chief Engineer, seek transfer from the projector report sick and stay away on medical leave.

CASE STUDY: 33

You are heading a leading technical institute of the country. The institute is planning to convene an interview panel shortly under your chairmanship for selection of the post of professors. A few days before the interview, you get a call from the Personal Secretary (PS) functionary seeking your intervention in favour of the selection of a close relative of the functionary for this post. The PS also informs you that he is aware of the long-pending and urgent proposals of your institute for grant of funds for modernization, which are awaiting the functionary's approval. He assures you that he would get these proposals cleared.

Questions

1. What are the options available to you?
2. Evaluate these options and choose the option which you would adopt, giving reasons.

CASE STUDY: 34

As a senior officer in the Finance Ministry, you have access to some confidential and crucial information about policy decisions that the government is about to announce. These decisions are likely to have far-reaching impact on the housing and construction industry. If the builders have access to this information beforehand, they can make huge profits. One of the builders has done a lot of quality work for the government and is known to be close to your immediate superior, who asks you to disclose this information to the said builder.

Questions

1. What are the options available to you?
2. Evaluate each of these options and choose the option which you would adopt, giving reasons.

CASE STUDY: 35

You are posted as a senior Labour Enforcement Officer in Sivakashi in Tamil Nadu. Sivakashi is known for its manufacturing clusters on firecrackers and matches. The local economy of the area is largely dependent on firecrackers industry. It has led to tangible economic development and improved standard of living in the area.

So far as child labour norms for hazardous industries like firecrackers industry are concerned, International Labour Organization (ILO) has set the minimum age as 18 years. In India, however, this age is 14 years.

The units in industrial clusters of fire crackers can be classified into registered/non-registered units, and it does not include household-based works. Household-based works mean children working under supervision of their parents/relatives. To evade child labour norms, several units project themselves as household-based works but employ children from outside. Needless to say that employing children saves the costs for these units leading to higher profits to the owners.

On your visit to one of the units which have about 10-15 children below 14 years of age, the owner tells you that in this household-based unit, all the children are his relatives. You notice that several children smirk, when the owner tells you this. On deeper inquiry, you figure out that neither the owner not the children are able to satisfactorily establish their relationship with each other.

Questions

1. What would be your reaction after the visit?
2. Bring out and discuss the ethical issues involved in the above case.

CASE STUDY: 36

A Public Information Officer (PIO) has received an application under the RTI Act. Having gathered the information, the PIO discovers that the information pertains to some of the decisions taken by him, which were found to be not altogether right. There were other employees also, who were party to these decisions. Discloser of the information is likely to lead to disciplinary action, with possibility of punishment against him as well as some of his colleagues. Non-disclosure or part disclosure or camouflaged discloser of information will result either into lesser punishment or in no punishment.

The PIO is otherwise an honest and conscientious person, but this particular decision, on which the RTI application has been filed, turned out to be wrong. He comes to you for advice.

The following are some suggested options:

i. PIO could refer the matter to his superior officer and seek his advice and act strictly in accordance with the advice, even though he is not completely in agreement with the advice of the superior.

ii. The PIO could proceed on leave and leave the matter to be dealt by his successor in office or request for transfer of the application to another PIO.

iii. The PIO could weigh the consequences of disclosing the information truthfully, including the effect on his career, and reply in a manner that would not place him or his career in jeopardy, but at the same time a title compromise can be made on the contents of the information.

iv. The PIO could consult his other colleagues who are party to the decision and take action as per their advice.

Questions

1. Evaluate the merits and demerits of each of the above options.
2. Also please indicate (without necessarily restricting to the above option) what you would like to advise, giving proper reasons.

CASE STUDY: 37

You have taken charge of Block-level officer. You are made in-charge of developmental works in the Block. During your travel through the area, you found that people are living in inhuman conditions, deprived of basic sanitation and drinking water facilities. The commercial banks have not any sympathy towards the farmers, so that the business of money lenders is flourishing. Local MLA also ignores the people who had not voted in favour of him.

Question

1. What should you do as a Block-Level Officer, so that the following points can be addressed?
   a. It can be assured that poor and needy people get help from the Banks.
   b. Drinking water and sanitation service provided by the Panchayati Raj Institution can be made effective especially for the weaker section people.
   c. Ill effect of development project selected in bipartisan manner by local M.L.A. can be mitigated.
   d. The people become aware about their rights and various government schemes of welfare and development.

CASE STUDY: 38

Mid-Day Meal (MDM) is a government programme which deals with supplementary nutrition support through educational Institutions. It took its root in India when Madras Corporation developed a school lunch programme in 1925. In Post-Independent India, the State of Gujarat also started the school lunch programme in 1984. In 1995, a Programme of Nutritional Support of Primary Education was launched at the national level. In 2004, this programme was revised and was popularly known as MDM. Government of India emphasized MDM's implementation in its Common Minimum Programme. It envisaged the provisions of cooked nutritional mid-day meal to primary and secondary school children. This initiative became the world's biggest school lunch program with following objectives:

(a) To improve health and education
(b) To increase school enrolment

(c) To improve socialization
(d) To solve malnutrition problem among young children
(e) Social empowerment of women by employment generation

However, problems of MDM currently include:

(a) poor infrastructure facilities
(b) repetition of same menu
(c) disruption of classroom as teachers are required to oversee the operation
(d) poor quality of food
(e) poor hygiene
(f) inadequate payments to contractors
(g) insufficient budgetary allocation
(h) caste and religious bias
(i) limited parental participation
(j) irregular and delayed delivery
(k) low quality supplies by Food Corporation of India (FCI)
(l) lack of maintenance

The fact remains that, in India, the welfare economies do not work properly. It works for people who create it and for the subordinates who are in position to implement such policies in the public. Political party in power creates such bogus schemes which also benefit the bureaucrats and politicians in power. The current Government, which was in opposition at the time of the implementation of this scheme, never revoked these bogus schemes of the previous government as it did not want to hurt the vote bank.

Questions

1. Should such similar Govt. schemes launched in India in future?
2. How corrupt practices could be prevented most effectively in the case of MDM scheme?

CASE STUDY: 39

Mid-Day Meal (MDM) is a government programme which deals with supplementary nutrition support through educational Institutions. Government of India emphasized MDM's implementation in its Common Minimum Programme. It envisaged the provisions of cooked nutritional mid-day meal to primary and secondary school children. It is also designed to boost school attendance and children's participation in school. This initiative became the world's biggest school lunch programme.

Recently, a State Government constituted a special team to effectively implement the MDM scheme. The mandate of the team is to look into infrastructure issues that include storage facilities, kitchens and quality drinking water. The team comprised of nutritionist, food inspector, dietician, doctor and members from drug-testing laboratories. Mr. Harish is the doctor and his close friend Mr. Mahesh is the food inspector in the said team. The team is supposed to send feedback to the Government after an inspection drive. Both Mahesh and Harish have a lackadaisical approach towards their work. Neither of them is sensing his responsibility properly. They enjoy political patronage in the State. In contrast to them, other team members are quite conscious of their duties and responsibilities. However, they don't have any political connection. Occasionally, the team decision was getting affected by the opinions of the doctor and the food inspector as the duo has close nexus with concerned political boss in the State. Despite some of the lacunae in the infrastructure issues in MDM, positive feedback was sent to the Govt.

Due to the above irresponsible act, quality of food was not ensured and sometimes even contaminated food was served to the children, which resulted in hospitalization of many school children in the State recently.

Questions

1. According to you, who is responsible for the problem highlighted in the above case—both Mahesh and Harish, or team as a whole? Also give reasons.
2. What are the ethical concerns involved in the case?

CASE STUDY: 40

You are the administrative head of a Government Office which deals with the public on a large scale. People regularly come to the office for their routine problems like pension claims, insurance claims, scholarship claims, etc. There is an assistant in the office who deals with these subjects. There is a complaint that he does not clear the claims without extracting a bribe for the same. So far, he has escaped disciplinary action because he has the backing and patronage of a local influential politician. Other assistants of the office are looking towards you for a decisive action. The work culture of the organization has reached to an all-time low efficiency. You have decided to act in the given situation.

Questions

1. What are the various options available to you?
2. Examine the merits and demerits of each option and suggest the best course of action under the given situation.

CASE STUDY: 41

You have recently retired as the financial head of a Public Sector company (PSU) and have joined a private firm as its financial advisor. The PSU has floated tenders for a long-term contract which your firm is interested in. As the financial head of the PSU, you regularly deal with the tender and contract process, and are well aware of the various criteria and parameters on which the PSU awards such contracts. The CEO of your present firm has requested you to use that knowledge in ensuring that the firm bags this contract with PSU, which will significantly boost the firm's revenues. On the other hand, failure to bag the contract may mean shutting down of the firm. The entire team is also looking up to you to disclose the parameters on which the PSU will award contracts to the bidders and is asking you to lead the bidding process.

Questions

1. What are the ethical dilemmas involved in this case?
2. What are the various options available to you? Also examine the merits and demerits of each option and suggest the best course of action under the given situation.

CASE STUDY: 42

You are the Executive Engineer of a road construction department and in charge of construction and maintenance of Major District Roads (MDRs) in a particular district. You have joined this Department recently. In course of your field inspections, you found large-scale misuse of funds in both construction, and in repair and maintenance of MDRs. You have started putting accountability on the concerned Assistant Engineers (AEs) and Junior Engineers (JEs). As a mark of protest, all AEs and JEs have started a 'go-slow' campaign by delaying the work. The financial year is going to close soon and still about 50% of the funds remain un-utilized. Your senior officers have suggested you to explore other options to ensure faster utilization of the funds.

Questions

1. What are the various options available to you?
2. Examine the merits and demerits of each option and suggest the best course of action with reasons.

CASE STUDY: 43

You are an RTI activist. There is a poor person living in a rural area and he wants to get his son admitted to a public school in a city. The public school asks for Transfer and Character Certificates and sets out a deadline for submission, otherwise the boy will not get admission. The father makes desperate attempts to procure the concerned documents, but could not get within the stipulated timeframe and the son is denied of admission. In running from pillar to post, the father met with an accident and lost his two legs. His son meets you and requests to help in redressal of his grievances, including fixing accountability regarding injury to his father. You want to use provisions under RTI Act, 2005.

Questions

1. How would you respond to his request?
2. Suggest some options through which you can help the grieved child.

CASE STUDY: 44

You are the District Magistrate of a backward district, which is ignominious for rampant child labour. One day in your office, an old friend from same school visits you and tells you that he has opened a small restaurant in the town and wants you to come for its inauguration. When you reach there, you notice 2-3 under-fourteen children washing utensils and taking orders. When you enquire from the children, they say that they are very grateful to the hotel owner for employing them, as they are very poor and their parents are too old to support and feed them. The children also tell you that the hotel owner treats them very well and gives them timely food and wages. When you enquire from your friend about employing underage children, he admits to it, but says that if he does not employ them then these children will have no option but to beg on streets.

Questions

1. What are the ethical and legal dilemmas involved in this case?
2. What would be the course of action in the above case? Give reasons.

CASE STUDY: 45

Ramesh is a misogynist from his childhood. However, he is a very diligent and scholar student. He was aspiring to become an IAS Officer from his childhood. By dint of his hard labour, he could fulfil his dream of becoming an IAS Officer. He got posted as a Sub-Divisional Magistrate (SDM) in a District. He was highly committed to and competent in his work. Incidentally, he has to work with a female colleague named Reema, who has been working in the same SDM office for long time now as Private Secretary. Reema has a track record of being one of the most productive employees in that office. But even after being an IAS Officer, Ramesh could not wipe out his misogynistic attitude towards women. He still holds a misperception that women tend to putrefy work culture and have a tendency of social loafing. Because of his inherent stereotyping, he always attributes all misdoings towards Reema. Many a times, Reema has been criticized even for small mistakes.

Questions

1. What are the steps by which Ramesh could be treated for his discriminating attitude?
2. After having known his inherent problem since childhood, what Reema should do to bring him on the right path?
3. Should persons with such perceptions be allowed to hold such high public posts?

CASE STUDY: 46

Read the Passage carefully and answer the followings:

In a recent tragedy, a cinema hall in your city caught fire leading to death and severe injuries to more than 50 persons. The state orders an immediate inquiry into the incident. You are in charge of the inquiry in your capacity as the district commissioner. In your inquiry, you discover severe lapses made by the cinema hall owners. They had violated norms with respect to safety. They had also violated regulations governing the construction of cinema halls with enough exit doors and emergency exits. The norms on safety from accidental fires were also not met. In other words, if you indict the cinema owners for lapses, they would be charged with homicide, not amounting to murder. However, several state agencies and the officers serving them could also become victims of the report because they let these lapses to continue and were a party to the crime because they allowed the cinema owners or gave them license to operate even when the conditions were not met. You find that you are responsible for the incident because you either did not inspect the cinema hall periodically as required or you couldn't identify the lapses in your inspections.

Question

1. What will you do in such a situation? Some of the options are given below. Evaluate the merits and demerits of each of these options and finally suggest what course of action you would like to take, giving reasons.
   i. You will make a detailed report indicting everyone, including yourself.
   ii. You will seek a legal advice that exonerates you legally and then make a report exonerating yourself.
   iii. You will request to be relieved of your inspection duties, citing your personal responsibility in the accident as a reason.
   iv. You will make a report that holds the cinema owners solely responsible for the case.
   v. You will make a report highlighting the fact that this is one of accident of rarest of rare kind that could not have been avoided thereby minimizing the responsibility on everyone.

CASE STUDY: 47

You are newly posted as a collector in the Malkangiri district of Odisha which is a Naxalite belt. You have empathy to poor and disadvantaged. The district is tribal inhabited and underdeveloped. After having taken charge as the Collector of the District, you noticed that the root cause of Naxalism is the deprivation and backwardness of that district. The government is slightly indifferent to the district. In a recent violence, some Maoists have damaged the public property also. However, one Maoist was caught and confessed that the extreme poverty compelled him to opt for the path of violence.

Questions

1. Would you accept his statement? Why?
2. What course of action you will take against him?

CASE STUDY: 48

You are the Principal of a Government College. One of your close aide named Rajan is a faculty of mathematics. The faculty is highly respected and known for his positive traits.

But one day, a girl student complained of sexual harassment against him. She alleged that the faculty also threatened her that it would harm her studies, if she complained against him. But the girl is neither good in studies nor an obedient student. Several complaints have been registered, many a times, against her. It has been seen in some cases that she was making many false allegations against some students as well as teachers.

Questions

1. Being the Principal of the college, what would be your initial reaction to the girl's statement?
2. How will you proceed with this situation?

CASE STUDY: 49

Suppose you are a Superintendent of Police in a District. You are a highly religious and an ardent supporter of Hindu belief system. In your District, a person, a self-styled godman, started preaching the people regularly in a particular place and persuaded the local people to adopt his principles and follow him as their Guru. With the passage of time, he became very popular and many more became his devotees. In the process, you also became one of his ardent devotees. The self-styled godman has built an ashram too in his name. Suddenly, you hear that the self-styled godman is a fraud and has accumulated much wealth by cheating his devotees. By now, the news has spread among the masses and the mob has turned violent.

Question

1. What steps will be taken by you? Also evaluate the merits and demerits of each step taken by you.

CASE STUDY: 50

The Odisha State Chief Minister seems to be determined to root out corruption in the State and plans to shame those involved in graft cases rather publicly. The CM has decided to post a list of the 'corrupt persons' on the State Vigilance Department's website.

You are the State Vigilance Department chief. You have to cooperate with the CM in this endeavour actively. Among the many featured in the list, there is the name of a Journalist called Chandrabhanu Patnaik, the editor of a local television channel against whom a vigilance case was already filed. Chandrabhanu Patnaik is a friend of your brother, and to your cognizance, he is an honest man. After hearing that his name is in the list to be posted, Chandrabhanu Patnaik comes to you and pleads before you not to make his name public on the website, as he was honest. He also assured you that he was not involved in any corrupt practices and the case in which he was sued was a conspiracy against him.

Question

1. What would be your step in this situation? Give reasons for the step taken by you.

CASE STUDY: 51

You are working with an NGO. You had travelled to one of the villages where your programme is running. In the programme, your funds were fully spent, although your calculations showed that this should not be so. You found that a locally employed Christian accountant had manipulated the accounts. He had grown rich and had many friends. He paid hefty tithes and offerings in the local church. After being confronted about the misappropriation of said funds of NGO, he repaid some money he had taken, but sadly, after more losses were discovered, he committed suicide. His fellow members thought his misdeeds have been reported by their senior most local colleague and were intensely angry with that colleague. Group loyalty was felt more strongly than their obligation to protect institutional funds and, more importantly, the Christian integrity. You boasted that you had detected the fraud and helped rebuild relationships. When you said at his funeral that, 'I had liked and admired our accountant and appreciated his efforts to make good with the losses, and that at the end all of us will need forgiveness'. But you learnt the moral strength of personal loyalty within a group possibly exacerbated because group members thought of themselves as 'poor' nationals dealing with expatriates from a rich country'.

Questions

1. Suggest what could have been done to avoid the scandal in the office?
2. What could have been done by the Church to mitigate the impact of the scandal?

CASE STUDY: 52

You are the Director of Durgapur Ispat Main Hospital. In an incident, four patients, who were admitted to Durgapur Ispat Main Hospital in Burdwan with various problems, became critical after receiving a blood transfusion. In all four cases, the blood was supplied by the hospital's blood bank and the patients' condition deteriorated after the transfusion.

They were shifted to a private facility where they died. The post-mortem report of one patient concluded that she had gone into septic shock following the transfusion. So far, none of the three patients' families have lodged any written complaint with the health department. But, as the news of the deaths of the three spread, the families of other patients started alleging that the hospital's blood bank was supplying contaminated blood. They also accused the hospital of gross negligence, prompting it to set up the probe committee.

Questions

1. Do you think the in-charge of blood bank is responsible for this incident?
2. How will you proceed with the case?

CASE STUDY: 53

You are posted as the District Magistrate (DM) of a Naxal-affected town. One day, while you were on your way to a village to oversee some development work, a group of armed Naxals surrounded the village and abducted you. They blindfolded you and took you to their hideout in the forest. Fortunately, the blindfold was not very tight, and you were able to secretly see through it, without the Naxals knowing. Noticing the path the abductors took, you have managed to identify the exact location of their hideout.

The Naxals kept you kidnapped for one week, after which the State government was able to secure your release safely. However, during your stay with the Naxals, they treated you very nicely. They also discussed with you their problems, and how the government is not doing enough for development of tribal villages. You come to realize that their issues are very genuine. Now, once you have been released, the government is asking for your help in locating the Naxals, so that armed action can be taken against them. You are well aware that if you disclose the location of the Naxals, they would definitely be killed by the Central Police Forces.

Questions

1. Would you disclose the location of the Naxals? Why or why not?
2. What are the other options available before you? Evaluate each of the options with their merits and demerits.

CASE STUDY: 54

You are posted as the Commissioner of Income Tax of an industrial town. A large proportion of the town's population is engaged in business activity, still the tax revenue generated from the town is very minimal—which clearly indicates evasion of taxes by the businessmen. You have decided to take action in this regard and have put an advertisement in the local newspapers that such businessmen should voluntarily pay their tax dues in a 10-day window, after which you will take action against the defaulters. The very next day, representatives of the business association meet you in the office and invite you for inaugurating a new shopping mall in the town. They also give you an idol of Lord Krishna—made in pure gold—as a gift. You suspect that this is a signal for you to go soft on the tax-disclosure front.

Question

1. Below are some of the options available to you. Identify the merits and demerits of each. Which option would you choose and why?
   (a) File a police complaint against the businessmen for attempting to bribe you.
   (b) Take their gift, because it is of a divine God. But you decide not to go to the mall opening.
   (c) Do not accept the gift, but decide to go to the mall opening ceremony.
   (d) Accept their gift and send your junior to the mall opening ceremony.

CASE STUDY: 55

You have recently qualified the Civil Services Exam. with a rank good enough to get into the IPS. Now you are about 32 years old, your parents are eager to get you married. They arrange a match, which is agreeable to you too. However, they are keen on taking on a large sum of money as dowry, and the girl's family has also agreed to the same. When you object to your parent and tell them that taking dowry is illegal, they say your thinking is impractical. They also highlight that you have two unmarried younger sisters, and arranging marriage for them would involve dowry payment. As a brother, you should be responsible to your sisters and even if you don't use your dowry money on yourself, at least it can be used later for the marriage of your sisters. You discuss this issue with your prospective wife, and she tells you not to worry about dowry as her parents have enough money and can easily pay the amount.

Questions

1. What would you do? Evaluate the below options –
   (a) Take the dowry, as it will help in your sisters' marriage.
   (b) Refuse to take the dowry, and lodge a police complaint against your parents and the girl's parents.
   (c) Cancel the marriage and look for another match.
2. How do you think can the young generation of today convince their parents for not taking dowry for their sons' marriage? Give pragmatic solutions.

CASE STUDY: 56

You are an upright and honest police officer, posted in a State infamous for political interference in bureaucracy. As you start taking strict action against crimes in the city, local MPs, MLAs and other local politicians start to victimize you by often talking against you in the media. They are putting lot of pressure on you to let off the arrested criminals. The final straw was when the MLA indirectly hinted that your family might not be safe if you choose not to tow their line. You decide not to remain silent any longer and talk to the media about this victimization. But you are also aware that as per the Civil Service Conduct Rules, going to media in such cases is prohibited.

Questions

1. What are the options available to you?
2. Identify the merits and demerits of each of them, and choose the best one, with justifications.

CASE STUDY: 57

You are posted as the District Magistrate of a town bordering Nepal. After the new Constitution has been adopted in Nepal, the border districts of Nepal are seeing lot of unrest by some groups. Some of this unrest has also spilled over to your town, and the local Nepali-community people are engaging in anti-India protests and sloganeering against alleged lack of action by the Indian government in resolving the crisis in Nepal. Last week, they burnt the Indian flag and even resorted to stone-pelting on the police. The police was forced to open fire in which two Nepali protestors lost their lives. The Central government has asked the state to take immediate measures to bring the situation in control, as it is negatively impacting Indo-Nepal diplomatic ties.

Questions

1. What steps would you take to tackle the situation?
2. Can resorting to firing by the state police be justified in the above case? Give reasons.
3. What long-term measures can you take so that such situations do not recur?

CASE STUDY: 58

You have been recently posted as the District Magistrate of a coastal town in Odisha. There is a warning from the Meteorological Department that a very strong cyclone is coming towards the town and will make a landfall in three days. As you plan to convene an emergency meeting of the District Disaster Management Authority (DDMA), you notice that many of its positions are vacant. Also, the DDMA had not carried out any preparatory or mitigation plans in the town, due to which there is a complete lack of awareness among the people about the 'dos and don'ts' during a cyclone. In the meanwhile, the state government has directed you to ensure that there is no loss of life due to the cyclone.

Questions

1. In this situation, what immediate steps would you take to minimize the damage due to impending cyclone?
2. What are the long-term measures that need to be taken?

CASE STUDY: 59

You have been recently posted as the Station Manager of a major railway station, which handles hundreds of trains per day, and has a daily footfall of over one lakh passengers. However, to your surprise, you notice that the station is drowned in filth, with overflowing dustbins and severe lack of cleanliness in the toilets. When you enquire about this from your staff, they say that they are underpaid and overworked, and they can't possibly handle such a large station. They also complain that the passengers have very poor civic sense and are used to throwing garbage and filth on the station. Meanwhile, under the Swachh Bharat campaign, the Indian Railways has decided to improve cleanliness standards in the platforms, and station managers will be held accountable for any poor implementation of the scheme.

Questions

1 How will you make use of the funds under Swachh Bharat to improve cleanliness at your station? Identify two priority areas for action.
2 Many passengers have a habit of littering on railway platforms. How can it be minimized? Give one innovative solution.

CASE STUDY: 60

You are posted in Uttarakhand as a District Magistrate (DM). The state had recently witnessed a devastating environmental disaster due to reckless construction of buildings and hotels in ecologically fragile regions. As a follow-up measure, the state government has asked all the DMs to re-verify the construction permits of all residential and commercial buildings in such regions. During such re-verification in your district, you come across numerous violations of the norms and decide to take strong action against these builders – including demolition of these illegal structures. However, you notice that many of these illegal buildings are running charitable hospitals and educational institutions also, and demolishing them would take a heavy toll on the health and educational security of the district. Moreover, there is not much alternative land available in the district where these hospitals and schools could be relocated.

Questions

1. What would you do in this situation? Explain the ethical and moral dilemma involved.
2. Is this case a trade-off between social development and environment-protection? Examine.

CASE STUDY: 61

You are posted as the Development Commissioner of a backward state which is running a high budget deficit. After several attempts, the state has managed to convince an international multilateral financial institution to give it a long-term loan at low interest rates. However, financial institution says that the loan is on the condition that the state government would reduce public spending in critical sectors such as education and health, and promote private players in these areas. Additional condition is that private companies should be able to lease land in the state at below-market rates. The state government is strongly opposed to these conditions, but sees no other alternative. As a last-ditch effort, a negotiating team is constituted to convince the financial institution that its demands are unrealistic. You have been appointed the head of this negotiating team.

Questions

1. How would you go about preparing your team for the negotiation? What are the areas you would focus upon during the negotiation?

2. Suppose that despite your best efforts, the lending institution is adamant on the conditions. Now, what would you recommend to the state government – to accept the conditions and take the loan, or to reject the conditions and stay in revenue shortage? Explain.

CASE STUDY: 62

You are the District Magistrate of a town. During your routine inspection to different government offices of the district, you notice that the quality of public service delivery is very poor. Many departments have not put up Citizen's Charters in their offices, and even in those offices where such a charter is present, it is incomplete, not updated and never followed. Public discontent is very high, and for valid reasons. All this is despite the fact that the State government had mandated all public offices to have Citizen's Charters two years ago. You have decided to take this issue on priority.

Questions

1. What are the contents of a good Citizen's Charter?
2. How will you go about the process of ensuring that all public departments have a good Citizen's Charter? Outline the key steps.

CASE STUDY: 63

You are Director and head of an autonomous organization working under a Ministry of Government of India. One of your Joint Directors is very competent and honest to his job. You also liked his way of working. One day he came to you for an important discussion regarding his junior officer recently posted as Deputy Director in his division. During the discussion, the Joint Director has mentioned that the Deputy Director is arrogant and ill tempered. He belonged to SC category and involved in groupism. He is very poor in disposal of his duties and never complete assignments given to him on time. Further, the Joint Director pointed out that the work in the division suffering a lot and immediate action in this matter is required for smooth functioning of the organization.

You sought an explanation about the charges levelled against him from the Deputy Director. The Deputy Director has denied all the charges put against him. On the contrary, he has been alleged of discrimination on the basis of caste. Further, he suspected that the Joint Director will spoil his ACR which will hamper his promotion and seniority. He has demanded action against the Joint Director. He has also threatened that if action is not taken in a week, he will go to SC Commission for seeking justice.

Questions

1. What steps will you take to solve the problem?
2. What will you do to convince both the officers and how?
3. As the matter is sensitive enough, what kind of strategy will you adopt to make conducive environment in the organization?

CASE STUDY: 64

You are head of a project. You appoint several people to complete the related tasks. One of the workers in the team is, however, a troublemaker. He tries to instigate other team members not to devote so much time to finish the assigned tasks in time. He tries to convince his colleagues saying that if they do not delay the project work, the boss will not increase the project duration, and in that case, they will lose their jobs. The trouble is also that, as their boss, you know his clout too to create further troubles in the said project.

Questions

1. What are the options available with you?
2. Which one option you will opt for to rectify the situation? Give reasons.

CASE STUDY: 65

You are an Administrative Officer in an organization. One day, a female worker came to you and she complained that the Assistant Administrative Officer is harassing her. And, the fact remains that the Officer in question is also close to the Head of your organization. The female worker is not a permanent worker, and she is quite vulnerable. She is not covered by the existing labour laws and job security provisions.

She knows that she may be fired if she lodges a written complaint. Your problem is that you cannot do anything without any written complaint from her.

Question

1. In this situation, how you will proceed with her complaint?

CASE STUDY: 66

You are an incharge of a police station. One day, you come to know that one of your junior officer has arrested a boy for committing a murder. The officer has produced the boy before Magistrate in the adult court/session court. As the age of the boy was recorded as more than 18 years in the police report, he was produced in that court. As a result, he was sent to jail. After one year of this incident, one day you come to know the fact that the boy was 17 years old when he committed the said crime and he was wrongly sent to jail. Being a sensitive and committed police officer towards child rights, you enquired into it. You found that the initial mistake was made by your junior officer in your police station. You also come to know that your junior officer was totally ignorant about rules, procedures, roles and responsibilities pertaining to the Juvenile Justice Act. Further, you observed that wrong reporting in the court was mainly responsible for this adverse situation in this case. As a matter of fact, this wrong reporting became the basis of the punishment involved in this case. As per Juvenile Justice Act, if a person found to be below 18 years of age on the date of offence, his case will be transferred to the Juvenile Justice Board and his custody to the Observation Home and he will not be sent to adult court in any case. But unfortunately the action of police was against the law in this case.

Questions

1. How will you ensure that the boy gets justice?
2. What action will you take against your officer?

CASE STUDY: 67

Ratan, a 15-year-old son of an auto driver, was taken to a different village by his friend in pursuit of work. He was employed as a domestic help and he planned to earn some money and return home. He was told that his salary was sent to his father at home, which was not true. After 2 years of enduring hard labour and abuse, Ratan ran away to his village. To his astonishment, he found that his father had expired a year back which was informed to his employer. Being frustrated and confused, Ratan tried to commit suicide, but one of his friends stopped him and took him to an NGO working for the welfare of child labour. Ratan told the incident in detail and requested for action against his employer. The representative of NGO has brought the case before District Labour Welfare Department where you are working as a labour welfare officer.

Questions

1. What will you do in such situation?
2. What are the issues involved in Ratan's case?

CASE STUDY: 68

You recently joined as head of the department in Government of India and responsible for implementation of Support to Training & Employment Programme for women (STEP) of your department. Under this project, your department has already given a grant of 3 crore rupees to an NGO for implementation of this scheme for a period of three years. Just after completion of the project, your department has given an order for evaluation of the project. By this time, the implementing agency has requested to extend the project period for six months. Thereafter, an independent agency has evaluated the project and given its report. The following issues emerged from the findings and recommendations of the report:

i. The project has achieved its objectives to some extent. In terms of number of beneficiaries, selection of target groups has been achieved as per the guidelines.
ii. As envisaged in the scheme, neither monitoring committee of senior officials from state government was formed nor was the implementation of the project monitored.
iii. Support services to the beneficiaries were not provided. The existing available infrastructure could not be utilized due to lack of efforts on the part of the implementing agency.

iv. Federation of SHGs was found formed only on papers while it was necessary to make the federation functional and the involvement of the implementing agency could be minimized and restricted to consultancy only after completion of the project. Thus, sustainability of the project was neglected.

v. As many children of beneficiary families were found engaged in handloom work under the project, they deprived from their education, there is an urgent need to address the child labour problem as well as the educational need of these children.

vi. Cost of administrative expenses of the project was found on higher side. It should be reduced to make the project economic and purposeful.

Questions

1. In view of the above, what steps will you take?
2. What provisions need to be made in the scheme to ensure education for children of beneficiaries?

CASE STUDY: 69

Mohan is the president of the Resident Welfare Association RWA of a society. He has recently received a complaint from a family residing in one of the houses in your society. A religious group has recently rented the ground floor of a house. As a result of their practices, a lot of noise is coming from the house, which is causing disturbance to the family's daily peace. Mohan communicated the problem to the group, and he was assured that they would keep it in control. However, the situation is still the same.

Question

1. What should be the Mohan's next step? Evaluate the below options with merits and demerits:
   (a) Talk to group once again and issue a final warning.
   (b) You would not do anything as every community has the right to follow its religious practices.
   (c) Go to the police and lodge a complaint against the religious group.
   (d) Ask the group to vacate the premises as soon as possible.

CASE STUDY: 70

You are a junior manager at one of the major automobile companies in India. The company has recently introduced some policies, which have adversely affected the wages of the labour force. When you take up this matter with the senior management, they convey to you that such changes were necessary because of the recent losses suffered by the firm. The workers are very aggrieved due to this decision and the trade union has decided to call a strike. Repeated attempts by the senior management to ask the workers to join work have failed, and they now have chosen you as a mediator to negotiate with the workers.

Questions

1. What are the various options available to you by which you can balance the interests of workers and the firm?
2. Evaluate each of these options and choose the best one, with justifications.

CASE STUDY: 71

You are working as a software engineer in a leading software development firm. You were part of a global team working on a very critical module, with very stringent timelines. One day before the project deadline, during routine testing of the module, you notice that there are some issues in the code written by your team, which could adversely affect the functionality of the module. Fixing this issue will take at least a week. You report this issue to the project manager, but he insists that since the affected functionality will be used very rarely, we must go ahead with the module launch. Moreover, he says that the module must be delivered on time; otherwise, the delay will have a very poor impact on the future of the Indian development centre of the firm.

Questions

1. What are the various dilemmas in the above case?
2. What are the various options available? Which one will you choose and why?

CASE STUDY: 72

You are the district officer of a large city. Because of greater opportunities for employment and sources of living, lot of people from the rural areas comes to this city to work as daily-wage labourers. They have set up temporary tents and slums in the outskirts of the city and have been living so for 8 to 10 years, with their families. Recently, the state government has taken a decision to launch metro services in the city, and the land on city's outskirts (including the tents and slums) has to be cleared to make way for a metro station. You have been asked to start an anti-encroachment drive to clear this land of tents and slums. But you also know that such a move will leave these poor people and their family homeless.

Question

1. What will you do? Evaluate the below options, with merits and demerits:
   (a) Write to Chief Secretary, asking him to stop the plan of launching a metro in the city.
   (b) Ask the slum-dwellers to go back to the villages and try to earn a living there.
   (c) Ask your superiors for guidance.
   (d) Ask your sub-ordinate officers to take charge of the demolition drive and thus delegate the responsibility to your juniors.

CASE STUDY: 73

You are posted as the Superintendent of Police of a district infamous for robbery and extortions. One day, during your morning walk, you notice that a group of people is mercilessly beating up an alleged extortionist whom they apprehended from their neighbourhood. Since you are not in police uniform, the mob does not recognize you and continue to beat the accused. When you question the mob that why are they not taking the culprit to the police station, they say that they are fed up with the slow judicial process of the country and are sure that once taken to police station, the culprit will be soon out on bail and will again start engaging in robbery and extortion.

Questions

1. What will be your immediate reaction in this situation?
2. In long term, how will you make sure that justice-delivery in your district is speeded up?

CASE STUDY: 74

You are the Civil Surgeon of a backward district, which is recently seeing a lot of dengue cases. More than 20 children have died so far in the district hospital, and the situation is very grim. Families of the patients are complaining that there are insufficient beds in the hospital, because of which they are being denied admission. They allege that the attitude of the doctors and medical staff is also very rude towards the patients. You have issued a directive to the doctors and staff to cancel their leaves and be present in the hospital at all times. However, the medical staff and doctors are complaining that they are being overworked and that they need adequate rest to perform at their best. The doctors are threatening to go on a strike if they are forced to work for long hours.

Questions

1. Do you think that in professions like medicine, doctors should be allowed to go on strike?
2. How will you tackle this situation?
3. What are the options available to you? Evaluate each of them, with merits and demerits.

CASE STUDY: 75

You are an evaluating officer with Mid-Day Meal (MDM) programme. You made a visit to a government school to evaluate the mid-meal service in the school. The mid-day meal was being received from centralized kitchen and was being served to the children during mid-morning break. Children who brought their own lunch from home were not interested in taking the meal. Children who didn't bring lunch had no other option but to take the mid-day meal. You noticed that children were not enthusiastic about taking the food. They were just taking it out of obligation. They were not enjoying the food and some of them were even wasting it. The school authorities offered you to taste the food and you did the same. You found the taste of the food as bad and not delectable. Looking at the amount of money being put in the scheme and the manpower employed to facilitate the service you feel it's going in waste since children are not enjoying it as it is meant for them only.

The mid-day meal menu is planned keeping in mind the nutritional requirements of children. A variety of dishes are served through MDM. The objective of MDM is to improve school retention among children. In spite of planning this scheme by giving importance to all the aspects, it fails to meet its goal.

Question

1. In this scenario, what will you do on your part to find a solution to the above problem?

CASE STUDY: 76

You are a District Child Protection Officer and Head of The District Labour Committee for Child Protection under Integrated Child Protection Scheme (ICPS) Of Govt. of India, Implemented by State Government through Child Care Institutions (CCIs). CCIs are funded by the Government and meant for the children who are either orphan or left to be on their own. Major Job of these institutions is to provide care and protection to these children and act as their guardians. You make a visit to one of these institutions to collect data for an ongoing project. As part of the project, you interact with both the children and various stakeholders of these CCIs. During your interaction with children, they disclose to you that the authorities are physically abusing them severely. The children wanted something to be done in this regard, but at the same time they were scared of authorities and they did not want them to find out that they have complained about them. Children expressed their hope in you and you also want to help them.

Question

1. By keeping the children's interest and safety in view, how will you handle the situation?

CASE STUDY: 77

You are posted as a Director, Social Welfare Department of State Govt. Being head of the department, you are getting many complaints against Child Development project Officer (CDPO) who is a drawing and disbursing officer/Head of Office for the ICDS project under your control. CDPO is engaging in corrupt practices like taking commission from suppliers of supplementary nutrition for children at Anganwadi centres. CDPO is making money, and she does not hesitate to compromise with quality and quantity of supplementary nutrition. You talk to this officer many times to stop such malpractices, but she does not change her mind. You are scared to complain about her as she has a good nexus with higher authorities. You are also afraid of her as complaining about her can hamper your promotion which you deserve and is due shortly, given the number of years of experience you hold.

Questions

1. In such a situation, what action is required on your part?
2. What steps are required to run the supplementary nutrition program smoothly?

CASE STUDY: 78

You are working as a District Protection Officer under Protection of Women against Domestic Violence Act. The domestic help working in your house faces violence at the hands of her sister-in-law and her husband. She shares the same residential facility with them. They also put some false allegations against her elder son (aged 15 years). When she complains about them to the elders of her family, they do not support her. Instead, they believe in what her sister-in-law and her husband say. She also files a police complaint against them, but the police also do not believe her.

Her husband is not in a condition to make a living for the family or to look after his children, as he does not keep well. She has no choice but to work in different houses to earn a living and leave her two children at home under the care of same family members who did not support her. She is scared that they may also physically abuse her children in her absence.

Question

1. In the above situation, how will you help your domestic help to get justice?

CASE STUDY: 79

You are a teacher in a school. You notice that one of the female students of your class is behaving differently. She has become quite, inattentive in class, looks outside through window and her grades in exams are also going down. You decide to talk to her. However, she does not disclose anything to you but you doubt that something is definitely wrong with her. After trying for a number of times, you win her confidence and she shares that her grandfather has been sexually abusing her. Her parents were employed and after school she was under the care of her grandfather. In her parent's absence, her grandfather abused her and also threatened her not to disclose to anyone. You want to bring the matter into the knowledge of her parents, but you are scared for the child. You do not want her to go through the same ordeal of narrating the story to her parents and loose her confidence as she was excellent in her studies, but this incident has left a mark in her life. Grandfather is a close family member, and the situation might take an ugly turn in house, which might further traumatize the child. You want the parents to believe in you and not involve the child too much.

Questions

1. In the above situation, what are the options available before you?
2. What will you do to get the confidence of the child back?

CASE STUDY: 80

In villages of a tribal development block in the district where you are posted as D.C., local administration has taken all the grazing land of villagers for social forestry programme. As a result, animal husbandry has reduced to a great extent. As money making mono culture trees were planted in the grazing land to meet out the requirement of industries, it was not considered fruitful. Consequently, the villagers opposed it. In spite of consensus, local administration wanted to maintain the status quo. As a result, the opposition was on the increase. Villagers started taking out sapling to destroy the plantation. On account of this, villagers were arrested by the police daily. The Block Development Officer (BDO) tries his best but failed as the matter was a policy-related one. The decision in this regard was still awaited. The administration as well as villagers continued destroying the plantation, administration found itself helpless and the matter is lying with you.

Questions

1. Since the grazing land is not in use, what immediate action is required?
2. What will be your role in solving the case?
3. What action do you suggest for promoting social forestry programme in the district?

CASE STUDY: 81

A high school girl of 15 years was promised a job by a friendly uncle of her town. The girl left her home with this uncle. On the way, the uncle repeatedly assaulted her sexually and sold her to a brothel. One day there was a raid on that brothel. She was rescued and sent to a shelter home run by an NGO in the partnership of Child Welfare Department of State Government under Integrated Child Protection Scheme (ICPS). The role of this shelter home was to provide the girl and other such girls' specialized medical care and schooling and happiness in life. But she was sexually assaulted by the in-charge of the shelter home like other girls and was threatened not to tell anybody about this. The abuse at the shelter home came to light after an employee telephoned Child line. The children were rescued and the in-charge of the shelter home was arrested by the police.

The girl and other children were presented before the District Child Welfare Committee under ICPS as per Juvenile Justice Act to decide how and where they should be looked after. The Child Welfare Committee sent them to a Children Home run by Child Welfare Department of State Government.

Once again the girl landed in another abusive situation just after three months in the Children Home. One day an investigation team discovered the girl and six other girls had complained of being sexually abused by the caretaker, and other staff members of the Home resorted to physical abuse and torture. The similar situation is prevailing in most of the Child Care Institutions under Child Welfare Department of State Government headed by you.

Questions

1. In such situations, being the head of the department, what will be your role in ultimate rehabilitation of the girl and other such girls living in Children's Homes/Shelter Homes?
2. What strategy will you adopt to ensure the proper implementation of POCSO Act and Juvenile Justice Act in the Child Care Institutions under your control?

CASE STUDY: 82

Recently you are posted as Block Development Officer in a far-flung Tribal Development Block. You found that tribal forest villagers are facing many problems due to illegal activities such as:

1. Commercial dealings between the local forest administration and the owners of Tile factories. A dozen of forest villages have become labour camps of the forest department. The villagers have been deprived not only of the wood for agricultural instruments but of firewood also. On the other hand, more than a thousand quintal of wood is burnt daily in the ovens of the tile factories located in the forest area. The wood consumption in these factories is increasing day by day and became so high that it cannot be fulfilled by legal means. Thus, illegal cutting of trees with the help of local forest administration is going on. Illegal wood stocks in huge quantity can be seen in these factories.
2. Similarly, illegal mining of soil in this area has become a big problem. The tile factories get clay for making kilns by illegal mining of soil in these forest villages with the help of local mines department. As per rule, pits should not be deeper than 10 feet, but 20 feet deep pits can be seen in this forest area. When the soil is removed from the roots of trees, either they fall down or they dry up. During the last 10 years wherever forest land has been dug up, pits can still be seen, where even grass doesn't grow.
3. Huge amount has been spent on various welfare plans/schemes for tribal villagers, but the people concerned have not benefited from these plans. These villagers were given loans for agricultural equipment, digging of wells, construction of houses, etc. It is found that those who could obtain loan for oxen did not get it for carts and those who had carts did not get loan for oxen. Loan could never be obtained on time, because of the delaying tactics of the officials. This loan was given through rural banks. The thumb impressions of the illiterate villagers were taken on the blank papers, without telling them the cause. They came to know about the consequences only when the concerned official visited their houses for the recovery of the instalments.
   By giving full exemption to these tribal villagers on gobar gas plants, about 150 families have been provided with this facility, out of which more than 100 families did not have sufficient gobar (cow dung) and those had sufficient cow dung were not given this facility.
4. Under the Tribal Housing Scheme for the landless and homeless tribes, 10 families of a village were given 15×10 feet plot each of which was quite insufficient for the family

and their cattle. For this reason, plot has been covered by wooden huts. A few non-tribal influential people of these villages took the benefit in the name of these tribal, completing the formalities in collusion with the local administration.

5. Villages have school buildings but without students. On paper there are schools for these villages but without teachers.
6. These tribal villagers are not comfortable and found themselves unfitted in the existing model of development. Their social values and concepts of development are quite different from nontribes, but they are treated in the same way.

Questions

1. Would it be possible for you to look into the linkages of their concepts of development with their needs and quality of life?
2. If yes, what kind of action plan is required?
3. What direct action would you take on your part to resolve the problems?

CASE STUDY: 83

Mr. Manoj Kumar is recently appointed as the Chairman of Tobacco Board. He is a very sincere and committed officer. Also, previously he has held various high-level positions.

Tobacco is an important commercial crop grown in India. It occupies the third position in the world with an annual production of about 800 million kg Tobacco and tobacco products earn approximately ₹ 20,000 crores to the national exchequer by way of excise duty, and approximately ₹ 5,000 crores by way of foreign exchange every year. But recently, the tobacco production in some parts of the country suffered from setback. Farmers and farm-labourers committed suicide because of crop failures and mounting debt. Also the farmers have gone for strikes and dharnas against economic policies of the Government.

Mr. Kumar has a very close relative who stays in Canada. He has always shown his presence in almost every functions of this particular relative. He does not have an attitude to say 'NO' to his family members and relatives.

Recently, he got a call from Canada to attend a marriage party of this particular relative there. But, amidst the ongoing suicide crisis of farmers and related agitations in the country, he fled to Canada to attend his relative's marriage.

Questions

1. Do you think Mr. Kumar is a responsible officer? Justify your viewpoint.
2. What you would have done if you were in place of Mr. Kumar?

CASE STUDY: 84

Mr. Ashok Kumar is the Deputy Superintendent of Police (DSP) of the Prohibition Enforcement Wing in a State. He has a very close childhood friend, named Naresh, who has now become a red sanders logs smuggler. Both are still good friends.

DSP led a four-member team to track down a prohibition offender and his associates. Mr. Kumar and his team seized around 4,000 litres of rectified spirit and confiscated a van during the raid recently. But the notorious bootlegger and his associates managed to escape.

DSP, however, instigated by Naresh, led the team comprising of the same four officers and raided a poultry farm. Naresh had given ₹ 3.5 crore worth of red sanders logs to owner of the poultry firm, and he was refusing to pay for it or return it.

Upon finding a huge haul of red sanders logs, the DSP told the four policemen that he must inform the appropriate authorities to take further course of action against the owner of the poultry firm. He also told the policemen to wait inside the police vehicle.

They were not aware that DSP has already informed Naresh about this raid. After the DSP and his team left the farm, Naresh and his men, who were waiting outside the farm, took the logs away.

Questions

1. Does Mr. Kumar's action reflect the integrity of the public office he holds?
2. How should Mr. Kumar have dealt with Naresh?

CASE STUDY: 85

You are the academic dean of a reputed college. You have recently received complaints from many parents that one of the senior professors is very rude to the students, and even resorts to severe physical punishments. The professor in question is a highly regarded academician with excellent teaching record and has won numerous awards, including the President's Award for Excellence in Teaching. When you confront the professor, he admits, but says that he feels punishment is necessary to make students focus on studies.

Questions

1. Evaluate each of the below options available to you:
   (a) Ask the professor for resignation.
   (b) Go to the students and tell them that professors need to be strict with them for the good of the students.
   (c) Transfer the professor to another department.
   (d) Resign yourself from the position of dean.
2. Also mention any other option which you have, and which one will you choose, with justification.

CASE STUDY: 86

You are the in-charge of the office that supervises the allotment of official residences to the incumbent Members of Parliament (MPs). You are finding it very challenging to issue allotment for all MPs because there is a crunch of appropriate bungalows. In the meanwhile, it has been brought to your notice that some of the ex-MPs are not vacating the official residences allotted to them, even after they are no longer entitled for the same. Numerous notices have been served to these ex-MPs, but there has been no response. Some of these ex-MPs are very influential and one of them has even threatened your office not to bother him with notices—he plans to stay in his residence for at least 2 years. Meanwhile, incumbent MPs are quickly demanding allocation of official residences.

Questions

1. Evaluate the below options:
   (a) Forcibly evict the erring ex-MPs.
   (b) Approach your superiors and ask for guidance.
   (c) Send a final notice to all the ex-MPs regarding the dates by which the residences have to be vacated and the charges that would be levied after such last date.
2. Also mention any other option that you have. Which option will you choose? Give justifications.

CASE STUDY: 87

You have recently been promoted as an Executive Engineer of a state road construction department, and the first assignment is construction of an all-weather road in a district, which connects a big but remote village to the state highway. There is an old dirt road that exists and is to be replaced by the new, broader road. During your inspection on site, you find that there is encroachment on either side of the road. Many villagers have built their house and business on the government land meant for the road. When you discuss this issue with the local Gram Panchayat, they understand the issue involved, but reject any proposal for demolition of the illegal contractions on the road.

Questions

1. What precautions should you take before you start the project and why?
2. What are the problems you anticipate and how do you plan to address them?

CASE STUDY: 88

You are the District Development officer of a drought-prone district. As a part of your responsibilities, you are required to send a report to the Chief Secretary of the state, declaring whether your district is affected by drought or not, and if yes, the extent of drought in the district. Only then is the compensation released for the affected people. For the past few years, your district has been drought-affected. However, this year, most areas in your district have received sufficient rainfall and you want to send an accurate report to the Chief Secretary. The MLA of your district, however, has asked you to send a report which declares the district as drought-affected, so that the compensation so received can be utilized in other development programmes which are facing funds shortage. The

Tehsildars and the Sub-Divisional Magistrate are not sure whether conditions in the district can be rightly classified as drought-affected.

Questions

1. What are the ethical and moral dilemmas in this case?
2. What are the options available to you? Identify the merits and demerits of each and choose the best option, with justifications.

Right to Public Services Legislation in India

1 APPENDIX

Right to Public Services legislation in India comprises statutory laws which guarantee time bound delivery of services for various public services rendered by the Government to citizen and provides mechanism for punishing the errant public servant who is deficient in providing the service stipulated under the statute. Right to Service legislation are meant to reduce corruption among the government officials and to increase transparency and public accountability. Madhya Pradesh became the first state in India to enact Right to Service Act on 18 August 2010 and Bihar was the second to enact this bill on 25 July 2011. Several other states like Bihar, Delhi, Punjab, Rajasthan, Himachal Pradesh, Kerala, Uttarakhand, Haryana, Uttar Pradesh, Odisha and Jharkhand have introduced similar legislation for effectuating the right to service to the citizen.

Framework

The common framework of the legislations in various states includes, granting of "right to public services", which are to be provided to the public by the designated official within the stipulated time frame. The public services which are to be granted as a right under the legislations are generally notified separately through Gazette notification. Some of the common public services which are to be provided within the fixed time frame as a right under the Acts, includes issuing caste, birth, marriage and domicile certificates, electric connections, voter's card, ration cards, copies of land records, etc.

On failure to provide the service by the designated officer within the given time or rejected to provide the service, the aggrieved person can approach the First Appellate Authority. The First Appellate Authority, after making a hearing, can accept or reject the appeal by making a written order stating the reasons for the order and intimate the same to the applicant, and can order the public servant to provide the service to the applicant.

An appeal can be made from the order of the First Appellate Authority to the Second Appellate Authority, who can either accept or reject the application, by making a written order stating the reasons for the order and intimate the same to the applicant, and can order the public servant to provide the service to the applicant or can impose penalty on the designated officer for deficiency of service without any reasonable cause, which can range from ₹ 500 to ₹ 5000 or may recommend disciplinary proceedings. The applicant may be compensated out of the penalty imposed on the officer. The appellate authorities has been granted certain powers of a Civil Court while trying a suit under Code of Civil Procedure, 1908, like production of documents and issuance of summon to the Designated officers and appellants.

Implementing states

State	Act title	Status
Punjab	Right to Public Service Act, 2011	Notified
Uttarakhand	The Uttarakhand Right to Service Act, 2011	Notified
Madhya Pradesh	Madhya Pradesh Lok Sewaon Ke Pradan Ki Guarantee Adhiniyam, 2010	Enacted
Bihar	Bihar Lok Sewaon Ka Adhikar Adhiniyam, 2011	Enacted
Delhi	Delhi (Right of Citizen to Time Bound Delivery of Services) Act, 2011	Notified
Jharkhand	Right to Service Act, 2011	Notified
Himachal Pradesh	Himachal Pradesh Public Services Guarantee Act, 2011	Notified
Rajasthan	Rajasthan Public Service Guarantee Act, 2011	Notified
Uttar Pradesh	Janhit Guarantee Act, 2011	Enacted
Kerala	The Kerala State Right to Service Act, 2012	Enacted
Karnataka	The Karnataka (Right of Citizens to Time Bound Delivery of Services) Bill, 2011	Notified
Chhattisgarh	Chhattisgarh Lok Seva Guarantee Bill, 2011	Notified
Jammu and Kashmir	The Jammu and Kashmir Public Services Guarantee Act, 2011	Notified
Odisha	Odisha Right to Public Services Act, 2012	Notified
Assam	Assam Right to Public Services Act, 2012	Notified
Central Government	Citizen's Charter and Grievance Redressal Bill 2011	Proposed
Gujarat	Gujarat (Right of Citizens to Public Services) Bill, 2013	Enacted
West Bengal	West Bengal Right to Public Services Bill, 2013	Notified
Goa	The Goa (Right to Time-Bound Delivery of Public Services) Act, 2013	Notified
Haryana	The Haryana Right to Service Act, 2014	Notified
Maharashtra	Maharashtra Right to Public Services Ordinance, 2015	Notified

The Right of Citizens for Time Bound Delivery of Goods and Services and Redressal of Their Grievances Bill, 2011

2 APPENDIX

The Bill was introduced in the Lok Sabha on 20 December 2011. The Bill was referred to the Department Related Standing Committee on Personnel, Public Grievances, Law and Justice (Chairperson: Mr. Shantaram Naik). The Report was submitted on 30 August 2012.

AIMS OF THE BILL

- The Bill seeks to create a mechanism to ensure timely delivery of goods and services to citizens.
- Every public authority is required to publish a citizens charter within six months of the commencement of the Act. The Charter will detail the goods and services to be provided and their timelines for delivery.
- A citizen may file a complaint regarding any grievance related to: (a) citizens charter; (b) functioning of a public authority; or (c) violation of a law, policy or scheme.
- The Bill requires all public authorities to appoint officers to redress grievances. Grievances are to be redressed within 30 working days. The Bill also provides for the appointment of Central and State Public Grievance Redressal Commissions.
- A penalty of up to ₹ 50,000 may be levied upon the responsible officer or the Grievance Redressal Officer for failure to render services.

KEY POINTS

- Parliament may not have the jurisdiction to regulate the functioning of state public officials as state public services fall within the purview of state legislatures.
- This Bill may create a parallel grievance redressal mechanism as many central and state laws have established similar mechanisms.
- Companies that render services under a statutory obligation or a licence may be required to publish citizens charters and provide a grievance redressal mechanism.
- The Commissioners may be removed without a judicial inquiry on an allegation of misbehaviour or incapacity. This differs from the procedure under other legislations.

- Appeals from the Commissions' decisions on matters of corruption will lie before the Lokpal or Lokayukta. The Lokpal and some Lokayukta have not been established.
- Only citizens can seek redressal of grievances under the Bill. The Bill does not enable foreign nationals who also use services such as driving licenses, electricity, etc., to file complaints.

PART A: HIGHLIGHTS OF THE BILL

Context

The Bill refers to a 'citizens charter' which is a document that defines the standard of services to be provided by an entity. The citizens charter will also provide the time frame within which goods and services are to be provided. The concept of citizens charter was introduced in the United Kingdom in 1991 and subsequently was adopted by various countries such as Belgium (1992), Malaysia (1993) and Australia (1997).

In 1997, at a chief ministers' conference, an Action Plan was approved requiring the central and state governments to formulate citizens charters for enterprises with a large public interface. In 2007, the Second Administrative Reforms Commission recommended that citizens charters should stipulate penalties for non- compliance. In 2008, the Standing Committee on Personnel, Public Grievances, Law and Justice recommended giving statutory status to grievance redressal mechanisms. The Central Information Commission also recommended that grievance redressal systems should be strengthened to reduce the use of the Right to Information Act, 2005 to redress grievances.

The President, in her address to Parliament in June 2009, had stated that the government would focus on ensuring effective delivery of public services. The Standing Committee that had examined the Lokpal Bill, 2011 recommended the creation of a separate legislation to deal with citizens charter and grievance redressal. The Parliament on 27 August 2011 while adopting the 'Sense of the House' Resolution on Lokpal, agreed in principle to the establishment of a citizens charter.

Currently, government departments deal with grievances internally. Persons may also approach the High Court through writ petitions. As of January 2011, 131 citizens charters were finalized by the central government departments and 729 citizens charters were finalized by state government departments. Additionally, by March 2012, several states had enacted laws providing for grievance redressal mechanisms.

KEY FEATURES

The Bill requires public authorities to publish a citizens charter within six months of enactment of the Bill. The charter should specify the services and the quality of services to be provided by the public authority. The head of departments are responsible for disseminating and updating the citizens charter.

Public Authority

- Public authorities include: (a) constitutional and statutory authorities; (b) entities established under a notification; and (c) public-private partnerships. They also include NGOs that are substantially government funded, government companies, and companies that provide services under a licence or a statutory obligation.

- Public authorities are required to establish Information Facilitation Centres for efficient and effective delivery of services and redressal of grievances. Information Facilitation Centres may include customer care centres, call centres, help desks and people's support centres.

Public Grievance Redressal Commissions

- The Bill establishes Central and State Grievance Redressal Commissions. Each Commission would consist of a Chief Commissioner and up to 10 Commissioners. The Commissioners would be appointed by the President (Governor) on the recommendation of a selection committee. This committee would consist of the Prime Minister (Chief Minister), the Leader of the Opposition in the Lok Sabha (Legislative Assembly) and a sitting Supreme Court (High Court) judge.
- The Commissioners should be: (a) present or former Secretaries to the central (state) government; or (b) present or former Supreme Court judges or Chief Justices of a High Court (district court judges for 10 years, or High Court judges); or (c) eminent persons with at least 20 years (15 years) of experience in social sectors with a postgraduate degree in a relevant sector. The Commissioners may be removed by an order of the President (Governor) under certain conditions.

COMPLAINT MECHANISM

- ***Complaint***: Any citizen may file a complaint for (a) failure in delivery of goods or services listed in the citizens charter; (b) the functioning of the public authority; and (c) any violation of a law, policy, programme, order or scheme. Complaints have to be redressed within 30 working days.
- Complaints have to be made to the Grievance Redressal Officer (GRO). GROs are to be appointed by each public authority at the central, state, district, sub-district, municipality and panchayat levels. The GRO is required to: (a) ensure that grievances are redressed within 30 working days; (b) ensure that disciplinary action is taken against a defaulting officer if he has acted negligently; and (c) recommend penalties and compensation where an individual has wilfully neglected to deliver services or there is a prima facie ground for a case under the Prevention of Corruption Act, 1988. The GRO has to inform the complainant about the action taken on the complaint.
- ***Appeal***: The orders of the GRO may be appealed before the Designated Authority (DA). The DA shall be an officer above the rank of the GRO and outside the concerned public authority. (According to a statement made by the Minister of State for Personnel, Public Grievances and Pensions, the DA shall be an officer at the district level. The DA shall dispose of appeals within 30 working days of their receipt. If a complaint with the GRO is not redressed within 30 working days, the GRO has to forward it as an appeal to the DA. The DA may penalize the defaulting officers.
- ***Second Appeal***: The DA's orders may be appealed before the Central or State Public Grievance Redressal Commission within 30 working days. Appeals relating to

complaints arising out of functioning of the central (state) departments would lie before the Central (State) Commission. The Commissions have to dispose of the appeal within 60 working days.

- *Third Appeal*: In relation to an offence under the Prevention of Corruption Act, 1988, an appeal against the decision of the Commissions shall lie with the Lokpal or the Lokayukta.
- *Suo moto mechanism*: The Central and State Commissions can *suo moto* refer matters related to non- delivery of goods and services to the heads of government departments. The Commissions may also initiate *suo moto* inquiry if they believe that there are reasonable grounds to inquire into the matter.
- Complaints may also be made to the Commissions in certain cases. It is the duty of the Commissions to inquire into complaints by persons: (a) who are unable to file appeals before the DA; (b) who are refused redress of grievances; (c) whose complaints are not disposed of within 30 days; and (d) who are denied access to the citizens charter because it has not been prepared or has not been widely disseminated.

Penalties

- **GRO:** The Bill requires the GRO to recommend penalties to the DA when: (a) he is convinced that the default was due to wilful neglect by an officer; or (b) when there is prima facie evidence of corruption.
- **DA and Commissions:** The Bill empowers the DA and the Commissions to impose a maximum penalty of ₹ 50,000 upon the defaulting officer and the GRO. Penalties may be imposed upon the defaulting officer when he has acted in a mala fide manner or has failed to discharge his responsibility in a proper manner.

A portion of the penalty may be awarded as compensation to the complainant.

- If there is evidence of corruption against the defaulting officer, the DA and the Commissions would have to refer the matter to appropriate authorities. Additionally, the DA may initiate proceedings in such cases.
- Disciplinary proceedings may be initiated by the GRO, DA and the Commissions against the defaulting officer if there is evidence of mala fide action.
- In any appeal proceeding, where it is alleged that the grievance has not been redressed by the GRO, the burden of proof shall be on the GRO.

PART B: KEY ISSUES AND ANALYSIS

Parliament's Jurisdiction to Regulate State Public Officials

The Bill regulates the functioning of departments and public officials at the central and state level. It also establishes Commissions at the central and state level. 'State public services; State Public Service Commission' is included in the State List (Entry 41) of the Seventh Schedule of the Constitution. This implies that the power to make laws to regulate the functioning of state public officials lies solely with state legislatures. Thus, Parliament may not have jurisdiction to enact laws governing such services and officials.

In this regard, the Ministry has stated that the provisions of the Bill relate to 'actionable wrongs' which comes under the concurrent list. This view was accepted by the Standing Committee.

The Supreme Court has held that, "Wrong means an actionable wrong and it must consist of: (a) an act or omission amounting to an infringement of a legal right of a person or a breach of legal duty towards him; and (b) the act or omission must have caused harm or damage to that person in some way, the damage being either actual or presumed". Under the Bill, complaints may be filed for violation of any policy or scheme. The claims under these schemes and policies may be non-justiciable (unenforceable by courts). It is unclear whether schemes and policies which are not justiciable would fall under the meaning of 'actionable wrong'.

Several states such as Delhi, Punjab and Bihar have also enacted their own grievance redressal laws. The mechanism provided under these laws is different from that provided under the Bill.

Lack of Clarity on the Meaning of Public Authority

Clause 2(n)

It is not clear whether the Bill applies to private entities only if they are established or constituted under a notification. The term 'public authorities' has been defined broadly to mean authorities constituted under: (a) the Constitution or under any central or state law; (b) an agreement between the government and a private entity as a PPP; and (c) any entity established under a notification or order of the government. This definition also includes: (i) non-governmental organizations that receive government finances either directly or indirectly, and (ii) other companies that are supplying goods or services to fulfil a statutory obligation, or under a license or authorization by law. It is not clear if these organizations are required to be established under a notification.

It is pertinent to note that the Right to Information Act, 2005 includes private entities as long as they are controlled or financed by the government. Private sector companies are covered by other laws such as Consumer Protection Act, 1986 and the Competition Act, 2002. Inclusion under this Bill may lead to multiple dispute settlement forums being available for the same dispute. For instance, grievances related to services to be provided under a contract would fall under the Consumer Protection Act and this Bill.

Multiplicity of Grievance Redressal Forums

Clause 2(f)

This Bill provides grievance redressal under several circumstances including violation of any law, policy or scheme. Some existing and proposed laws provide their own grievance redressal mechanisms, for instance, the Mahatma Gandhi National Rural Employment Guarantee Act, 2005, Right of Children to Free and Compulsory Education, 2009, National Food Security Bill, 2011, and the Public Procurement Bill, 2012.

There could be an overlap of jurisdictions in some cases, as grievances under these legislations may be covered under this Bill as well. It is unclear as to which mechanism may be approached first, and whether seeking relief under one law bars remedies under the other.

Furthermore, the commissions established under these legislations are specialized in nature. They comprise persons of eminence in the field to which the laws relate. For instance, commissions under the National Food Security Bill, 2011 comprise persons with experience in the field of food security, agriculture and health.

Exclusion of non-citizens

Clause 2(f)

A complaint may only be filed by a citizen. However, certain services may be used by both citizens and foreign nationals. For example, a foreign national is eligible to apply for a driving license under Indian law. The rationale for excluding foreign nationals from the purview of the redressal mechanism is unclear.

Under some state laws, the criterion for accessing grievance redressal mechanism is the eligibility of the complainant and not his citizenship. The Punjab Right to Services Act, 2011 and the Rajasthan Guaranteed Delivery of Public Services Act, 2011 provide access to the redressal mechanism to all 'eligible persons'. Under these Acts an 'eligible person' is defined as 'any person who is eligible for the notified services'. The Standing Committee has recommended that the Ministry review whether non-citizens can be brought under the Bill.

Inconsistencies in the Appeals Procedure

Clause 47, 28 and 44

Under the Bill, if the Commission is satisfied that a prima facie case of corruption exists, it will refer the matter to the 'appropriate authority'. The Bill also provides that the Commissions' decisions related to corruption may be appealed before the Lokpal or the Lokayukta. This raises three issues.

First, under the Bill, the Commission is not empowered to adjudicate matters related to corruption. It is only empowered to refer the matter to the appropriate authority. It is unclear how an appeal may be made before the Lokpal or the Lokayukta in the absence of the Commissions' power to decide on cases of corruption.

Second, the Bill does not provide a process to appeal against the Commissions' orders that do not relate to corruption. Third, the Lokpal is yet to be instituted at the centre and a number of states have not yet established Lokayukta.

The Standing Committee has recommended that appeals to the Lokpal and Lokayukta should not be provided. It observed that the Lokpal and Lokayukta are anti-corruption agencies, whereas, the Bill addresses the issue of delivery of services. It also noted that the Bill already provided for three levels of appeal, and that a fourth appeal to the Lokpal or the Lokayukta is not required.

Removal of Members of the Central and State Grievance Commissions

Clause 20 and 37

Members of the Commissions can be removed by an order of the President or the Governor. The Bill states that the government may by rules regulate the investigation procedure for removal of the Commissioners for misbehaviour or incapacity. However, it does not require a judicial inquiry to be conducted in case there is an allegation of misbehaviour (acquisition of financial or such other interest) or incapacity of the Commissioners.

This is different from the process provided under some legislations. For example, the Competition Act, 2002, the Right to Information Act, 2005 and the Protection of Human Rights Act, 1993 require a judicial inquiry to be conducted before removal of the Commissioners when there is an allegation of misbehaviour or incapacity against them. The Electronic Delivery of Services Bill, 2011 and the Lokpal and Lokayukta Bill, 2011 also have a similar inquiry procedure.

Inconsistency between the Powers of the DA and the Commissions

Clause 11(10) and 28

The Bill provides for two levels of appeals by a complainant: first to the DA, and then to the Commission. There is an inconsistency between the powers of the two. If there is a prima facie indication of corruption, the DA may either refer the matter to the appropriate authority or initiate proceedings. However, if the complainant appeals against the DA's decision to the Commission, it can only refer the matter to the appropriate authority. Unlike the DA, the Commission does not have the power to initiate proceedings.

India's Citizen's Charter and Grievance Redressal Bill, 2011

3 APPENDIX

The Citizen's Charter and Grievance Redressal Bill, 2011 in India is also known as The Right of Citizens for Time Bound Delivery of Goods and Services and Redressal of their Grievances Bill, 2011 or Citizens Charter Bill. It was tabled by V. Narayanasamy, Minister of State for Personnel, Public Grievances and Pensions, in Lok Sabha in December 2011.

The Bill seeks to confer on every citizen the right to time-bound delivery of specified goods and services and to provide a mechanism for grievance redressal. The Bill makes it mandatory for every public authority to publish a Citizen's Charter within six months of the commencement of the Act, failing which the official concerned would face action, including a fine of up to ₹ 50,000 from his salary and disciplinary proceedings.

The bill came after Anna Hazare asked for its provisions to be included in the Jan Lokpal Bill.

JAN LOKPAL BILL

The Jan Lokpal Bill, also referred to as the Citizen's Ombudsman Bill, is an anti-corruption bill drafted and drawn up by civil society activists in India seeking the appointment of a Jan Lokpal, an independent body to investigate corruption cases. This bill also proposes improvements to the Lokpal and Lokayukta Bill 2011, which was to be passed by Lok Sabha in December 2011. The Jan Lokpal Bill aims to effectively deter corruption, compensate citizen grievances and protect whistle-blowers. The prefix *Jan* (translation: citizens) signifies that these improvements include inputs provided by "ordinary citizens" through an activist-driven, non-governmental public consultation.

The word *Lokpal' was coined in 1963 by L.M. Singhvi, a Member of Parliament during a debate mechanisms. His son Dr. was head of the Parliament reviewing the bill but later resigned from the post after a sex-tape controversy.* In order to draw the attention of the government, a focused campaign "India Against Corruption" (IAC) was started in 2011. Anna Hazare is the head of civil society and the IAC movement, being a foreground for Jan Lokpal campaign. Through these collaborative efforts till August 2011, IAC was able to upload the 23rd version of the Jan Lokpal Bill draft.

Lokpal Bill

The Lokpal Bill was first introduced by Shanti Bhushan in 1968 and passed the 4th Lok Sabha in 1969. But before it could be passed by Rajya Sabha, the Lok Sabha was dissolved and the bill lapsed. Subsequent versions were re-introduced in 1971, 1977, 1985, 1989, 1996, 1998, 2001, 2005 and in 2008, but none of them were passed. In 2011, during the Parliament's Winter Session, the Lok Sabha passed the controversial Lokpal Bill, but could not be passed by Rajya Sabha due to shortage of time in the winter session of 2011. Government has not put Lokpal bill again in Rajya Sabha.

Timeline and cost

The Lokpal Bill has been introduced in the Parliament a total of eight times since 1968.

- 1968 – 3 lakh (300,000)
- 1971 – 20 lakh (2 million)
- 1977 – 25 lakh (2.5 million)
- 1985 – 25 lakh
- 1989 – 35 lakh (3.5 million) – PM under Lokpal
- 1996 – 1 crore (10 million) – PM under Lokpal
- 2001 – 35 crore (350 million) – PM under Lokpal
- 2011 – 1700 crore (17 billion)
- 2012 – 2000 crore (20 billion)

Current Anti-Corruption Laws and Organizations

While India currently has a number of laws intended to stem corruption, supporters of the Jan Lokpal Bill have argued that the current laws are inadequate in light of the large number and size of scandals in India.

Central Vigilance Commission (CVC)

CVC has a staff strength of between 200 and 250 employees. If one went by international standards, India needs 28 anti-corruption staff in CVC to check corruption of 57 lakh employees. There has been considerable delay in many cases for grant of sanction for prosecution against corrupt government officials. The permission to prosecute such officials acts as a deterrent in the drive to eradicate corruption and bring transparency in the system.

Central Bureau of Investigation (CBI)

Because the CBI is under the control of the central government, it needs a go-ahead from central agencies to initiate criminal proceedings. By then, the accused can take advantage of such a situation. He can get time to pressure the complainant and intimidate him so that the case be withdrawn. In the Jan Lokpal Bill, it is proposed that both of these wings be merged into the Lokpal. This would enable the Lokpal to be completely independent of the government and free from ministerial influence in its investigations.

Inspiration

The bill was inspired by the Hong Kong Independent Commission Against Corruption (ICAC). In the 1970s, the level of corruption in Hong Kong was seen so high, that the government created the commission with direct powers to investigate and deal with corruption. In the first instance, the ICAC sacked 119 out of 180 police officers.

Key Features of Proposed Bill

Some important features of the proposed bill are:

1. To establish a central government anti-corruption institution called *Lokpal*, supported by *Lokayukta* at the state level.
2. As is the case with the Supreme Court of India and Cabinet Secretariat, the *Lokpal* will be supervised by the Cabinet Secretary and the Election Commission. As a result, it will be completely independent of the government and free from ministerial influence in its investigations.
3. Members will be appointed by judges, Indian Administrative Service officers with a clean record, private citizens and constitutional authorities through a transparent and participatory process.
4. A selection committee will invite short-listed candidates for interviews, the video recordings of which will thereafter be made public.
5. Every month on its website, the *Lokayukta* will publish a list of cases dealt with, brief details of each, their outcome and any action taken or proposed. It will also publish lists of all cases received by the *Lokayukta* during the previous month, cases dealt with and those which are pending.
6. Investigations of each case must be completed in one year. Any resulting trials should be concluded in the following year, giving a total maximum process time of two years.
7. Losses to the government by a corrupt individual will be recovered at the time of conviction.
8. Government office-work required by a citizen that is not completed within a prescribed time period will result in *Lokpal* imposing financial penalties on those responsible, which will then be given as compensation to the complainant.
9. Complaints against any officer of *Lokpal* will be investigated and completed within one month and, if found to be substantive, will result in the officer being dismissed within two months.
10. The existing anti-corruption agencies [CVC], departmental vigilance and the anti-corruption branch of the [CBI] will be merged into *Lokpal* which will have complete power authority to independently investigate and prosecute any officer, judge or politician.
11. Whistle-blowers who alert the agency to potential corruption cases will also be provided with protection by it.

Difference between Government's and Activists' Drafts of Jan Lokpal Bill

Highlights

Difference between Jan Lokpal Bill and Draft Bill, 2010

Jan Lokpal Bill (Citizen's Ombudsman Bill)	Draft Lokpal Bill (2010)
Lokpal will have powers to initiate *suo moto* action or receive complaints of corruption from the general public.	*Lokpal* will have no power to initiate suo moto action or receive complaints of corruption from the general public. It can only probe complaints forwarded by the Speaker of the *Lok Sabha* or the Chairman of the *Rajya Sabha*.
Lokpal will have the power to initiate prosecution of anyone found guilty.	*Lokpal* will only be an Advisory Body with a role limited to forwarding reports to a "Competent Authority".
Lokpal will have police powers as well as the ability to register FIRs.	*Lokpal* will have no police powers and no ability to register an FIR or proceed with criminal investigations.
Lokpal and the anti-corruption wing of the CBI will be one independent body.	The CBI and *Lokpal* will be unconnected.
Punishments will be a minimum of 1 year and a maximum of up to life imprisonment.	Punishment for corruption will be a minimum of 6 months and a maximum of up to 7 years.

Governments Approach about Whistleblower Protection & Citizen-charter

In a bid to narrow differences on the anti-graft legislation and provide itself some political cover against the threat of a public protest, the Government introduced Citizen's Charter and Grievance Redressal Bill 2011 or *Citizen-charter Bill in Dec 20, 2011* along with the already introduced Whistleblower Protection Law or *Public Interest Disclosure (Protection of Information) Bill, 2010* back in August 2011. Responding to this move, Team Anna issued a statement that: "The government proposes to remove CBI, judiciary, citizen charter, whistle blower protection, Group C and Group D employees from the Lokpal jurisdiction. Wouldn't that reduce Lokpal to an empty tin box with no powers and functions?" This issue remains open between Team Anna & Government.

Campaign for the Jan Lokpal Bill

The first version of the Lokpal Bill drafted by the Government of India headed by United Progressive Alliance in 2010 was considered ineffective by anti-corruption activists from the civil society. These activists, under the banner of India Against Corruption, came together to draft a citizen's version of the Lokpal Bill later called the Jan Lokpal. Public awareness drives and protest marches were carried out to campaign for the bill. However, public support for the Jan Lokpal Bill draft started gathering steam after Anna Hazare, a noted Gandhian announced that he would hold an indefinite fast from 5 April 2011 for the passing of the Lokpal/Jan Lokpal bill. The government has however accepted it. To dissuade Hazare from going on an indefinite hunger strike, the Office of the Prime Minister directed the personnel and law ministries to see how the views of social activists can be included in the bill. On 5 April, the National Advisory Council rejected the Lokpal bill drafted by the government. Union Human Resource Development Minister Kapil Sibbal then met social activists Swami Ganesh and Arvind Kejriwal on 7 April to find ways to bridge differences over the bill. However, no consensus could be reached on 7 April owing to several differences of opinion between the social activists and the Government.

Fast & Agitation—Phase 1

On 7 April 2011, Anna Hazare called for a *Jail Bharo Andolan* (translation: Fill jail movement) from 13 April to protest against the Government's rejection of their demands. Anna Hazare also claimed that his group had received six crore (60 million) text messages of support and that he had further backing from a large number of Internet activists. The outpouring of support was largely free of political overtones; political parties were specifically discouraged from participating in the movement. The fast ended on 9 April, after 98 hours, when the Government accepted most demands due to public pressure. Anna Hazare set a deadline, 15 August, for the passing of the bill in the Parliament, failing which he would start a hunger strike from 16 August. The fast also led to the Government of India agreeing to set up a Joint Drafting Committee, which would complete its work by 30 June 2011.

Fast & Agitation—Phase 2

According to Anna and his team, the Government's version of the Lokpal bill was weak and would facilitate the corrupt to go free apart from several other differences. To protest against this, Anna Hazare announced an "Indefinite Fast" (not to be confused with "Fast until death"). Anna and his team asked for permission from Delhi Police for their fast and agitation at Jantar Mantar or JP Park. Delhi Police gave its permission with certain conditions. These conditions were considered by team Anna as restrictive and against the fundamental constitutional rights and they decided to defy the conditions. Delhi Police imposed Sec 144 CrPC. On 16 August, Anna Hazare was taken into preventive custody by Delhi Police. Senior officers of Delhi Police reached Anna Hazare's flat early in the morning and informed him that he could not leave his home. However, Hazare turned down the request following which he was detained. Anna in his recorded address to the nation before his arrest asked his supporters not to stop the agitation and urged the protesters to remain peaceful. Other members of "India Against Corruption", Arvind Kejriwal, Kiran Bedi, Kumar Vishwas and Manish Sisodia were also taken into preventive custody. Kiran Bedi described the situation as resembling a kind of Emergency (referring to the State of Emergency imposed in 1975 by the Indira Gandhi Govt.). The arrest resulted in a huge public outcry and under pressure, the government released him in the evening of 16 August.

However, Anna Hazare refused to come out of jail, starting his indefinite fast from Jail itself. Manish Sisodia explained his situation as, "Anna said that he left home to go to JP Park to conduct his fast and that is exactly where he would go from here (Tihar Jail). He has refused to be released till he is given a written, unconditional permission".

Unwilling to use forces owing to the sensitive nature of the case, the jail authorities had no option but to let Anna spend the night inside Tihar. Later on 17 August, Delhi Police permitted Anna Hazare and team to use the Ramlila Maidan for the proposed fast and agitation, withdrawing most of the contentious provisions they had imposed earlier. The indefinite fast and agitation began in Ramlila Maidan, New Delhi, and went on for around 288 hours (12 days from 16 August 2011 to 28 August 2011). Some of the Lokpal drafting committee members became dissatisfied with Hazare's tactics as the hunger strike went on for the 11th day: Santosh Hegde, a member of Hazare team who headed the Karnataka Lokayukta, strongly criticized Hazare for his insistence of *"having his way"*, concluding *"I feel I am not in Team Anna any more by the way things are going. These (telling Parliament what to do) are not democratic things."* Swami Ganesh, another central figure in the Hazare group also distanced himself.

Logjam of Lokpal and Lokayukta Bill, 2011

On 27 December 2011, Lok Sabha Parliament winter session passed controversial Lokpal Bill under title of Lokpal and Lokayukta Bill, 2011, but without constitutional status. Before passing this bill it was introduced in Lok Sabha with key amendments moved. The 10-hour house debate, number of opposition parties claimed introduced bill is weak and wanted it withdrawn. Key amendments that were discussed but defeated were following:

- Including corporates, media and NGOs receiving donations
- Bringing CBI under the purview of Lokpal

Amendments that the house agreed upon were:

- Keeping the defence forces and coast guard personnel out of the purview of the anti-graft ombudsman
- Increasing the exemption time of former MPs from five to seven years

Team Anna rejected the proposed bill describing it as "anti-people and dangerous" even before the Lok Sabha gave its assent. The key notes Team Anna made about rejection were:

- Government will have all the control over Lokpal as it will have powers to appoint and remove members at its will.
- Only 10 per cent political leaders are covered by this Bill.
- Bill was also covering temples, mosques and churches.
- Bill was offering favour to corruption accused by offering them free lawyer service.
- Bill was also unclear about handling corruption within Lokpal office.
- Only five per cent of employees are in its ambit, as Class C & D officers were not included.

Team Anna was also disappointed over following inherent exclusions within tabled government bill.

- Central Bureau of Investigation (CBI) should be merged with the Lokpal, and the anti-corruption bureaus and the Vigilance Departments of the State governments with the Lokayukta.
- The Lokpal and the Lokayukta should have their own investigative wings with exclusive jurisdiction over cases filed under the Prevention of Corruption Act.

- The Lokpal should have administrative and financial control over the CBI, and the appointment of the CBI Director should be independent of any political control.
- The jurisdiction of the Lokpal and the Lokayukta should cover Class C and D officers directly.

This bill was then presented in Rajya Sabha where it hit logjam again.

Parliamentary Actions on the Proposed Legislation

On 27 August 2011, a special and all exclusive session of Parliament was conducted and a resolution was unanimously passed after deliberations in both the houses of Indian Parliament by sense of the house.

The resolution, in principle, agreed on the following subjects and forwarded the Bill to a related standing committee for structure and finalize a report:

- A citizen charter on the bill
- An appropriate mechanism to subject lower bureaucracy to Lokpal
- The establishment of Lokayukta (ombudsmen at state level) in states

On being informed of this development, Anna Hazare, civil rights activists along with protestors at the site of the fast welcomed this development, terming it as a battle "half won" while ending the protest.

THE LOKPAL BILL, 2011

The Lokpal Bill, 2011, also referred to as The Lokpal and Lokayukta Bill, 2011, is a proposed anti-corruption law in India which "seeks to provide for the establishment of the institution of Lokpal to inquire into allegations of corruption against certain public functionaries and for matters connecting them". The bill was tabled in the Lok Sabha on 22 December 2011 and was passed by the house on 27 December 2011 as The Lokpal and Lokayukta Bill, 2011. The bill was subsequently tabled in the Rajya Sabha on 29 December 2011. After a marathon debate that stretched until midnight of the following day, the vote failed to take place for lack of time. On 21 May 2012, the bill was referred to a Select Committee of the Rajya Sabha for consideration. The bill was introduced in parliament following massive public protests led by anti-corruption crusader Anna Hazare and his associates. The bill is one of the most widely discussed and debated bills in India, both by the media and the People of India at large, in recent times. The protests were named among the "Top 10 News Stories of 2011" by the magazine *Time*. The bill received worldwide media coverage. Corruption is an emotional issue in India, where at least 12 whistle blowers were killed and 40 assaulted after seeking information under a new Right to Information Act aimed at exposing local graft, according to data compiled by Bloomberg L.P. from January 2010 through mid-October 2011. Enacted by Singh six years ago, the legislation became the most powerful tool for fighting wrongdoing in politics and business, with 529,000 requests filed in the year through March. In 2011, India ranked 95th in the Corruption Perceptions Index of Transparency International. A recent survey estimated that corruption in India had cost billions of dollars and threatened to derail growth. India lost a staggering $462 billion in illicit financial flows due to tax evasion, crime and corruption post-Independence, according to a report released by Washington-based Global Financial Integrity.

Union Cabinet Approved Bill

The government moved its version of the bill in the Lok Sabha on 4 August, the ninth such introduction. The bill was introduced by the Minister of State in the Prime Minister's Office, V. Narayanasamy. Leader of Opposition Sushma Swaraj opposed the exclusion of the prime minister from the purview of the proposed Lokpal. V. Narayanasamy told the House that Prime Minister Manmohan Singh was in favour of bringing his office under the purview of the Lokpal, but the Cabinet rejected the idea after deliberation. Anna Hazare burnt copies of the bill, to protest the government's lack of sincerity. The bill was referred to the Parliament's Standing Committee on Personnel, Public Grievances and Law and Justice on 8 August. The committee was headed by Congress Rajya Sabha MP Abhishek Manu Singhvi. The committee of 31 members from across parties was given three months to submit its report. On 27 August the Lok Sabha and Rajya Sabha passed a Pranab Mukherjee-proposed resolution conveying the sense of the House on the Lokpal Bill. The House agreed 'in principle' on a Citizen's Charter, placing the lower bureaucracy under the Lokpal and establishing the Lokayukta in the States.

A high point was noticed on 27 August 27, 2011 when the historic debate leading to the 'Sense of the House' in Parliament on the Lokpal Bill was held. The event reinforced the inviolable primacy of the Indian Constitution. It was also an event of relief and reassurance to the vast and silent majority who constitute India's core civil society.

Journey through The Lok Sabha

The Lokpal was tabled in the Lok Sabha on 22 December 2011 and passed by voice voting on the first day of the three day extended session of the Winter session of the Lok Sabha, on 27 December 2011, after a marathon debate that lasted over 10 hours. The Lokpal body was not given the constitutional status as the Constitutional Amendment Bill, which provided for making the Lokpal a constitutional body, was defeated in the house. The Prime Minister described this as "a bit of disappointment" and added:

We have, however, fulfilled our objective of bringing these bills to Parliament as we had promised.

The bill passed by the house was termed as "useless" by Team Anna and held its view that there was no need of giving such a weak Lokpal a constitutional status. The government withdrew its previous version and had introduced a newer version of the bill. RJD leader Lalu Prasad, along with the support from the other parties like SP, AIMMM and LJP, demanded an inclusion of candidates from minorities in the nine member Lokpal Bench. The government gave in to the demands of parties. The principal opposition party, the BJP, objected to it, classifying that such a move was illegal and asked the government to withdraw the bill. BJD, JDU, RJD, SP, TDP and Left said the bill was weak and wanted it to be withdrawn.

The bill passed by the house deleted the provision that gave presiding officers the power to act against ministers and MPs, even before trial, but the exemption time of former MPs was increased from five to seven years. It excluded armed forces and coast guard from the purview of the anti-graft body. The Lokpal would take complaints against the prime minister after the consent of two-thirds of the Lokpal panel. The consent of state governments is mandatory for the notification to set up Lokayukta in the states, but the setting up of them in the states was made mandatory. The appointment panel is loaded in favour of the government. Mr. Mukherjee also said, during the discussion in the house, that the government has agreed that the Leader of the Opposition and the Chief Justice of India will now be asked to select the chief of the CBI with the Prime Minister. The Lokpal Bill was passed under Article 252 of the constitution of India. Opposition parties objected to this saying that bill could be passed only by Article 253 as the law pertains to public services. The bill didn't relinquish administrative control of the CBI to the Lokpal. The BJP, Left, BSP and SP, all wanted the government should loosen its grip over the CBI. The rationale of such parties was that as long as the government decides the CBI's budget, and the postings and transfers of its officers, the agency is vulnerable to governmental influence. The Prime Minister, making it clear the government's stand on the issue of CBI:

We believe that the CBI should function without interference through any Government diktat. But no institution and no individual, howsoever high he may be, should be free from accountability.

The Bharatiya Janata Party (BJP) abstained from voting on the amendment moved by Basudeb Acharia on bringing corporate houses and the act of the Prime Minister signing commercial agreements under the Lokpal. A number of amendments moved by Opposition to bring the media and NGOs receiving donations were also defeated. The Left, Samajwadi Party and BSP staged a walkout during voting of the bill, protesting that their demands were not being met. With a strength of 277 in the Lok Sabha, the UPA managed to obtain only 243 votes. At least 15 Congress members and close to a dozen belonging to UPA allies were not present at the time of voting. The house also secured the passage of the Whistleblowers Bill.

Journey through The Rajya Sabha

Winter Session, 2011

The ombudsman debate was taken up by The Rajya Sabha during the last day of the three day extension of the winter session of Parliament, but the body recessed on 29 December without voting. The bill was debated for over 12 hours ending abruptly at midnight as the House ran out of scheduled time. The House was adjourned sine die by Chairman Hamid Ansari. A verbal duel marred proceedings as some members including UPA ally Trinamool Congress interrupted V. Narayanasamy's defence of the Bill and a lawmaker snatched papers from a minister and flung them across the chamber. A vociferous opposition insisted on a vote while the government maintained it needed time to reconcile the 187 amendments/confusion marked the proceedings. Ansari asked for the national anthem Jana Gana Mana to be played, signalling the end of the proceedings and told the house:

"This is an unprecedented situation…there appears to be a desire to outshout each other. There is a total impasse. The House cannot be conducted in the noise that requires orderly proceedings, I am afraid the Chair has no option…most reluctantly…I am afraid I can't and..."

After a 15-minute adjournment between 11.30 and 11.45 PM, Pawan Kumar Bansal said that the decision on extension of the House was the government's prerogative. Leader of the Opposition Arun Jaitley charged that the government was running away from Parliament and that the House should decide how long it should sit. He added: You are creating an institution where you control the appointment mechanism, where you control the removal mechanism. We will support the appointment of the Lokpal procedures, but we cannot be disloyal to our commitment to create an integrity institution. Sitaram Yechury (CPI-M) said the House had expected the bill on Wednesday, but it came only on Thursday, the last day of the session. Derek O'Brien, a Trinamool upper house lawmaker, stated that his party could not back the bill because it infringed on states' autonomy. He said "This is a shameful day for India's democracy. The government handled this situation very badly. As the Opposition insisted on a vote, Bansal said the government was willing provided that the House passed the Bill voted by the Lok Sabha on Tuesday. This meant that the proposed amendments would have to be set aside. As stalemate and wrangling continued, the Chairman called an end to the proceedings. Chidambaram defended the deferment of Lokpal and Lokayukta Bill, 2011 in Rajya Sabha on December 29 contending that it was the "only prudent course" before the government and that it had ensured that the Bill remained alive. He continued to attack the BJP and called the amendments an "ingenious" method to scuttle the bill Hazare called off his hunger strike prematurely, blaming poor health.

Budget Session, 2012

Activists pushing hoped that the House would approve the bill towards the end of the second half of the budget session of 2012. The bill was re-introduced in the Rajya Sabha on 21 May 2012. While moving the bill, the minister said that the differences had been narrowed. He said that the government proposed to bring the lower bureaucracy under the Lokpal, which would have investigation and prosecution powers. CVC would monitor Lokpal-referred investigations by the CBI. There would be provisions for attaching properties and a time-frame for investigations. The government proposed that the Bill would be amended to give states the right to pass the bill in their own assemblies. So the national law would not be forced upon states. After the amended bill was introduced, Narayanasamy, Samajwadi Party member Naresh Agrawal sought to send the bill to a *select committee*. This was strongly objected to by BJP, the Left parties and BSP, with their members arguing that only the minister concerned (Narayanasamy) could do so and accusing the ruling coalition of "using the shoulder" of a "friendly opposition" party. After high drama the government yielded and Narayanasamy moved the motion, which immediately passed by voice vote.

The committee met on 25 June and decided on "wider consultations" with the government officials and the public. The panel invited public comments and called representatives of various ministries for recording evidence. The meeting was headed by senior Congress MP Satyavrat Chaturvedi. Law Secretary B. A. Agarwal was summoned to clarify various matters. The committee met again on 19 July 2012. The director of the CBI aired his views in the meeting. He made it clear that the CBI is open to changes in the Lokpal bill that strengthen the agency's autonomy by enhancing the proposed Lokpal's role in key appointments like those of director, head of prosecution and lawyers who represent CBI. He also mentioned in the meeting that the Lokpal should be given a significant say in appointing the director of the prosecution wing instead of the process being controlled by the law ministry as is currently the procedure, the persistent criticism about CBI's investigations being throttled by political directives could be addressed as well. He opposed making the prosecution or the anti-corruption wings subservient to the Lokpal. The select committee had in its earlier sittings examined senior law officials who agreed with the members that the prescription for Lokayukta under Article 253 that refers to fulfilment of international obligations— in this case the UN convention against corruption - might not be feasible. Recourse to international treaties to frame a law that impact the federal structure is not within the ambit of the law. The Select committee referred the Bill for Public Suggestions in July 2012. In reply hundreds of responses were received to the Rajya Sabha. The committee took a view and shortlisted certain recommendations and took Oral Evidence in physical presence of the Members. Committee considered some of the most valid suggestions being done by the Members. Mr. Deepak Tongli of Hyderabad had come with a proposal of setting up the lower most unit to keep regular check on Anti-Corruption in petty cases at District Level. In addition few other members also shared their views in this regard. Mr. Tongli, 26 yrs. aged happened to be the youngest person to appear before the Parliamentary committee for Oral Evidence at Rajya Sabha.

Monsoon Session, 2012

The monsoon session of parliament was to be held in August 2012. Hence, a bill that is pending before the upper house whether or not it was passed by the Lok Sabha, does not lapse on its dissolution. Hence, the bill is still alive in its present form. The bill was not expected to be tabled in the Rajya Sabha before the first day of the last week of the session.

LOKAYUKTA

The Lokayukta (also Lok Ayukta) is an anti-corruption ombudsman organization in the Indian states. The Administrative Reforms Commission (ARC) headed by Morarji Desai submitted a special interim report on "Problems of Redressal of Citizen's Grievances' in 1966. In this report, the ARC recommended the setting up of two special authorities designated as 'Lokpal' and 'Lokayukta' for the redressal of citizens' grievances. The Lokayukta, along with the Income Tax Department and the Anti-Corruption Bureau, mainly helps people bring corruption amongst the politicians and officers in the government service to public attention. Many acts of the Lokayukta have not resulted in criminal or other consequences for those charged. Maharashtra was the first state to introduce the institution of Lokayukta through *The Maharashtra Lokayukta and Upa-Lokayuktas Act in 1971*. This was followed by similar acts being enacted by states of Rajasthan, Bihar, Uttar Pradesh, Karnataka, Madhya Pradesh, Andhra Pradesh, Gujarat and Delhi. Maharashtra Lokayukta is considered as weak due to lack of powers, adequate staff, funds and no independent investigating agency. Karnataka Lokayukta is considered as the most powerful Lokayukta in the country.

Constitutional Amendment for Effectiveness

An amendment to the Constitution has been proposed to implement the Lokayukta uniformly across Indian States. The proposed changes will make the institution of Lokayukta uniform across the country as a three-member body, headed by a retired Supreme Court judge or high court chief justice and comprising the state vigilance commissioner and a jurist or an eminent administrator as other members.

Lokayukta/Lokpal/Lokaayog Acts in Indian States

- Lokayukta, Andhra Pradesh
- Lokayukta, Assam
- Lokayukta, Bihar
- Lok Aayog Adhyadesh (ordinance), Chhattisgarh
- Lokayukta, Delhi
- Lokayukt, Goa
- Lokayukta, Gujarat
- Lokayukta, Haryana
- Lokayukta, Himachal Pradesh
- Lokayukta, Jharkhand
- Lokayukta, Karnataka
- Lokayukta, Kerala
- Lokayukta, Madhya Pradesh
- Lokayukta, Maharashtra
- Lokpal, Orissa
- Lokpal, Punjab
- Lokayukta, Rajasthan
- Lokayukta, Uttarakhand—adopted from Uttar Pradesh
- Lokayukta, Uttar Pradesh

There are no Lokayukta in Arunachal Pradesh, Jammu and Kashmir, Manipur, Meghalaya, Mizoram, Nagaland, Sikkim, Tamil Nadu, Tripura and West Bengal. The latest Lokayukta was established in Goa.

Reforms

In November 2012, after conclusion of the 11th *All India Lokayukta Conference*, as many as 16 Lokayukta sent many recommendations to the Government of India. The recommendations were as follows:

- Make Lokayukta the nodal agency for receiving all corruption complaints.
- Accord Lokayukta jurisdiction over State-level probe agencies.
- Bring bureaucrats under the ambit of the Lokayukta.
- Accord powers of search and seizure and powers to initiate contempt proceedings.
- Provide Lokayukta administrative and financial autonomy.
- Bring Non-Governmental Organizations (NGO) funded by the government under Lokayukta's jurisdiction.

FOCUS ON NATIONAL COMMISSION TO REVIEW THE WORKING OF THE CONSTITUTION

Probity in governance is an essential and vital requirement for an efficient and effective system of governance and for socio-economic development. An important requisite for ensuring probity in governance is absence of corruption. The other requirements are effective laws, rules and regulations governing every aspect of public life and, more important, an effective and fair implementation of those laws, etc. Indeed, a proper, fair and effective enforcement of law is a facet of discipline. Unfortunately for India, discipline is disappearing fast from public life and without discipline, as the Scandinavian economist- sociologist, Gunnyar Myrdal, has pointed out, no real progress is possible. Discipline implies *inter alia* public and private morality and a sense of honesty. While in the West a man who rises to positions of higher authority develops greater respect for laws, the opposite is true in our country. Here, the mark of a person holding high position is the ease with which he can ignore the laws and regulations. We are being swamped by a culture of indiscipline and untruth; morality, both public and private, is at a premium. This paper explores whether some legislative measures can be designed to ensure probity in governance. It is true that instilling a sense of discipline among the citizens is more the function of the society, its leaders, political parties and public figures and less a matter which can be legislated upon. Even so, things have come to such a pass that measures need to be contemplated.

Menace of Corruption in Public Life

Corruption is an abuse of public resources or position in public life for private gain. The scope for corruption increases when control on the public administrators is fragile and the division of power between political, executive and bureaucracy is ambiguous. Political corruption which is sometimes inseparable from bureaucratic corruption tends to be more widespread in authoritarian regimes where the public opinion and the Press are unable to denounce corruption. The paradox of India, however, is that in spite of a vigilant press and public opinion, the level of corruption is exceptionally high. This may be attributed to the utter insensitivity, lack of shame and the absence of any sense of public morality among the bribe-takers. Indeed, they wear their badge of corruption and shamelessness with equal élan and brazenness. The increase of opportunities in State intervention in economic and social life has vastly increased the opportunity for political and bureaucratic corruption, more particularly since politics has also become professionalized. We have professional politicians who are politicians on a full time basis, even when out of office. India is rated at 73 out of 99 countries in the corruption perception index prepared by a non-governmental organization, Transparency International. Corruption today poses a danger not only to the quality of governance but is threatening the very foundations of our society and the State. Corruption in defence purchases, in other purchases and contracts tend to undermine the very security of the State. Some of the power contracts are casting such financial burden upon some of the States that the very financial viability of those States has fallen into doubt. There seems to be a nexus between terrorism, drugs, smuggling, and politicians, a fact which was emphasized in the Vohra Committee Report.

Corruption has flourished because one does not see adequately successful examples of effectively prosecuted cases of corruption. Cases, poorly founded upon, half-hearted and incomplete investigation, followed by a tardy and delayed trial confluence a morally ill-deserved but a legally inevitable acquittal. The acceptance of corruption as an inexorable reality has led to silent reconciliation and resignation to such wrongs. There needs to be a vital stimulation in the social consciousness of our citizens—that is neither has a place in the personal nor social. It is true that the present process of withdrawing the State from various sectors in which it should have never entered or in which it is not capable of performing efficiently may reduce the chances of corruption to some extent but even if we migrate to a free market economy, there has to be regulation of economy as distinct from restrictions upon the industrial activity. The requirements of governance would yet call for entering into contracts, purchases and so on.

The Scandinavian economist-sociologist, Gunnyar Myrdal, had described the Indian society as a 'soft society'. He also clarified what the expression 'soft society' means. According to him, a soft society is: (a) one which does not have the political will to enact the laws necessary for its progress and development and/or does not possess the political will to implement the laws, even when made, and (b) where there is no discipline. In fact, he has stressed the second aspect more than the first. According to him, if there is no discipline in the society, no real or meaningful development or progress is possible. It is the lack of discipline in the society—which expression includes the administration and structures of governance at all levels—that is contributing to corruption. Corruption and indiscipline feed upon each other. One way of instilling the discipline among the society may be to reduce the chances of corruption and to deal with it sternly and mercilessly wherever it is found. For this purpose, the inadequacies in the criminal judicial system have to be redressed. Corruption is also anti-poor. Take, for example, the Public Distribution System (PDS) and the welfare schemes for the poor including Scheduled Castes (SCs) and Scheduled Tribes (STs). It is well-known that a substantial portion of grain, sugar and kerosene oil meant for PDS goes into black-market and that hardly 16% of the funds meant for STs and SCs reach them—all the rest is misappropriated by some of the members of the political and official class and unscrupulous dealers and businessmen. The famous economist, Late Mehbub-Ul-Haq succinctly and poignantly set out the ill-effects of corruption in a South Asian country like ours. He said:

"Corruption happens everywhere. It has been at the center of election campaigns in Italy and the United Kingdom, led to the fall of governments in Japan and Indonesia, and resulted in legislative action in Russia and the United States. But, if corruption exists in rich, economically successful countries, why should South Asia be worried about it? The answer is simple: South Asian corruption has four key characteristics that make it far more damaging than corruption in any other parts of the world.

First, corruption in South Asia occurs up stream, not down stream. Corruption at the top distorts fundamental decisions about development priorities, policies, and projects. In industrial countries, these core decisions are taken through transparent competition and on merit, even though petty corruption may occur down stream.

Second, corruption money in South Asia has wings, not wheels. Most of the corrupt gains made in the region are immediately smuggled out to safe havens abroad. Whereas there is some capital flight in other countries as well, a greater proportion goes into investment. In other words, it is more likely that corruption money in the North Asia is used to finance business than to fill foreign accounts.

Third, corruption in South Asia often leads to promotion, not prison. The big fish—unless they belong to the opposition – rarely fry. In contrast, industrialized countries often have a process of accountability where even top leaders are investigated and prosecuted. For instance, former Italian Prime Minister Bettino Craxi was forced to live in exile in Tunisia to escape extradition on corruption charges in Rome. The most frustrating aspect of corruption in South Asia is that the corrupt are often too powerful to go through such an honest process of accountability.

Fourth, corruption in South Asia occurs with 515 million people in poverty, not with per capita incomes above twenty thousand dollars. While corruption in rich rapidly growing countries may be tolerable, though reprehensible, in poverty stricken South Asia, it is political dynamite when the majority of the population cannot, but to massive human deprivation and even more extreme income meet their basic needs while a few make fortunes through corruption. Thus corruption in South Asia does not lead to simply Cabinet portfolio shifts or newspaper headlines inequalities. Combating corruption in the region is not just about punishing corrupt politicians and bureaucrats but about saving human lives. There are two dimensions of corruption. One is the exploitative corruption where the public servant exploits the helpless poor citizen. The other is collusive corruption where the citizen corrupts the public servant by a bribe because he gets financially better benefits. Collusive corruption depends on black money."

It may be recalled that the Supreme Court had given certain directions in the case of Vineet Narain vs. Union of India (AIR 1998 SC 889) for conferring statutory status upon the Central Vigilance Commission and to insulate the Central Bureau of Investigation and the Enforcement Directorate from political control and pressures. In the said decision, the Supreme Court referred with approval the recommendations of Lord Nolan Committee on Standards in Public Life in the United Kingdom. The following principles of public life, of general application, were commended by the court:

Principles of public life: The general principles of conduct which underpin public life need to be restated. We have done this. The seven principles of selflessness, integrity, objectivity, accountability, openness, honesty and leadership are set out (later on).

Codes of conduct: All public bodies should draw up codes of conduct incorporating these principles.

Independent scrutiny: Internal systems for maintaining standards should be supported by independent scrutiny.

Education: More needs to be done to promote and reinforce standards of conduct in public bodies, in particular through guidance and training, including induction training."

The Seven Principles of Public Life stated in the Report by Lord Nolan

Selflessness: Holders of public office should take decisions solely in terms of the public interest. They should not do so in order to gain financial or other material benefits for themselves, their family, or their friends.

Integrity: Holders of public office should not place themselves under any financial or other obligation to outside individuals or organizations that might influence them in the performance of their official duties.

Objectivity: In carrying out public business, including making public appointments, awarding contracts, or recommending individuals for rewards and benefits, holders of public office should make choices on merit.

Accountability: Holders of public office are accountable for their decisions and actions to the public and must submit themselves to whatever scrutiny is appropriate to their office.

Openness: Holders of public office should be as open as possible about all the decisions and actions that they take. They should give reasons for their decisions and restrict information only when the wider public interest clearly demands.

Honesty: Holders of public office have a duty to declare any private interests relating to their public duties and to take steps to resolve any conflicts arising in a way that protects the public interest.

Leadership: Holders of public office should promote and support these principles by leadership and example.

The Supreme Court observed further:

"These principles of public life are of general application in every democracy and one is expected to bear them in mind while scrutinizing the conduct of every holder of a public office. It is trite that the holders of public offices are entrusted with certain powers to be exercised in public interest alone and, therefore, the office is held by them in trust for the people. Any deviation from the path of rectitude by any of them amounts to a breach of trust and must be severely dealt with instead of being pushed under the carpet. If the conduct amounts to an offence, it must be promptly investigated and the offender against whom a prima facie case is made out should be prosecuted expeditiously so that the majesty of law is upheld and the rule of law vindicated. It is the duty of the judiciary to enforce the rule of law and, therefore, to guard against erosion of the rule of law."

An instance and consequence of the adverse effects of corruption on Indian economy can be gauged from the following statement by Prem Shankar Jha, a keen observer of Indian economy:

"So far, despite adopting some of the most liberal foreign investment laws in Asia, India has not succeeded in seducing even one major international corporation into using it as a global production platform. All the Foreign Direct Investment that has come has been bent upon exploiting the domestic market for consumer goods and durables. In a frank discussion in Singapore, fund managers and corporate executives revealed that the main reason why they were not prepared to mesh India into their global production plans was that even after they had obtained all the clearances from the Central and State Governments, they remained at the mercy of local bureaucrats and politicians. Any one of them could stop their operations, and threatened to do so if they were not given an adequate 'inducement'. Every change of government in a state led to a fresh set of demands and a fresh set of negotiations with the new incumbents. To sum it up, the Chinese took larger bribes, but delivered security of investment in return. Petty bureaucrats who transgressed this principle received a bullet in the back of the head in a football stadium. In India, by contrast, they prospered while the enterprise sickened or died.".

Certain measures required to be taken for ensuring probity in governance. For ensuring probity in governance, several measures are necessary, some of which are mentioned herein below:

A. Need for enforcing section 5 of the Benami Transactions (Prohibition) Act, 1988

While many provisions of the Benami Transactions (Prohibition) Act, 1988 are salutary, it is necessary to take note of some of the anachronisms in the said Act. The expression "benami transaction" is defined in clause (a) of section 2 of the said Act. The said clause reads as under:

'(a) "benami transaction" means any transaction in which property is transferred to one person for a consideration paid or provided by another person;'.

This definition appears to be susceptible to unchartered application taking in *bona fide* transactions which do not injure public interest—say, a father buying a flat for his child, paying the price in instalments. If the money for purchase is accounted for and it is a transaction of advancement, it should not be voided. This is the true meaning and purport of the definition. The Act, a statute containing nine sections, perhaps requires to be modified and strengthened. Section 3 prohibits a person from entering into any benami transaction. Be that as it may, the Act prohibits "benami transactions" and disables any person from claiming that though the property stands in another's name, he himself is the real owner. This Act, enacted as far back as 1988 by Parliament, contains a very salutary and much desired provision in section 5 which reads thus:

Property held benami liable to acquisition: (1) All properties held benami shall be subjected to acquisition by such authority, in such manner and after following such procedures, as may be prescribed.

For the removal of doubts, it is hereby declared that no amount shall be payable for the acquisition of any property under sub-section (1).

It is evident from a reading of section 5 that it can become effective and operational only when rules are made under section 8 prescribing the authority, the manner and procedure following which benami properties can be acquired by the State (without paying any compensation). In fact, section 8 expressly contemplates rules being made by the Central Government for carrying out the purposes of the Act. It is surprising that the Central Government has not so far thought it fit to make rules for the above purpose. The Act is of general application; it applies to every benami transaction, whether the persons concerned are public servants or not. It is imperative that this is done forthwith, thus fulfilling the legislative mandate.

Perhaps, it may be safer to have a separate and exhaustive law relating to public servants. A law in relation to "public servants" as defined by section 2(c) of the Prevention of Corruption Act, 1988 and section 21 of the Indian Penal Code is a prime necessity. Such an Act must be comprehensive in nature and must also deal with acquisition of assets of public servants. The law must provide the manner in which properties can be held by the wife, minor children, near relations of a public servant and should stipulate that if circumstances show that they are benamidars of the public servants (which expression should be defined in the same manner as in section 2(c) of the Prevention of Corruption Act, 1988 and section 21 of the Indian Penal Code), the same should warrant a special provision which would declare the effects of holding of such assets. The statute may also provide that if proper statutory procedures of reporting and verification are not followed, the burden of proof may be placed on the holder of the property to show that the same was not acquired by him benami. It is also suggested that amendments to the Transfer of Property Act, 1882 and the Registration Act, 1908 should be made by which acquisition or transfer of property in favour of or by a public servant would only be through registered instruments warranting prior scrutiny or post-transaction scrutiny. (In Delhi, majority of property transactions are done only on the basis of power of attorney and wills; no registered documents are ever executed—which incidentally means a substantial loss of public revenue by way of stamp duty and registration charges). This may be made applicable even in relation to transactions by which even though a final conveyance may not be executed, yet interest in property may be sought to be passed *de facto*. The provisions may cover not only the public servants but all those within the family of the public servant. There must exist a clear definition of the family of the public servants. The Companies Act, 1961, which has enabled the near and dear ones of the corrupt to float fabulously rich companies through complex cyclical money in poring also needs to be amended. The status—financial and property matters—of a public servant needs to be brought under the proposed comprehensive law relating to public servants. We suggest that in the law, there should be a monitoring mechanism not composed of officials of the executive government (since the executive government can misuse such provisions to retaliate against unwilling civil servants) but an independent Ombudsman who will regulate the civil service. It is needless to add that in addition to stringent provisions relating to public servants, public opinion should encourage concurrent inward digestion of the principles.

It may be recalled that the Benami Transactions (Prohibition) Act, 1988 was made by Parliament about thirteen years ago. It conferred the rule-making power upon the Central Government for the purpose *inter alia* to make rules prescribing the requisite matter contemplated by section 5. The Government has singularly failed in discharging the duty placed upon it by Parliament. It is true that Parliament has not prescribed any time limit for the purpose, but this is no answer. It is never done. In any event, the Central Government must have made the rules within a reasonable time. A period of thirteen years is too long. Central Government cannot frustrate the intent and object of the Parliament by its inaction. Indeed, it is under a statutory obligation to take measures to effectuate the said provision, if the same has not yet been done.

We must also clarify that the principle of the decision of the Supreme Court in A. K. Roy has no application here. Firstly, that was a case of 'conditional legislation' (power to bring a constitutional provision/enactment into force). Secondly, the matter related to the constitutional amendment (to Article 22) effected in 1979 and the case before the Supreme Court came up in 1981 i.e., within about two years. But when the very same question came up before the Supreme Court in 1994 in A.G. of India vs. Amratlal Prajivandas, the nine-Judge Constitution Bench made certain pertinent observations. While observing that it was not necessary to decide the said question for the purpose of that case, the Court noted with approval the argument of the Counsel that such delay on the part of Central Government was not reasonable and that the Parliament while enacting the said amendment Act could never have contemplated that it would be converted into a dead letter by the Central Government by its inaction—deliberate or otherwise.

We are, therefore, of the opinion that at least now the Central Government should enact a comprehensive law on public servants. Such a measure would act as a salutary check—a deterrent—upon corrupt public servants and would certainly be a measure to ensure probity in governance.

In this connection, it is necessary to point out the inadequacies in the existing law, namely, the Prevention of Corruption Act, 1988 and the Indian Penal Code. Mere prosecution under the IPC or the Prevention of Corruption Act (PCA) is not sufficient, apart from the fact that such prosecutions are very rarely launched and even when they are, the conviction is much too rare. Unless the fruits of corruption are taken away, you would not be fighting the corruption truly and effectively. A law for forfeiture of property of corrupt public servants otherwise then through the route of conviction is absolutely essential. In other words, wherever a public servant is found to have screened the illegally acquired assets in the name of a benamidar, action should be taken under this Act and the Rules framed thereunder, and those assets acquired by State without any compensation, as indeed provided for expressly by the Act. For this purpose, the appropriate authority (like the one specified under section 5 of PCA) should be clothed with the necessary powers of investigation, verification, enquiry and the power to gather and receive information from any source, authority, institution or organization. So far as the public servants are concerned, different authorities may be specified in the States and at the Centre. So far as Union and State Ministers are concerned, appropriate authorities have to be created. For non-public servants, appropriate authorities may also have to be specified. The only obligation of such authorities should be to observe the principles of natural justice. It would not be a case of conviction by criminal courts—it would be a purely civil remedy—against corruption. The burden of proving that the property is not held 'benami' should be placed upon the holder of such property/asset.

B. Misfeasance in Public Office—A Remedy

The Supreme Court in an innovative exercise, examined executive actions of two former Union Ministers. It found that one of them allotted petrol pumps in favour of fifteen persons which were plainly vitiated by lack of transparency, nepotism and arbitrariness. The allotments made mostly in favour of the relations of the Ministers or members of his staff. In the case of the other Minister, the Court found that illegal allotments had been made in relation to occupation of Government accommodation. The Court, while taking the view that no public servant could arrogate himself the power to act in a manner which was plainly arbitrary, observed:

"It is high time that the public servants should be held personally responsible for their mala fide acts in the discharge of their functions as public servants. With the change in socio-economic outlook, the public servants are being entrusted with more and more discretionary powers even in the field of distribution of government wealth in various forms. We take it to be perfectly clear, that if a public servant abuses his office either by an act of omission or commission, and the consequence of that is injury to an individual or loss of public property, an action may be maintained against such public servant. No public servant can say "you may set aside an order on the ground of mala fide but you cannot hold me personally liable". No public servant can arrogate to himself the power to act in a manner which is arbitrary." On the question of allotments, the Court opined how the Minister who was executive head of the department held a position of trust. The court observed:

"The government today—in a welfare State—provides large number of benefits to the citizens. It distributes wealth in the form of allotment of plots, houses, petrol pumps, gas agencies, mineral leases, contracts, quotas and licences, etc. Government distributes largesse in various forms. A Minister who is the executive head of the department concerned distributes these benefits and largesse. He is elected by the people and is elevated to a position where he holds a trust on behalf of the people. He has to deal with the people's property in a fair and just manner. He cannot commit breach of trust reposed in him by the people. A transparent and objective criteria/procedure has to be evolved....".

The Supreme Court directed one Minister to pay a sum of ₹ Fifty lakhs by way of exemplary damages to the government. Likewise, the other Minister was asked to pay a sum of ₹ Sixty lakhs by way of exemplary damages. The Court, in both the cases, concluded that the actions of the Ministers amounted to a misfeasance of public property.

The Supreme Court relied upon the well stated position in Ramana Deyaram Shettey and Lucknow Development Authority to hold that in the matter of grant of largesse, the Government and its officials were expected to act in a fair, just and transparent manner and that if they acted in a malicious and deliberate manner causing injury to the citizens of the State, they could be held liable for damages. Rookes v. Barnard was relied upon to hold that exemplary damages could be awarded for "oppressive, arbitrary and unconstitutional action by the servants of the government.". The Supreme Court then concluded:

"We are of the view that the legal position that exemplary damages can be awarded in a case where the action of a public servant is oppressive, arbitrary or unconstitutional is unexceptionable". The same principle was reiterated in the decision concerning the other Minister. It would not be out of place to mention that the Supreme Court followed several other English decisions besides Rookes v. Barnard in arriving at its decision. Indeed the Court pointed out that the principle of Rookes v. Barnard was expressly affirmed by the House of Lords in Broome v. Cassell (1972 AC 1027). The Court also referred to the decision of the Court of Appeals in A. B. v. South West Water Services Ltd. (1993 (1) All E. R. 609) as following and affirming the rule in Rookes v. Barnard. It may also be mentioned that as late as 1996, the U.K. High Court has held in Three Rivers District Council v. Bank of England (1996 (3) All E. R. 558), following earlier decisions that:

"The tort of misfeasance in public office was concerned with a deliberate and dishonest wrongful abuse of the powers given to a public officer and the purpose of the tort was to provide compensation for those who suffered loss as a result of improper abuse of power. It was not to be equated with torts based on an intention to injure, although it had some similarities to them. The tort could be established in two alternative ways: (a) where a public officer performed or omitted to perform an act with the object of injuring the plaintiff (i.e. where there was targeted malice); and (b) where he performed an act which he knew he had no power to perform and which he knew would injure the plaintiff. Accordingly, malice, in the sense of an intention to injure the plaintiff or a person in a class of which the plaintiff was a member, and knowledge by the officer both that he had no power to do the act complained of and that the act or omission would probably (but not that it would necessarily or inevitably) injure the plaintiff or such a person, were alternative, not cumulative, ingredients of the tort. To act with such knowledge was to act in a sufficient sense maliciously.".

This statement of law is indeed a faithful reiteration of the law laid down by the Court of Appeals in Bourgoin S.A. v. Ministry of Agriculture (1985 (3) All E. R. 585).

These decisions, certainly, were welcome and enhanced the image of the Supreme Court in the public eye. The decisions established that courts were concerned with public servants and ministers could not escape consequences of their mala fide acts and orders. The decisions, in substance, demonstrated the adage that "howsoever high you may be, the law is above you". The decisions reinforced the rule of law and not that of men and further that public servants must develop a respect for public property and, above all, that public office is a trust and not a charter of corruption, nepotism and personal gain.

However, the principle enunciated in the above decisions were overruled in a subsequent decision of the Supreme Court in a review petition filed by one of the Ministers. A reading of the judgment (reported in AIR 1999 SC 2979) discloses that the review petition was allowed on the following grounds:

The petitioner before the court "Common Cause", a registered society, was not one of the applicants for allotment of petrol outlets and therefore has not suffered any legal injury by the unlawful allotments made by the Minister. If so, "how could then a finding of commission of misfeasance in public office by the petitioner (the Minister) be recorded in proceedings under Article 32 and that too at the instance of "Common Cause" on the basis of a Press report". Maybe, Common Cause was justified in agitating the said question by way of public interest litigation but that effort has already succeeded inasmuch as the 15 illegal allotments were quashed. But the Court was not entitled to go further and hold that the Minister has committed the tort of misfeasance in public office and to award exemplary damages on that basis.

Damages can be awarded for a tortious act to a particular plaintiff who has suffered loss on account of the said tortious action; "mere allotment of petrol outlets would not constitute 'misfeasance' unless other essential elements were present". True, it is that allotment of 15 outlets by the Minister was wholly unjustified and was an instance of wanton misuse of power, yet "it falls short of 'misfeasance in public office' which is a specific tort and the ingredients of that tort are not wholly met in the case". Hence, there was no occasion to award exemplary damages. Exemplary damages can no doubt be awarded against the public servants in certain situations but not in a case like this. The decision of the House of Lords in Rookes v. Bernard as affirmed in Broome v. Cassell cannot be accepted; "if we were to apply the rule in Rookes v. Bernard as upheld in Cassell and Company Limited v. Broome invariably and unhesitatingly and were to award exemplary damages in every case involving government officers or government servants, the result would be appalling". The Court further observed: "The petitioner does not on becoming the Minister.... assume the role of a 'trustee' in the real sense nor does a 'trust' come into existence in respect of the government properties".

Examined from the point of view of criminal breach of trust as defined in section 405 of the Indian Penal Code, the 'power to allot' cannot be treated as 'property' within the meaning of section 405 IPC that is capable of being misutilized and misappropriated. The direction to initiate criminal proceedings against the Minister concerned was violative of the right to life and liberty guaranteed to him by article 21 of the Constitution. In exercise of its powers under Article 32 of the Constitution, it was not permissible for the Supreme Court "to direct the government to pay the exemplary damages to itself". (This was so held obviously on the footing that a Minister of the government is part of the Government and therefore the Government cannot be directed to pay damages to itself.)

While the moral vigour of the decisions rendered in the aforesaid cases needs to be respected. Whether the principle of damages for a tort of misfeasance must necessarily involve an ingredient of injury to an agreed individual needs to be re-examined. The principle on which liability can be placed on public servants must be clear and must also be a fair principle consistent with need to act fearlessly and must not be capable of comprehending *bona fide* actions, though may be concerned, of civil servants. It is necessary that the principle must promote good governance. By way of example, we may refer to the Andhra Pradesh Cooperative Society's Act, 1964. Section 60 thereof provided that when an office bearer who was entrusted with the organization, affairs of management of the society, misappropriated or fraudulently retained any money or was guilty of any breach of trust, his conduct could be inquired into and an order requiring him to repay or restore the money or property by way of compensation would follow. It is necessary to enact as a part of a comprehensive law relating to public servants, the principles on the basis of which misfeasance can be rendered punishable. The principle must ensure that the wrong-doing is palpably evident, and given the barest standards of foreseeability, no two views are possible. It is then, and then alone, that the public servant is exposed to damages. Likewise, the principle may deal with both the situations, i.e., a situation where a definite injury had been caused to a third person and secondly where a declaration of wanton abuse of power can be arrived at by satisfying judicially manageable standards. Public servants in both the cases must be visited with the imposition of damages. Likewise, the principles of quantification of damages need to be defined since arbitrariness in arriving at figures may well become an area (of non-liquet) where 'no human law and justice may ever reach'. While drafting the legal provisions, there must be an examination of the basic power structure, the composition of the elite, of their fundamental structures in [see W. Michael Reisman, Folded Lies: Bribery, Crusades and Reforms, 69–73 (1973)]. It is necessary that the principles must be clear and achieve the desired result since there have been far too many moral crusades but few successful prosecutions. While adjusting the *bona fide*s or mala fides of an executive act, the matter should be one which is determinable contemporaneously with reference to clear standards of foreseeability.

Section 60 of the Andhra Pradesh Cooperative Societies Act, which carries the heading "Surcharge" reads as follows:

"Surcharge.- (1) Where in the course of an audit under section 50 or any inquiry under section 51 or an inspection under section 52 or section 53, or the winding up of a society, it appears that any person who is or was entrusted with the organization, affairs or management of the society or any past or present officer or servant of the society has misappropriated or fraudulently retained any money or other property or has been guilty of breach of trust in relation to the society or has caused any deficiency in the assets of the society by breach of trust or willful negligence or has made any payment contrary to the provisions of this Act, the rules or the bye-laws, the Registrar himself, or any person specially authorized by him in this behalf, of his own motion or on the application of the committee, liquidator or any creditor or contributory, may inquire into the conduct of such person or officer or servant and make an order requiring him to repay or restore the money or property or any part thereof with interest at such rate as the Registrar or the person authorized as aforesaid thinks just or to contribute such sum to the assets of the society by way of compensation in respect of the misappropriation, misapplication of funds, fraudulent retainer, breach of trust or willful negligence as the Registrar or the person authorized as aforesaid thinks just:

Provided that no order shall be passed against any person referred to in this sub-section unless the person concerned has been given an opportunity of making his representation.

(2) This section shall apply notwithstanding that such person or officer or servant may have incurred criminal liability by his act."

It may be remembered that a cooperative society has an elected managing committee to run and manage its affairs/business and also staff appointed to assist the persons in management in their duties. Both elected members and the employees so appointed are within the ambit of the above section. There is no reason why this principle cannot be extended to the governing machinery at the Union and State level, where too elected members form the government and run and manage the affairs of the State with the assistance of a permanent bureaucracy. Even the statutory authorities should be within the purview of this rule. The protective clauses usually found in enactments only save the authorities from any suit or prosecution in respect of acts done by them in 'good faith'. The protection does not and should not extend to acts done mala fide. Where the mala fide action causes loss to the State, i.e. people as such, the State must be entitled to recover the loss from the concerned official/ authority.

Several other enactments concerning the cooperative societies enacted by the various States too contain similar provisions.

A comprehensive law needs to be enacted to provide that where public servants cause loss to the State by their mala fide actions or omissions of a palpable character to be defined, they should be made liable to make good the loss caused by him to the State and, in addition, would be open to the imposition of exemplary damages. The principles must include cases of misuse of official position and acts outside authority. The expression 'public servant' must be extended to 'all public servants as defined in the Indian Penal Code and in the Prevention of Corruption Act, 1988, which expression has been interpreted to include Members of Parliament, Members of State Legislatures and Councils and Ministers. Such a law would have the merit of obviating several questions like whether Government can be asked to pay damages to itself, whether the power to grant or allot some benefit can be called 'property', whether such action of the public servant constitutes a 'tortuous action', whether damages/ exemplary damages can be awarded for such acts, and if so, on what basis and to what extent, whether public office is a trust and questions of 'locus standi' and so on. It would also contribute to avoidance of multiplicity of proceedings and would be more effective than a mere criminal prosecution, whether under IPC or PC Act. The law must, however, provide that proceedings thereunder can be taken on the basis of information received including an audit report or a report of any commission, committee or body competent to examine the relevant facts. The authority empowered to take proceedings must be an independent high level officer/agency whose tenure, conditions of service and independence should be firmly and fully guaranteed as has been done in the case of Central Vigilance Commissioner. Different authorities may be prescribed for different classes of public servants. For example Ministers and Legislators may constitute one category, Group A officers may constitute another category and so on. Classification can also be done department-wise. This is, however, a matter for the

Parliament/Legislature to decide. It may be appropriate for the Parliament and also State Legislatures on similar lines to enact a new comprehensive law to deal with public servants with reference to their public functions, relationship with the State as well as the examination of their personal effects and private properties. The fact, however, remains that such a course has become absolutely essential and urgent.

The public servants must be put on notice that they will be responsible to make good the loss caused by them to the State by their mala fide acts, to use a comprehensive expression to done the grounds mentioned herein above—that they should no longer be under the cozy impression that all that would happen in such a case is that their mala fide order or action would be set aside by the Court but that nothing would happen to them personally. They should be made aware that a mala fide act or action on their part carries the liability for damages/compensation. Creating personal liability of this kind would contribute greatly to good governance and would emphasize the need for transparent, fair and honest exercise of power. It would in no way dampen the initiative of the Ministers or officials nor would it inhibit them in any manner in effective discharge of their functions. A responsible government and the concept of accountability are not antithetical to good governance; on the contrary they promote it—they contribute to public good. Mere errors of judgment or *bona fide* mistakes would certainly not expose the public servants to such a consequence but where their actions are mala fide, i.e., falling within any of the six grounds mentioned hereinabove, they should be held responsible. If such acts result in loss to the State, they must be made liable to make good the same.

C. Necessity for a law providing for confiscation of illegally acquired assets of public servants

In the decision reported in Delhi Development Authority v. Skipper Construction Co. (P) Ltd. (AIR 1996 SC 2005), the Supreme Court made the following observations:

"... a law providing for forfeiture of properties acquired by holders of 'public office' (including the offices/posts in the public sector corporations) by indulging in corrupt and illegal acts and deals, is a crying necessity in the present state of our society. The law must extend not only to—as does SAFEMA—properties acquired in the name of the holders of such property but also to properties held in the names of his spouse, children or other relatives and associates. Once it is proved that the holder of such office has indulged in corrupt acts, all such properties should be attached forthwith. The law should place the burden of proving that the attached properties were not acquired with the aid of monies/properties received in the course of corrupt deals upon the holder of that property as does SAFEMA whose validity has already been upheld by this Court in the aforesaid decision of the larger Constitution Bench. Such a law has become an absolute necessity, if the canker of corruption is not to prove the death-knell of this nation. According to several perceptive observers, indeed, it has already reached near-fatal dimensions. It is for the Parliament to act in this matter, if they really mean business."

Indeed, in the above case the Supreme Court followed the law laid down by a nine-judge Constitution Bench in Attorney General of India vs. Amratlal Prajivandas [1994

(5) SCC 54] while dealing with the constitutional validity of the Smugglers and Foreign Exchange Manipulators (Forfeiture of Property) Act, 1976 (13 of 1976) which provided a similar forfeiture of illegally acquired assets of smugglers and foreign exchange violators. The nine-judge Bench, in a unanimous decision observed that the laudable object behind the said enactment was:

"to forfeit the illegally acquired properties of the convict/detenue irrespective of the fact that such properties are held by or kept in the name of or screened in the name of any relative or associate as defined in the said two Explanations. The idea is not to forfeit the independent properties of such relatives or associates which they may have acquired independently but only to reach the properties of the convict/detenue or properties traceable to him, wherever they are, ignoring all the transactions with respect to those properties.".

SAFEMA, it may be pointed out, placed the burden of proof squarely upon the smuggler and foreign exchange manipulator to establish that the assets owned by him or by the members of his family have been lawfully acquired. It was pointed out in the said nine-judge Bench decision that such a course was inevitable in the light of the fact that only the person who acquired properties can explain how he has come to acquire those properties and that it is not possible for the authority to do so. It was observed in the said decision:

"... The violation of foreign exchange laws and laws relating to export and import necessarily involves violation of tax laws. Indeed, it is well known fact that over the last few decades, smuggling, foreign exchange violation, tax evasion, drugs and crime have all got mixed-up. Evasion of taxes is integral to such activity. It would be difficult for any authority to say, in the absence of any accounts or other relevant material that among the properties acquired by smuggler, which of them or which portions of them are attributable to smuggling and foreign exchange violations and which properties or which portions thereof are attributable to violations of other laws (which the Parliament has the power to make). It is probably for this reason that the burden of proving that the properties specified in the show cause notice are not illegally acquired properties is placed upon the person concerned. May be this is the case where a dangerous disease requires a radical treatment. Bitter medicine is not bad medicine. In law it is not possible to say that definition is arbitrary or is couched in unreasonably wide terms...."

It is, therefore, quite appropriate that even in the proposed legislation to forfeit the properties of corrupt public servants, the burden of proof should be placed upon the holders of the property. This indeed is the principle of section 106 of the Indian Evidence Act, 1872. The said section along with the illustration appended to it reads as follows:

"Burden of proving fact especially within knowledge: When any fact is especially within the knowledge of any person, the burden of proving that fact is upon him.

Illustrations

(a) When a person does an act with some intention other than that which the character and circumstances of the act suggest, the burden of proving that intention is upon him.

(b) A is charged with traveling on a railway without a ticket. The burden of proving that he had a ticket is on him."

It is on this principle that in prevention of corruption statutes, the burden of proof is very often laid upon the accused. It has been held by the Supreme Court in C. S. D. Swami *versus* State (AIR 1960 SC 7) that "... the Legislature has, thus, deliberately cast a burden on the accused not only to offer a plausible explanation as to how he came by his large wealth, but also to satisfy the Court that his explanation was worthy of acceptance". This case was decided with reference to section 5(3) of Prevention of Corruption Act, 1947. The Court observed further "... section 5(3) of the Act does not create a new offence but only lays down a rule of evidence, enabling the Court to raise a presumption of guilt in certain circumstances" – and thus an exception to the general rule of burden of proof in criminal cases. To the same effect is the decision in State of Maharashtra *versus* Wasudeo (1981 SC 1186). Construing section 5, the Court held: "When section 5(1)(e) uses the words "for which the public servant is unable to satisfactorily account", it is implied that the burden is on such public servant to account for the sources for the acquisition of disproportionate assets", and that if he fails to satisfactorily account for his assets, he is liable to be convicted.

It is pointed out by some that where the property has been acquired several years ago, the person called upon to prove the sources of such acquisition may be under a severe handicap, inasmuch as he may not have kept or preserved the records relating to sources of such acquisition. This is however an aspect which the Court or Tribunal would certainly keep in mind while determining whether the person has discharged the burden that lay upon him.

The philosophical basis for such confiscation was explained by the Supreme Court in, the Attorney General of India, by invoking the concept of 'implied trust'. The relationship between the government and the public servant is of a fiduciary nature. In such a case, it was held, any benefit obtained by a fiduciary through a breach of duty belongs in equity to the beneficiary. It was further observed that a gift accepted by a person in a fiduciary position as an incentive for breach of his duty constituted a bribe and although in law it belonged to the fiduciary, in equity he not only became a debtor for the amount of the bribe to the person to whom the duty was owed, but he also held the bribe and any property acquired therewith on 'constructive trust' for that person. Any increase in the value of such property belonged to the person injured/beneficiary and that in case of any diminution in the asset, the wrong-doer was liable in person. It was also observed that unless there is a law providing for prompt forfeiture of illegally acquired assets, they would be spirited away beyond our shores to safe havens and numbered accounts.

Acting upon the observations of the Supreme Court in the above two judgments, the Law Commission of India submitted its 166th Report on "the Corrupt Public Servants (Forfeiture of property) Bill" recommending to the Central Government to introduce a Bill in Parliament for forfeiture of illegally acquired properties of corrupt public servants. A draft Bill was also enclosed to the said Report. It is again a matter of regret that the government has not thought it fit to take the desired steps.

We are of the opinion that a law as recommended hereinabove, has become absolutely inescapable in today's situation. It would clothe the State with an effective means of checking corruption. Nobody suggests that such an enactment would by itself check corruption. But even if a handful of cases concerning some notoriously corrupt persons are dealt with under such enactment, it will have a sobering effect upon other wrong-doers.

D. Enactment of a Public Interest Disclosure Act

One of the measures adopted in several western countries to fight corruption and mal-administration is enactment of Public Interest Disclosure Acts, which are popularly called Whistle-blower Acts. The object of such enactments is to improve accountability in government and public sector organizations by encouraging people not to turn a blind eye to malpractice taking place in their organizations and to report the same to the specified authority. The motto of the British Act (Public Interest Disclosure Act, 1998) is "Address the message rather than the messenger; and resist the temptation to cover up serious malpractices". The Act provides for protection of Whistle-blowers from dismissal and victimization by making appropriate provisions in that behalf.

An experienced corrupt public servant knows how to circumvent internal control proceedings. Such person indulges in such activity either by himself or in collusion with others, whether employees or outsiders. Even so, wherever corruption or malpractice takes place, it cannot but be that some or the other person in the organization knows it or comes to know of it. The Act enables such person to lay such information before the specified authority and thus promote public interest. It is true that such Whistle-blowing has been looked upon until now with some kind of disfavour, but recently a growing recognition has dawned upon all concerned that the persons who sound the alarm of serious malpractice, corruption or fraudulent activity in government or public sector organizations deserve public thanks and support rather than punished and humiliated for being 'disloyal' to their employers or colleagues.

The Act is really aimed at improving accountability within the government and public sector by allowing the employees to inform the appropriate authorities of organizational or individual wrong doing either in a confidential manner or by a public report. The Act should provide that the authority receiving such information should be an independent person and not be a part of the concerned government or public sector organization. If any information is received by him confidentially containing some allegations, he must investigate the same without publicly humiliating the suspect or the Whistle-blower. He must adopt appropriate methods to ensure the same. It must also be ensured that the persons who lay correct and true information about such illegalities should be rewarded which need not necessarily be financial in nature. It is equally necessary to ensure that this Whistle-blowing facility is not abused by malicious employees, out to achieve their personal grievance or vendetta.

Indeed, it is now believed that the law and the society must help create a culture wherein honest interchanges are respected and valued rather than punished. The Act must ensure that the informants are protected against retribution and any form of discrimination for reporting what they perceived to be wrong doing, i.e., for *bona fide* disclosures which may ultimately turn out to be not entirely or substantially true. It must be recognized, at the same time, that there are certain pitfalls in such a measure in the sense that it is liable to be abused by persons out of vindictiveness or for the purpose of retaliation or for claiming rewards. It must, however, be left to the appropriate authority to determine whether information laid before him confidentially is substantially correct information or whether the informant was acting *bona fide* or whether it is a totally false information actuated by malice or vindictiveness. There must be a provision for punishing persons who lay false information out of such inadmissible motives. It is believed in many developed countries that while there are certainly some risks inherent in such a legislative measure, it is better to run these risks rather than allow corruption and fraud to continue or to leave the Whistle-blower to go to an outside agency. Undoubtedly, the balance between asking people to blow the whistle and telling them that they themselves could be subject to proceedings for laying incorrect information, is a fine one. The situations arising under such a legislative measure, if handled sensitively, may certainly prove a step forward rather than a step backward in the fight against corruption and mal-administration.

In the British Act, the person/authority specified to receive complaints of the above nature is called a regulator.

As the London Borough, Lambeth says in its Whistle Blowing Charter, "if you believe something is wrong, speak out".

In this connection, it would not be out of place to refer to an organization in U.K., "Public Concern At Work", active in this field which has received the recognition of the government of the U.K. In their White Paper, 'The Governance of Public Bodies', the government has accepted the important role Whistle-blowing can play in ensuring probity and accountability and in that connection referred to the said organization as 'the leading organization in this field'. The said organization has published a number of papers espousing the cause of Whistle-blowing including some case studies. It is stated in one of their papers as below:

Standards in Public Life

In policy terms the most important development in recent years has been the Nolan Committee's endorsement of whistle-blowing as a means of ensuring and demonstrating high standards in public bodies. Nolan's 1996 recommendations, which are reproduced on the back cover, were accepted by the Major Government in its 1997 White Paper on The Governance of Public Bodies. The work of the Committee has also clarified the meaning of whistle-blowing. As the White Paper remarks, "The Nolan Committee used the term 'whistle-blowing' to mean the confidential raising of problems within an organization or within an independent review structure associated with that organization, not in the popular pejorative sense of leaking information to the media."

We have also looked into the whistle-blower Acts enacted by various countries viz., U.K., Australia, State of Michigan (USA) and Canada. We find that the Australian Act can serve as a model for our country, no doubt, with appropriate changes. In this connection, we may refer to the episode relating to "Pentagon Papers" which ultimately resulted in the decision of the U.S. Supreme Court in New York Times v. United States (1971) 403 U.S. 713 = 29 L. Ed. 2d. 822. One of the employees, Daniel Ellsberg, working in the defence department, came across a classified study entitled "History of the U.S. Decision-making Process on Vietnam Policy". The study disclosed that the U.S. government has been withholding from public true and correct information regarding its involvement in Vietnam and that it has been guilty of misrepresenting to the American people the issues and the facts relating to their involvement in Vietnam conflict and other relevant facts vitally affecting the American lives and interests. He did not know whom to complain. There was no authority outside the government to whom he could turn. He therefore approached the two leading U.S. dailies, The New York Times and The Washington Post with the material (he had secretly made copies of it). The employee was arrested and harassed for allegedly compromising the national security. The government tried unsuccessfully to block the publication of the said study, popularly known as 'Pentagon Papers' in the aforesaid dailies. The affair turned out to be a serious embarrassment to the U.S. government, and to its successive Presidents responsible for the American involvement in Vietnam.

It is obvious that had there been an independent authority ('Regulator') to whom the employee could have turned with the information in his possession and had such authority been empowered to enquire into the matter and make necessary orders—and if called for in public interest, gone public with it, the proceedings would have ended in an orderly manner and public interest served much better and more promptly. It could also have saved many lives, both American and Vietnamese. It goes without saying that these disclosures led to public disenchantment with—nay, opposition to—Vietnam war in U.S. and to its ultimate withdrawal from Vietnam on 30th April, 1975.

It is understood that the Law Commission of India is in the process of drafting a Public Interest Disclosure Bill, for forwarding it to the Government of India.

E. Enactment of a Freedom of Information Act

Right to receive and the right to impart information has been held to be a part of freedom of speech and expression guaranteed by sub-clause (a) of clause (1) of article 19 of the Constitution subject of course to the reasonable restrictions, if any, that may be placed on such right in terms of and to the extent permitted by clause (2) of the said article. It has been held by the Supreme Court in Secretary, Ministry of I&B vs. Cricket Association of Bengal (1995 (2) SCC 161) that:

"The freedom of speech and expression includes right to acquire information and to disseminate it. Freedom of speech and expression is necessary, for self-expression which is an important means of free conscience and self-fulfillment. It enables people to contribute to debates on social and moral issues. It is the best way to find a truest model of anything, since it is only through it that the widest possible range of ideas can circulate. It is the only vehicle of political discourse so essential to democracy. Equally important is the role it plays in facilitating artistic and scholarly endeavours of all sorts. The right to communicate, therefore, includes right to communicate through any media that is available whether print or electronic or audio-visual such as advertisement, movie, article, speech, etc. That is why freedom of speech and expression includes freedom of the press. The freedom of the press in turn includes right to circulate and also to determine the volume of such circulation. This freedom includes the freedom to communicate or circulate one's opinion without interference to as large a population in the country, as well as abroad, as is possible to reach.".

The fundamental values underlying the concept of freedom of speech, and the functions that the freedom serves in a democratic society, are widely accepted. They can be summarized in the following form:

(i) First, freedom of speech is essential to the development of the individual personality. The right to express oneself and to communicate with others is central to the realization of one's character and potentiality as a human being. Conversely, suppression of thought or opinion is an affront to a person's dignity and integrity. In this respect freedom of speech is an end in itself, not simply an instrument to attain other ends. As such it is not necessarily subordinate to other goals of the society.

(ii) Second, freedom of speech is vital to the attainment and advancement of knowledge. As John Stuart Mill pointed out, an enlightened judgment is possible only if one is willing to consider all facts and ideas, from whatever source, and to test one's conclusion against opposing views. Even speech that conveys false information or maligns ideas, has value, for it compels us to retest and rethink accepted positions and thereby promotes greater understanding. From this function of free speech, it follows that the right to express oneself does not depend upon whether society judges the communication to be true or false, good or bad, socially useful or harmful. All points of view, even a minority of one, are entitled to be heard.

(iii) Third, freedom of speech is a necessary part of our system of democratic government. Sovereignty resides in the people; in other words, the people are the masters and the government is their servant. If the people are to perform their role as sovereign and instruct their government, they must have access to all information, ideas, and points of view. This right of free speech is crucial not only in determining policy but in checking the government in its implementation of policy. The implication of this position is that the government has no authority to determine what may be said or heard by the citizens of the community

(iv) Fourth, freedom of speech is vital to the process of peaceful social change. It allows ideas to be tested in advance before action is taken, it legitimizes the decision reached, and it permits adaptation to new conditions without the use of force. It does not eliminate conflict in a society, but it does direct conflict into more rational, less violent, channels. In the words of Justice William J. Brennan in New York Times v. Sullivan (1964), speech may often be "uninhibited, robust, and wide-open".

It would not be out of place to quote from the oft-quoted judgment of Brandies J. in Whitney v. California, the following observation:

"... that the greatest menace to freedom is an inert people; that public discussion is a political duty; and that this should be a fundamental principle of the ... government.".

It must be recognized at the same time that today the freedom of expression and in particular the freedom of information is under a grave threat. The "free market-place of ideas"—an expression used in several U.S. Supreme Court judgments to denote freedom of speech and expression—is analogous to the more general argument for a "free market economy", as is opined by Milton Friedman and Jane Friedman in their book "Free to Choose". As indeed pointed out by Jerome Barron (Access to Press—A new First Amendment Right—80 Harvard Law Review 1641-1967) "... if ever there were a self-operating market place of ideas, it has long ceased to exist.... There is inequality in the power to communicate ideas just as there is inequality in economic bargaining power; to recognize the latter and deny the former is quixotic.... Changes in the communications industry have destroyed the equilibrium in that market place. While it may have been still possible in 1925 to believe with Justice Holmes that every idea is "acted on unless some other belief outweighs it or some failure of energy stifle the movement at its birth", it is impossible to believe it now. Yet the Holmesian theory is not abandoned, even though the advent of Radio and television has made even more evident that philosophy's unreality...." Another jurist Herbert Marcuse similarly argues that "under the rule of monopolistic media—themselves the mere instruments of economic and political power—a mentality is created from which right and wrong, true and false are pre-defined whenever they affect the vital interests of society" (Repressive Tolerance by Herbert Marcuse). How much more true all this sounds today when the television and other means of mass communication have become all-pervasive and all-encompassing. What they represent passes for information and truth and our ideas and views are imperceptibly formed by what we hear on television or read in newspapers. It is true that Press and media perform an important and essential function in a democratic society and that notwithstanding their ownership being in the hands of business tycoons and notwithstanding their dependence on government-sponsored advertisements, they are performing a highly valuable and useful function as guardian of the citizens' right to know and their right to impart their ideas and views to the government and the public. As has been rightly observed:

"The functions that freedom of the press performs in a democratic society are, in general, the same as those served by the system of freedom of expression as a whole. Freedom of the press enhances the opportunity to achieve individual fulfillment, advances knowledge and the search for understanding, is vital to the process of self-government, and facilitates social change by the peaceful interchange of ideas. More particularly the press has been conceived as playing a special role in informing the public and in monitoring the performance of government. Often referred to as the "fourth estate," or the fourth branch of government, an independent press is one of the principal institutions in our society that possesses the resources and the capacity to confront the government and other centers of established authority. This concept of a free press was forcefully set forth by Justice Hugo L. Black in his opinion in New York Times Co. v United States (1971) (The Pentagon Papers case): "In the first Amendment, the Founding Fathers gave the free press the protection it must have to fulfill its essential role in our democracy. The press was to serve the governed, not the governors. The government's power to censor the press was abolished so that the press would remain forever free to censure the government. The press was protected so that it could bare the secrets of government and inform the people. Only a free and unrestrained press can effectively expose deception in government."

The Press is thus an important agent in ensuring the citizens' right to receive and impart information as a measure of ensuring probity in governance.

Realising the importance of the freedom of speech and expression including the freedom to receive and impart information, some of the advanced countries have enacted Freedom of Information Acts. The object behind these enactments is to ensure that the governmental activity is transparent, fair and open. Except in matters of defence, atomic energy and matters concerning the security of the country, there is no room for secrecy in the affairs of the government. Whether it is a matter of taking a decision affecting the people or whether it is a transaction involving purchase or sale of government property or whether the matter relates to entering into contracts—in all these matters, the government should act in a transparent manner which means that any and every citizen who wishes t o obtain any information with respect to any of those matters should be entitled to receive it. In this connection, we may usefully refer to the Freedom of Information Act, 2000 enacted by the British Parliament on 30 November, 2000. The main purpose of the Act is to implement the principles set out in the White Paper insofar as it is appropriate to do so by primary legislation. Other matters will be dealt with in secondary legislation, codes of practice or by administrative action. The Act provides a right of access to recorded information held by public authorities, creates certain exemptions from the duty to disclose information and establishes arrangements for enforcement and appeal. The Act amends the Data Protection Act, 1998 and the Public Records Act, 1958. Since the Act purports to implement the principles set out in the White Paper which was issued in December 1997, it may be appropriate to briefly refer to them. In the White Paper entitled "Your Right to Know: the Government's Proposals for a Freedom of Information Act", the following scheme of the Act was indicated:

The new Act will provide for any individual, company or other body to have a right of access to records or information of any data held by a wide range of public bodies. Applicants need not state their purpose in applying for information. The authorities are bound to make certain information public as a matter of course. Indeed, the authorities covered by the Act are required to make certain information publicly available without request (these include facts and analyses which the government considers important in framing major policy proposals, explanatory material on dealing with the public, operational information on costs, standards, targets and complaints procedures of public servants) and further give reasons for administrative decisions. There should be no ministerial veto to prevent disclosures.

What is more, there is no exclusion in favour of the Cabinet or Cabinet Committees from the purview of the Act. Access will be allowed to documents and not merely to information. Of course, security and intelligence services are excluded from the purview of the Act.

There is a similar exclusion—which has attracted a lot of criticism—in favour of criminal and civil enforcement proceedings and the investigation and prosecution functions of the police, prosecutors and "other bodies carrying out law enforcement work such as the Department of Social Security or the Immigration Service", as well as the public sector employment records. There are certain other exemptions too. In view of the above scheme of the English Act, it may not be necessary to refer to its provisions at any length. The Government of India too has recognized the importance of this right and has accordingly introduced a Bill called the Freedom of Information Bill, 2000 (Bill No. 98 of 2000) in Lok Sabha on 25 July 2000. The Bill, as it stands, does ensure to a large extent the freedom of information to citizens with respect to the functioning of the government. It casts an obligation upon public authorities to furnish such information wherever asked for. It would have been better if the said Bill had also provided for the government making information public, without a request therefor from anyone, concerning matters involving major policy proposals and the major multilateral agreements proposed to be entered into. This is for the reason that very often the people who are really going to be affected by such policies and agreements are not even aware of them. The experience of WTO Agreements signed by the Government of India in 1994, without taking the Parliament or the States or the people into confidence, and without a national debate on the pros and cons of the said Agreements, is a telling example. Purporting to exercise their power under article 73 read with article 253 and entry 14 of List I of the Seventh Schedule to the Constitution, the Union Government has concluded several agreements covering not only the subjects in Lists I and III of the said Schedule but also with respect to subjects in List II, which are in the exclusive domain of the States—for example, Agriculture and Public Health. The negative effects of the said Agreements are becoming evident with each passing day and are seriously eroding the viability of the domestic industries (which were built up with huge public funds), agriculture and trade. Be that as it may, the said Bill fills a great void though, it is true, several improvements are possible in it. It is understood that the said Bill has been referred to a Standing Committee. We are enclosing herewith a copy of the recently enacted South African Freedom of Information Act (the promotion of Access to Information Act, 2000) (Annexure) which covers both the public bodies and private bodies. It can indeed serve as a model enactment for any country committed to concept of freedom of information. The necessity and importance of an early enactment in terms of the said Bill—with some improvements—cannot be over-emphasized. It would be useful to notice the various provisions of the English Act and the South African Act before finalizing the draft of the proposed Indian legislation.

F. Necessity for enacting a Lok Pal Bill in addition to the Central Vigilance Commission Act

Institution of Lok Pal

Another measure for ensuring probity in governance is the enactment of a Lok Pal Act and a Central Vigilance Commission Act. It would be appropriate to deal with the Lok Pal Act first. In their interim report on the "Problem of Redress of Citizens' Grievances" submitted in 1966, the Administrative Reforms Commission recommended *inter alia* the setting up of the institution of Lok Pal. To give effect to this recommendation, a Bill called the Lok Pal and Lokayukta Bill, 1968 was introduced in the fourth Lok Sabha in 1968. It was referred to a Joint Committee of the two Houses of Parliament and on the basis of its Report, the Bill was passed by Lok Sabha in 1969. But while the Bill was pending in the Rajya Sabha, the fourth Lok Sabha was dissolved with the result that the Bill lapsed.

In 1971, the Bill passed by the previous Lok Sabha was reintroduced in Lok Sabha under the same title but this Bill also lapsed on the dissolution of the fifth Lok Sabha. The Bills introduced in 1968 and 1971 covered complaints in respect of not only allegations of misconduct but also grievances as to mal-administration. Lok Pal was thought of as a single member body who could be described roughly as a person who would combine in himself the functions of ombudsman as known to the western countries such as Norway, Sweden, UK and the functions of the Central Vigilance Commission as it was constituted under an administrative order of the Central Government. Complaints could be made under the said Bill against the union ministers, union civil servants, union territory ministers and persons in the service of local authorities and corporations, owned or controlled by the Central Government. However, Members of Parliament and the State Chief Ministers were not covered by the Bill. In short, these Bills were designed to check abuse of power, corruption and other instances of mal-administration; liberty was given to the aggrieved persons to approach specified authorities.

In the year 1977, a fresh Bill called the Lok Pal Bill, 1977 was introduced in Lok Sabha. It was again referred to a Joint Committee of both Houses of Parliament which submitted its Report in July 1978. While this Bill was under consideration of the Lok Sabha, it was prorogued first and subsequently dissolved. Accordingly, this Bill also lapsed. It may be mentioned that the 1977 Bill did not take in grievances as to mal-administration; it was confined to complaints as to misconduct or corruption against specified categories of persons including Union Ministers, Members of Parliament, State Chief Ministers and so on. This Bill brought within its purview the Prime Minister and MLAs of Union Territories as well. Civil servants were excluded from its purview. The definition of 'misconduct' was widely worded to include instances of abuse of power wherein a public man—if we can use that expression to denote the persons brought within the purview of the Act—directly or indirectly, allows his position to be taken advantage of by his relatives or associates. The Bill also provided that a public man would be guilty of misconduct if he fails to act in accordance with norms of integrity and conduct which ought to be followed by the class of public men to which he belongs. Of course, the Joint Committee to which this Bill was referred had recommended that the said requirement be omitted. Be that as it may, this Bill also lapsed. In the year 1985, another Lok Pal Bill was introduced in Lok Sabha on the pattern of the 1977 Bill. However the office of the Prime Minister was excluded from its purview. The Lok Pal was to be a single member body and its jurisdiction was confined to cases of corruption leaving out mal-administration and grievances. Be that as it may, this Bill also lapsed for the same reason as in the case of other such Bills. In the year 1989, another Lok Pal Bill was introduced. Under this, the Lok Pal was to be a three-member body and the office of the Prime Minister was also brought within its purview. There were some changes in the matter of eligibility for appointment and removal which it may not be necessary to mention here.

In the year 1996, yet another Lok Pal Bill was introduced in the Lok Sabha on 13th September, 1996. It was referred to the Department related Parliamentary Standing Committee on Home Affairs for examination. The Standing Committee submitted its report to the Parliament on 9th May, 1997. But before the government could finalize its thinking on the various recommendations of the Committee, the Lok Sabha was dissolved on 4 December 1997. Consequently, the Bill lapsed.

Another attempt at enacting the Lok Pal Act was made by the introduction of a Lok Pal Bill in the Lok Sabha on 3 August 1998, being Bill No. 90 of 1998. This Bill sought to provide for setting up the office of Lok Pal with a chairperson and two members with a fixed term. To ensure the members of their independence, it is provided that they shall not be removed from their office except by an order made by the President on the ground of proved misbehaviour or incapacity after an inquiry made by a committee consisting of the Chief Justice of India and two other judges of the Supreme Court, next to the Chief Justice in seniority, in which inquiry the member has been informed of the charges against him and given a reasonable opportunity of being heard in respect of those charges. The chairman and members are to be appointed by the President on the recommendation of the committee consisting of the Vice President of India (chairman), Prime Minister, Speaker of Lok Sabha, Minister of Home Affairs, Leader of the House to which the Prime Minister does not belong, Leader of the Opposition in the Lok Sabha and Leader of the Opposition in the Rajya Sabha. The jurisdiction of the Lok Pal under this Bill is to inquire into allegations constituting an offence punishable under the Prevention of Corruption Act, 1988. The Prime Minister, Union Ministers and Members of Parliament are within its purview. Clause 12 of the Bill provided that any person other than a public servant may make a complaint under that legislation to the Lok Pal (the expression 'complaint' is defined by sub-clause (c) to clause 2 to mean "a complaint alleging that a public functionary has committed any offence punishable under the Prevention of Corruption Act, 1988". The expression 'public functionary' means the Prime Minister, Union Ministers and Members of Parliament, both past and present). If it becomes necessary in the course of its inquiry, the Lok Pal is also empowered to inquire into any act or conduct of any person other than a public functionary insofar as it is necessary for an effective disposal of the matter within his jurisdiction. Clause 13 provides for preliminary scrutiny of complaints by Lok Pal whereas clause 14 provides for the procedure to be followed by Lok Pal in conducting any inquiry. Clause 15 clothes the Lok Pal with the power to summon any person or document from any person or authority. The Lok Pal is also vested with the powers of search and seizure by clause 16. Chapter IV of the Bill which contains only one clause, namely, clause 18, creates an obligation on every Member of Parliament to furnish a return of all assets owned by him and members of his family and all liabilities incurred by him and the members of his family, before the Lok Pal, within a period of 90 days from the date he enters upon his office and continue to do so every year within 90 days of the commencement of each financial year. The declaration has to be filed in the prescribed form. The expression 'family' is defined to include the spouse and dependent children of such member. This is certainly a defect. It would be more appropriate if the net is spread wider to include even major children and close relatives like father-in-law, mother-in-law, brothers, brothers-in-law and close associates.

While examining the provisions of the Bill, we have come to believe that while bringing the Prime Minister within the purview of the Lok Pal may be a desirable step, it is necessary at the same time to regulate and circumscribe that power. In our Constitutional system, i.e., under the parliamentary form of government, the Prime Minister occupies a unique position. He is the kingpin of the entire governmental structure. It is his image, his reputation and his personality that pervades the entire government. The image of the government is very often identified with the image of the Prime Minister. Because of the extraordinary power a Prime Minister wields in a parliamentary system like ours, it is sometimes referred to by jurists as 'prime ministerial form of government'. A Prime Minister is normally the leader of the majority party in the Lok Sabha or the leader of the coalition, if a coalition forms the government. Because of his very position and the power he wields, he attracts a good amount of opposition, criticism, allegations and what not. If a Lok Pal were to take up each and every allegation or accusation made against the Prime Minister by a political party or a group or a person, it would hobble the Prime Minister in an effective discharge of his functions. He cannot afford to remain under a cloud all the time nor can the nation afford a Prime Minister under a cloud all the time. Probably for this reason, in some of the earlier Bills, the Prime Minister was kept out of the purview of the Lok Pal. But, as we have said earlier, while it may be a desirable step to bring the Prime Minister within the purview of Lok Pal, it should at the same time be provided that before the Lok Pal undertakes any investigation, inquiry or any other proceeding against the Prime Minister, he should first obtain the permission in writing of the President therefor. It means that the Lok Pal shall place all the relevant material before the President and must satisfy the President with the facts and circumstances which call for an investigation and inquiry into those allegations and charges. The requirement of obtaining President's permission would be in the nature of a check upon a routine or mechanical initiation of inquiry by Lok Pal against the Prime Minister. One has to keep in mind in this behalf the distinction between legitimacy and legality. Legitimacy is a political concept. The Prime Minister normally represents the will of the majority of the people, being the leader of the majority of elected representatives. The legitimacy to rule belongs to him and his Council of Ministers. As against this, Lok Pal, a mere appointee, cannot be so empowered as to erode the image, reputation and personality of the Prime Minister by seeking to investigate or inquire into each and every allegation. The requirements of President's prior permission or sanction as it may be called would ensure that an investigation or inquiry into an allegation against the Prime Minister is taken up only where it is backed by substantial and acceptable evidence. The nation cannot afford to have a Prime Minister under a cloud, unless there are real and substantial grounds to believe that he may have been guilty of some serious misconduct. There is also a belief that the Prime Minister of a country should not be subjected to Lok Pal as this would severely impair his independence and freedom of judgement. The Prime Minister should have a free hand and absolute independence which is most necessary. Even if a particular Prime Minister is inclined that he should be subjected to Lok Pal, his readiness should not weigh with the Commission. There is a need to reconcile national interest and public interest and keeping in view how prime ministerial discretion is exercised, it would be a retrograde step. Anyhow, a new Bill titled The Lok Pal Bill, 2001 covering the Prime Minister also was introduced in Lok Sabha on 14th August, 2001.

In this connection, it would not be out of place to refer to the institution of the Independent Counsel created by Title VI of the Ethics in Government Act in USA. The Independent Counsel Act provides for appointment of an "independent counsel" to investigate and if appropriate prosecute certain high ranking government officials for violations of federal criminal laws. The Act requires the Attorney General, if he is satisfied on receipt of information that it is "sufficient to constitute grounds to investigate whether any person (covered by the Act) may have violated any federal criminal law", to conduct a preliminary investigation of the matter. When the Attorney General has completed this investigation, or 90 days has elapsed, he is required to report to a special court (the Special Division) created by the Act "for the purpose of appointing independent counsels". If the Attorney General determines that "there are no reasonable grounds to believe that further investigation is warranted", he must notify the Special Division of this result. In such a case, "the Division of the court shall have no power to appoint an independent counsel". If the Attorney General determines that there are "reasonable grounds to believe that further investigation or prosecution is warranted," then, he "shall apply to the Division of the court for the appointment of an independent counsel". The Attorney General's application to the court shall contain sufficient information to assist the court in selecting an independent counsel and in defining that independent counsel's prosecutorial jurisdiction. Upon receiving such information, the Special Division "shall appoint an appropriate independent counsel and shall define that independent counsel's prosecutorial jurisdiction".

The independent counsel's jurisdiction is very wide. He is vested with the full power and independent authority to exercise all investigative and prosecutorial functions and powers of the Department of Justice, the Attorney General and any other officer or employee of the Department of Justice. He can conduct grand jury proceedings and other investigations, he can participate in civil and criminal court proceedings and litigation and is also empowered to file appeals against any decision in any case in which he has participated in an official capacity. His powers include initiating and conducting prosecutions in any court of competent jurisdiction, framing and signing indictments, filing information and handling all aspects of any case in the name of the United States. He is entitled to call for assistance from any department or authority. Moreover, when a matter is referred to an independent counsel under the Act, the Attorney General in the Justice Department is required to suspend all investigations and proceedings with respect to the said matter. The validity of the Independent Counsel Act was challenged in the federal courts. The matter ultimately reached the United States Supreme Court. While a majority of seven judges led by Rehnquist C. J. upheld the validity of the Act holding that it does not curtail or infringe the powers of the President vested in him by clause 2 of section 2 of Article II of the U.S. Constitution, Scalia J. dissented (another Judge Kennedy J. took no part in the decision of the case)—Morrison v. Olson, 487 U.S. 654 (1988). Though the dissenting opinion of Scalia J. was criticized at that time as highly conservative, the events since then have proved him right. The manner in which an independent counsel appointed to investigate the Whitewater affair allegedly implicating President Bill Clinton and his wife was hijacked to take in unrelated issues is an instructive instance. Not able to find any substance against the President in the Whitewater issue, the Independent Counsel picked upon a case of suicide by a member of the White House staff and finding nothing therein shifted to Paula Jones' affair. While investigating the Paula Jones' affair, the independent counsel, Kenneth Starr, stumbled upon the Monica Lewinsky affair and everyone knows how the whole thing was blown up beyond all sensible and reasonable proportions leading to the impeachment proceedings and trial of President Clinton in Senate. The following observations of Scalia J. in the aforementioned case are pertinent:

"What every prosecutor is practically required to do is to select the cases for prosecution and to select those in which the offense is the most flagrant, the public harm the greatest, and the proof the most certain. If the prosecutor is obliged to choose his case, it follows that he can choose his defendants. Therein is the most dangerous power of the prosecutor; that he will pick people that he thinks he should get, rather than cases that need to be prosecuted. With the law books filled with a great assortment of crimes, a prosecutor stands a fair chance of finding at least a technical violation of some act on the part of almost everyone. In such a case, it is not a question of discovering the commission of a crime and then looking for the man who has committed it; it is a question of picking the man and then searching the law books, or putting investigators to work, to pin some offense on him. It is in this realm—in which the prosecutor picks some person whom he dislikes or desires to embarrass, or selects some group of unpopular persons and then looks for an offense, that the greatest danger of abuse or prosecuting power lies. It is here that law enforcement becomes personal, and the real crime becomes that of being unpopular with the predominant or governing group, being attached to the wrong political views, or being personally obnoxious to or in the way of the prosecutor himself… The mini-Executive that is the independent counsel, however, operating in an area where so little is law and so much is discretion, is intentionally cut off from the unifying influence of the Justice Department, and from the perspective that multiple responsibilities provide. What would normally be regarded as a technical violation (there are no rules defining such things) may in his or her small world assume the proportions of an indictable offense. What would normally be regarded as an investigation that has reached the level of pursuing such picayune matters that it should be concluded, may to him or her be an investigation that ought to go on for another year. How frightening it must be to have your own independent counsel and staff appointed, with nothing else to do but to investigate you until investigation is no longer worthwhile – with whether it is worthwhile not depending upon what such judgments usually hinge on, competing responsibilities. And to have that counsel and staff decide, with no basis for comparison, whether what you have done is bad enough, willful enough, and provable enough, to warrant an indictment... The notion that every violation of law should be prosecuted, including—indeed, especially—every violation by those in high places, is an attractive one, and it would be risky to argue in an election campaign that is not an absolutely overriding value. *Fiat justitia, ruat coelum.* Let justice be done, though the heavens may fall. The reality is, however, that it is not an absolutely overriding value....".

It is in the context of all the above circumstances, that we are inclined to suggest that there ought to be a proviso to clause 12 of the Lok Pal Bill in the following terms:

"Provided that before taking up any investigation or inquiry against the Prime Minister on the basis of any complaint or information received, the Lok Pal shall obtain the prior permission in writing of the President therefor."

Coming back to the Bill, it is difficult to predict whether the present Bill succeeds in becoming an Act or would it meet the same fate as its predecessors. But so far as it goes, the Bill is welcome though in certain respects it requires to be strengthened. The Bill rightly provides that a proceeding before the Lok Pal shall to be deemed to be a judicial proceeding within the meaning of section 193 of Indian Penal Code (clause 15(2)) and further that it is not necessary for the Lok Pal to maintain secrecy or other restriction upon the disclosure of information as provided in the Official Secrets Act, 1923 or any other provision of law. But, the Bill does not say that the conclusions arrived at by the Lok Pal shall be final and that if any public functionary is found guilty he should resign from his office including his membership of the Parliament/Legislature forthwith. Instead of doing that, section 17 merely speaks of the conclusions of the Lok Pal being communicated to the competent authority. (The expression "competent authority" is defined by sub-clause (b) in clause 2 of the Bill to mean (i) in the case of Prime Minister, the House of People; (ii) in the case of a member of the Council of Ministers other than Prime Minister, the Prime Minister and (iii) in the case of a Member of Parliament other than a minister, Rajya Sabha or Lok Sabha, as the case may be). Maybe, the Constitution may have to be amended to provide for an effective Lok Pal, with his own machinery of investigation.

Central Vigilance Commission

So far as the Central Vigilance Commission (CVC) is concerned, it has a long antecedent history. Pursuant to the recommendations of the Santhanam Committee constituted by the Government of India to advise the government in respect of matters pertaining to maintenance of integrity in administration, the CVC was established in 1964. The jurisdiction of CVC extended to all public servants and employees of central public sector undertakings, nationalized banks and autonomous organizations *vide* the resolution dated February 11, 1964 of the Government of India, Ministry of Home Affairs. It continued to function as such but without much effect until the Supreme Court directed in Vineet Narain vs. Union of India (1997 (7) SCALE 656) [AIR 1998 SC 889], on 18th December, 1997, to give a statutory shape to the CVC and to endow it with wider powers including supervision over Central Bureau of Investigation (CBI) and the Enforcement Directorate (ED). Indeed the Supreme Court, while giving the said directions had relied upon the report of the Independent Review Committee (IRC) comprising Shri B. G. Deshmukh, former Cabinet Secretary, Shri N. N. Vohra, Principal Secretary to the PM and Shri S. V. Giri, Central Vigilance Commissioner, which Committee was constituted under the Government Order dated 8th September, 1997. The directions of the Supreme Court are quite elaborate and they extend to the appointment, powers and functioning of CVC, CBI and ED, all designed to insulate the said institutions from political control and to invest them with good amount of independence coupled with accountability. (Those interested in perusing the said directions may refer to the aforementioned decision of the Supreme Court.) Pursuant to the said directions, the Central Government has drafted a Bill, being Bill No. 137 of 1999, called the Central Vigilance Commission Bill, 1999 and has introduced the same in Lok Sabha on 20 December 1999. It appears to be still pending before the Parliament. Meanwhile, the CVC is acting under the authority of the decision of the Supreme Court referred to above. It is imperative that the Parliament passes the said Bill as early as possible, keeping in mind the directions contained in the decision of the Supreme Court in Vineet Narain.

Civil Services Commission Board

An ancillary suggestion in this behalf that can be implemented without much ado, but which may have extremely beneficial results, is the constitution of a Civil Services Commission Board for overseeing appointment and transfer to senior posts. The idea is to take away the power of transfer from the political executive which, according to the universally held opinion, has not only been abused but has also been used in such a manner as to make the bureaucracy, including the IAS, plaint, toothless and corrupt. Maybe a Constitutional amendment is called for to provide for the composition of such a Board. The composition of the Board need not be exclusively non-political. It can be headed by the Prime Minister or the Home Minister and its jurisdiction restricted to certain high-level posts in the bureaucracy.

Suggestions of Central Vigilance Commission

Yet another ancillary idea floated by Shri N. Vittal, Central Vigilance Commissioner is to make the corruption-free governance, a fundamental right of the citizen. He has suggested that an article be inserted in Part III declaring such a right of the citizens. At any rate, Shri Vittal suggests, a provision to that effect must be included in Part IV (the Directive Principles of State Policy). He is of the opinion that such a provision would enable the Central and State Governments to legislate standards of probity and the rules governing the delivery of services to consumers of those services and in the matter of transfer of public employees. He is also of the opinion that insertion of such a right will provide an avenue for the civil society to demand transparency, fair procedures and decent behaviour on the part of the officials as also to demand public involvement in all matters affecting the public.

Ethics in Government Act of the United States of America

In this context, it would not be out of place to refer to certain provisions of the Ethics in Government Act enacted by the US Congress in 1978. Section 101 which carries the heading "persons required to file" says that (a) within 30 days of assuming the position of an officer or employee described in sub-section (f), an individual shall file a report containing the information described in section 102(b) unless the individual has left another position described in sub-section (f) within 30 days prior to assuming such new position or has already filed a report under this title with respect to nomination for the new position or as a candidate for the position. Sub-section (f) includes the President, the Vice President, each officer or employee in the executive branch, all government servants, members of the congress, officers or employees of the Congress, judicial officers and employees of the judiciary. Section 102 provides the matters which such declaration should contain.

It is a very lengthy section and it is not feasible to extract the whole of it. Suffice it to mention that the section provides for a full, true and complete disclosure of all kinds of assets including mortgages, movable assets, benefits under trusts and so on. Section 103 prescribes the time within which the report should be filed and the person before whom they should be filed. Section 104 empowers the Attorney General to bring a civil action in an appropriate US district court against any individual who knowingly and wilfully files a false declaration. Section 105 provides for custody of the declarations; it expressly provides that public shall have access to such declarations. Any US citizen is entitled to use the said reports for any lawful purpose. Section 106 provides for review and scrutiny of these reports by specified authorities. Section 108 declares that the Comptroller General shall have access to financial disclosure reports filed under the Act for the purpose of effectively discharging his statutory functions.

It is a matter for consideration whether it would be advisable for the Parliament to enact a legislation similar to the said U.S. Act.

G. Strengthening of the Criminal Judicial System

This is one of the most important requisites for ensuring probity in governance. The criminal judicial system consists of the police/investigating agency, the prosecuting agency, the advocates, witnesses and finally the judiciary. Inasmuch as this topic is dealt with in another paper, the same is not being dilated upon in this Consultation Paper.

Official Secrets Act of India, 1923

4 APPENDIX

The Official Secrets Act, 1923 is India's anti-espionage act held over from British colonization. It states clearly that any action which involves helping an enemy state against India. It also states that one cannot approach, inspect, or even pass over a prohibited government site or area. According to this Act, helping the enemy state can be in the form of communicating a sketch, plan, model of an official secret, or of official codes or passwords, to the enemy. The disclosure of any information that is likely to affect the sovereignty and integrity of India, the security of the State, or friendly relations with foreign States, is punishable by this act.

Prosecution and Penalties

Punishments under the Act range from three to fourteen years imprisonment. A person prosecuted under this Act can be charged with the crime even if the action was unintentional and not intended to endanger the security of the state. The Act only empowers persons in positions of authority to handle official secrets, and others who handle it in prohibited areas or outside them are liable for punishment. In any proceedings against a person for an offence under this Act, the fact that he has been in communication with, or attempted to communicate with a foreign agent, whether within or without India is relevant and enough to necessitate prosecution. Journalists also have to help members of the police forces above the rank of the sub-Inspector and members of the Armed forces with investigation regarding an offence, up to and including revealing his sources of information (If required).

Under the Act, search warrants may be issued at any time if the magistrate feels that based on the evidence in front of them there is enough danger to the security of the state. Uninterested members of the public may be excluded from court proceedings if the prosecutions feels that any information which is going to be passed on during the proceedings is sensitive. This also includes media; so the journalists will not be allowed to cover that particular case. When a company is seen as the offender under this Act, everyone involved with the management of the company including the board of directors can be liable for punishment. In the case of a newspaper, everyone including the editor, publisher and the proprietor can be jailed for an offence.

International NGO Accountability Charter

5 APPENDIX

The International Non-Governmental Organizations Accountability Charter (INGO Accountability Charter) is a charter, founded in 2006 by a group of independent non-profit organizations, which is intended to foster accountability and transparency of non-governmental organizations, as well as stakeholder communication and performance. NGOs are today more than ever before important participants in framing the social, political and economic environment. On the national level they provide disaster relief and social service, promote self-help and self-governance in developing countries where they are operating. In addition, they enhanced a strong international Civil society by creating informal but important normative regimes which are influencing international institutions in their decision-making. This greater involvement of NGOs also raises the question of how they justify their activities. NGOs have a particular interest in meeting standards on accountability and transparency in view of the responsibilities towards not only the cause which they are meant to serve, but also stakeholders of various types, including donors and sponsors (possibly comprising corporations and governments), intended programme beneficiaries, staff and the general public.

The charter is considered a contributing element to underscoring the legitimacy of NGOs.

Origin

The Development of the Charter

At the International Advocacy Non-Government Organizations (IANGO) Workshop hosted by Transparency International in June 2003, the importance of promoting accountability and legitimacy was discussed by its participants. As they recognized their growing involvement in international issues the need of promoting accountability was highlighted. The Hauser Center for Non-Profit Organizations at the Harvard University was asked for a research paper on the topic to provide a foundation for following discussions. At the following annual meetings in 2004 and 2005, the participants analysed their own concepts of accountability, set up an initial draft and with the help of independent consultant specialists revised the draft until a final version was ready to launch.

Adoption

Signed in June 2006 by eleven leading international NGOs active in the area of human rights, environment and social development, the INGO Accountability Charter has been referred to as "the first ever set of international and cross-sector guidelines for the NGO sector" and the "first global accountability charter for the non-profit sector".

Founding Members

The founding members are Action Aid International, Amnesty International, Civicus World Alliance for Civic Participation, Consumers International, Greenpeace International, Oxfam International, International Save the Children Alliance, Survival International, International Federation Terre des Hommes, Transparency International and World YWCA.

Articles

The Charter is *based on nine core principles and aimed at enhancing accountability and transparency, encouraging stakeholder communication, and improving organizational performance and effectiveness*. It documents the commitment of international NGOs to these aims.

The Charter requires its members to submit an annual report according to the Global Reporting Initiative's NGO Sector Supplement. The reports are then reviewed by an Independent Review Panel that provides feedback to the organization, before the reports and the feedback are published to the Charter website.

Governance

The Board of Directors of the Charter has representatives from Amnesty International, CBM International, CIVICUS: World Alliance for Citizen Participation, Greenpeace International, Oxfam International, and World Vision International. The current Chairman of the Board of Directors is Jeremy Hobbs, Executive Director of Oxfam International. In July 2010 the Berlin Civil Society Center took over the Secretariat role of the Charter from CIVICUS.

Related Codes of Conduct

In 1997, the One World Trust had created an *NGO Charter*, a code of conduct comprising commitment to accountability and transparency.

Previous Years' Questions of IAS GS Mains Paper IV: Ethics, Integrity and Aptitude

UPSC Mains 2017

Paper 4: Ethics Integrity and Aptitude

Question 1. Conflict of interest in the public sector arises when

(a) Official duties,
(b) Public interest, and
(c) Personal interest

are taking priority one above the other.

How can this conflict in administration be resolved? Describe with an example.

(150 Words, 10)

Answer: The conflict of interest is the situation when the public duty of an individual comes in conflict with his personal interest. An individual may use it to amass benefit to himself and his associated party. This creates moral as well as legal dilemma. Any advantage seeking may lead to loss of public trust, miscarriage of justice and is against the virtue of an individual.

This is evident in following examples:

1. The Justice Lodha panel pointed in the recent case of BCCI that Mr. Srinivasan was the head of the BCCI as well as owner of the IPL team Chennai Super Kings. This may prevent him from taking any decision that may be adversial to his franchise.
2. In the case of Appointment of Chief Election Commissioner and other ECs, the government has discretion to appoint any person. The government may place person who favours the party. This may affect the idea of free and fair election, which is the basis of democracy.
3. The appointment of ex-Chief Justice of India as Governor of a State just after retirement raises question on the independent justice delivery, wherein 80% of cases in Supreme Court are against the government.

4. The awarding spectrum to the company of the relative in the recent spectrum scam case shows how nepotism and personal interest have cost dearly to exchequer.

The conflict of interest can be resolved by following ways:

1. **Merit-based Appointment**: The appointments on government posts must be based on merit and open competition, and any favouritism must be avoided. For example, in appointment of Central Vigilance Commissioner, a collegium of Prime Minister and Leader of Opposition decide who shall be appointed for post from the list of individuals.
2. **Recuse from the Case**: When the deciding authority is stakeholder of the case or he is deciding the case of person-known to him, he must recuse himself from the case. This is provided in the Code of Ethics of Judiciary.
3. **Declaration of Conflict of Interest** to the relevant authority. For example, a minister must declare his interest to Prime Minister if any of his relative is involved in the projects being undertaken by government.
4. **Integrity Pacts** in government projects allotment. Here, the third party is brought in to oversee if any case of corruption or wrongs is done during allocation and execution of project.
5. Fixing **Responsibility and Accountability of Individual** for each work. He must be open to any scrutiny and question regarding project. Also, the data must be put on **Public Domain** so that public awareness is done.

Thus, conflict of interest must be resolved such that the decisions are transparent and made in public interest. **"Justice must not only be done, but it must also be seen to be done."**

Question 2. Examine the relevance of the following in the context of civil service. ***(150 Words, 10)***

(a) Transparency
(b) Accountability
(c) Fairness and justice
(d) Courage of conviction
(e) Spirit of service

Answer:

(a) Transparency: It implies **openness of the decision-making process** and freedom of information to the members and the media. The people have the right to know how decisions are made and what effect it has on beneficiaries, i.e., work procedure and objectives accomplished.

The relevance it has in public service is as follows:

- It helps in merit-based appointment.
- It helps in curbing corruption.
- It maintains public trust in government.
- It encourages public participation in governance.
- Better utilisation of public funds.

(b) **Accountability:** Holders of public office are accountable for their decisions and actions to the public and must submit themselves to whatever scrutiny is appropriate to their office. It means answerability.

The relevance in public service is as follows:

- It helps achieve ethical standards in governance system.
- Civil servants made accountable for their commissions and omissions.
- This helps to curb corruption and misuse of power.

(c) **Fairness and Justice:** It is similar treatment to people when placed in similar situation. It means absence of any privileges or differentiation based on caste, religion or economic status.

The relevance in public services is as follows:

- Positive discrimination and reservation for weaker sections.
- Instrument of good and ethical governance.
- Bring empathy and compassion in public service delivery.
- Better implementation of Social Welfare measures.
- Inclusive development of nation.

(d) **Courage of Conviction:** It is doing action without fear. It is conviction of upholding justice and virtues at all situations. It is having firm belief that the moral values cannot be compromised.

Its relevance in public service is as follows:

- Whistleblowing of any wrongdoing in public service delivery.
- Holding firm to values despite having discretion to spend public funds and better utilisation of funds.
- Conviction to work in adverse situation and remote locations. For example, CRPF working in Naxalite areas.
- Prevents corruption
- Courage to maintain integrity despite political pressure.

(e) **Spirit of Service:** It is working towards efficient public service delivery such that the good governance reaches the last mile to the last person. It is keeping aside the self-interest and working selflessly in public interest.

Its relevance in public service is as follows:

- Good governance
- Working selflessly for the underprivileged.
- Efforts to reduce inequality
- Better implementation of schemes

Question 3. Young people with ethical conduct are not willing to come forward to join active politics. Suggest steps to motivate them to come forward. (150 Words, 10)

Answer: To bring about change in the system, one must be the part of the system. Politics provides an excellent opportunity to get involved in identifying problems and provide a sustainable and constructive solution to such problems.

The youth are not willing to join the politics because of problems like criminalisation of politics, money power and corruption, nepotism and perception of politics as dirty game instead of public service.

Some of the ways to motivate young people to make them come forward and join politics are following:

1. There must be effort to bring about behavioural change by projecting people, like Jawaharlal Nehru, Sardar Patel, Dr. Bhimrao Ramji Ambedkar, who acted as beacons of public service delivery.
2. The Youth must be motivated to take politics as career and must be involved in Youth Parliament, PRIs models in schools and colleges, clean election in colleges, etc. such that they may take to politics at national level.
3. Nelson Mandela and Mahatma Gandhi have shown the path how the system can be cleaned and problems of people addressed when one takes to politics. Their autobiographies may be taught to build a mind-set of how a single person can change the course of nation.
4. Media and social media can be used to motivate people to take to politics and make them aware of situation, and initiate them to take action.
5. Create platform to bring together the like-minded people to initiate a party which upholds values and public service as integral to the politics.
6. NGOs can help in motivating people at lowest level to take part in election of PRIs and ULBs.

These efforts will help in bringing the youth to politics. **Plato rightly says that the only price that people pay by not joining the politics is to get ruled by their inferiors.**

Gandhiji said, "Be the change you wish to see in the world." So the youth must come forward to bring about change in the system and help build India into a thriving democracy.

Question 4 (a). One of the tests of integrity is complete refusal to be compromised. Explain with reference to a real life example. ***(150 Words, 10)***

Answer: Integrity means adopting similar standards or principles in similar situations across time and parties. It is personal sense of wholeness coming from honesty and consistent uprightness of character.

The test of integrity comes when a person in placed in such situation where he is put under pressure or is at loss of personal comfort, but he declines to compromise with his values and virtues.

For example, Mr. Ashok Khemka has been transferred for 51 times to different departments and locations but has refused to come under political pressure to compromise his integrity. He exposes corruption and wrong doings that has harmed public service delivery in each department he is transferred. His resolve to bring about good governance helps us learn that whatever the situation may be one cannot compromise with the moral values of public welfare that one holds.

We also see this in lives of great leaders. For example, Mahatma Gandhi even after the provocative Jalianwala Bagh tragedy where many people were fired upon and killed, upheld peace and non-violence as the solution to achieve independence despite many Indians suggesting the path of revolutionary overthrow of British.

In personal life, I worked as an Asst. Engineer with a reputed company as Quality Analyst. In my survey of the road I found poor quality material used which was not as per the standard. I was offered bribe by contractor and calls from superior to show the quality as good and not report it. Despite this, I presented a detailed report to the NHAI about the poor quality. The NHAI cancelled the contract of the company showing negligence and awarded the contract to different contactor.

The idea is that integrity cannot be compromised at any cost. It is rightly said that if your values are right, you would not face any dilemma in decision-making.

Question 4 (b). Corporate social responsibility makes companies more profitable and sustainable. Analyse. ***(150 Words, 10)***

Answer: Corporate Social responsibility is based on idea of giving back to the society. It is in the idea of trusteeship theory where one is not the owner of resources but the trustee and must utilise it for public welfare.

It is two-way process of benefitting both the society and the company. It brings benefit to society in form of CSR in education, health, poverty alleviation, green development, renewable energy, etc. which in turn builds a good name for the company itself.

It makes companies more profitable and sustainable in following ways:

1. It builds a brand value of the company. For example, the hospital and schools opened by TATA that have helped build and save many lives have made it a home name in India.
2. It benefits all the stakeholders' right from individual, employees and their family and builds up a social capital for the company.
3. It creates more public trust of the company and in turn builds its consumer base and increases its profit.
4. CSR also includes training of individual, which creates better skill in individual and a pool of efficient employee who may benefit company in the long run.
5. It builds human capital by education and health and better loyalty of the employee to the company and hence growth.
6. The CSR also includes environment protection. A good environment will produce better standard of living and conducive condition to set up industry in such area.
7. There will be less protests by the employees, and better satisfaction will lead to higher work efficiency and more profit to company.

Thus, CSR makes companies more profitable and sustainable.

Question 5 (a). "Great ambition is the passion of a great character. Those endowed with it may perform very good or very bad acts. All depends on the principles which direct them." – Napoleon Bonaparte.

Stating examples mention the rulers (i) who have harmed society and country, and (ii) who worked for the development of society and country. ***(150 Words, 10)***

Answer: Ambition is one of the prerequisites of success. It is the virtue which enables men to aspire and dream big and helps them achieve their goals. Great people have usually been seen to be ambitious as it helps them stay motivated and confident. Ambition adds purpose to their life and helps them work hard towards their desired goals.

But sometimes being ambitious makes them obsessed towards their goals and success, and this might make them choose the wrong path. As such which path he chooses depends on the character of the person and values inculcated by him/her over a period of time.

Man builds up his principles and value systems during his lifetime based on his experiences and socialisation. These principles guide them to choose the right path in future.

For example, territorial ambitions of rulers like Genghis Khan and Alexander the great were followed by bloodshed in each of their expeditions. Autocratic rulers like Adolf Hitler had visions and big plans for Germany to see it as a prosperous and great state. But in his desire to rule Germany, he became a tyrant and dictator and led to killing of thousands of people, especially Jews during holocaust. His ideas of racial cleansing were unjust ways of making Germany great. He waged a war which engulfed people across the world and led to huge suffering even after the world war.

Dictators like Mussolini in Italy and Saddam Hussein in Iraq too massacred anyone who came in their way of rule.

On the other hand, rulers like Akbar worked for development and welfare of his people. He is seen as a tolerant ruler who advocated for peace and harmony among religions. The most important attribute of Akbar was his liberal religious views. Though he was a Muslim, he never let religion become a part of his jurisdiction.

Leaders like Mahatma Gandhi helped India to attain freedom and establish democracy, apart from promoting welfare of general masses and eradicating social evils.

Nelson Mandela fought apartheid and injustice to gift South Africa with equality and democracy.

Question 5 (b). "If a country is to be corruption free and become a nation of beautiful minds, I strongly feel there are three key societal members who can make a difference. They are father, the mother and the teacher." – A. P. J. Abdul Kalam. Analyse.

(150 Words, 10)

Answer: Parents and teachers are the first sphere which a child encounters while growing up. They have the maximum impact in shaping the values of a child as they get to spend maximum time with a child and are in a contact with him in his initial years, when his thoughts and attitudes starts forming.

Thus, they have the maximum impact in shaping a child.

Role of Father

A child considers his father as a role model. He usually follows his father and observes his behaviour. For a growing child his father's behaviour is the ideal behaviour. Qualities of father, like discipline, punctuality, honesty, are gradually imbibed in his children.

For example, if father respects women, child will also start to respect women. Whereas if a child sees domestic violence there are chances that he will perceive women as weak in future.

If a child is familiar that his father brings corruption money home, he might get adapted to the fact that it is alright to be a part of the corrupt system.

Role of Mother

A mother is referred to as the first teacher and guide for a child. Children are most familiar and close to their mothers. She teaches him love, care, emotional intelligence, empathy and compassion .She provides the moral support needed to an individual. It is often the mother who guides our perception of what is right and wrong. Her teachings through stories, daily conversations become the base of values of a person.

For example, Mother has a great impact on the way an individual behaves in a family or society. She scolds his child if he rudely behaves with his friends.

She influences our religious beliefs, cleanliness habits. If mother rewards child for stealing, child might continue it in future.

Role of Teacher

Outside home, teacher has the maximum influence on him. For a young kid, a teacher is a person who knows everything. A teacher shares the wisdom he acquired through his experiences of life. Whenever we hear about great leaders and achievers, we also hear about their teachers like Aristotle and Alexander, Kautilya and Chandragupta.

For example, Teachers are the ones who constantly observe the growth and behaviour of children, monitors his company and tendencies. A check at an early stage helps in improving a child's conduct.

Teachers are the prime motivators of an individual and encourage them to take up the right path to be successful in life.

Teacher teaches us in school that discipline and hard work will get us good grades, and being lazy will only harm us. We apply this lesson in all our life afterwards.

Thus, mother, father and teacher play a great role in building and transforming a child's conduct in society.

Question 6 (a). How will you apply emotional intelligence in administrative practices?

(150 Words, 10)

Answer: Emotional intelligence according to Goleman is "Capacity for recognising our own feelings and those of others, for motivating ourselves and for managing emotions well in ourselves and in our relationships."

Emotional intelligence has five components of self-awareness, self-motivation, self-regulation, empathy and handling relationship with patience, harmony, tactfulness and agreeableness.

Emotional intelligence can be applied in administrative practises in following ways:

1. **Focus on Resocialisation:** It is a restructuring exercise which helps recognise the fault and substitute it with the right component. It is by feedback mechanism from public

participation and awareness generation. For example, the social audit has helped curb corruption in MGNREGA.

2. **Role-Playing and Active Participation:** The public servant understands the local problem and takes genuine efforts to solve them. For example, in Manipur, the District Collector Armstrong Palme realised the inappropriate connectivity and lack of roads that lead to huge economic loss and wastage of agricultural perishable projects and took to public funding and local labour to build the entire road. This has changed the economy of area and restored people's trust in government.
3. **Training of Civil Servants:** The civil servant must be trained in communication skill whereby he connects to the people to understand their problem and take efforts to solve them with best available resources.
4. Emotional intelligence will help increase the capacity to handle work pressure and conflicts within self. It helps to bounce back from the problems and setbacks and helps them handle properly.
5. Emotional intelligence will help us take the leadership role and become the catalyst of change.
6. It will help build a better work environment and better relation between the people and the administration.
7. It will increase social capital by building trust in governance, mutual respect and higher participation in people in administration. This can be achieved by associating locals in administration and implementation of schemes.
8. Political pressure can also be handled by emotional intelligence, whereby it helps in maintaining integrity for public welfare.
9. Work-family conflict can be reduced by using emotional intelligence by giving time for both and handling relationship.

Thus, the emotional intelligence holds key to good governance where a sustainable relation is built between people and the government.

Question 6 (b). Strength, peace and security are considered to be the pillars of international relations. Elucidate. ***(150 Words, 10)***

Answer: In the international arena, there is no single power to maintain world order, and it has to be based on strength, peace and security of all the members.

The early chaos has been due to the continuous wars including the world war that led to massive loss to human and civilisations. However, with changing times the threat is from both the state and non-state actors.

North Korea has posed nuclear threat to the neighbouring countries and threatened peace in the region.

Terrorism is another major threat in the region. The growth of Al-Qaeda and ISIS and the violence due to intolerance in religion has led to problems of international relation. India and Pakistan suffers from relationship and trust crisis on issue of state-led terrorism.

In this background we understand the importance of strength, peace and security as pillars of International relations.

The idea of creating a common group of nation to fight terrorism of ISIS and the UNSC taking the role to foster relation between opposing powers like USA and Russia shows how important security dimension has become for relation between nations.

With Great Power Comes Great Responsibility: China in the South China Sea has created problems where it has denied rights of other nations. But this needs to change. It must, being a great power, respect the rights of other smaller nation and create good will to bring peace and prosperity of all in the region.

The countries with higher economic strength taking the role for environment protection in Paris summit and also ensuring the peace and security around the world have defined international relation between nations.

In India, the idea of Vasudev Kutumbakam shows that India sees entire world as single home of citizens and promotes peace and tolerance among all.

The religious tolerance and protection of minorities are also evident from the teachings and philosophies of great leaders like Swami Vivekananda who said that all religions equally promote peace and harmony and love for fellow beings.

Question 7 (a). The crisis of ethical values in modern times is traced to a narrow perception of the good life. Discuss. ***(150 Words, 10)***

Answer: In the present-day world, there is a very shallow concept of what is regarded as a good life. We have started emphasizing more on materialistic things acquired as a measure of prosperity. This can be partly attributed to consumerism influenced by globalisation. Today's notion of good life is flawed due to wrong parameters by which we measure our happiness and success. This behaviour causes us crises and conflicts of ethics values in long run.

Priority of material over values: While measuring success or happiness of an individual, we always give more priority to money, property, likeability and power over the goodwill and strength of character. A person with more wealth will be perceived to be more successful and happy than a person with good character.

Materialistic ambition of more cars, homes, more gadgets, etc. leads to preference given to greed over need.

Preference to Shortcuts: People want instantaneous success. They are not ready to be patient. This sometimes diverts them to wrong practices.

For example, a good life today is measured by a good job or a good designation/ promotions, sometimes lead to lack integrity and honesty when take shortcut measures for the above.

For example, Instead, for working for long hours in offices some prefer to earn money by gambling, crime, etc.

Tolstoy once said that "True happiness is pleasure without repentance."

A materialistic interpretation of happiness and good life might bring happiness for a short time, but it will cause depression and misery in the long run. At some point of time, it will lead to internal conflicts and crisis. For example, a corrupt person might earn a lot of money and manage to arrange a comfortable life for his family, but will lose goodwill and reputation in his organisation. He will be seen as a corrupt man and will lose respect in society and in front of his children. Also, he will be at a constant risk of getting caught which will degrade his mental peace.

Question 7 (b). Increased national wealth did not result in equitable distribution of its benefits. It has created only some "enclaves of modernity and prosperity for a small minority at the cost of the majority." Justify. ***(150 Words, 10)***

Answer: India was a poor country at the time of independence, but recent decades have seen rapid growth in the nation's wealth, especially after LPG reforms. Our leaders assumed that this growth in the nation's wealth will trickle down to the lowermost level and uplift the masses from poverty. But it failed to deliver, and today the result is abject inequality, India is facing.

Growth coupled with poor redistribution had led to creation of islands of prosperity in a sea of poverty. The inequality is evident, as 59% of the total wealth in India is owned by just 1–2% of the people. While we have become the third largest economy (in PPP terms), we also continue to have the largest number of poor and malnourished population. Two hundred seventy million people are under abject poverty, 100 million homeless, and 38% of the children stunted and underweight.

The traditional classes like moneylenders and proprietor prospered, and after the independence, their influence in governance continued, as evident from the failure of the land reform movements, bonded labour, etc. Also the politician-criminal-businessman class prospered during license raj, and money was made from money by those who had it.

This brings us to a situation where we see development made at the cost of majority who are poor and devoid of basic amenities, whereas its fruits are enjoyed by a handful of rich influential class. This is evident through the stark difference of landscape we see when we look out of the window of a five star hotel and find nothing but slums, where people are living in inhuman conditions.

We see large dams built and their water going through pipes to cities where it meets wastage at multiple levels, whereas a tribal whose land was acquired for the construction of the same dam walks mile to get just drinking water.

In a country with high malnutrition, food wastage and consumerism are rampant.

The growing inequality can be attributed to various reasons ranging from non-inclusiveness, lack of willpower and commitment of political and bureaucratic class, apathy and negligence towards poor.

The constitution of India under DPSP (Article 39b and 39c) clearly mentions the need for State to check "that the ownership of resources and control of means of production are distributed equitably and are not concentrated in hands of few." In India where our Constitution explicitly declares our socialist goals, such stark difference in economic and social status of people is unwelcome and needs to be tackled.

Question 8 (a). Discipline generally implies following the order and subordination. However, it may be counter-productive for the organisation. Discuss. (150 Words, 10)

Answer: Discipline is required to regulate human behaviour to maintain order in an organisation, family or society. Since it is the practice of training people to obey rules or a code of behaviour, using punishment to correct disobedience is perceived to be an act of following order and subordination. Usually, discipline is regarded as a virtue and considered essential for smooth functioning of an organisation. It helps people to be formal, punctual and efficient, and promotes favourable work culture in an organisation. It ensures hierarchy in the organisation and allows seniors to have respects among subordinates.

For example, discipline is one of the pillars of Army, and it has led to the success of the institution.

Disciplined approach of E Sreedharan has led to the timely completion of Metro projects in the country.

But too much strict disciplinary norms may affect the productivity of an organisation. It can prove detrimental in the following ways:

1. Discipline may lead to too much strict behaviour of seniors with subordinates, which may demoralise the later and may affect the organisation's welfare adversely.
2. Sometimes in an organisation, maintaining discipline becomes priority, and public welfare takes a back seat due to rigidity of procedures.
3. Discipline sometimes creates distance between the head and subordinates, and it may lead the later suppress his ideas and not present before the former.
4. Strict norms of discipline is sometimes tyrannical, might lead to following of unjust orders.
5. Discipline may be counter-productive to innovative ideas, creativity and expression of one's views which may keep the organisation aloof from the benefits of diversified ideas. It might lead to failure of an individual to question the status quo and thus promote mediocrity in procedures.
6. Overemphasis on discipline sometimes results in protest and revolt, and also hinders productivity of the organisation.
7. The fear of disciplinary action may lead to lackadaisical approach of officials.

Thus, there is a need to optimise discipline such that it serves the purpose of enhancing work culture without affecting its productivity.

Question 8 (b). Without commonly shared and widely entrenched moral values and obligations, neither the law, nor democratic government, nor even the market economy will function properly.

What do you understand by this statement? Explain with illustration in the contemporary times.

(150 Words, 10)

Answer: We understand the importance of moral values and obligations when it comes to maintaining order in society. Morals, values, rights and obligations are derived from collective conscience of the citizens so that smooth functioning of the society and its institutions are maintained. Without them none of the institutions made up in society can smoothly function.

Laws are rules that bind all people living in a community. **Laws** protect our general safety and ensure our rights as citizens against abuses by other people, by organizations, and by the government itself. They place everybody on equal footing and ensure fair conduct, thus maintaining social structure. But in the absence of values in individuals, laws might prove ineffective. For example, state machinery or the criminal justice system will not prove sufficient if everybody starts violating law. It is the moral values and obligations of individuals towards the society, which make them accountable to it and prevent crime or violation of laws. In addition, in the absence of morals, one may find loopholes in the present legal system to commit crime.

When we talk about democratic government, we mean a system of governance where people make decisions for themselves directly or through their representatives. Absence of values gives rise to criminalisation of politics, autocracy, nepotism, lobbyism, etc. A politician may succumb to his private interests in absence of values and side-line the very cause of his representation. Politicians fuelling communal hatred, giving hate speeches can be seen as manifestation of lack of values.

Similarly, lack of values in market economy leads to issues in corporate governance, unfair practices of trade, hoarding and black marketing, predatory pricing, surrogate advertising, etc. Somewhere failure of market economy to tackle inequality can be attributed to lack of value system. Recent scams like Satyam scam and Saradha chit fund scam are examples.

Thus without commonly shared and widely entrenched moral values and obligations, neither the law, nor democratic government, nor even the market economy will function properly.

Question 9. You are an honest and responsible civil servant. You often observe the following:

(a) There is a general perception that adhering to ethical conduct one may face difficulties to oneself and cause problems for the family, whereas unfair practices may help to reach the career goals.

(b) When the number of people adopting unfair means is large, a small minority having a penchant towards ethical means makes no difference.

(c) Sticking to ethical means is detrimental to the larger developmental goals.

(d) While one may not involve oneself in large unethical practices, but giving and accepting small gifts makes the system more efficient.

Examine the above statements with their merits and demerits. ***(250 Words, 20)***

Answer:

(a) Merits of the Statement

1. It may help to reach career goal and easy promotions.
2. It will help avoid difficulties of transfer to oneself and family.

Demerits of the Statement

1. Dedication to the public service is the value to be upheld by the public servant.
2. Transfers are part and parcel of service and must be seen as opportunity to work in different departments and areas. For example, Mr. Ashok Khemka has been

transferred 51 times in 24 years of his service. He believes it's a part of job and his integrity to public service cannot be compromised.

3. In the long-term unethical practises will definitely get caught and the short-term gains will perish. So, one must work ethically which has long-term sustenance.
4. Ethical practise will not lead to conflict between values and action and no crisis of conscience will be created. Thus, moral attitude will be upheld.
5. Fair practises will also achieve career goals. Also, there is a sense of satisfaction to have served a large number of people.

(b) Merits of the Statement

1. Ease of working in the path where a majority of people work.
2. Will not be isolated in the system.
3. No problem associated with whistle blowing.

Demerits of the Statement

1. My path of action should be correct even though the majority is in wrong path. Gandhiji has shown a path when he says to walk alone in path of truth and justice even when everyone is against you.
2. Since most of people are dishonest, it is more essential for me to be honest as I may act as the guiding light to the ones who does not want to be dishonest.
3. My honesty may help in exposing dishonesty and bring about systemic reforms which will create an ethical system.
4. Small minority has always led to revolution against tyranny, against ill practises of discrimination, etc. For example, Martin Luther King Jr. opposed the racial discrimination and led the movement and so did Nelson Mandela against white dominance against black.
5. Journey of the thousand miles starts with a single step.

(c) Merits of the Statement

1. This may help in achieving higher economic progress in short-run.
2. People may benefit from development.

Demerits of the Statement

1. Development without ethics will be unsustainable in the long run. For example, if development projects are cleared without taking environmental concerns then it may bring more harm than benefit.
2. Though there may be economic benefit in the short run, but even then the development will not be inclusive and may not reach to large sections of people. It will create problems of inequality.
3. Development with ethics will bring social equity, inclusive growth, public participation and overall development.

(d) Merits of the Statement

1. Small gifts may act as incentive for him to work more.
2. It does not affect his values at large.

Demerits of the Statement

1. Wrong deeds cannot be justified based on value. If accepting and giving gifts is wrong and not permitted, it cannot be justified on size or its value.
2. It will set a wrong precedence and may justify corruption which is ethically, legally and morally wrong.
3. The gifts can be given by the rich whose work will be done while the poor who cannot give gifts may be neglected. This is against the idea of inclusive development and effective public service delivery.

Question 10. You are aspiring to become an IAS officer and you have cleared various stages and now you have been selected for the personal interview. On the day of the interview, on the way to the venue you saw an accident where a mother and child who happen to be your relatives were badly injured. They needed immediate help. What would you have done in such a situation? Justify your action. ***(250 Words, 20)***

Answer: The **stakeholders** of the case are: Myself, my relatives who have met accident, UPSC and society.

The **facts** of the case are:

- I have been called for the interview.
- Saw accident where the lives of mother and child are in danger and need immediate help.

The **ethical dilemma** is between my professional goal of becoming IAS officer and empathy and compassion of saving the life of a relative who have met an accident.

I would have taken the following steps in such a situation:

1. Immediately go to the spot to analyse the situation and call for an ambulance from the nearest hospital.
2. I would provide for preliminary first aid and make them stable.
3. I would call police and relatives' family to come for support. I would also call UPSC to apprise them of the situation and seek suggestions.
4. Local people who are nearby will be asked for support to take the person to hospital.
5. When the relatives are admitted to hospital, I would go for my interview.

The justifications of the steps are:

1. Life of the person is more important than anything else.
2. Being a future civil servant I must help the person who is in immediate need.
3. I will inform police as it is case of accident and the relatives so that they may come to hospital and
4. Will call UPSC because any plea of getting late and reschedule of interview can be sought.
5. Local help for reaching the relative to hospital immediately so that their lives are saved.

Thus, to become a good civil servant, I need to be a good human being and serve the people who need my help and support.

Question 11. You are the head of the Human Resources Department of an organisation. One day, one of the workers died on duty. His family was demanding compensation.

However, the company denied compensation because it was revealed in investigation that he was drunk at the time of the accident. The workers of the company went on strike demanding compensation for the family of the deceased. The chairman of the management board has asked for your recommendation.
What recommendation would you provide the management?
Discuss the merits and demerits of each of the recommendations. *(250 Words, 20)*

Answer: The stakeholders of the case are:

- The worker's family
- Organisation
- Workers of the company

The facts of the case are:

- The worker died on duty and his family is demanding compensation.
- The worker was drunk on duty at the time of the accident and so the company has denied compensation.
- Workers went on strike demanding compensation for the family.

The recommendations and their merits and demerits are:

(a) Compensation Should Be Given

Merits

1. Worker was the part of the company and family must be compensated. This will build the trust of workers on the company. Also, family of deceased will be helped.
2. This will end the strike and functioning of company may be started.

Demerits

1. It will set a wrong precedence that workers even with their mistake and not due to some mishap is compensated.
2. The workers will strike and get their demands met.

(b) Compensation is not given

Merits

1. The company will show no tolerance towards unethical behaviour.
2. The law will take its course and facts will be revealed in investigation.

Demerits

1. The victim's family will suffer as they lost their man and also a working hand.
2. The company might seem to be non-concerned about worker's welfare.
3. The strike will disrupt its functioning.

(c) Alternative methods to help the family

Merits

1. The help to family may be through employment or welfare fund as voluntary contribution and not as compensation.
2. The strike may end and functioning may begin.

My recommendations will be based on the following:
1. I will investigate the matter and prepare a report on lapses on part of the worker and the company.
2. I will find why the person was drunk. Whether due to behaviour or due to work stress and seek occurrence of such behaviour in other workers also.

My recommendations will be:
1. To provide alternative help to family immediately in form of employment or monetary help.
2. Compensation in case there are lapses on the part of company in not ensuring that drunken person is allowed to work.
3. Measures to be taken and technology installed such that a drunken person is not allowed to work.
4. Work stress of workers and ways to address them.

Question 12. You are the manager of a spare parts company A and you have to negotiate a deal with the manager of a large manufacturing company B. The deal is highly competitive and sealing the deal is critical for your company. The deal is being worked out over a dinner. After dinner the manager of manufacturing company B offered to drop you to the hotel in his car. On the way to hotel, he happens to hit motorcycle injuring the motorcyclist badly. You know the manager was driving fast and thus lost control. The law enforcement officer comes to investigate the issue and you are the sole eyewitness to it. Knowing the strict laws pertaining to road accidents you are aware that your honest account of the incident would lead to the prosecution of the manager and as a consequence the deal is likely to be jeopardised, which is of immense importance to your company.

What are the dilemmas you face? What will be your response to the situation?

(250 Words, 20)

Answer: The stakeholders of the case are:
- Me as manager of the spare parts company
- The manager of a large manufacturing company who is accused
- Motorcyclist who is injured badly
- Police and society
- My organisation

The dilemmas faced are:
1. **Professional benefits vs. Justice:** To get the deal for my organisation or to provide justice to the individual.
2. **Personal Conscience vs. Organisational Benefit:** My duty towards society and values of justice as against the benefits of the organisation to get the deal.
3. **Organisational Interest vs. Societal Interest:** The values of organisation towards society or profit making
4. **Values of Individual**: Justice, value of life, upholding the law, compassion.

My response to situation will be: **I will become witness to the case** because:

1. Innocent person has been injured because of rash driving and he must get justice. So, it is my responsibility as civic duty to help the person in crisis.
2. It would uphold the law and order of the system. It should not be tweaked for personal benefits.
3. The accused was driving rash and must be punished for his deed. If left unpunished, he may again violate law.
4. From point of view of organisation, my organisational value of standing by the truth in crisis situation may come in question if I don't help the victim. It is in interest of the ethical principles that my company follows.
5. Even my response may not affect the deal as it is in economic interest of both.

My moral values of justice and upholding law in all circumstance will be practised in this and every other such situation and it cannot be compromised for self-interest or economic gains.

Question 13. A building permitted for three floors, while being extended illegally to 6 floors by a builder, collapses. As a consequence, a number of innocent labourers including women and children died. These labourers are migrants of different places. The government immediately announced cash relief to the aggrieved families and arrested the builder. Give reasons for such incidents taking place across the country. Suggest measures to prevent their occurrence. (250 Words, 20)

Answer: The following are the reasons for such incidents taking place in the country:

1. Greed to earn more profit by the builders leads to illegal construction.
2. Poor and multiple laws related to construction of buildings.
3. Poor implementation of laws and poor public service by officials to avoid such situation. Apathy on parts of officials.
4. Collusive corruption and nexus between builders and government officials in tweaking rules for profit.
5. Safety measures not taken and rules not followed.
6. Quality of material may be poor and checks may not have been done.
7. The lack of awareness among the buyers of illegal construction and norms relating to it.
8. Lack of planned urbanisation and lack of housing also leads to buying of illegal constructions.

The following measures can be taken to prevent such occurrence:

IMMEDIATE STEPS

1. The builders of such buildings with illegal construction must be caught and punished under law.
2. People living in such construction must be evacuated and compensated by the builders for the danger to their lives.
3. Proper investigation for accountability must be fixed and crony capitalism and corruption is exposed.

LONG-TERM STEPS

1. Proper laws must be made and multiple rules and laws must be converged. E.g. Real Estate Regulation Act, 2016.
2. Effective implementation of laws must be ensured by quality checks, integrity pacts, preventing any construction not allowed by law.
3. Corruption must be checked by putting projects in public domain and opening grievance redressal cells.
4. Online complaint mechanism must be set up and public awareness must be done for reporting of illegal construction.
5. Proper mechanism to prevent forced labour for migrant workers and humane condition of work must be ensured for them.
6. Long-term urban planning must be done so that Housing for All can be provided within the ambit of law.

Question 14. You are a Public Information Officer (PIO) in a government department. You are aware that the RTI Act 2005 envisages transparency and accountability in administration. The act has functioned as a check on the supposedly arbitrarily administrative behaviour and actions. However, as a PIO you have observed that there are citizens who filed RTI applications not for themselves but on behalf of such stakeholders who purportedly want to have access to information to further their own interests. At the same time there are these RTI activists who routinely file RTI applications and attempt to extort money from the decision makers. This type of RTI activism has affected the functioning of the administration adversely and also possibly jeopardises the genuineness of the applications which are essentially aimed at getting justice.

What measures would you suggest to separate genuine and non-genuine applications? Give merits and demerits of your suggestions. (250 Words, 20)

Answer: The Right to Know is the fundamental right of any citizen and must not be denied. Everyone has the right to seek information and question the wisdom of decision making. It brings more public participation in governance and feedback helps in framing better laws and effective implementation of existing ones.

Following are the options available:

(a) Denial of the information to third party

Merits

1. Frivolous applications will be rejected.
2. Only the rightful use of RTI is made
3. Problem of extortion solved.

Demerits

1. It is against the spirit of RTI, which seeks to provide information to all.
2. The illiterate may not be able to seek information who had earlier option to take help of third party.

(b) Reasons can be sought along with information and details of applicant

Merits

1. Only for genuine reasons, the information may be provided.
2. Person can be held responsible for misuse of information.

Demerits

1. Person may not furnish the correct reason.
2. Extortion problem unresolved.
3. Against the rule of RTI to provide proactive information.

(c) Fast track records of applicants

Merits

1. The frivolous seekers will be denied information.
2. Only genuine cases will be addressed.

Demerits

1. The right to seek information denied.
2. Third party may be used to seek information in his place.

The steps taken by me are the following:

1. I would use technology and data of previous applicants to see who misuses the data and deny them information.
2. Anyone seeking extortion will be handed over to police as it is punishable under law.
3. I will make efforts to make disclosure of maximum information on public domain.
4. The function of the organisation will be made transparent and open such that events leading to seeking extortion does not arise at first instance.

Topic: Ethics and Human Interface (essence, determinants, consequences of ethics in human actions); Dimensions of ethics; Ethics in public & private relationships

- Explain how ethics contributes to social and human well-being. **(2016)**
- Law and ethics are considered to be the two tools for controlling human conduct so as to make it conducive to civilized social existence. (a) Discuss how they achieve this objective. (b) Giving examples, show how the two differ in their approaches. **(2016)**
- What is meant by 'environmental ethics'? Why is it important to study? Discuss any one environmental issue from the viewpoint of environmental ethics. **(2015)**
- Differentiate between the following (200 words); a) Law and Ethics; b) Ethical management and Management of ethics; c) Discrimination and Preferential treatment; d) Personal ethics and Professional ethics **(2015)**
- Human beings should always be treated as 'ends' in themselves and never as merely `means'. Explain the meaning and significance of this statement, giving its implications in the modern techno-economic society. **(2014)**
- What do you understand by 'values' and 'ethics'? In what way is it important to be ethical along with being professionally competent? **(2013)**

- Some people feel that values keep changing with time and situation, while others strongly believe that there are certain universal and eternal human values. Give your perception in this regard with due justification. **(2013)**

Emotional Intelligence & Allied Topics

Syllabus Topic: Emotional Intelligence (concepts, utility & application in administration & governance)

- Anger is a harmful negative emotion. It is injurious to both personal life and work life. (a) Discuss how it leads to negative emotions and undesirable behaviours. (b) How can it be managed and controlled? **(2016)**
- All human beings aspire for happiness. Do you agree? What does happiness mean to you? Explain with examples. **(2014)**
- What is 'emotional intelligence' and how can it be developed in people? How does it help an individual in taking ethical decisions? **(2013)**
- What do you understand by the term 'voice of conscience'? How do you prepare yourself to heed to the voice of conscience? **(2013)**
- What is meant by 'crisis of conscience'? Narrate one incident in your life when you were faced with such a crisis and how you resolved the same. **(2013)**

Thinkers and Reformers

Syllabus Topic: Contributions of Moral Thinkers & Philosophers from India and world; human value lessons from great leaders, reformers & administrators

- Discuss Mahatma Gandhi's concept of seven sins. **(2016)**
- Analyze John Rawls's concept of social justice in the Indian context. **(2016)**
- Corruption causes misuse of government treasury, Administrative inefficiency and obstruction in the path of national Development. Discuss Kautilya's views. **(2016)**
- Max Weber said that it is not wise to apply to public administration the sort of moral and ethical norms we apply to matters of personal conscience. It is important to realize that the State bureaucracy might possess its own independent bureaucratic morality. Critically analyze this statement. **(2016)**
- "The weak can never forgive; forgiveness is the attribute of the strong." **(2015)**
- We can easily forgive a child who is afraid of the dark; the real tragedy of life is when men are afraid of the light. **(2015)**
- Which eminent personality has inspired you the most in the context of ethical conduct in life? Give the gist of his/her teachings giving specific examples. Describe how you have been able to apply these teachings for your own ethical development. **(2014)**
- There is enough on this earth for every one's need but for no one's greed. —Mahatma Gandhi. **(2013)**
- Nearly all men can withstand adversity, but if you want to test a man's character, give him power—Abraham Lincoln **(2013)**
- I count him braver who overcomes his desires than him who overcomes his enemies. —Aristotle **(2013)**

Attitude

Syllabus Topic: Attitude (content, structure, function, influence & relation with thought & behaviour); Moral and Political Attitudes

- In the context of defense services, 'patriotism' demands readiness to even lay down one's life in protecting the nation. According to you, what does patriotism imply in everyday civil life? Explain with illustrations and justify your answer. **(2014)**
- It is often said that 'politics' and 'ethics' do not go together. What is your opinion in this regard? Justify your answer with illustrations. **(2013)**

Family, Society

Syllabus Topic: Role of family, society, educational institutions in inculcating values

- Our attitudes towards life, work, other people and society are generally shaped unconsciously by the family and social surroundings in which we grow up. Some of these unconsciously acquired attitudes and values are often undesirable in the citizens of modern democratic and egalitarian society. (a) Discuss such undesirable values prevalent in today's educated Indians. (b) How can such undesirable attitudes be changed and socio-ethical values be cultivated in the aspiring and serving civil servants? **(2016)**
- Social values are more important than economic values. Discuss the above statement with examples in the context of inclusive growth of a nation. **(2015)**
- The current society is plagued with widespread trust-deficit. What are the consequences of this situation for personal well-being and for societal well-being? What can you do at the personal level to make yourself trustworthy? **(2014)**
- What factors affect the formation of a person's attitude towards social problems? In our society, contrasting attitudes are prevalent about many social problems. What contrasting attitudes do you notice about the caste system in our society? How do you explain the existence of these contrasting attitudes? **(2014)**
- We are witnessing increasing instances of sexual violence against women in the country. Despite existing legal provisions against it, the number of such incidences is on the rise. Suggest some innovative measures to tackle this menace. **(2014)**

Society Attitude Case Study: Promoting Girl education while ensuring their safety (2015)

You are recently posted as district development officer of a district. Shortly thereafter you found that there is considerable tension in the rural areas of your district on the issue of sending girls to schools.

The elders of the village feel that many problems have come up because girls are being educated and they are stepping out of the safe environment of the household. They are of the view that the girls should be quickly married off with minimum education. The girls are also competing for jobs after education, which have traditionally remained in boys' exclusive domain, adding to unemployment amongst male population.

The younger generation feels that in the present era, girls should have equal opportunities for education and employment, and other means of livelihood. The entire locality is divided between the elders and the younger lot and further sub-divided between sexes in both generations. You come to know that in Panchayat or in other local bodies or even in busy crossroads, the issue is being acrimoniously debated.

One day you are informed that an unpleasant incident has taken place. Some girls were molested, when they were en route to schools. The incident led to clashes between several groups and a law and order problem has arisen. The elders after heated discussion have taken a joint decision not to allow girls to go to school and to socially boycott all such families, which do not follow their dictate.

- What steps would you take to ensure girls' safety without disrupting their education?
- How would you manage and mould matriarchic attitude of the village elders to ensure harmony in the inter-generational relations? **(250 words) (25 Marks)**

Family Matter Case Study: Wife-beater Boss: To do something or not? (2016)

You are a young, aspiring and sincere employee in a Government office working as an assistant, to the director of your deportment. Since you've joined recently, you need to learn and progress. Luckily your superior is very kind and ready to train you for your job. He is a very intelligent and well-informed person having knowledge of various departments. In short, you respect your book and are looking forward to learn a lot from him.

Since you've good tuning with the boss, he started depending on you. One day due to ill health he invited you at his place for finishing some urgent work. You reached his house and you heard shouting noises before you could ring the bell. You waited for a while. After entering, boss greeted you and explained the work. But you were constantly disturbed by the crying of a woman. At last, you inquired with the boss but his answer did not satisfy you. Next day, you were compelled to inquire further in the office and found out that his behavior is very had at home with his wife. He also beat up his wife.

His wife is not well educated and is a simple woman in comparison to her husband. You see that though your boss is a nice person in the office, he is engaged in domestic violence at home. In such a situation, you are left with the following options. Analyze each option with its consequences.

- Just ignore thinking about it because it is their personal matter.
- Report the case to the appropriate authority.
- Your own innovative approach towards the situation. **(250 words)**

Social influence

Syllabus Topic: Social Influence and Persuasion

- How could social influence and persuasion contribute to the success of Swatchh Bharat Abhiyan? **(2016)**

Sarkaari Job Values

Syllabus Topic: Civil Service aptitude & foundational values (integrity, impartiality, non-partisanship, objectivity, dedication to public service)

- Why should impartiality and non-partisanship be considered as foundational values in public services, especially in the present day socio-political context? Illustrate your answer with examples. **(2016)**
- Public servants are likely to confront with the issues of 'Conflict of Interest'. What do you understand by the term 'Conflict of Interest' and how does it manifest in the decision making by public servants? If faced with the conflict of interest situation, how would you resolve it? Explain with the help of examples. **(2015)**
- How do the virtues of trustworthiness and fortitude get manifested in public service? Explain with examples. **(2015)**
- A mere compliance with law is not enough, the public servant also has to have a well-developed sensibility to ethical issues for effective discharge of duties." Do you agree? Explain with the help of two examples, where (i) an act is ethically right, but not legally and (ii) an act is legally right, but not ethically. **(2015)**
- Two different kinds of attitudes exhibited by public servants towards their work have been identified as the bureaucratic attitude and the democratic attitude. A) Distinguish between these two terms and write their merits and demerits. B) Is it possible to balance the two to create a better administration for the faster development of our country? **(2015)**
- What does 'accountability' mean in the context of public service? What measures can be adopted to ensure individual and collective accountability of public servants? **(2014)**
- Integrity without knowledge is weak and useless, but knowledge without integrity is dangerous and dreadful. What do you understand by this statement? Explain your stand with illustrations from the modern context. **(2014)**
- There is a heavy ethical responsibility on the public servants because they occupy positions of power, handle huge amounts of public funds, and their decisions have wide-ranging impact on society and environment. What steps have you taken to improve your ethical competence to handle such responsibility? **(2014)**
- What do you understand by the following terms in the context of public service? (5 terms x 3 marks each: a) Integrity b) Perseverance c) Spirit of service d) Commitment e) Courage of conviction f) Personal opinion **(2013)**
- Indicate two more attributes which you consider important for public service. Justify your answer. **(10 marks/100 words) (2013)**

Work Culture at Office

Syllabus Topic: Work Culture

From this topic, case studies are formed instead of theoretical question. These case studies are usually related to sexual harassment, work deadline, Chalta hai mindset, pressure from above, etc.

Case Study: Engineer: Bogus flyover vs. deadline (2013)

You are working as an Executive Engineer in the construction cell of a Municipal Corporation and are presently in-charge of the construction of a flyover. There are two Junior Engineers under you who have the responsibility of day-to-day inspection of the site and are reporting to you, while you are finally reporting to the Chief Engineer who heads the cell. While the construction is heading towards completion, the Junior Engineers have been regularly reporting that all construction is taking place as per design specifications. However, in one of your surprise inspections, you have noticed some serious deviations and lacunae which, in your opinion, are likely to affect the safety of the flyover. Rectification of these lacunae at this stage would require a substantial amount of demolition and rework which will cause a tangible loss to the contractor and will also delay completion. There is a lot of public pressure on the Corporation to get this construction completed because of heavy traffic congestion in the area. When you brought this matter to the notice of the Chief Engineer, he advised you that in his opinion it is not a very serious lapse and may be ignored. He advised for further expediting the project for completion in time. However, you are convinced that this was a serious matter which might affect public safety and should not be left unaddressed.

What will you do in such a situation? Some of the options are given below. Evaluate the merits and demerits of each of these options and finally suggest what course of action you would like to take, giving reasons. **(20 marks/250 words)**

- Follow the advice of the Chief Engineer and go ahead.
- Make an exhaustive report of the situation bringing out all facts and analysis along with your own viewpoints stated clearly and seek for written orders from the chief Engineer.
- Call for explanation from the Junior Engineers and issue orders to the contractor for necessary correction within targeted time.
- Highlight the issue so that it reaches superiors above the Chief Engineer.
- Considering the rigid attitude of the Chief Engineer, seek transfer from the project or report sick.

Case Study: Favouritism in Job Recruitment (2013)

You are heading a leading technical institute of the country. The institute is planning to convene an interview panel shortly under your chairmanship for selection of the post of professors. A few days before the interview, you get a call from the Personal Secretary (PS) of a senior government functionary seeking your intervention in favour of the selection of a close relative of the functionary for this post. The PS also informs you that he is aware of the long pending and urgent proposals of your institute for grant of funds for modernization, which are awaiting the functionary's approval. He assures you that he would get these proposals cleared. **(20 marks/250 words)**

- What are the options available to you?
- Evaluate each of these options and choose the option which you would adopt, giving reasons.

Case Study: Sexual Harassment (2013)

You are the Executive Director of an upcoming InfoTech Company which is making a name for itself in the market.

Mr. A, who is a star performer, is heading the marketing team. In a short period of one year, he has helped in doubling the revenues as well as creating a high brand equity for the Company so much so that you are thinking of promoting him. However, you have been receiving information from many corners about his attitude towards the female colleagues; particularly his habit of making loose comments on women. In addition, he regularly sends indecent SMS's to all the team members including his female colleagues.

One day, late in the evening, Mrs. X, who is one of Mr. A's team members, comes to you visibly disturbed. She complains against the continued misconduct of Mr. A, who has been making undesirable advances towards her and has even tried to touch her inappropriately in his cabin. She tenders her resignation and leaves your office.

(20 marks/250 words)

- What are the options available to you?
- Evaluate each of these options and choose the option you would adopt, giving reasons.

Case Study: Bogus Rape Complaint (2014)

You are a no-nonsense, honest officer. You have been transferred to a remote district to head a department that is notorious for its inefficiency and callousness. You find that the main cause of the poor state of affairs is the indiscipline of a section of employees. They do not work themselves and also disrupt the working of others. You first warned the troublemakers to mend their ways or else face disciplinary action. When the warning had little effect, you issued a show cause notice to the ringleaders. As a retaliatory measure, these troublemakers instigated a woman employee amongst them to file a complaint of sexual harassment against you with the Women's Commission. The Commission promptly seeks your explanation. The matter is also publicized in the media to embarrass you further. Some of the options to handle this situation could be as follows:

- Give your explanation to the Commission and go soft on the disciplinary action.
- Ignore the Commission and proceed firmly with the disciplinary action.
- Brief your higher-ups, seek directions from them and act accordingly.
- Suggest any other possible option(s). Evaluate all of them and suggest the best course of action, giving your reasons for it.

Case Study: Ethics not Essential (2014)

Suppose one of your close friends, who is also aspiring for civil services, comes to you for discussing some of the issues related to ethical conduct in public service. He raises the following points:

In the present times, when unethical environment is quite prevalent, individual attempts to stick to ethical principles may cause a lot of problems in one's career. It may also cause hardship to the family members as well as risk to one's life. Why should we not be pragmatic and follow the path of least resistance, and be happy with doing whatever good we can?

When so many people are adopting wrong means and are grossly harming the system, what difference would it make if only a small minority tries to be ethical? They are going to be rather ineffective and are bound to get frustrated.

If we become fussy about ethical considerations, will it not hamper the economic progress of our country? After all, in the present age of high competition, we cannot afford to be left behind in the race of development.

- It is understandable that we should not get involved in grossly unethical practices, but giving and accepting small gratifications and doing small favours increases everybody's motivation. It also makes the system more efficient. What is wrong in adopting such practices?
- Critically analyze the above viewpoints. On the basis of this analysis, what will be your advice to your friend? **(250 words)**

Case Study: Disillusioned UPSC Topper **(2014)**

Rameshwar successfully cleared the prestigious civil services examination and was excited about the opportunity that he would get through the civil services to serve the country. However, soon after joining the services, he realized that things are not as rosy as he had imagined.

He found a number of malpractices prevailing in the department assigned to him. For example, funds under various schemes and grants were being misappropriated. The official facilities were frequently being used for personal needs by the officers and staff. After some time, he noticed that the process of recruiting the staff was also not up to the mark. Prospective candidates were required to write an examination in which a lot of cheating was going on. Some candidates were provided external help in the examination. Rameshwar brought these incidents to the notice of his seniors. However, he was advised to keep his eyes, ears and mouth shut and ignore all these things which were taking place with the connivance of the higher-ups. Rameshwar felt highly disillusioned and uncomfortable. He comes to you seeking your advice.

- Indicate various options that you think are available in this situation. How would you help him to evaluate these options and choose the most appropriate path to be adopted? **(250 words)**

Case Study: Dubious Plot acquired for School **(2015)**

You are heading a district administration in a particular department. Your senior officer calls you from the State Headquarters and tells you that a plot in Rampur village is to have a building constructed on it for a school. A visit is scheduled during which he will visit the site along with the chief engineer and the senior architect. He wants you to check out all the papers relating to it and to ensure that the visit is properly arranged. You examine the file which relates to the period before you joined the department. The land was acquired from the local Panchayat at a nominal cost and the papers show that clearance certificates are available from the two of the three authorities who have to certify the site's suitability.

There is no certification by the architect available on file. You decide to visit Rampur to ensure that all is in order as stated on file. When you visit Rampur, you find that the plot under reference is part of Thakurgarh Fort and that the walls, ramparts, etc., are running across it. The fort is well away from the main village, therefore a school here will be a serious inconvenience for the children. However, the area near the village has potential to expand into a larger residential area. The development charges on the existing plot, at the fort, will be very high and the question of heritage site has not been addressed. Moreover, the Sarpanch, at the time of acquisition of the land, was a relative of your predecessor. The whole transaction appears to have been done with some vested interest.

- List the likely vested interests of the concerned parties.
- Some of the options for action available to you are listed below. Discuss the merits and demerits of each of the options :
- You can await the visit of the superior officer and let him take a decision.
- You can seek his advice in writing or on phone.
- You can consult your predecessor/colleagues, etc., and then decide what to do.
- You can find out if any alternate plot can be got in exchange and then send a comprehensive written report.
- Can you suggest any other option with proper justification? **(250 words)**

Compassion for others while on job

Syllabus Topic: empathy, tolerance & compassion towards weaker sections

From this topic, case studies are formed, e.g. old lady needing social welfare, child labourers etc.

Compassion Case Study: Child Labourers in Sivakasi (2013)

Sivakasi in Tamil Nadu is known for its manufacturing clusters on firecrackers and matches. The local economy of the area is largely dependent on firecrackers industry. It has led to tangible economic development and improved standard of living in the area.

So far as child labour norms for hazardous industries like firecrackers industry are concerned, International Labour Organization (ILO) has set the minimum age as 18 years. In India, however, this age is 14 years.

The units in industrial clusters of firecrackers can be classified into registered and non-registered entities. One typical unit is household-based work. Though the law is clear on the use of child labour employment norms in registered/non-registered units, it does not include household-based works. Household-based work means children working under the supervision of their parents/relatives. To evade child labour norms, several units project themselves as household-based works but employ children from outside. Needless to say that employing children saves the costs for these units leading to higher profits to the owners.

On your visit to one of the units at Sivakasi, the owner takes you around the unit which has about 10-15 children below 14 years of age. The owner tells you that in his household-based unit, the children are all his relatives. You notice that several children smirk, when the owner tells you this. On deeper enquiry, you figure out that neither the owner nor the children are able to satisfactorily establish their relationship with each other.

- Bring out and discuss the ethical issues involved in the above case.
- What would be your reaction after your above visit?

Compassion Case Study: Dalit Cook in Mid-day Meal (2015)

You are the Sarpanch of a Panchayat. There is a primary school run by the government in your area. Mid-day meals are provided to the children attending the school. The Headmaster has now appointed a new cook in the school to prepare the meals. However, when it is found that the cook is from Dalit community, almost half of the children belonging to higher castes are not allowed to take meals by their parents. Consequently the attendance in the school falls sharply. This could result in the possibility of discontinuation of midday meal scheme, thereafter of teaching staff and subsequent closing down the school.

- Discuss some feasible strategies to overcome the conflict and to create right ambience.
- What should be the responsibilities of different social segments and agencies to create positive social ambience for accepting such changes?

Compassion Case Study: Poor Woman without Documentary Proof? (2016)

Suppose you are an officer in-charge of implementing a social service scheme to provide support to old and destitute women. An old and illiterate woman comes to you to avail the benefits of the scheme. However, she has no documents to show that she fulfils the eligibility criteria. But after meeting her and listening to her you feel that she certainly needs support. Your enquiries also show that she is really destitute and living in a pitiable condition. You are in a dilemma as to what to do. Putting her under the scheme without are documents would clearly be violation of rules. But denying her the support would be cruel and inhuman.

- Can you think of a rational way to resolve this dilemma?
- Give your reasons for it. **(250 words)**

Public Organizations

Syllabus: probity in public organization

Public Org- Theory

Syllabus Topic: Public service values & Ethics in Public Administration; Strengthening of ethical & moral values in governance; Accountability & ethical governance; Philosophical basis of governance and probity

- What do you understand by the terms 'governance', 'good governance' and 'ethical governance'? **(2016)**
- What do you understand by 'probity' in public life? What are the difficulties in practicing it in the present times? How can these difficulties be overcome? **(2014)**
- What does ethics seek to promote in human life? Why is it all the more important in public administration? **(2014)**
- The good of an individual is contained in the good of all. What do you understand by this statement? How can this principle be implemented in public life? **(2013)**

Public Org-Dilemma

Syllabus Topic: problems, dilemmas in Public Administration and public service.

From this topic, mainly case studies are formed- related to land acquisition; environmental conservation vs. economic development, etc.

Case Study: Environment Degradation (2014)

Now-a-days, there is an increasing thrust on economic development all around the globe. At the same time, there is also an increasing concern about environmental degradation caused by development. Many a time, we face a direct conflict between developmental activity and environmental quality. It is neither feasible to stop or curtail the development process, nor it is advisable to keep degrading the environment, as it threatens our very survival.

- Discuss some feasible strategies which could be adopted to eliminate this conflict and which could lead to sustainable development. **(250 words)**

Case Study: Why Villagers Migrate? (2014)

In our country, the migration of rural people to towns and cities is increasing drastically. This is causing serious problems both in the rural as well as in the urban areas. In fact, things are becoming really unmanageable. Can you analyse this problem in detail and indicate not only the socio-economic but also the emotional and attitudinal factors responsible for this problem? Also, distinctly bring out why—

- Educated rural youth are trying to shift to urban areas;
- Landless poor people are migrating to urban slums;
- Even some farmers are selling off their land and trying to settle in urban areas taking up petty jobs.
- What feasible steps can you suggest which will be effective in controlling this serious problem of our country?

Case Study: Disaster Management (2015)

There is a disaster-prone State having frequent landslides, forest fires, cloudbursts, flash floods and earthquakes, etc. Some of these are seasonal and often unpredictable. The magnitude of the disaster is always unanticipated. During one of the seasons, a cloudburst caused devastating floods and landslides leading to high casualties. There was major damage to infrastructure like roads, bridges and power generating units. This led to more than 1,00,000 pilgrims, tourists and other locals trapped across different routes and locations. The people trapped in your area of responsibility included senior citizens, patients in hospitals, women and children, hikers, tourists and ruling party's regional president along with his family

- As a civil services officer of the State, what would be the order in which you would rescue these people and why? Give justifications.

Case Study: Draft Better Land-acquisition Policy (2016)

Land needed for mining, dams and other large-scale projects is acquired mostly from Adivasis, hill dwellers and rural communities. The displaced persons are paid monetary compensation as per the legal provisions. However, the payment is often tardy. In any case, it cannot sustain the displaced families for long. These people do not possess marketable skills to engage in some other occupation. They end up as low paid migrant labourers. Moreover, their living is destroyed. Thus, the benefits of traditional ways of community development go to industries, industrialists and urban communities whereas the costs are passed on to these poor helpless people. This unjust distribution of costs and benefits is unethical.

- Suppose you have been entrusted with the task of drafting a better compensation-cum-rehabilitation policy for such displaced persons, how would you approach the problem and what would be the main elements of your suggested policy? **(250 words)**

Public Org- Code of Conduct/Ethics

Syllabus Topic: Codes of Ethics; Codes of Conduct; Laws, rules, regulations, conscience as sources of ethical Guidance.

- Discuss the Public Services Code as recommended by the 2nd Administrative Reforms Commission. **(2016)**

Public Org-Charter

Syllabus Topic: Citizens Charters; Quality of Service Delivery; Probity in Governance, concept of public service;

Nothing directly asked so far.

Public Org-Corruption

Syllabus Topic: Challenges of Corruption; Utilization of public funds

- It is often said that poverty leads to corruption. However, there is no dearth of instances where affluent and powerful people indulge in corruption in a big way. What are the basic causes of corruption among people? Support your answer with examples. **(2014)**

Case Study: "Shivaji—the Boss": Movie plot (2016)

Saraswati was a successful IT professional in USA. Moved by the patriotic sense of doing something for the country she returned to India. Together with some other like-minded friends, she formed an NGO to build a school for a poor rural community.

The objective of the school was to provide the best quality modern education at a nominal cost. She soon discovered that she has to seek permission from a number of Governments agencies. The rules and procedures were quite confusing and cumbersome. What frustrated her most was the delays, callous attitude of officials and constant demand of bribes. Her experience and the experience of many others like her has deterred people from taking up social service projects.

- A measure of Government control over voluntary social work is necessary. But it should not be exercised in a coercive or corrupt manner. What measures can you suggest to ensure that due control is exercised but well meaning, honest NGO efforts are not thwarted? **(25 marks)**

Public Org-RTI

Syllabus Topic: Information (sharing & transparency in government); RTI;

- Some recent developments such as introduction of RTI Act, media and judicial activism, etc., are proving helpful in bringing about greater transparency and accountability in the functioning of the government. However, it is also being observed that at times the mechanisms are misused. Another negative effect is that the officers are now afraid to take prompt decisions. Analyze this situation in detail and suggest how this dichotomy can be resolved. Suggest how these negative impacts can be minimized. **(2015)**
- Today we find that in spite of various measures like prescribing codes of conduct, setting up vigilance cells/commissions, RTI, active media and strengthening of legal mechanisms, corrupt practices are not coming under control. (A) Evaluate the effectiveness of these measures with justifications. (B) Suggest more effective strategies to tackle this menace. **(2015)**

Case Study: RTI: To hide or not to hide **(2013)**

In the following questions, carefully study the cases presented and then answer the questions that follow:

A Public Information Officer has received an application under RTI Act. Having gathered the information, the PIO discovers that the information pertains to some of the decisions taken by him, which were found to be not altogether right. There were other employees also who party to these decisions were. Disclosure of the information is likely to lead to disciplinary action with possibility of punishment against him as well as some of his colleagues. Non-disclosure or part disclosure or camouflaged disclosure of information will result into lesser punishment or no punishment.

The PIO is otherwise an honest and conscientious person but this particular decision, on which the RTI application has been filed, turned out to be wrong. He comes to you for advice.

The following are some suggested options. Please evaluate the merits and demerits of each of the options:

- The PIO could refer the matter to his superior officer and seek his advice and act strictly in accordance with the advice, even though he is not completely in agreement with the advice of the superior.
- The PIO could proceed on leave and leave the matter to be dealt by his successor in office or request for transfer of the application to another PIO.

- The PIO could weigh the consequences of disclosing the information truthfully, including the effect on his career, and reply in a manner that would not place him or his career in jeopardy, but at the same time a little compromise can be made on the contents of the information.
- The PIO could consult his other colleagues who are party to the decision and take action as per their advice.
- Also please indicate (without necessarily restricting to the above options) what you would like to advise, giving proper reasons. (20 marks/250 words)

Case Study: Leaking information (2013)

As a senior officer in the Finance Ministry, you have access to some confidential and crucial information about policy decisions that the Government is about to announce. These decisions are likely to have far-reaching impact on the housing and construction industry. If the builders have access to this information beforehand, they can make huge profits. One of the builders has done a lot of quality work for the Government and is known to be close to your immediate superior, who asks you to disclose this information to the said builder. **(20 marks/250 words)**

- What are the options available to you?
- Evaluate each of these options and choose the option which you would adopt, giving reasons.

IR and Funding

Syllabus Topic: Ethical issues in international relations and funding

- At the international level, the bilateral relations between most nations are governed on the policy of promoting one's own national interest without any regard for the interest of other nations. This leads to conflicts and tensions between the nations. How can ethical consideration help resolve such tensions? Discuss with specific examples. **(2015)**

Private Organizations

Corporate Governance

Syllabus Topic: Corporate Governance; Ethical concerns and dilemmas in government & private institutions

Case studies have been asked from this topic, rather than direct questions. Theme is usually bribing, displacement, environmental degradation.

Case Study: Give Bribe or End Career (2014)

Suppose you are the CEO of a company that manufactures specialized electronic e quipment used by a government department. You have submitted your bid for the supply of this equipment to the department. Both the quality and cost of your offer are better than those of the competitors. Yet the concerned officer is demanding a hefty bribe for approving the tender. Getting the order is important both for you and for your company. Not getting the order would mean closing a production line. It may also affect your own career. However, as a value-conscious person, you do not want to give bribe.

- Valid arguments can be advanced both for giving the bribe and getting the order, and for refusing to pay the bribe and risking the loss of the order. What those arguments could be? Could there be any better way to get out of this dilemma? If so outline the main elements of this third way, pointing out its merits. **(250 words)**

Case Study: Trade Union Issue

(2015)

A private company is known for its efficiency, transparency and employee welfare. The company though owned by a private individual has a cooperative character where employees feel a sense of ownership. The company employs nearly 700 personnel and they have voluntarily decided not to form a union.

One day suddenly in the morning, about 40 men belonging to a political party gatecrashed into the factory demanding jobs in the factory. They threatened the management and employees, and also used foul language. The employees feel demoralized. It was clear that those people who gatecrashed wanted to be on the payroll of the company as well as continue as the volunteers/members of the party. The company maintains high standards in integrity and does not extend favours to civil administration that also includes law enforcement agency. Such incidents occur in public sector also.

- Assume you are the CEO of the company. What would you do to diffuse the volatile situation on the date of gatecrashing with the violent mob sitting inside the company premises?
- What could be the long-term solution to the issue discussed in the case?
- Every solution/action that you suggest will have a positive and a negative impact on you (as CEO), the employees and the performance of the employees. Analyse the consequences of each of your suggested actions. **(250 words)**

Case Study: To do Drug Research on non-profitable Disease or not?

(2015)

One of the scientists working in the R & D laboratory of a major pharmaceutical company discovers that one of the company's bestselling veterinary drugs, B has the potential to cure a currently incurable liver disease that is prevalent in tribal areas. However, developing a variant of the drug suitable for human beings entailed a lot of research and development having a huge expenditure to the extent of 50 crores rupees. It was unlikely that the company would recover the costs as the disease was rampant only in poverty-stricken area having very little market otherwise.

If you were the CEO, then—

- Identify the various actions that you could take;
- Evaluate the pros and cons of each of your actions.

Case Study: To Whistleblow against Polluting Industry or not? (2016)

A fresh engineering graduate gets a job in a prestigious chemical industry. She likes the work. The salary is also good. However, after a few months accidentally discovers that a highly toxic waste is being secretly discharged into a river nearby. This is causing health problems to the villagers downstream who depend on the river for their water needs. She is perturbed and mentions her concern to her colleagues who have been with the company for longer periods. They advise her to keep quite as anyone who mentions the topic is summarily dismissed. She cannot risk losing her job as she is the sole bread-winner for her family and has to support her ailing parents and siblings.

At first, she thinks that if her seniors are keeping quiet, why should she stick out her neck. But her conscience pricks her to do something to save the river and the people who depend upon it. At heart, she feels that the advice of silence given by her friends is not correct though she cannot give reasons for it. She thinks you are a wise person and seeks your advice.

- What arguments can you advance to show her that keeping quiet is not morally right?
- What course of action would you advise her to adopt and why?

Case Study: New Project hurting lifestyle of locals? (2016)

ABC Ltd. is a large transnational company having diversified business activities with a huge shareholder base. The company is continuously expanding and generating employment. The company, in its expansion and diversification programme, decides to establish a new plant at Vikaspuri, an area which is underdeveloped. The new plant is designed to use energy efficient technology that will help the company to save production cost by 20%. The company's decision goes well with the Government policy of attracting investment to develop such underdeveloped regions. The Government has also announced tax holiday for five years for the companies that invest in underdeveloped areas. However, the new plant may bring chaos for the inhabitants of Vikaspuri region which is otherwise tranquil. The new plant may result in increased cost of living, aliens migrating to the region, disturbing the social and economic order. The company sensing the possible protest tried to educate the people of Vikaspuri region and public in general that how its Corporate Social Responsibility (CSR) policy would help overcome the likely difficulties of the residents of Vikaspuri region. In spite of this the protests begin and some of the residents decided to approach the judiciary as their plea before the Government did not yield any result. **(25 marks)**

- Identify the issues involved in the case.
- What can be suggested to satisfy Company's goal and to address the resident's concern. **(300 words)**

Model Questions of IAS GS Mains Paper IV: Ethics, Integrity and Aptitude

Question 1. What is meant by environment Ethics? Why is it important to study? Discuss any one environmental issue from the viewpoint of environmental ethics.

Answer: Environmental ethics is a branch of ethical philosophy which studies the relation of humans and non-human world and conceived as the project of pushing the bounds of moral consideration beyond humans to encompass other entities by the use of values. It takes into account not just human beings but also other living beings like plants and animals. It includes moral obligation of human beings towards environment.

It is important to study the Environmental ethics because:

(i) *Environmental impact:* Environmental impact of anthropogenic activities which shows a negative effect on environment and we can take steps to design environment friendly projects and technologies.

(ii) *Better policy formulation and implementation:* For ensuring inclusive and sustainable development, we will be able to formulate and implement better policies.

(iii) *Changing attitude of people:* Conservation and sustainable use of environmental resources can be achieved only when we succeed in changing attitude of people. For this environmental ethics is crucial.

Pollution—Serious Environmental Issue

Air, water and soil pollution, are major environmental issue concerning human and environment. Various initiatives environment laws, various policies and regulations are implemented, but all show a limited success. Greed and negligence, reduced value for environment.

To resolve environmental pollution, ethical perspective is required to save our environment. This moral obligation will change the attitude of people from apathy to compassion and this encourage them to actively curb pollution. It will also make us aware of carbon footprint. New innovation and green technology, which makes environment sustainable.

Question 2. Differentiate between the following:

(i) Law and Ethics
(ii) Ethical Management and Management of Ethics
(iii) Discrimination and Preferential Treatment
(iv) Personal Ethics and Professional Ethics.

Answer:

(i) *Law and Ethics:* Laws are system of rules that are enforced through social institutions, in order to govern our behaviour. Laws are made by Legislature, or by executive (ordinances). It prescribes what one must do. Violation of law may involve penalty or punishment. Law can be enforced by various agencies or through court of law.
Ethics are standards of right and wrong that prescribe what humans ought to do. There are various sources for ethical standards like the organization, profession, social norms, religion etc. Not adhering to ethical principles may or may not involve punishment. Ethics are enforced in an informal manner through processes like conformity, social reflections etc.

(ii) *Ethical Management and Management of Ethics:* Ethical Management refers to inclusion of ethical dimension in management of institutions like government, NGO's and private firms. For example training of Managers and workers to make them ethically literate and professional Management of Ethics refers to creating a code, norms or policy for members of society or institutions, to assure their compliance towards ethical behaviour. For example formulating Code of Conduct for organization or profession like civil services, law etc.

(iii) *Discrimination and Preferential Treatment:* Discrimination is a negative concept, which involves denial of social participation of certain categories of people, based on prejudices. It violates the basic Human Rights of the individual. It is against the concept of social justice. Our Constitution prohibits any kind of discrimination, like practicing untouchability is discriminatory.
Preferential treatment on the other hand is a positive concept which involves favouring certain sections of society which are at disadvantage and cannot compete at equal level. It may be for rectifying some historical disadvantages suffered by the community. It promotes social justice. Our Constitution provides for preferential treatment under certain circumstances. For example, provisions related to reservation.

(iv) *Personal Ethics and Professional Ethics:* Personal Ethics refers to the morals and values, which we hold as a standard for governing our life. They help in shaping our character. They determine our behaviour and attitude with the people we know personally. For example, speaking truth, respecting elders.
Professional Ethics involves adherence to code of conduct laid down at workplace. Our personal views and concerns about any topic are overshadowed by the protocol of the organization. They influence our professional career. For example Punctuality, equality in treatment, fairness in delivering justice etc.

Question 3. Given out are two quotations of moral thinkers/philosophers. For each of these bring out what it means to you in the present context.

(a) "The weak can never forgive; forgiveness is the attribute of the strong."
(10 Marks) (150 words)

(b) "We can easily forgive a child who is afraid of the dark; the real tragedy of life is when men are afraid of the light."

Answer:

(a) "The weak can never forgive; forgiveness is the attribute of the strong.": Mahatma Gandhi had given this beautiful quotation. The weak can never forgive. He is bound by extreme emotions which prevent him from forgiving. This weakness is also the source of our negative attitude, anger, sense of revenge etc. By not forgiving others, we are inclined to think that we are taking revenge from the person who has done harm to us. But in fact it harms us, more than it does to other. Our mind remains occupied with such negativity that it hampers our own personality development. A person with weak personality always believes that forgiving someone is in itself a sign of incapability to punish the culprit.

However, for forgiveness, one needs moral fortitude to overcome the strong emotions which prevent us from forgiving. One needs to transcend the distinction between good and bad. This way we can free our soul of the chains and hence, ensure our all-round personality development. So by inculcating the value of forgiveness, we are helping ourselves as much as we are helping others. We need to always remember that forgiveness doesn't change our past but it does change our future.

So for society to prosper and humanity to progress, we need to inculcate the value of forgiveness, as forgiving someone even when you have the power to punish him needs patience and compassion towards mankind.

(b) "We can easily forgive a child who is afraid of the dark; the real tragedy of life is when men are afraid of the light."

The problem is not that we are inadequate. The problem is that we don't want to come out from our comfort zone and improve on our limitations. It is the light and effort to achieve it, not our darkness that frightens us the most. Our fear of our weaknesses can be removed by working on the weak areas. For example, a person having poor level of integrity can improve by constantly working upon it. However, those who fear their weaknesses can never realize their potential fully and hence can never excel in life. They just keep justifying their wrongs without accepting them.

We have infinite potential, but we tend to seek comfort and pleasure. We restrict our world, to places where we are comfortable. We are afraid of the pain, which we may get, while trying to realize our true potential. However, we forget that pain is temporary. It may last for an hour, a day or a month. For realizing our true potential we need to overcome this fear and only then we'll be able to reach the stage of enlightenment. We need to accept what we are and shall pursue excellence in every Endeavour of life.

Question 4. (a) Mere compliance with law is not enough; the public servant also has to have a well-developed sensibility to ethical issues for effective discharge of duties. Do you agree? Explain with the help of two examples, where (i) an act is ethically right but not legally and (ii) an act is legally right, but not ethically.

Answer:

A civil servant needs to have ethical literacy, ethical competency and moral reasoning abilities, for effective discharge of his duties.

It is significant due to following reasons.

(i) Better interpretation of law and its enforcement

(ii) Ethics fill the gap which is left by law. It caters to the dynamic nature of administration.

(iii) Better understanding of needs of people.

(iv) Effective and holistic approach towards problem solving.

(v) Bridging the gap between people and administration.

(vi) Better policy formulation and implementation.

(vii) Optimum utilization of available resources.

So, both compliance with law and ethical sensibility are needed for a civil servant. However, there are situations when only one of them is fulfilled.

(i) Ethically right, legally wrong: A doctor may wish to administer euthanasia to a terminally ill patient, to relive him of the unbearable pain. Though it is morally right for him, he can't do it as it is not permitted legally in India.

(ii) Legally right, ethically wrong: Legally it may be right for army personnel to conduct raid and even kill a suspect in states where AFSPA is applicable. But ethically it is wrong. It involves depriving the citizens their basic human rights including their right to get justice from the court of law.

So, for effective public service delivery, a public servant must be ethically sensitive along with complying with the law.

(b) How do the virtues of trustworthiness and fortitude get manifested in public service? Explain with examples.

Answer: Virtues of trustworthiness and fortitude are needed for effective public service delivery. It gets manifested in the following form:

- *Upholding principles of Fidelity*: Government is all about relationships. If trust is lost, everything is lost. Fulfilling our commitments, and being responsible in our inter-personal relationship, builds trust in the team. This trust is reflected when commitments are fulfilled.
- *Maintaining confidentiality of information in public interest*: Like not disclosing budget details before formal announcement.
- Transparency and participative approach which can develop credibility and trust among people. Like Panchayati Raj Institution enhances trust and teamwork between people and administration.

- *Upholding Rule of Law*: There may be challenging circumstances when it becomes difficult to uphold the law. It requires moral fortitude to uphold the rule of law and to work for realizing the values enshrined in the constitution. So upholding it reflects our virtue of fortitude. Like not taking into account the inappropriate influence by the political boss which can hurt public interest.
- *Dedication to service*: There are many temptations to make personal gains at the cost of public interest. It requires moral fortitude, to overcome these temptations, and remain dedicated to the service of the people. So our dedication to service reflects our fortitude.

Question 5.

(a) "Social Values are more important than economic values". Discuss the above statement with examples in the context of inclusive growth of a nation.

Answer: *Social Values*: They are the standards of social behaviour derived from social interaction and accepted as constituent facts of social structure. Social values form an important part of the culture of the society. Values account for the stability of social order. They provide the general guidelines for social conduct and help in choosing between alternative courses of action. For example, respect for human dignity, equality, justice etc. are some of the social values even enshrined in our constitution.

Economic value: They are the worth of a good or service as determined by people's preferences and the trade-offs they choose to make. Making economic choices involve trade-off in allocating resources. Economic values like efficiency, economy, and profits are helpful in guiding us when we make economic choices. Measures of economic values are based on preferences of the people.

Focusing only on economic values and neglecting social values can lead to large-scale deprivation and inequality. For example, the capitalist system which arose during Industrial revolution caused large scale inequality in the society. Their main focus was creating economic value rather than fulfilling social goals.

For improving the social capital, we need to focus on social values. It will also help in improving quality of life of an individual. For example, current-day welfare states focus on social values, along with economic values. It tries to minimize inequality.

So for a balanced, inclusive and sustainable development, we need to focus more on the social values than the economic values. In fact, social values provides the foundation over which a strong economy can be built upon.

(b) Some recent developments such as introduction of RTI Act, media and judicial activism, etc., are proving helpful in bringing about greater transparency and accountability in the functioning of the government. However, it is also being observed that at times the mechanisms are misused. Another negative effect is that the officers are now afraid to take prompt decisions.

Analyse this situation in detail and suggest how this dichotomy can be resolved. Suggest how these negative impacts can be minimized.

Answer: Any participatory approach has its limitations, but it can't be an excuse for an opaque system. RTI and activism through different institutions has led to:

- Helped in unearthing many scams like 2G, coal block allocation, etc.
- Bringing greater degree of transparency and accountability by bringing even political parties under the ambit of RTI.
- Increasing participation of citizens in governance process However, they have also led to some negative repercussions like:
  - Misuse of these provisions for vested interests
  - Interference and pessimism in decision making process of public servants
  - Reluctance on part of officers to take bold decisions

There is a need to resolve the dichotomy between the need for transparency and accountability and protecting honest civil servants from undue harassment. It can be done by:

- Providing monitoring mechanisms for ensuring transparency in program implementation.
- Providing adequate safeguards to officers such autonomy and accountability can be balanced.
- Encouraging officers to take decisions by rewarding them for success.
- Defining standard operating procedure and code of conduct for officers
- Encouraging voluntary disclosure of information
- Value education for all
- Encouraging participation of people in governance through trust building measures.
- Penalty for those who use measures for personal interests.
- Bringing media under regulations through propagating positive values.
- Judiciary can restrict itself in crossing the boundaries by coming out with norms for judicial activism. In this way, the dichotomy can be resolved and the negative impact can be minimized.

Question 6. Two different kinds of attitudes exhibited by public servants towards their work have been identified as the bureaucratic attitude and the democratic attitude.

(a) Distinguish between these two terms and write their merits and demerits.

(b) Is it possible to balance the two to create a better administration for the faster development or our country?

Answer:

(a) Bureaucratic Attitude: The attitude of public servants to strictly follow decision making process according to the laid down rules and guidelines is the Bureaucratic attitude. Some basic attributes of this attitude involves objectivity, neutrality, secrecy, elite approach etc.

Merits

- Strict compliance of standard operating procedure.
- Since consultation with public is not needed so decision can be taken quickly.

- It is easier to fix responsibility of decisions because of hierarchical decision making process.

Demerits

- Red-tapism, as there is no urgency in achieving targets.
- They are opposed to changes in the system, leading to stagnation.
- It is rigid; hence public service delivery may not be effective.
- Apathy towards common people

Democratic Attitude: The attitude of public servants to encourage participation of people in decision making process and delegate authority to other members of the team. It involves values like compassion, tolerance, responsiveness etc.

Merits

- It ensures participation of people in governance.
- It improves effectiveness of public service delivery as it is according to the 'felt needs' of the people.
- It allows flexibility in program designing and implementation.

Demerits

- Since it involves wider consultation, so it may be time consuming.
- It becomes difficult to arrive at wide consensus on certain issues.
- It slows down decision making process.

(b) Yes, it is possible to balance the two. It can be achieved by following methods:

(i) Demarcating separate areas: In certain areas of governance we need democratic attitude of Bureaucrat and in other areas we need bureaucratic attitude. These should be demarcated. For Example, Areas having larger public interface requires democratic attitude. Like in case of field posting. Whereas areas needing quicker decision making needs bureaucratic attitude. Like in day to day functioning of administration at higher levels.

(ii) Laying down of guidelines with provisions for flexibility: Guidelines and standard operating procedures should be issued at macro level while at micro level there should be provisions for flexibility. This will ensure bureaucratic attitude at macro level and democratic attitude at micro level.

In this way both these can be balanced for creating a better administration for faster and inclusive development of the country.

Question 7. Today we find that in spite of various measures like prescribing codes of conduct, setting up vigilance cells/commissions, RTI, active media and strengthening of legal mechanisms, corrupt practices are not coming under control.

(a) Evaluate the effectiveness of these measures with justifications.

(b) Suggest more effective strategies to tackle this menace.

Answer: (a) The present initiative have met with limited success in curbing corruption. The main reasons are:

- *Code of Conduct*: They have been defined comprehensively, but lack enforcement mechanism. Use of legal language and different interpretations make them of little use. Lack of revision is another problem.
- *Vigilance cells/commissions*: The have been effective in unearthing many corruption cases, but due to lack of autonomy and limited powers they have not been able to make much difference. CBI for example was recently referred as a caged parrot by the Supreme Court.
- *RTI, Active media*: They have been successful in unearthing many scams like 2G scam, coal block allocation scam, etc. But they are also misused sometimes. Also killing of RTI activists pose a challenge. This has limited their effectiveness.
- *Legislative Measures*: Though with time amendments have been done to curb various types of corrupt practices, but implementation is weak. This provides loopholes to the corrupt people.

(b) To tackle this menace we need to take following steps.

- *Changing attitude of people*: We need to change attitude of both the bribe giver and taker, through methods of social influence. Social proof, liking, reciprocity etc. can play a significant role in this.
- Strict implementation of law and passing new laws like whistle-blowers bill.
- *Inculcating values*: We need to focus on inculcating positive values in children, who are our future generation. Role of family and school is very important in this. Also, we need to protect them from negative impact of internet and social media.
- *Mid-career Training*: It will help in keeping them motivated and dedicated towards service.
- *Comprehensive performance appraisal mechanism*: Performance appraisal of public servants should be conducted by neutral observers, along with the present hierarchical mechanism.
- *Leading by example*: Public servants must lead by example so that they can motivate their sub-ordinates. So, by following these steps, along with the present mechanism, we can curb the menace of corruption.

Question 8. At the international level, the bilateral relations between most nations are governed on the policy of promoting one's own national interest without any regard for the interest of other nations. This leads to conflicts and tensions between the nations. How can ethical consideration help resolve such tensions? Discuss with specific examples.

Answer: Foreign policy of a country is governed by a number of factors. A country has economic, political and strategic interests, which determine its foreign policy. Countries try to promote their national interest at the cost of interest of other nations. Colonialism, World wars, bio-prospecting etc. are some of the examples (like tension between littoral states of South China Sea).

However such an approach has led to conflicts and tensions between the countries. These issues can be resolved by ethical considerations in the foreign policy. It can help in the following manner:

- *Principle of Vasudhaiva Kutumbakam*: Our principle of Vasudhaiva Kutumbakam, i.e. World is a global village, can help in establishing peace and harmony in the world. It gives us the message that we need to look beyond these man-made boundaries, for the larger good of humanity.
- *Principle of peaceful co-existence (Panchseel)*: Instead of mutual antagonism, our foreign policy should be driven by idea of peaceful co-existence. Countries can prosper only in peaceful global order. We need to understand that the present path leads us only to the destruction of the whole world. We need to change our course.
- *Respecting Humanity*: Instead of dividing people among various identity groups and then discriminating among them, we need to see the larger picture. We need to ensure basic human rights for everyone. We should strive to improve quality of life of people around the world.
- *Shared responsibility*: If we want to save this world for our future generations, we need to take the responsibility collectively. We must ensure conservation and sustainable use of available environmental resources.
- Refurbishing policies like Non-alignment movement.
- So, for the progress of humanity and for preserving our planet for future generations, we must include these ethical considerations in our foreign policy.

Question 9. Public servants are likely to confront with the issues of 'Conflict of Interest'. What do you understand by the term "Conflict of Interest' and how does It manifest in the decision making by public servants? If faced with the conflict of Interest situation, how would you resolve it? Explain with the help of examples.

Answer:

Conflict of interest: It refers to a set of circumstances that creates a risk that professional judgment or action regarding a primary interest may be unduly influenced by a secondary interest. In public service it involves a conflict between public interest and private interests. It may directly or indirectly compromise the performance of the public servant.

There are various ways in which it manifest in the decision making process.

- Public interest v/s private interest
- Public interest v/s interest of family or friends
- Public interest v/s interest of particular community

For resolving conflict of interest following steps can be taken:

- *Keeping Public interest above private interest*: A public servant should always work in public interest. In situations involving conflict of interest he should take a principled stand.
- *Making voluntary disclosure*: A public servant should voluntarily declare in situations involving conflict of interest. It will help in taking suitable steps for avoiding the conflict.
- *Recuse from the situation/case*: often done by judges to resolve conflict of interest.
- *File noting*: Public servants should always mention the reason for taking particular decision, in the files. This ensures greater degree of transparency and accountability.

- *Identifying "risk-areas"*: It will help in providing clear cut guidelines to the public servants, in order to tackle conflict of interest in those situations.
- *Developing organizational culture*: It will help in addressing such situations in a better manner. It will also help in motivating public servants to disclose the potential conflict of interest.

So in this manner conflict of interest situation can be tackled, for providing efficient public service.

Question 10. A private company is known for its efficiency, transparency and employee welfare. The company though owned by a private individual has a cooperative character where employees feel a sense of ownership. The company employs nearly 700 personnel and they have voluntarily decided not to form a union.

One day suddenly in the morning, about 40 men belonging to a political party gate-crashed into the factory demanding jobs in the factory. They threatened the management and employees, and also used foul language. The employees feel demoralized. It was clear that those people who gate-crashed wanted to be on the payroll of the company as well as continue as the volunteers/members of the party.

The company maintains high standards in integrity and does not extend favors to civil administration that also includes law enforcement agency. Such incidents occur in public sector also. (20 Marks) (250 Words)

(a) Assume you are the CEO of the company. What would you do to diffuse the volatile situation on the date of gate-crashing with the violent mob sitting inside the company premises?

(b) What could be the long-term solution to the issue discussed in the case?

(c) Every solution/action that you suggest will have a positive and a negative impact on you (as CEO), the employees and the performance of the employees. Analyze the consequences of each of your suggested actions.

Answer:

(a) As the CEO of the company, I would take the following steps to diffuse the volatile situation:

- *Use of Emotional intelligence*: To tackle such volatile situation it is important to use ones' emotional intelligence, to appraise the situation in a better manner. I will call the leader of mob, and will try to manage and regulate his violent emotions. This may help in bringing the situation under control.
- *Informing Police*: Since the situation involves law and order problem, I will inform the police about it. If issue is resolved peacefully then fine, otherwise police may take suitable action.
- *Calling the political leader*: I will call the political leader, informing my inability to provide jobs to the men.

  I will also request him to call back his party members, as on his direction they will agree to leave.

(b) In the long-term, following steps can be taken:

- I will get court orders, for police protection of our factory. It will help in keeping the mob away from our factory in future.
- I will also put additional barriers at the main entrance of the factory. It will restrict the entry of unwanted elements.
- Further, I will issue strict guidelines regarding recruitment policy of the company. This will sensitize the people regarding our organizational values.
- I will also take help of media, to make the issue public. It will help in preventing any such attempt in future.

(c) Evaluation of the consequences:

(i) Option 1: Getting Court orders for police protection

Merits

- It will boost the morale of employees, as there will be a sense of security.
- It will help in maintaining the performance of the company at highest standards.
- I will also be able to work with full dedication for the company.

Demerits

- It may increase cost of company due to extra security requirements.

(ii) Option 2: Putting additional barriers

Merits

- It will also boost morale of employees because of a sense of security.
- Performance of company will remain at highest standards.

Demerits

- Will cause some inconvenience to employees who commute on daily basis.

(iii) Option 3: Issuing guidelines

Merits

- It will instil a sense of confidence among the employees.
- Our organizational values will be clearly spelt out for everyone.

Demerits

- It may not be that much effective for outside people.

(iv) Option 4: Taking help of media

Merits

- Will sensitize outside people regarding our organizational values.

Demerits

- May also annoy the political party concerned.

Question 11. You are the Sarpanch of a Panchayat. There is a primary school run by the government in your area. Midday meals are provided to the children attending the school. The Headmaster has now appointed a new cook in the school to prepare the meals. However, when it is found that the cook is from Dalit community, almost half of the children belonging to higher castes are not allowed to take meals by their parents. Consequently the attendance in the school falls sharply. This could result in the possibility of discontinuation or midday meal scheme, thereafter of teaching staff and subsequent closing down the school. **(20 Marks) (250 Words)**

(a) Discuss some feasible strategies to overcome the conflict and to create right ambience.

(b) What should be the responsibilities of different social segments and agencies to create positive social ambience for accepting such changes?

Answer:

(a) At the root of the problem lies the caste discrimination prevalent in the village. So for overcoming the conflict and creating the right ambience following strategies can be implemented:

- *Changing attitude of people*: The caste discrimination prevalent in the village can be eliminated through changing attitude of people. I will use social influence and persuasion techniques for achieving this. For example, social proof, reciprocity, liking, dissemination of information, breaking stereotypes etc. can be used.
- *Inter-community cultural festivals*: The barriers dividing society into various segments can be overcome only when there is more interaction among people. Festivals provide an opportunity to bring people closer.
- *Defining shared goals*: Village should work together for achieving certain shared goals. Defining such goals like in education and health sector can help in ensuring collective effort of people.
- *Leading by Example*: As Sarpanch of the village, I will lead by example. It will help in influencing people, and bringing change.

(b) The various social segments and agencies like family, school and Gram Sabha have certain responsibilities for creating right ambience.

(i) Responsibility of Social segments: People must promote shared values like equality, fraternity, justice etc. It is our responsibility to respect every individual in the manner we expect respect from others. We need to persuade people for attitude change if they discriminate against anyone.

(ii) Responsibility of Social Agencies: Law enforcement agencies must ensure proper enforcement of laws which prohibit discrimination. Also, Civil servants need to remain pro- active in order to detect early warning signs of such discrimination and take corrective steps. They should also launch various awareness campaigns in this regard. They should lead by example, which will help in influencing people.

So, for bringing social change and creating right kind of ambience, above steps can be taken.

Question 12. One of thc scientists working in the R & D laboratory of a major pharmaceutical company discovers that one of the company's bestselling veterinary drugs. B has the potential to cure a currently incurable liver disease that in prevalent in tribal areas. However, developing a variant of the drug suitable for human beings entailed a lot of research and development having a huge expenditure to the extent of ₹ 50 crores. It was unlikely that the company would recover the costs as the disease was rampant only in poverty-.stricken area having very little market otherwise.

(20 Marks) (250 Words)

If you were the CEO, then

(a) Identify the various actions that you could take;

(b) Evaluate the pros and cons of each or your actions.

Answer:

(a) The various actions which can be taken are –

- Taking support of Government
- Raising money through equity market
- Collaborating with foreign company
- Appealing common people through media and NGO's for collaboration and funds through sale of products

(b) Evaluation of the options:

(i) Option 1: Taking support of government

Merits

- It will solve the funding issue.
- Poor people will benefit. Justice will be done to them.
- Government machinery can be utilized for better service delivery.

Demerits

- It will put Subsidy burden on government.
- Company's ownership of product will be diluted.

(ii) Option 2: Raising money through Equity market

Merits

- It will solve the problem temporarily.
- Poor people will benefit.
- Corporate Social Responsibility will be fulfilled

Demerits

- Investors may lose money in future.
- My company might come under severe financial stress.

(iii) Option 3: Collaborating with foreign company

Merits

- Not just poor of India, but of whole world will benefit.
- The problem can be solved in holistic manner.

Demerits

- Issues of Intellectual property rights may hamper this collaboration.
- Foreign company may sell the drug at higher prices.

(iv) Option 4: Appealing common people through media and NGO's for collaboration and funds through sale of products

Merits

- Pool for social activities will be created.
- Good publicity of company will be done.
- Increase in sales and profits which then are transfer to the project.

Demerits

- It may also decrease the sale as price of company's products will be increased.
- May take a long time to collect necessary funds.

Considering all the above three options, I will go for the first option, of taking support of government.

Question 13. There is a disaster-prone State having frequent landslides, forest fires, cloudbursts, flash floods and earthquakes, etc. Some of these are seasonal and often unpredictable. The magnitude of the disaster is always unanticipated. During one of the seasons, a cloudburst caused devastating floods and landslides leading to high causalities. There was major damage to infrastructure like roads, bridges and power generating units. This led to more than 100000 pilgrims, tourists and other locals trapped across different routes and locations. The people trapped in your area of responsibility included senior citizens, patients in hospitals, women and children, hikers, tourists, ruling party's regional president along with his family, additional chief secretary of the neighbouring State and prisoners in jail.

As civil services officer of the State, what would be the order in which you would rescue these people and why?
Give justifications.

Answer: I will follow the following sequence for rescue operation.

1. Patients in Hospitals
   - They are highly vulnerable during disasters, because of their inability to take care of themselves. So they should be rescued even before women and children.
   - Since their number is less and position known, it will be easy to evacuate them with less effort.
2. Senior citizens
   - They are valuable members of society, and cannot be left without help for too long. They are also vulnerable because of their old age and physical handicap. People have tendency to leave behind the old, thus priority shall be given to them.
3. Women and children
   - Children are our future generation, and hence they must be rescued first of all.
   - Women and Children are highly vulnerable during disasters, not just physically but emotionally as well.
4. Prisoners in jail
   - Since they are in jail, so their mobility is highly restricted. This makes them vulnerable in disaster situation.
   - Even though they are prisoners, but still they are human beings. So, they must be rescued, considering their vulnerability.
5. Tourists
   - Next I will rescue tourists, because they lack any means to tackle the disaster themselves. Also, they know very less about the local conditions.
   - But, since they are healthy, so they can wait till other more vulnerable people are rescued.

6. Ruling Party's regional president and his family
   - Since he has political linkages, he can make temporary arrangements for safety of his family till other vulnerable people are rescued.
   - Once vulnerable people are rescued, he and his family will be rescued.
   - Since he has a family with him, which include women and children, so I will rescue him before the hikers and Chief Secretary.
7. Chief Secretary of the other state
   - He has been well trained to handle such situations. So he can wait till others are rescued.
   - Instead, he can also help, in rescue operation since he has experience in this regard. This is a part of his duty.
8. Hikers
   - I will rescue them at last, as they have both the training as well as equipment with them, to deal with challenging terrain.
   - They can easily wait till others are rescued.

So, I will conduct the rescue operation according to above mentioned priority list. However, in some cases, simultaneous rescue mission can be launched for different categories as they are not mutually exclusive.

Question 14. You are heading a district administration in a particular department. Your senior officer calls you from the State Headquarters and tells you that a plot in Rampur village is to have a building constructed on it for a school. A visit is scheduled during which he will visit the site along with the chief engineer and the senior architect. He wants you to check out all the papers relating to it and to ensure that the visit is properly arranged. You examine the file which relates to the period before you joined the department. The land was acquired from the local Panchayat at a nominal cost and the papers show that clearance certificates are available from the two of the three authorities who have to certify the site's suitability. There is no certification by the architect available on file. You decide to visit Rampur to ensure that all is in order as stated on file. When you visit Rampur, you find that the plot under reference is part of Thakurgarh Fort and that the walls, ramparts, etc. are running across it. The fort is well away from the main village, therefore a school here will be a serious inconvenience for the children. However the area near the village has potential to expand into a larger residential area. The development charges on the existing plot, at the fort, will be very high and the question of heritage site has not been addressed. Moreover, the Sarpanch, at the time of acquisition of the land, was a relative of your Predecessor. The whole transaction appears to have been done with some vested interest. (250 words) (25 Marks)

(a) List the likely vested interests of the concerned parties.

(b) Some of the options for action available to you are listed below. Discuss the merits and demerits or each of the options:

(i) You can await the visit of the superior officer and let him take a decision.

(ii) You can seek his advice in writing or on phone.

***(iii)* You can consult your predecessor/colleagues, etc. and then decide what to do.**
***(iv)* You can find out if any alternate plot can be got in exchange and then send a comprehensive written report. Can you suggest any other option with proper justification?**

Answer:

(a) The likely vested interest of the parties involved are:
- Grabbing the heritage land illegally by village and previous government authorities.
- The two certifying authorities, certifying the suitability of plot, for some monetary or in kind gains.
- Vested interest of Sarpanch, in keeping the area near village for residential purpose, instead of using it for school. He might be considering the monetary gains which can be made by this.
- The predecessor providing undue advantage to Sarpanch, by misusing his authority.

(b) Evaluation of the actions which can be taken.

(i) Option 1: Awaiting the visit of the superior officer and let him take a decision.

Merits
- It will help in maintaining the line of hierarchy in decision making process.
- Seniors will take a holistic view of the whole issue, considering the best available evidence.
- It will help in solving the problem and punishing the guilty.
- I will also perform my duty efficiently.

Demerits
- It will delay the solution of the problem.
- It will be like transferring my duty to my seniors.

(ii) Option 2: Seeking his advice in writing or on phone.

Merits
- It will help in appraising the seniors, of the situation.
- It will also help in quicker decision making.
- I will perform my duties efficiently.
- It may help in solving the issue before seniors visit the site.

Demerits
- Seeking advice will again be like shifting responsibility on seniors.
- Getting written orders will delay the process of solving the issue.

(iii) Option 3: Consulting my predecessor/colleagues, etc. and then decide what to do.

Merits
- I can know about the exact reasons behind the decisions of predecessor.
- I will have a democratic and legal approach towards problem resolution.
- It will help in proving the wrongs done by predecessor.

Demerits
- It may not help in solving the problem, because of the vested interest of the predecessor.

- It will delay the decision making process.
- I will have to bear the responsibility for the actions based on their advice.

(iv) Option 4: I can find out if any alternate plot can be got in exchange and then send a comprehensive written report.

Merits

- It will help in solving the problem, as school cannot be constructed at present location.
- Sending detailed report will help in appraising seniors on every aspect of the issue.
- Standard operating procedure will be followed in resolving the issue.
- I will perform my duty efficiently.
- Children will benefit if plot for school is near the village.

Demerits

- It may cause some delay in resolving the problem.

Considering the above four options, I will go with the fourth option as it resolves the issue in a holistic manner, while maintaining the line of duty.

Question 15. You are recently posted as district development officer of a district. Shortly thereafter you found that there is considerable tension in the rural areas of your district on the issue or sending girls to schools.

The elders of the village feel that many problems have come up because girls are being educated and they are stepping out of the safe environment of the household. They are or the view that the girls should be quickly married off with minimum education. The girls are also competing for jobs after education, which have traditionally remained in boys' exclusive domain, adding to unemployment amongst male population.

The younger generation feels that in the present era, girls should have equal opportunities for education and employment, and other means of livelihood. The entire locality is divided between the elders and the younger lot and further sub-divided between sexes in both generations. You come to know that in Panchayat or in other local bodies or even in busy crossroads, the issue is being acrimoniously debated.

One day you are informed that an unpleasant incident has taken place. Some girls were molested, when they were en route to schools. The incident led to clashes between several groups and a law and order problem has arisen. The elders after heated discussion have taken a joint decision not to allow girls to go to school and to socially boycott all such families, which do not follow their dictate. (250 words) (25 Marks)

(a) What steps would you take to ensure girls' safety without disrupting their education?

(b) How would you manage and mould patriarchic attitude of the village elders to ensure harmony in the inter-generational relations?

Answer:

(a) The issue involves ensuring safety of girls, without disrupting their education. It also involves ironing out the difference of opinion between the two generations. Following steps can be taken for safety and education of girls:

- *Social influence and persuasion techniques*: For bringing social change through attitude transformation, we need to use different techniques of social influence and persuasion. Elders should be persuaded for allowing education of girls, while assuring them of their safety. Social proof, reciprocity, role models, etc. can play a significant role in this.
- *Changing Socialization process*: Gender stereotypes need to be broken by changing the socialization process of children. This is important to remove the gender discrimination face by girls. Child rearing practices can be modified.
- *Security arrangement and combat training*: Police roundups can be increased during opening and closure time of schools. Girls can also be taught in self-defence techniques.
- *Infrastructural improvements*: Safety of girls in rural area is compromised because of lack of adequate infrastructure, like street light, toilet facilities etc. Bridging these gaps will help in providing a sense of security to girls. Constructing toilets, providing them cycles etc. are some of the steps.

(b) For managing and mouldings the patriarchal attitude we need to use the following methods:

- *Using persuasion techniques*: Elder people must be persuaded with all due respect, in order to change their attitude towards girl education. Sarpanch of the village can play a significant role in this, since his position has authority to influence behaviour of people.
- *Leadership skills*: The situation requires leadership skill on my part to influence the attitude of elderly people. I can do it my demonstrating them the benefits of girl education, through various examples. It is a powerful method of social influence.
- *Emotional intelligence*: It also requires emotional intelligence on my part, in order to understand and manage the emotions of the village elders. This is crucial for success of other steps. The issue has lot of emotional component which need to be managed properly.
- *Attitude change*: Stereotypes and prejudice can be broken through adult education and dissemination of information regarding the benefits of girl education.

So, in this manner social change can happen, and ensure that there is inter-generationa harmony.